Mountains & Man

Mountains

UNIVERSITY OF CALIFORNIA PRESS

& Man

A Study of Process and Environment

Berkeley · Los Angeles · London

Larry W. Price

University of California Press
Berkeley and Los Angeles, California
University of California Press, Ltd.
London, England
© 1981 by
The Regents of the University of California

Printed in the United States of America

1 2 3 4 5 6 7 8 9

Library of Congress Cataloging in Publication Data

Price, Larry W.
  Mountains and man.

  Bibliography: p. 443.
  Includes index.
  1. Mountains.   2.   Alpine environments.
  3. Mountain landuse.   I.   Title.
GB501.2.P74   551.4'32   76–14294

ISBN 0–520–03263–2

This book is dedicated to the students of the geography summer field camp at Portland State University who shared good times and bad in the mountains and taught me more than they learned.

Contents

Foreword

This is a most important and timely book. It is destined to become a standard text on mountain processes and environments.

Man's relations with mountains predate the beginnings of recorded history. Mountains have influenced art, religion, philosophy, politics, and social institutions. This man-mountain relationship has never been more important than during the final quarter of this century. As governments, societies, and individuals gradually exhaust the earth's limited resources, and as populations continue to expand, the prospects for man's survival become increasingly dubious. That survival may depend on preserving mountains.

Erik Eckholm has observed that Nepal exports to India and Bangladesh the one commodity that it cannot afford to lose and that the receiving countries can acquire only with disastrous consequences: silt carried by the floodwaters of its mountains. At the same time, growth in the mountains has brought on alarming deforestation and pushed agricultural terracing onto steeper and higher slopes, threatening Nepal's economic stability and political independence. Indeed, the threat is not just to Nepal: many countries that rely on mountains for their economic stability suffer from this. Himalayan India, Sikkim, Afghanistan, Ethiopia, Ecuador, and Colombia are each losing valuable mountain soil daily. Papua, New Guinea, Bhutan, Northern Thailand, and many other mountain countries and provinces are being similarly impoverished.

The threat to the Alps also derives from overuse, but that stemming from uncontrolled tourism. Over the last two or three centuries, the treeline has lowered dangerously; the more recent construction of roads, hotels, and ski facilities in avalanche zones has obliged the Alpine countries to devote enormous sums over the last thirty years to protect themselves from natural hazards caused by man.

Northern Thailand has recently commanded attention because of its burgeoning population and prolific opium crop. The traditional forest *swidden* (slash and burn/ shifting agriculture) economies of this rugged mountain region of monsoon forests have collapsed. Today Northern Thailand's once-splendid mountain forest that connected Burma, Laos, and Yunnan is burned over, extensively deforested, and badly eroded. This devastation is upsetting the hydrologic cycle of the major rivers and damaging the productivity of the fertile rice-producing plains and valleys that lie below.

While only 200 million people inhabit the world's mountain regions (about 20 to 30 percent of the world's land area), many times this number are adversely affected by degeneration that begins in the mountains and spreads to the adjacent lowlands. In the Himalayas, for instance, environmental degradation threatens the lives of 300 million people on the Indo-Gangetic Plain. By any standard, this is a problem of worldwide importance, and it has prompted worldwide action. Recently the urgency of this man-mountain problem was recognized by the UNESCO Man and the Biosphere (MAB)

program. In collaboration with UNESCO, the Austrian government invited experts to meet in Salzburg in January 1973. This meeting, called to develop a design for applied research, formally initiated MAB Project 6, a study of the impact of human activities on mountain ecosystems. Other meetings followed: Lillehammer, Norway, November 1973; Vienna, Austria, December 1973; La Paz, Bolivia, June 1974; Boulder, Colorado, July 1974; Lima, Peru, December 1974; Kathmandu, Nepal, October 1975; Bogotá, Colombia, June 1976; and Briançon, France, May 1977.

The Lillehammer meeting established an International Working Group for MAB Project 6, which I was privileged to chair. Since that time, national committees have designed and initiated crucial applied mountain research in more than fifteen countries. In 1977, the United Nations University (UNU) inaugurated a special project whose ambitious title was "Highland-Lowland Interactive Systems in the humid tropics and sub-tropics." Areas of initial concern have been Papua, New Guinea, Northern Thailand, and Nepal. Moreover, the collaboration between UNESCO and UNU has brought forth a program for mapping mountain hazards in Nepal in association with the newly founded Regional Centre for Integrated Mountain Development in Katmandu. Four young Nepali specialists received special training in mountain geoecology in the Colorado Front Range, and this past summer they were incorporated into the Himalayan mapping project.

UNESCO and UNU, in conjunction with other agencies and institutions (especially the Arbeitgemeinschaft für Hochgebirgsforschung, Munich, and the Commission on Mountain Geoecology of the International Geographical Union [IGU]), are planning a new journal to deal with mountain environmental problems, research, and development.

Let us not become complacent because of this enormous burst of activity over the past seven years. As we attempt to formulate applied research projects and influence political and land-use decisions, we learn the extent of ignorance in the natural and human sciences concerning mountain environments and mountain processes. Synthesizing and publicizing current knowledge is an immense first step. In taking this step Professor Price has made a most important contribution, and he is to be congratulated for his dedication, insight, and courage. I say courage because the scope of our work will render an initial study inadequate and incomplete. Ten or twenty or more volumes are needed, aimed at different sectors of society and various levels of education. The interdisciplinary, multilingual, and multinational nature of the work exceeds the capacity of one individual. But collaborating to achieve such objectives will be no less difficult.

Where, then, do we go from here? This is not a rhetorical question; furthermore, I am certain Professor Price will approve my asking it in this unconventional foreword, because he shares my own commitment and concern. The need for combined activity among scientists, educators, politicians, government agencies, and the people of the mountains themselves is critical. We need many simultaneous undertakings: publicity, education, and training; long-term and short-term research and monitoring; and the intelligent application of existing and new knowledge to decision-making at all levels.

This task, or series of interrelated tasks, may appear so formidable that we should all despair. Such shunning of responsibility must be avoided. Some of the more serious threats to world civilization and environment are complacency, lethargy, and despair—a conviction that the problems are too great, the time too short, and our environmental and cultural losses irrecoverable. We probably have the expertise to make a worthy beginning, although political issues may overpower us unless we muster considerable determination. Individual communities, as well as national governments and international organizations of many hues, must be induced to think and act collectively. We cannot be sure that all of these needs will be met, but neither can we shrink from attempting to influence the outcome.

I have read this book carefully in my own mountain fastness at 3,000 meters in the Colorado Front Range. I felt admiration, enthusiasm, and joy. It is the best synthesis and analysis of mountain processes and environments available. The author's breadth of interest and understanding and, above all, his obvious devotion to solving the problems of mountains and man are to be commended. *Mountains and Man* will not only provide a vital text for courses that have lacked one far too long, but it should also unify and mobilize the mountain scientific community, which is dedicated to working with the mountain peoples for the preservation and balanced development of our mountain heritage.

Jack D. Ives
Chairman, IGU Commission on
Mountain Geoecology
Mountain Research Station
Colorado Front Range
15 July 1979

Preface

The idea of this book first came to me in 1973 while I was preparing for a new course at Portland State University entitled "Mountains," to be an introductory general-interest course oriented toward the study of mountain processes and environments. I soon discovered that much of the information had to be taken from journal articles and symposium papers; there were no books that covered the various topics adequately. This was no problem for me, but what could I assign my students? Nothing in English seemed appropriate. The available texts were either too old and out of print (e.g., Peattie 1936, *Mountain Geography*), regional in focus (e.g., Pearsall 1960, *Mountains and Moorlands*), or too detailed and selective (e.g., Wright and Osburn 1967, *Arctic and Alpine Environments*). At the other extreme was the Time-Life Nature Library publication by Milne and Milne (1962), entitled *The Mountains*. This thin volume is wonderfully illustrated and well-written but too elementary for use as a college text. Several books have appeared since, most notably the huge and beautiful *Arctic and Alpine Environments* (1974), by Ives and Barry, but they also tend to fall into one of the above molds.

The need for a good introductory synthesis on mountains is accentuated by a strong and growing interest in mountains. Mountains are at the heart of the wilderness mystique that has developed in this country; they are viewed as one of the last refuges of wild and untamed nature, and, equally, as one of the last remaining retreats in which man may escape the pressures of civilization. This is especially important in an urbanized society where opportunities to be alone and to feel the pulse and flow of nature are becoming ever fewer. In many people's minds, mountains represent all that is good in nature; they are the antithesis of the city. This increasing interest in mountains, coupled with burgeoning population and land-use pressures, makes the need to understand the nature of such landscapes and their susceptibility to disturbance all the more immediate.

I have tried to write this book for three types of use: first, as a college text for courses dealing with the environment and natural processes in mountains; second, for naturalists, hikers, climbers, and others interested in mountains; finally, I hope that the synthesis of ideas and extensive bibliography will make it of value as a reference volume for more advanced students in the natural and physical sciences.

I have striven to avoid unnecessary use of technical or scientific jargon, but it has not been possible, or desirable, to eliminate all technical words. Those used are italicized and defined in context upon first use, and the page numbers are italicized in the index. Measurements are given in metric units, with English equivalents; while this slows the reading in some contexts, it was felt that most users of the book will find the English values a helpful addition. Most illustrations are identified in metric units; a few, where the original was too awkward to change, are in English units. In cases where precision is required, the exact equivalents are shown,

but large numbers are generally rounded to the nearest appropriate figure.

The book focuses on the processes and environments of high mountains. The choice and depth of treatment of specific topics has depended upon the information available in general texts, my own interests, strengths, and priorities, and a general conception of what would be most useful and interesting to the average reader. There also had to be a stopping point. Regrettably, for example, there is no separate discussion of mountain lakes. On the other hand, there is fairly extensive coverage of mountain insects. Arthropods are extremely important organisms in mountains and their characteristics and survival strategies exemplify and reflect the problems of life, generally, in this environment. For the same sorts of reasons, some sections are far longer and more detailed than others: for example, the chapter on mountain climate is three times as large as the one on the origin of mountains. Much is already readily available in introductory texts about the geology of mountains, while an understanding of climate is more fundamental to an understanding of specific landscape processes operative in mountains. Similarly, glaciers are covered in less detail than vegetation, wildlife, and soils, because information on mountain glaciation is readily available in introductory books.

I have attempted to document the text completely without being pedantic, and I hope the bibliography will be found to be one of the major strengths of the book. Whenever information was taken directly, the source was cited, whether from a popular magazine or a scholarly journal. The focus has been on the most recent publications, and those containing good bibliographies are cited at the expense of older but perhaps more classic sources. I have tried to limit the references to those that are available in college libraries. Dissertations, theses, and in-house publications are generally not cited, nor have I identified in the text the many cases where information was acquired through personal communications from colleagues. The emphasis is on English-language citations; consequently, many of the classic works in mountain geography have been omitted, especially those in French and German dealing with the Alps. Fortunately, most of these ideas have been reported in English publications as translations or by European scholars publishing in English.

I have had a great deal of help while writing this book and am indebted to a number of people. Foremost among them are Ted M. Oberlander and Will F. Thompson, who read each chapter as it was written and returned the pages covered with criticisms, comments, and ideas. Both were enthusiastic and helpful mentors, and this thank-you is poor payment for their considerable contributions to the book. Other colleagues who critically read one or more chapters are listed in alphabetical order: L. C. Bliss, R. S. Hoffmann, Peter Höllermann, Jack Ives, Martin Kaatz, Fritz Kramer, David Lantis, and Melvin Marcus. I thank each of them.

I also appreciate the kindness of the many people who sent me reprints of their publications, answered my queries, provided original photographs, and allowed use of their published illustrations. I am very proud of the linework, most of which was drafted by Ray Hudnut. Out of the goodness of his heart, Ted Oberlander produced the accomplished renditions in Figures 5.14 and 5.18. Ron Cihon and Terry Storms worked overtime filming and developing prints: their efforts are gratefully acknowledged. Several students took an active interest in the project and were helpful in many ways. I especially thank Gary Beach, Katherine Hanson, Michael Deatherage-Newsom, Robert Voeks, and Delores McClarin for their assistance and ideas.

I thank the members of the geography department at Portland State University, who have been supportive of me during what seemed an interminable period when I carried less than my share of the load. I especially wish to acknowledge James Ashbaugh who, as department chairman, had the foresight and courage to allow me to teach the geography field camp with a focus on the mountains of the Pacific Northwest during the summers of 1970, 1971, 1973, 1974, 1977, and 1978. This greatly helped to focus my interest in mountains. I am indebted to the University for the sabbatical year in which the book was begun, and to the University library and the interlibrary loan system, whose services were invaluable in dealing with such a diverse literature.

The departmental secretaries bore the burden of typing and retyping the manuscript; they added their own flavor to the effort. I am especially grateful to Nadine White, who shepherded the first version carefully and conscientiously to completion. Carolyn Perry expedited many logistical problems and typed parts of the manuscript when she had time. Betty Froen and Marion Bradley typed much of the final copy. To all of these people, I offer my thanks.

Grant Barnes, sponsoring editor at the University of California Press, had faith in the project during its early development, and was an enthusiastic and helpful supporter throughout. Karen Reeds critically read and edited the book; she provided many valuable suggestions on the content as well as its written expression. I am greatly appreciative of their help.

Finally, I thank my wife, Nancy, and my children, Laura, Mark, and Jennifer, for sacrificing and doing without a proper husband and father for far too long. Nancy provided a receptive sounding-board for ideas and problems. Her enthusiasm, unswerving patience, and strength were a constant source of encouragement and comfort during the occasional days of frustration and doubt. The book is as much hers as mine.

Introduction

. . . lofty mountains are most worthy of deep study.
For everywhere you turn, they present to every
sense a multitude of objects to excite and delight
the mind. They offer problems to our intellect; they
amaze our souls. They remind us of the infinite
variety of creation, and offer an unequaled field
for the observation of the processes of nature.

> Josias Simler
> *De alpibus commentarius*
> (1574)

The presence of mountains fundamentally transfigures the earth and greatly alters the character and distribution of natural phenomena. The extent to which this is true can perhaps best be seen by thinking momentarily about what the world would be like without mountains or hills. Imagine a land surface with no slopes or inequalities except for coastlines, and how this would affect the nature and distribution of environments. Probably the major change would be the homogenization of the earth's surface and of its habitats. There would be fewer climatic-biotic regions; they would occupy vast areas and merge imperceptibly into one another. Mountains serve to delineate, accentuate, and modify the global patterns of climate, vegetation, soil, and wildlife.

Mountains establish the fundamental scenery of the earth and set the stage upon which the terrestrial play takes place. The ebb and flow of wind and water, of life and living processes, are expressed against this backdrop. Limitations to human activities are imposed and potentials are provided as the scenario unfolds. Natural resources may be concentrated or diffused, multiplied or reduced. For example, the Himalayas and Alps separate north from south, a division reflected in a thousand ways by the differences in the natural and cultural landscapes between one side and the other. The Andes, Cascades, and Ghats run north and south and create enormous environmental contrasts between east and west. One side is rainy, the other is dry; lush forests are juxtaposed with scrublands and deserts. Settlement and land use follow accordingly, with vast differences in productivity and value.

Mountains result in the creation of original and unique phenomena. Without mountains there would be no alpine plants or animals. There would be no mountain snows or rushing brooks, no folded rocks or motherlodes. There would be no Tahiti or Martinique, which, like most other islands, are but the exposed summits of oceanic mountains. Plains would rule supreme, with no elevated and rugged skylines to add interest to the view. We could not look to the "everlasting hills from whence cometh our strength." There would be no mountain gods, no Fujiyama or Everest to ascend and appreciate. Machu Picchu and Kathmandu would not exist; there would be no Andean or Sherpa guide. The course of history would be changed in countless ways: think of Khyber Pass, Thermopylae, Hannibal and the Alps. There would be fewer languages, cultures, and nationalities; there would be no Switzerland or Montenegro. The world would be a poorer place.

Fortunately, we do not have to worry about any of these imagined situations because mountains are a very real part of our world and always will be. The Biblical verse "Lo, the valleys will be exalted and the mountains made low" is beautifully prophetic. The creation and destruction of mountains are eternal processes; the forces to destroy are more than adequately matched by forces to construct. Mountains are created from the interior of the earth, but upon reaching the surface the material be-

comes so altered in composition that it can never return to its source. Every earthquake and volcanic eruption attests to continuing mountain-building. Mountains are the progeny of the earth, and continents are the bones of old mountains.

The creation of mountains provides massive physical structures that not only modify the character and distribution of terrestrial environments, but also produce habitats and life forms unlike those found in lowlands. By projecting upward into the encapsulating air, mountains create the potential for land organisms to experience the conditions that exist at high altitudes: the air becomes thinner, the sun more intense, the wind stronger, the temperature lower. Organisms adapt to the conditions at different levels, evolving, innovating, developing, and using the various niches and components of the mountain landscape for the production of distinctive life forms and communities. A mountain slope will often display altitudinal belts or zones into which plants and animals have preferentially arranged themselves. One by one, species reach their upper limit and drop out. Those that do persist become progressively less productive. The environments become more compressed and life processes more deliberate. Organisms become more directly tied to the environment, less complicated, and more exposed to view. At the very highest levels there is only the cold, and snow, and glacial ice.

Mountains exist as microcosms, like islands amid surrounding lowland seas. They serve as refugia for the production and maintenance of original genetic material. They offer sanctuary for endangered species, provide unique habitats, and serve as natural laboratories for investigation, experimentation, and education.

Mountains occupy the far end of the continuum from cities and the works of man to the natural and the unchanged. Many mountains remain among the least altered of the earth's landscapes, while cities represent almost total modification. And even though most of us spend our lives in cities, it is not a complete existence. We are increasingly finding that there is something about the distant woods and rocky slopes that fills a primeval and mystic need. Mountains provide an opportunity to escape from one world to another, to commune with nature. They offer solitude and stand lonely among the last bastions of "wildness" on the earth. This quality, becoming ever more important as population pressures grow and human activities intensify, is also becoming increasingly difficult to maintain as more and more people utilize mountains. There is unlimited demand for limited resources. All cannot be accommodated. To make wilderness more available is, paradoxically, to make it less so. These are problems of resource management that must be dealt with if the attributes of this environment which we find attractive are to persist.

Mountains stand like barometers of change. They feel the effects of pollution or alteration more acutely than lowlands, and they are less resilient in their response, more fragile and susceptible to irreversible damage than lowlands. The harm done is not contained, however; damage to highlands invariably finds its way to lowlands. These effects are additive and compound the problems that sea-level regions already face.

This book is an investigation into the nature of mountain environments, their characteristic features and dominant processes, and their significance to man. It is a journey into the world of the inclined, the unstable, the harsh, the abrupt, the catastrophic, the awesome, the beautiful. It is a tribute to the existence of mountains and to the diversity and challenge that they present. It is an invitation to explore and to learn about the mountain milieu.

I told him his nerves were affected: Every mole-hill was a mountain.

Thomas Hutchinson,
Diary (1778)

What Is a Mountain?

During the 1930s it became fashionable among members of various alpine clubs in the United States to travel about, climbing the highest point in each of the 48 states. The highest of all was Mount Whitney in California, at 4,418 m (14,496 ft.), the lowest, Iron Mountain in Florida, at 100 m (330 ft.) (Sayward 1934). No one would doubt that Whitney is truly a mountain, but there is considerable question about Iron Mountain. Webster's dictionary defines a mountain as "any part of a land mass which projects conspicuously above its surroundings." By this definition Iron Mountain may be properly named, but most of us would judge this as euphemism. At the opposite extreme, there is the story about a British climber in the Himalayas who asked his Sherpa guide the names of several of the surrounding 3,500 m (11,500 ft.) peaks. The guide shrugged his shoulders, saying that they were just foothills with no name.

The difference between the two situations is one of conspicuousness. The lesser peaks were lost in the majesty of the high Himalayas, while even a small promontory on a plain may be a "mountain" to the local people. Thus, Iron Mountain in Florida or landforms of only slightly larger stature, such as the Watchung Mountains in New Jersey, are important local landmarks to which the name "mountain" apparently does not seem inappropriate even though they may not exceed 150 m (500 ft.) in elevation. Nevertheless, calling a feature a mountain does not make it one.

Roderick Peattie in his classic *Mountain Geography* (1936, p. 3) suggests several subjective criteria for defining mountains: mountains should be impressive; they should enter into the imagination of the people who live within their shadow; and they should have individuality. He cites Fujiyama and Mount Etna as examples. Both are snow-capped volcanic cones that dominate the surrounding landscapes, and both have been immortalized in art and literature. They produce very different responses in the minds of the people who live near them, however. Fujiyama is benign and sacred, a symbol of peace and strength. Etna, on the other hand, is a devil, continually sending out boiling lava and fire to destroy farms and villages.

> To a large extent, then, a mountain is a mountain because of the part it plays in popular imagination. It may be hardly more than a hill; but if it has distinct individuality, or plays a more or less symbolic role to the people, it is likely to be rated a mountain by those who live about its base. (Peattie 1936, p. 4)

Although many mountains meet these requirements, it is difficult to include such intangibles in a workable definition. A more objective basis for defining mountains is elevation. A landform must attain at least a certain altitude (e.g., 300 m) to qualify. While this is an important criterion, by itself it is still insufficient. The Great Plains of North America are over 1,500 m (5,000 ft.) high, and the Tibetan Plateau reaches an elevation of 5,000 m (16,500 ft.), but neither is classified as mountainous. In Bolivia, the Potosi railway line reaches an elevation of 4,800 m (15,750 ft.) near the station of El Condor, high enough to make your nose bleed, but it is situated in fairly level country with only occasional promontories exceeding 5,000 m (16,500 ft.) (Troll 1972a, p. 2). By contrast, western Spitsbergen, situated only a few hundred meters above sea level, has the appearance of a high mountain landscape with its glaciers, frost debris, and tundra vegetation.

An objective definition of mountainous terrain should include local relief, steepness of slope, and the amount of land in slope, in addition to elevation. *Local relief* is the elevational distance between the highest and lowest points in an area. Its application depends upon the context in which it is applied. Several early European geographers believed that for an area to be truly mountainous there should be at least 900 m (3,000 ft.) of local relief. If this standard is used, only the major ranges such as the Alps, Pyrenees, Caucasus, Himalayas, Andes, Rockies, Cascades, and Sierra Nevada qualify. Even the Appalachians would fail under this approach. On the other hand, American geographers working in the eastern and midwestern United States have thought that 300 m (1,000 ft.) of local relief is sufficient to qualify as mountainous. Various landform classifications have been proposed with specifications ranging between these figures (Hammond 1964).

Local relief by itself is, like elevation, an incomplete measure of mountains. A plateau may display spectacular relief when incised by deep valleys (e.g., the Grand Canyon). Such features are, essentially, inverted mountains, but we are accustomed to looking up at mountains, not down. (On the other hand, if one were at the bottom of the Grand Canyon looking up, the landscape might very well appear mountainous.) Still, the area of high local relief is of limited extent and is surrounded on either side by relatively flat-lying surfaces. An opposite but comparable landscape is that of the Basin and Range Province in the western

United States: most of the area is in plains, but occasional ridges protrude 1,500 m (5,000 ft.) above their surroundings. Such landscapes are problematic, since they do not fit nicely into the category of either plain or mountain.

Mountains are usually envisaged as being both elevated and dissected landscapes. The land surface is predominantly inclined and the slopes are steeper than those in lowlands. While this is true as a generalization, the actual amount of steeply dissected land may be rather limited. Much depends upon geological structure and landscape history (see pp. 168–69). In mountains such as the Alps or Himalayas, steep and serrated landforms are the dominant features; in other regions, these features may be more confined. The southern and middle Rocky Mountains display extensive broad and gentle summit uplands, and similar conditions exist in the Oregon Cascades. It is the young Pleistocene volcanoes sticking above the upland surface that give distinctiveness to the Cascades. The Sierra Nevada of California contains many strongly glaciated and spectacular features, but there are also large upland areas of only moderate relief. Yosemite Valley is carved into this undulating surface, and most of the impressive relief in this region derives from the occurrence of deep valleys rather than from the ruggedness of the upland topography. While the world of mountains is basically one of verticality, slope angles of 10° to 30° are characteristic; it is the intermittent cliffs, precipices, and ridges that give the impression of great steepness. Nevertheless, the horizontal distances between ridges and valleys, which establish the texture and framework for slope steepness, are just as fundamental to the delineation of mountains as are the vertical distances that establish the relief.

Mountains may be delimited by geologic criteria, in particular, faulted or folded strata, metamorphosed rocks, and granitic batholiths (Hunt 1958). Most of the major mountain chains have these features, and they are also important in identifying former mountains. Good examples are found along the south shore of Lake Superior in Michigan and throughout much of southeastern Canada, where all of these characteristics are present but erosion has long since removed the ancient peaks that once were mountains. Implicit in this definition is the idea that mountains are features of construction, that they are built and produced by some internal force. This is certainly true of the major ranges, but mountainous terrain may also result from destructive processes, i.e., erosion. For example, a strongly dissected plateau may take on a mountainous character although it contains none of the geologic characteristics listed above. Certain areas of the southwestern United States do in fact display such dissection. Curiously, these landscapes are often perceived very differently from those of constructional origin. They are viewed as ruins, pathetic features, rather than as initial expressions of grand nature. They evoke "the sentiment of melancholy" (Tuan 1964).

Another basis for defining mountains is by their climatic and vegetational characteristics. An essential difference between hills and mountains is that mountains have significantly different climates at successive levels (Thompson 1964). This climatic variation is usually reflected in the vegetation, giving mountains a vertical change in plant communities from bottom to top that hills lack. It is argued that 600 m (2,000 ft.) of local relief in most parts of the world suffices to bring about a distinct vegetation change. This is not always evident, because some plants (e.g., sagebrush—*Artemisia spp.*) have great altitudinal range and may cover entire mountains; however, even if the vegetation is homogeneous, there are climatic changes with altitude which are measurable (Thompson 1964). The major advantage of this approach is that it recognizes ecology as well as topography. Clearly, one of the most distinctive characteristics of mountains, in addition to high relief and steepness of slope, is great environmental contrast within a relatively short distance.

HIGH MOUNTAIN LANDSCAPES

German-speaking peoples differentiate between the *hochgebirge* (high mountains) and *mittelgebirge* (medium mountains). The Hartz Mountains and the Black Forest are *mittelgebirge*, while the Alps are the classic example of the *hochgebirge* (Troll 1972a, p. 2). French has the comparable terms *hautes montagnes* and *moyennes montagnes*; and in English we speak of the High Sierra or the High Cascades, as opposed to the Sierra or the Cascades. The coastal ranges are low mountains and the Rockies are high mountains, but what distinguishes high mountains from low? Elevation alone is not sufficient: compare the high plateaus of Tibet with the modest elevations of western Spitsbergen. High relief is not reliable, either: the California coastal ranges are on the whole probably more rugged than are most parts of the Rockies. Climate is the best determinant of where the alpine zone begins. For this reason, high mountain landscapes occur at different altitudes under different environmental conditions. In Java, the volcano Pangerango, which rises from sea level to 3,000 m (10,000 ft.) is covered with tropical rainforest to its summit. "It is a high mountain without a high mountain landscape" (Troll 1972a, p. 2).

The word *alpine* comes from the Alps and refers to a cold and windy zone above continuous forest, with rocky ridges and scattered tundra vegetation (Love 1970). The upper edge of the forest (the timberline) is generally lowest in the polar regions and rises in elevation toward the equator. This is not a simple, straightline relationship, however. The highest elevations at which trees grow occur at about 30° latitude in the arid zones of the Andes and Himalayas, rather than in the humid tropics (Troll 1973a, pp. 10–13). Timberline

also tends to rise from coastal areas toward the continental interiors. Thus, on Mount Washington in New Hampshire, the alpine zone begins at 1,500 m (5,000 ft.); in the Rockies of Wyoming it occurs at over 3,000 m (10,000 ft.); and in the Oregon Cascades it declines again to 1,800 m (6,000 ft.) (Daubenmire 1954, p. 121). Although the upper timberline is probably the major criterion for determining where the high mountain environment begins, it should not be the sole determinant. Since different tree species have different climatic requirements, contrasting abilities and potentials are involved in different regions (see p. 288). Geological or other natural factors may result in abnormally low timberlines. In addition, many timberlines have been greatly affected by human interference, especially through the agency of fire, so they are not easily compared (Hedberg 1972).

Accordingly, a geoecological approach has been suggested for determining the lower limit of high mountain environments. There are three main criteria: high mountains should rise above the Pleistocene snow line, the zone of rugged and serrated topography associated with mountain glaciers and frost action; high mountains should extend above the regional timberline; high mountains should display *cryonival* processes such as frost-heaving and solifluction (see pp. 190–91) (Troll 1972a, 1973b). Although each of these may exist at various altitudes, and one may be more important in some areas than in others, when considered together they provide a fairly good basis for delimiting high mountain environments (Fig. 1.1). "According to this concept, high mountains are mountains which reach such altitudes that they offer landforms, plant cover, soil processes, and landscape character which in the classical region of mountain geography in the Alps is generally perceived as high-alpine" (Troll 1972a, p. 4).

It is clear why opinions vary as to what a mountain is, let alone concerning the differ-

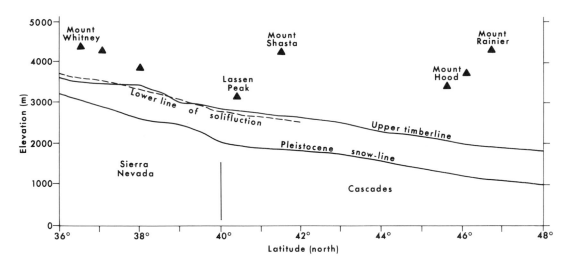

Fig. 1.1. Generalized location of altitudinal lines for delimiting high mountain environments on a north-south basis through the Cascades and Sierra Nevada. (From Höllermann 1973, p. A151)

ence between high and low mountains. Perhaps at our present state of knowledge it is best to leave considerable flexibility in the establishment of definitions. For our purposes, a mountain will be defined as an elevated landform of high local relief, e.g., 300 m (1,000 ft.), with much of its surface in steep slopes, usually displaying distinct variations in climate and associated biological phenomena from its base to its summit. A high mountain landscape is the area above the climatic timberline where glaciation, frost action, and mass-wasting are the dominant processes.

Attitudes Toward Mountains

Theology, philosophy, geology, astronomy—
basic and radical changes in all these occurred
before the "Mountain Gloom" gave way to
"Mountain Glory."

> Marjorie H. Nicolson,
> *Mountain Gloom and Mountain*
> *Glory* (1959)

Mountains today are almost universally viewed with admiration and affection. Positive attitudes toward mountains are relatively new, however. In the Western world, they date back only three or four centuries, although they have a much longer history in the Orient and Middle East. Man has been attracted by mountains for millennia; he has traveled through them, used different altitudinal environments on a seasonal basis for hunting and gathering and the grazing of his animals, and he has built permanent homes in them and tilled the soil. But throughout most of human history the predominant feeling toward mountains has been one of fear, suspicion, and awe. In order to understand our present love of mountains it is necessary to trace the development of these ideas through time and to place them in historical perspective.

THE PREHISTORIC ERA

Very little is known about primitive man's view of mountains. Much of the evidence is based on the study of primitive societies before major contact with Europeans. Many of these groups lived in regions of active volcanoes, and attitudes toward the fiery and destructive peaks were largely negative. The mountains were viewed as the homes of beneficent deities or of devils, and volcanic eruptions were interpreted as signs of the gods' displeasure with the people. Accordingly, various cultures established elaborate taboos, ceremonies, and sacrifices to appease the wrath of the gods. In non-volcanic areas, mountains were also viewed with awe. They towered above the plains and were remote and distant, a place where earth met sky, a place of communion with the heavens. Earthquakes often replaced volcanic eruptions as evidence of the violence and power of the gods who dwelled in the mountains and of their displeasure with mortals.

Primitive peoples often closely identified mountains with the weather. Mountains are the homes of storms, lightning, strong winds, cold, and clouds. The tops of mountains are frequently shrouded in clouds, hidden from view and mysterious. Mountains are also associated with snow, a phenomenon which may or may not occur in the lowlands; in any event, snow is much more persistent at high altitudes, and it transforms the mountain peak into an unearthly site (and sight), a natural abode of spirits and gods. The magnification of sounds and haunting vibrato of echoes in the mountains must have added an eerie sensation to an already frightening experience. Another observation doubtless made by early visitors to mountain peaks was of the reaction that took place within their bodies. Symptoms of high-altitude sickness such as stomachache, vomiting, dizziness, and shortness of breath must have been difficult for travelers to ascribe to natural causes. The explanation was obvious: they were transgressing on hallowed ground. While many of the features associated with mountains and weather evoked terror, mountains did also have positive attributes. For example, mountains were considered givers of life, since they were a source of water through rainfall and mountain streams.

Mountains were often considered the home of strange (sometimes mythical) and dangerous beasts. Some of these beasts were real enough, animals that lived in the dense mountain forests but occasionally wandered into the snow zone, for example, the snowy leopard and other large cats, bears, eagles, wolves, monkeys, and apes. Many were large predators that were elusive and seldom seen in the lowlands, made larger than life in legends and superstitions. Some of the legends, like that of the Yeti (Abominable Snowman) of the Himalayas and the Sasquatch (Bigfoot) in the mountains of western North America, have persisted to the present day.

We do not know just when human settlement of the mountains began. In the Alps and the mountains of the Middle East, archeological sites indicate the presence of humans since at least the Stone Age (100,000 years ago). These include the alpine components of the so-called Mousterian and Paleolithic cultures (Charlesworth 1957, p. 1035; DeSonnerville-Bordes 1963, p. 354; Young and Smith 1966; Schmid 1972). These mountain groups were composed primarily of transient hunting parties, but some also made permanent settlements. They lived in caves and manufactured stone hunting tools; later (about 40,000 years ago) they used tools of bone, ivory, and antlers. Eventually they began to paint on cave walls and to make a custom of burying their dead (often preserved by mummification in the dry alpine air). A steady cultural development continued in Eurasian mountains down through the Bronze and Iron Ages (Anati 1960), but our knowledge of them is so scanty that all we can say with confidence is that they chose to live in the mountains.

Man came to the New World by way of the Bering Strait 20,000 to 50,000 years ago. It is possible that Eurasian mountain cultures, accustomed to cold and harsh environmental conditions, helped lead this movement. Radiocarbon dating of bone, shells, and artifacts indicates human presence in the Rocky Mountains of Colorado by 10,000 to 11,000 years ago (Husted 1965, 1974; Benedict and Olson 1973, 1978). The alpine tundra zone was used primarily by summer hunting parties, who apparently employed a technique of driving game which resembled that used in the Arctic. The target of the game drives was probably mountain sheep. Since, unlike the caribou of the Arctic, it is next to impossible to corral mountain sheep, it is thought that the drives were designed to direct the sheep to concealed hunters (Husted 1974, p. 869). Permanent dwelling sites were established at mid-elevations, but these were occupied and abandoned many times over the centuries (Wedel et al. 1968, p. 184; Benedict 1975).

In North America it seems fairly clear that migration to and from the mountains depended on favorable climatic conditions and the availability of food. The major influx to the mountains coincided with the *altithermal*, a climatic period 5,000 to 9,000 years ago when warmer and drier conditions prevailed in the Great Plains and Great Basin (Fagan 1973; Husted 1974; Benedict 1975; Morris 1976; Benedict and Olson 1978). Similarly, during cooler, wetter periods with glacial advance in the mountains, general migration to the lowlands took place. In addition to these periodic migrations between the mountains and the plains based on major climatic incursions, there is also evidence that some groups (e.g., the Ute and Shoshoni) utilized the mountains and the plains on an annual cycle according to the resources available. In winter they hunted the plains for bison and antelope and in summer went to the mountains for deer and mountain sheep. Such a relatively full exploitation of environments foreshadows much more modern approaches to mountain land-use.

Mountains played an important role in the religion and imagination of American Indians (Bent 1913; Jackson 1930; Clark 1953). Many mountains have Indian names:

among the most famous are Denali (Mount McKinley) and Tacoma (Mount Rainier). The Blackfeet sang of "Going to the Sun Mountain," where the sun, a principal deity, made its home. The Zuni of New Mexico considered Mount Tsikomo to be the center of the universe and the most sacred of all places (Müller 1969, p. 194). The Nez Percé of the Pacific Northwest lived in the Wallowa Mountains adjacent to "Hell's Canyon" and the group of mountains immediately to the east in Idaho they called the "Seven Devils." The volcanic peaks in the Cascades inspired many legends (Clark 1953). Several deal with Tacoma, "the mountain that was God" (Williams 1911).

Only a few North American alpine archeological remains have religious significance. One possible candidate is located above timberline at an altitude of 2,940 m (9,640 ft.) in the Big Horn Mountains of northern Wyoming. It consists of a crude circle of stones 25 m (80 ft.) in diameter with a central cairn 4 m (13 ft.) across from which 28 spokes radiate to the rim (Eddy 1974) (Fig. 2.1). Early observers thought that the structure was a medicine wheel constructed as a replica of the Medicine Lodge to allow the observance of the Sun Dance ceremony in the mountains (Grinnell 1922, p. 299). However, Eddy (1974) believes it is a primitive astronomical observatory, but with some mystical and/or aesthetic connotations as well, since its astronomical purpose could just as easily have been served on the plains. Whatever the eventual verdict, it seems clear that this was an artifact constructed for a special purpose in what the Indians considered a special place.

Perhaps the most spectacular display the world has ever known of human settlement in mountains is found in the Andes of South America. Here, several thousand years before the birth of Christ, at elevations up to 4,500 m (15,000 ft.), there flourished civilizations that are still a wonder to the modern world. The culmination of these cultures is reflected in the ruins of Tiahuanaco and Machu Picchu (Fig. 2.2). Even today it is

Fig. 2.1. Stone medicine wheel located above timberline in the Big Horn Mountains, Wyoming. Exact age and purpose unknown. Thought by some to be built by Blackfeet as a replica of the Medicine Lodge to allow observance of the Sun Dance ceremony in the high mountains; others believe it to be a primitive astronomical observatory. (Western History Research Center, University of Wyoming)

Fig. 2.2. Machu Picchu, ancient Inca settlement and religious site at 2,300 m (7,500 ft.) amid precipitous terrain in the Peruvian Andes. Extensive terracing has increased the amount of usable land. Even the high peak on right displays terracing near the summit. This was used as a look-out; soldiers stationed there grew their own food. (Leonard Palmer, Portland State University)

difficult to imagine the logistics of habitation in this environment, let alone the techniques involved in the building of their famous stone structures (Heizer 1966).

In the Andes, early peoples preferred the highlands to the densely forested tropical lowlands or the coastal deserts (Mayer-Oakes 1963; MacNeish 1971). Although the Andeans were initially hunters and gatherers—food was reasonably plentiful at the higher elevations—the basis for the civilizations to come was agriculture. Several plant species, including potatoes, corn, squash, and beans, were first domesticated in the highlands of Central and South America (Sauer 1936; Linares et al. 1975). The production of food, which released man from the constant burden of hunting, allowed greater numbers of people to settle in a small area and, eventually, to evolve the highly organized and complex cultures of the Tiahuanaco and Inca.

What attitude did these people have toward the mountains that were their home? We know that among their many deities were the sun, the moon, stars, and mountains. Like the ziggurats of Near Eastern cultures, their stepped pyramids were essentially man-made mountains (Quaritch-Wales 1953). It was usually in these artificial mountains that the high priest lived and carried out sacrifices of foodstuffs, precious metals, llamas, and humans.

Mountains were frequently linked in legend with the origin of the tribe. The Panzaleo of highland Ecuador traced their descent from the volcano Tungurahua. Another tribe, the Puruha, believed that they were created by the union between two volcanoes, the feminine Tungurahua and the masculine Chimborazo (Trimborn 1969, p. 97). Many cultures have viewed mountains as phallic symbols or in other ways associated them with fertility. An Algonquin Indian legend from the northeastern United States provides a typical example: There was once an Indian girl gathering blueberries on Mount Ktaadn and, being lonely, she said,

"I would that I had a husband." Seeing the great mountain in all its glory rising on high, with red sunlight on the top, she added: "I wish Ktaadn were a man, and would marry me." Her wish came true, and she gave birth to a son who used his great supernatural powers to help his people (Bent 1913, p. 263). In addition to the phallus, mountains are often compared to the female breast: the name of the spectacular Grand Tetons of Wyoming comes from the French for "big breasts."

Most of the higher peaks of the Andes were considered to be the home of spirits. In a modern study of the cosmology of a remote village located east of Cuzco, Peru, at 4,265 m (14,000 ft.), a number of the surrounding peaks were found to have special religious significance. The villagers still made offerings of coca and foodstuffs every August to the gods of the mountains, as protection against disease and to insure good crops. According to local legend, the god of hail and lightning lives on the highest peak, Ausangate, at 6,400 m (21,000 ft.); if he is not given enough food he becomes angry and wraps the mountain in clouds, sending down lightning and hail to destroy the fields (Mishkin 1940, p. 237).

Although mountains had some religious connotations for many tribes, to other primitive peoples, mountains were simply a natural part of their world. Mountains demanded special attention primarily because of their size and dominance in the landscape. Early peoples must have felt an attraction and a curiosity about the distant peaks, but if they went there to live it was probably out of necessity, to search for food or escape from enemies. The attitude developed toward mountains must have depended in part upon the relationship with the land. Where conditions in mountains were harsh and unpredictable, people were likely to ascribe those same qualities to the spirits who dwelt there. Where the peaks were accessible, the weather mild, and food abundant, people were apt to see the mountain gods as benign. It is not surprising that belief in the holiness of mountain places should have been carried over into the written traditions of the West.

THE WESTERN TRADITION

The Biblical Period

Mountains were objects of veneration and symbols of strength and peace to the Hebrews of the Old Testament. God often chose a mountain as the place to meet with one of his prophets. David said, "I will lift up mine eyes unto the hills, from whence cometh my help" (Psalms 121:1). Every Bible-school child knows the story of Moses receiving the Ten Commandments on Mount Sinai (Exodus 19, 20, 24) and how Abraham took his only son, Isaac, to a mountain in the land of Moriah to sacrifice him to Jehovah (Genesis 22:2). David established his capital on Mount Zion, now one of the hills on which Jerusalem is located (Psalms 78:68–70). Lot and his family fled from Sodom and Gomorrah to the refuge of a mountain (Genesis 19:17, 19, 30). Noah and the ark came to rest on Mount Ararat as the flood subsided (Genesis 8:4). Many other mountains—e.g., Mount Carmel, Lebanon, Tabor, Calvary, Horeb, Pisgah, and the Mount of Olives—were considered sacred by the Israelites (Headley 1855). It is important to realize that many of these are no more than hills. Ancient Near Eastern religions referred to mountains as "the center of fertility, the primeval hillock of creation, the meeting place of the gods, the dwelling place of the high god, the meeting place of heaven and earth, the monument effectively upholding the order of creation, the place where god meets man, a place of theophany" (Clifford 1972, p. 5).

The New Testament places much less emphasis on mountains: they are mentioned in 509 verses in the Old Testament, but in only 64 in the New Testament (Strong 1894, pp. 696–97). Part of this disparity is due to the greater length of the Old Testament, but it is also a result of fundamental differences in philosophy. When Jesus retreats to the mountains, as he does many times, the New Testament states it simply as fact. The beauty, strength, and peace of the everlasting hills are no longer considered worthy of comment. Christ takes center stage, and his teachings dwell on the philosophy epitomized by Isaiah's prophecy: "Every valley shall be exalted, and every mountain and hill shall be made low" (Luke 3:5). Whether in nature or in society, what was high or proud or rich was suspect, and what was low or humble or poor was worthy. This is well expressed in the Beatitudes (Matthew 5:3–11). Marjorie Nicolson, in *Mountain Gloom and Mountain Glory* (1959, pp. 42–43), argues that this heritage partially accounts for the revulsion against mountains displayed in medieval Europe.

Classical Heritage

Greeks

The contributions of classical antiquity to later Western attitudes toward mountains are hard to define. Although Greece is a mountainous country, its art and literature rarely refer to mountains. Victorian art critic and essayist John Ruskin pointed out that the Greeks "did not seem as artists to know that such things were in the world. They carved, or variously represented, men, and horses, and beasts, and birds, and all kinds of living creatures, — yes, even down to cuttle-fish; and trees, in a sort of way; but not so much as the outline of a mountain" (1856, vol. 4, ch. 11, sec. 3). Homer's *Iliad* mentions mountains chiefly in contexts that evoke their wildness and isolation. They are the haunts of nymphs, wild beasts, and centaurs; the only men to frequent the lonely slopes are hunters and woodcutters. Homer is very much aware of mountain weather and describes its force vividly:

In spring, snow-water torrents risen and flowing down the mountainsides hurl at a confluence their mighty waters out of gorges, filled by tributaries, and far away upon the hills a shepherd hears the roar. As south wind and the southeast wind, contending in mountain groves, make all the forest thrash . . . swaying their pointed boughs toward one another in roaring wind, and snapping branches crack. (*Iliad*, Book 16)

The mountain that figures most prominently in Greek mythology and literature is, of course, Mount Olympus in Thessaly, the home of the gods. *Olympus*, a word that predated the Greeks, apparently meant "peak" or "mountain" in a generic sense, for there are a number of other Greek mountains named Olympus. Several of these, like Olympus in Thessaly, were associated with weather cults. Olympus is often mentioned as the home of Zeus in his role as the god of storms and weather. By his ability to strike with lightning and thunder, Zeus controls both gods and men from the mountaintop (Nilsson 1972, pp. 220–51).

The Greeks of course recognized the wild, rugged, and untamed nature of mountain scenery, but they preferred the more harmonious aspects of nature. They were engrossed with man and his works. Socrates, for example, was totally absorbed by the perplexities of the city. He is quoted as answering the reproach of his friend Phaedrus, who complained that he never left the city, by saying "he was fond of knowledge and could learn nothing from the trees and the country, but only from the people in the city" (in Hyde 1915, p. 71). The human form was considered the highest level of beauty, and even their gods appeared in human form. What was good in nature was that which provided comfort and harmony for man. Beauty was symmetry and order. Ruskin, in his interpretation of Greek art and literature, says, "Thus, as far as I recollect without a single exception, every Homeric landscape, intended to be beautiful, is composed of a fountain, a meadow, and a shady grove" (1856, vol. 4, ch. 13, sec. 15).

By the fourth century B.C., from the time of Homer onward, the Greeks began to take an active interest in mountains. They settled the valleys and slopes; they appreciated the mountain springs and cool forests; they built watchtowers and signaling stations on promontories; they cut mountain timber to build their ships (A.C. Merriam 1980). The observations of mountain weather in the *Iliad* prefigure the scientific curiosity of later Greeks about the origins of mountains and the causes of phenomena associated with them. Herodotus, for example, commented on the work of rivers and their ability to erode and deposit. To him is attributed the saying, "Egypt is the gift of the river." Having discovered fossil marine shells in the mountains, he speculated that the peaks had at one time been under water. He also thought it likely that earthquakes—rather than the wrath of the gods—were responsible for breaking apart the earth and uplifting mountains. Aristotle observed the unequal distribution of mountains, the significance of springs flowing from mountainsides, and the changes in climate that occurred with altitude. He believed that earthquakes and volcanoes were closely related and that they were involved in the formation of mountains. One of Aristotle's students, Theophrastus, investigated mountain plants and another, Dicaearchus, attempted to calculate the heights of mountains. In his famous geography, Strabo described mountains of the ancient world (Tozer 1935).

Romans

Italy, like Greece, is a mountainous country: the Apennines run its entire length and the Alps form its northern border. Although some Romans—notably, the philosopher Seneca and the encyclopedist Pliny—made important observations concerning mountains, on the whole the Romans did not share the Greeks' appreciation of mountains, except perhaps as distant vistas to be seen from the porches of their villas. Among the Latin poets, only Lucretius discerned a sublime beauty in the Alps (Geikie 1912, p. 287; Nicolson 1959, p. 40). These practical people viewed mountains primarily as wastelands and as obstacles to commerce and conquest. The Romans were regularly crossing the Alps by Caesar's time, but apparently never overcame their initial dread of them. To appease the deities of the Alpine passes and to commemorate safe journeys, they made offerings of coins and small bronze tablets inscribed with the names of the deity and the traveler. The hospice museum at the Great St. Bernard Pass has gathered a large collection of these offerings from the surrounding pass area.

The prevailing Roman attitude toward mountains was aptly expressed by Silius Italicus in his description of Hannibal's famous crossing of the Alps in 218 B.C.:

As the soldiers drew near to the mountains the recollection of their previous toils was forgotten in face of the far more serious trials that now confronted them. Here everything is wrapped in eternal frost, white with snow, and held in the grip of primeval ice. The mountain steeps are so stiff with cold that although they tower up into the sky, the warmth of the sunshine cannot soften their hardened rime. Deep as the Tartarean abyss of the underworld lies beneath the ground, even so far does the earth here mount into the air, shutting out with its shade the light of heaven. No Spring comes to this region, nor the charms of Summer. Misshapen Winter dwells alone on these dread crests, and guards them as her perpetual abode. Thither from all sides she gathers the sombre mists and the thunder-clouds mingled with hail. Here, too, in this Alpine home, have the winds and the tempests fixed their furious dominion. Men grow dizzy amidst the lofty crags, and the mountains disappear in the Clouds. Were Athos piled on Taurus, Rhodope on Mimas, Ossa on Pelion, and Othrys on Haemus, they would all yield to the Alps. (*Punica* III:479–95, in Geikie 1912, p. 293)

Literally thousands of pages have been written concerning Hannibal's crossing, many of which debate the question of his exact route. DeBeer (1946, p. 405) mused:

I often wonder whether Polybius and Livy realized what a blessing they conferred on humanity by couching their accounts of Hannibal's passage of the Alps on a level of precision insufficient to make the tracing of his route obvious, but just enough to encourage their readers to think that there is sufficient internal evidence to give them a sporting chance of solving the puzzle of where he went.

The titles of works published by Freshfield are typical: "The Pass of Hannibal" (1883) and "Further Notes on the Pass of Hannibal" (1886) (both in the *Alpine Journal*), and his book *Hannibal Once More* (1914). DeBeer could not resist the temptation himself: he produced *Alps and Elephants: Hannibal's March* (1955), which, as might be expected, immediately spawned more controversy (McDonald 1956).

The Roman opinion of mountains remained almost consistently negative. They apparently never acquired a taste for alpine scenery, as did the Greeks. The implicit dualism in the attitudes of these two peoples toward mountains, in some ways reminiscent of that between the Old and New Testaments, became the legacy for Western Europe (Nicolson 1959, p. 42). Ultimately, as we know, the nobler spirit of the Greeks, who worshipped their gods on Mount Olympus, and the Children of Israel, who lifted up their eyes to the everlasting hills, would triumph, but not before several centuries of antipathy toward mountains had elapsed.

From Medieval Fears to Romantic Enthusiasm

During the Middle Ages superstition held sway, and mountains were considered no better than grotesque wastelands. Medieval people, like their Roman predecessors, paid little attention to the grander aspects of nature, and there are few favorable references to mountains in either their literature or their graphic art. What does exist is often grossly distorted by allegory, abstraction, and moralization. In paintings of the period, mountains are usually shown emblematically or symbolically as dark, twisted mounds rising out of the plains (Rees 1975a, p. 306). Dante made mountains the guardians of hell (although some have argued that this was allegory and Dante was, in fact, one of the earlier admirers of mountains) (Freshfield 1881; Noyce 1950, pp. 23–33).

Medieval travelers disliked mountains, but nevertheless traversed them regularly. To ease the journey, Alpine villages provided inns and supplied guides; churches and hospices were constructed along the most popular routes. Pilgrims on their way to Rome from western and northern Europe favored the Great St. Bernard Pass, where a monastery has stood since 812 A.D., and a hospice since 859 (Coolidge 1889, p. 3). Although August was considered the best month for mountain travel, the passes were attempted at all seasons (Tyler 1930, p. 27). Master John de Bremble, a monk of Christ Church, Canterbury, England, who had been sent to Rome on business, sent a letter home describing his passage of the Great St. Bernard in February 1188:

Pardon me for not writing. I have been on the Mount of Jove [the Roman name for the Great St. Bernard Pass]; on the one hand looking up to the heavens of the mountains, on the other shuddering at the hell of the valleys, feeling myself so much nearer heaven that I was more sure that my prayer would be heard. "Lord," I said, "restore me to my brethren, that I may tell them, that they come not into this place of torment." Place of torment, indeed, where the marble pavement of the stony ground is ice alone, and you cannot set your foot safely; where, strange to say, although it is so slippery that you cannot stand, the death (into which there is every facility for a fall) is certain death. I put my hand in scrip, that I might scratch out a syllable or two to your sincerity — lo, I found my ink-bottle filled with a dry mass of ice; my fingers too refused to write; my beard was stiff with frost, and my breath congealed into a long icicle. I could not write the news I wished. (In Coolidge 1889, pp. 8–9)

Tales of monsters and supernatural perils added to the fears of travelers and mountain dwellers. King Peter III of Aragon (born 1236) set out to prove it was possible to climb Pic Canigou—2,785 m (9,135 ft.)—then believed to be the highest peak in the Pyrenees. Resting by a small lake near the summit, he absently threw a stone into the water. Suddenly "a horrible dragon of enormous size came out of it, and began to fly about in the air, and to darken the air with its breath." The full account may be found in Gribble's *The Early Mountaineers* (1899, pp. 16–17). Gribble concludes: "For many centuries after Peter's death, men of enlightenment believed in dragons as firmly as they believed in God; while men of less enlightenment, but equal integrity, swore affidavits before magistrates to the effect that they had encountered dragons in the mountains."

Perhaps the most famous legend is that of Mount Pilatus, 2,129 m (6,985 ft.) in the Swiss Alps. As the story goes, Caesar was angry with Pilate for crucifying Jesus, so he had Pilate brought to Rome to be put to death. His body was tied to a stone and dropped into the Tiber River, where it caused a great turmoil. The body was therefore retrieved, and was eventually placed in a small lake on Mount Pilatus, in the Swiss territory of Lucerne. From that time on, if anybody shouted or threw a stone into the lake, Pilate would avenge himself by stirring up a great tempest. He also rose from the water on each Good Friday and sat on a nearby rock; if anybody saw him, that person would surely die. So great was their fear of the tempests he might cause that the government of Lucerne forbade anybody to approach the lake; in 1387 six men who broke this regulation were actually imprisoned (Coolidge 1889, pp. 11–12; Gribble 1899, pp. 43–50). The natural history museum of Lucerne possesses a "dragon stone" (supposedly dropped by a passing dragon) that has been preserved since the dark ages (DeBeer 1930, p. 97).

An excellent collection of these beliefs is

contained in Johann Jacob Scheuchzer's *Itinera per Helvetia Alpina regiones*, published in 1723. Scheuchzer, a professor at the University of Zurich, was a highly respected botanist who was credited with being the first to attempt to formulate a theory of glacier formation and movement (Gribble 1899, p. 69). He had a penchant for the extraordinary, however, and firmly believed that dragons lived in mountains. His book is a mixture of the real and unreal, containing many accounts of sightings of these creatures, with several illustrations of the various dragon forms (Fig. 2.3). A sampling of these may be found in Gribble (1899, pp. 70–81) and in DeBeer (1930, pp. 76–97).

Belief in dragons had almost died out before the time of Scheuchzer, however. In 1518 four scholars climbed Mount Pilatus and visited the lake with no ill effects, and in 1555 Conrad Gesner, a professor of medicine at the University of Zurich, climbed the mountain, by special permission of the Lucerne magistrates, to prove that there was nothing to fear. Only thirty years later, a group of villagers, led by the pastor of Lucerne, climbed to the lake, threw stones, and defiantly mocked the spirit of Pilate, chanting *"Pilat, wirf aus dein kath!"* (Pilate, cast out your crud!) (Gribble 1899, pp. 46–50).

It is probably fair to say that most medieval people who had any acquaintance with mountains feared them, or, at the very least, would have considered it a waste of time to climb to the top of one, but there were exceptions. In 1336 the poet Petrarch, inspired by the Roman historian Livy's mention of a king of Thrace who had climbed a mountain overlooking the Adriatic and Black Seas just for the view, climbed Mont Ventoux in Provence simply "for the sake of seeing the remarkable altitude of the place" (Gribble 1899, pp. 18–19). Petrarch's climb is often cited as the first evidence of Renaissance appreciation of natural beauty, but much of his account has so allegorical a cast that some scholars have suspected he never made the climb at all (Noyce 1950, p. 45).

Fig. 2.3. A winged dragon in the mountains, as depicted in a book published in Switzerland in 1723. The belief that such creatures lived in mountains was apparently very common during the Middle Ages. (From DeBeer 1930, p. 90)

Much more clearcut evidence of a new interest in natural beauty and natural phenomena is Leonardo da Vinci's observations of mountains, both in his art and in his scientific notebooks, at the end of the fifteenth century.

The person usually credited as being the first to appreciate and love mountains for their own sake is the sixteenth-century Swiss naturalist Conrad Gesner. In a letter to a friend in 1541, Gesner wrote:

I am resolved henceforth, most learned Avienus, that as long as it may please God to grant me life, I will ascend several mountains, or at least one, every year, at the season when the flowers are in their glory, partly for the sake of examining them, and partly for the sake of good bodily exercise and of mental delight. For how great a pleasure, think you, is it, how great delight for a man touched as he ought to be, to wonder at the mass of the mountains as one gazes on their vastness, and to lift up one's head as it were amongst the clouds? The understanding is deeply moved, I know not wherefore, by their amazing height, and is driven to think of the Great Architect who made them. (In Coolidge 1889, pp. 12–13)

He not only carried out this resolve, but took other Renaissance naturalists along on his Alpine excursions, awakening their interest in mountain plants and opening their eyes to the glories of the mountains. His student and successor at the University of Zurich, Josias Simler, published a learned treatise in 1574 on snow and ice travel; in it, he discussed such things as crampons, alpine sticks, use of eye shades, and how to cross crevasses (Gribble 1899, pp. 62–68).

The hold of theology on science and philosophy was very strong throughout the Middle Ages, and the general repugnance felt toward mountains by most people was reinforced by religious sanctions. Many medieval and early modern theologians regarded the presence of mountains as evidence of the world's having fallen from grace. An influential post-medieval spokesman for this idea was Thomas Burnet, who asserted in his book, *The Sacred Theory of the Earth* (1684), that the earth was originally a perfectly smooth sphere, the "Mundane Egg"; as punishment for man's sins, the surface was ruptured and the interior fluids boiled out as "vast and undigested heaps of stones and earth." Others proposed a cataclysmic origin for mountains—e.g., the Biblical flood (Nicolson 1959, p. 78).

By the end of the seventeenth century, on the verge of the Enlightenment, publications began to appear which supported the idea of a purposefully designed earth and the usefulness of mountains. Mountains were recognized as being valuable for wildlife preserves, as sources of minerals, and as a means of converting salt water to fresh (Rees

1975a, p. 307). But mountains were still not generally appreciated for their beauty. The wild disarray of mountains and their utter lack of symmetry and proportion were difficult for the early modern mind to accept. Mountains represented confusion, and were quite unlike the order and uniformity these thinkers sought in the natural world. Their ideals were the classical ones of order, reason, and restraint. Yet, appalled as they were at these "warts, wens, blisters, and imposthumes" on the fair face of the earth, they were also profoundly impressed by the vastness and enormity of mountains. This is well expressed in Burnet's *The Sacred Theory of the Earth*:

The greatest objects of nature are, methinks, the most pleasing to behold; . . . there is nothing that I look upon with more pleasure than the wide sea and the mountains of earth. There is something august and stately in the air to these things, that inspires the mind with great thoughts and passions; we do naturally, upon such occasions, think of God and his greatness: And whatsoever hath but the shadow and appearance of the infinite, as all things have that are too big for our comprehension, they fill and overbear the mind with their excess and cast it into a pleasing kind of stupor and admiration.

Still, . . . although we justly admire its greatness, we cannot at all admire its beauty or elegancy for 'tis as deformed and irregular as it is great. (In Nicolson 1959, pp. 214–15)

The feelings of "delightful horror" and "terrible joy" expressed by Burnet and his contemporaries are the first signs of the romantic enthusiasm that has typified European attitudes toward mountains ever since the eighteenth century. In 1732 Albrecht Haller published *Die Alpen*, a book of poems in praise of the Alps and their inhabitants which became something of a best-seller in Europe. The journals and letters of another poet, Thomas Gray, describing his tour of the Alps in 1739, evoked a similar response in England. The most influential writer of all was Jean-Jacques Rousseau (Hyde 1917, p. 117; Noyce 1950, pp. 47–55). In his *La*

Nouvelle Héloise, published in 1759, he enthuses:

The nearer I came to Switzerland, the more were my feelings moved. The moment when from the heights of Jura I descried the Lake of Geneva was a moment of ecstasy and rapture. The sight of my country, that so-beloved country, where torrents of pleasure had overwhelmed my heart, the wholesome, pure air of the Alps; the soft air of home, sweeter than the perfumes of the East; this rich and fertile soil; this unrivaled landscape, the most beautiful that human eye has ever seen; this charming spot of which I had never beheld the like in my journey; the sight of a happy and free people; the softness of the season; the gentleness of the climate; a thousand delicious memories that recalled all the emotions I had felt, — all these things threw me into transports that I cannot describe. (In Perry 1879, p. 305)

Rousseau's writings had an almost revolutionary impact. Although the love of nature was not new, Rousseau's expression of it, particularly with respect to mountains, greatly increased popular appreciation of Switzerland as a place of beauty. Among those who came under Rousseau's spell were the famous German philosopher and poet, Goethe, and the English poet Wordsworth, who was perhaps the greatest interpreter of nature in all literature. Rousseau also influenced Horace Benedict de Saussure, the first great Swiss alpinist and scientist, who attempted to climb Mont Blanc four times between 1760 to 1787, before succeeding in 1787. (He knew so little about mountain climbing that on his first attempt he brought along a sunshade and smelling salts!) De Saussure initiated a great boom in scientific interest in mountains; in the following half-century, for scientific purposes Swiss alpinists ascended many other mountains never before climbed (Noyce 1950, pp. 57–67). By the middle of the nineteenth century, however, the scientific focus gave way to the English sense of sport. When Hudson, Hadlow, and Lord Douglas lost their lives on the Matterhorn in 1865, the disaster seemed

to serve as a challenge rather than a deterrent, and in the years that followed, English climbers and tourists swarmed into the remote regions of the Alps (Peattie 1936, p. 5). The modern period of mountain adoration had begun.

THE FAR EAST

The development of attitudes toward mountains in the Far East contrasts greatly with that of the West. Attitudes in both civilizations changed from initial feelings of awe and aversion to admiration and love (Tuan 1974, p. 71), but in the Far East, the appreciation of mountains began very early. In Japan, China, Tibet, and India, mountains have long been adored and worshipped. Mountains were considered sacred in China at least 2,000 years before the birth of Christ (DeSilva 1967, p. 40; Sullivan 1962, p. 1). Buddhism, Taoism, Confucianism, Shintoism, and Hinduism all incorporated mountain worship into their beliefs.

The impact of mountains on early Chinese culture was profound. The mountain was considered to be the body of God, the rocks his bones, the water his blood, the vegetation his hair, and the clouds and mists his breath (Sullivan 1962, p. 1). This belief probably sprang from the ancient cult of the earth and, although largely replaced by other concepts since, it remains basic to Chinese philosophy. Man is viewed as an integral part of nature. Inanimate objects have spirits and souls, just as do animate objects: it is from this point of view that mountains, being so dominant in the landscape, have come to be seen as sacred.

At first there were five sacred mountains in China: the central, western, northern, southern, and eastern or T'ai Shan, which is the most holy and famous (Chavannes 1910). These mountains are usually associated with Taoist and Confucian thought, but were worshipped as far back as the Hsia Dynasty (2205–1176 B.C.) (Sowerby 1940, p.

154). There are also four mountains of special significance to Buddhism, of which Omei Shan in Szechuan Province is the most famous (Shields 1913; Mullikin and Hotchkis 1973). Omei Shan alone is reputed to have over 50 pagodas and temples.

Many other mountains have local religious significance. One such peak is Dragon Mountain near the ancient city of Anking, celebrated in this poem:

> There is a dragon mountain in Hsu
> With a spring which waters the fields
> On the mountain is the spring
> And upon the hillsides are tilled fields
> From the earliest ages the men of Hsu have
> received this help,
> In time of trouble all heads are turned toward
> the mountain.
> High above the hills float the clouds,
> And within them is a spirit who changes their
> shapes continually.
> The people wondered who the spirit was
> Until they found that it was the Lung Wang.
> Hence they rebuilt the temple,
> So that sacrifices might be made for a thousand
> years.
> These sacrifices are still continued
> And the people reap the reward.
> (Shryock 1931, p. 118)

The mountain as a source of water is a religious motif found in many cultures: it was central to the Israelites of the Old Testament and to the Babylonians, as well as throughout the Orient and Indonesia (Quaritch-Wales 1953; Van Buren 1943). Clouds have a special fascination for the Chinese, and appear in their earliest art. Mountains are frequently shown rising out of clouds or enshrouded by them, not as a symbol of gloom or dreariness, but of beauty (Fig. 2.4). Sometimes clouds are shown as dragons: the two are associated as

humid elements. To the Oriental mind, dragons—their menacing appearance aside—do not generally have an evil connotation as they do to the Westerner; they are benevolent creatures controlling the elements (Sowerby 1940, p. 154).

Perhaps it is only natural, given Oriental sentiments toward mountains, that mountains should occupy a dominant position in their art. The very word for landscape in Chinese is *Shan Shui*, literally, "mountains and water." Painting is considered a branch of calligraphy; the Chinese character for mountain (山) is a pictorial representation of a mountain (DeSilva 1967, p. 40). The mountain motif appears on the earliest known Chinese pottery and stone carvings, and in landscape paintings from the Han Dynasty (206 b.c.–220 a.d.) onward (DeSilva 1967, pp. 53–74).

The Japanese also view mountains as symbols of strength and of the eternal. The use of stones to represent mountains is an ancient art form practiced in both Chinese and Japanese gardens. The culmination of this is what the Japanese call *Ishiyama*: a natural stone about 15 cm (6 in.) high is placed vertically on a small wooden base. This simple piece of nature sculpture, a mountain landscape in miniature, is kept inside the house on a shelf or table, and often has great value and meaning to its owner. Japan has several holy mountains, of which Fujiyama is by far the most famous; it is still climbed annually by thousands as a sacred pilgrimage (over 25,000 per day climb the mountain during the summer). When a commercial proposal was made for constructing a funicular railway to the summit, the Japanese angrily rejected the idea as a desecration of the holy mountain (Fickeler 1962, p. 110).

The people of Cambodia, Thailand, Bali, Java, and the Philippines also practice mountain worship (Quaritch-Wales 1953). Mount Popa in Burma has been considered sacred for over 2,000 years (Aung 1962, pp. 61–81). Mountains also have a special significance in India. Although India is basi-

---

Fig. 2.4. Cloud-enshrouded mountains in fourteenth-century Chinese landscape painting, "Poetic Conception of Evening Clouds" by Ma Wan (Ming Dynasty). (Shanghai Museum)

cally a plains country, the Himalayas extend for 2,500 km (1,500 mi.) along its northern border. These mountains have many religious and mythological associations. They are the source of the three great holy rivers, the Indus, Brahmaputra, and Ganges. The source of the Ganges is considered especially holy and is visited by many as a sacred pilgrimage. The Himalayas are the home of several Hindu gods, the most important of whom is Siva, the great god of the mountains, who resides on Mount Kailas. Siva's wife, Parvat, is the daughter of the Himalayas (Basak 1953, p. 114). Another Himalayan peak, Mount Meru, is considered the center of the universe. The Vindhya and Kaimur ranges to the south also play a part in Hindu religion (Crooke 1896).

In Tibet, as well as in the smaller Himalayan principalities of Kashmir, Nepal, Sikkim, and Bhutan, mountains have been natural shrines since very ancient times, even before the advent of Buddhism and Hinduism (Nebesky-Wojkowitz 1956). Cultural influences from both China and India are now evident but the inhabitants have retained many of their indigenous beliefs. Thus, it is common for persons to make such pious gestures as tying strips of cloth on bushes, or placing stones or pieces of wood in sacred heaps at a vista they have reached after a steep climb along a mountain trail (Shaw 1872) (Fig. 2.5). Circumambulation of mountains is also widely practiced by Buddhists, particularly in Tibet. The two most famous Tibetan mountains are Am-

Fig. 2.5. Monastery at Thyangboche in the Nepal Himalayas at 3,873 m (12,715 ft.). Note the carved motif stones placed along the roadside as a pious gesture. (Pradyumna P. Karan, University of Kentucky)

nye-rMachen (translated as "Hail Ancient One," "Great Peacock") and Tisegangs (Mount Kailas). Tisegangs, also sacred to the Hindus, is a pyramidal peak of singular beauty and a favorite for circumambulation. The trip over the rocky trail around the mountain takes two days; many people also use a higher trail that is quite treacherous and upon which accidents are common (Ekvall 1964, p. 242).

Many of the higher peaks are still considered sacred by the people of the Himalayas. With the onslaught of modern mountain climbers, governments have had to restrict activities in certain areas. In Nepal, for example, Machapuchare and Kangchenjunga are both off-limits for religious reasons (Siiger 1952). Airplane flights are also prohibited over these peaks. This prohibition has been eased somewhat with familiarity and with the advent of high-altitude jets, but when aviation first began, a planned flight over Mount Everest (the sacred Chomolungma) in 1934 by two English airplanes raised quite a stir in India and Tibet (Fickeler 1962, p. 110). Transcending the pure worship of ancient times is the zest for life in the mountains. This is exemplified by the Sherpa dance ceremony "Mani-Rimdu," a three-day festival held during full moon in the spring. This ceremony has religious aspects, but it is primarily a vehicle for exhilaration and glorification of the way of life of a very proud people in the highest mountains in the world (Jerstad 1969).

THE MODERN PERIOD

The beginnings of the modern period —romantic adoration of mountains— can be found in the writings of Albrecht von Haller, Thomas Gray, Jean-Jacques Rousseau, and Horace Benedict de Saussure. By the nineteenth century, the beauty of mountains was a common theme for poets and philosophers; scientists began to take a serious interest in the origins of mountains and alpine phenomena and popular accounts of scientific findings were published in newspapers and periodicals; and mountains became a favorite of landscape painters (Ruskin 1856; Lunn 1912; Rees 1975a, 1975b). By 1856 railways provided relatively easy access to the Alps. Tourist resorts sprang up, and sanitariums were built to accommodate sufferers from consumption (tuberculosis), since the dry clean air of the mountains was found to have excellent therapeutic results (*Alpine Journal* 1871). The popular image of mountains was no longer that of a cold, inhospitable land of horrors, but that of an attractive, healthy environment.

In 1857 the British Alpine Club was formed, and shortly thereafter other mountaineering clubs were established on the Continent. It was the British, however, who inundated the Alps during the ensuing decades. An article on the history of the British Alpine Club states: "It is impossible to dwell in detail on this wonderful period, and a mere enumeration of its first ascents and first passages would be intolerably tedious. At the end of it hardly any of the greater summits of the Alps remained unconquered, and of the new ascents made, a very large share had fallen to the British climbers" (Mumm 1921, p. 8). The Matterhorn tragedy of 1865 gave the Alpine Club, and the world, pause for thought, but after a few years other younger members took up the challenge of unconquered peaks with renewed zeal.

Alpine clubs gradually spread around the world (the first in the United States, the Appalachian Mountain Club, was formed in 1876), and many of these were quite exclusive: one had to be invited to join, and the requirements for admission were not easily met. Mountaineering became a consuming passion, almost a religion. Peattie (1936, p. 6) called the development a "cult of mountains," a modern, more conscious phase of the ancient worship of mountains. An article entitled "Mountaineering as a Religion" was typical of this extreme point of view:

[W]e must seek for some homogeneous and inward spiritual characteristics marking us off as a caste apart from other men. For myself, I find these characteristics in a certain mental predisposition, a distinct individual and moral bent, common to all mountaineers, but rarely found in those who are not addicted to mountain climbing. The true mountaineer is not a mere gymnast, but a man who worships the mountains. (Strutfield 1918, p. 242)

A comparatively recent article, "The Love of Mountains," puts the sentiment more moderately:

Primitive peoples who live among great mountains worship them through awe and fear, conceiving them to be gods and goddesses, or at least their dwelling-places. Modern civilised mountain-loving men, too, have often spoken of worshipping them: and true worship does, in fact, consist of that mingled love and awe which such men feel in their presence. Great snow-mountains by reason of their purity, seem especially worthy to be regarded as objects of worship. . . . The trouble about mountains, for us mountain-lovers, is that when we see them in their glory we are apt to throw reason to the winds, and to be possessed by a sort of frenzy. Mountain-worship cannot, in the long run, be a satisfactory religion. But, for some of us, "the unreasoned, uncovetous, unworldly love of them" can, I think, be a stepping-stone, as it were, toward a truer worship. (Vandeleur 1952, p. 509)

The cult of mountains had many prophets and a large following. The journals published by the various alpine clubs are full of articles praising mountains (e.g., Freshfield 1904; Fay 1905; Godley 1925; Lunn 1939, 1950; Young 1943; Howard 1949; Thorington 1957). Perhaps the most far-reaching claim of any zealot is that advanced by Geoffrey W. Young, a respected and long-time member of the British Alpine Club, at a lecture before the University of Glasgow in 1956—that mountains have been influential in the development of human intelligence:

It is a bold claim to make for mountains, that they contributed a third dimension, of height and depth, to man's intelligence; and, by means of it, adumbrated even a fourth dimension, that of spirit, not permeating it but placed above it. And yet, when mind first grew capable of comparison, when man's mastery began to move upon the earth, and he was released from labour only and from a surrounding darkness of fear, a mountain peak first sighted upon the skyline must indeed have seemed to belong to some sphere "visited all night by troops of stars." Just as the first flash of sunrise upon a snow summit, for the first time realised, must have revealed the golden throne of a god. (Young 1957, pp. 14–15)

Further, in discussing the various components of landscape, he argued:

In all this visual balance, and in the influence it has exercised, the mountains play, and have played, the principal part. It is the heights which have given the measure. They are set like upright rulers, to mark the scale, against the perspectives of plain and sea and sky. In their constant contemplation, illuminated by a lighting definite and brilliant, upon colour and shadow positive and luminous, primitive mind had no alternative but to acquire, as part of its growth, laws of measure, of order, of proportion, in thought no less than in vision. From the acquired ability to compare, to discriminate, reasoning, speculation, with measure and proportion, dawning upon the human mind in the genius of the first Greek philosophers and in the sculpture and building of the first Greek artists, began or hastened the beginnings of civilisation and culture in every western race. (Young 1957, pp. 24–25)

These are very strong statements, and they are perhaps too deterministic for most of us to accept. After all, trees and rocks also have a third dimension and provide perspective; mountains simply provide a greater impression of dimension. Moreover, the physical environment is only one of several factors (and probably not the most important) in a child's—or a society's—development (Keenlyside 1957).

Some of the alpine clubs became very powerful financially, socially, and politically. The British Alpine Club has supported a large number of projects, from polar exploration to the search for the Abominable

Snowman. Its members have traditionally been among the elite in British society. Hillary and Hunt, after climbing Mount Everest, were knighted by the Queen. Most of these clubs have diversified now, but they are still powerful. A good example in the United States is the Sierra Club, which has a membership of over 144,000. It employs five full-time lobbyists in Washington, D.C., and has considerable political clout. Its most impressive achievement has been (with the assistance of several other groups) to cause the construction of the Alaskan pipeline to be delayed for almost three years, until sufficient safeguards were taken for protection of the environment.

Mountains are no longer the private preserve of elitist clubs or of special-interest groups, but a "cult of mountains" continues. This has been beautifully expressed by René Dubos:

Man has now succeeded in humanizing most of the earth's surface but paradoxically, he is developing simultaneously a cult for wilderness. After having been for so long frightened by the primeval forest, he has come to realize that its eerie light evokes in him a mood of wonder that cannot be experienced in an orchard or a garden. Likewise, he recognizes in the vastness of the ocean and in the endless ebb and flow of its waves a mystic quality not found in humanized environments. His response to the thunderous silence of deep canyons, the solitude of high mountains, the luminosity of the deserts is the expression of an aspect of his fundamental being that is still in resonance with cosmic events. (Dubos 1973, p. 772)

As the world becomes increasingly populated and urbanized and the need to escape the pressures of the city grows, mountains become more and more a focus of attention. Mountains are now almost universally viewed as havens of retreat and symbols of freedom. The city is no longer viewed as Socrates saw it, as the center of action where everything good happens, but more and more as the center of evil. This is particularly evident in the return-to-nature movement that has taken place among the young within the last two decades, with its emphasis on casting off the artificiality of modern urbanized life. This trend, reminiscent of that advocated by Rousseau two hundred years ago and by Thoreau a century later, is an important influence in our times.

Mountains are a favorite refuge for those seeking to commune with nature, whether they be motor tourists or backpackers. This influx of tourists has created unprecedented pressures on mountain landscapes. Permits and other restrictions are being imposed in some areas, and the day may not be far off when there will be waiting lists and reservations. Mountains have never been in such demand or regarded with such favor in all the history of man. They comprise a major and praiseworthy theme in our art, literature, and music. Mountains are considered the embodiment of the good, the beautiful, and the sublime. During a recent class discussion I asked my students what the attraction of mountains was for them. One young person's answer perhaps echoes a larger feeling: "I go to the mountains," she said, "to get high."

Origin of Mountains

What caus'd the Mountains? whence, and when
their birth?
Are they indeed coeval with the Earth?
Or, as some learned Theorists declare,
The rugged Ruins of a delug'd Sphere?

> James Kirkpatrick,
> *The Sea-Piece: A Narrative*
> *Philosophical and Descriptive*
> *Poem* (1749)

Like attitudes toward mountains, views about the origin of mountains have changed a great deal through time. During the Middle Ages and early modern period in Western Europe, mountains were regarded as "monstrous excrescences of nature"; one of the prevailing views was that they had been created by God for punishment after man's expulsion from the Garden of Eden. This idea apparently had its origin in the fact that the story of creation in Genesis makes no mention of mountains. Explanations of the precise method of mountain creation differed: some said that interior fluids ruptured the spherical surface and piled up in great heaps, while others leaned toward a cataclysmic origin brought about by the Biblical flood (see epigraph, above). Although more advanced ideas than these had been developed by the ancient Greeks and by medieval Arab scholars, such was the power of theology in Western Europe that geological science had retrogressed. It was not until this intimate bond between religion and science was severed, in the seventeenth and eighteenth centuries, that major scientific advances began to be made. Once begun, scientific progress developed rapidly, and a number of plausible theories were postulated to account for the origin of mountains. We have, for the most part, built on these and improved them, but a virtual geologic revolution has taken place in the last twenty years, based on discoveries from the ocean floor. The newly developed theory of *plate tectonics* maintains that the earth's crust is divided into rigid plates which are moving in different directions; new crustal material is being created where the plates are pulling apart, and where the plates are colliding they are buckling into mountains and undergoing destruction by descending back inside the earth's mantle. Before discussing the mechanics of these processes, however, it is appropriate to establish some of the basic characteristics of mountains on a global scale.

CHARACTERISTICS OF THE MAJOR MOUNTAIN RANGES

The two most important clues to the origin of mountains are the distribution of mountain ranges over the globe and the structure and material composition of mountains. Both point to a fundamental association between oceans and mountains. A glance at any relief map of the world will show that mountain ranges tend to run in long, linear belts along the margins of continents (Fig. 3.1). One exceptionally long belt extends around the perimeter of the Pacific Ocean, and another runs east-west along the "underbelly" of Eurasia. This distribution of mountains follows closely the distributions of earthquakes, fault zones, volcanic activity, ocean trenches, and certain curved chains of islands (island arcs) (Figs. 3.6, 3.8, 3.10, and

Fig. 3.1. Generalized distribution of mountain belts (grey) and shield areas (black). The solid lines within the grey pattern represent mountains of Cenozoic age (the last 65 million years); dotted lines represent mountains of Mesozoic age (65–225 million years ago); and dashed lines represent mountains of Paleozoic age (225–600 million years ago). (Adapted from various sources)

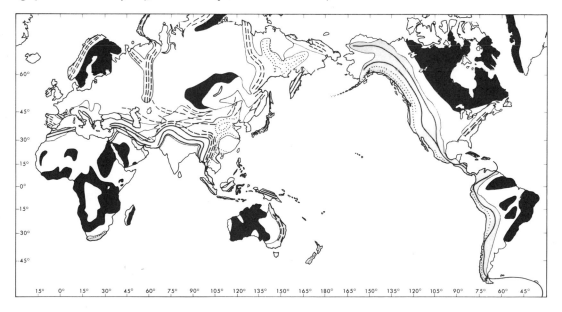

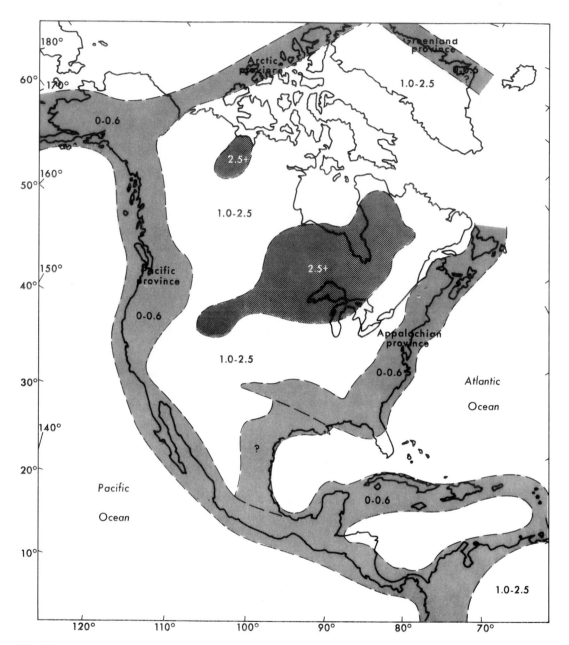

Fig. 3.2. Generalized distribution and ages of geologic provinces in North America, as defined by the major granite-forming and mountain-building events. Note that the interior of the continent is the oldest area, while the coastal areas are the youngest, indicating growth by accretion. (After Engel 1963, p. 145)

3.15). There must be something about these zones to make them particularly active geologically. The interiors of continents, by contrast, are relatively stable.

The coastal zones, as well as being less stable than the interiors, are made of much younger rock. Most continental interiors are composed of ancient crystalline cores of Precambrian granitic and metamorphic rock surrounded by roughly concentric rings of younger sedimentary rocks (Fig. 3.2; cf. Fig. 3.1). The primary method for adding new land to the continental cores is by mountain-building.

The great mountain belts are made up chiefly of marine sediments (although the rocks have often been metamorphosed and injected with volcanic material during the course of mountain-building). The sediments that compose these mountain rocks are undeniably of marine origin, as proven by the presence of fossil seashells high up in mountains. This fact has confounded everyone who has theorized about the genesis of mountains. How did the fossils typical of the muds of shallow seas make their way to the mountaintops? Marine fossils are also found deep in the earth, far below the foot of the mountains. Indeed, the sediments underlying mountains go far deeper than the sedimentary accumulations under the surrounding lowlands. In the United States, for instance, it was observed more than a century ago that the sedimentary rocks in Illinois and Iowa (which were covered by ancient shallow seas) were not as thick as those under the Appalachians in Pennsylvania and New York.

The presence of deeper accumulations of sedimentary rock under mountains than under the surrounding lowlands reveals a great deal about the nature of mountains. Geologists had long puzzled about whether the great weight and mass of mountains were simply piled on top of the surface as excess load and were therefore in an unstable condition, or whether mountains have "roots" or foundations that are less dense

than the surrounding strata so that a relatively balanced condition exists. In addition to the depth of the sedimentary rock, evidence for the presence of mountain roots came during the middle 1800s from northern India, where a team of surveyors was establishing precise land-measurements. At survey stations near the Himalayas, they noticed that their plumb line (a string with a pointed weight attached to one end to make the string hang vertically) did not hang straight down: the line was deflected slightly toward the mountains, away from the earth's center of gravity. This had been expected, considering the great mass of the Himalayas; in fact, the deflection was not as great as it should have been, according to their calculations. It was concluded, correctly, that the low degree of deflection was due to the mountain mass being composed of lighter rocks that extend into the earth, displacing the heavier substrata (Holmes 1965, p. 28). In other words, mountains float on the earth's surface somewhat like icebergs in water. The larger the mountain and the higher it rises, the deeper its roots will extend into the earth. This situation, called *isostasy* (from the Greek for "equal standing"), suggests that the earth's crust always strives to maintain a state of gravitational equilibrium: a mountain mass rising high above the surrounding surface is compensated for by a deep root that displaces denser rocks (Fig. 3.3).

The height mountains can achieve is limited by the nature of the physical processes that create mountains and by the ability of the base to support the accumulated mass. The type and intensity of tectonic activity determine the specific processes involved in mountain origin, and the support capacity of the base is determined by the weight of the mountain mass and the pressure melting-point of the basal material —that is, at some point the basal material will begin to melt and flow (Weisskopf 1975, p. 608). The maximum height is not known, but from a quick survey of mountain eleva-

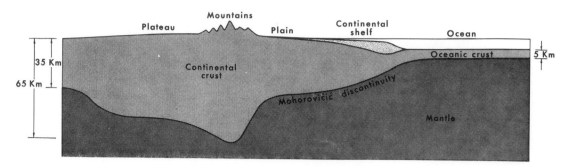

Fig. 3.3. Idealized representation of crustal thickness under continents and oceans. Note that the greatest thickness occurs under plateaus and mountains, while the thinnest crust exists under the oceans. (Adapted from Holmes 1965, p. 30)

tions it is apparent that 6,000 m (20,000 ft.) must be close to the upper limit. The Himalayas, an obvious exception, stand as high as they do because of the way in which they were formed. Portions of two continental masses were compressed together with the deposits of an ancient sea caught in between (Fig. 3.12), which resulted in an exceedingly thick accumulation of low-density rock. This thick blanket of sedimentary rock probably also explains why there has been very little volcanic activity in the Himalayas: volcanic material does lie beneath the mountains but it cannot push through the thick layer of sedimentary rock.

Just as the height (mass) of a mountain determines the depth of its roots, thereby maintaining a balance with the surroundings, the earth's crust continues to adjust to changing load-conditions as erosion or gravity-sliding (see p. 54) takes place: as the load on the base is lightened, the mountain tends to rise to compensate for this loss of weight. The reaction of the earth's crust to vast applications of weight can be seen in areas that were covered to a depth of several kilometers by the Pleistocene ice sheets, the weight of which must have been immense. For example, Hudson's Bay—the center for the accumulation of continental glaciation in North America—is now rebounding from being depressed under this great weight at a rate of about 1 m (3.3 ft.) per century (Andrews 1970).

The continents themselves adhere to the principle of isostasy: they are composed of lighter rocks floating on a substratum of denser rocks. This was confirmed by the Yugoslavian seismologist Mohorovičić, who observed that shock waves from earthquakes travel at a fairly low velocity until they reach a certain distance below the earth's surface, where they speed up abruptly. He concluded that this was due to the denser rocks in the earth's mantle, and that the point of increased velocity marked the base of the earth's crust (the outer layer of the earth). The zone of density contrast between crustal and mantle material was subsequently named the *Mohorovičić discontinuity*, or as it is popularly known, the *Moho* (Fig. 3.3). Seismologic studies show that the earth's crust underneath the continents has an average thickness of 20–30 km (12–19 mi.), but that it is only 5–10 km (3–6 mi.) thick under the oceans. The deep roots or foundations under the major mountain ranges, where the earth's crust reaches its greatest thickness, descend to 60 km (37 mi.).

A fundamental question at this point is: What accounts for the great accumulations of marine sediments that are present in the major mountain belts? Fossils collected near the summit of Mount Everest at 8,840 m (29,000 ft.), as well as in many other high mountain areas, indicate that these rocks were originally deposited as sediments in a shallow sea. How is it possible for thick rock accumulations to have been continually deposited in shallow water? The answer seems to be that these sediments were eroded from the land and deposited in coastal areas. As their weight increased, it gradually depressed the underlying rock, allowing sedimentation to continue in shallow water— some deposits eventually reached thicknesses of up to 12,000 m (40,000 ft.) in huge, linear, troughlike depressions. Such features, known as *geosynclines,* are thought to be intimately related to mountain-building. Through the study of ancient folded mountains such as the Appalachians, it was discovered that a typical geosyncline is divided into two parallel components: the inner or more continental part is composed of gently folded sedimentary rocks, termed the *miogeocline;* the outer or seaward part, the *eugeocline,* is much more intensely deformed, with abundant volcanic material interjected into the folded and faulted rocks (Fig. 3.4).

Until very recently, information about geosynclines had to be derived entirely from the study of folded strata in mountains because no examples of modern geosynclines had been recognized. In recent years, however, oceanographic research has discovered geosynclines actively forming in shallow water. Along the eastern seaboard of the United States, for example, a wedge of sediments 250 km (155 mi.) wide and 2,000 km (1,245 mi.) long composes the *continental shelf.* This is considered to be a "living" miogeocline. The *continental rise,* which ascends from the ocean deep, is thought to be a "living" eugeocline (Fig. 3.4a). The sediments on the continental shelf thicken to seaward, attaining depths of 3 to 5 km (1.8–3 mi.) and consist of heterogeneous deposits that result from muddy suspensions and turbidity currents (dense flows along the bottom slope of water bodies). These suspensions occasionally flow down the continental rise and deposit at its base great fans of sediments having thicknesses of up to 10 km (6 mi.). The recent sediments on

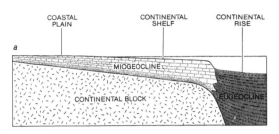

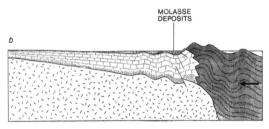

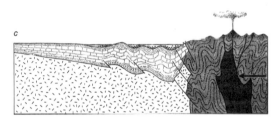

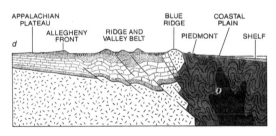

Fig. 3.4. One interpretation of the sequence of events that resulted in crumpling a former geosynclinal couplet into the Appalachian Mountains. These deposits were apparently laid down during the late Precambrian (about 450 million years ago). The miogeocline, or landward section of the geosyncline, was folded into a series of ridges between the Blue Ridge line and the Allegheny front. The eugeocline, composed of rocks altered by great heat and pressure associated with volcanism, was elevated and deformed into a large mountain range whose crest lay to the east of the Blue Ridge line. Erosion has taken its toll, however; all that remains are the present Appalachians, as shown in the bottom illustration. (From Dietz 1972, p. 36; courtesy of *Scientific American*)

both the continental shelf and continental rise resemble very closely the ancient rocks found in the fold belts of the Appalachians (Fig. 3.4d). It is reasoned, therefore, that these deposits are the stuff of which mountains are made, and that similar examples of living geosynclines exist off the coasts of the other major continents today. The mechanism causing their eventual deformation and uplift into mountains, however, has yet to be explained.

THEORIES OF MOUNTAIN ORIGIN

The ultimate cause for the origin of mountains has been one of the great enigmas of science. Even as late as the 1950s, geologists subscribed to at least half a dozen major theories. One of these was that mountains were created by the rise of *batholiths* (from the Greek for "deep rock"). Batholiths are huge masses of molten material which come from below and intrude into rocks near the earth's surface and then solidify into granite. Since batholiths are found at the core of most mountain ranges, it was thought that they were also responsible for the initial uplift and deformation of the surface. The sliding of rock strata through gravity down the flanks of slopes was considered instrumental in the folding and distortion of the overlying rocks (Bucher 1956). Another major theory, proposed 150 years ago but still held valid by some, is that the earth is contracting (since it was thought to have been originally a molten planet formed from material ejected by the sun and now gradually cooling). As the earth cooled and contracted, the outer shell would shrivel and wrinkle like the skin of a drying apple. Another proposed theory, that the earth was expanding, was suggested to account for the huge rift valleys and fault zones and to explain continental drift (Carey 1958). One idea envisioned giant convection currents within the earth; under this theory, mountains develop where the rising currents from two

opposing systems converge, resulting in great compressional forces causing folding and deformation of the surface (Holmes 1931). Yet another theory held that mountain-building took place through continental drift, as the leading edge of a continent encountered resistance from the material through which it was moving and buckled under the pressure.

Most of these theories are not mutually exclusive, and elements of each are still retained in one form or another, but now no one believes that they adequately explain the primary initiating mechanisms for creating mountains. The revolutionary discoveries of the last twenty years have replaced them with the new unifying concept of plate tectonics. This concept is proving to be one of the most significant developments in the history of science. Its immediate predecessor, continental drift, was not so well received.

The theory of continental drift was proposed in 1910 by Alfred Wegener, a young German meteorologist who was struck by the complementarity of the continental outlines of Europe, Africa, and the Americas. It seemed to him that if these continents were pushed together they would fit like pieces of a jigsaw puzzle (Fig. 3.5). Others had observed this before but had made nothing of it; Wegener, however, was curious enough to follow up on his hunch. He soon uncovered evidence of identical plant and animal fossils from coastal areas in Brazil and Africa. This strengthened his conviction that there were former land connections, and from that point on he devoted much of his life to searching for evidence to support the idea that the continents had drifted apart (Hallam 1975). Wegener's book, *The Origin of Continents and Oceans* (translated into English in 1924), contains compelling evidence that there was once a single supercontinent which later broke into the separate units that now exist.

Wegener's evidence for former land

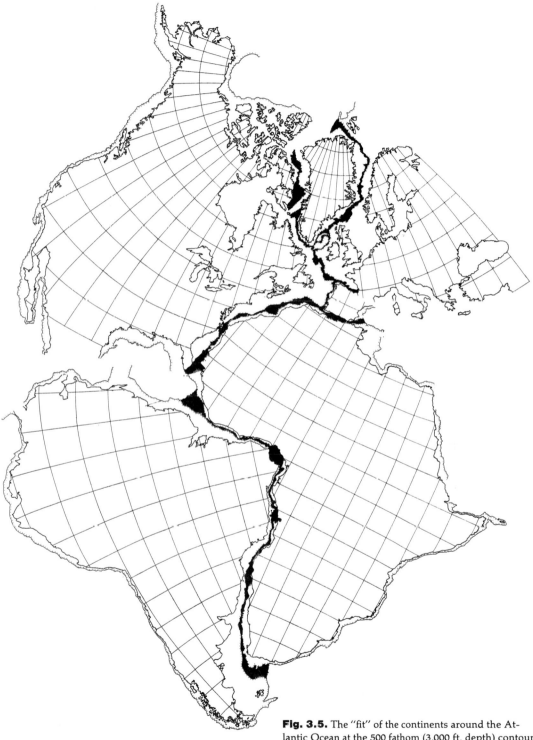

Fig. 3.5. The "fit" of the continents around the Atlantic Ocean at the 500 fathom (3,000 ft. depth) contour. Black areas are gaps or zones of overlap. (From Bullard et al. 1965, p. 48)

connections included matching fossils and rock types, alignment of fault zones, matching former areas of glaciation, and the presence of similar mountain-types in Europe and North America. Most geologists at the time regarded his theory as fantastic. The connections and similarities Wegener pointed out were interesting but could not be proved, and all could be explained by other means. The major objection, however, was to the mechanism he offered to account for such spectacular movements of entire continents—the tidal attractions of the sun and moon. In the succeeding years, interest in continental drift waxed and waned as new theories were proposed and symposia were held to discuss the theory, but by and large the scientific community remained unconvinced. As late as the 1960s, when I was a graduate student at the University of Illinois, the idea of continental drift was still scoffed at by some of my professors. The discoveries of the last two decades, however, have piled one type of evidence upon another so heavily that the conclusion becomes inescapable—the continents have indeed moved apart (Wilson 1976).

One of the **first** of these modern discoveries was made in the early 1950s by geophysicists studying the paleomagnetism of rocks. When molten volcanic rocks with traces of iron solidify, the rocks are slightly magnetized in the direction of the earth's magnetic field. It follows that molten rocks formed at about the same time on different continents should be like compasses with their needles frozen in the direction of the earth's magnetic pole, but it was discovered that the orientation of similar ancient rocks on different continents do not line up with the earth's present magnetic field. This suggests that either the poles have "wandered," or the continents have moved with respect to the magnetic pole. Since it is generally believed that the earth's magnetic and rotational poles have always been very close to each other (within 15°), the continents were

assumed to have moved (Hurley 1968; Dietz and Holden 1970).

The mechanism for this movement was still unknown. It was hypothesized that convection currents within the earth were driving the continents about, like huge floating rafts, on a viscous sea. Under this hypothesis, in North America the Pacific coast would be the leading edge, plowing against other rocks and buckling and breaking them into mountains: the Atlantic coast would be the relatively stable trailing edge, having as its primary activity the accumulation of sediments into a great geosyncline. But most geologists, unable to envision the continents moving through solid crustal material in this manner, refused to embrace the theory of continental drift until a more satisfactory mechanism could be brought forward.

Plate Tectonics

Plate tectonics embodies the idea that the earth's surface is broken into several rigid plates, like a huge cracked sphere. The plates consist of portions of both continents and oceans and are moving in various directions (Fig. 3.6). Where the plates are pulling apart, new molten volcanic material from depth fills the void created by their separation. Where the plates come together, the continental rocks are often squeezed and buckled into mountains; eventually one plate descends under the other and is absorbed back inside the earth.

The initial evidence for plate tectonics came from the sea floor. Systematic surveys in the 1950s and 1960s revealed that the globe is virtually encircled by spectacular undersea mountain ranges or mid-ocean ridges. The development of sophisticated seismic, sonar, and computerized equipment allowed detailed sampling and analysis of the ocean bottom. It soon became evident that the undersea mountain ranges are, like those on land, the loci of frequent volcanic and earthquake activity, and that they are areas of abnormally high heat flow

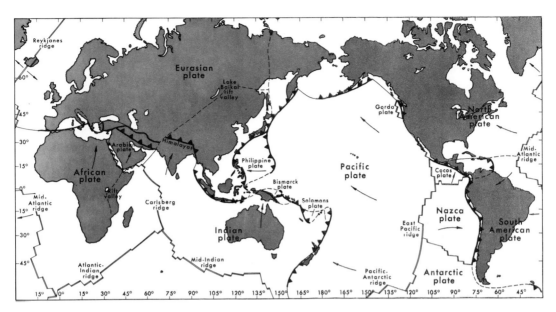

Fig. 3.6. Distribution of major plates and mid-ocean ridges. Double lines represent ridge axes; connecting single lines indicate displacement along transform faults. The heavy line and triangular symbols represent subduction zones. Dashed lines show uncertain plate boundaries and areas of extension within continents. Arrows indicate the general direction of plate movement. (Adapted from Dewey 1972, pp. 56–57, and Toksoz 1975, pp. 90–91)

(Figs. 3.6, 3.8, and 3.15). The largest and best-known undersea range is the Mid-Atlantic Ridge, which extends north-south for several thousand kilometers roughly parallel to the coastlines of Europe, Africa, and the Americas (Orowan 1969). The new island of Surtsey, which first appeared above the water in 1963, and other volcanic activity near Iceland are associated with this ridge.

A corollary discovery based on dating of rocks from the sea floor revealed that the youngest rocks are near the center of the ridge; rock age increases with distance from the ridge in both directions. This led to the theory of *sea-floor spreading*, which postulates that new crust is being created at the mid-ocean ridge and that it spreads outward (Hurley 1968, p. 57). In addition, studies made by towing sensitive magnetometers behind ocean research vessels revealed the presence of distinct magnetic strips of rock paralleling the axis of the mid-ocean ridge. These strips occur as symmetrically distributed pairs, with the pattern on one side of the ridge forming a mirror image of that on the other. The magnetic orientation of iron particles contained in the formerly molten rock in these strips reveals opposite headings. It is well-known that the earth's magnetic field has reversed itself repeatedly throughout geologic time—north has become south and south has become north (although the poles have stayed in about the same locations). When lava was erupted along the mid-ocean crest, it became magnetized in the direction of the prevailing magnetic field. As the sea floor spread, the rock was carried away from the center in both directions. Later eruptions deposited new material which was in turn magnetized in the direction of the prevailing magnetic field and then transported away from the ridge axis. By dating the rocks in these strips, it has been possible to calculate the rate of sea-floor spreading, which has been found to be several centimeters per year (Heirtzler 1968).

While these discoveries fitted into the context of continental drift as it was conceived in the early 1960s, they also raised new questions. If new material was being created and moving away from the mid-ocean ridges, what was happening at the other end? Either the earth was indeed expanding, or material somewhere else was being destroyed. Since most evidence indicates that the earth is not expanding to any appreciable extent, the material was apparently being destroyed (but see Carey 1976). Shortly afterward, in the mid-1960s, the theory of plate tectonics was postulated. The process of plate destruction and consumption is called *subduction* and takes place mainly at the deep sea trenches (Fig. 3.7). The evidence for this process has come largely from seismology (Isacks et al. 1968).

Most volcanic and earthquake activity occurs in the vicinity of the deep sea trenches and island arcs (Fig. 3.8; cf. Figs. 3.6, 3.10, 3.15). Both volcanism and earthquakes are now known to be direct by-products of plate movement and subduction.

There are four basic regions of earthquake occurrence. One is along the mid-ocean ridges, where high heat flow and volcanic activity occur, caused by the stretching of the earth's surface. These mid-ocean earthquakes are usually shallow-focus, originating at depths of less than 70 km (44 mi.). The second area of earthquake occurrence is along *transform fault* zones—where one section of the earth's crust is sliding by another—such as the San Andreas Fault in California or the Anatolian Fault in northern Turkey. Earthquakes here are also shallow but without associated volcanic activity. Third, a belt of shallow-focus earthquakes extends from the Himalayas to the Alps; it is apparently associated with the compressive forces responsible for the creation of these mountains. In general, shallow-focus earthquakes pose the greatest danger to human populations, since they are most numerous and involve the greatest release of energy (see pp. 383–88). The last earthquake area is the deep sea trenches and volcanic island arcs that surround the Pacific Ocean. Earthquake foci occurring in this region may be shallow, intermediate, or as deep as 700 km (440 mi.), depending on their exact location

Fig. 3.7. Schematic view of plate movement through sea-floor spreading and subduction. New crustal material is being created at the mid-ocean ridges (accreting plate margin), while oceanic crust and lithosphere are being consumed back into the earth at the deep sea trenches (converging plate boundary). Accordingly, the central ocean in this sketch is growing in size while the one on the left is closing. (Compiled from various sources)

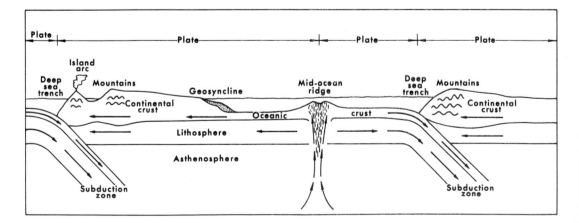

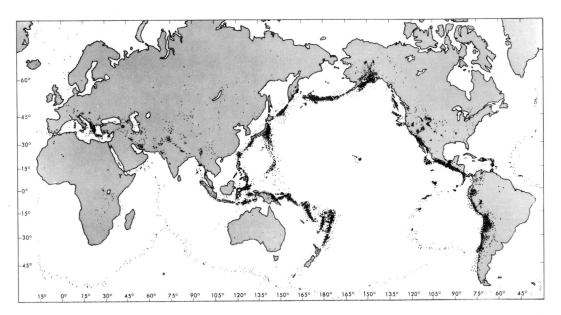

Fig. 3.8. Epicenters of all earthquakes recorded from 1957 to 1967. The greatest frequency of occurrence is found around the Pacific Ocean, where major subduction and crustal movement is taking place. There is a lesser east-west extension from the Himalayas to the Alps. A distinct pattern of earthquake occurrence can also be seen along the plate boundaries in the Atlantic and southern hemisphere oceans (see Fig. 3.6). (After Barazangi and Dorman 1969, plate I)

in the subduction zone (Dewey 1972). The tracing of earthquake foci in these areas has revealed that the deeper earthquakes occur in an inclined zone that dips away from the deep sea trench. Therefore, by using a network of sensitive seismographs around the earth to locate the foci of these earthquakes, it is possible to establish the position and steepness of the subduction zone (Fig. 3.9). Earthquakes do not occur below a depth of 700 km (440 mi.), because the descending *lithosphere* becomes molten and behaves more like a plastic than a brittle solid (Toksoz 1975). The lithosphere is the solid outer shell of the earth, the material of the plates. It is 60–150 km (40–90 mi.) thick and includes the earth's crust and the uppermost rigid layer of the mantle.

What exists, then, is essentially a conveyor-belt system involving the creation of new crustal material at the mid-ocean ridges and the reincorporation of the plate's leading edge back into the mantle at the

subduction zones (Fig. 3.7). The material in between is slowly transported from one point to another. The continents do drift, but they do not, as formerly envisaged, float about like rafts in a viscous sea (a picture which had always been one of the major obstacles to broad acceptance of continental drift). Plate tectonics provides an acceptable mechanism for continental movement: the continents are now considered to be passengers on lithospheric plates which are pushing outward from oceanic ridge systems and which may include oceanic crust as well as continental crust. The exact number of plates is unknown, but at least seven large ones and several small ones have been identified (Fig. 3.6). The largest, the Pacific Plate, carries most of the Pacific Ocean. The North American Plate consists of that continent and the western half of the Atlantic Ocean; the entire unit is moving to the west, where it is colliding with the Pacific Plate. The eastern side of the Atlantic is part of the

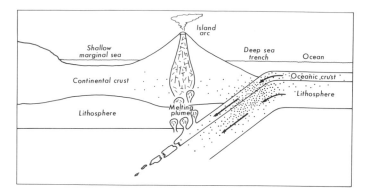

Fig. 3.9. Generalized view of subduction taking place at deep sea trench. Dots represent earthquake epicenters. The deepest ones occur at 400–700 km (250–438 mi.), where the descending lithosphere melts owing to the great heat and pressure at that depth. The melting plume that results is responsible for building the island arc, with its characteristic string of composite cones, between the deep sea trench and the continent. (Adapted from various sources)

Eurasian Plate, which is moving in the opposite direction and colliding with the western edge of the Pacific Plate. Thus, the Atlantic Ocean is opening and the Pacific Ocean is closing. Since continental crust is composed of low-density materials and is more buoyant than ocean crust, it cannot be subducted. Consequently, the Pacific Plate, which is composed of oceanic crust, is descending under the North American and Eurasian Plates carrying continental crust, and undergoes subduction into the deep sea trenches, i.e., the Aleutian, Kuril, Japan, and Marianas trenches. The driving mechanism for plate movement is unknown, but is still thought to involve huge convection currents of some sort (Anderson 1962; Wyllie 1975).

Plate tectonics has suddenly become everybody's darling. Although the details are far from settled, it provides a broad and unifying framework into which virtually all aspects of earth science fit. It explains the movement of continents as well as such formerly perplexing problems as the youthfulness of oceans. The origin of the oceans had long been one of the great enigmas: they

are thought to be coterminous with the earth and yet sea-floor rocks are less than 180 million years old, as opposed to 4 billion years for the earth. This disparity is now explained by the theory of plate tectonics. New sea-floor crust is continually being produced at the mid-ocean ridges and simultaneously being destroyed at the subduction zones; as a result, it can never be very old (Bullard 1969). The continents, on the other hand, may be broken apart and reassembled in various ways as plates divide and/or collide, but since they cannot be subducted, the basic amount of continental material stays about the same or even increases (Moorbath 1977). Erosion may wear down the land and transport sediments to the sea, but these materials are eventually reconstituted and added to the existing continental masses through mountain-building. Thus, the continents display accretion and active tectonism at their margins, while their interiors are older and more stable (Figs. 3.1 and 3.2).

The essential feature in mountain-building through plate tectonics is the plate boundary, of which there are three main types. *Divergent plate boundaries* are located at the rift zones, where plates are pulling apart. Mountainous topography can be created in these areas through volcanic activity, as well as through faulting caused by tensional stresses. Examples are the Mid-Atlantic Ridge and the Rift Valley of East Africa with its associated topography. In a *transform plate* boundary, plates converge but no subduction occurs; instead, the plates simply slide by each other along a transform fault, as is occurring along the San Andreas Fault in California (Fig. 3.19c). Mountains produced through wrenching and buckling along a fault are relatively minor features. The most important plate boundary for mountain-building is the *convergent plate boundary*, where plates converge and subduction takes place. Mountains are thought to be created along convergent plate boundaries in at least four major ways: where the oceanic lithosphere underthrusts island arcs; where the oceanic lithosphere underthrusts a continental margin; where a continent collides with another continent; and where a continent collides with an island arc (Dewey and Bird 1970; Dewey and Horsfield 1970).

Island Arc

An *island arc* is a chain of islands curved in a convex arc toward the ocean, with a deep sea trench immediately offshore to the seaward side and a small ocean basin between the arc and the continent. Island arcs are created at plate margins where an oceanic plate begins to be consumed and a trench is formed in the ocean at some distance from the continental margin. Upthrusting and doming occur on the continental side of the trench. The great heat created by the descending oceanic plate causes melting of the rocks, and the resultant *magma* (molten material within the earth) moves upward to build a platform of basalts and andesites (Fig. 3.9). Island arcs contain most of the world's destructive volcanoes. These are primarily composite cones (see pp. 337–83) built from silica-rich lavas (andesites) created in association with plate consumption in deep sea trenches (Dewey and Bird 1970).

Island arcs, and the volcanoes they contain, are largely restricted to the Pacific Ocean, where they occur around the periphery in a zone known as "the ring of fire" (Fig. 3.10). Curiously, there are no island arcs along the American coasts except

Fig. 3.10. Distribution of island arcs (solid lines) and deep sea trenches (dash-dot lines). Note that both phenomena are located almost entirely around the Pacific, a closing ocean. (From various sources)

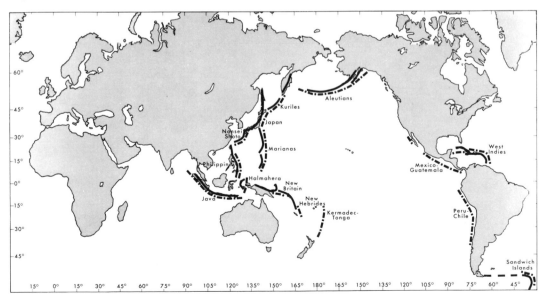

for the Aleutians off the Alaska coast and the West Indies and Sandwich Islands off the Atlantic Coast. Apparently, any island arcs that existed along the Pacific coast of North and South America have collided with and become incorporated into the continent. The Andes are thought to be partially composed of a former island arc and the Cascades and Sierra Nevada may be, too. There are still deep sea trenches off the coasts of Central and South America (e.g., the Peru-Chile Trench), but none exists off the western coast of the continental United States. There is, instead, a transform fault (the San Andreas), where the Pacific Plate is moving to the northwest and being subducted into the Aleutian Trench (Anderson 1971).

The construction of island arcs is an effective way of adding land to the continents. Volcanic liquids, originating deep within the earth, expand and crystallize upon reaching the earth's surface to form rocks of about the same density as that of continental crust. Since island arcs lie on the

Fig. 3.11. Schematic sections showing relationships among lithospheric plates, continents, oceans, island arcs, deep sea trenches (subduction zones), and mountain-building. (Adapted from Dewey and Bird 1970, p. 2627, and Dewey and Horsfield 1970, p. 523)

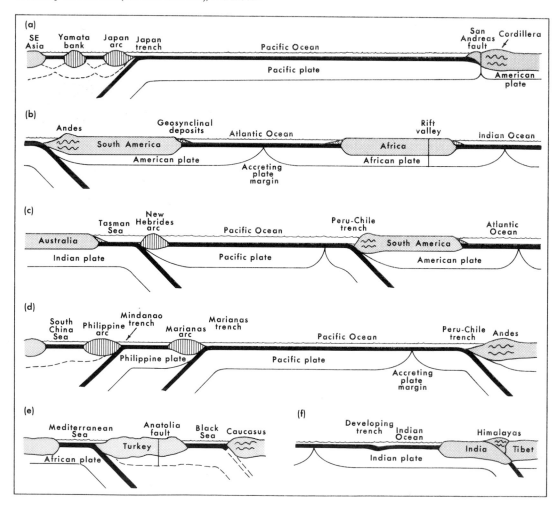

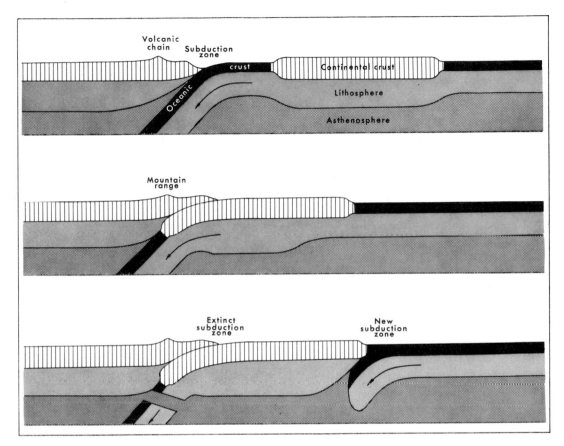

Fig. 3.12. One interpretation of sequence of events in continent/continent collision. A subduction zone develops between two plates each carrying continental material, allowing them to converge and combine. Since the lighter continental crust cannot be subducted, the entire mass is compressed and buckled into high mountains (e.g., the Himalayas). The former subduction zone eventually becomes inactive; another zone may form somewhere else. (From Dewey 1972, p. 64)

leading edge of oceanic plates and eventually collide and mesh with the adjacent continent, this material eventually becomes incorporated into the continent. The sediments contained in the small ocean basin between the island arc and the continent will also be squeezed up onto the land through mountain-building. A prime candidate for this process at the present time is the Sea of Japan, which lies between the Japan arc and China (Fig. 3.11a; cf. Fig. 3.10).

Cordilleran Type

Cordillera is the Spanish term for a large mountain system such as the great mountain region of western North America that includes the Rockies, the Cascades, the Sierra Nevada, and associated ranges. The word is used here to designate a special type of mountain origin through plate tectonics. When a subduction zone forms offshore close to the continental margin, the marine sediments contained on the continental shelf and continental rise will eventually be pushed up onto the continent and deformed into mountains (miogeocline). Volcanic activity may also take place as the area is up-domed, resulting in the emplacement of a batholith (eugeocline) (Fig. 3.4). Andesitic volcanoes may also develop in association with deep subduction. The cordilleras of North and South America are thought to have been formed in this way, and perhaps the Appalachians also. It is probable that all gradations exist between the cordilleran and island-arc types of mountain origin; that is, if the trench forms far enough away from the continent, an island arc may result with an ocean basin in between, but if the trench forms closer to the continent, a cordilleran type of mountain belt may develop (Dewey and Bird 1970, p. 2640).

Continent/Continent Collision

Mountains can be created when two plates, each carrying a continent, are consumed in such a way as to bring the continents on a collision course (Fig. 3.12; cf. Fig. 3.11f). The intervening ocean is squeezed as the continents close upon each other and the marine deposits are shoved upward onto the continent that is riding on the descending plate. Neither the continent nor the sediments can sink very far into the subduction zone, however, because of their low density. As a result, the two continents are pressed together, crushing, buckling, and thickening their combined continental crusts until a suture or subduction zone develops somewhere else and the pressure is relieved. The general lack of intermediate-focus and deep-focus earthquakes in zones where continents are thought to have collided indicates that the original subduction zone becomes inactive (Dewey 1972). The best example of mountains that originated in this way is that of the Himalayas, which were formed by the collision of what are now India and China. The Alps, Pyrenees, and Caucasus were probably created in a similar manner by the collision of Africa and Europe, although the situation there is more complex (Dewey and Bird 1970, p. 2641). In fact, it is thought that the small ocean basins here, such as the Mediterranean and Black Sea, may be remnants of once larger oceans that are now being squeezed in the closing vise between Africa and Europe (Figs. 3.6

and 3.11e). The Appalachian mountains may have been created by a continent/continent collision. In order for this to have occurred, the Atlantic Ocean would have to have closed and reopened again. As fantastic as it sounds, this is the most favored theory at present (Dietz 1972) (Fig. 3.13).

Continent/Island-Arc Collision

If a deep sea trench or subduction zone develops between an island arc and a continent and consumption of oceanic crust takes place in this zone, the island arc may eventually be pressed against the continent. The mountains of New Guinea are thought to have been created in this way. A present-day example of this process is the Tasman Sea to the west of the New Hebrides arc, which may eventually press against Australia (Fig. 3.11c). If collision occurs, the sediment on the continental shelf generally underthrusts the island arc, but not to any great extent, due to the buoyancy of the low-density rocks. Consequently, the continent and the island arc are simply squeezed together, deforming and folding the rocks. A new trench may then develop on the oceanic side of the arc (Dewey and Horsfield 1970, p. 525).

It is important to stress that these processes are transitional; they merge and recombine in infinite ways. Sea-floor spreading proceeds at right angles to divergent plate boundaries, but the plates may be subducted into the trench at any angle. Plate consumption depends upon the shape of the plates as well as the speed of movement; therefore, the rate of crustal consumption and the amount of deformation may vary a great deal from place to place. The leading segments along an uneven continental outline will collide first and will exhibit the earliest and most intense deformation—on this basis, the Klamath Mountains of southern Oregon are thought to have suffered the initial deformation along the western coast of North America (Dewey and Bird 1970, p. 2640). On the other hand, in-

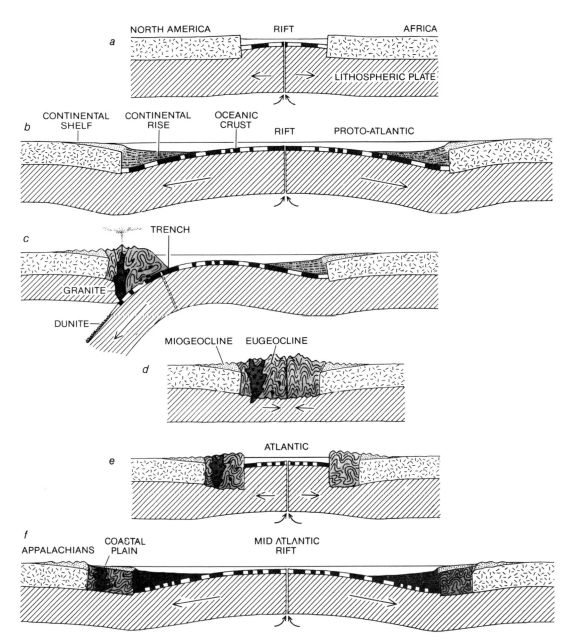

Fig. 3.13. Schematic interpretation of events leading to creation of the Caledonian-Hercynian-Appalachian mountains, and their eventual separation by creation of the Atlantic Ocean. (a and b) A rift develops initially between the two continents and the ancient Atlantic Ocean forms, complete with continental shelves and geosynclines. (c and d) A subduction zone develops as the plates begin to converge. The geosynclinal deposits are thrown up as mountains and eventually the two continents collide, increasing the mountain mass. (e and f) A suture develops and the plates begin to diverge, separating the once-connected mountains and creating the present Atlantic. That this process is continuing is demonstrated by the fact that the Atlantic is still growing at the rate of 3 cm (1.2 in.) per year. (From Dietz 1972, p. 37; courtesy of *Scientific American*)

dented portions of the continental margins may never collide, and will show considerably less deformation.

Many questions with respect to plate tectonics and the origin of mountains are still unanswered. For example, it seems clear now that the idea of one or two original supercontinents is oversimplified. These continents may have existed at one time, but they were only temporary sets on a stage of continually changing scenery. We assume that the processes we see active today must have extended throughout the geologic past: plates must always have moved around and rearranged themselves, oceans must always have opened and closed, continents must have split and recombined many times. It is virtually certain that the Atlantic did not exist 200 million years ago (Wilson 1966). Long before that, perhaps 500 million years ago, there was an older ocean in which the sediments forming the rocks in the Caledonian–Hercynian–Appalachian mountains of Europe and North America were laid down. The closing of this ocean created these mountains, and its subsequent reopening separated them by what is now the Atlantic Ocean (Fig. 3.13).

This raises intriguing questions about some of the world's present mountain ranges that are situated far from oceans. The Urals, clearly produced by tectonic compression, are located deep in the interior of a continent. Some geologists believe that they may have been formed near the coastal margin of an ocean that once divided Siberia from western Russia. Lake Baikal in Siberia is thought to be the site of a new rift zone developing within the Eurasian Plate. The Rockies, largely composed of vertical uplift of ancient continental crust, are also located in the interior of a continent, and although they are generally considered part of the total mountain-building that created the cordillera, their location raises questions as to where the oceans were at the time of their formation (Bullard 1969, p. 75).

Such mega-thinking is great fun, of course, but it is a heady business. Much remains to be solved. The theory of plate tectonics is still in its infancy and only time will tell if it can stand the test of subsequent discoveries. What we have is a broad outline with very little detail. Nevertheless, even this outline does much to explain many aspects of mountain origin that were formerly obscure. It must also be admitted that the objects of our affection pale in the light of the processes that created them. This knowledge should heighten rather than lessen our appreciation of mountains, as we begin to look more closely at the different mountain types.

PRINCIPAL MOUNTAIN TYPES

Some mountains are created by the extrusion of volcanic material; others result from the deformation of pre-existing rocks into folded or faulted structures. Mountainous relief can also be created by processes receiving their motive power from the sun and expressed through erosion, but this is generally a secondary process: mountains are fundamentally features of construction produced by energies originating inside the earth. The major mountain types, classified according to mode of origin, are volcanic; faulted; folded; and combinations of these.

Volcanic Mountains

Volcanoes result from molten material issuing from within the earth and accumulating on the surface as lava, ash, and other volcanic debris. They are generally singular features resulting from localized deep-seated activity expressed along fissures or fault zones where the superheated material finds access to the surface. Volcanoes may occur in groups or in linear extensions, as in the Cascades or Aleutians, but they do not form the continuous and formidable ridges found in the major folded and faulted ranges like the Rockies

Fig. 3.14. Paricutín Volcano, Mexico, in 1944, while still actively growing: time-exposure photo taken during late evening. Incandescent bombs and molten material can be seen flying through air and down sides of cone. Volcanic ash covers surrounding area. (Ted Nichols)

or Himalayas. Volcanic eruptions provide spectacular evidence of their ongoing construction. In some cases they can develop with incredible speed. Paricutín in Mexico emerged from a farmer's field in 1943 and grew 140 m (460 ft.) in one week. By the end of the first year it had grown to a height of 325 m (1,065 ft.) (Bullard 1962, p. 272) (Fig. 3.14). While evidence (e.g., earthquakes, surface flexure, and fault scarps) may also be seen of the continued construction of folded and faulted mountains, these ranges are relatively inactive compared to many volcanic mountains.

Volcanoes occur on all continents and comprise a substantial percentage of the world's mountains (Fig. 3.15). The number becomes even more impressive if we include those hidden by oceans—most islands are nothing more than the summits of undersea volcanoes. If one includes the submerged as well as the visible part, the world's tallest and largest peak is a volcano—Mauna Loa in Hawaii (Fig. 3.18). Although the above-water portion of this gently domed 4,169 m (13,680 ft.) mountain is not particularly impressive, it rises 9,100 m (30,030 ft.) from a sea-floor base that is over 100 km (60 mi.) in diameter (Macdonald 1972, p. 275). The highest

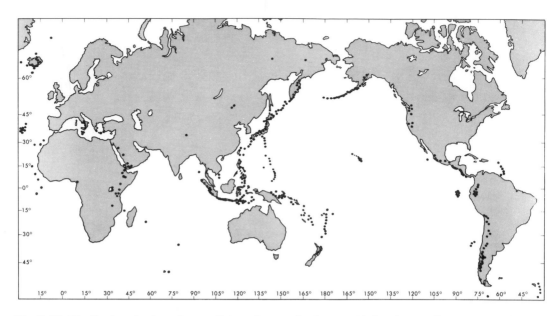

Fig. 3.15. Distribution of active volcanoes. Points of known submarine eruptions are shown; probably an even greater number are still unknown. Compare this distribution with that shown in Figs. 3.6, 3.8, and 3.10. (From Macdonald 1972, p. 346)

volcano on land, at 6,267 m (20,556 ft.), is Mount Chimborazo in the Andes of Ecuador.

Volcanoes are linked with two basic regions on the earth: subduction zones, and "hot spots" or thermal centers where molten material rises from deep within the mantle. The hot spots are relatively fixed and tend to produce a string of volcanoes as a plate drifts over them. For example, the Hawaiian islands (which are really mountains on the sea floor) are a northwest-southeast string, with the oldest islands to the northwest and the youngest to the southeast. This pattern is a result of the Pacific Plate moving to the northwest and the islands continually being moved away from the hot spot. The youngest island, Hawaii, now overlies the hot spot (Burke and Wilson 1976). If the present tendency continues, Hawaii too will eventually drift to the northwest, and the activity of Mauna Loa and Kilauea volcanoes will subside, while another volcano will presumably form

immediately to its southeast over the hot spot.

Some geologists believe that hot spots may be the loci of developing plate margins and serve as the source of energy that drives the plates from place to place. Such a hot spot is thought to underlie the Snake River basalts of the western United States. Called the Yellowstone Plume, this hot spot has resulted in huge outpourings of lava in this region. It may in fact be the location of a future plate boundary that will cause the break-up of North America 50 to 60 million years from now (Morgan 1972).

Volcanoes are generally divided into two basic types, composite cones and shield volcanoes. As their names suggest, they have different shapes and different kinds of eruptions, according to the method of production of the lava involved. Composite cones develop primarily around the margins of the continents, along convergent plate boundaries where subduction is taking place. As the oceanic plate descends into the mantle, it heats and, at great depths, begins to melt; the molten material rises in a "melting plume" to build island arcs and the volcanoes they contain (Fig. 3.9). Although molten, this material has relatively low temperatures and therefore is more viscous, acidic, and gas-rich than the hotter, more liquid lavas of shield volcanoes. Shield volcanoes are associated with boundaries where the plates are pulling apart, and with hot spots where molten material rises from deep within the mantle. Consequently, shield volcanoes are composed of basaltic (basic) lavas and are most often found in oceanic areas. Rarely, the two kinds of volcanoes may occur together; for example, the high peaks of the Cascades (e.g., Mount Rainier, Mount Hood) are composed of composite cones built on a platform of basaltic shield volcanoes. This platform is of Miocene age (20 million years old), while

the composite cones, many of which are still active, are of Pleistocene age (less than 2 million years old). The reasons for this peculiar pattern are unknown, but are thought to be related to the timing and specific developments associated with the movement of the North American Plate westward over the Pacific Plate (Lipman et al. 1971).

Composite Cones

The *composite cone* is one of the most beautiful mountain forms. The typical form is of a cone with a circular base, sloping gently in its lower reaches and then more steeply toward its summit to create a balanced and well-proportioned edifice. This mountain form has long fascinated people of many cultures. Fujiyama, Kilimanjaro, and Vesuvius are classic examples (Fig. 3.16). Composite cones are also known as stratified volcanoes, since they are com-

Fig. 3.16. View of Fujiyama, 3,754 m (12,388 ft.) high, from Ashi-no-ko, 34 km (21 mi.) to the southeast. Observe the classic form of the volcano, gentle near the base and steeper near the summit. (Naka Rhynsburger)

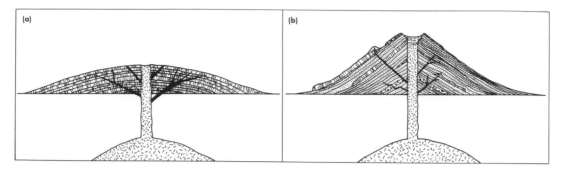

Fig. 3.17. Idealized cross-sections of (a) shield volcano and (b) composite cone. The shield volcano is built primarily of outpourings of basaltic lava, which tend to produce a gently arched dome. The composite cone is built of alternating layers of andesitic lava, volcanic ash, and other pyroclastic debris whose interlayering and imbrication provides greater strength and results in the construction of a steeper, conelike form. (Adapted from Macdonald, 1972)

posed of alternate layers of lava and aerially ejected material (Fig. 3.17b). This alternation between fluid rock and solidified debris is responsible for creating and maintaining the relatively steep form of the composite cone: the interleaving of the different materials provides greater strength. These are sometimes referred to as explosive volcanoes, because the silica-rich lavas (*andesites*), characteristic of composite cones, become viscous and solidify quickly upon reaching the surface, capping the underlying material. This prevents the gas and steam from escaping, and pressure builds until it is suddenly released by the explosive ejection of vast amounts of superheated steam, gas, lava, and other volcanic debris. Once activity ceases, the lava solidifies and reseals the volcano until sufficient pressure again builds to uncap it. Eruptions may occur every few years as a series of minor disturbances, or the volcano may lie somnolent for centuries and then awaken violently one day.

Composite cones are the most dangerous and unpredictable volcanoes. They have been responsible for some of the greatest disasters in human history: the 1815 eruption of Tamboro in the East Indies, in which 56,000 people perished; that of Mount Pelee on the island of Martinique in 1902, in which 30,000 were destroyed in a matter of minutes (Fig. 10.18); and the most famous eruption of all time, that of Vesuvius in 79 A.D., which killed 16,000 people and completely buried the town of Pompeii (Williams 1951). Literally hundreds of other examples could be given of the destruction of property and lives either directly or indirectly by volcanic activity, and yet the toll is relatively low compared to what it might have been. Many of the greatest eruptions have occurred in more or less unpopulated regions, such as the eruption of Mount Mazama (now Crater Lake) in the Oregon Cascades 6,000 years ago; that of Mount Katmai in Alaska in 1912, which deposited over 50 cm (20 in.) of ash in the streets of Anchorage, 160 km (100 mi.) away; and the huge eruption of Bezymianny in Kamchatka in 1956. As the population of the world increases and larger numbers of people settle nearer to volcanoes, the potential for disaster also increases (see pp. 377–83).

Shield Volcanoes

Shield volcanoes are gently arched domes with slopes of less than 10°; their bases merge imperceptibly into the surrounding landscape (Fig. 3.18). They were named by the Vikings, who likened the domed volcanoes of Iceland to circular battle shields

(Macdonald 1972, p. 271). They are also known as "quiet volcanoes," because they are built by successive outpourings of lava rather than by explosive ejection of solidified material (Fig. 3.17a). This does not mean that their eruptions are benign or gentle; they can be truly spectacular, spewing fountains of fiery lava up to 500 m (1,600 ft.) into the air. Unlike composite cones, however, the gases in shield volcanoes remain dissolved in hotter, less siliceous, more fluid lavas which do not form caps to seal in great pressure.

The most famous and best-documented shield volcanoes are Mauna Kea, Mauna Loa, and Kilauea on the island of Hawaii (Fig. 3.18). Mauna Loa and Kilauea are among the most active volcanoes in the world and are continuing to add land to the island. They have been studied inten-

sively since 1912, when an observatory was established near the Kilauea crater. From the first recorded eruption in 1832 to the present, Mauna Loa and Kilauea have erupted on an average of every 3.6 years. A typical eruption is preceded by a series of earthquakes as the fissures open and allow the magma to reach the surface. In a matter of days or hours, hot lava fountains spew skyward along the fissures, and great quantities of smoke and gas fill the air. Rivers of superheated lava flow down the slopes at speeds reaching 15–40 km (10–25 mi.) per hour before they begin to cool and slow in their distal parts. The longest flow, observed in 1859, continued for ten months and flowed into the ocean 53 km (33 mi.) away. In 1881 an eruption flowed 46 km (29 mi.), stopping just short of the city limits of Hilo (Bullard 1962, p. 213). The most recent ma-

Fig. 3.18. Mauna Loa, a shield volcano on the island of Hawaii. Although it looks like a gentle dome, its vital statistics are impressive: it rises to an altitude of 4,169 m (13,680 ft.) above a base that exceeds 100 km (60 mi.) in diameter. The foreground is occupied by a recent lava flow upon which vegetation and soil are slowly developing. (Courtesy of Hawaii Visitors Bureau)

jor eruption, on Kilauea in 1960, has been
beautifully documented by the United
States Geological Survey in a film entitled
Eruption of Kilauea, 1959–60.

Faulted and Folded Mountains

The major mountain chains were caused
by the breaking, folding, and crumpling of
pre-existing rock strata into features of
high relief. This process is known as *orogenesis* (from the Greek meaning "mountain
origin"), a term that includes the uplift as
well as the deformation of the earth's crust
into mountains. The force comes from
plate movement: continental crust and sediments are squeezed or stretched at the
plate margins. Most geologists differentiate
between the intense deformational forces
that cause the faulting and folding, and
the more general uplift that elevates the
landscape (Billings 1956). It is generally believed that much of the deformation takes
place first, often deep within the earth,
and the rocks are then uplifted to produce
mountainous elevations.

There are two basic kinds of uplift; one is
that of lifting relatively large areas, often
without deformation taking place (e.g.,
creating plateaus); the other is of concentrated and intensive uplift (e.g., creating
mountains). The two are generally interconnected, however, since most plateaus
abut mountains. Geologists have long puzzled over the question of why the rocks
of one area are so deformed and altered
while those on adjacent, similarly elevated
plateaus remain flat-lying and unaltered.
This difference in geologic processes is still
far from understood; apparently, the crust in
plateau regions is more rigid and the uplift
more gentle and widespread, so no significant deformation results. In any case, it is
clear that the basic structure displayed in the
major mountain ranges is produced primarily by faulting and folding. These processes
act singly and in concert to create distinctive
landscapes.

Faulted Mountains

Faulted mountains result from the displacement of segments of the earth's surface along fracture zones. This movement is
generally very slow, taking place in short
jerks over thousands of years. The displacement may be vertical or horizontal, but
the result is the elevation of one block in
relation to another (Fig. 3.19). Features
associated with faulting include: the juxtaposition of different types of material;
raised escarpments; jointing and fracturing;
local alteration or crushing of rocks in the
movement zone; and various sorts of surface
disturbances, such as the damming or re-
arrangement of stream flow. Another common surface expression of faulting is the
presence of *lineaments*—topographic features that form straight lines. These are
apparently the result of abrupt earth movements wherein the rock behaves as a brittle
substance and tends to fracture into straight
segments. Since straight lines are uncommon in nature, lineaments are often diagnostic of fault zones and earthquake activity.

Forces that stretch the crust (tension) and
forces that squeeze it (compression) each
produce their own characteristic forms of
faulting. Tensional forces tend to create
abrupt and spectacular fault scarps, drop-
ping or raising crustal blocks with respect to
one another: this is known as *normal faulting* (Fig. 3.19a). If a central block drops in
relation to the land on both sides of it, a
fault trough or *graben* (from the German for
"grave") is created. The higher blocks on
either side are called *horsts* (from the German for "eagle's nest") (Fig. 3.19e). The
Rhine Valley of Germany is an example of a
graben; the Vosges and Black Forest ranges
on either side of it are horsts. Such down-
faulting is one of the few processes that can
create landscapes below sea level. For example, Death Valley, a graben in California,
lies 86 m (282 ft.) below sea level between
two horsts, the Panamint and the Black
mountains.

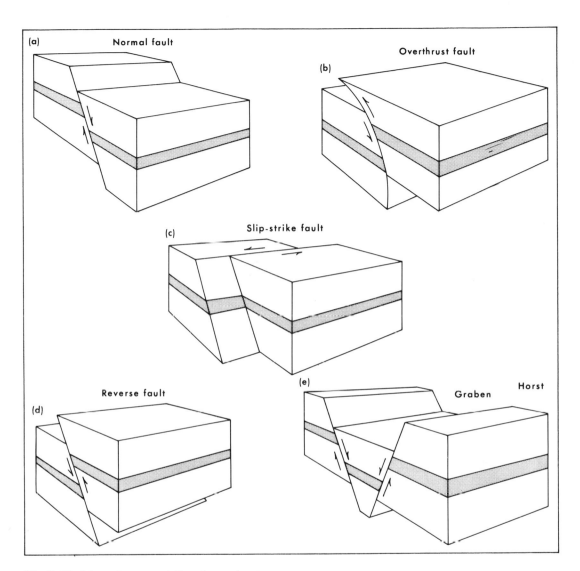

Fig. 3.19. Schematic representation of several major types of faulting associated with mountain-building. (Adapted from *California Geology* 1971, p. 209)

Much of the basin and range mountains of the western United States are considered to be a result of tensional forces. This region, centered in Nevada, has been broken into a series of fault zones oriented roughly northwest-southeast, and the resulting blocks have been tilted, lifted, and dropped relative to one another to create more or less parallel ridges and valleys. Many of the blocks occur as asymmetric massifs with

one side (fault scarp) rising as much as 1,500 m (5,000 ft.) above the adjacent surface, while the other side dips gently into the surrounding lowlands. Some who have studied this landscape believe that the surface expressions come not so much from faulting per se as from differential erosion along the fault lines at places where rock types of different resistances are in contact. Probably both processes are important, with some

Fig. 3.20. East face of the Sierra Nevada as viewed from the air over the Owens Valley looking west. Mountain front rises over 3,350 m (11,000 ft.) above the valley floor. Mount Whitney, 4,418 m (14,496 ft.), is in center. (U.S. Geological Survey)

scarps resulting directly from displacement along fault zones while others are produced by erosion. In either case, it is faulting that has created the structural framework and given the area its distinctive character.

The Sierra Nevada of California is a spectacular example of faulting. This range consists of several individual segments which have tilted more or less in unison to present a block 650 km (400 mi.) long by 80 km (50 mi.) wide. This huge block dips gently to the west, while east-facing slopes rise abruptly along fault scarps and present the highest mountain front in the continental United States (Fig. 3.20). In a horizontal distance of less than 10 km (6 mi.) there is a drop of 3,350 m (11,000 ft.) between the higher peaks of the Sierra Nevada and the Owens Valley (which is a graben). Other spectacular fault scarps in the United States include those of the Grand Tetons in Wyoming and the Wasatch Range in Utah, both of which display abrupt mountain fronts rising as much as 1,800 m (6,000 ft.) above the surrounding plains (Fig. 10.19).

In another major type of faulting, one piece of the land surface is displaced horizontally (sometimes vertically as well) past another to create *slip-strike* or transform *faults* (Fig. 3.19c). This type of fault is less important to mountain-building than those that primarily produce vertical displacement, but it is nevertheless an important geological process. The San Andreas Fault of California, extending in a northwesterly direction from Mexico to the northern Pacific Ocean for 3,000 km (1,800 mi.), is a highly active slip-strike fault that is the source of the region's most violent earthquakes. The western section (the Pacific Plate, on which Los Angeles is located) is moving northward at the rate of 5.8 cm (2.3 in.) per year. Past movement is estimated to have been 1,100 km (700 mi.), and if the present trend continues, Los Angeles may one day (several million years from now) be a suburb of San Francisco (Anderson 1971). Although movement along the fault is primarily horizontal, some buckling and vertical displacement have taken place, resulting in mountainous terrain (e.g., the San Gabriel and San Bernardino mountains). Other major slip-strike (transform) faults such as the Anatolian Fault in Turkey, the Alpine Fault in New Zealand, and the Great Glen Fault of the Scottish Highlands have also produced mountainous topography. The first two of these are still extremely active loci of earthquakes and mountain-building; the third is older and less active. A string of long, narrow, and extremely deep lakes, including the famous Loch Ness, now occupies the Great Glen Fault (Holmes 1965, p. 230).

Although normal and transform faulting can be quite complex processes, the structures they produce through displacement and deformation of strata are relatively simple compared to the bewildering disarray produced by *reverse* and *overthrust faulting* (Figs. 3.19b and d). These are caused by compressive forces that tend to squeeze and push one segment of the earth's surface over another. The movement may take place along either high or low-angle faults. *High-angle faulting* tends to produce a more or less vertical stacking of beds which often erode

differentially into a series of parallel ridges and valleys. The result is sharp and rugged topography, as in the Sawtooth Range of Montana, where thrust faulting has produced juxtaposed harder and softer rocks (Fig. 3.21).

Low-angle faulting tends to produce horizontal displacement as low-lying older rocks are pushed over younger strata. The rock units involved may vary from a few tens to hundreds of meters in thickness, and they can override the adjoining surface for distances of up to 80 km (50 mi.). Erosion may then remove the weaker strata, leaving the more resistant portions as isolated remnants. Extremely confusing stratigraphic relationships are often produced: a mountain peak may be composed of rocks that are older than the underlying strata and are not found elsewhere in the vicinity; alternatively, a mountain peak may be composed of rocks identical to those exposed far below in an adjacent valley, while sandwiched in between are several hundred meters of younger rock.

There are many overthrust faults in the

Fig. 3.21. Cross-sections of rock structures resulting from high-angle thrust faulting in the Sawtooth Range of Montana. This often results in the juxtaposition of rocks of varying resistance and produces an extremely rugged landscape. Length of cross-section is 16 km (10 mi.). (After Deiss 1943, in Thornbury 1965, p. 391)

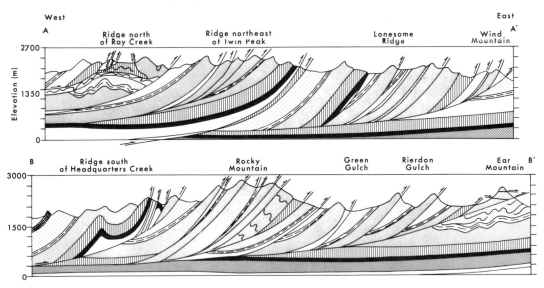

world's major mountain ranges. A famous example in the Rockies is the Lewis Overthrust near Glacier National Park, Montana. Here ancient Precambrian rocks were uplifted and thrust a distance of 24 km (15 mi.) over younger shales and sandstones of Mesozoic age. Chief Mountain is an ero-sional remnant of that overthrust sheet (Fig. 3.22) (Thornbury 1965, p. 389). Results similar to overthrust faulting may also be accomplished through other processes, e.g., gravity sliding and overturned folding (to be discussed in the following section). All three of these processes may be interrelated, and

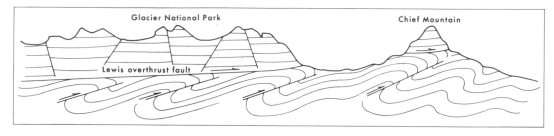

Fig. 3.22. Generalized east-west cross-section of the Lewis Overthrust, located near the Canadian border in northern Montana. Older rocks were thrust over younger rocks along the low-angle fault (as shown in this section) for at least 24 km (15 mi.). Chief Mountain is an erosional remnant of the overthrust sheet, which at one time was probably much more extensive. (After Alt and Hyndman 1972, p. 165)

Fig. 3.23. Spectacular folding displayed near the Sullivan River in the southern Rockies of British Columbia. (Geological Survey of Canada)

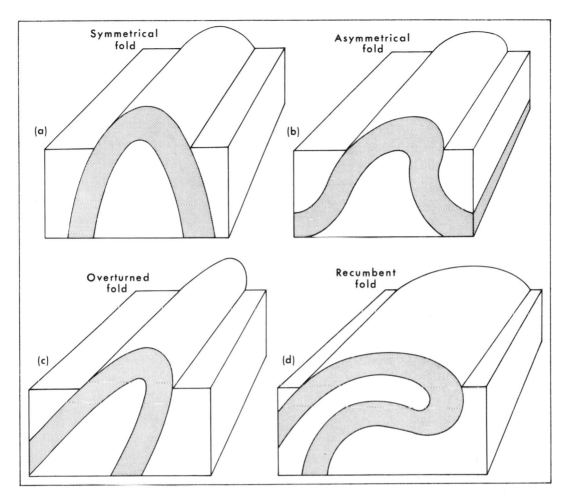

Fig. 3.24. Schematic representation of various types and degrees of folding. (Adapted from Putnam 1971, p. 392)

it is often difficult to identify the relative influence of each in a given situation.

Folded Mountains

Folding compresses rock strata into a series of wave-like troughs and ridges without significantly fracturing or breaking the rock layers. This plastic deformation of the rock layers takes place slowly over thousands or millions of years. When the deforming forces are only mildly compressive, the amplitude and spacing of the *synclines* (troughs) and *anticlines* (ridges) resemble a gently rippled sea, but under extreme pressures the rock strata can take on the appearance of a tempestuous sea crystallized at the point of greatest fury (Fig. 3.23), as in most complex mountains, where the strata have been extruded, overturned, and intertwined in many ways (Fig. 3.24).

The major orogenic belts are folded mountains, consisting of thick accumulations of marine sediments (geosynclines) that have been altered and deformed in various ways. This is generally thought to result from large-scale compressive forces

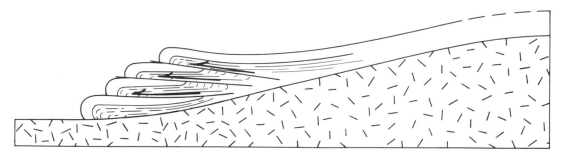

Fig. 3.25. Graphic representation of gravity-sliding. Rock beds slide slowly downslope and deform under their own weight to produce local folding and faulting.

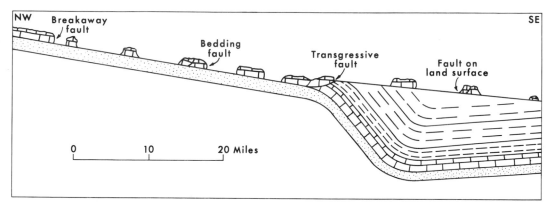

Fig. 3.26. The Heart Mountain detachment fault, located in northwestern Wyoming near Yellowstone National Park. Huge blocks up to 8 km (5 mi.) across appear to have broken away from the strata at upper left and to have slid down the gentle incline so that older strata now rests upon younger rock surfaces. (After Pierce 1957, and Garner 1974, p. 194)

shortening certain sections of the earth's crust so that the strata become thickened and pile up as mountainous accumulations of deformed rock. However, similar effects may result from local processes; if an area is domed upward, for example, the beds on either side of the dome may slide downslope under their own weight through *gravity sliding* (Fig. 3.25). There is evidence to support both processes; strongly metamorphosed rocks indicate that folding took place at considerable depths within the earth under great heat and pressure; rocks with little or no metamorphosis suggest that folding occurred at the surface under normal atmo-

spheric temperatures, and may be due to gravity sliding.

Gravity sliding is being discovered to be much more important in the folding of mountains than was formerly thought. Evidence includes the fact that while the most intense rock metamorphosis occurs near the axis of a range (usually occupied by a granitic-core batholith), the most complex folding is displayed around the margins. As huge rock masses are transported downslope through gravity sliding, the central area typically undergoes uplift to compensate for its loss of weight. When this happens, the central core achieves the highest point of relief, both because it undergoes greater uplift and because the crystalline rocks of which it is composed are more resistant to erosion. For example, Mount McKinley, the highest mountain in North America, is carved from the granitic core of the batholith that underlies the Alaska Range. Gravity sliding may also account for the displacement of older strata over younger rock in overthrust faults: Figure 3.26 shows a series of huge earth blocks that have slid down a slight incline to lie unconformably on younger rocks. Chief Mountain, mentioned as an example of an overthrust remnant, may actually have been formed by gravity sliding. The most famous example of displacement from gravity sliding is the Rock of Gibraltar in the Mediterranean: it consists of older limestones and shales overlying younger sedimentary rocks. This huge monolith is apparently carved from a larger mass that moved laterally from the east to its present location (Garner 1974, p. 194).

The most spectacular and complex feature associated with folded mountains is the *nappe* (from the French for "tablecloth"). Nappes are enormous slablike masses of rock, bulbous protrusions that have been extruded into or over other rock strata for considerable distances, in some cases up to 100 km (60 mi.). Closely associated with overthrust faults, nappes are usually attributed to *overturned* and *recumbent folding*, where the axis of the anticline is strongly

asymmetrical and is often forced laterally over the adjacent strata for some distance (Fig. 3.24). Nappes, found in most of the major mountain ranges, are an integral part of orogenesis. The entire suprastructure of the Alps is dominated by a series of huge overlapping nappes that were displaced to the northwest from their point of origin near present-day Italy, as Africa collided with Europe causing the creation of these mountains from the sediments of an ancient intervening sea (Fig. 3.27). Millions of years of erosion have removed many of the displaced rock sheets entirely, and only remnants remain of others. The famous Swiss Matterhorn is a remnant of one of these nappes; it consists of older, more resistant rocks overlying younger rock (Bailey 1935, p. 115).

The Alps today are only the skeletal remains of a formerly more robust mountain body. Theoretical reconstruction of the original is a matter of exceeding complexity, and several schools of thought have arisen from different interpretations of nappe formation. Early workers had difficulty in rationalizing the great horizontal displacements involved. A study in 1841 near Glarus, Switzerland, revealed that for a distance of over 50 km (30 mi.) the mountain peaks are composed of older rocks than the valleys. The original explanation for this anomalous situation was that the older rock had been transported to its present location by two recumbent folds coming from opposite directions (Fig. 3.28a). Even this rela-

Fig. 3.27. Generalized cross-section of the eastern Alps based on the theory that they were formed from great recumbent folds and nappes that were driven northward from the ancient Mediterranean Sea geosyncline by the closing of Africa and Europe. (After Holmes 1965, p. 1151)

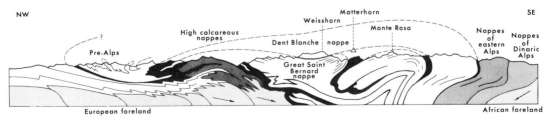

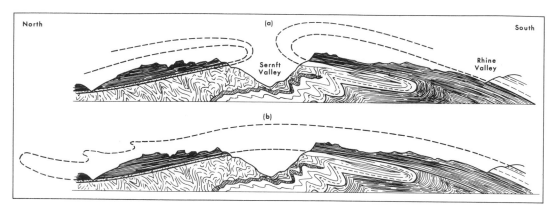

Fig. 3.28. Two interpretations of the mechanism responsible for emplacing older strata over younger in the Alps near Glarus, Switzerland. The lower illustration, of one huge overthrust sheet or nappe, is the usually accepted view. Length of section is 40 km (25 mi.). (After Holmes 1965, p. 1163)

tively cautious speculation was so revolutionary at the time that its author would not allow publication of the work: "No one would believe me if I published my sections; they would put me in an asylum" (Vanderlinth 1841, cited in Holmes 1965, p. 1162). In 1884, one gigantic overthrust was postulated for the entire region (Fig. 3.28b). This eventually became the more widely accepted view, although controversy persists.

It can be seen that geologic interpretation of mountain structures requires not only careful study and mapping of rock strata, but also an ability to see the larger picture, with an imagination to match the fantasy of the landscape under investigation, which in mountains reaches the largest proportions known. The importance of these qualities can be seen in the progression of ideas concerning the origin of mountains; the theory of plate tectonics is a fantastic and spectacular culmination of human ingenuity. While much remains to be learned, it has provided a logical and acceptable framework into which most observations fit. It is a quantum advance in knowledge that has virtually revolutionized the earth sciences. The perspectives gained from this examination of the origin of mountains should be retained as we move to the central concern of this book—the processes that characterize present-day mountain landscapes.

Mountain Climate

*The cosmic cold of space drains the radiant
energy from the alpine tundra through brilliantly
clear skies at night and the dawn breaks with the
suddenness and intensity of an avalanche as the
sun's rays from the east penetrate the transparent
sky. The discontinuity of the dawn is dramatic;
figures and forms on the surface suddenly receive
the stimulus of light and heat; everything is
clearly alive and vital. In phase and out of phase,
leading and lagging, life renews as the sunlight
penetrates every nook and cranny.*

> David M. Gates
> and Robert Janke,
> *"The Energy Environment of the
> Alpine Tundra"* (1966)

Climate is the fundamental factor in
establishing a natural environment; it sets the
stage upon which all physical, chemical, and
biological processes operate. This becomes
especially evident at the margins of the
earth, i.e., desert and tundra. Under temperate conditions, the effects of climate are
often muted and intermingled so that the
relationship between stimulus and reaction
is difficult to isolate, but under extreme
conditions the relationship becomes more
evident. Extremes constitute the norm in
many areas within high mountains; for this
reason, a basic knowledge of climatic processes and characteristics is a prerequisite to
an understanding of the mountain milieu.

The climate of mountains is kaleidoscop-
ic, composed of myriad individual segments
continually changing through space and
time. Great environmental contrasts occur
within short distances as a result of the diverse topography and highly variable nature
of the energy flux within the system. While
in the mountains, have you ever sought
refuge from the wind in the lee of a rock?
If so, you have experienced the kind of
difference that can occur within a small area.

Near the margin of a species' distribution, such differences may decide between life and death; thus, plants and animals reach their highest elevations by taking advantage of microhabitats. Great variations also occur within short time-spans. When the sun is shining it may be quite warm, even in winter, but if a passing cloud blocks the sun, the temperature drops rapidly. Therefore, areas exposed to the sun undergo much greater and more frequent temperature contrasts than those in shade. This is true for all environments, of course, but the difference is much greater in mountains because the thin alpine air does not hold heat well.

In more general terms, the climate of a slope may be very different from that of a ridge or valley. When these basic differences are compounded by the infinite variety of combinations created by the orientation, spacing, and steepness of slopes, along with the presence of snow patches, vegetation, and soil, the complexity of climatic patterns in mountains becomes truly overwhelming. Nevertheless, predictable patterns and characteristics are found within this heterogeneous system; for example, temperatures normally decrease with altitude while precipitation increases, it is usually windier in mountains, the air is thinner and clearer, and the sun's rays are more intense.

Mountains also have important effects on the climates of adjacent regions. Their influence may be felt for hundreds or thousands of kilometers, making surrounding areas warmer or colder or wetter or drier than they would be if the mountains were not there. The exact effect of the mountains depends upon their location, size, and orientation with respect to the moisture source and the direction of the prevailing winds. The 2,400-kilometer-long (1,500 mi.) natural barrier of the Himalayas permits tropical climates to extend farther north in India and southeast Asia than they do anywhere else in the world. One of the heaviest rainfall records in the world also occurs at Cherrapunji, near the base of the Himalayas in Assam. This famous weather station has an annual rainfall of 10,871 mm (428 in.). Its record for a single day is 1,041 mm (41 in.)— as much as Chicago or London receives in an entire year (Kendrew 1961, p. 173)! On the north side of the Himalayas, however, there are extensive deserts and the temperatures are abnormally low for the latitude. This contrast in environment between north and south is due almost entirely to the presence of the mountains, whose east-west orientation and great height prevent the invasion of warm air into central Asia just as surely as they prevent major invasions of cold air into India. It is no wonder that the Hindus pay homage to Siva, the great god of the Himalayas!

MAJOR CLIMATIC CONTROLS

Mountain climates occur within the framework of the surrounding regional climate and are controlled by the same factors, including latitude, altitude, continentality, and regional circumstances such as ocean currents, prevailing wind direction, and the location of semipermanent high and low-pressure cells. As we have seen, mountains themselves, by acting as a barrier, affect regional climate. Our primary concern is in the significance of all these more or less independent controls to the weather and climate of mountains.

Latitude

The distance north or south of the equator governs the angle at which the sun's rays strike the earth, and the length of the day. In the tropics, the sun is always high overhead at midday and the days and nights are of nearly equal length throughout the year. As a result, there is no winter or summer; one day differs from another only in the amount of cloud cover. There is an old adage, "Night is the winter of the tropics." With increase in latitude, however, the height of the sun changes during the course of the year, and days and nights become

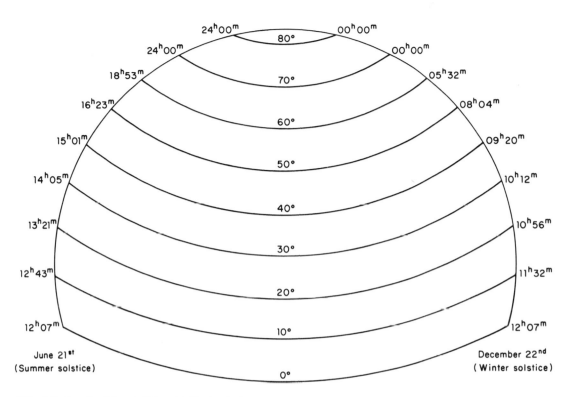

Fig. 4.1. Length of day at different latitudes during summer and winter solstice in the northern hemisphere. (From Rumney 1968, p. 90)

longer or shorter depending on the season (Fig. 4.1). Thus, during summer solstice in the northern hemisphere (June 21) the day is 12 hours and 7 minutes long at Mount Kenya on the equator; 13 hours and 53 minutes long at Mount Everest in the Himalayas (28° lat.); 15 hours and 45 minutes long at the Matterhorn in the Swiss Alps (41° lat.); and 20 hours and 19 minutes long at Mount McKinley in Alaska (63° lat.) (List 1958, pp. 507–11). During the winter, of course, the length of day and night at any given location are reversed. Consequently, the distribution of solar energy is greatly variable in space and time: in the polar regions, the extreme situation, up to six months of continuous sunlight follow six months of continuous night.

Although the highest latitudes receive the lowest amounts of heat energy, middle latitudes frequently experience higher temperatures during the summer than do the tropics. This is due to moderate sun heights and longer days. Furthermore, mountains in middle latitudes may experience even greater solar intensity than lowlands, both because the atmosphere is thinner and because the sun's rays strike slopes oriented toward the sun at a higher angle than level surfaces. A surface inclined 20° toward the sun in middle latitudes receives about twice as much radiation during the winter as a level surface. It can be seen that slope angle and orientation with respect to the sun are vastly important and may partially compensate for latitude.

The basic pattern of global atmospheric-pressure systems reflects the role of latitude. These systems are known as the equatorial low (0°–20° lat.), subtropical high (20°–40° lat.), subpolar low (40°–70° lat.), and polar high (70°–90° lat.). The equatorial low and subpolar low are zones of relatively heavy precipitation while the subtropical high and polar high are areas of low precipitation. Therefore, the distribution of mountains in the global pressure areas has a major influence on their climate. Mountains near the equator—such as Mount Kilimanjaro in East Africa, Mount Kinabalu in Borneo, or Mount Cotopaxi in Ecuador—are under the influence of the equatorial low and receive precipitation almost daily. By contrast, mountains located at 30° latitude may experience considerable aridity—for example, the northern Himalayas and Tibetan highlands, as well as the Puna de Atacama in the Andes, the most arid high-mountain region in the world (Troll 1968, p. 17). It is also evident in the Atlas mountains of North Africa and in the mountains of the southwestern United States and northern Mexico. Farther poleward, the Alps, the Rockies, the southern Andes, and the southern Alps of New Zealand again receive heavy precipitation, especially on westward slopes facing prevailing winds from the sea.

Altitude

Fundamental to mountain climatology are the changes that occur in the atmosphere with increasing altitude, especially the decrease in temperature, air density, water vapor, carbon dioxide, and impurities. The sun is the ultimate source of energy, but very little heating of the atmosphere takes place directly. The earth absorbs the shortwave energy coming from the sun, converts it to longwave energy, and the earth itself becomes the radiating body. The atmosphere, therefore, is heated directly by the earth, not by the sun. This is why the highest temperatures usually occur next to the earth and decrease outward. Mountains are part of the earth, too, but they present a smaller land area at higher elevations, so they are less able to modify

the temperature of the surrounding air. A mountain peak is analogous to an oceanic island. The smaller the island and the farther it is from large land masses, the more its climate will be like that of the surrounding sea. By contrast, the larger the island or mountain area, the more it modifies its own climate. This *mountain mass effect* is a major factor in the local climate (see pp. 77–81).

The density and composition of the air control its ability to hold heat. The weight or density of the air at sea level (standard atmospheric pressure) is generally expressed as 760 mm (29.92 in.) of mercury. Near the earth, pressure decreases at a rate of approximately 30 mm for every 300 m (1 in. per 1,000 ft.) of increased altitude; above 5,000 m (20,000 ft.), though, atmospheric pressure begins to fall off exponentially. Thus, half the weight of the atmosphere occurs below an altitude of 5,500 m (18,000 ft.) and the pressure is halved again in the next 6,000 m (Fig. 4.2).

The ability of air to hold heat is a function of its molecular structure. At higher altitudes, molecules are spaced farther apart, so there are fewer molecules in a given parcel of air to receive and hold heat. Similarly, the composition of the air changes rapidly with altitude, losing water vapor, carbon dioxide, and suspended particulate matter (Tables 4.1 and 4.2). These constituents, important in determining the ability of the air to hold heat, are all concentrated in the lower reaches of the atmosphere. Water vapor is the chief heat-absorbing constituent, and half of the water vapor in the air occurs below an elevation of 1,800 m (6,000 ft.). It diminishes rapidly above this point and is barely detectable at elevations above 12,000 m (40,000 ft.).

The importance of water vapor as a reservoir of heat can be seen by comparing the daily temperature range of a desert and a humid area. Both areas may heat up equally during the day but, due to the rel-

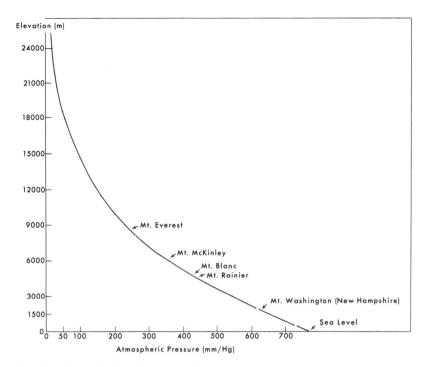

Fig. 4.2. Generalized profile showing decrease of atmospheric pressure with altitude. (Adapted from several sources)

ative absence of water vapor to absorb and hold the heat energy, the desert area cools down much more at night than the humid area. The mountain environment's response is similar to that of a desert but is even more accentuated, because the thin pure air of high altitudes cannot hold heat. Mountains depend for warmth almost entirely on the sun, not on the surrounding air (although some mountains receive considerable heat from precipitation processes). The sun's rays pass through the high thin air with negligible heating. Consequently, although the temperature at 1,800 m (6,000 ft.) in the free atmosphere changes very little between day and night, next to a mountain peak, the sun's rays are intercepted and absorbed. The soil surface may be quite warm but the envelope of heated air is usually only a few meters thick and displays a steep temperature gradient.

In theory, every point along a given latitude receives the same amount of sunshine; in reality, of course, clouds interfere. The amount of cloudiness is controlled by distance from the ocean, direction of prevailing winds, dominance of pressure systems, and altitude. Precipitation normally increases with altitude, but only up to a certain point. Precipitation is generally heaviest on middle slopes where clouds first form and the moisture is greatest; it often decreases at higher altitudes. Thus, the lower slopes can be wrapped in clouds while the higher slopes are sunny. In the Alps, for example, the outer ranges receive more precipitation and less sunshine than the higher interior ranges. The herders in the Tien Shan and Pamir Mountains of Central Asia traditionally take their flocks higher in the winter than in summer to take advantage of the lower snowfall and sunnier conditions at the higher altitudes. High mountains have another advantage with respect to possible sunshine: in effect, they lower the horizon. The sun shines earlier in the morning and later in the evening on mountain peaks than on the surrounding lowlands.

Continentality

The relationship between land and water has a strong influence on the climate of a region. Generally, the more water-dominated an area is, the more moderate its climate. An extreme example is a small oceanic island, on which the climate is essentially that of the surrounding sea. The other extreme is a central location on a large land mass such as Eurasia, far removed from the sea. Water heats and cools more slowly than land, so the temperature ranges between day and night and between winter and summer are smaller in marine areas than in continental areas.

The same principle applies to alpine landscapes, but is intensified by the barrier effect of mountains. We have already noted this effect in the Himalayas between India and China. The Cascades in the Pacific Northwest of the United States provide another good example. This range extends north-south at right angles to the prevailing westerly wind off the Pacific Ocean. As a result, western Oregon and Washington have a marine-dominated climate characterized by moderate temperatures, cloudiness, and persistent winter precipitation. The eastern side of the Cascades, however, experiences a continental climate characterized by hot summers and cold winters with a minimum of precipitation. In less than 85 km (50 mi.) across the Cascades the vegetation changes from lush green forests to dry-land shrubs and grasses (Price 1971a). This spectacular transect provides eloquent testimony to the vast differences in climate that may occur within a short horizontal distance. The presence of the mountains increases the precipitation in western Oregon and Washington at the expense of that received on

the east side. Additionally, the Cascades inhibit the invasion of cold continental air to the Pacific side. At the same time, their obstruction of mild Pacific air allows the continental climate to extend much closer to the ocean than it otherwise would (Church and Stephens 1941). It must be stressed that the significance of mountains in accentuating continentality depends upon their orientation with respect to the ocean and prevailing winds. Western Europe has a climate similar to the Pacific Northwest, but the east-west orientation of the European mountains allows the marine climate to extend far inland.

The effect of continentality on mountain climate is much like that on climate generally. Mountains in the interior of continents experience more sunshine, less cloudiness, greater extremes in temperatures, and less precipitation than mountains along the coasts. This would seem to add up to a more rigorous environment, but there may be extenuating circumstances. The extra sunshine in continental regions tends to compensate for the lower ambient temperatures, while the greater cloudiness and snowfall in coastal mountains tend to make the environment more rigorous for certain organisms than is suggested by the moderate temperatures of these regions. The fact that trees generally grow to higher altitudes on continental mountains than coastal mountains is a good, if rough, indication of the importance of these compensating circumstances to regional mountain climate and ecology (see pp. 277–82). People, too, find that the bright sunshine typical of high mountain slopes can make the low air temperatures of the alpine environment tolerable. During the winter in the Alps, for instance, when it is cloudy and rainy in the surrounding lowlands and foggy in the lower valleys, the mountain slopes and higher valleys may bask in brilliant sunshine. It is for this reason that lodges and tourist facilities in the Alps are generally located higher up on the slopes and in high valleys. Health resorts and sanatoriums also take advantage of the intense sunlight and clean dry air of the high mountains (Hill 1924).

Barrier Effects

Several examples of how mountains serve as barriers have already been given. The Himalayas and Cascades are both outstanding climatic divides that create unlike conditions on their windward and leeward sides. All mountains serve as barriers to a greater or lesser extent, depending on their size, shape, orientation, and relative location. Specifically, the barrier effect of mountains can be grouped under the following subheadings: (1) damming, (2) deflection, (3) blocking, (4) disturbance of the upper air, (5) forced ascent, and (6) forced descent.

Damming

Damming of stable air occurs when the mountains are high enough to prevent the passage of an air mass across them. When this happens, a steep pressure-gradient may develop between the windward and leeward sides of the range. The effectiveness of the damming depends upon the depth of the air mass and the elevation of the lowest valleys or passes. A shallow, ground-hugging air mass may be effectively dammed, but a deep one is likely to flow through higher gaps and transverse valleys to the other side. Of course, sea-level valleys permit even shallow air masses to penetrate the mountain barrier. In the Cascades, for example, two low-level valleys transect the range—the Fraser River Valley in British Columbia and the Columbia River Gorge between Washington and Oregon. They are foci of extreme weather conditions, since they serve as release valves for the unlike pressure conditions that develop on the east and west side of the mountains (Lawrence 1939; Lynott 1966).

Deflection

When an air mass is dammed by a mountain range, the winds are usually deflected by the mountains. In winter, polar continental air coming down from Canada across the central United States is channeled to the south and east by the Rocky Mountains. Consequently, the Great Plains experience more severe winter weather than does the Great Basin (Church and Stephens 1941; Baker 1944). Similarly, as the cold air progresses southward, the Sierra Madre Oriental prevents it from crossing into the interior of Mexico. The east coast of Mexico also provides an excellent example of deflection in the summer: the northeast trade winds blowing across the Gulf of Mexico cannot cross the mountains and are deflected southward through the Isthmus of Tehuantepec, where they become northerly winds of unusual violence (Hurd 1929).

Blocking

High-pressure areas prevent the passage of storms. Large mountain ranges such as the Rockies and Himalayas are very efficient at blocking storms: since they are often the foci of anticyclonic systems (because the mountains are a center of cold air), the storms must detour around the mountains. The jet streams may also split to flow around the mountains; they rejoin to the lee of the range, where they often intensify and produce storms (Reiter 1963, pp. 379–91). In North America these storms, known as "Colorado Lows" or "Alberta Lows," reach their greatest frequency and intensity in the spring season, sometimes causing heavy blizzards on the Great Plains and Prairie provinces. The tornadoes and violent squall lines that form in the American Midwest also result from the great contrasts in air masses which develop in the confluence zone to the lee of the Rockies (McClain 1958; Henz 1972).

Mountains have additional influence on the location and intensity of the jet streams, which, as we are increasingly discovering, have vastly important effects on the kind of weather experienced at any particular place and time. The splitting of the jet streams by the Himalayas has the effect of intensifying the barrier effect in this region and produces a stronger climatic divide. In addition, the presence of the Himalayas reverses the direction of the jet streams in early summer. The Tibetan Highlands act as a "heat engine" in the warm season, with a giant chimney in their southeastern corner through which heat is carried upward into the atmosphere. This causes a gradual warming of the upper air above the Himalayas during the spring, which weakens and finally eliminates the subtropical westerly jet; it is then replaced by the tropical easterly jet during the summer. Thus, the Himalayas are intimately connected with the complex interaction of the upper air and the development of the Indian monsoon (Flohn 1968; Hahn and Manabe 1975).

Disturbance of the Upper Air

In addition to the effect of blocking, mountains cause other perturbations to upper-air circulation. This occurs on a variety of scales: locally, with the wind immediately adjacent to the mountains; on an intermediate scale, creating large waves in the air; and on a global basis, with the larger mountain ranges actually influencing the motion of planetary waves (Bolin 1950; Gambo 1956; Kasahara 1967) and the transport momentum of the total circulation (White 1949). (Beyond the mere mention of it, this largest level will be disregarded here, since it is beyond the scope of our concern.)

Disturbance of the air by mountains generally creates a wave pattern much like that found in the wake of a ship. This may result in the kind of clear-air turbulence feared by airline pilots (Alaka 1958; Colson 1963) or it may simply produce lee waves with their beautiful lenticular (standing-wave) clouds, associated with mountains the world over (Scorer 1961) (Fig. 4.40). The new art of satellite photography has greatly aided in the study of large-scale waves to the lee of mountains (Fig. 4.42).

An area of low precipitation immediately surrounds the San Francisco Mountains of Arizona for up to 16 km (10 mi.); farther away the precipitation increases. The ring of low precipitation is thought to coincide with the trough of the wave created by the air passing over the mountains, while the heavier precipitation coincides with the ridge (Fujita 1967). A similar situation exists in the lee of the Rocky Mountains: the area immediately to the lee is frequently cloud-free and receives low precipitation, while regions farther east are cloudy and wetter. This pattern corresponds to an intermediate-scale wave whose trough is located close to the lee of the mountains and whose ridge is located over the eastern United States (Reiter et al. 1965; Dirks et al. 1967).

A very interesting consequence of the frictional modification of atmospheric circulation is the relationship between topography and the occurrence of tornadoes. It has long been known that tornadoes appear less frequently in mountains than in lowlands. An investigation of tornadoes in Wisconsin and Arkansas has revealed the existence of "tornado alleys" separated by "shunt zones" (Asp 1956; Gallimore and Lettau 1970). The main areas of tornado occurrence in Arkansas are the coastal plain and the Arkansas River Valley, while the shunt zones are in the Ozark and Ouachita mountains (Fig. 4.3). Although these low mountains probably do not affect the direction of tornado movement in progress, they apparently have a very real influence on their inception, through the creation of surface roughness and turbidity in the boundary layer (Lettau 1967, p. 4).

Forced Ascent

When moist air blows perpendicular to a mountain range, the air is forced to rise; as it does, it is cooled. Eventually the dew point is reached, condensation occurs (clouds), and precipitation results (see p. 94). Some of the rainiest places in the world are mountain slopes in the path of winds blowing off relatively warm oceans. Examples are legion

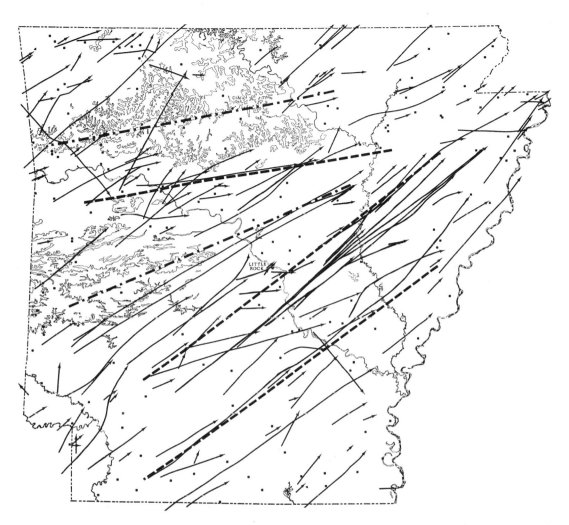

Fig. 4.3. Tornado paths in Arkansas, 1879–1955, with Ouachita and Boston mountains shown by contours. Arrows indicate direction and length of individual tornado movement. Dots show paths too short to track. Heavy dashed lines designate areas of greatest occurrence or "tornado alleys," and heavy dash-dot lines indicate areas of infrequent occurrence or "shunt zones." (After Asp 1956, p. 144, and Lettau 1967, p. 5)

and could be given from every continent, but the mountainous Hawaiian Islands will serve as an illustration. The precipitation over the water around Hawaii averages about 650 mm (25 in.) per year, while the islands average 1,800 mm (70 in.) per year. This is largely due to the presence of mountains, many of which receive over 6,000 mm (240 in.) per year. At Mount Waialeale on Kauai, the average annual rainfall reaches the extraordinary total of 12,344 mm (486 in.), i.e., 12.3 m (40.5 ft.)! This is the highest recorded annual average in the world (Blumenstock and Price 1967). In the continental United States, the heaviest precipitation occurs on the western side of the Olympic Mountains in Washington, where an average of 3,800 mm (150 in.) or more is received annually (Phillips 1972).

Although heavy precipitation may take place on the windward side of mountains where the air is forced to rise, the leeward side may receive considerably less precipitation because the air is no longer being lifted and much of the moisture has already been removed. To the lee of Mount Waialeale, Kauai, precipitation decreases at the rate of 3,000 mm (118 in.) per 1.6 km (1 mi.) along a 4 km (2.5 mi.) transect to Hanalei Tunnel. This still leaves a total of 5,080 mm (200 in.), but the gradient is nevertheless extreme (Blumenstock and Price 1967). In the Olympic Mountains, precipitation decreases from 3,800 mm (150 in.) on the windward side to less than 430 mm (17 in.) at the town of Sequim on the leeward, a distance of only 48 km (30 mi.) (Phillips 1972). Since both of these leeward areas are maritime, they are still quite cloudy; under more continental conditions, there would be a corresponding increase in sunshine as precipitation decreases, especially where the air is forced to descend on the leeward side.

Forced Descent

Atmospheric-pressure conditions determine whether the air, after passing over a mountain barrier, will maintain its altitude or whether it will be forced to descend. If the air is forced to descend, it will be heated by compression (*adiabatic heating*) and will result in clear, dry conditions. This is a characteristic phenomenon in the lee of mountains and is responsible for the famous foehn or chinook winds (see pp. 114–19). The important point here is that the descent of the air is induced by the barrier effect and results in clear dry conditions that allow the sunshine to reach the ground with much greater intensity and frequency than it otherwise would. This can produce "climatic oases" in the lee of mountain ranges, e.g., in the Po Valley of Italy (Thams 1961).

MAJOR CLIMATIC ELEMENTS

The discussion so far has covered the more or less independent climatic controls of latitude, altitude, continentality, and the barrier effect of mountains. These factors, along with ocean currents, pressure condi-

tions, and prevailing winds, control the distribution of sunshine, temperature, humidity, precipitation, and local winds. The climatic elements—e.g., sunshine, temperature, and precipitation—are essentially dependent variables reflecting the major climatic controls; they interact in complex ways to produce the day-to-day weather conditions experienced in different regions.

Solar Radiation

The sun is the primary climatic factor in high mountains. The effect of the sun becomes more exaggerated and distinct with altitude. The time lag, in terms of energy flow, between stimulus and reaction is greatly compressed. Looking at the effect of the sun in high mountains is like viewing its effects at lower elevations through a powerful magnifying glass. The alpine environment has perhaps the most extreme and variable radiation climate on earth. The thin clean air allows very high solar intensities, and the mountain landscape provides diverse surfaces at different exposures. Although the air next to the ground may heat up very rapidly under the direct rays of the sun, it may cool just as rapidly if the sun's rays are blocked. Thus, in the sun's daily and seasonal march through the sky mountains experience a continually changing pattern of sunshine and shadow, of energy flux in the ecosystem. The major factors to consider are the amount of sunlight received, the quality or kinds of rays, and the effect of slopes upon this energy.

Amount of Solar Radiation

The most striking aspect of the vertical distribution of solar radiation in the atmosphere is the rapid depletion of short-wavelength energy (ultraviolet radiation) at lower elevations. This diminution results from the increased density of the air and the greater abundance of water vapor, carbon dioxide, and particulate matter (Tables 4.1 and 4.2).

Table 4.1. *Average density of suspended particulate matter in the atmosphere with changing elevation (Landsberg 1962, p. 114).*

Elevation (m)	Number of Particles (cu. cm)	Number of Particles (cu. in.)
0–500	25,000	435,000
500–1,000	12,000	209,000
1,000–2,000	2,000	34,800
2,000–3,000	800	14,000
3,000–4,000	350	6,100
4,000–5,000	170	3,000
5,000–6,000	80	1,400

The atmosphere acts as a filter, reducing the intensity of some wavelengths and screening out others altogether. Consequently, the amount of energy reaching the earth at sea level is only about half that at the outer reaches of the atmosphere (Fig. 4.4). High mountains protrude through the lower atmospheric blanket and thus have the potential for receiving much higher levels of solar radiation, as well as cosmic-ray gamma radiation (Solon et al. 1960).

The first, and very vital, screening of solar energy takes place in the high atmosphere (stratosphere) where most of the deleterious rays of the sun are absorbed by the ozone layer. It is probable that life on earth could not exist if it were not for the presence of ozone in the atmosphere. The shortwave energy is further reduced by *scattering* when it strikes tiny molecules of air, water, and dust. Scattering is a selective process that takes place when the diameter of the obscuring particle is less than that of the wavelength. Scattering principally affects the wavelengths of blue light; when scattering is in full operation, it can be recognized by the deeper blue of the sky. Have you ever noticed how much bluer or darker the sky looks in high mountains than it appears at lower elevations? That is because there is more shortwave energy at higher altitudes and because scattering is the principal atmospheric process affecting the incoming radiation. At lower altitudes, *reflection* is the primary process of radiation return. Reflection is a non-selective process caused by the larger obscuring molecules of water and impurities. It affects all wavelengths, so no color change takes place. Clouds, of course, are the single most important factor in controlling variable receipt of solar energy at any given latitude.

Because of the atmosphere's filtering action on solar radiation, the more atmosphere the sunlight has to pass through, the greater

Table 4.2. *Average water-vapor content of air with elevation in middle latitudes (Landsberg 1962, p. 110).*

Elevation (m)	Volume (percent)
0	1.30
500	1.16
1,000	1.01
1,500	0.81
2,000	0.69
2,500	0.61
3,000	0.49
3,500	0.41
4,000	0.37
5,000	0.27
6,000	0.15
7,000	0.09
8,000	0.05

the attenuation. Consequently, the sun is most intense when it is directly overhead (90°) and its rays concentrated in the smallest area. When the sun is only 4° above the horizon, solar rays have to penetrate an atmosphere more than twelve times as thick as when the sun is directly overhead. This explains why it is possible to look directly at the orange ball of the sun at sunrise and sunset without being blinded. It also ex-

plains why the sun's rays are much more intense in mountains: there is less atmosphere to pass through, and mountains stand above the lower reaches of the atmosphere which provide the most effective filtering action (Fig. 4.5).

Table 4.3 gives figures for daily global radiation received at different elevations in the Austrian Alps. Solar intensity increases with altitude under all conditions, but the

Fig. 4.4. Spectral distribution of direct solar radiation at the outside of the atmosphere and at sea level. Calculations are for clear skies with the sun directly overhead. Also shown is the spectral distribution of cloud light and sky light. The graph is plotted on a wavenumber scale in cm^{-1} that is the reciprocal of the wavelength and is directly proportional to the frequency of light, to allow display of the full spectrum (a wavelength plot has difficulty including the visible and infrared together). The total area under the upper curve is the solar constant, 2.0 cal. cm^{-2} min^{-1}. (After Gates and Janke 1966, p. 42)

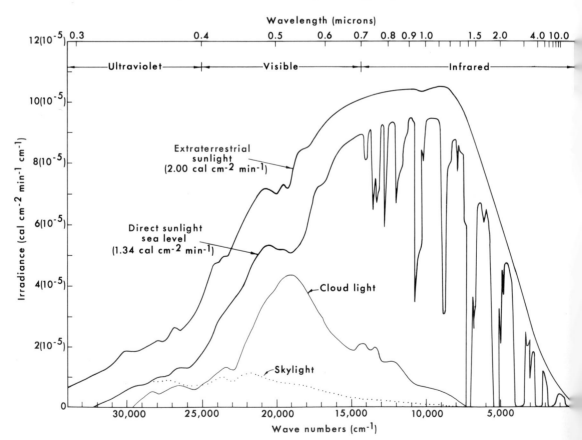

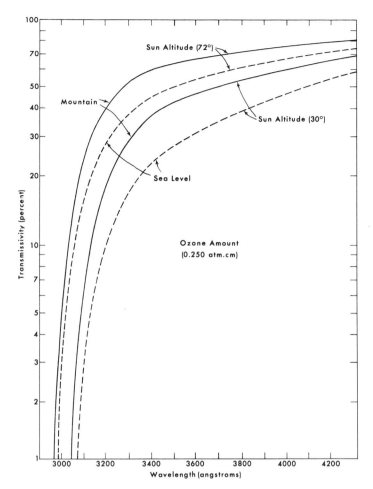

Fig. 4.5. Spectral transmissivity of the atmosphere at 4,200 m (14,000 ft.) and at sea level for a latitude of 40° at summer and winter solstice. The attenuation shown here is for clear skies and is due entirely to ozone absorption. When the effects of dust, water vapor, and other impurities are included, the difference in transmissions between high and low elevations becomes considerably greater. (After Gates and Janke 1966, p. 45)

greatest differential between high and low-level stations occurs when skies are overcast. In summer, when skies are clear, there is 21 percent more radiation at 3,000 m (10,000 ft.) than at 200 m (650 ft.); but when skies are overcast, there is 160 percent more radiation at the higher elevation. Overcast skies are much more efficient at filtering out short-

wave energy, so less reaches the lower elevation (Geiger 1965, p. 443).

The *solar constant* is defined as the average amount of total radiation energy received from the sun at the outside of the atmosphere on a surface perpendicular to the sun's rays (Fig. 4.4). This is approximately two calories per square centimeter per min-

Table 4.3. *Average daily global-radiation totals (cal. cm⁻² d⁻¹) received on a horizontal surface at different elevations in the Austrian Alps. (Data include diffuse and reflected energy as well as direct solar radiation) (Geiger 1965, p. 444).*

Elevation (m)	Cloudless		Overcast	
	June	December	June	December
200	691	130	155	30
400	708	136	168	32
600	723	141	180	34
800	735	146	192	36
1,000	747	150	205	38
1,200	759	154	220	40
1,400	771	157	236	43
1,600	782	160	253	47
1,800	791	163	272	50
2,000	799	166	293	54
2,200	807	168	314	58
2,400	814	169	336	62
2,600	821	170	358	66
2,800	828	171	380	70
3,000	834	171	403	75

ute (2.0 cal. cm⁻² min⁻¹). At midday under clear, transparent skies the total calorie flux from the sun in mountains may almost equal the solar constant. Angstrom and Drummond (1966, p. 801) have calculated the theoretical upper limit on high mountains to be 1.85 cal. cm⁻² min⁻¹, but several investigations have recorded readings near or even slightly above the solar constant (Turner 1958a; Gates and Janke 1966; Bishop et al. 1966; Terjung et al. 1969a, b; Marcus and Brazel 1974). The conditions under which the highest values have been recorded are clear and transparent skies with occasional scattered cumulus clouds. Under these conditions the surface not only receives direct radiation from the sun but also receives radiation reflected from clouds. Turner (1958a) measured instantaneous values as high as 2.25 cal. cm⁻² min⁻¹ in the Alps. This is 112 percent of the solar constant! If there are drifting clouds, the sun may be blocked for varying lengths of time, which causes great fluctuations in the amount of sunshine received. Variations in global radiation up to seven times the value of the solar constant in one minute and up to fif-

teen times its value in eleven minutes have been observed in the Alps, exemplifying the spectacular changes that may occur in short lengths of time in high mountains (Turner 1958b, in Geiger 1965, p. 443).

Quality of Solar Radiation

The relatively greater quantity of shorter wavelengths received at high elevations has special significance for life and for biological processes. An old proverb in the Andes says, *"Solo los gringos y los burros caminan en el sol"* ("Only foreigners and donkeys walk in the sunshine"). This saying indicates the respect the Andeans give to the efficacy of the sun at high altitudes (Prohaska 1970). Ultraviolet light has been cited for numerous harmful effects, ranging from retardation of growth in tundra plants (Lockart and Franzgrote 1961) to cancer in humans (Blum 1959). Some of the deleterious effects on plants have been questioned (Caldwell 1968), but there is no question that the greater quantity of ultraviolet light in mountains does create additional stress in an environment already extreme. Solar energy in the ultraviolet spectrum is mainly responsible for the deep tans of mountain dwellers and the painful sunburns of neophytes who expose too much of their skin too quickly. The wavelengths responsible for sunburn occur primarily between 2,800 and 3,200 Å., while those responsible for darkening the skin occur between 3,000 and 4,000 Å. Wavelengths less than 3,200 Å. are known to cause skin cancer.

The alpine environment receives considerably more ultraviolet energy than low elevations. If only wavelengths shorter than 3,200 Å. are considered, alpine areas receive 50 percent more ultraviolet light during summer solstice than do areas at sea level (Fig. 4.6). Later in the year, when the sun is lower in the sky (and therefore passes through denser atmosphere), alpine areas receive 120 percent more ultraviolet energy than areas at sea level (Gates and Janke 1966, p. 47).

Caldwell (1968, pp. 250–52), believes that these calculations of ultraviolet light are too high; he found an increase of only 4 to 50 percent from sea level to 3,650 m (12,000 ft.). His investigations in the Colorado Rockies indicate that while direct-solar-beam ultraviolet light increases with altitude, sky

Fig. 4.6. Spectral distribution of total sunlight (direct and diffuse) on a horizontal surface at 3,650 m (12,000 ft.) and at sea level. This is shortwave ultraviolet radiation measured as a function of area under the curve. Calculations are made for a latitude of 40° N. at summer and winter solstice. Alpine environments (solid lines) receive substantially more ultraviolet energy than does the surface at sea level. (After Gates and Janke 1966, p. 47)

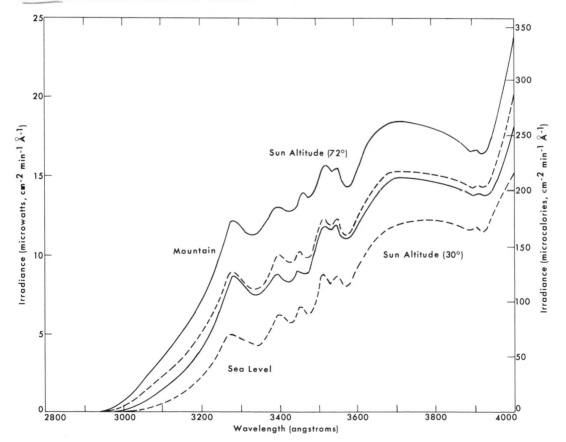

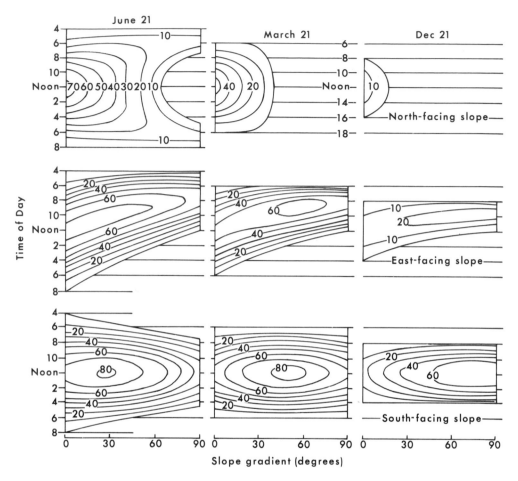

Fig. 4.7. Direct solar radiation (cal. cm^{-2} hr^{-1}) received on different slopes during clear weather at 50° N. lat. Three slopes are shown: north, south, and east-facing (west would be a mirror image of east), for summer and winter solstice and equinox (vernal is a mirror image of autumnal). The lefthand side of each diagram shows the distribution of solar energy on a horizontal surface (0° gradient) and is therefore identical for each set of 3 in the same column. The righthand side of each diagram represents a vertical wall (90° gradient). The top of each diagram shows sunrise and the bottom shows sunset. As can be seen, the north- and south-facing slopes experience a symmetrical distribution of energy, while the east and west reveal an asymmetrical distribution. Thus, on the east-facing slope during summer solstice the sun begins shining on a vertical cliff at about 4:00 A.M and highest intensity occurs at 8:00 A.M. By noon the cliff passes into shadow. The opposite would hold true for a west-facing wall: it would begin receiving the direct rays of the sun immediately past noon.

The bottom row of diagrams illustrates a south-facing slope. During equinox days and nights are equal, so the distribution of energy is equal. During winter solstice the sun strikes south-facing slopes of all gradients at the same time (sunrise), but during summer the sun rises farther to the northeast, so some time elapses before it can shine on a south-facing slope. This difference in time increases with steeper slopes: for example, a 30° south-facing slope would receive the sun at about 5:00 A.M. and would pass into shadow at about 6:30 P.M., while a 60° south-facing slope would receive the sun at 6:30 A.M. (1 1/2 hrs. later) and the sun would set at 5:30 P.M. (1 hr. earlier). On a north-facing slope (top row of diagrams) during summer, slopes up to 60° receive the sun at the same time, but if the slope is greater than 60°, the sun cannot shine on it at noon; hence the "neck" cut out of the righthand margin. Steep north-facing slopes at this latitude would only receive the sun early in the morning and late in the evening. During the winter solstice only north-facing slopes with gradients of less than 15° would receive any sun at all. (After Geiger 1965, p. 374) ultraviolet light decreases, owing to reduced scattering of the thinner atmosphere. The net result is only a modest increase in ultraviolet light with elevation. His study shows a 26 percent increase in ultraviolet light between elevations of 1,670 and 4,350 m (5,500–14,300 ft.) on a cloudless summer day. Caldwell also believes that many high mountain areas do not receive more total solar radiation than lowland areas, because of the increased cloud cover. This, of course, depends upon the mountain area and the time of year. Nevertheless, there is no question that mountains generally have greater cloudiness and feel the impact of passing storms more than lowlands do. The contradiction between these findings points to the great variability of mountain climates and also to the fact that we still have a great deal to learn about them.

Effect of Slopes on Solar Radiation

The play of the sun on the mountain landscape is like a symphony. As the hours, days, and seasons follow one another, the sun bursts upon some slopes with all the strength of crescendo while the shadows lengthen and fade into diminuendo on others. The melody is continuous and ever-changing, with as many scores as there are mountain regions, but the theme remains the same. It is a study of slope angle and orientation.

The closer to perpendicularly the sun's rays strike a surface, the greater their intensity. The longer the sun shines on a surface, the greater the heating that takes place. In mountains, every slope has a different potential for receiving the sun. This amount can be measured if the following facts are known: latitude, time of year (height of sun), time of day, slope angle, and slope orientation (Garnier and Ohmura 1968, 1970; Swift 1976). There are many problems associated with this, however, depending on the kind of information desired, i.e., point measurements, daily or monthly totals, or simply duration of sunlight on any particular slope

(Geiger 1965, p. 369; 1969, p. 105). The basic characteristics of solar radiation on slopes are illustrated in Figure 4.7. This very useful diagram shows the situation for one latitude at four times of the year, at four slope orientations. Other diagrams could be constructed for combinations of these conditions, but they would still not include the effects of clouds, diffuse sky radiation, or the receptiveness of different slopes to the sun's rays. The diagram also fails to reveal the shadow climate caused by the presence of one ridge or peak above another.

Most mountain slopes receive fewer hours of sunshine than a level surface, although slopes facing the sun may receive more energy than a level surface (this is particularly true at higher latitudes). In the tropics, level surfaces usually receive a higher solar intensity than slopes because the sun is always high in the sky. Whatever the duration and intensity of sunlight, the effects are generally clearly evident in the local ecology. In the northern hemisphere, south-facing slopes are warmer and drier than north-facing slopes and, under humid conditions, are more favorable for life. Timberlines go higher on south-facing slopes, and the number and diversity of plants and animals are greater. Man, too, takes advantage of the sunny slopes. In the east-west valleys of the Alps most settlements are located on south-facing slopes. Houses are seldom found within the mid-winter noonday shadow area, although they may go right up to the shadow line (Garnett 1935, 1937) (Fig. 4.8). In spring north-facing slopes may still be deep in snow while south-facing slopes are clear. As a result, north-facing slopes have traditionally been left in forest while south-facing slopes are used for high pastures (Fig. 4.9). The environmental differences are so great between the sunny and shady sides of the valley that each mountain speech or dialect in the Alps has a special term for these slopes (Peattie 1936, p. 88). The most frequently used are the French *adret* (sunny) and *ubac* (shade).

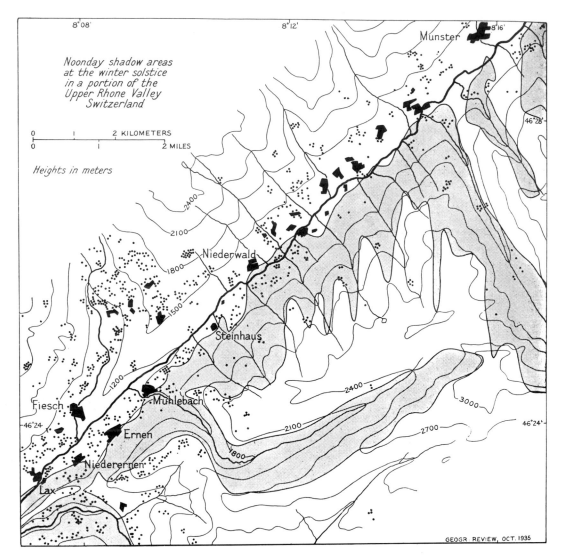

Fig. 4.8. Settlement in relation to noonday shadow areas during winter in the upper Rhône Valley, Switzerland. (From Garnett 1935, p. 602)

The east and west-facing slopes are also affected differently by the sun's rays. Soil and vegetation surfaces are frequently moist in the morning, owing to higher humidity at night and the formation of dew or frost. On east-facing slopes the sun's energy has to evaporate this moisture before the slope can heat appreciably. By the time the sun reaches the west-facing slope, however, the moisture has already evaporated, so the sun's energy more effectively heats the slope. The driest and warmest slopes are, therefore, those which face toward the southwest rather than strictly south (Blumer 1910).

Cloud cover, which varies from season to season and according to time of day, can make a great deal of difference in the amount of solar energy received on slopes. During storms the entire mountain may be wrapped in clouds; even during relatively clear weather, mountains may still experience local clouds. In winter, stratus clouds and fog are characteristic on intermediate slopes and valleys, but these frequently burn off by midday. In summer, the mornings are typically clear but convection clouds (cumulus) build over mountains by mid-afternoon. Consequently, convection clouds result in east-facing slopes receiving greater sunlight while stratus clouds, as described above, allow greater sun on west-facing slopes. Scattered convection clouds do not block the sun as effectively as stratus clouds, but on the other hand, stratus clouds do not affect the higher slopes, while cumu-

lus clouds do. The exact conditions depend upon the region, but it is clear that local clouds often have a marked effect upon the amount of solar energy received by mountains (Fig. 4.10).

A last major factor to consider is the effect of the surface itself upon incoming solar radiation. This is a major consideration in local energy budgets (Miller 1965, 1977). The effects of two factors, groundcover and topographic setting, will illustrate this. Snow-fields, glaciers, and light-colored rocks have a high reflectivity (*albedo*), so much of the incoming shortwave energy is lost. If the snow is in a valley or on a concave slope, reflected energy may bounce from slope to slope, increasing the energy budget of the upper slopes. The opposite occurs on a

Fig. 4.9. View of an east-west valley near Davos, Switzerland, showing settlement and clearing on the sunny side (south-facing), while the shady side (north-facing) is left in forest. (Author)

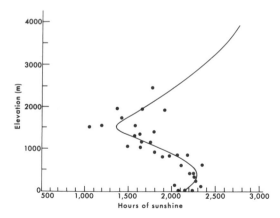

Fig. 4.10. Relationship between total hours of sunshine and altitude in the mountains of Japan. The decrease at about 1,500 m (5,000 ft.) results from the greater presence of clouds and fog at this level. (After Yoshino 1975, p. 185)

mountain ridge or convex slope: the energy is reflected back out into space. Consequently, valleys and depressions are areas of heat build-up and generally experience greater temperature extremes than do ridges and convex slopes. Dark-colored features in the path of reflected sun rays receive increased amounts of energy. You may have experienced this process yourself while skiing—you are likely to sunburn much faster on a snowcovered surface than on bare ground because of the additional shortwave energy striking your body. Reflected energy is an important source of heat for trees in the high mountains. Snow typically melts faster around trees because the increased heat is transferred, as longwave thermal energy, to the adjacent surface. On a larger scale, the presence of forests adds significantly to the heat budget of snowcovered areas. The shortwave energy from the sun can pass through a coniferous forest canopy, but very little of it escapes again to outer space. The absorbed energy heats the tree foliage and produces higher temperatures than in open areas. This results in rapid melting rates for the regional snowpack (Miller 1959).

Temperature

The decrease of temperature with elevation is one of the most striking and fundamental features of mountain climate. Those of us who are fortunate enough to live near mountains are constantly reminded of this fact, either by spending time in the mountains or by viewing the snowcapped peaks from a distance. Nevertheless, there are many subtle and poorly understood characteristics about the nature of temperature in mountains. Alexander Von Humboldt was so struck by the effect of temperature on the altitudinal zonation of climate and vegetation in the tropics that he proposed the terms *tierra caliente*, *tierra templada*, and *tierra fría* for the hot, temperate, and cold zones. These terms, commonplace in the tropics today, are still valid for this region. Their extension to higher latitudes by others, however—under the mistaken assumption that the same basic kinds of temperature conditions occur in belts from the equator to the poles—has been unfortunate. This simplistic approach is still used in some modern textbooks.

Vertical Temperature-Gradient

Change of temperature with elevation is called the *lapse rate* or vertical temperature-gradient. The lapse rate varies according to many factors. De Saussure, who climbed Mount Blanc in 1787, was one of the first to measure temperature at different elevations. Since his time many temperature measurements have been made in mountains throughout the world—and almost every one of them has been different. Nevertheless, by averaging the temperatures at different levels, as well as those measured in the free air by balloon, radiosonde, and aircraft, average lapse rates have been established, ranging from 1° C. to 2° C. (1.8° F. to 3.6° F.) per 300 m (1,000 ft.). Aside from purposes of gross generalization, however, average lapse rates have little value in moun-

Table 4.4. *Temperature conditions with elevation in the eastern Alps (after Geiger 1965, p. 444).*

Elevation (m)	Mean Air Temperature (°C.)			Annual Range	Annual Number of		
	January	July	Year		Frost-Free Days	Frost Alternation Days	Continuous Frost Days
200	− 1.4	19.5	9.0	20.9	272	67	26
400	− 2.5	18.3	8.0	20.8	267	97	1
600	− 3.5	17.1	7.1	20.6	250	78	37
800	− 3.9	16.0	6.4	19.9	234	91	40
1,000	− 3.9	14.8	5.7	18.7	226	86	53
1,200	− 3.9	13.6	4.9	17.5	218	84	63
1,400	− 4.1	12.4	4.0	16.5	211	81	73
1,600	− 4.9	11.2	2.8	16.1	203	78	84
1,800	− 6.1	9.9	1.6	16.0	190	76	99
2,000	− 7.1	8.7	0.4	15.8	178	73	114
2,200	− 8.2	7.2	−0.8	15.4	163	71	131
2,400	− 9.2	5.9	−2.0	15.1	146	68	151
2,600	−10.3	4.6	−3.3	14.9	125	66	174
2,800	−11.3	3.2	−4.5	14.5	101	64	200
3,000	−12.4	1.8	−5.7	14.2	71	62	232

tains. There is no constant relationship between altitude and temperature. Instead, the lapse rate changes continually with changing conditions. For example, the vertical temperature-gradient is normally greater during the day than at night, and greater during the summer than in winter. The gradient is steeper under clear than cloudy conditions, steeper on sun-exposed slopes than shaded ones, and steeper on continental mountains than on maritime mountains (Peattie 1936; Dickson 1959; Tanner 1963; Yoshino 1964a, 1975; Coulter 1967; Marcus 1969). There is also a difference between the characteristics of free-air temperature and that measured on a mountain slope (the latter tends to have a lower mean temperature). Of course, the higher and more isolated a mountain peak is, the more closely its temperature will approach that of the free atmosphere (Schell 1934, 1935; Eide 1945; Samson 1965).

Table 4.4 lists figures for the average decrease of temperature with changing elevation in the Alps, and Figure 4.11 illustrates the temperature changes with altitude in the southern Appalachians of the United States.

The temperatures shown are averages, with some interpolation between stations; the actual decrease with elevation is much more variable. A station located on a sunny slope will have a temperature regime different from that of a shaded slope. The disposition of winds and clouds is equally important, as is the nature of the slope surface—whether it is snowcovered, wet or dry, bare or vegetated. A convex slope has qualities of heat retention different from those of a concave slope. A high valley will heat up more during the day (and cool down more at night) than an exposed ridge at the same elevation will. Nevertheless, broad averages will smooth out the extremes and individual differences, generally showing a steady and progressive decrease in temperature with increase in elevation.

Mountain Mass Effect

Large mountain systems create their own surrounding climate (Ekhart 1948). The greater the surface area or land mass at any given elevation, the greater effect the mountain area will have on its own environment. Mountains serve as elevated heat

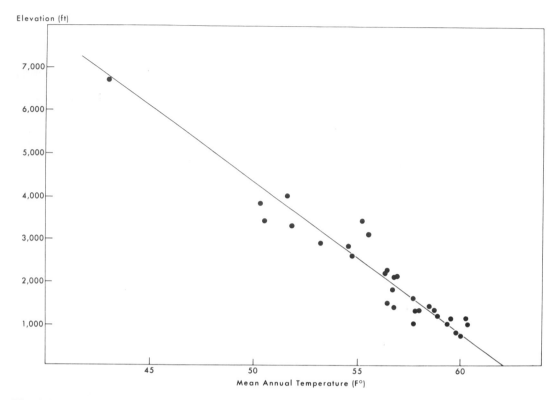

Elevation (ft)

Mean Annual Temperature (F°)

Fig. 4.11. Mean annual temperature with altitude in the southern Appalachian Mountains. Dots represent U.S. Weather Bureau First Order Stations in Tennessee and North Carolina. Temperatures were calculated for period 1921–1950. (Adapted from Dickson 1959, p. 353)

islands where solar radiation is absorbed and transformed into longwave heat energy, resulting in much higher temperatures than those found at similar altitudes in the free air (Gutman and Schwerdtfeger 1965; Flohn 1968). Accordingly, the larger the mountain mass, the more its climate will vary from the free atmosphere at any given elevation. This is particularly evident on some of the high plateaus, where agriculture is possible at greater elevations than on isolated peaks at the same altitude. On the broad general level of the Himalayas, at 4,000 m (13,100 ft.) it seldom freezes during summer, while on the isolated peaks at 5,000 m (16,400 ft.) it seldom thaws (Peattie 1936, p. 18).

An excellent example of the heating effect of large high-altitude land masses is the Mexican Meseta (Fig. 4.12). Radiosonde data indicate higher temperatures in the free atmosphere over the plateau than over the Pacific and Gulf coasts up to an elevation of almost 6,000 m (20,000 ft.). The mean annual temperature over the central plateau at 3,000 m (10,000 ft.) is about 3° C. (5.4° F.) warmer than that over coastal stations (Hastenrath 1968, pp. 122–23). This is largely due to the heating effects of the sun on the larger land mass exposed at higher elevations.

In establishing the relationships between mountain mass and the heat balance, continentality, latitude, amount of cloud cover, winds, precipitation, and surface conditions must all be considered. A persistent cloud cover during the summer can prevent a large mountain mass from showing substantial warming. Also, the presence of a heavy snow cover can retard the warming of a mountain area in spring because of surface reflectivity and the amount of initial heat required to melt the snow. The high Sierra Nevadas of California are relatively warm compared with other mountain areas, in spite of very heavy snowfalls there (Miller 1955, pp. 16–20). This is partially because the extreme clarity of the skies over this region in late summer allows maximum reception of the sun's energy. In general, the effect of greater mountain mass on climate is somewhat like that of increasing continentality. The ranges of temperature are greater than on small mountains, i.e., the winters are colder and the summers warmer, but the average of these temperatures will generally be higher than the free air at the same altitude. The effective growing climate, especially, is more favorable at the soil surface

than in the free air, owing to higher soil temperatures. This is particularly true when there is a high percentage of sunshine (Peattie 1931; Yoshino 1975).

Generally, the larger the mountain mass, the higher the elevation at which vegetation grows. The most striking example of this is found in the Himalayas, where plants reach their absolute highest altitude (Zimmermann 1953; Webster 1961). In the Alps (where the influence of mountain mass, *massenerhebung*, was first observed) the timberline is higher in the more massive central area than on the marginal ranges (Imhof 1900, in Peattie 1936, p. 18). At a more local level, the effects of mountain mass on vegetation development can be observed in the Oregon Cascades. Except for Mount McLoughlin in southern Oregon, timberline is highest and alpine vegetation reaches

Fig. 4.12. Distribution of mean annual temperature (°C.) in a transect across the Mexican Meseta from Mazatlán to Veracruz. The temperature over the plateau at 3,000 m (10,000 ft.) is about 3° C. (5.4° F.) higher than over the coastal stations, owing to greater heating of the elevated land mass. (Adapted from Hastenrath 1968, p. 123)

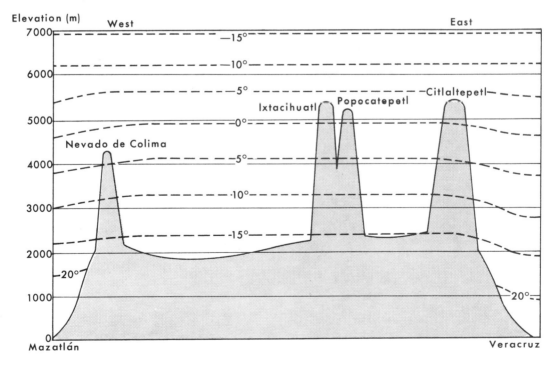

Fig. 4.13. Rice terraces on steep slopes in the Himalayas, near the upper limit for rice cultivation. Most are dry terraces; those in lower left are fed by a spring in the slope and are used for growing wet rice. A village is situated among the dry terraces in the upper part of the slope. The somewhat muted terraces to the right are apparently former terraces that have been abandoned. (Harold Uhlig, University of Giessen)

its best development in the Three Sisters Wilderness area, where three peaks join to form a relatively large land mass above 1,800 m (6,000 ft.) (Price 1978). On the higher but less massive peaks of Mount Hood and Mount Washington a few kilometers to the north, the timberline is 150–300 m (500–1,000 ft.) lower and the alpine vegetation is considerably more impoverished. The development of vegetation involves more than climate, of course, since plant adaptations and species diversity are related to the size of the gene pool and other factors (Van Steenis 1961). Nevertheless, vegetation is a useful indicator of environmental conditions and a positive correlation between vegetational development and mountain mass can be observed in most mountain areas (see pp. 266–67).

An interesting practical consequence of the mountain mass effect is that rice, basically a tropical plant, can grow at higher altitudes in the subtropics than in the tropics. Rice cultivation goes up to 2,500 m (8,250 ft.) in the high interior valleys of the Himalayas (Fig. 4.13) but only reaches about 1,500 m (5,000 ft.) in the humid tropics. The lower tropical limits are due to the lower cloud level, whereas the higher elevations reached in the Himalayas are due to the greater mountain mass and reduced cloudiness, permitting greater possible sunshine, higher temperatures, and a longer growing season than would otherwise be expected. In general, the upper limit of rice cultivation corresponds closely to the limit of frost during the growing season. At the highest levels in the Himalayas, rice seedlings are germinated and grown inside the houses, since it takes eight months for complete production at this altitude but the growing season is only seven months long (Uhlig 1978).

Temperature Inversion

Temperature inversions are ubiquitous in landscapes with marked relief, and anyone who has spent time in or around mountains is certain to have experienced their effects. They are the exception to the general rule of decrease in temperature with elevation. During a temperature inversion the lowest temperatures occur in the valley and increase upward along the mountain slope. Eventually, however, the temperatures will begin to decrease again, so that an intermediate zone, the *thermal belt*, will experience higher night temperatures than either the valley bottom or the upper slopes.

Cold air is heavier than warm air so, as slopes are cooled at night, the colder air begins to move downward, flowing underneath and displacing the warm air in the valley. Temperature inversions are best developed under calm, clear skies, where there is no wind to mix and equalize the temperatures and the transparent sky allows the surface heat to be rapidly radiated and lost to space (Blackadar 1957). Consequently, the surface becomes colder than the air above it, and the air next to the ground is cooled and flows downslope. The cold air will continue to collect in the valley until an equilibrium between the temperatures of the slopes and the valleys has been established. If the valley is enclosed, a pool of relatively stagnant colder air may collect, but if the valley is open there may be a continuous movement of air to the lower levels. The depth of the inversion depends on the characteristics of the local topography and the general weather conditions, but it is generally not more than 300–600 m (1,000–2,000 ft.) in depth.

The downslope flow of cold air is analogous to that of water, since it follows the path of least resistance and always gravitates toward equilibrium, but water has a density 800 times greater than air. Even with a temperature difference of 10° C. (18° F.), the density of cold air is only 4 percent greater than warm air; unlike the rapid flow of water due to gravity, the displacement of warm air by cold air is a relatively slow process (Geiger 1969, p. 122). On broad and gentle slopes the movement of cold air downward

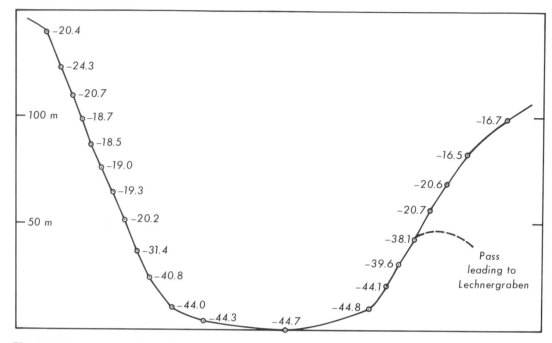

Fig. 4.14. Cross-section of an enclosed basin, Gstett-neralm, in the Austrian Alps, showing a temperature inversion in early spring. Altitude of valley bottom is 1,270 m (4,165 ft.). Note increase in temperature (°C.) with elevation above valley floor, especially the rapid rise directly above the pass. This results from the colder air flowing into a lower valley at this point. (After Schmidt 1934, p. 347)

at night is generally not very noticeable (unless you happen to be sitting on the downslope side of a smoky campfire). The movement of the colder air on gentle slopes may be retarded or temporarily blocked by obstacles such as vegetation, topography, inflow from side valleys, or even man-made fences (Hough 1945; Suzuki 1965; Bergen 1969). In the wine-producing regions of Germany, hedges are frequently planted above the vineyards to deflect cold air from upslope (Geiger 1969, p. 123). In steep terrain, air drainage can be very impressive and not easily blocked, particularly when it is funneled along narrow valleys (Hales 1933; A. H. Thompson 1967). Under certain topographic or vegetative conditions a pulsating flow may be established: the cold air builds up behind obstacles and then surges forth in sporadic "avalanches" (Scaëtta 1935; Geiger 1969, p. 122).

Figure 4.14 demonstrates a temperature inversion in Gstettneralm, a small enclosed basin at an altitude of 1,270 m (4,165 ft.) in the Austrian Alps, about 100 km (62 mi.) southwest of Vienna. Because of the local topographic situation and the "pooling" of cold air, this valley experiences some of the lowest temperatures in Europe, even lower than the high peaks (Schmidt 1934, p. 348). The lowest temperature recorded at Gstett-neralm is –51° C. (–59.8° F.) while the lowest temperature recorded at Sonnblick at 3,100 m (10,170 ft.) is –32.6° C. (–26.7° F.).

As might be expected, distinct vegetational patterns are associated with these extreme temperatures. Normally, valley bottoms are forested and trees become stunted on the higher slopes, eventually being replaced by shrubs and grasses still higher up, but the exact opposite occurs here. The valley floor is covered with grass, shrubs, and stunted trees, while the larger trees occur higher up. An inversion of vegetation matches that of temperature (Schmidt 1934, p. 349). A similar vegetative pattern has been found in the arid mountains of Nevada, where valley bottoms support sagebrush, while higher up is a zone of Pinyon and Juniper woodland. Higher still the trees again disappear (Billings 1954). The Pinyon-Juniper zone, the thermal belt, is sandwiched between the lower night temperatures of the valley bottom and those which occur higher up on the slopes.

Human populations have taken advantage of thermal belts for centuries, particularly in the cultivation of frost-susceptible crops such as vineyards and orchards. In the southern Appalachians of North Carolina, the effect of temperature inversions is beautifully displayed by the distribution of the fruit orchards (Cox 1920, 1923; Dickson 1959; Dunbar 1966). During the winter, the valleys are often brown with dormant vegetation, while the mountain tops at 1,350 m (4,430 ft.) may be white with snow. In between is a strip of green that marks the thermal belt.

Frost is common in the valley, but in the thermal belt they cultivate a sensitive Isabella grape which has apparently grown for years without danger from frost (Peattie 1936, p. 23). A similar situation exists in the Hood River Valley of Oregon, on the north side of Mount Hood. Cherries are grown on the slopes of this valley in a sharply delimited thermal belt between the river and the upper slopes. With increased demand, more fruit trees are being planted in marginal areas, but their success is questionable, since the risk of frost is much greater.

Temperature Range

The temperature difference between day and night and between winter and summer generally decreases with elevation (Fig. 4.15). This is because of the relatively greater distance from the heat source—the broad level of the earth's surface. Like the analogy of a marine island and the dom-

Fig. 4.15. Diurnal temperature range at different elevations on Mount Fuji, Japan. The difference between high and low altitudes is much more exagger- ated in winter (left) than in summer (right). (After Yoshino 1975, p. 193)

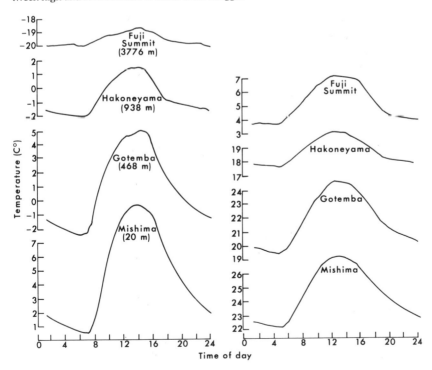

Temperature (C°)

Time of day

inating influence of the ocean, the higher
and more isolated a mountain, the more
its temperature will reflect that of the surrounding free air. Temperature in mountains
is largely a response to sunshine. The free
air, however, is essentially non-responsive
to the heating effects of the sun, particularly
at higher elevations. A mountain becomes
heated at the surface but there is a rapid
temperature-gradient in the surrounding
air. As a result, only a thin boundary layer
or thermal shell surrounds the mountain,
its exact thickness depending on a variety
of factors (e.g., solar intensity, mountain
mass, humidity, wind velocity, surface
conditions, and topographic setting).

Ambient temperatures are normally measured at a standard instrument-shelter
height of 1.5 m (5 ft.). Such measurements
generally show a progressive decline in
temperature and a lower temperature range
with elevation (Table 4.4; Figs. 4.11, 4.15).
There is a vast difference between the temperature conditions at a height of 1.5 m
(5 ft.) and immediately next to the soil surface, however. Paradoxically, the soil surface in alpine areas may experience higher
temperatures (and therefore a greater temperature range) than the soil surface of low
elevations, due to the greater intensity of
the sun at high altitudes. (This statement
only holds true for well-drained surfaces
with adequate exposure to the sun's rays.)
At an elevation of 2,070 m (6,800 ft.) in the
Alps, temperatures up to 80° C. (176° F.)
were measured on a dark humus surface
near timberline on a southwest-facing slope
with a gradient of 35° (Turner 1958b, in
Geiger 1965, p. 446). This is comparable to
the maximum temperatures recorded in hot
deserts! At the same time, the air temperature at a height of 2 m (6.5 ft.) was only 30°
C. (86° F.), a difference of 50° C. (90° F.).
Such high surface temperatures may occur
infrequently and only under ideal conditions, but temperatures somewhat less extreme are characteristic, and demonstrate
the vast differences that may exist between

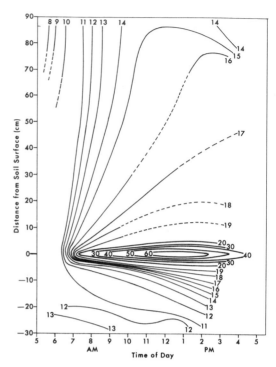

Fig. 4.16. Vertical profile of soil and air temperatures
(°C.) under clear skies on a well-drained alpine tundra
surface at 3,580 m (11,740 ft.) in the White Mountains
of California. Note the tremendous gradient occurring
immediately above and below the soil surface. The
slightly higher temperatures at a depth of 25–30 cm
(10–12 in.) are a result of the previous day's heating and
are out of phase with present surface conditions. (After
Terjung et al. 1969a, p. 256)

the surface and the overlying air (Fig. 4.16).
The soil surface in the alpine tundra will
almost always be warmer during the day
than the air above it. It may also become
colder at night, although the differences are
far less at night than during the day. The low
growth of most alpine vegetation may be
viewed as an adaptation to take advantage of
these warmer surface conditions. In fact,
several studies have shown that tundra
plants may suffer more from high temperatures than from low temperatures (Dahl
1951; Mooney and Billings 1961).

Temperature ranges vary not only with
altitude, but on a latitudinal basis as well.
The contrast in daily and annual tempera-

ture ranges is one of the most important distinguishing characteristics between tropical and mid-latitude or polar climates. The average annual temperatures of high tropical mountains and polar climates are similar. The average annual temperature of El Misti in Peru at 5,850 m (19,193 ft.) is –8° C. (18° F.), which is comparable to many polar stations. The use of this figure alone is grossly misleading, however, since there are vast differences in the temperature regimes. Tropical mountains experience a temperature range between day and night that is relatively greater than any other mountain area, due to the strongly positive heating effect of the sun in the tropics. On the other hand, changes in temperature from month to month or between winter and summer are very small. This is in great contrast to middle-latitude and polar mountains, which experience lower daily temperature ranges with latitude, but are increasingly dominated by strong seasonal gradients. A knowledge of the differences between these temperature regimes is essential to an understanding of the nature and significance of the physical and biological processes at work in each latitude.

Figure 4.17a depicts the temperature characteristics of Irkutsk, Siberia, a subpolar station with strong continentality. The most striking feature of this temperature regime is its marked seasonality. The daily range is only 5° C. (9° F.), while the annual range is over 60° C. (108° F.). This means that during winter, which lasts from October to May, the temperatures are always below freezing, while in summer they are consistently above freezing. The period of stress for organisms, then, is concentrated into one extended block of time—the winter. An alpine station at this latitude would have essentially the same temperature regime except for a relatively longer period with negative temperatures and a shorter period with positive temperatures. More poleward stations would show an even smaller daily temperature range (Troll 1968, p. 19).

Such a temperature regime stands in great contrast to that of tropical mountains. Figure 4.17b shows the temperature characteristics of Quito, Equador, located on the equator at an elevation of 2,850 m (9,350 ft.). The isotherms on the graph are oriented vertically, indicating very little change between winter and summer, but with a marked contrast between day and night. The average annual range is less than 1° C. (1.8° F.), while the average daily range is approximately 11° C. (19.8° F.). This beautifully demonstrates the saying, "Night is the winter of the tropics"; night is indeed the only winter the humid tropics experience. This is particularly true if the station is high enough for freezing to occur.

The lower limit of frost is determined principally by latitude, mountain mass, continentality, and the local topographic situation. In the equatorial Andes it exists at about 3,000 m (10,000 ft.). This elevation decreases with latitude; the point where frost begins to occur in the lowlands is normally taken as being the outer limits of the tropics. In North America the frostline runs through the middle of Baja California and eastward to the mouth of the Rio Grande, although it is highly variable from year to year. The frost line in tropical mountains is much more sharply delineated. In Quito, Ecuador, at 2,850 m (9,350 ft.), frost is practically unknown. The vegetation consists of tropical evergreen plants which blossom continuously; farmers plant and harvest crops throughout the year. By an altitude of 3,500 m (11,500 ft.), however, frost becomes a limiting factor (Troll 1968, pp. 19–23). At an elevation of 4,700 m (15,400 ft.) on El Misti in southern Peru, it freezes and thaws almost every day of the year.

The fundamental relationships between these disparate freeze-thaw regimes are demonstrated in Figure 4.18. Each of the sites selected has a similar average annual temperature of –8° C. to –2° C. (18° F. to 28° F.) but the daily and annual ranges are markedly different. Yakutsk, Siberia, experi-

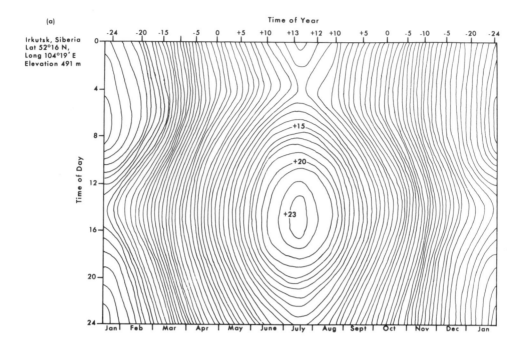

(a)

Irkutsk, Siberia
Lat 52°16 N,
Long 104°19' E
Elevation 491 m

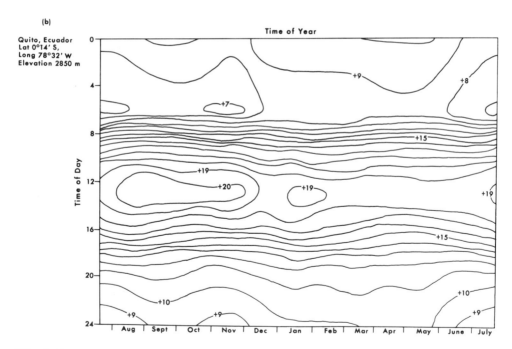

(b)

Quito, Ecuador
Lat 0°14' S,
Long 78°32' W
Elevation 2850 m

Fig. 4.17. Daily and seasonal temperature distribution in a subarctic continental and alpine tropical climate. The opposite orientation of the isotherms reflects the fundamental differences in daily and seasonal temperature ranges in the two contrasting environments. The subarctic continental station (a) experiences a small daily temperature range (read vertically) but a large annual range (read horizontally). Conversely, the high altitude tropical station (b) experiences a much greater daily temperature range than the annual range. (Adapted from Troll 1958a, p. 11)

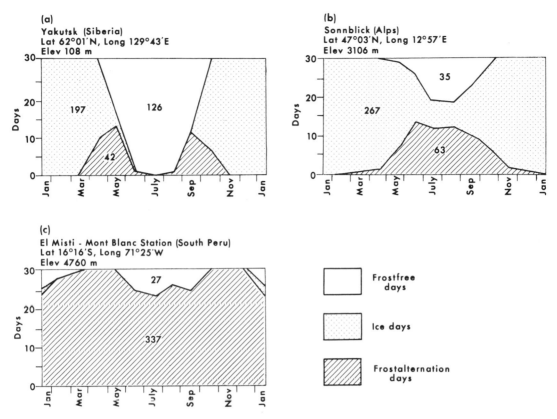

Fig. 4.18. Freeze-thaw regimes at different latitudes and altitudes. *Frost-free days* indicate the number of days when freezing did not occur, *ice days* are those when the temperature was continually below freezing, and *frost alternation days* are the days when both freezing and thawing occurred. Note that the greatest number of these occur in tropical mountains. (Adapted from Troll 1958a, pp. 12–13)

ences strong seasonality, with a frost-free summer period of 126 days, but in winter the temperatures remain below freezing for 197 days. Alternating freezing and thawing take place during 42 days in the spring and fall. At Sonnblick in the Alps, the winter season is much longer (276 days), with a very short summer during which freezing and thawing can occur at any time. El Misti, however, is dominated by a freeze-thaw regime which operates almost every day throughout the year. This type of weather has been characterized as "perpetual spring": the sun melts the night frost every morning and the days are quite pleasant. The twelve-hour day adds to the impression of spring (McVean 1968, p. 378). It can be seen that these different systems provide greatly contrasting frameworks for the survival of plants and animals, as well as for the development of landscapes.

Humidity and Evaporation

Water vapor constitutes less than 5 percent of the atmosphere but it is by far the single most important component with regard to weather and climate. It is highly variable in space and time. Water vapor provides energy for storms and its abundance is an index of the potential of the air for yielding precipitation; it absorbs infrared energy from the sun and reduces the amount of shortwave energy reaching the earth; it serves as a buffer from temperature

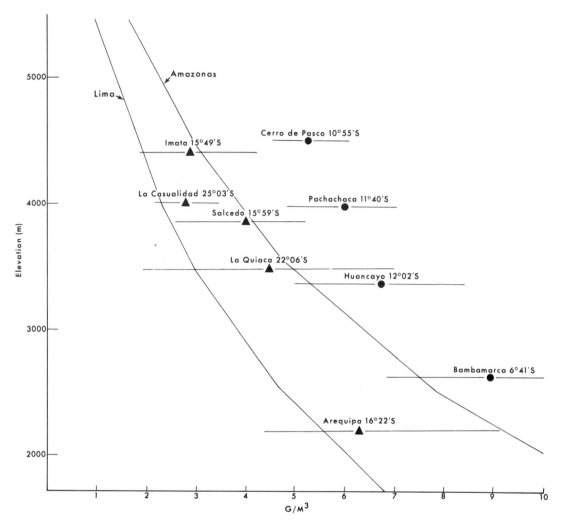

Fig. 4.19. Average annual absolute humidity (mass of water vapor per unit volume, g/m³) with elevation on the humid eastern and arid western side of the tropical Andes. Triangles indicate west-side and altiplano stations; circles indicate east-side stations. Horizontal lines provide a measure of the annual range of the monthly means of absolute humidity. The extremes are largely a reflection of the wet and dry seasons. Profiles are calculated as a function of height, according to starting values at Lima and Amazonas, based on empirical formulas obtained from observations in the Alps. The tropical-station data indicate that the decrease in vapor density with height is less pronounced than in middle latitudes. (Adapted from Prohaska 1970, p. 3)

extremes; and it is important biologically, since it controls the rate of chemical reactions and the drying power of the air.

The moisture content of the atmosphere decreases rapidly with increasing altitude. At 2,000 m (6,600 ft.) it is only about 50 percent of that at sea level; at 5,000 m (16,400 ft.) it is less than 25 percent; and at 8,000 m (26,200 ft.) the water-vapor content of the air is less than 1 percent of that at sea level (Table 4.2). Within this framework, however, the presence of moisture is highly variable. This is true on a temporal basis—between winter and summer, day and night, or within a matter of minutes, as when the saturated air of a passing cloud shrouds a mountain peak. It is also true on a spatial basis—between high and low latitudes, a marine and a continental location, the windward and leeward sides of a mountain range, or north and south-facing slopes. The general upward decrease in water-vapor content, and the variations that occur, are illustrated by the east and west sides of the tropical Andes (Fig. 4.19). The contrast in absolute humidity between these two environments is immediately apparent, although the difference decreases with elevation and probably disappears altogether above the mountains. Imata, Salcedo, and Arequipa on the west have only about half the water-vapor content of stations on the east (Cerro do Pasco, Pachachaca, Huancayo, Bambamarca). Values similar to those at Arequipa occur at elevations 2,000 m (6,600 ft.) higher on the east side (e.g., at Pachachaca). During the wet season, however, the absolute humidity at Arequipa may be two to three times higher than during the dry season. This corresponds to an elevational difference of up to 3,000 m (10,000 ft.).

The decrease in water vapor with altitude may seem somewhat difficult to explain, since it is well-known that precipitation increases with altitude. The two phenomena are not directly related, however. Precipitation is caused by air from lower elevations (with greater moisture content) being forced upward into an area of lower temperature. Increasing precipitation does create a more humid environment in mountains, at least for part of the year and up to certain elevations, but eventually signs of aridity increase (although this may be as much due to lower barometric pressure, stronger winds, porous well-drained soils, and the intense sunlight as to the lower absolute humidity).

The greater aridity of high altitudes is evident from the plants and animals, many of which are either desert-related or have adapted to a dry environment. Thick, corky bark and waxy leaves are common in alpine plants. Mountain sheep and goats and their cousins, the llama, guanaco, alpaca, chamois, and ibex, are all able to live for prolonged periods on little moisture. Geomorphologically, aeolian processes become relatively more important than fluvial processes in higher landscapes, and the low availability of moisture is reflected in soil development. Surface salt accumulations and drying cracks are often present. One of the physiological stresses reported by climbers on Mount Everest is a dryness of the throat and a general desiccation. The establishment of sanatoriums in alpine areas to utilize the intense sunlight and clean, dry air was mentioned earlier (Hill 1924). Air-dried meat is a provincial dish in the high Engadine, and pemmican and jerky were both important in the mountains of western North America. In the Andes, an ancient method exists for the production of dried potatoes (*chuño*) in the high dry air above 3,000 m (10,000 ft.). Permanent settlement of the higher elevations apparently depended upon the development of this technique of food preservation (Troll 1968, p. 32). Mummification of the dead was practiced in the Andes and in the Caucasus.

The lower absolute humidities and the tendency toward aridity at higher altitudes suggest greater evaporation rates with elevation. However, this may not be true. Several early studies do indicate an increase of evaporation with elevation, but these were largely empirical or based on short-term observations (Hann 1903; Church 1934; Matthes 1934; Peattie 1936). For example, Matthes (1934), in discussing the development of the dimpled surfaces (sun cups) of snowfields above 3,600 m (12,000 ft.) in the Sierra Nevada of California, states that *ablation* (the combined processes of wasting away of snow and ice) is caused entirely by evaporation, since melting does not occur at this elevation. Similar results were reported

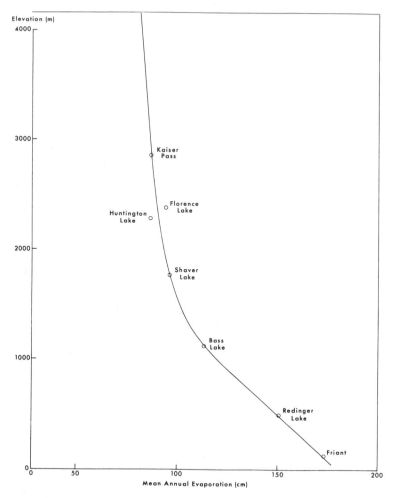

Fig. 4.20. Mean annual evaporation from reservoirs at different elevations in the Sierra Nevada of central California. (After Longacre and Blaney 1962, p. 42)

in a recent study in the alpine zone of the White Mountains of California (Beatty 1975). However, other studies in the same area have shown that evaporation does not exceed 10 percent of the total ablation (Kehrlein et al. 1953). Whichever of these observations is accepted as being the more general, it should be noted that these particular alpine areas are exceptionally, if not uniquely, dry environments, with high solar intensities, strong winds, and persistent subfreezing temperatures. The bulk of investigations on snowfields and glaciers in other regions has tended to show that evaporation is relatively unimportant in total ablation. In some cases, evaporation may actually inhibit ablation, owing to the heat it extracts (Howell 1953; Martinelli 1960; Hoinkes and Rudolph 1962; Platt 1966). In addition, long-term studies of evaporation in measurement pans and lakes at different altitudes in the western United States have shown that evaporation decreases with elevation (Shreve 1915; Blaney 1958; Longacre and Blaney 1962; Peck and Pfankuch 1963) (Fig. 4.20).

Evaporation and the factors that control it in a natural environment are exceedingly complex (Horton 1934; Montieth 1965; Gale 1972; Miller 1977). The rate depends upon temperature, sun intensity, atmospheric pressure, the available quantity of water, the degree of saturation of the air, and the wind. One of the problems in measuring the rate of evaporation is the availability of moisture. In a lake or evaporating pan, the available moisture is for all practical purposes unlimited, but this is not true for most surfaces in high mountains. Rainfall is generally lost to the surface by drainage through porous soil or by runoff on steep slopes. As a result, there is frequently little surface moisture available for evaporation, no matter how great the measured rates are from an evaporation pan. For this reason, the determination of *evapotranspiration*, the loss of water to the air from both plant and soil surfaces, has become an increasingly attractive approach (Thornthwaite and Mather 1951; Tanner and Fuchs 1968; Rao et al. 1975). Unfortunately, very few measurements of evapotranspiration have been made in the alpine environment (Terjung et al. 1969a; Le Drew 1975).

The single most important factor in controlling the decrease of evaporation with altitude is temperature, both of the evaporation surface and of the air directly above it. While it is true that soil surfaces exposed to the sun at high altitudes may reach exceptionally high temperatures, this is a highly variable condition. During peak periods of high sun intensity and high soil temperatures, the potential for evaporation may be considerable, especially when the wind is blowing. Generally, however, the lower temperatures of higher altitudes are more than sufficient to compensate for the decreasing water-vapor content and lower barometric pressure, so that the vapor-pressure gradient is likewise decreased. In other words, the relative humidity (ratio of water vapor in the air to the maximum amount it could hold at that temperature)

increases with decreasing temperature, and it is the relative humidity which really determines the rate of evaporation. This is illustrated by the surprising fact that the water-vapor content of the air in the Sahara Desert is two to three times greater than that over the Rocky Mountains during clear summer weather. Owing to the higher temperatures in the Sahara, however, the relative humidity is usually not more than 20–30 percent, compared to 40–60 percent for the Rockies. Consequently, the evaporation rate in the Sahara far exceeds that of the Rockies, even though there is more actual moisture in the desert.

An inverse relationship holds between temperature and relative humidity. This can be seen by comparing mountains during day and night and at various slope exposures (Fig. 4.21). The greatest contrasts occur on south-facing slopes in the northern hemisphere. Under the higher temperatures that prevail during the day, relative humidity varies very little with elevation, although it is lowest in the valley bottom. At night there is considerable contrast because of the temperature inversion that develops in the valley, resulting in lower temperatures and high relative humidities. The lowest relative humidity occurs immediately above the temperature inversion, in the thermal belt, where temperatures are higher (Hayes 1941). The difference in relative humidity between the two slopes gradually decreases with elevation.

Local wind circulation can also greatly affect water-vapor content: descending air brings dry air from aloft, while ascending air carries moist air upward from below. At night colder air tends to descend through air drainage, but during the day the slopes are warmed and the air rises. Under these conditions, the normal inverse temperature/relative-humidity relationship may be overridden. Even though the summit air is cool at night, the motion of the descending air lowers the relative humidity. During the day, however, when temperatures are higher

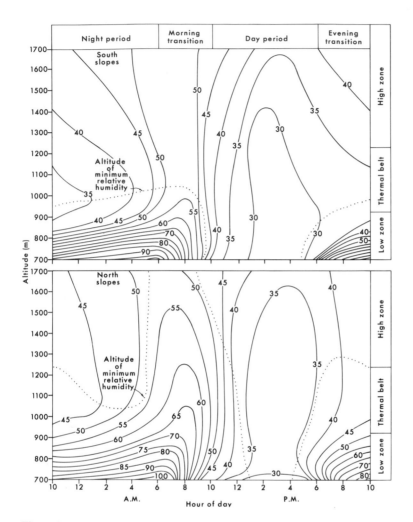

Fig. 4.21. Diagrammatic representation of daily changes in relative humidity with altitude on north- and south-facing forested slopes during August in the mountains of northern Idaho. Dotted line represents the altitude where minimum relative humidities occur at different times during the twenty-four-hour cycle. Note that both the highest and lowest relative humidities occur in the valley bottoms, where the greatest temperature extremes are also found. (Adapted from Hayes 1941, p. 17)

and relative humidity would normally decrease, it may actually increase, because the valley breezes carry moist air up the mountain slopes. This frequently results in afternoon clouds and precipitation (Schell 1934).

Precipitation

The increase of precipitation with altitude is well-known. It is demonstrated in every country of the world, even if the landforms involved are only small hills. In many regions an isohyetal map with its lines of equal precipitation will look very much like a topographic map composed of lines of equal altitude. Of course, the data on which most precipitation maps are based are scanty, so that considerable interpolation may be necessary, particularly in the areas of higher relief (Peck and Brown 1962). Like other natural phenomena in and around mountains, great variations in precipitation occur within short distances; one slope may be excessively wet while another is relatively dry. The terms "wet hole" and "dry hole" are frequently used in this regard. Jackson Hole, Wyoming, is located in a protected site at the base of the Grand Tetons. The mountains receive 1,400 mm (55 in.) but Jackson Hole, only 16 km (10 mi.) away, receives 380 mm (15 in.).

Precipitation does not always correspond to landforms. In some cases, maximum precipitation may occur at the foot or in advance of the mountain slopes (Reinelt 1968). In some regions and under certain conditions, valleys may receive more rainfall than the nearby mountains. In the higher alpine areas, precipitation may actually decrease beyond a certain elevation, with the peaks receiving less than the lower slopes. Wind direction, temperature, moisture content, depth of the air mass and its relative stability at different elevations with respect to the altitude, orientation, and configuration of the landforms are all contributing factors in determining location and amount of precipitation.

The most fundamental reason for increased precipitation with altitude is that landforms obstruct the movement of air and cause it to rise. This is part of a complex of processes known as the *orographic effect* (from the Greek *oros*, meaning "mountain," and *graphein*, "to describe"). Forced ascent of air is most effective when mountains are oriented perpendicular to the prevailing winds; the steeper and more exposed the slope, the more rapidly air will be forced to rise. As the air is lifted in its journey over the mountains it is cooled by expansion and by coming into contact with the air at higher elevations, where temperatures are lower. The ability of air to hold moisture depends primarily upon its temperature—warm air can hold much more moisture than cold air. The temperature, the pressure, and the presence of hygro-

scopic nuclei in the atmosphere tend to concentrate the water vapor in its lower reaches. This is why most clouds occur below 9,000 m (30,000 ft.), and why those that do develop higher than this are usually thin and composed of ice particles and yield little or no precipitation.

When the air holds as much moisture as it can (when its relative humidity is 100 percent), it is said to be saturated. Condensation is a common process in saturated air, and the temperature at which condensation takes place is called the *dew point*. Ground forms of condensation, i.e., fog, frost, and dew, are caused by cooling of the air in contact with the ground surface, but condensation in the free air, i.e., clouds, can only result from rising air. The key to forming clouds and creating precipitation, therefore, is to cause the air to rise. This may be brought about by one of several ways. The driving force may be convection—the sun warms the earth's surface and warm air rises until clouds begin to form, usually at about mid-morning. Such clouds may grow to great size since they are fed from below by relatively warm, moist rising air, until the moisture content within the clouds becomes too great and it is released as precipitation. Convectional rainfall is best displayed in the humid tropics but it occurs in all climates. The air may also be forced to rise by the passage of cyclonic storms—warm or cold fronts mechanically lift and cool the air. This takes place primarily in the middle latitudes. Although both of these processes can operate without the presence of mountains, their effectiveness is greatly increased (or decreased) by mountains. For example, a passing storm may drop a certain amount of precipitation on a plains area, but when the storm reaches the mountains, a severalfold increase in precipitation typically occurs on the windward side, while a marked decrease generally takes place on the leeward side.

One has only to compare the distribution of world precipitation with the location of mountains to see their profound influence.

Almost every area of heavy rainfall is associated with landforms. In general, any area outside the tropics receiving more than 2,500 mm (100 in.) and any area within the tropics receiving more than 5,000 mm (200 in.) is experiencing a climate affected by mountains. The examples of Cherrapunji, Assam; Mount Waialeale, Hawaii; and the Olympic Mountains were given earlier. Many others could be added: Mount Cameroon, West Africa, the Ghats along the west coast of India, the Scottish Highlands, the Blue Mountains of Jamaica, Montenegro in Yugoslavia, and the Southern Alps of New Zealand. The list could go on and on. The reverse is also true, for to the lee of each of these ranges is a rain-shadow in which precipitation decreases drastically. The western Ghats receive over 5,000 mm (200 in.) but immediately to their lee on the Deccan Plateau the average amount of precipitation is only 380 mm (15 in.). The windward slopes of the Scottish Highlands receive over 4,300 mm (170 in.) but the amount decreases to 600 mm (24 in.) on the lowlands around the Moray Firth. The Blue Mountains on the northeast side of Jamaica face the trade winds and receive over 5,600 mm (220 in.), while Kingston, 56 km (35 mi.) to the leeward, receives only 780 mm (31 in.) (Kendrew 1961, p. 516). Mountains, therefore, not only cause increased precipitation, but also have the reciprocal effect of decreasing precipitation. One of the classic questions of mountain climatology is whether the presence of mountains increases or decreases the total precipitation received on the earth. The alternative would be a smooth surface with only coast lines to break the monotony. On balance, it is generally felt that mountains do increase precipitation, but the question is almost philosophical (Bonacina 1945).

The movement of air up a mountain slope, creating clouds and precipitation, may be due simply to the wind, but it is usually associated with convection and frontal activity. Rising air cools at a rate of 3.05° C.

(5.5° F.) per 300 m (1,000 ft.) (dry adiabatic rate) until the dew point is reached and condensation occurs. Thereafter, the air will cool at a slightly lower rate (wet adiabatic rate) because of the release of the latent heat of condensation. If, upon being lifted, the air has a high relative humidity, it may take only slight cooling to reach saturation, but if it has a low relative humidity it may be lifted considerable distances without reaching the dew point. Conversely, if the air is warm, it often takes considerable cooling to reach dew point but then may yield copious amounts of rainfall, whereas cool air usually needs only slight cooling to reach dew point but also yields far less precipitation. After the air has passed over the mountains precipitation ceases (or at least decreases) and the air may then be forced to descend; as it does, it gains heat at the same rate at which it was cooled initially—3.05° C. per 300 m (5.5° F. per 1,000 ft.)—since it is now being compressed and moving into warmer air. Such conditions are not, of course, conducive to precipitation.

The orographic effect involves several distinct processes: (1) forced ascent, (2) blocking (or retardation) of storms, (3) the triggering effect, (4) local convection, and (5) condensation processes.

Forced Ascent

Forced ascent seems to be the most important precipitation process in mountains; after all, rainfall increases with altitude and is greater on windward than on leeward slopes. The process may be most clearly seen in coastal mountains, like the Cascades, that lie athwart moisture-laden winds. Other processes contribute to the total precipitation, of course, and differentiation among them is difficult. In order to explain the amount and distribution of rainfall caused strictly by forced ascent it is necessary to consider the atmospheric conditions from three different perspectives (Sawyer 1956; Sarker 1966). First is the large-scale synoptic pattern that determines the characteristics of the air mass crossing the mountains—its depth, stability, moisture content, windspeed, and direction. Second is the microphysics of the clouds—the presence of hydroscopic nuclei, the size of the water droplets, and their temperature, which will determine whether the precipitation will fall as rain or as snow or will evaporate before reaching the ground. Third, and most important, is the air motion with respect to the mountain. Will it blow over, or around, the mountain? This will determine to what depth and extent the air mass at each level is lifted. It is not realistic, for example, to assume that the air is lifted the same amount at all levels. The solution to these problems involves atmospheric physics and the construction of dynamic models (Myers 1962; Barker 1966, 1967).

The simplest system is that of coastal mountains: the moisture-laden winds are predominantly from the ocean and they approach at low elevations, so the resulting precipitation is clearly due to the landforms. Exceptions may occur in areas where the mountains are oriented parallel to the prevailing winds and/or where the frontal systems resist lifting. In southern California, for example, precipitation is often heavier in the Los Angeles coastal lowlands than in the Santa Inez and San Gabriel mountains. The orographic component of precipitation increases only when the approaching air mass is unstable; under stable conditions, the wind simply flows around the mountains (which are oriented east-west), so there is no significant orographic lifting and the precipitation is due entirely to frontal lifting. The mountains apparently receive less rainfall than the lowlands under these conditions because the shallow cloud-development does not allow as much depth for falling precipitation particles to grow by collision and coalescence with cloud droplets before reaching the elevated land.

The situation becomes even more complex in interior high-altitude areas where there is more than one source region and

storms enter the area at various levels in the atmosphere. Such a situation exists in the Wasatch Mountains of Utah (Williams and Peck 1962; Peck 1972a). It has long been known that precipitation in this region is highly variable; the valleys may receive greater amounts than the mountains during any given storm or season (Clyde 1931). The average over a period of years, however, does show an increase with altitude (Price and Evans 1937; Lull and Ellison 1950). The greater precipitation in valleys is apparently associated with certain synoptic situations, particularly when a "cold low" is observed on the upper-air charts. These occur as closed lows on the 500-millibar pressure chart, i.e., at a height of about 5,500 m (18,000 ft.), and are associated with large-scale upward (vertical) movement of air which is not displayed in normal cold or warm-front precipitation. Under these conditions, precipitation may occur with relatively little dependence on orographic lifting, compared to other storm types (Williams and Peck 1962).

Blocking of storms

By retarding or hindering the free movement of frontal systems, mountains can cause increased precipitation. Storms often linger for several days or weeks and produce a steady downpour. This is best displayed in the middle latitudes with high-barrier mountains. Winter storms linger with amazing persistence in the Cascades and in the Gulf of Alaska before they pass across the mountains or are replaced by another warm front. Storms of similar character in the Great Plains travel much more rapidly, since there are no restrictions to their movement. The countries surrounding the Alps are ideally located with respect to storm blocking. Switzerland frequently experiences lingering torrential rains during the summer (Bonacina 1945). In northern Italy, between the Alps and the Apennines, heavy and persistent rains are associated with the "lee depressions" caused by the interception of polar air by the Alps (Grard and Mathevet 1972). Tennyson's poem "The Daisy" evokes the legendary spring and winter rains in Lombardy:

And when we crossed the Lombard Plain
Remember what a plague of rain.

The Triggering Effect

Although little mention has so far been made of it, one important variable influencing the amount of precipitation is the stability of the air, that is, its resistance to vertical displacement. This is controlled primarily by temperature: when there is a low lapse-rate, i.e., less than 1.4° C. per 300 m (2.5° F. per 1,000 ft.), as there frequently is at night in mountains, the air is stable. During the day, when the sun warms the slopes and the surface air is heated, the lapse rate increases and the air will have a tendency to rise, frequently producing afternoon clouds. When the lapse rate exceeds the dry adiabatic rate—3.05° C. per 300 m (5.5° F. per 1,000 ft.)—a condition of absolute instability prevails. Under these conditions even slight lifting of the air by a landform may be enough to "trigger" it into continued lifting on its own accord. If it then begins to feed upon itself through the release of latent heat of condensation, it will yield considerable precipitation (Bergeron 1965; Thornthwaite 1961). As a result of this effect, small hills in the path of moist unstable air often receive surprisingly heavy precipitation even though their role in an orographic sense is minimal.

Local Convection

Clouds commonly form over mountains during the day, especially in summer, when nights and early mornings are clear but by mid-morning clouds begin to build, often culminating in thunderstorms, hail, and rain. Mountains serve as elevated heat-islands during the day, since they may be warmed to almost the same temperature as the surrounding lowlands. As a result, the air at a given altitude is much warmer over the mountains than over the valley (MacCready 1955). The lapse rate above the peaks, therefore, is considerably greater than in the surrounding free air, resulting in actively rising air. Glider pilots have long taken advantage of this fact (Scorer 1952, 1955; Ludlam and Scorer 1953). Airline pilots, on the other hand, make every effort to avoid the turbulence associated with unstable air over mountains (Reiter and Foltz 1967; Colson 1963, 1969).

Perhaps the most intensely studied mountain convection phenomena anywhere are those found in the San Francisco and Santa Catalina mountains of Arizona. A number of studies have traced the initiation and development of convection and cumulus clouds over the range (Braham and Draginis 1960; Orville 1965; Fujita 1967). Figure 4.22 shows the change in temperature and moisture content over the Santa Catalina Mountains from early morning to mid-morning. Note that the south-facing slopes show considerably more thermal convection than the north-facing slopes. On this particular day the base of the clouds was about 4,500 m (15,000 ft.), so the sun was not blocked and could continue to shine on the slopes to feed the thermal convection (Braham and Draginis 1960, p. 2).

The height of the cloud base is very important to the development of convection in mountains, since once the sun is blocked the

Fig. 4.22. Cross-section of atmosphere above the Santa Catalina Mountains near Tucson, Arizona, on a summer day in 1965. Measurements were made by flying transects across the range with an instrument-equipped airplane. Profiles show changes in mixing ratio (which is a measure of humidity) (upper) and temperature (°K.) (lower) at the different altitudes between 6:15 A.M. (left) and 10:41 A.M. (right). Note the considerable warming, increased humidity, and increased instability of the air as the sun shines, especially on the south side of the range. This leads to convectional lifting, cloud formation, and localized precipitation over the mountains. (After Braham and Draginis 1960, pp. 2–3)

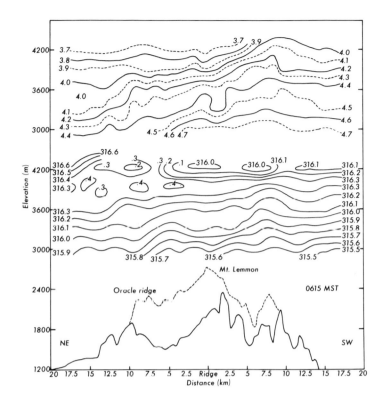

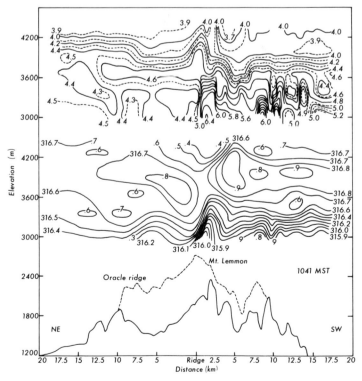

positive effect of solar heating is eliminated. The height of the cloud base is also critical to the distribution of precipitation, as is demonstrated in the San Gabriel Mountains, California (see p. 95). Obviously, if the cloud base is below the level of the peaks, as it usually is in the winter, when forced ascent occurs, cloud growth and precipitation will take place mainly on the windward side. In summer, however, the base of convection clouds is generally much higher.

Mountains are cloud breeders by day but cloud dissipators by night. During the day in summer, clouds typically form over the peaks and produce thunderstorms and locally heavy precipitation (Fuguay 1962; Baughman and Fuguay 1970). This has been well-documented for the base of the Colorado Rockies, where the higher peaks of the Front Range provide a "heated chimney effect" in the initiation of thunder and hailstorms (Harrison and Beckwith 1951; Beckwith 1957). I experienced one of these storms while driving from Denver to Cheyenne. It was early afternoon and the hailstorm hit with such ferocity that we had to stop the car. Within a matter of minutes the road was covered by a blanket of hailstones 2–3 cm (1 in.) thick. I grew up in the Midwest, where hail and thunderstorms are common, but I have never experienced a hailstorm before or since to match the intensity of that mountain hail.

Clouds and thunderstorms initiated in the Front Range frequently drift eastward, continuing to develop as they move onto the plains, and producing locally heavy precipitation. A study in the San Francisco Mountains north of Flagstaff, Arizona, suggests that clouds may increase in volume by as much as ten times after drifting away from a mountain source (Glass and Carlson 1963). Most of the clouds observed in this area were small cumuli that eventually dissipated once removed from their supply of moist, rising air, but a large cumulonimbus could maintain itself independently of the mountains and result in storms at some distance away. Fujita (1967) found that there was a ring of low precipitation about 24 km (15 mi.) in diameter encircling these mountains, with an outer ring of heavier precipitation. During the day the rainfall is over the mountains but at night it falls over the lowlands because the mountains are then relatively cold. A "wake effect" due to wave action created by air flow over the mountains may be partly responsible for the inner ring of light precipitation (Fujita 1967). A similar phenomenon occurs adjacent to the Rockies, on the Great Plains, where there is a second peaking of thunderstorm activity in the early evening (Bleeker and Andre 1951).

The role of mountains in the development of these nighttime thunderstorms is not fully understood, but has led to some interesting speculation. Some believe, for example, that increased heating on mountain slopes under certain circumstances may lead to less, not more, precipitation (Lettau 1967). Studies in the coastal desert west of the Peruvian Andes and in the Great Plains, where nighttime lightning and thunderstorms are characteristic, suggest that they may be caused by the development of a local circulation system in which air moves downward and away from the mountains at night and converges on the plains, resulting in nocturnal thunderstorms. During the day, the reverse situation exists: air moves away from the mountains at higher levels and diverges over the plains. This pattern of circulation results from a complex interaction between the thermally induced pressure-gradient, surface friction, and coriolis force. It is not known how widespread such systems are, but where they are present, the intensification of heating on slopes may lead to increased aridity (Lettau 1967). This is particularly interesting with regard to certain recommendations for increasing precipitation in deserts. The proposal is to asphalt large areas in coastal deserts to simulate "thermal mountains" and thereby increase the rainfall (Black and Tarmy 1963). We must be very careful, however, to understand not only the general processes but also the special conditions that exist in certain areas. In coastal deserts, the use of asphalt may intensify the very condition it is trying to ameliorate (Lettau 1967). These are isolated circumstances, however, and exceptions to the general rule. The increased thermal activity over mountains during the day normally leads to localized convection, clouds, and precipitation (Flohn 1974, pp. 66–68.)

Mountains are sites of natural atmospheric instability, and as such are ideal areas for artificial stimulation of precipitation. The considerable efforts that have been made in this regard have met with varied success, depending upon technique and local atmospheric conditions (Mielke et al. 1970; Chappell et al. 1971; Hobbs and Radke 1973; Grant and Kahan 1974). Most of the projects have been aimed at increasing the snowpack for runoff during the summer. This appears to be a desirable objective, but the ecological implications of such undertakings are very far-reaching (Weisbecker 1974; Steinhoff and Ives 1976). To illustrate: the Portland General Electric Company of Portland, Oregon, hired a commercial firm during the winter of 1974/75 to engage in cloud-seeding on the eastern side of the Cascades. The objective was to increase the snowpack in the Deschutes River watershed, where they have two dams and power-generating plants. Considerable success was apparently achieved, but problems arose when residents of small towns at the base of the mountains were suddenly faced with a marked increase in snow. There were new problems of transportation and of snow removal, as well as other hardships for the local people. Greater snowfall meant greater profits for the power company but it also meant greater expenses for the local people. Objections were raised in the courts, and the project was eventually halted. The positive effects of such programs must always be balanced against the negative. In our efforts to manipulate nature we are made increas-ingly aware of how little we understand the effects of our actions on natural systems. This is especially true of the mountain environment (Steinhoff and Ives 1976).

Condensation Processes

The presence of fog or clouds near the ground may result in increased moisture. Water droplets in fog and clouds are usually so small that they remain suspended, and even a slight wind will carry them through the air until they strike a solid object and condense upon it. You have experienced this, if water droplets have ever formed on your hair and eyebrows as you passed through a cloud or fog. Fog drip and rime deposits, which form at subfreezing temperatures, are responsible for an appreciable amount of the moisture in mountains, since elevated slopes are often in contact with clouds.

Fog Drip. Fog drip is most significant in areas adjacent to oceans with relatively warm, moist air moving across the windward slopes. In some cases, the moisture yield from fog drip may exceed that of mean rainfall (Nagel 1956). The potential of clouds for yielding fog drip depends primarily upon their liquid content, the size of the cloud-droplet spectrum, and the wind velocity (Grunow 1960). The amount that occurs at any particular place depends upon the nature of the obstacles encountered and their exposure to the clouds and wind. For example, a tree will yield more moisture than a rock, and a needleleaf tree is more efficient at "combing" the moisture from the clouds than a broadleaf tree. A tall tree will yield more moisture than a short one, and a tree with front-line exposure will yield more than one surrounded by other trees. The tiny fog droplets are intercepted by the leaves and branches and grow by coalescence until they become heavy enough to fall to the ground, thereby increasing soil moisture and feeding the ground-water table. If the trees are removed, of course, this

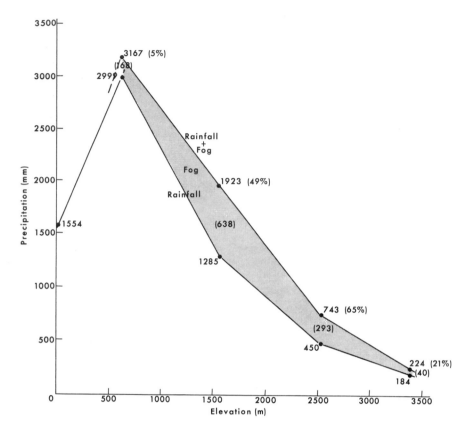

Fig. 4.23. Contribution of fog drip to precipitation during twenty-eight-week study period (October 1972 to April 1973) on the forested northeast slopes of Mauna Loa, Hawaii. Numbers show precipitation amounts in millimeters. Those in parentheses indicate fog drip. Percentages are the relative amounts contributed to the total by fog drip at each station. (After Juvik and Perreira 1974, p. 24)

source of moisture is also eliminated.

Many tropical and subtropical mountains sustain so-called "cloud forests," which are largely controlled by the abundance of fog drip. Along the east coast of Mexico in the Sierra Madre Oriental, luxuriant cloud forests occur between 1,300–2,400 m (4,300–7,900 ft.). The coastal lowlands are arid by comparison, as is the high interior plateau beyond the mountains. Measurements in both of these drier areas show little increase in available moisture due to fog drip, whereas on the middle and upper slopes the process boosts moisture by more than 50 percent—at one site located at 1,900 m (6,200 ft.), the increase over rainfall was 103 percent. These cloud forests were at one time much more extensive, but they have been severely disturbed by man and are now in danger of being eliminated (Vogelmann 1973).

On the northeast slopes of Mauna Loa, Hawaii, at 1,500–2,500 m (5,000–8,200 ft.), above the zone of maximum precipitation, fog drip is likewise a major ecological factor in the floristic richness of the forests. During a twenty-eight-week study, fog drip was found to provide 638 mm (25.3 in.) of moisture at an elevation of 1,500 m (5,000 ft.); and at 2,500 m (8,200 ft.) it provided 293 mm (11.5 in.), which was 65 percent of the direct rainfall (Juvik and Perreira 1974; Juvik and Ekern 1978) (Fig. 4.23).

The contribution of fog drip on middle and upper mountain slopes in the lower latitudes is clearly a major factor in the mois-

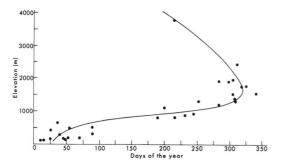

Fig. 4.24. Relationship between the number of foggy or cloudy days and altitude in the mountains of Japan. (Dots represent data from weather stations at various altitudes.) The altitude of greatest cloudiness is 1,500–2,000 m (5,000–6,000 ft.), where clouds develop almost daily, especially in August. This is caused by the inflow of cool marine air at these levels. The actual height of maximum cloudiness varies from one season to another and from one mountain range to another, even in Japan. (After Yoshino 1975, p. 205)

Fig. 4.25. Rime accumulation on newly constructed Palmer ski lift at 2,380 m (7,800 ft.) on the south side of Mount Hood, Oregon. The heavy rime resulted in discontinuation of lift construction until the following summer. (Bob McGown, December 1977)

ture regime. The relationship between the cloud forest and fog drip is essentially reciprocal. The trees cause additional moisture in the area. At the same time, the trees apparently need the fog drip in order to survive. This is particularly true in areas with a pronounced dry season, at which time fog drip provides the sole source of moisture for the plants. In the middle latitudes, fog drip is less critical to the growth of trees, but it can still be important (Grunow 1955; Costin and Wimbush 1961; Vogelmann et al. 1968). This can be seen in the mountains of Japan, where there is heavy fog at intermediate altitudes (Fig. 4.24).

Rime Deposits. Rime is formed at subfreezing temperatures when supercooled cloud droplets, blown against solid obstacles, freeze on them. Rime deposits tend to accumulate on the windward side of objects: the greater the wind velocity, the more rapid the rate of growth (Fig. 4.25). In extreme

cases the rate of growth may exceed 2.5 cm (1 in.) per hour, although the average rate is usually less than 1 cm (0.4 in.) per hour. Rime deposits can reach spectacular dimensions and, by their weight, cause considerable damage to tree branches, especially if followed by snow or freezing rain. Trees at the forest edge and at timberline frequently have their limbs bent and broken by this process; power lines and ski lifts are also greatly affected. One study in Germany measured a maximum hourly growth of 230 g per m (8.1 oz. per 3.3 ft.) on a power-line cable (Waibel 1955, in Geiger 1965, p. 350). The stress caused by this added weight may cause a power failure if the supporting structures are not properly engineered.

Rime accumulation is a severe obstacle to the maintenance of mountain weather stations because instruments become coated, making accurate measurements extremely difficult. Some instruments can be heated or enclosed in protected housing, but the logistical problems of accurately monitoring the alpine environment are very great. The problems encountered are exemplified by the U.S. Weather Bureau Station on Mount Washington, New Hampshire, where rime-forming fogs are frequent and the wind is indefatigable. This mountain has been nominated as having the worst weather in the world (Brooks 1940). It is foggy over 300 days a year, or about 87 percent of the time; wind velocities there average 18 m/sec. (40 mph) with frequent prolonged spells of 45 m/sec. (100 mph) and occasional extremes of over 90 m/sec. (200 mph) (Pagliuca 1937).

Few investigations have been made concerning the moisture contribution of rime. It is known to be generally somewhat less than fog drip, but it may nevertheless be significant. A study in the eastern Cascades of Washington indicates that timbered areas above 1,500 m (5,000 ft.) receive an added 50–125 mm (2–5 in.) of moisture per year from this source (Berndt and Fowler 1969). Considerably greater amounts have been measured in Norway (Table 4.5). Rime is found primarily in middle-latitude and polar mountains, although it also occurs at the highest altitudes in the tropics. Like fog drip, it is most effective on forest-covered slopes that provide a large surface area for its accumulation. At very high altitudes and at latitudes where total precipitation is low, rime deposits on glaciers and snowfields may constitute the primary source of the water taken from the air.

Zone of Maximum Precipitation

Precipitation is generally thought to increase only up to a certain altitude, beyond which it decreases. The argument is that the greatest amount of precipitation will usually

Table 4.5. *Accumulation of rime deposits near Haldde Observatory, Norway. The larger amounts at Talviktoppen and Store Haldde are due to higher wind velocity and cloud frequency at these elevations (Köhler 1937, in Landsberg 1962, p. 186).*

Station	Elevation	Rime Deposit (water equivalent)
Haldde Plateau	860 m	35 mm
Haldde Observatory	904 m	70 mm
Talviktoppen	989 m	590 mm
Store Haldde	1,141 m	1,310 mm

occur immediately above the cloud level because most of the moisture is concentrated here. As the air lifts and cools further, the amount of precipitation will eventually decrease, because a substantial percentage of the moisture has already been released on the lower slopes. In addition, the decreased temperature and pressure at higher elevations reduce the capacity of the air to hold moisture. The water-vapor content at 3,000 m (10,000 ft.) is only about one-third that at sea level. Forced ascent also plays a part, since the air, seeking the path of least resistance, will generally move around the higher peaks rather than over them.

The concept of a zone of maximum precipitation was developed over a century ago from studies in tropical mountains and in the Alps (Hann 1903). Other studies seemed to confirm the concept and its application to other areas (Lee 1911; Henry 1919; Peattie 1936). The existence of such a zone has been challenged in recent decades, however. Calculations of the amount of precipitation necessary to maintain active glaciers in high mountains and observations of relatively heavy runoff from small alpine watersheds seem to call for more precipitation in certain mountain areas than climatic station data would indicate (Court 1960; Anderson 1972; Slaymaker 1974). Currently, the situation is moot, the problem being one of measurement. There are very few weather stations in high mountains, and even where measurements are available, their reliability is questionable. As one author says, "Precipitation in mountain areas is as nearly unmeasureable as any physical phenomenon" (Anderson 1972, p. 347). This is particularly true at high altitudes with strong winds. Not surprisingly, many studies have shown that wind greatly affects the amount of water collected in a rain gauge (Court 1960; Brown and Peck 1962; Hovind 1965; Rodda 1971) (Fig. 4.26). Considerable effort has been made to alleviate this problem by the use of shields on gauges, by location in protected sites, by use of horizontal or inclined gauges, and by the use of sophisticated radar techniques (Storey and Wilm 1944; Harrold et al. 1972; Peck 1972b; Sevruk 1972).

To measure snow is even more difficult, since the wind not only drives falling snow but redistributes it after it is on the ground. There are also problems in storage and melting of snow for water equivalency, as well as the losses due to evaporation. The major problem, however, is accurate monitoring of snowfall. Small clearings are used in conifer forests, and above timberline snow fences are increasingly being used to enclose and shield the gauges. This still does not guarantee accurate measurements, but shielded gauges (whether for rain or snow) do record greater amounts of precipitation than unshielded gauges in the same location. For example, the University of Colorado has since 1952 operated a series of weather stations in the Front Range of the Rocky Mountains (Marr 1967; Marr et al. 1968a, b). The measured precipitation amounts from the two highest sites above treeline increased abruptly in 1964 when snow fences were erected around the recording gauges. Before the gauges were shielded, the average annual amount was 655 mm (25.8 in.); it jumped to 1,021 mm (40.2 in.) and 771 mm (30.3 in.), respectively, after the snow fence was installed (Barry 1973, pp. 95–96). The data now show an absolute increase in precipitation with increasing elevation (Table 4.6). More reliable instrumentation in the Alps has apparently led to similar results, at least up to an elevation of 3,000 m (10,000 ft.) (Flohn 1974, p. 56). Studies of snow accumulation at still higher elevations, in the Saint Elias Mountains, Yukon Territory, indicate decreasing amounts beyond 3,000 m (10,000 ft.), although there is a steady increase at lower elevations at least up to 2,000 m (6,000 ft.) (Murphy and Schamach 1966; Keeler 1969; Marcus and Ragle 1970; Marcus 1974b).

Another problem with precipitation analysis in mountains is that many weather

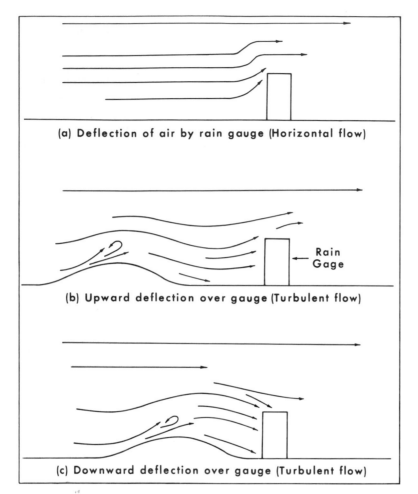

(a) Deflection of air by rain gauge (Horizontal flow)

(b) Upward deflection over gauge (Turbulent flow)

Rain
Gage

(c) Downward deflection over gauge (Turbulent flow)

Fig. 4.26. The effects of a precipitation gauge on surface wind-flow. In the first case (a) the wind may tend to speed up next to the gauge since it must travel farther to get around the obstacle. The lower illustrations (b and c) show that turbulence caused by surface roughness may result in upflow or downflow at the gauge orifice, depending on its location with respect to surrounding topography and wind direction. (Adapted from Peck 1972b, p. 8)

Table 4.6. *Average annual precipitation at four ridge sites in a transect up the Front Range of the Colorado Rockies during 1965–1970 (Barry 1973, p. 96).*

Station	Elevation (m)	Amount (mm)
Ponderosa	2,195	579
Sugarloaf	2,591	578
Como	3,048	771
Niwot Ridge	3,750	1,021

stations are located in valleys. Uncritical use of these data may lead to erroneous results. Valleys oriented parallel to the prevailing winds may receive as much or more precipitation than the mountains on either side, while valleys oriented perpendicular to the prevailing winds may be "dry holes." In addition, local circulation systems between valleys and upper slopes may result in valleys being considerably drier than the ridges (see p. 111). For example, in parts of the Hindu Kush, Karakoram, and Himalayas, many valleys are distinctly arid (Schweinfurth 1972; Troll 1972b). These contrast sharply with the adjacent mountains, where large glaciers exist. Some glaciologists have estimated an average annual precipitation of over 3,000 mm (120 in.) for the glacial area, compared to 100 mm (4 in.) in the valleys—figures that seem to support the idea of a steady increase of precipitation with elevation (Flohn 1968, 1969a, 1970). On the other hand, it is argued that little precipitation is required to maintain a glacier under such low temperatures, owing to the relatively small losses to be expected through ablation. Several studies have provided evidence for a zone of maximum precipitation at about 2,000 m (6,600 ft.) along the southern slope of the Himalayas (Dhar and Narayanan 1965; Dalrymple et al. 1970; Khurshid Alam 1972). The high, sheltered inner core of the Himalayas is most certainly arid (Troll 1972c), but the exact precipitation relationships for the range as a whole must await more precise measurement and analysis before the controversy can be resolved.

In the tropics, decrease of precipitation above a certain elevation is much better established. The precipitation falls principally as rain, with snow or rime on the highest peaks, and tropical mountains experience considerably less wind than in middle latitudes. As a result, simple rainfall measurements are more dependable. The zone of maximum precipitation varies according to location. In the tropical Andes and in Central America it lies between 900–1,600 m

(3,000–5,300 ft.) (Hastenrath 1967; Weischet 1969; Herrmann 1970). Mount Cameroon in West Africa near the Gulf of Guinea receives an annual rainfall of 8,950 mm (355 in.) on the lower slopes but less than 2,000 mm (80 in.) at the summit. The zone of maximum precipitation occurs at 1,800 m (6,000 ft.) (Lefevre 1972). In East Africa, measurements on Mount Kenya and Mount Kilimanjaro show an increase up to the montane forest belt at 1,500 m (5,000 ft.) and then a sharp decrease (Fig. 4.27). The maxi-

Fig. 4.27. Average annual rainfall on the southeast slope of Mount Kilimanjaro, 1959–1967. The zone of maximum precipitation is clearly identified at about 1,500 m (5,000 ft.). (Adapted from Flohn 1970, p. 254)

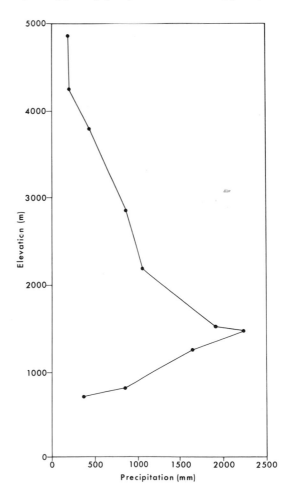

Fig. 4.28. The "alpine desert" at 4,400 m (14,500 ft.) on Mount Kilimanjaro. View is toward the east from the saddle between Kibo and Mawenzi (pictured). (O. Hedberg, 1948, University of Uppsala)

mum zone receives about 2,500 mm (100 in.) but less than 500 mm (20 in.) falls on the summit areas. The effects of low rainfall, high sun-intensity, and porous soils give the alpine belt a desert-like appearance, although both summit areas support small glaciers (Hedberg 1964; Thompson 1966; Coe 1967). Desert-like conditions exist at the summits of many tropical mountains (Fig. 4.28). On the islands of Indonesia and on Ceylon the zone of maximum precipitation varies between 900–1,400 m (3,000–4,600 ft.) (Domrös 1968; Weischet 1969), while it lies between 600–900 m (2,000–3,000 ft.) in Hawaii (Blumenstock and Price 1967; Juvik and Perreira 1974). Weischet (1969) maintains that on a general basis the belt of maximum precipitation in the humid tropics occurs between 900–1,400 m (3,000–4,600 ft.); above this level annual precipitation decreases at a rate of approxi-

mately 100 mm (4 in.) per 100 m (330 ft.). The decrease immediately above the zone of maximum precipitation is counteracted somewhat by the presence of fog drip, however, since this is a zone of frequent cloudiness (Fig. 4.23).

The vertical distribution of precipitation illustrates yet another environmental distinction between tropical and extratropical mountains. The presence of a zone of maximum precipitation is well established for the tropics, but the existence of such a zone in the middle latitudes is being increasingly questioned. Although there are insufficient measurements to settle the question categorically, evidence from mass-balance studies on glaciers, runoff from mountain watersheds, and improved methods of instrumentation seem to indicate that precipitation continues to increase with altitude in middle latitudes at least up to 3,000–3,500 m

(10,000–11,500 ft.). The decrease beyond moderate elevations in the tropics is explained by the dominance there of convection rainfall, which means that the greatest precipitation occurs near the base of the clouds. Where forced ascent is important the level may be somewhat higher, but it does not vary over a few hundred meters. In many tropical areas an upper air inversion composed of dry, stable air tends to restrict the deep development of clouds. This is the case on Mount Kenya and on Kilimanjaro, as well as on Mauna Loa and Mauna Kea in Hawaii (Juvik and Perreira 1974).

The continued increase of precipitation with elevation in the middle latitudes is somewhat more difficult to explain. The water-vapor content of the air decreases at the higher levels just as it does in the tropics. Precipitation in middle-latitude mountains is caused primarily by forced ascent rather than convection, however. Orographic lifting becomes stronger as the wind grows stronger, and wind velocity increases markedly in middle latitudes. Apparently, this factor is more than enough to compensate for the absolute decrease in water content. The water-vapor transport is at its maximum in the westerlies at about the 700-millibar level, i.e., at 3,000 m (10,000 ft.). Consequently, it is postulated that precipitation continues to increase at least up to this level (Havlik 1969). In tropical mountains, however, the wind tends to decrease with elevation above 1,000 m (3,300 ft.), so the decrease in water content of the air becomes more effective and precipitation decreases beyond this point (Weischet 1969; Flohn 1974).

Winds

Mountains are among the windiest places on earth. They protrude into the high atmosphere, where there is less friction to retard air movement. There is no constant increase in windspeed with elevation, but measurements from weather balloons and aircraft show a persistent increase at least up to the troposphere where, in middle latitudes, the wind culminates in the jet stream. A famous example of increasing windspeed with elevation is at the Eiffel Tower in Paris. The windspeed at the top—305 m (1,000 ft.)—averages about four times greater than at the base. Similar increases occur in mountains, although the conditions at any particular site are highly variable. Windspeeds are greater in middle latitudes than in tropical or polar areas, in marine than in continental locations, in winter than in summer, during the day than at night, and, of course, the velocity of the wind is dependent on the local topographic setting and the overall synoptic conditions. The wind is usually greatest in mountains oriented perpendicular to the prevailing wind, on the windward rather than the leeward side, and on isolated, unobstructed peaks rather than those surrounded by other peaks. The reverse situation may exist in valleys, since those oriented perpendicular to the prevailing winds are protected while those oriented parallel to the wind may experience even greater velocities than the peaks, owing to channeling and intensification. Table 4.7 lists the mean monthly windspeeds during the winter for several representative mountain stations in the northern hemisphere.

Mountains greatly modify the normal wind patterns of the atmosphere. Their effect may be felt for many times their height in both horizontal and vertical distance. The question of whether the windspeed is greater close to mountains or in the free air has long been problematic. It is generally believed that the wind near mountains is greater, because of compression and forcing of the air around the peak like water around a rock in a stream (Schell 1935, 1936; Conrad 1939). However, a recent study in the Alps indicates that the windspeed on these mountain summits averages only about one-half that of the free air (Wahl 1966, in Lettau 1967). Both of these

Table 4.7. *Mean monthly windspeeds during winter at selected mountain weather-stations, in order of decreasing velocity. Readings were taken above treeline or in treeless areas in all cases (after Judson 1965, p. 13).*

Location	Elevation (m)	Monthly Windspeed (mph)					
		Nov.	Dec.	Jan.	Feb.	Mar.	Apr.
Mount Fujiyama, Japan	3,776	42	42	47	37	43	34
Mount Washington, N.H.	1,909	25	36	39	49	41	36
Jungfraujoch, Switzerland	3,575	27	29	25	24	26	25
Niwot Ridge, Colo.	3,749	21	25	26	24	22	21
Pic du Midi, France	2,860	15	19	20	17	20	17
Sonnblick, Austria	3,106	22	16	18	15	18	15
Berthoud Pass, Colo.	3,621	15	15	17	17	16	17
Mauna Loa, Hawaii	3,399	15	12	19	15	13	10

situations may in fact occur; much depends upon the stability of the air mass and the size and configuration of the mountain. Generally, the more stable the air, the greater the compression, because the air will resist lifting in its passage, and this will result in increased windspeeds near the surface. On the other hand, if the air is unstable, it will tend to rise on its own accord as it is forced up over the mountain, and this will result in greater windspeeds aloft. The vertical velocity-gradient of the wind is largely a function of the interplay between compressional and frictional effects. Compression tends to create greater velocities near the surface, decreasing upward, whereas friction tends to cause lower velocities near the surface, increasing upward (the normal increase with height is not at question here). Consequently, the windspeeds in any given mountain area may have very different distributions in time and space (Schell 1936).

The sharpest gradient in windspeed usually occurs immediately above the surface. Windspeed doubles or triples within the first few meters, but the vegetation and surface roughness make a great difference in the absolute velocity (Fig. 4.29). At a height of 1 m (3.3 ft.) the windspeed in a closed forest immediately below timberline is less than half that in the open tundra just above timberline. The low-lying foliage of alpine vegetation does not produce much frictional drag on the wind, so the wind can reach quite high velocities close to the ground. There is nevertheless a sharp gradient within the first few centimeters of the surface, and most alpine plants escape much of the wind.

A reciprocal and reinforcing effect is operative here: taller vegetation tends to re-

Fig. 4.29. Wind velocity with height above a tundra surface. Note how windspeed increases with distance above the ground—one reason why alpine plants stick so close to the ground. (From Warren-Wilson 1959, p. 416)

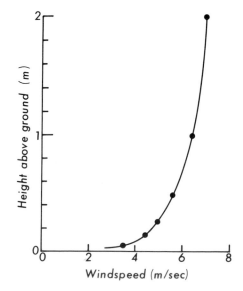

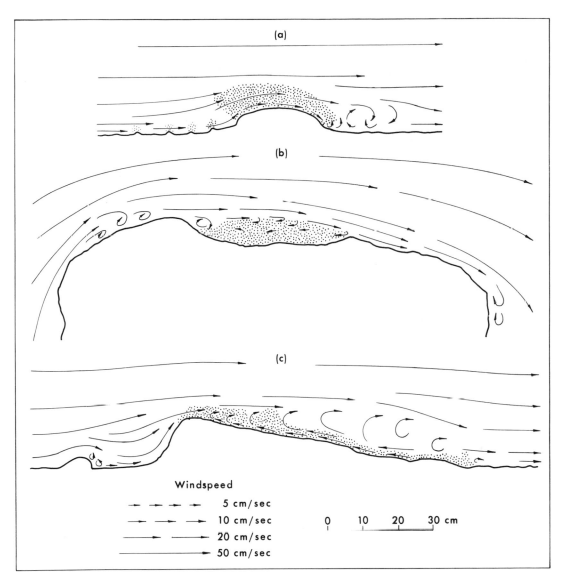

Fig. 4.30. Wind behavior in relation to microtopography in the Cairngorm Mountains, Scotland. The stippled area represents vegetation. Vertical scale is roughly equivalent to the horizontal. (a) Air movement across a grassy tussock. (b) The movement of air over a rock with a depression occupied by vegetation. (c) A wind-eroded bank. Note the eddies that develop to the lee of small obstacles: windspeed is greatly reduced in these areas and vegetation is better-developed. (Adapted from Warren-Wilson 1959, pp. 417–18)

duce the windspeed and provide a less windy environment for plants, while low-lying alpine vegetation provides little braking effect, so the wind blows freely and becomes a major factor of stress in the environment. Under these conditions the presence of microhabitats becomes increasingly important.

Surface roughness caused by clumps of vegetation and rocks creates turbulence and hence great variability in windspeed near the surface (Fig. 4.30). In the illustration, windspeed at a height of 1 m (3.3 ft.) above the grass tussock is 390 cm/sec., while closer to the ground it is 50 cm/sec. on the exposed side of the tussock and 10 cm/sec. on the lee side (Fig. 4.30a). Similar conditions exist with the eroded soil bank, except that windspeeds are higher on the exposed side and there is more eddy action and reverse flow to the lee. The restriction of the vegetation to the lee of the soil bank is largely due to the reduced windspeed there (Fig. 4.30b). The wind follows a similar pattern across the rock, with small eddies developing in depressions and to the lee. A mat of vegetation occupies the center depression where windspeeds are less (Fig. 4.30c).

Wind is clearly an extreme environmental stress; in many cases it serves as the limiting factor to life. What may be the two most extreme environments in mountains are caused by the wind: late-lying snowbanks, where the growing season is extremely short; and windswept, dry ridges. Both of these environments become more common and more extreme with elevation, until eventually the only plants are mosses and lichens—or perhaps nothing at all (but see p. 292).

There are two overall groups or types of winds. One type originates within the mountains themselves. These are local, thermally induced winds given distinct expression by the topography. The other type is caused by obstruction and modification of winds originating from outside the mountain area. The first type is a relatively predictable, daily phenomenon, while the second is more variable, depending as it does on the vagaries of changing regional wind and pressure patterns.

Local Wind Systems in Mountains

Winds that blow upslope and upvalley during the day and downslope and downvalley at night are common. Albrecht von Haller, author of *Die Alpen*, observed and described these during his stay in the Rhône

Valley of Switzerland from 1758 to 1764; since then many studies—summarized by Defant (1951), Geiger (1965), and Flohn (1969b)—have been made. The driving force for these winds is differential heating and cooling, which produces air density differences between slopes and valleys and between mountains and adjacent lowlands. During the day, slopes are warmed more than the air at the same elevation in the center of the valley; the warm air, being less dense, moves upward along the slopes. Similarly, mountain valleys are warmed more than the air at the same elevation over adjacent lowlands, so the air begins to move up the valley. These are the same processes that give rise to convection clouds over mountains during the day and provide good soaring for glider pilots (and birds). At night, when the air cools, it moves downslope and downvalley. This is the flow responsible for the development of temperature inversions. Although they are interconnected and part of the same system, a distinction is generally made between slope winds and mountain and valley winds (Fig. 4.31).

Slope Winds. Slope winds consist of thin layers of air, usually less than 100 m (330 ft.) thick, moving up the slope during the day and down at night. The wind typically begins to blow uphill about one-half hour after sunrise and reaches its greatest intensity shortly after noon (Fig. 4.31a). By late afternoon the wind abates and within a half hour after sunset reverses to blow downslope (Fig. 4.31c). Since slope winds, like mountain and valley winds, are entirely thermally induced, they are better developed in summer than in winter, in clear weather than in clouds, during the day than at night, and on sun-exposed than on shaded slopes. Local topography is important; greater windspeeds will generally be experienced in ravines and gullys than on the ridges in between (Defant 1951). Slope winds reach their greatest velocities on the upper slopes and, although generally quite moderate,

(a)

(b)

(c)

(d)

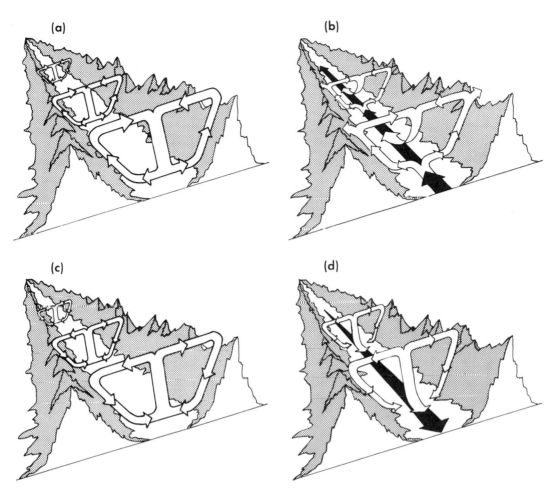

Fig. 4.31. Schematic representation of slope winds (open arrows) and mountain and valley winds (black arrows). (a) and (b) Early morning and day conditions.

(c) and (d) Early evening and night conditions. (After Defant 1951, p. 665, and Hindman 1973, p. 199)

they may be impressive when the slope terminates in a steep cliff or headwall. I have seen a small stick, thrown over a cliff, be carried upward for several meters before falling. The upslope wind does not rise far above the ridge tops, however, since it is absorbed and overruled by the regional prevailing wind.

The upward movement of two slope winds establishes a small convection system in which a return flow from aloft descends in the center of the valley (Figs. 4.32, 4.33; cf. Fig. 4.31a). This descending flow brings

from aloft drier air that has been heated slightly by compression and thus is strongly opposed to cloud formation. For this reason the dissipation of low-lying fog and clouds generally takes place first in the center of the valley. If the valley is deep enough, the dry descending air can produce markedly arid zones. In the dry gorges and deep valleys of the Andes of Bolivia and in the Himalayas, the vegetation ranges from semi-desert shrubs in valley bottoms to lush forests on the upper slopes where clouds form (Troll 1952, 1968; Schweinfurth 1972).

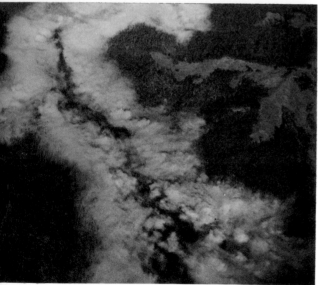

Fig. 4.32. Valley fog in the Coast Range of northern California beginning to dissipate as slope winds strengthen and the return flow develops in the center of the valley. Top photo taken at 9:58 A.M.; bottom photo taken at 10:07 A.M. (Edward E. Hindman, U. S. Navy)

Mountain and Valley Winds. Mountain and valley winds operate on a somewhat larger scale than slope winds, blowing longitudinally up and down the main valleys, essentially at right angles to the slope winds. They are all part of the same system, however, and are controlled by similar thermal responses. The valley wind (blowing from the valley toward the mountain) is interlocked with the upslope winds, and both begin shortly after sunrise (Buettner and Thyer 1962, 1965) (Fig. 4.31b). Valley winds involve greater thermal contrast and a larger air mass than slope winds, however, so they attain higher windspeeds. In the wide and deep valleys of the Alps, the smooth surfaces left by glaciation allow maximum development of the wind. The Rhône Valley has many areas where the trees are wind-shaped and flagged in the upvalley direction (Yoshino 1964b). Temperature contrasts are much smaller at night so, except where the air is channeled by deep and narrow valleys, the velocity of the mountain wind is far lower than that of the valley wind during the day (Fig. 4.31d).

As with slope winds, a circulation system is established in mountain and valley winds. The return flow from aloft (called an *antiwind*) can frequently be found immediately above the valley wind (Bleeker and Andre 1951; Defant 1951). This concept was formerly only theoretical, but a recent study of valley winds near Mount Rainier, Washington, using weather balloons, clearly identified the presence of antiwinds (Buettner and Thyer 1965). The model of the valley wind in Figure 4.33 is based on that investigation. This discovery beautifully demonstrates the three-dimensional aspects of mountain climatology: next to the surface are the slope and mountain-valley winds; above them is the return flow or antiwind; and above this is the prevailing regional gradient wind. During clear weather all of these may be in operation at the same time, each moving in a different direction.

Other Local Mountain Winds. An important variant of the thermal slope wind is the

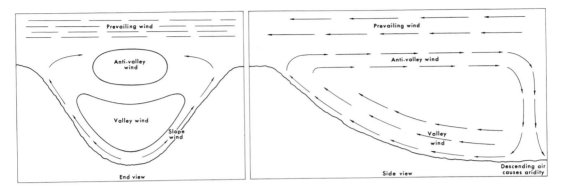

Fig. 4.33. Graphic representation of slope and valley winds. The view on the left is looking upvalley at mid-day. Slope winds are rising along the slopes, while the valley wind and antiwind are moving opposite each other, up and down the valley. The illustration on right provides a vertical cross-section of the same situation, viewed from the side. The valley wind and antiwind essentially establish a small convection system. The regional gradient wind is shown blowing above the mountains. If the regional wind is very strong, of course, it may override and prevent development of the slope and valley winds. (Adapted from Buettner and Thyer 1965, p. 144)

glacier wind, which arises as the air adjacent to the icy surface is cooled and moves downslope due to gravity. The glacier wind has no diurnal period but blows continuously, since the refrigeration source is always present. It reaches its greatest depth and intensity at mid-afternoon, however, when the thermal contrast is greatest. At these times the cold air may rush downslope like a torrent. During the day the glacier wind frequently collides with the valley wind and slides under it (Fig. 4.34). At night it merges with the mountain wind that blows in the same direction (Defant 1951). In mountains like the Rockies or Alps, with small valley glaciers, the glacier winds are fairly shallow, but when glaciers are as extensive as they are in the St. Elias Mountains or the Alaska Range, the wind may be several hundred meters in depth (Marcus 1974a). Glacier winds have a strong ecological effect, since the frigid temperatures are transported downslope with authority and the combined effect of wind and low temperatures can make the area they dominate quite inhospitable.

Another famous local wind in mountains is the "Maloja Wind," named after the Maloja Pass in Switzerland between the Engadine and Bergell valleys (Hann 1903; Defant 1951). This wind blows downvalley both day and night and results from the valley wind of one valley reaching over a low pass into another valley, where it overcomes and reverses the normal upvalley windflow. This anomaly occurs in the valley with the greater temperature-gradient and the ability to extend its circulation into the neighboring valley across the pass. Thus, the wind ascends from the steep Bergell Valley and

Fig. 4.34. Idealized cross-section of wind movement in a valley with a glacier near its head. Glacier wind is shown moving downslope in a thin zone immediately next to the ice. Valley wind blows upslope and rides over the glacier wind. At elevations above the mountains the regional gradient-wind may be blowing in still another direction. (After Geiger 1965, p. 414)

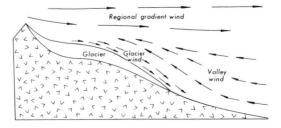

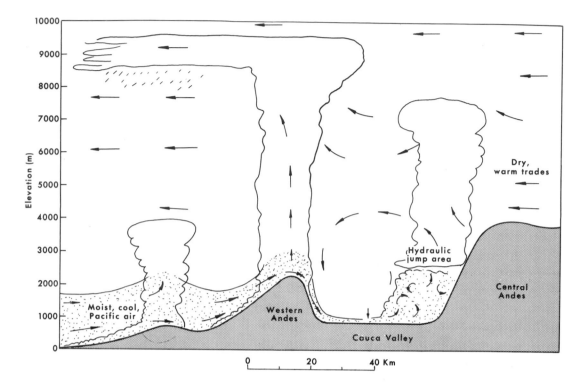

Fig. 4.35. Diagrammatic representation of typical late-afternoon weather conditions along the western slopes of the Colombian Andes, 5° N. Lat. The Andes provide a barrier to the prevailing easterly wind flow, allowing a thin layer of cool, moist Pacific air to move inland. This causes much cooler conditions and also transports moisture for the formation of clouds as it moves over the ridges. In the Cauca Valley, thunderstorms often result from air flowing down the slopes of the western Andes with enough velocity so that it is forced up the adjoining slopes of the central Andes. This produces an "hydraulic jump" that provides the impetus for cloud formation and thunderstorm activity. (After Lopez and Howell 1967, p. 31)

extends across the Maloja Pass downward into the Engadine Valley to St. Moritz and beyond. A similar situation exists in the Davos Valley, Switzerland (Flohn 1969b).

A related phenomenon occurs in coastal areas where a strong sea-breeze moves inland and over low passes in such a way that the wind blows down the lee mountain-slope during the day. This is well-developed on the asymmetric escarpments of the Western Ghats in India. In the equatorial Andes, cool air from the Pacific moves inland in a shallow surface layer overflowing the lower passes into the valleys beyond, producing relatively cool flows down the east side of the range (Lopez and Howell 1967).

In some cases these winds are forced up the opposite slopes in an hydraulic-jump phenomenon, producing afternoon rainfall (Fig. 4.35). Other examples of local winds could be given, since every mountainous country has its own peculiarities, but those mentioned suffice to illustrate their general nature.

Mountain Winds Caused by Barrier Effects

Foehn Wind. Of all the transitory climatic phenomena of mountains the *foehn wind* (pronounced "fern") is the most intriguing. Many legends, folklore, and misconceptions have arisen about this warm, dry wind that descends with great suddenness from mountains. The foehn, known in the Alps for centuries, is a feature common to all major mountain regions. In North America it is called the "chinook," in the Argentine Andes the "zonda," in New Zealand the "north-wester"; other mountain regions have their own local names for it.

The foehn produces distinctive weather: gusts of wind, high temperatures, low humidity, and very transparent and limpid air. When viewed through the foehn, mountains frequently take on a deep blue or violet tinge and seem unnaturally close and high, because light rays are refracted upward through layers of cold and warm air. The bank of clouds that typically forms along the crest line is associated with the precipitation falling on the windward side. This bank of clouds remains stationary in spite of strong winds and is known as the *foehn wall* (when viewed from the lee side).

The following is an early naturalist's description of the foehn in Switzerland:

In the distance is heard the rustling of the forests on the mountains. The roar of the mountain torrents, which are filled with an unusual amount of water from the melting snow, is heard afar through the peaceful night. A restless activity seems to be developing everywhere, and to be coming nearer and nearer. A few brief gusts announce the arrival of the foehn. These gusts are cold and raw at first, especially in winter, when the wind has crossed vast fields of snow. Then there is a sudden calm, and all at once the hot blast of the foehn bursts into the valley with tremendous violence, often attaining the velocity of a gale which lasts two or three days with more or less intensity, bringing confusion everywhere; snapping off trees, loosening masses of rock; filling up the mountain torrents; unroofing houses and barns—a terror in the land. (Quoted in Hann 1903, p. 346)

The primary characteristics of the foehn are a rapid rise in temperature, gustiness, and an extreme dryness that puts stress on plants and animals and creates a fire hazard. Forests, houses, and entire towns have been destroyed during foehn winds. For this rea-

son, smoking and fires (even for cooking) have traditionally been forbidden in many villages in the Alps during the foehn. In some cases special guards (*Föhnwächter*) were appointed to enforce the regulations. The foehn is purported to cause various psychological and physiological reactions, including a feeling of depression, tenseness, and irritability, and muscular convulsions, heart palpitations, and headaches. The suicide rate is said to rise during the foehn (Berg 1950). These symptoms have rarely been observed in North America, and medical explanations remain elusive.

In spite of its disadvantages, the foehn is generally viewed with favor, since it provides respite from the winter's cold and is very effective at melting snow (Ashwell and Marsh 1967), a fact reflected in many local sayings from the Alps: "If the foehn did not interfere, neither God nor his sunshine would ever be able to melt the winter snows"; "The foehn can achieve more in two days than the sun in ten"; "The wolf is going to eat the snow tonight" (De La Rue 1955, pp. 36–44). In North America, the value of the chinook for the Great Plains was poignantly illustrated by the painting "Waiting for a Chinook," by Charles M. Russell. During the winter of 1886, cattle and sheep died by the thousands in Montana in one of the worst snowstorms on record. Russell, a cowboy on a large ranch there, received a letter from his alarmed employers in the East, asking about the condition of their stock. Instead of writing a reply, he made a watercolor sketch of a nearly starved steer standing in deep snow unable to find food, with coyotes waiting nearby (Fig. 4.36). The picture soon became famous and so did Russell; "Waiting for a Chinook" remains his best-known painting (*Weatherwise* 1961).

The causes of the foehn are complex. One of the early explanations in the Alps was that the warm dry wind came from the Sahara Desert. The wind was usually from the south, so this seemed a perfectly logical

This is the real thing painted the winter of 1886 at the OH ranch C M Russell

This picture is Chas. Russell's reply to my inquiry as to the condition of my cattle in 1886. L E Kaufman

Fig. 4.36. "Waiting for a Chinook," by Charles M. Russell. This small watercolor was sent in a letter to Russell's employers in 1886 to announce the emaciated condition of their cattle. (Courtesy of Montana Stock-growers Association)

solution—until one day somebody climbed to the side of the mountain from which the foehn was coming and found that it was raining there, a very unlikely effect for a Saharan wind to produce! The Austrian climatologist Julius Hann (1866, 1903) is given credit for the true explanation. When air is forced up a mountain slope, it is cooled at the dry adiabatic rate, 3.05° C. per 300 m (5.5° F. per 1,000 ft.) until the dew point is reached and condensation begins. From this point on, the air is cooled at a lower rate (wet adiabatic rate) of approximately 1.7° C. (3° F.), because latent heat from condensation is being added to the air (Fig. 4.37). On the lee side of the summit, precipitation ceases and the ascending air now begins to descend. Under these conditions, the air is warmed at the dry adiabatic rate, 3.05° C. per 300 m (5.5 ° F. per 1,000 ft.) the entire length of its descent. Consequently, the air has the potential for arriving at the valley floor on the leeward side much warmer than its original temperature at the same elevation on the windward side.

The foehn develops only under specific pressure conditions. The typical situation is a ridge of high pressure on the windward side and a trough of low pressure on the leeward, creating a steep pressure-gradient across the mountain range. Under these conditions the air may undergo the thermo-dynamic process just described in a relatively short time. In order for there to be a true foehn, however, the wind must be absolutely warmer than the air it replaces

(Brinkman 1971). Either side of the mountains may experience a foehn, depending upon the orientation of the range and the development of the pressure systems. In the Alps there is a south foehn which affects the north side of the mountains and comes from the Mediterranean, and a north foehn which comes from northern Europe and affects the south side of the Alps. Because of its original warmth, the south foehn is much more striking and more frequent than the north foehn, which has to undergo much greater warming to make itself felt (Defant 1951). Similarly, in western North America most chinook winds occur on the east side of the mountains, because of the prevailing westerly wind and its movement over the Pacific Ocean, which is considerably warmer in winter than the continental polar air characteristic of the Great Basin and High Plains. Chinooks do occur, although less frequently, on the western side of the mountains (Ives 1950; Cook and Topil 1952; McClain 1952; Glenn 1961; Longley 1966, 1967; Ashwell 1971; Riehl 1974).

Although Hann's account (1866, 1903) of precipitation occurring on the windward slopes and the foehn developing on the lee slopes is valid, it is now known that the foehn can take place without the presence of precipitation. This is particularly true for the chinook wind of the Rockies. The processes responsible have been divided into four subtypes (Cook and Topil 1952; Glenn 1961; Beran 1967). In the first type, the air is forced to descend on the lee side of a mountain without precipitation occurring on the windward side (Cook and Topil 1952). This happens when certain stability conditions develop on the windward side. The lower levels of the wind are blocked by the mountain, creating drag, and the subsequent wave-action causes the upper levels to descend on the lee side of the mountain (Beran 1967, p. 867). The warming of the air in this type of chinook is due entirely to compressional heating at the dry adiabatic rate of 3.05° C. per 300 m (5.5° F. per 1,000 ft.) (Fig. 4.38a). The second type is that originally proposed by Hann, where precipitation occurs and latent heat of condensation is added to the air in addition to the heat of compression as it descends the leeward side (Fig. 4.38b). The third type is really an indirect effect: the night wind creates turbulence and prevents colder air from settling into the valleys, so temperature inversions do not occur (Fig. 4.38c). Consequently, the temperature contrasts between chinook conditions and normal conditions are often

Fig. 4.37. Diagrammatic representation of classical development of a foehn (chinook) wind. Temperatures at different locations are based on the assumption that air at the base of mountain on windward side is 10° C.

(50° F.). By the time the air has undergone the various thermodynamic processes indicated in its journey across the mountains it reaches the base on the leeward side at 18.1° C. (64.6° F.). (Author)

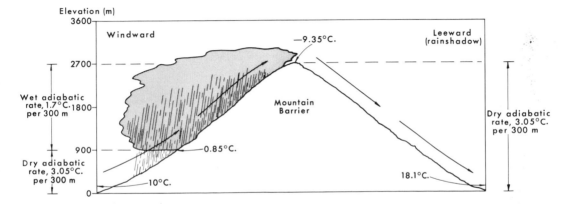

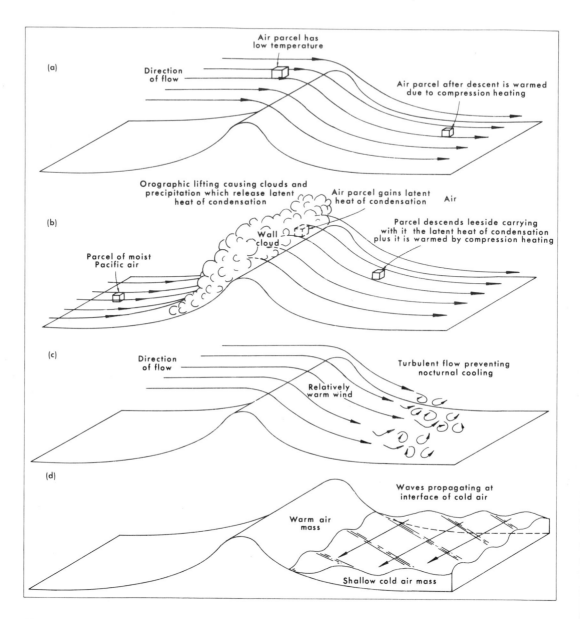

Fig. 4.38. Graphic representation of different types of chinook along the eastern slopes of the Rocky Mountains. (Adapted from Beran 1967, pp. 866–67)

more pronounced at night than during the day (Cook and Topil 1952).

The fourth and last type involves the replacement of a cold air mass by a warm air mass along a mountain front. Some spectacular changes in temperature can occur under these conditions. The arche-

typal situation is that of a shallow cold continental polar air mass from northern Canada stretched along the east side of the Rockies and an advancing low-pressure area of warmer air ascending the west side of the Rockies. The cold air mass may be likened to a lake: the lowlands and valleys are cold but the ridges are in warmer air. The warm air moves out over the cold air, and in the contact zone between the two unlike air masses, waves are often created. The cold air reacts like a giant sloshing liquid—stations near the "shore" may periodically be submerged by the wave action and undergo rapid temperature changes as they are alternately in and out of the cold air (Fig. 4.38d) (Math 1934; Hamann 1943).

Lee Waves. When wind passes over an obstacle, its normal flow is disrupted and a train of waves may be created that extends downwind for considerable distances (Fig. 4.39). The major mountain ranges produce large-amplitude waves that extend around the globe (Hess and Wagner 1948; Bolin 1950; Gambo 1956; Nicholls 1973). On a smaller scale, these waves take on a regional significance reflected in their relationship to the foehn, in distinctive cloud forms, and in upper-air turbulence (Scorer 1961, 1967; Reiter and Foltz 1967; Wooldridge and Ellis 1975; Smith 1976). The amplitude and spacing of lee waves depends on the windspeed and the shape and height of the mountains, among other factors. An average wavelength is between 2–40 km (1–25 mi.) and the vertical amplitude is usually between 1–5 km (0.6–3 mi.). The waves of greatest practical concern to man occur at altitudes of 300–7,600 m (1,000–25,000 ft.) (Hess and Wagner 1948). Windspeeds within lee waves are quite strong, frequently exceeding 160 km (100 mi.) per hour (Scorer 1961, p. 129).

The most distinctive features of lee waves are the lens-shaped (lenticular) clouds that form at the crests of waves (Fig. 4.40). These are created when the air reaches dew point and condensation occurs as the air moves upward in the wave. The clouds do not form in the troughs of the waves, since the air is descending and warming slightly (Fig. 4.39). The relatively flat cloud-bottoms represent the level of condensation, and the smoothly curved top follows the outline of the wave

Fig. 4.39. Lee waves resulting from air passing across a mountain barrier. Lee-wave clouds often form at the ridge of the waves. Rotors may develop nearer the ground in the immediate lee of the mountain. (Adapted from Scorer 1967, p. 93)

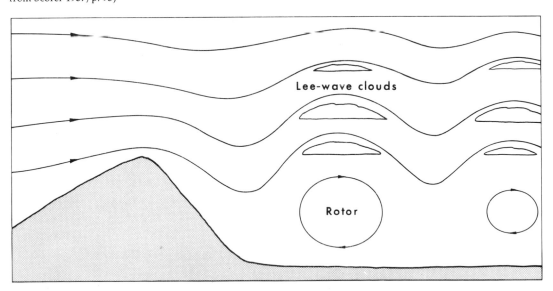

Lee-wave clouds

Rotor

Fig. 4.40. Lee-wave clouds forming over the Front Range of the Colorado Rockies. View is toward the west, so wind is southwesterly (from left to right). (Robert Bumpas, National Center for Atmospheric Research)

Fig. 4.41. Multi-storied lee-wave clouds forming to the lee of the Front Range of the Colorado Rockies. Formation of lenticular clouds above one another in this fashion indicates different wave amplitudes and increasing instability of the air. (Robert Bumpas, National Center for Atmospheric Research)

crest. The clouds are restricted in vertical extent by overlying stable air. *Lee-wave clouds* are relatively stationary (hence the name "standing-wave clouds"), although the wind may be passing through them at high speeds. Their habit of forming and staying in one place can be irritating if you happen to be in the shadowed area. I experienced this unpleasantly while carrying out field research in a small mountain range to the lee of the St. Elias Mountains, Yukon Territory. During the occasional clear sunny days, a standing-wave cloud seemed invariably to form over our slope, blocking out the sun for hours. Lee-wave clouds frequently develop above one another, as well as in horizontal rows (Fig. 4.41; cf. Fig. 4.39). They typically consist of 1–5 clouds and extend only a few kilometers downwind, but satellite photography has revealed series of 30–40 clouds extending for several hundred kilometers (Fritz 1965) (Fig. 4.42).

Much of the early knowledge about lee waves was acquired by glider pilots who found to their surprise that there was often greater lift to the lee of a hill than on the windward side. The pilots had long made use of upslope and valley winds, but by this method could never achieve a height of more than a couple of hundred meters above the ridges. In southern England, the members of the London Gliding Club had soared for years in the lift of a modest 70 m (230 ft.) hill, never achieving more than 240 m (800 ft.). After discovering the upcurrents in the lee wave, however, one member

Fig. 4.42. Satellite photo of the northwestern United States, showing extensive lee-wave cloud development from the lee of the Cascades in Washington and Oregon through the intermountain west of Idaho and Utah. Photo was taken 8 December 1977 from a permanently stationed weather satellite at an altitude of 4,320 km (2,700 mi.) at 40° N. lat. and 140° W. long. Resolution, or size of features which may be identified, is 1.6 km (1 mi.). (National Oceanic and Atmospheric Administration)

soared to a height of 900 m (3,000 ft.), thirteen times higher than the hill producing the
wave (Scorer 1961, p. 129). German pilots
were the first to explore and exploit lee
waves fully. In 1940, one pilot soared to
11,300 m (37,400 ft.) in the lee of the Alps.
Since then, sailplane pilots have taken advantage of lee waves in many mountainous
regions. The world's altitude record of
13,410 m (44,255 ft.) was set in 1952 in the
lee of the Sierra Nevada of California. This
range has one of the most powerful lee-
waves in the world, owing to its great altitudinal rise and the clean shape of its east
front (Scorer 1961, p. 129).

Another aspect of lee waves is the development of *rotors*. These are awesome roll-
like circulations that develop to the immediate lee of mountains, usually forming
beneath the wave crests. The rotor flow
moves toward the mountain at the base and
away from it at the top (Fig. 4.39). It is
marked by a row of cumulus clouds but,
unlike ordinary cumulus, they may contain
updrafts of 95 km (60 mi.) per hour (Fig.
4.43). The potential of such a wind for damage to an airplane can well be imagined; at
the very least it would provide an exciting
ride! The height of the rotor clouds is about
the same as that of the crest cloud or foehn

Fig. 4.43. A rare photograph of a rotor along the east
face of the Sierra Nevada, California. This powerful
roll-like circulation of the air is operating beneath the
flat, thin clouds. Dust is being lifted from the floor of
Owens Valley to a height of 4,800 m (16,000 ft.). (Robert
Symons, courtesy of R. S. Scorer)

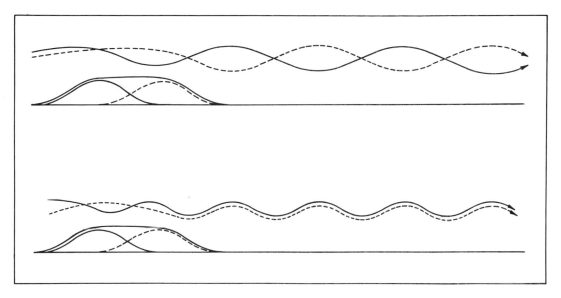

Fig. 4.44. Air current over mountains, showing superposition of lee-wave trains. The mountain ridge (indicated by dashed line of mountain form) produces a certain wave pattern (dashed streamline) and the other mountain (solid line) produces a different wave pattern (continuous streamline). Together the mountains have the effect of creating an obstacle (indicated by the continuous line). In the upper diagram the wavelength is such that the wave trains cancel out; in the lower diagram the amplitude is doubled. Since the wavelength is determined by the flow of air across the ridge, the same air-stream could produce either large-amplitude lee-waves or none at all, depending on its direction. (After Scorer 1967, p. 76)

wall. The rotating motion is thought to be created when the lee waves reach a certain amplitude and frictional drag causes a roll-like motion in the underlying air (Fig. 4.39) (Scorer 1961, 1967).

Several other kinds of turbulence may be associated with lee waves, particularly when the wave train produced by one mountain is augmented by that of another situated in the right phase relationship (Fig. 4.44). In some cases they cancel each other; in others they reinforce each other. Wind strength and direction are also important, since a small change in either one can alter the wave length of two superposed wave trains so that they become additive and create violent turbulence (Scorer 1967; Lilly 1971; Lester and Fingerhut 1974). One example of this is where the energy in standing waves is caused to "cascade" down from a wavelength of 10 km (6 mi.) to only a few hundred meters (Reiter and Foltz 1967). The exact kinds of turbulence are beyond the scope of the present discussion, except to point out that they are often directly related to mountains and the airflow across them (Fig. 4.45).

Bora, Mistral, and Similar Winds. Like the foehn, these winds descend from mountains onto adjacent valleys and plains but, unlike the foehn, they are cold. Compressional heating occurs, but it is insufficient to appreciably warm the cold air that blows from an interior region in winter across the mountains to an area which is normally warmer. These winds and others like them are basically caused by the exchange of unlike air across a mountain barrier.

The *bora* is a cold, dry north wind on the Adriatic coast of Dalmatia. It reaches its most intense development in winter and orig-

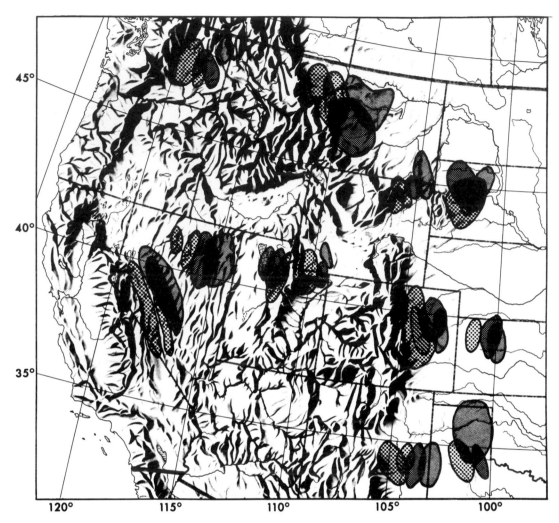

Fig. 4.45. Areas of most frequent occurrence of clear-air turbulence in the western United States. The patterns represent severe, moderate to severe, moderate, and light to moderate turbulence, with the area closest to the mountain crest being most severe (largest dots) and the area farthest away the least severe (smallest dots). (Adapted from Reiter and Foltz 1967, p. 556)

inates from high-pressure, cold continental air in southwestern Russia which results in air movement southward across Hungary and the Dinaric Alps. Ideal conditions for the bora exist when a southerly wind has brought exceptionally warm conditions to the Adriatic coast, and relatively large temperature- and pressure-differentials exist between the coast and the interior. Under these conditions, the cold continental air may move down the pressure gradient, steepened by the presence of the mountains, with extraordinary violence (Yoshino 1975, p. 361). It frequently reaches gale force, especially when channeled through narrow valleys and passes. The bora has been known to overturn haywagons, tear off roofs, and destroy orchards. It is even claimed that it once overturned a train near the town of Klis (De La Rue 1955).

The *mistral*, similar to the bora, occurs in Provence and on the French Mediterranean coast. It is caused by the movement of cold air from high-pressure areas in the north and west of France toward low-pressure areas over the Mediterranean between Spain and Italy in the Gulf of Lyon. It is as violent as the bora, or more so, since it must pass through the natural constriction between the Pyrenees and the western Alps (Defant 1951, p. 670). The mistral was known in ancient times. The Greek geographer Strabo called it "an impetuous and terrible wind which displaces rocks, and hurls men from their chariots" (De La Rue 1955, p. 32). Its effects extend throughout Provence and may be felt as far south as Nice. Like the bora, the mistral poses a major problem for fruit production, and great expenditures of human labor have gone into constructing stone walls and other windbreaks to protect the orchards (Gade 1978). The greatest wind velocities occur in the Rhône Valley, where windspeeds of over 145 km (90 mi.) per hour have been clocked.

Although the bora and mistral are the most famous, similar cold dry winds occur in many mountain areas. The *bise* (breeze) at Lake Geneva between the Alps and the French Jura is of the same type, and numerous examples could be cited from the large mountain gaps and passes of Asia (Flohn 1969b). In North America, the "northers" of the Gulf of Tehuantepec, Mexico, are a similar phenomenon (Hurd 1929). Another example is the exchange of the cold air during winter between the east and west sides of the Cascade Mountains along the Columbia River Gorge and the Fraser River Valley. This is most pronounced when an outbreak of cold Arctic air moves southward and banks up against the east side of the Cascades, causing great temperature- and pressure-contrasts between the cold continental air and the relatively warm Pacific air. At these times cold air is forced through these sea-level valleys at high velocities and brings some of the clearest and coldest weather of the winter to the cities of Vancouver, British Columbia, and Portland, Oregon (both located at valley mouths). At other times the cold air may force the warm coastal air aloft and produce locally heavy snowfall. The most dominant feature, however, is the cold and ferocious wind which leaves its mark on the landscape in the brown and deadened foliage of needleleaf trees and in the strongly flagged and wind-shaped trees on exposed sites (Lawrence 1938).

Snow, Glaciers, and Avalanches

The instant a [snow]flake has sunk to earth, changes in its structure begin to take place. As we gaze at the whitened woods stilled to silence or look through the tiny window of the alpine hut upon the dazzling snowfields, conveying to us the false message of an inert nature standing still, we are really looking upon a supremely busy laboratory in which, in sum total, vast energy is at work inducing all kinds of physical changes, so that in a short time nothing is left of the original flake of yesterday's blizzard save its whiteness.

G. Seligman,
Snow Structure and Ski Fields
(1936)

The presence of snow is fundamental at high altitudes and provides the essential ingredient for the development of glaciers and avalanches. These three interrelated phenomena, which contribute much to the distinctiveness of mountain landscapes, offer a considerable challenge to the inhabitants, both plant and animal, of these regions.

SNOW

Snow is precipitation in the solid form that originates from freezing of supercooled water around tiny nuclei of foreign matter, especially clay minerals, in the air. Once formed, snow crystals are subject to continual change. They may grow through condensation and accretion or diminish through evaporation and melting, and they may be fragmented and recombined in numerous ways. Snowflakes are generally small and simple when first formed in the cold dry air of high altitudes, but they become larger and more complex when formed at or when falling through lower elevations where temperatures are higher and there is more moisture. Thus, snow received at the summits of mountains is often quite different from that received on middle slopes of ranges. Most snowflakes follow a hexagonal pattern, although their individual shapes display infinite variety: any child who has ever played in the snow knows that every snowflake is different. The principal forms of snow crystals are generally grouped into ten main types (Fig. 5.1). These are only applicable to falling snow; a very different range of forms is present in fallen snow. Upon reaching the ground, snowflakes quickly lose their original shapes as they become packed together and undergo metamorphism (Alford 1974). Snow, then, displays continual change

Fig. 5.1. The principal types of snow crystals. (From LaChapelle 1969, p. 11)

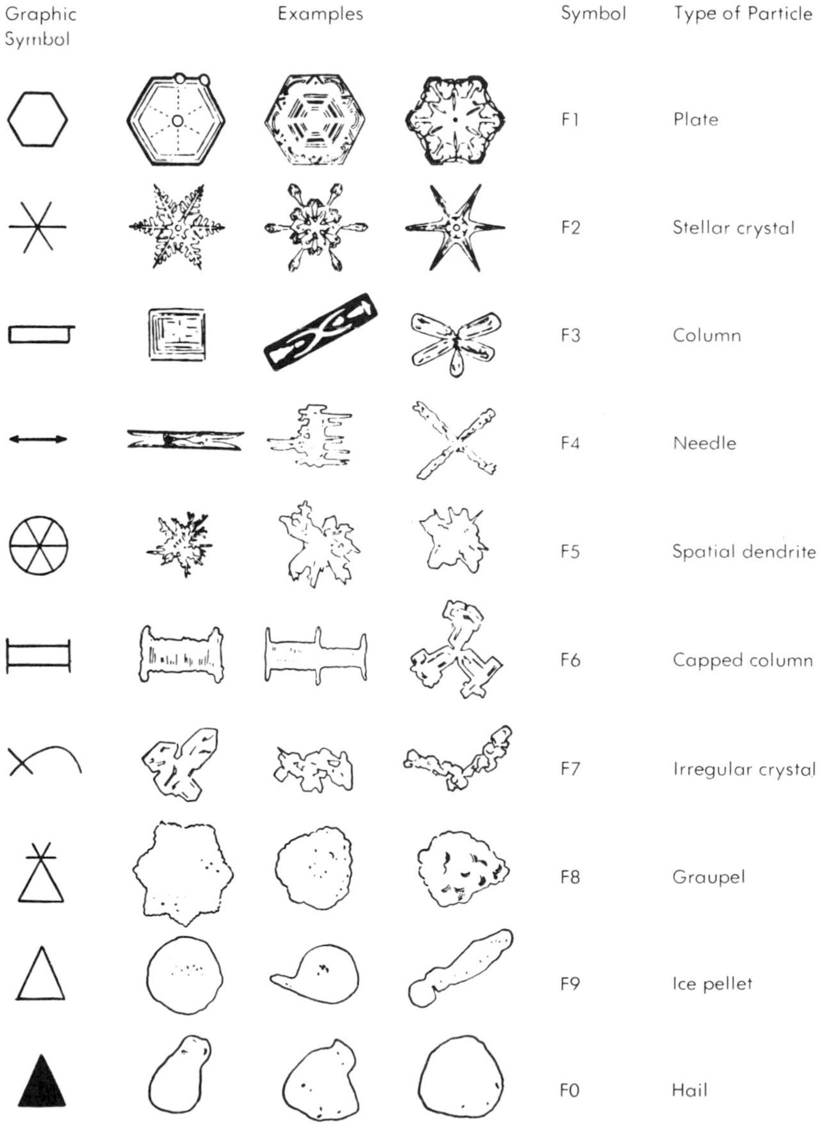

Graphic Symbol	Examples			Symbol	Type of Particle
				F1	Plate
				F2	Stellar crystal
				F3	Column
				F4	Needle
				F5	Spatial dendrite
				F6	Capped column
				F7	Irregular crystal
				F8	Graupel
				F9	Ice pellet
				F0	Hail

during formation, falling, and accumulation on the ground, until it eventually melts and returns to the sea.

Snow may form in the atmosphere at any latitude, but in order to maintain its identity it must fall to the earth in an area with sufficiently low temperatures to preserve it. Most fallen snow melts within a few days or months, depending upon the amount received and climatic conditions (Dickson and Posey 1967; McKay and Thompson 1972). For example, polar areas receive very little snow, owing to the extremely low temperatures there, but what does fall is preserved with great efficiency. On the other hand, snow may persist even in areas where temperatures are above freezing if sufficient amounts fall: the snowline in the Himalayas extends much lower on the southern side than on the northern side, because the greater precipitation received on the south more than compensates for the effects of higher temperature. A similar situation exists in the tropics, where snow often reaches lower elevations in tropical mountains during summer (the period of high sun) than in winter. The increased precipitation and cloudiness in summer overrule the effect of the higher sun.

Heavy snowpack is found mostly in middle-latitude and subpolar mountains, regions of relatively high precipitation and low temperatures. Consequently, after the snow has disappeared from the surrounding lowlands, vast amounts may still remain in the higher elevations. The mountain snowpack has become increasingly valuable as a source of water during the summer. In the western United States, the Snow Survey, which takes measurements and publishes reports monthly on the status of the snowpack in different regions, has become a vital operation (Davis 1965; U.S. Dept. Agriculture 1972). The increasing importance of the scientific aspects of snow and ice is reflected in annual symposia such as *The Role of Snow and Ice in Hydrology* and the *Western Snow Conference.* Considerable

research and effort have gone into methods of increasing the snowpack, e.g., installing fences in alpine grasslands, planting more trees, and an experimental method of timber-cutting that alternates cut with standing patches of trees to preserve the snow from wind drift (Martinelli 1967, 1975; Leaf 1975). Efforts toward artificial stimulation of precipitation have largely been focused on increasing the snowfall in mountains (Weisbecker 1974; Steinhoff and Ives 1976). The implications for man of mountain snow are discussed later (see pp. 348–53), but the importance of meltwater cannot be stressed enough. The Pacific Northwest of the United States is largely dependent upon hydroelectric power from streams that head in mountains, and California's bountiful farm production is derived largely from meltwater from the Sierra Nevada. In fact, the economy of the entire western United States is dependent upon meltwater from mountains.

The build-up of a snowcover is in many ways analogous to the formation of sedimentary rock. Snow accumulates as a sediment, with each layer reflecting the nature of its origin. Newly fallen snow has a very low density, somewhat like fluffed goose down, with vast amounts of air between the crystals, but as more snow accumulates and settling takes place, it becomes compressed. The exact behavior of fallen snow depends upon its temperature, moisture content, internal pressures, and age. The eventual tendency is for the snow to undergo metamorphosis (Bader and Kuroiwa 1962; de Quervain 1963; Sommerfeld and LaChappelle 1970). This includes the transformation of delicate snow crystals into amorphous rounded grains through compaction and through molecular processes which have their greatest effect on the projecting points of the snowflakes. These processes take anywhere from a few weeks to months, depending on temperature and moisture conditions (they occur most rapidly given warmth and moisture), and are responsible for the springtime "corn snow" so popular with skiers. Another process that occurs within the snow, particularly in very cold areas, is migration of water vapor through diffusion from warm layers to cold layers, causing new crystal growth. This frequently results in larger crystals with fewer bonding surfaces (*depth hoar*) and reduces the strength of the snow (see p. 163). Periodic melting and refreezing of the snow also produces increased densification. Upon thawing, snow loses much of its cohesion and strength, but refreezing brings about new intergranular bonds and greater strength. The process of repeated freezing and thawing causes compaction and consolidation and is responsible for the formation of *firn* or *névé*, which is dense snow at least one year old. The snow may now be as much as fifteen times heavier than when it first fell, and it is well on its way toward becoming glacial ice (de Quervain 1963, p. 378).

Snowline

The zone between seasonal snow which melts every summer and the permanent snow which does not is represented by the *snowline*. This zone has fundamental implications for environment and process. The varying disposition of the snowline in time and space has resulted in different interpretations of its significance and has caused considerable confusion in the literature, where such terms as climatic snowline, annual snowline, orographic snowline, temporary snowline, transient snowline, and regional snowline occur (Charlesworth 1957; Flint 1971; Östrem 1964, 1973, 1974). The use of *snowline* without definition of terms has become fairly meaningless. To appreciate the problem, consider the following conditions. At one extreme is the delineation between a snowcovered and snow-free area at any time of the year. Obviously, this snowline varies from day to day and will be lowest in the winter, reaching sea level in middle latitudes, and highest in summer. There is also a snow-

line establishing the lower limits of persistent snow in winter, a matter of great importance to the location of ski resorts and road maintenance (Rooney 1969). Our primary concern, however, is the location of the snowline after maximum melting in summer, since this is the level which establishes the glacial zone and largely limits the distribution of most plants and animals. The position of this line is likewise highly variable and difficult to delineate. For example, avalanches may transport large masses of snow to valley bottoms where, if shaded, they may persist for several years. Similarly, mountain glaciers occupy sheltered topographic sites and receive greater accumulations from drifting snow and avalanches than do the surrounding slopes. They also experience less melting because of their shadow climate and the natural cooling effect of the larger ice mass. As a result, snowline is generally lower on glaciers than in the areas between them. In mountains without glaciers, or on slopes between glaciers, the snowline is commonly represented by small patches of perennial snow whose distribution is largely controlled by slope orientation and local topographic sites.

The disparity of the various snow limits and the difficulty in establishing their exact locations have led to the use of several indirect methods of approximation. One of these is to use the elevation where the average temperatures are 0° C. (32° F.) or less during the warmest month of the year. Since this is determined primarily through the use of radiosonde and weather balloons, a snowline can be established even where there are no mountains. The resulting snowline, although only theoretical, is useful for purposes of generalization. This is particularly true when investigating temperatures during the glacial age. For example, if a glacier exists today at 2,000 m (6,600 ft.) but it at one time existed at 1,000 m (3,300 ft.), the difference in elevation can be converted to temperature (through use of the vertical lapse-rate) to get an approximate idea of the temperature necessary to produce the lower snowline. In general it is believed that temperatures during the Pleistocene were 4–7° C. (7–13° F.) lower than they are today (Flint 1971, p. 72; Andrews 1975, p. 5).

A more useful approach is to establish a zone or band about 200 m (660 ft.) wide to represent the "regional snowline," or the "glaciation level," as it is known, since it represents the minimum elevation in any given region where a glacier may form (Östrem 1964, 1974; Porter 1977). The location of this zone is based on the difference in elevation between the lowest peak in an area bearing small glaciers and the highest peak in the same area without a glacier (but with slopes gentle enough to retain snow). For example, if one mountain is 2,000 m (6,600 ft.) high but has no glacier, although its slopes are gentle enough to accommodate one, and another mountain 2,200 m (7,300 ft.) high does have a glacier, the local glaciation level and the regional snowline lie between these two elevations (Östrem 1974, pp. 230–33) (Fig. 5.2).

The regional snowline is lowest in the polar regions, where it may occur at sea level, and highest in the tropics, where it occurs between 5,000–6,000 m (16,500–19,800 ft.). This is not a straight-line relationship, of course, owing to the interplay of temperature and precipitation. The highest snowlines are found between 6,000–6,500 m (19,800–21,500 ft.) in the arid Puna de Atacama of the Andes (25° S. lat.) and the Tibetan Highlands (32° N. lat.). The greater precipitation and cloudiness experienced in the tropics depresses the snowline, while areas under the influence of the subtropical high at 20–30° N. and S. lat. receive less precipitation and fewer clouds, resulting in a higher snowline even though temperatures are lower (Fig. 5.3). At any given latitude, the snowline is generally lowest in areas of heavy precipitation, e.g., coastal mountains, and highest in areas of low precipitation, e.g., continental mountains. Accordingly, there is a tendency for snowlines to rise in elevation toward the west in the tropics and toward the east in middle latitudes, in accordance with the prevailing winds. The middle-latitude situation is illustrated by the snowline in the western United States, which rises from 1,800 m (6,000 ft.) in the Olympic Mountains, Washington, at 48° N. lat. to 3,000 m (10,000 ft.) in Glacier National Park, Montana, located in the Rockies, 800 km (480 mi.) to the east (Flint 1971, p. 66). A similar tendency for the snowline to rise

Fig. 5.2. Method of approximating the regional snowline or glaciation level for mountainous regions. The regional snowline occupies the zone lying between the highest peaks not supporting glaciers and the lowest peaks that do support glaciers. (After Flint 1971, p. 64, and Östrem 1974, p. 230)

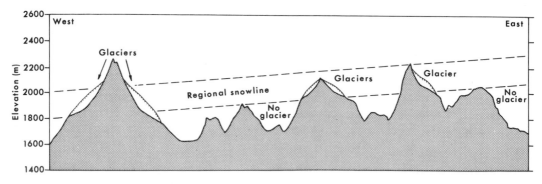

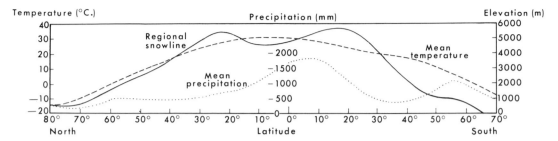

Fig. 5.3. Generalized altitude of snowline on a north-south basis. Reason for slightly lower snowline elevations in tropics is the increased precipitation and cloudiness in these regions. Mean temperature and precipitation are also given. (After Charlesworth 1957, p. 9)

from west to east exists in the mountains of Scandinavia, the Andes of southern Chile, and the Southern Alps of New Zealand (Östrem 1964; Porter 1975a).

GLACIERS

A glacier is a mass of moving ice created by the accumulation of snow. The transformation of snow into ice is basically a process of densification and expulsion of air. This is accomplished by sublimation, melting and refreezing, and compaction. Sublimation, melting, and refreezing are most important when the snow is still near the surface, and compaction becomes more important after the snow has been buried under successive annual accumulations. As the snow becomes harder and more dense, the air spaces between the particles are diminished and eventually closed. Once this stage is reached, it is considered to be glacial ice. The pattern of progression is clear, although the time needed to accomplish it depends upon the temperature, precipitation, and other conditions (the time is shorter where there is greater warmth and moisture). First, newly fallen snow turns into pea-sized ice crystals at the end of the season, i.e., corn snow; the corn snow then becomes firn. By this time the ice crystals are somewhat more dense, with smaller air spaces between them. Firn represents an

intermediate stage in the progress toward glacial ice, but several more years are required to complete the process. The difference between firn and glacial ice is not always clearly marked, but they can usually be distinguished by the color and density of the material. If there are air spaces between the ice crystals and the ice has a whitish color when viewed in mass, it is firn. On the other hand, if the material has a massive structure with no air spaces between the ice crystals, and a vitreous appearance reflecting a blue or greenish color, it is glacial ice (Seligman 1936, p. 118).

Today's glaciers are only a vestige of what existed during the height of the ice age a few thousand years ago. Nevertheless, active mountain glaciers still occur in all latitudes, and range from small *cirque glaciers* occupying isolated depressions on mountain slopes to major *icefields* covering all but the highest peaks (Figs. 5.4 and 5.5). Cirque glaciers are typical of tropical and middle-latitude mountains, while icefields are restricted to subpolar and polar areas. Intermediate between these is the *valley glacier*, which heads in an accumulation basin and extends downvalley for some distance (Fig. 5.6; cf. Fig. 5.8). Where the ice is sufficient to flow through the valley and accumulate at the base of the mountains, it may spread out upon reaching the

Fig. 5.4. Several small cirque glaciers along a northeast-facing ridge in the central Sierra Nevada, California. Photo was taken in late September 1972, and the snowline (firn line) is located on upper part of glaciers. The sinuous downslope depositional forms consist of material that has been eroded relatively recently from the cirque walls. The bare rock of the valley farther downslope results from strong ice-scouring in the past, when glacial development was more extensive. (Austin Post, U. S. Geological Survey)

Fig. 5.5. Icefield ranges in the St. Elias Mountains, southwestern Yukon Territory, Canada. Large massif in background is Mount Logan, 6,052 m (19,850 ft.) high, the second highest mountain in North America. View is to the southwest toward the Gulf of Alaska. The glacial ice here may extend to depths of 300–900 m (1,000– 3,000 ft.) or more. Peaks sticking above ice are called *nunataks*. The darker surface in immediate foreground represents the firn line, since the previous winter's snow has melted in this area. Picture was taken near the end of melt season in late August. (Author)

flats to form a spatulate tongue; this is a *piedmont glacier*.

The forms of alpine glaciers result from both topography and climate. A glacier cannot develop if the slopes are too steep, since the snow cannot accumulate, even if climatic conditions are favorable. At the opposite extreme, it is unlikely that one would develop on an exposed level upland of limited size, because of wind and sun exposure. Topography can be viewed as the initial mold into which the snow and ice must fit, while climate determines at what level and to what extent glaciers develop in any given topographic situation.

In the simplest terms, all that is required for a glacier to form is for more snow to fall than melts. This may be accomplished by various environmental combinations. Consider the differences in energy flux and temperature/precipitation regimes in mountains at various latitudes. Mid-latitude mountains receive heavy amounts of snow but summers are very warm, resulting in

Fig. 5.6. Kluane Glacier in the St. Elias Mountains, Yukon Territory. This large valley glacier flows toward the interior, while similar glaciers on the other side of the range flow to tidewater in the Gulf of Alaska. Note the extremely rough, crevassed surface. The rocky material on either side of the glacier is lateral moraine. To the extreme right is a small glacial tongue that was at one time connected with the larger valley glacier, but is now receding. (Author)

heavy melting and relatively rapid turnover within the system. By contrast, polar mountains receive so little precipitation that the contribution of rime and hoarfrost is often greater than that of snow. At the same time, there is little or no melting. Calving off of icebergs when glaciers move into the sea is the principal method of depletion. At the other extreme, tropical mountains often display a curious situation: the lower part of the glacier receives more precipitation than the higher part (owing to the zone of maximum precipitation), and melting may take place every day of the year rather than just during summer. Consequently, tropical glaciers are quite short.

There are also major differences in environmental conditions through time. The epoch of the ice ages (the Pleistocene) represents 2.5 million years of major fluctuation in environmental conditions (Boellstorff 1978). During this time at least four major advances of the ice have taken place: continental glaciers developed and moved into the middle latitudes of the northern hemisphere and mountain glaciers grew and spread into the surrounding lowlands. It is generally felt that each of the major glacial advances coincided with a period of lower temperatures, but the exact requirements for glacial growth are complex and may vary for different regions. Vastly different conditions can develop, depending on the deployment of moisture and temperature regimes between winter and summer. For example, lowering the winter temperature in continental areas may lead to less, not more, snow. This is confirmed by the very small amount of precipitation received in the polar regions. Consequently, if the winter temperatures are lowered in a continental area while the summer temperatures remain the same, the result may be glacial retreat. On the other hand, a small amount of summer cooling—from increased cloud cover, for instance—may allow the normal snowfall (which would otherwise have melted) to persist through the season. In some areas this change alone causes increased snow accumulation and glacial growth. Similarly, increased snowfall (with no marked change in temperature) permits some snow survival even under summer temperatures, when the regular amount would normally melt. It can be seen that glaciers are created not simply by the lowering of temperature but by the interplay of different climatic factors. Nevertheless, temperature remains the crucial factor, and there is evidence that temperatures were several degrees lower during the height of the ice ages (see p. 130).

Climatic Response

Once formed, a glacier responds to and reflects changing climatic conditions. Whether a glacier grows, retreats, or maintains itself depends upon its mass balance, or budget. This is determined by total snow accumulation as opposed to what is lost through ablation. A chief indicator of glacial status on a year-to-year basis is the location of the annual snowline or *firn limit*, which represents the maximum extent of summer melting (Fig. 5.7). Since firn is snow at least one year old, the firn limit is the zone dividing this year's snow from last (or, in some cases, fresh snow from glacial ice). The firn limit on a glacier is generally quite distinct near the end of the summer and can be identified by field examination or from aerial photographs (Fig. 5.8; cf. Fig. 5.4).

Fig. 5.7. Longitudinal section of typical valley glacier, showing areas of accumulation and ablation separated by the annual snowline. Long arrows within glacier represent streamlines of flow. (After Sharp 1960, p. 9, and Flint 1971, p. 36)

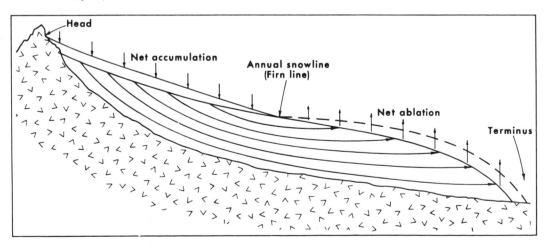

Fig. 5.8. Small valley glacier located in the North Cascades, Washington. Picture was taken near the end of summer, and the firn line is evident midway up the glacier. The lightest-colored snow had fallen within the previous few days. (Austin Post, 9 September 1966, U.S. Geological Survey)

A similar but more sophisticated approach to the study of glacial mass-balance is use of the *equilibrium line*. Since it is calculated from measurements of snow density, water equivalent, and other internal qualities, it does not always coincide with the firn limit. The equilibrium line marks the zone on the glacier where the mass of the glacier stays approximately the same during the year. Above the equilibrium line is an excess of winter snow, resulting in increased mass; below the equilibrium line ablation exceeds accumulation, so the glacier loses mass. If the mass gain above the line equals the mass loss below the line, the glacier is in a (rare) steady-state condition; if the mass gain above the equilibrium line exceeds the mass loss below the line, the result is mass transfer to lower levels and glacial growth, whereas if mass loss exceeds gain, the glacier is shrinking. The problems of establishing the mass balance of a glacier are discussed by Meier (1962).

Over a period of several years, the obvious standard for judgment is the advance or retreat of the glacial tongue itself (Posamentier 1977). The most striking fact of glacial behavior in the last century has been widespread glacial retreat. There have been periods of advance within this period, e.g., the 1920s (Hoinkes 1968), but the overriding tendency toward retreat has been documented by hundreds of investigations in mountainous areas throughout the world (Charlesworth 1957; Flint 1971). Climatic variations and glacial fluctuations such as this are the norm rather than the exception. It was formerly thought that the major ice advances had each lasted about 100,000 years and had been separated by somewhat longer interglacials with warmer and drier climates. However, it is now believed that the glacial and interglacial periods each lasted only 10,000 to 30,000 years (Emiliani 1972; Woillard 1978). The last major ice advance melted about 15,000 years ago; we are now in an interglacial period. (Shorter-term climatic fluctuations have continued to occur within this framework, however.)

The final melting of the continental ice was followed by a distinctly warm and dry period, known as the *hypsithermal*, which lasted from 4,000 to 10,000 years ago (Deevey and Flint 1957). The next major change was a widespread advance of mountain glaciers 2,000–4,000 years ago (Denton and Karlén 1973). Subsequent climatic fluctuations, most notably a warming trend about 1,000 years ago, were followed by a period of glacial advance during the Little Ice Age in the seventeenth and eighteenth centuries (Lamb 1965). Glacial advance during this period did considerable damage to farmland and villages in the Alps and in the mountains of Norway (Grove 1972; Messerli et al. 1978). The period of modern glacial retreat witnessed within the twentieth century apparently reflects warming and amelioration of conditions following the Little Ice Age. Since the 1940s, however, there has been a slight cooling trend and in some areas the glaciers are beginning to advance again (Meier 1965, p. 803). It is, of course, too soon to know where this will end. Is it just another small deviation from the norm, or are we in fact near the end of the interglacial period and on the verge of another ice age? This question was the topic of a recent symposium published in a volume of *Quaternary Research* (Vol. 2, No. 3, 1972).

Glacial Movement

Glacial movement is determined by the thickness of the ice, its temperature, the steepness of the glacial surface, and the configuration of the underlying and confining topography. In general, greatest movement of the ice takes place in the center of the glacier and decreases toward the edges. Movement is also greatest at the surface and decreases with depth. On a longitudinal basis, movement is greatest near the center at the equilibrium line and least at the head and terminus. The area above the equilibrium line is the zone of accumulation; the area below is the zone of ablation (Fig. 5.7). Therefore, if a glacier is to maintain its form and profile, transfer of mass must be greatest in this zone (Paterson 1969, p. 64). Movement in the accumulation area is generally greatest in winter because of increased snow load, while movement in the ablation zone is greatest in the summer because temperatures are higher and there is more meltwater to serve as lubrication. Velocities are highly variable, ranging from a few centimeters to several meters per day. In steep reaches of the glacier, particularly where the ice cascades over cliffs, velocities may be much higher. Greatest single velocities occur in the so-called "surges" of glaciers, where speeds exceeding 100 m (330 ft.) per day may occur for short periods of time. This still little-understood phenomenon has received increasing attention within the last decade or so (Meier 1969).

Glaciers are thought to move through two basic mechanisms—*plastic flow* and *basal sliding*. Historically, it was believed that glaciers flow much like a viscous liquid, but in recent years it has been realized that ice behaves more like a polycrystalline solid where there is deformation due to flow or creep, as in the creep of metals. Ice, of

Fig. 5.9. Glacial striations showing direction of ice movement on basalt bedrock at an altitude of 2,700 m (9,000 ft.) on Steens Mountain, southeast Oregon. (Author)

course, is much weaker than most crystalline solids and deforms easily through the action of gravity on its mass. The processes involved in plastic flow are still not completely agreed upon, but the favored theory, that of intragranular yielding, says that the ice crystals yield to shear stress by gliding over one another along basal planes within the lattices of the ice crystals. The individual ice crystals should become internally elongated, but since no such deformations of crystals is found in glaciers, a progressive recrystallization apparently accompanies the deformation (Sharp 1960, p. 46). The flow is largely a result of directional shear

stress, so the ice is equally plastic throughout (rather than being more plastic at the base owing to greater confining pressures, as is sometimes thought). The primary factors controlling the rate of flow are the depth of the ice and the surface slope of the glacier. The steepness of the bedrock slope beneath the ice is less important, since plastic flow may continue even where there are bedrock depressions and obstacles (Paterson 1969, p. 78).

The other major mechanism involved in glacier movement is that of basal sliding, which involves the slippage of ice en masse over the rock surface at its base. The abrasions and striations left on bedrock across which glaciers have moved are evidence for this kind of movement (Fig. 5.9). The processes involved are even less well understood than those of plastic flow, since the base of a glacier is inaccessible to direct observation. An important factor is the temperature of the ice at the base and the presence of water to serve as a lubricant. Basal sliding does not generally occur in polar glaciers, since the ice freezes to the underlying rock surface. In other regions the temperature of the glacial ice is higher and water may be present along the base. Water may also be released when ice reaches the pressure melting-point. This happens when an obstacle is encountered during glacial movement, the ice is compressed on the upstream side of the obstruction, and the increased pressure causes melting. The meltwater then flows around the obstacle and refreezes to the downstream side where the pressure is less. The process is maintained by the latent heat of fusion (given off upon refreezing), which is transmitted through conduction from the freezing area upglacier to the melting area, where it helps maintain the melting. This only operates on small obstacles 1–2 m (3–7 ft.) in length, however, because the heat cannot be effectively transmitted through larger features. On larger obstacles the ice undergoes greater deformation and movement is probably due mainly to plastic flow, since the ice immediately next to the obstacle must travel farther and faster in order to keep up with the surrounding glacier mass. The larger the obstacle, the more rapid the ice deformation and movement near the bedrock interface (Weertman 1957, 1964).

Glacier Structures

Glaciers contain a number of interesting features resulting from the transformation of snow to ice and from downslope movement. Most of these are beyond our present concern, but two of them, crevasses and moraines, require mention. A *crevasse* is a crack in the ice which may range up to 15 m (50 ft.) in width, 35 m (115 ft.) in depth, and several tens to hundreds of meters in length. Most are smaller than this, especially in temperate mountain glaciers, where the average crevasse is only 1–2 m (3–7 ft.) wide and 5–10 m (16–33 ft.) deep (Fig. 5.10). Crevasses are among the first structural features to appear on a glacier and may develop anywhere from the head to the terminus. Their formation is primarily in response to tensional stress, so their distribution, size, and arrangement provide useful information on the flow behavior of the ice (Sharp 1960, p. 48). They occur most often where the middle and the sides move at different rates, or where the ice curves around a bend, or where the slope steepens and the rate of movement increases (Figs. 5.6 and 5.8). Crevasses are most often transverse to the direction of flow, but they can be oriented in any direction. They are also largely restricted to the surface, where the ice is more brittle and fractures easily; the greater pressure at depth results in closure by plastic flow.

A special type of crevasse develops at the upslope end of the glacier where the ice pulls away from the rocky headwall. This is known as the *bergschrund* (Fig. 5.11). Rock debris from the headwall and valley sides falls into the bergschrund and other crevasses and becomes incorporated into the glacier, often not to be seen again until it is released by glacial melting at the terminus. The presence of crevasses, therefore, increases the efficiency of rock transport. Crevasses also hasten ablation by increasing the glacier's surface area, by the pooling of meltwater, and by disaggregating the ice near the terminus. Crevasses pose great danger to traffic across glaciers. This is particularly true after a fresh snow has bridged the surface, hiding the underlying chasms from view. For this reason glacial travel is usually attempted only by experienced teams using ropes (Manning 1970).

Fig. 5.10. A crevasse on Collier Glacier in the Three
Sisters Wilderness, Oregon Cascades. Downslope is to
the left. The rocky debris has fallen onto the ice from a
projecting ridge. (Author)

Fig. 5.11. Mount Assiniboine in the Canadian Rockies. This peak displays a classic glacial horn; small cirque glaciers are still present. Note the well-marked bergschrund at the glacier head. (Austin Post, U.S. Geological Survey)

Another conspicuous surface feature of mountain glaciers is the linear accumulation of rocky debris oriented in the direction of flow. Known as *lateral* and *medial moraines*, these accumulations result from rocks that have fallen onto the ice and from the debris input of tributary glaciers. When a smaller ice stream joins a larger glacier, it usually carries with it a load of rocky debris along its edges (lateral moraine) which becomes incorporated into the ice as a vertical partition between the two ice masses. The material then becomes a medial moraine on the main glacier (Fig. 5.12). What we see is only the surface expression of the rock debris, which extends into the ice, frequently all the way to the bottom (except for material contributed by smaller ice streams that join at shallower levels) (Fig. 5.13).

The presence of moraines on the ice alters the mass balance, since the rock material is dark in color and can absorb more of the sun's energy. On the other hand, if the rocky burden is thick enough it may serve as an insulative cover and inhibit local melting of the underlying ice. This results in the ice on either side melting more quickly, leaving the moraine exposed as a higher ridge. On very large glaciers, moraines can reach heights of up to 40 m (130 ft.) (Flint 1971, p. 108). As the ridge builds through differential melting, some of the rocky material may slide or tumble onto the ice; in this way the moraine is widened and the underlying ice is again exposed to melting. The moraines gradually widen toward the terminus, eventually ending up as a jumble of rock debris covering the terminus of the glacier (now called *ablation moraine*). If the glacier is retreating, the underlying ice may melt, leaving the rocks lying about in heaps. On the other hand, isolated masses of ice may be preserved indefinitely under the debris as ice-cored moraine. This is essentially the end of the journey for the larger rock material. The finer debris, however, can be transported farther through the action of glacial meltstreams and wind.

Glacial Erosion

When a glacier moves over an area, the ice undergoes plastic deformation to fill every nook and cranny. Movement at the ice-rock interface results in modification of the underlying surface through glacial erosion and transport. The primary processes are abrasion and plucking or quarrying. *Abrasion* is the scratching, gouging, and grooving of the surface as the ice, carrying rock particles as tools, moves across it. Obviously, this is most effective when the rocks in the ice are harder than the surface over which they are passing. Pure ice or ice containing softer rocks is relatively ineffective at abrasion, although it may produce smoothed and shiny surfaces (glacial polish). A bedload of fine material will result in tiny scratches and smoothing of surfaces, while large embedded rocks can produce scratches several centimeters deep. Striations are found in greatest abundance on gently inclined terrain where the ice was forced to ascend, since in that way greater pressure is placed on the glacial base. Striations provide good evidence for the direction of glacial movement; some caution should be used in their interpretation, however, since they can be caused by other processes, e.g., avalanches and mass movement.

Plucking or *quarrying* is generally considered to be a much more potent erosional force than is abrasion. It involves the lifting and incorporation of surface rubble and bedrock segments into the moving ice. Plucking is aided in its work by frost-weathering, which operates in front of the glacier, producing frost-shattered rock with many cracks and crevices. As the ice moves, it easily incorporates the loose material and the ice undergoes plastic deformation around the larger rocks until they too are swept along with the mass. This debris becomes part of the glacier's bedload and serves as a tool for abrasion. Plucking also operates when ice reaches the pressure melting-point

Fig. 5.12. Kennicott Glacier in the Wrangell Mountains of southeastern Alaska. This large glacier flows 43 km (27 mi.) to the southeast from Mount Blackburn, which is 5,000 m (16,390 ft.) high. Observe the ridges of rocky debris on the glacier. Those in the middle are medial moraines; those along the edges are lateral moraines. The latter are particularly well-developed along the lower left side. (Austin Post, August 1969, U.S. Geological Survey)

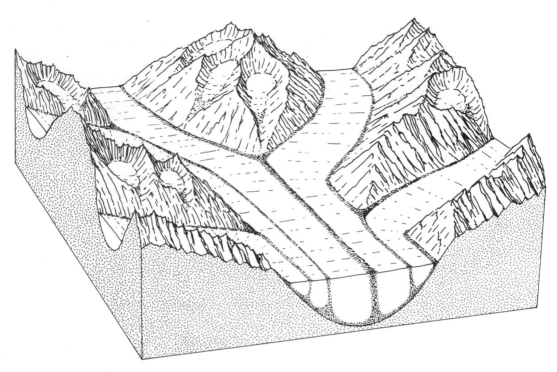

Fig. 5.13. Idealized cross-section of valley glacier showing lateral and medial moraines and their extension into the glacier. Note that the moraine from the small tributary glacier on the right maintains itself at the depth at which it joins the main glacier. (Drawn by Ted M. Oberlander, University of California)

on the upstream side of obstacles and the water moves downslope and refreezes in cracks in the bedrock, creating a bond between the glacial ice and the rock; the continued movement of the ice plucks the individual segments from the bedrock. This process gives an asymmetric profile to the underlying obstacles: the upstream side is smoothed and gentle, while the lee side becomes steep and irregular, owing to the quarrying which has taken place. Such features provide excellent evidence for the direction of glacial movement.

The landscape that extends above the glacial ice is a product of both frost-shattering and glacial erosion (Russell 1933). Frost-shattered rocks eventually tumble onto the ice surface for further transport. Glacial erosion constantly takes place as well. A glacier can be thought of as a huge malleable mass completely smothering the surface and picking up loose rock and soil as it moves along. In this way new surface is continually being exposed to the erosive power of the ice. The load a glacier can carry is almost unlimited; a large glacier can easily transport rocks as big as a house.

Mountain Glaciation

The landscapes of glaciated mountains are among the most distinctive and striking on earth. The features and forms created by ice sculpture are very different from those caused by running water, and glaciated mountains possess a ruggedness and grandeur seldom achieved in unglaciated mountains. For most of us, the visual image of high mountains is typified by glaciated landscapes with their pyramidal peaks, jagged sawtooth ridges, amphitheater-like basins, and deep elongated valleys where occasional jewel-blue lakes sparkle amid surrounding meadows. It is a landscape largely inherited from the past, when the ice was much more extensive than now. In the western United States alone there were over 75 separate high-altitude glacial areas (Fig. 5.14). Most of these were occupied by small cirque or valley glaciers, but in some

areas there were mountain ice-caps. The largest areas of former glaciation are in the Yellowstone–Grand Teton–Wind River ranges, the Sierra Nevada, the Colorado Rockies, and the Cascades (Flint 1971, pp. 471–74). Mountains farther north—the Canadian Rockies, the coast ranges, and

Fig. 5.14. Generalized areas of mountain glaciation in the western United States. The southern extent of continental ice is also shown. (Adapted from Flint 1971, p. 475)

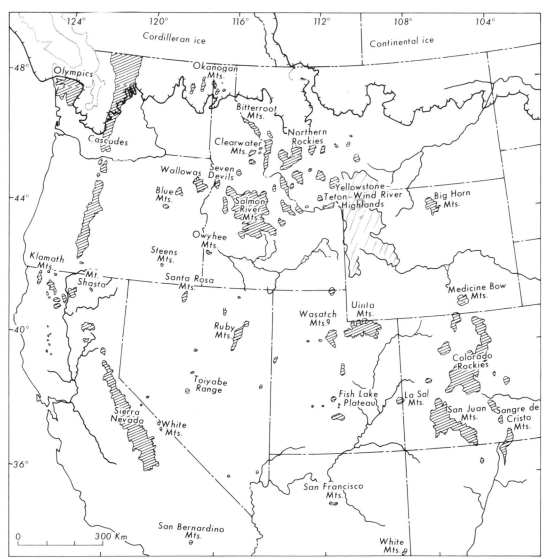

the Alaska and Brooks Range—were almost totally inundated.

The most characteristic and dominant feature of mountain glaciation is erosion. Glacial erosion in mountains is facilitated by the channeling of ice into pre-existing valleys which accentuate its depth and velocity. For this reason glaciers erode deeper in mountains than the former ice sheets did in continental areas; they often exceed depths of 600 m (2,000 ft.) (Flint 1971, p. 114). There is a sharp contrast between the appearance of glaciated uplands and valleys. The ice is thinner on upper surfaces and prone to earlier melting than that in the valleys, where the ice is deeper and more sheltered. The higher surfaces are thus exposed to prolonged weathering. Typical features include sharp, angular ridges and peaks, and accumulations of frost-loosened rock. By contrast, the valleys (glacial troughs) are so smoothed and shaped by the ice that very few sharp or rugged features remain. An exception occurs where the entire upland surface has been overrun by ice so that both upland and valley are smoothed by the ice. The Scottish Highlands and the Presidential Range in New Hampshire are examples (Goldthwait 1970). Features of deposition, moraines and glaciofluvial debris, are largely restricted to the lower elevations and generally mark the point of maximum extent of the ice or places where the glacier remained for the longest periods or where it readvanced slightly as it receded.

Erosional Features

The growth and decline of mountain glaciers lead to a predictable pattern of landform development (Fig. 5.15). Upon initial accumulation, the snow and ice adapt to the pre-existing topography. If the snow accumulation is sufficient, the mountains may be totally covered by glacial ice. When this happens the landscape is actually somewhat protected, since temperatures under the ice remain near the

freezing level and surfaces are not subject to intense frost-shattering. The rugged topography revealed in Figures 5.15b and c, however, is believed to develop under a partial ice cover; frost and mass-wasting processes attack the exposed surfaces while glaciers occupy the valleys and slope depressions to carve, deepen, and sculpture the topography into a distinctive landscape (Cotton 1942, 1968; Flint 1971; Embleton and King 1975a).

The dominant features of mountain glaciation are cirques, glacial troughs, horns, sawtooth ridges (*arêtes*), rock-basined lakes, and hanging valleys. A *cirque* is a semicircular bowl-like depression carved into the side of a mountain where a small glacier has existed (Fig. 5.16; cf. Figs. 5.4, 5.11, 5.15). Cirques are typically located at the heads of valleys, but they may develop anywhere along a mountain slope. They vary in size from shallow basins a few meters in diameter to the huge excavations several kilometers deep and wide found in Antarctica and the Himalayas. A well-developed cirque usually contains a headwall, basin, and threshold. The *headwall* is the steep and smoothed bedrock surface at the back of the cirque, extending concavely upward to the ridge. The *basin* is a circular or elongated depression at the base of the headwall, and the *threshold* is a lip or slightly elevated rampart at the outlet end of the basin. The threshold, composed of bedrock or depositional material, results from the decreasing glacial mass and rate of movement at the periphery, so that the intensity of erosion is less and deposition occurs. If the cirque was occupied by a valley glacier with ice flowing downward and away into the valley, a threshold may not form. Thresholds are typical of cirques occupied by small glaciers (either during their formation, or afterward, when a large glacier has shrunk). The presence of a threshold produces an enclosed basin where water collects, forming a lake. Such lakes are characteristically clear and blue, since the

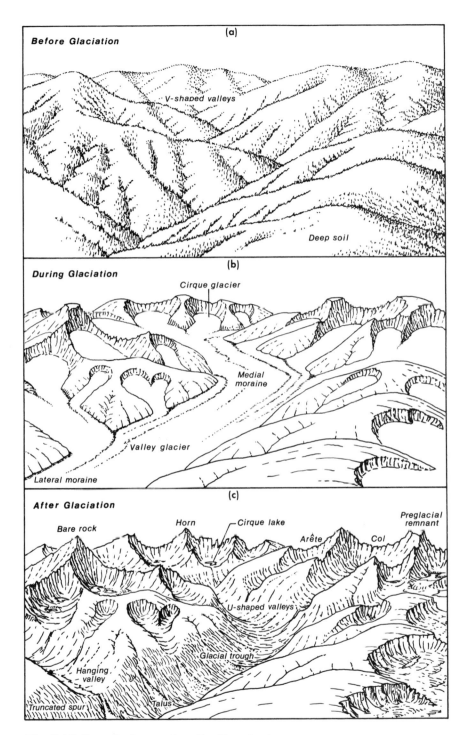

Fig. 5.15. Generalized conception of landform development before, during, and after glaciation. (Drawn by Ted M. Oberlander, University of California)

Fig. 5.16. Cirques and glacial lakes in the Wind River Mountains, Wyoming. The glacial features cut into an older erosional surface composed of subdued and gently rolling uplands. (Austin Post, U.S. Geological Survey)

glacier has removed most of the loose debris, leaving a smoothed bedrock depression. Depending on their age, size, and history, cirque lakes may or may not contain fish. Generally, they have to be at least several hundred years old before they support fish. The question of how fish get to the high mountain lakes has always been puzzling (aquatic birds are probably most important in transporting the fish and their eggs). Nowadays, of course, the fish population of high mountain lakes is largely maintained through intensive fish-stocking programs.

The origin of cirques involves at least two distinct processes: frost-shattering and glacial erosion. At the turn of the century there was a major controversy over the relative importance of these processes. Some subscribed to the "bergschrund theory," which attributed great efficacy to frost processes caused by the freezing and thawing of water in rock joints near the base of the crevasse (bergschrund). Others objected to this theory because many glaciers do not have bergschrunds and because many cirque headwalls far exceed the height of bergschrund depths. They argued that plucking and abrasion by the moving ice alone was sufficient to create cirques (Embleton and King 1975a, pp. 205–38). We need not choose between these theories, since both processes are important to a greater or lesser extent.

The distribution, orientation, and elevation of cirques reveal a great deal about their development (Derbyshire and Evans 1976; Graf 1976). They exist at lower elevations and are best developed on the windward side of mountains where precipitation is relatively heavy. As the snowline rises toward the interior or toward more continental conditions, so do the elevations at which cirques develop. Within this general pattern, however, cirques have preferred orientations. In the northern hemisphere they are found primarily on slopes facing north and northeast, while in the southern hemisphere they are found on south and southeast-facing slopes. This is largely in response to wind direction and shade. The prevailing wind in middle latitudes is westerly, so exposed west-facing slopes are typically blown free of snow, which is then redeposited on east-facing slopes (especially in continental climates with dry, powdery snow). Shade is also important, since protection from the direct rays of the sun allows the snow to persist in areas where it otherwise might melt. This is

the case even in mountains with oceanic climates receiving heavy amounts of snowfall. For example, the present distribution of glaciers in the Cascades is largely restricted to north-facing slopes, and cirque development follows the same pattern.

Since cirques require a glacier for their formation, the presence of cirques in areas not now glaciated indicates the former existence of glacial ice. It is generally estimated that the level of cirque floors roughly approximates the annual snowline that existed when the cirques were made. Plots of the elevation and orientation of cirques in different regions have provided a great deal of

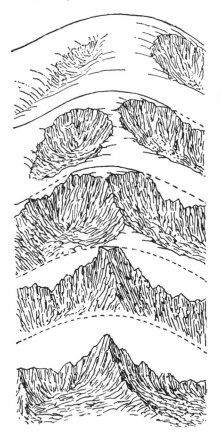

Fig. 5.17. Sequence of events showing headward erosion by cirque glaciers to create steep sawtooth ridges and glacial horns. (From Davis 1911; Lobeck 1939; Cotton 1942)

Fig. 5.18. A narrow rocky saddle separating two glacial cirques in the Ruby Range, Yukon Territory. Note the angular frost-shattered rocks. (Author)

information about past climatic conditions. As with all natural phenomena, however, caution must be used in their interpretation. For example, the formation of cirques may take a long time, and most areas have experienced more than one glaciation; cirques may have been occupied and reoccupied during several glacial periods. Once a depression is formed, it provides a greater reservoir for snow collection and greater protection from melting, so that more snow will accumulate and less will melt than on surrounding slopes. When one cirque sits

above the other, the two may coalesce to form one large cirque. This may be the reason why a single cirque exists at the head of many mountain valleys. In other cases, cirques are simply enlarged with each glaciation, so their present level is not a true representation of the most recent snowline but is, instead, a composite feature resulting from a combination of events. Despite these problems, cirques can provide excellent information about past conditions if care is used in their interpretation (Flint 1971, p. 138; Embleton and King 1975a, p. 223).

The headward erosion of cirque glaciers (along with frost processes and avalanching) is largely responsible for the rugged topography of glaciated mountains. When cirque glaciers develop on opposite sides of a ridge, they erode headward, and eventually meet to create a saddle or notch in the ridge crest (Figs. 5.17, 5.18). This also tends to reduce the thickness of the ridge, making it narrow and knife-like. The continuation of this process along the ridge creates sawtoothed arête ridges (Figs. 5.4, 5.15b, c). The headward erosion of cirque glaciers on all sides of a summit may result in a pyramidal peak called a *horn*. The Matterhorn in the Swiss Alps is the classic example, but such features are common in most glaciated mountains (Figs. 5.11, 5.15c).

Although cirque erosion is the dominant glacial process operating on upper slopes and depressions, the larger glaciers may overflow the cirque basins to form valley glaciers. The ice commonly inherits a pre-existing drainage system, and the former stream channels are soon transformed into glacial troughs (Fig. 5.19; cf. Figs. 5.15, 6.39). Most stream-cut valleys in mountain regions have roughly V-shaped cross-profiles, while a glaciated valley is typically U-shaped. Streams are limited to channel-cutting along their beds, while other processes, especially mass-wasting (see pp. 189–210), erode the valley slopes and transport material to the stream. A glacier, on the other hand, occupies the entire valley and its much greater mass and erosive capacity soon widen and deepen the valley into a semicircular or elliptical cross-section with steep rock walls. The valley floor may be bare rock, or it may be back-filled with glacial meltwater deposits, resulting in flat valley bottoms. In longitudinal profile, glacial valleys have a more irregular surface than stream valleys, often consisting of a series of steps and risers. Various origins have been postulated for the stepped nature of glacial valleys, including differential rates of erosion controlled by valley width, different rock types, more intensely fractured zones within the same rock type, greater erosion

occurring at the base of deep crevasses, and association with places where tributary glaciers join the main stream (Thornbury 1969; Flint 1971; Embleton and King 1975a). Whatever their exact cause, lakes frequently form in the depressions behind the treads; such lakes in a chain, because of their resemblance to beads on a rosary, are called *paternoster lakes* (Fig. 6.39). Massive erosion and excavation of material by the ice deepen, widen, and straighten the former stream valley along its axis so that the lower reaches of tributary streams and their interfluves are cut off, leaving them truncated at some height above the main valley. After the

Fig. 5.19. Glacial trough at Lauterbrunnen in the Swiss Alps. The deep and steep-walled valley was created by glacial erosion; the flat floor resulted from infilling and deposition during glacial retreat. (Author)

glacier melts, the water of these streams cascades down as waterfalls over the trough sidewall. Such tributary valleys with floors higher than the floor of the trunk valley, known as *hanging valleys*, are a scenic feature of glaciated mountains (Fig. 5.15c).

Depositional Features

Sooner or later, a glacier must put down the load of earth and rock it has picked up. The landforms created by glacial deposition, less spectacular than the features caused by glacial erosion, are nonetheless distinctive. Most glacial deposition takes place upon melting and retreat of the ice.

Morainal material is deposited directly by the ice, while glaciofluvial material is deposited by meltwater streams. Moraines typically consist of large and small particles mixed in an unsorted matrix. They may occur along the sides of the glacier as *lateral moraines*, or around the end of the glacial tongue as a *terminal moraine*, or as it recedes as *recessional moraines*. In other cases, the moraine may be less distinct, occurring as a jumble of rocky debris like the tailings from a deserted strip mine. Lateral and terminal moraines can be quite impressive, reaching heights of 100–300 m (330–1,000 ft.) or more (Fig. 5.20).

Fig. 5.20. Terminal moraine marking the furthest extent of the most recent advance of the Kaskawulsh Glacier, St. Elias Mountains, Yukon Territory. Debris-covered glacier tongue can be seen to right of picture. The glacial meltstream forms the Slims River (also shown in Figure 5.21). (Author)

The larger rock debris can only be transported directly by the glacier or by ice-rafting (chunks of ice floating in water), but the smaller material may be carried considerable distances by wind and glacial meltwater streams. The winds that blow off the glacier in summer (see p. 113) are often very effective at picking up and transporting the finely ground rock particles produced by grinding and scraping during glacial transport (glacial flour). In some valleys where glaciers exist, the development of such winds is an almost daily occurrence during clear weather in summer. I spent several weeks camped in one such valley in Yukon Territory, and the presence of afternoon dust storms made working conditions truly miserable. Dust and grit coated my hair, clothes, cooking utensils, and food. Ecologically, however, the deposition of this silt (called *loess*) is beneficial—it expedites soil development and greatly improves local productivity.

Glacial meltstreams are the main mechanism for transport of the smaller material. The amount a stream can carry depends primarily upon the stream's velocity, which in turn depends, among other factors, upon the volume. Glacial streams, of course, display great fluctuations in flow, between winter and summer as well as between day and night (Fig. 6.35). If you have ever hiked in glacierized mountains during the summer, you know that the best time to cross the meltstreams is in early morning, since by late afternoon they may become raging torrents following daytime melting. Such volume fluctuations produce an irregular pattern of erosion and redeposition; during periods of high velocity, the stream erodes and carries a large load of material, only to drop it again as the water volume subsides and the velocity decreases (R. J. Price 1973).

Glacial streams are characteristically choked with sediment, much of which is eventually deposited near the glacial terminus. Such deposits, called *valley train*, create flat-floored valleys and may reach

considerable depths and extend for several kilometers beyond the glacial terminus (Figs. 5.19, 5.20). An extreme example is the Yosemite Valley of California, where seismic investigations reveal that over 600 m (2,000 ft.) of deposits cover the original bedrock floor excavated by the glacier (Gutenberg et al. 1956).

Glacial and glaciofluvial deposits are important ecologically because soil and vegetation develop much more rapidly on aggregate material than on bare rock. Such areas frequently become locally important agricultural regions. The contribution of glacial meltwater streams to the runoff of watersheds in many cases amounts to millions of liters annually. On the negative side, glacial streams are commonly so choked with sediment that the water is not immediately usable by human populations. Very little life exists in the headwaters of these streams. The sediments can be transported long distances and provide increased deposition and infilling of the stream or lake into which they empty. A good example of this is Kluane Lake along the Alaska Highway in Yukon Territory. The meltstream of the Kaskawulsh Glacier (Fig. 5.20), located about 24 km (15 mi.) away in the Saint Elias Mountains, is building a delta into the lake (Fig. 5.21). The quality of the lake water is affected in several ways, but the most obvious are that the normal crystal-blue of the lake is transformed to a murky grey around the mouth of the stream and that the fishing near this end of the lake is very poor (Bryan 1974a, b).

AVALANCHES

The sudden release and movement of vast amounts of snow down a mountainside can be an awe-inspiring phenomenon. The avalanche is one of the great destructive forces in nature and every bit the equal of the hurricane, the tornado, and the earthquake. Thousands of persons have

Fig. 5.21. Slims River, a glacial meltstream draining the Kaskawulsh Glacier 26 km (16 mi.) upstream, empties into Kluane Lake, southwest Yukon Territory. The heavily silt-laden stream is building a delta into the lake. The Alaska Highway can be seen crossing the river at this point. (Author)

perished in avalanches over the centuries. If mountains were more heavily populated, the toll would be even higher. Untold numbers of avalanches occur every year but only a few are observed or recorded. With increasing population in the mountains, however, the potential for avalanche damage increases markedly. Early records of the Alps reveal considerable avalanche destruction. In the Davos Valley, Switzerland, avalanches became a problem between the sixteenth and eighteenth centuries when increased population and widespread cutting of the mountain forests coincided with the increasing snowfall and

glacial advance associated with the Little Ice Age. A chronicler described one such avalanche in 1602:

On 16 January, on a Saturday night, at 2400 hours, after it had been snowing for 3 weeks and the snow had reached a depth of over 12 shoes [*sic*], all at once powerful snow avalanches broke loose in Davos in several locations so that mountains and valleys trembled and roared. Entire larch and pine trees with their roots, much earth, and stone were torn away, the Lady Chapel with 70 houses and farm buildings were demolished or carried away and buried with all the inhabitants in the snow. (Cited in Frutiger 1975, p. 38)

Avalanches causing the death of 50 to 100 people are commonplace in early records from the Alps, but the greatest disaster awaited the twentieth century: during World War I on the Austrian-Italian Front in December 1916, a series of huge snow slides annihilated 10,000 soldiers in a single day (Atwater 1954).

In North America the first major problems with avalanches arose during the Gold Rush, when prospectors swarmed into the mountains of the west and numerous mining towns were established. Telluride and Aspen in the Colorado Rockies, Atlanta in the Sawtooths, Mineral King in the Sierra, and Alta and Brighton in the Wasatch are but a few of these. Many prospectors lost their lives and whole mining towns were destroyed by snow slides. One of the earliest reliable records is from Alta, Utah, where in 1874 the mining camp was buried and 60 lives were lost. During the next 35 years

Fig. 5.22. Modern snow-avalanche damage in Alta, Utah, an old problem area. This avalanche occurred 1 January 1974. Three ski lodges were damaged, two people were injured, and thirty-five cars were damaged or destroyed. (Ron Perla, Environment Canada)

avalanches killed 67 more persons in the same area (U.S. Dept. Agriculture 1968, p. 4). As mining decreased in importance, expansion of railroads and highways across the mountains raised the avalanche danger at other sites. In 1910 a huge snow slide at Stevens Pass in the Washington Cascades swept away three snowbound trains, killing 108 people and resulting in several million dollars in property loss. In 1926, 40 lives were lost when an avalanche buried the mining community of Bingham Canyon, Utah. More recently, the popularity of winter sports, particularly skiing, has attracted more people to mountains than ever before and there has been an equally rapid development of recreational facilities in mountains, often in the same areas as the old mining camps (e.g., Aspen, Colorado, or Alta, Utah) (Fig. 5.22). According to recent statistics, in the United States, an average of 140 persons are caught in avalanches each winter, 60 of whom are either partly or wholly buried, 12 injured, and 7 killed. In addition, an average of 30 vehicles are buried, and 10 buildings, 2 ski lifts, and 7 to 10 other structures are damaged, with an average property loss of $250,000 (Williams 1975a). It is ironic that despite our greater scientific understanding of avalanches and our considerable investment in their prediction and prevention, the number of accidents continues to increase, primarily because more and more people, especially recreationists, go to the mountains during the winter (Fig. 5.23). It will always be impossible to protect the foolhardy. This is graphically illustrated by an analysis of recent avalanche accidents in the United States. Each situation was evaluated with respect to whether the individuals acted wisely or foolishly; the episodes make very interesting reading (Williams 1975a).

Types of Avalanches

There are two principal types of avalanches—the *loose-snow avalanche* and the *slab avalanche*. The loose-snow avalanche is

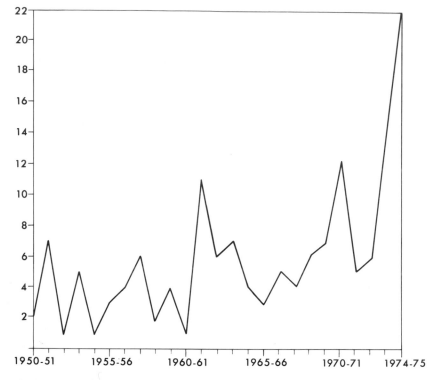

Fig. 5.23. Avalanche fatalities in the United States, 1950–1975. There were 147 avalanche deaths during this twenty-five-year period, an average of 6 per year. The United States had no avalanche disasters involving scores of people during this time, as other countries had. Avalanche fatalities are increasing, however; in the last five years the average number of deaths rose to 12 per winter. (After Williams 1975b, p. 1)

Fig. 5.24. Typical form displayed by loose-snow avalanches and slab avalanches. (After U.S. Dept. Agriculture 1968, p. 27)

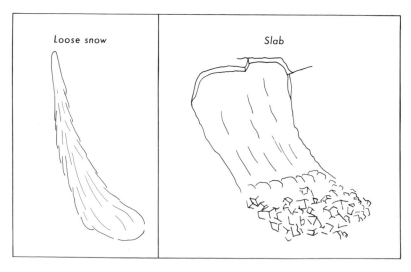

usually small and relatively harmless, *& terrain*
whereas a slab avalanche may involve large
amounts of snow and cause considerable
destruction. The distinction between the
two types is based on snow conditions at
the point of origin, since a snow slide may
lose its original identity by the time it
reaches the valley below. A loose-snow
avalanche has little internal cohesion and
tends to move as a formless mass starting at
a point and growing wider in its distal parts
as more snow becomes involved. Slab
avalanches, on the other hand, usually
consist of more cohesive snow which tends
to fracture along a broad front and begins
sliding downward as a single unit until it
breaks into smaller chunks (Fig. 5.24).
Types of avalanches are further subdivided
according to whether the snow is dry or
wet; whether the slide takes place on a
snow layer or extends all the way to the
ground; and whether the motion is on the
ground, in the air, or both.

Loose-Snow Avalanches

Loose-snow avalanches occur most frequently in newly fallen snow on steep
slopes, where the snow cannot maintain itself through internal strength. This is very
common when light fluffy snow falls and the
winds are gentle. The snow has little internal
cohesion, so slight disturbances may be
enough to cause it to slide until it reaches a
gentler slope. Loose-snow slides are by far
the most common kind of avalanche but
they are generally shallow and small and
cause little damage (Fig. 5.25). Scores of such
slides may take place during a single snowstorm. In fact, their occurrence may be a
stabilizing factor, since frequent small slides
provide a continual adjustment in the snow
and can prevent major slides. The harmless
loose-powder sluffs of newly fallen snow on
steep slopes are typical. The most dangerous
kind happens in the spring when the snow is
wet; these start on the high upper slopes as
loose-snow avalanches but gather momentum and mass as they move downward,

Fig. 5.25. Loose-snow avalanches in the Swiss Alps
near Davos. Such avalanches are usually small and
harmless sluffs, many of which take place during any
given storm. (Swiss Federal Institute for Snow and
Avalanche Research)

particularly when confined to gullies, so by
the time they reach the valley the heavy
weight of the snow can cause considerable
damage (U.S. Dept. Agriculture 1968, p. 21;
Perla and Martinelli 1976, p. 68).

Slab Avalanches

The very dangerous slab avalanches occur
much less frequently than loose-snow ava-

alla   *Cardiff Pass*   *Flagstaff*

Fig. 5.26. The breakaway zone of a slab avalanche. Note the clean snow fracture at the head and the smooth base over which the snow moved. (Ed LaChapelle, University of Washington)

lanches. Slab avalanches originate in all types of snow, from old to newly fallen and from dry to wet. The chief distinguishing characteristic is that the snow breaks away with enough internal cohesion to act as a single unit until it disaggregates during its journey downslope. In fresh new snow this cohesion may be relatively slight, but in hard older snow it may be so great that the snow is broken into chunks only by great force. The zone of release is usually marked by fracture lines that stand perpendicular to the slope and extend to a well-defined basal-slippage plane (Fig. 5.26). The size of the slab avalanche depends on many factors, but it is usually confined to a discrete zone on the slope. At times, though, the whole mountainside may become involved, with the fractures racing along the contour to release snow held in neighboring slide paths. The entire mass of a slab avalanche is generally set in motion at once and may reach its maximum velocity within seconds, so that full destructive power is attained from the point of origin (Atwater 1954, p. 27). The exact behavior, of course, depends upon the nature of the snow. If the snow is dry, a *powder-snow avalanche* may develop. These move as much in the air as on the ground, and their turbulent motion may create a dense dust-cloud of ice crystals which behaves like a body of heavy gas preceding the rapidly sliding snow. Such wind blasts may achieve a velocity of 320 km (200 mi.) per hour and cause damage well beyond the normal avalanche zone (Seligman 1936; LaChapelle 1966, 1968). On the other hand, wet-snow avalanches tend to slide at slower speeds with no particular dust-cloud, but their great mass and weight can still cause great damage.

Avalanche Triggers

A mass of unstable snow perched on a mountainside is like a loaded gun: it awaits only the triggering action to set it off. Many potential avalanches never fall because there was no trigger to release them, while relatively stable snow masses may be released because of external disruptions. The point of critical instability for avalanche release is reached when the component of force parallel to the slope exceeds the shear strength of the bond between the surface snow and the underlayer. This may be brought about in several ways, the most common of which is overloading by fresh snowfall. The weight builds up until it overcomes cohesion and the snow begins to slide (U.S. Dept. Agriculture 1968, p. 25). Another common factor affecting the stress-strength relationship between snow crystals is changing temperature. Warming of the snow usually decreases its internal cohesion, while lowering of the temperature retards settlement of the snow mass, increases its brittleness, and may create an equally if not more unstable situation.

A number of natural external factors can trigger an avalanche, e.g., the falling of an overhanging snow mass (a *cornice*), a rockfall, or even lumps of snow falling from tree branches. In modern efforts to control avalanches, artificial means such as artillery fire, dynamite, loud noises, or skiing are employed (Gardner and Judson 1970; Martinelli 1972; Perla 1978). Many of the accidentally triggered slides are released by the victims themselves; a good number of these avalanches would probably never have occurred if they had not been artificially released. In other cases, even the slightest perturbation may trigger an avalanche, e.g., the vibration of footsteps or the sound of voices. In the Alps, avalanches have reportedly been started by the bells of flocks of sheep or goats. There is said to be an ancient regulation in Switzerland against yodeling during the avalanche season (Allix 1924).

Avalanche Conditions

Ultimately, there are two main causes of avalanches—snow and slopes. The favored slope angle is between 30–45°. Anything less than this does not create enough downslope stress, while steeper slopes do not retain enough snow to cause large avalanches. Thus, the probability of avalanches increases with steeper slopes to a certain point and then decreases. Snow is a highly variable factor: it occurs under different environmental conditions; it displays vastly different characteristics with greater or lesser internal strength; and it is susceptible to constant modification once on the ground (Perla and Martinelli 1976).

Terrain

Many features of the terrain can favor or inhibit avalanches. A convex slope will be more prone to avalanches than a concave slope: the outward bend of a convex slope puts tensional stress on its snow cover, while a concavity of slope strengthens the snow's cohesion through compression. Slope orientation with respect to both the wind and

Fig. 5.27. Large snow cornices on the Jungfrau in
central Switzerland. (Andre Roch, Swiss Federal Institute for Snow and Avalanche Research)

the sun is critical. Windward slopes generally experience less avalanche danger because snow is blown off to the leeward, and what does accumulate on the windward is better compacted by the wind. Consequently, the avalanche danger is greater on leeward slopes, especially where cornices develop along ridge crests to overhang and fall (Fig. 5.27). Exposure to the sun greatly influences the behavior of snow. North-facing slopes receive little sun during the winter (in the northern hemisphere). This results in dry and cold conditions, with the accompanying constant danger of dry slides. On south-facing slopes, the sun strikes the surfaces at a higher angle, causing melting and metamorphism. South-facing slopes are frequently sites of instability and wet-snow avalanches (U.S. Dept. Agriculture 1968, pp. 29–31).

Other important variables in the landscape include its roughness and groundcover. A slope strewn with large boulders is not as susceptible to avalanching as a smooth surface (at least until the snow fills the depressions). On the other hand, a smooth grassy slope provides no major surface inequalities to be filled by the snow and offers little resistance to sliding. Forested slopes generally offer good protection, but many mountain forests have been cut or destroyed in recent centuries (Aulitzky 1967). In heavy snow years, avalanches may start above the timbered zone and destroy strips of the forest in their path (Fig. 5.28; cf. Fig. 8.25). Once this happens, these zones become more vulnerable to avalanching and it is extremely difficult for the forest to redevelop. Trees in the path of the avalanching are continually damaged or killed (Frutiger 1964; Schaerer 1972; Martinelli 1974).

Snow and weather factors

Given the framework of mountainous terrain, snow and weather conditions are the critical factors in avalanche occurrence. There are ten main factors (Seligman 1936; Atwater 1954; U.S. Dept. Agriculture 1968):

1. Old-snow depth.
2. Condition of the base.
3. New-snow depth.
4. New-snow type.
5. New-snow density.
6. Snowfall intensity.
7. Precipitation intensity.
8. Settlement.
9. Wind.
10. Temperature.

Old snow tends to fill surface inequalities and provide a smooth gliding plane. The initial surface roughness will determine how much old snow is needed, but in general the more old snow, the more likely avalanches are to form. Old snow also provides a bonding surface for new snow. If the surface snow is loose, it may provide good cohesion, while a crusted or wind-packed surface [Hoar layer] provides poor cohesion. Other factors include the amount of new snow and its rate of accumulation. It is estimated that 80 percent of all large slides occur either during or shortly after storms. The more snow, the more weight and the greater the downhill component of force. A given amount of snow received over several days may settle and become stabilized, but the same amount falling in only six hours may leave the snow in a highly unstable state. The stability of the snow depends, in turn, upon the character of the snow crystals and the moisture content. Fluffy stellar flakes provide an interlocking mesh with considerable internal strength, while such forms as small rounded pellets, graupel, and needle-like crystals provide little cohesion (Fig. 5.1). The moisture content of snow controls its packing ability: a moderate amount of moisture permits maximum coherence, whereas excessive meltwater acts as a lubricant. Whatever the rate of settlement and packing, the more rapid it is, the greater the stability. In general, a snow-settlement ratio of 20–30 percent or more indicates a trend toward stabilization. The one exception to this is when the underlying snow layer settles

Fig. 5.28. Treeless strips on forested slope near Davos, Switzerland, caused by snow avalanches. The forest has been greatly reduced by human activities in the Alps; this has increased the frequency of avalanching, making it very difficult for the forest to grow back. (Author)

downward and away from a rigid overlying layer, leaving the upper snowbase without support (U.S. Dept. Agriculture 1968, p. 34). The associated weather phenomena of wind and temperature are both critically important to the stability of the snow. Wind may very well be the single most important factor in the formation of slab avalanches because of its ability to transport, transform, and deposit snow in concentrated areas (Seligman 1936). Strong persistent winds are almost always certain to create favorable avalanche conditions. The minimum effective velocity is thought to be about 24 km (15 mi.) per hour. Warm winds such as the foehn or chinook (see pp. 114–19) can cause

rapid and intensive melting, so the snow loses cohesion and therefore slides.

Temperature affects the internal structure of both falling and accumulated snow. The temperature at the time of snow deposition controls the snow-crystal type, the moisture presence, the rate of settlement, and the general cohesion. After deposition, the temperature of the snow layer and of the air above is critical to the rate of settling, compaction, internal creep, and metamorphosis. In general, the avalanche hazard tends to be greater under lower temperatures in winter, because the snow is preserved in its unstable state for longer periods of time. On the other hand, high temperatures permit melting and the loss of cohesion among snow layers (U.S. Dept. Agriculture 1968, p. 35). A process responsible for many avalanches is a crystal transformation that takes place at depths of 1–2 m (3–7 ft.) within the snow. This process, known as *constructive metamorphism*, takes place when the air temperature is markedly lower than the snow temperature. Under these conditions, sublimation occurs in the lower, warmer snow and the water vapor moves upward to the colder snow layers, where it is redeposited as depth hoar—hollow, cuplike crystals arranged above one another in vertical stacks with a very fragile structure and little strength. A snow layer overlying a zone of depth hoar is very susceptible to avalanching (LaChapelle 1966; Perla and Martinelli 1976, p. 46).

Avalanche Control

The safest way to deal with avalanches is to avoid them. This will never be possible, however, so long as people remain in mountains through the winter. The control of avalanches, practiced in the Alps for centuries, is a relatively new endeavor in North America. There are two basic approaches to the problem—modification of terrain and modification of the snow. The first method is relatively effective but is expensive and requires continual maintenance, whereas the second is much less expensive but must be applied repeatedly. Terrain modification consists of placing structures—walls, pylons, dams, and wedges of various designs—either in the snow accumulation zone or immediately above the area to be protected (U.S. Dept. Agriculture 1975). The strategy in the snow accumulation zone is to break up the solid mass of the snow into smaller units, to anchor the snow base, and to create terraces so that there is less effective slope for each snow unit (LaChapelle 1968, p. 1024) (Fig. 5.29). In the runout zone the structures consist of barricades, walls, and wedges to dam or divert the avalanche. Roofs or sheds are frequently constructed over highways

Fig. 5.29. Avalanche fences in the snow accumulation zone above Davos, Switzerland. Such features tend to retain the snow and create a stair-stepped topography that stabilizes the snow slopes. (E. Wengi, Swiss Federal Institute for Snow and Avalanche Research)

and railway lines along avalanche paths (Fig. 5.30).

A relatively new technique, discovered quite by accident, is the use of alternately spaced mounds. About twenty years ago in Austria a construction firm, building diversion structures in an avalanche path near Innsbruck, left several mounds of rubble nearby after they finished the job. The following winter, the first avalanche came down the slope and broke up in the rubble mounds before reaching the diversion structures. The Austrians quickly

Fig. 5.30. Avalanche-protection structures over a highway in the Italian Alps. Snow is allowed to cover structures, and avalanches slide harmlessly over the top. Middle area between two structures is defended by a rocky bastion upslope that divides the snowy torrents, protecting the area immediately downslope. Nevertheless, a small snow fence has been placed next to the highway. Structures such as these exist by the hundreds in the Alps. (Author)

seized upon this idea and built several other mound systems (Fig. 5.31). Avalanche mound systems constructed at several places in North America have also been quite successful. The mounds apparently break up and slow the avalanche by dividing it into cross-currents that dissipate its kinetic energy (LaChapelle 1966, p. 96).

The other major approach to avalanche control is modification of the snow itself. The oldest, and perhaps still the most successful, method of this type is artificially to trigger the release of small avalanches to prevent the build-up of larger ones. This is generally done by using explosives, either placed directly on the slope or through artillery fire. The use of explosives allows the release of avalanches from a safe distance. The preferred weapons are recoilless rifles and mountain howitzers, since they have good range and accuracy. The release of an avalanche requires at least a 75 mm shell, although a 105 mm shell is better. Normal shells penetrate the snow and lose their effectiveness; hence they are generally equipped with fuses to detonate upon impact or slightly above the snow surface (Perla 1978). In some cases the weapons are pre-aimed and stationed at critical avalanche areas so that they can be blindfired during storms to release the snow from dangerous build-up. An undesirable side-effect of using such weaponry is the accumulation of shrapnel, scrap metal, and dud shells on the mountainside (Perla and Martinelli 1976).

Another method of snow stabilization is simply to pack the snow down. This is used in many ski resorts, where skiers and tracked vehicles are constantly packing the newly fallen snow. In ski areas where depth hoar is likely to form and greater pressure is needed to discourage its development, the ski lodge operators may hire several persons during the early snow season to pack critical zones on foot. It has also been found that the crisscrossing of a few skiers through the soft snow may be enough to break up the formation of a large single slab by bonding the new snow to the old and effectively establishing smaller snow units. One of the newer methods of combatting avalanches is by the use of organic chemicals (e.g., benzaldehyde) that inhibit the growth of depth-hoar crystals. The chemical is sprayed on the ground before the first snowfall in late autumn; it then moves upward through the snow, coating the crystals and preventing depth hoar from developing. This method, although

it holds considerable promise, has not yet been used extensively enough to determine its real potential or its potential ecological effects (LaChapelle 1966). Other innovations include the use of pre-installed vibrators and the inflation of preplanted airbags. Initial experiments with these methods are encouraging, especially where the snowpack is relatively thin (LaChapelle et al. 1976, 1978). Research is constantly being done to discover new ways of controlling avalanches, and has already significantly reduced the potential hazards of many areas. The control of avalanches is expensive, however, and it will never be possible to tame the snowy torrents entirely. In the long run, the best defense is careful planning and location of activities and facilities to avoid areas of high avalanche danger.

Fig. 5.31. Avalanche diversion mounds located above Innsbruck, Austria. (U.S. Forest Service)

6

Landforms and Geomorphic Processes

Every valley shall be exalted, and every mountain and hill shall be made low.

Isaiah 40:4

The mountain landscape is the product of both constructive and destructive processes. Mountains are created by forces originating from within the earth but they are soon modified, and are eventually destroyed, by forces from without. The one builds up; the other tears down. In the history of the earth, many mountain ranges have been created and destroyed. We can see this at work today. The Sierra Nevada, the Cascades, and the Alaska Range are very young mountains; in fact, they are still growing. The frequent occurrence of earthquakes and volcanic eruptions in these areas may have locally destructive effects but they are also fundamental acts of construction, reflecting the growing pains of young mountains. It is estimated that present rates of orogeny in western North America exceed rates of erosion by about 7.5 m (25 ft.) per 1,000 years (Schumm 1963). The Appalachians, on the other hand, are old mountains. At one time they were possibly as high as the Alps, but they are now worn and low. Erosion has taken its toll. They have barely sufficient relief and elevation to be called mountains. In more extreme cases, all evidence of relief and elevation may be erased, but the roots of the former mountain range remain as mute testimony of a more glorious past. Such an example is the Canadian shield of eastern Canada.

While mountain ranges display different ages and degrees of development, they are all relatively young compared to the vastness of geologic time and the age of the earth. One reason for this is the increased effectiveness of erosion at higher altitudes. Mountains are rapidly worn away and, consequently, can never be very old. The geologist J. W. Powell observed this many years ago in the western United States: "We may now conclude that the higher the mountain, the more rapid its degradation; that high mountains cannot live much longer than low mountains, and that mountains cannot remain long as mountains: they are ephemeral topographic forms. Geologi-

cally all existing mountains are recent; the ancient mountains are gone" (Powell, 1876, p. 193).

A recent study has attempted to reconstruct the rates of erosion at various altitudes on a volcanic cone in northeastern Papua, New Guinea (Ruxton and McDougall 1967). This region has a humid tropical climate with heavy rainfall and a fairly complete cover of tropical forest. By reconstructing the former mountain form through use of generalized contours and dating of the rocks by the potassium-argon method, it was possible to calculate erosional rates for various altitudinal zones for the last 650,000 years. *Denudation* (wearing away of the land) rates range from 8 cm (0.26 ft.) per 1,000 years at 61 m (200 ft.) above sea level to 52 cm (1.70 ft.) per 1,000 years at an altitude of 533 m (1,750 ft.) (Fig. 6.1). These rates are exceptionally high, and may be as much a

Fig. 6.1. The relationship between denudation rates and the amount of local relief (vertical difference between ridge crests and valley floors) in the Hydrographers Range, northeastern Papua, New Guinea. Data from more dissected areas are shown as solid circles; data from less dissected areas are shown as open circles. (After Ruxton and McDougall 1967, p. 557)

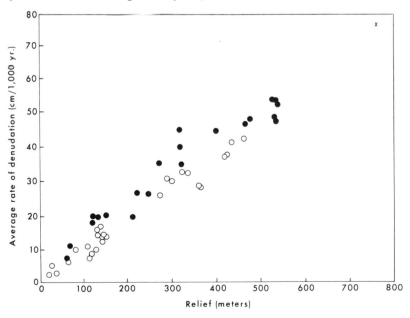

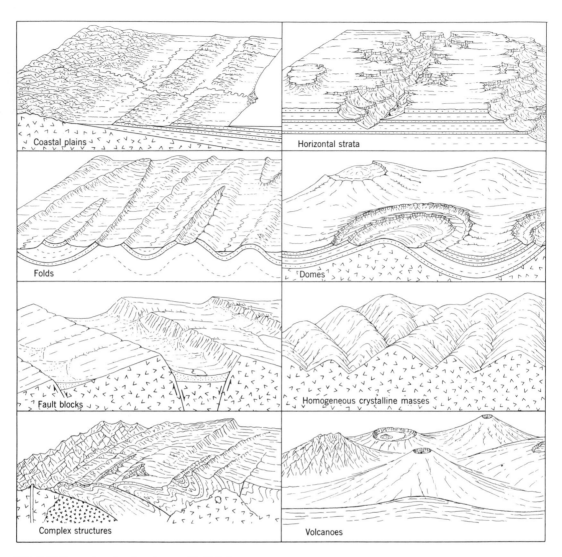

Fig. 6.2. Examples of various types of initial structures and rock types on surface forms. (From Strahler 1965, p. 364)

result of the methodology used as of the humid tropical conditions, where erosion is rapid. The exact rates of erosion would vary in different parts of the world under different climatic and vegetation types, but the general rule, of erosion increasing with altitude, holds true. Recognition of this fact makes estimates of total removal of material from the upper surface of mountain regions somewhat more comprehensible. Many

modern-day mountain landscapes are built on rocks that were formerly buried 20 km (12.5 mi.) or more deep. The Alps are estimated to have suffered 30 km (18.8 mi.) of denudation in the last 30 million years. This eroded material now largely composes the Rhône River delta, an area of 460,000 km³ (287,500 mi.³) (Clark and Jäger 1969).

The form, structure, and material composition of mountains greatly affect the rate and type of geomorphic processes. Horizontally oriented rock, volcanic features, and folded, faulted, and domal structures with strata dipping in various directions all present very different surfaces and starting points for erosional processes (Fig. 6.2). Because water, earth, snow, and ice tend to follow the path of least resistance, the processes of erosion tend to reinforce and exaggerate existing slopes and structures.

The kinds of landscapes that develop in different mountain regions depend upon the rate of uplift and deformation, the nature and reaction of various rock surfaces, and the intensity and kinds of erosional processes. These combined circumstances result in a wide variety of conditions and end products. To illustrate: the structural modification of rock units often involves their compression in some areas and their stretching in others, producing alternating resistant and susceptible zones. Thus, in folded rock the anticlines are areas of extension and therefore weak, while the synclines are areas of compression with greater strength. As a result, valleys often develop in anticlinal ridges, where stretching has made the strata more susceptible to breaching by erosion, and the elevated anticlines are worn away more rapidly than the synclines (Twidale 1971, p. 173). This paradoxical situation is due to the more aggressive and prolonged erosion of topographic promontories, as well as to the structural modifications associated with folding. The relationships are not everywhere the same; in some places the streams occupy the synclinal valleys and the anticlines form the ridges, but this is less common. Where folding is extremely rapid and the rock strata resistant, the structure may be so little modified by erosion that it is expressed directly in the form of the land surface (Fig. 6.3). Such features are, again, more often the exception than the rule. Much depends upon whether the geologic structure is passive or active. If the area is passive or stable, with no uplift or deformation taking place,

the major controls are the existing differences in bedrock, topography, and structure; but if the area is tectonically active, a much more dynamic relationship exists between form and process, because erosion is taking place simultaneously with uplift and deformation. Under these conditions, for example, streams may sometimes cut across the structural grain of the land with seeming indifference to the underlying structural conditions (see pp. 222–24).

The nature of the rock type itself has a major impact on landscape development. Massive and resistant crystalline rocks, such as granite or quartzite, have the potential for producing outliers and ridges, while landforms formed in weak and friable rocks, such as limestone or shale, often form valleys. The exact developments depend upon local circumstances, but the more resistant the rock, the more likely it is to produce salients, peaks, and ridges. Joints, fractures, and fault lines provide ingress for water and weathering and are zones of weakness. Streams exploit such features and develop preferentially along them; the resultant stream pattern often provides a good indicator of the structural framework of an area (Fig. 6.40).

While structure and rock type exert significant control on landform development and are normally expressed to a greater or lesser extent in the landscape, they are also largely innate and unique in their character and distribution, depending as they do upon processes originating from within the earth. On the other hand, subaerial processes operating at the surface of the earth have their ultimate origin in solar energy, and display a very different distribution (although the presence of mountains strongly influences this pattern). Climate exists over broad zones and provides the basic framework into which all natural phenomena must fit. It is obvious that environmental conditions are very different depending upon whether the climate is tropical or polar, desert or marine. Therefore, although

Fig. 6.3. Folded structures in the Grande Chartreuse north of Grenoble in the French Alps. Note the clear relationship between the synclines and valleys and anticlines and ridges. Displacement of the rockbeds in the synclinal valley denotes a fault. (Swissair photo)

there are widespread regional differences in the character of mountains, many pervasive and overriding similarities suggest that similar geomorphic processes operate under comparable environmental conditions and give rise to similar kinds of landforms.

The basic components of the mountain landscape are the upland surfaces, the valley bottoms, and the slopes between them. Slopes are the primary consideration, since they occupy the greatest area and result in a high degree of energy transfer through their effect on gravity. Great environmental contrasts occur within small areas and within short periods of time. Geomorphic processes are intensified in the presence of steep slopes and a mountain climate. While precipitation is often the major factor at intermediate altitudes, low temperatures become the dominant environmental feature at higher altitudes and give rise to *glacial, niva-*

tional, and *periglacial* regimes (Davies 1969; Price 1972; Washburn 1973; Embleton and King 1975b) (Fig. 6.4). The glacial system has already been discussed; it is one in which ice acts directly to shape the land. It generally occurs on the highest part of the mountains. Nivation is a combination of frost action and the downslope movement of earth material by gravity (mass-wasting) resulting from the presence of snow patches.

Fig. 6.4. The three major process systems of high-mountain landform development. The glacial system is dominated by glacial ice, while the periglacial system is dominated by frost action and mass-wasting. Nivation is an intermediate process occurring at the snowline, where snow-patch erosion and snowmelt transport are important. (After Davies 1969, p. 16)

Nivation is best developed at snowline and occupies the narrow transitional zone between the glacial and periglacial environments. In the glacial system the ice itself is the mode of transport, but nivation depends upon snow-patch erosion and snow-melt transport. The periglacial system, peripheral to both glacial and nivation systems, is characterized by cold climate, frost action, and mass-wasting. Of the three, the periglacial regime occupies by far the greatest area in high mountains and is the primary focus of this section.

The mountain landscape is characterized by instability and variability. Rock-strewn surfaces resulting from rapid physical weath-

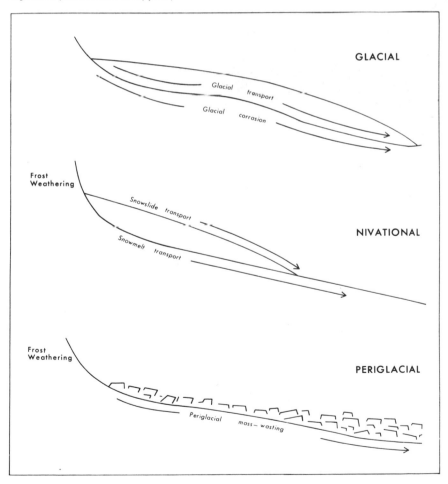

ering processes are common, and earth materials are continually being transported downslope. This can be seen in the rushing waters of mountain streams and in the instability and movement of entire slopes. If you have ever spent much time above the timberline in mountains, you know that a very common sound is that of falling rocks. Large-scale features such as mudflows, landslides, and avalanches can reach catastrophic dimensions and do more geomorphic work in a matter of minutes than day-to-day processes accomplish in centuries. Such spectacular phenomena epitomize the inherent instability of the mountain system (Hewitt 1972; Caine 1974). The process begins, however, with the weakening and breakdown of the bedrock.

WEATHERING

Weathering is the alteration and reduction of rock into finer particles. It involves both physical and chemical processes and is usually antecedent to erosion and soil development. A mountaintop is a far cry from the place of origin of most rocks, which were created deep within the earth under great heat and pressure and in the absence of water and air. Many rocks, particularly those that are highly metamorphosed and recently formed through mountain-building, tend to be unstable in their new environment and to yield more or less easily to the processes of alteration. This provides yet another example of the ultimate tendency toward equilibrium in all natural systems. The processes of rock breakdown are normally divided into chemical and physical weathering. Although in nature they merge and combine in various ways, one generally dominates over another in the more extreme environments. Chemical weathering refers to those processes that break the rock down by altering its chemical composition, by dissolving minerals, or by depositing crystals which exert pressure as they grow. Physical weathering refers to the physical forces—chiefly mechanical—that pry apart rocks or make their surfaces disintegrate.

Chemical Weathering

Very little research has been done on the role of chemical weathering in mountains. This is partly because of the apparent dominance of frost action, which tends to mask the more subtle effects of chemical action, and also because of the difficulty in measuring and studying the chemical processes. Like many chemical reactions, the processes of chemical weathering require the compounds to be in solution and a certain amount of heat to be supplied for activation. Not surprisingly, in dry and cold places—deserts, polar regions, and most mountaintops—these preconditions are hard to meet, so that chemical weathering is reduced in importance (Fig. 6.5). Mountains in the humid tropics or near oceans generally show more active chemical weathering than mountains in continental and arid regions. Nevertheless, there is evidence of some chemical weathering even in arctic and desert mountains (Washburn 1969, pp. 11–32; Marchand 1971, 1974). Certain types of chemical processes—e.g., *carbonation* (the alteration of minerals that contain basic oxides, such as lime, soda, and potash, to carbonate salts by action of carbonic acid)—may actually be accelerated in cold climates because of the greater solubility and concentration of carbon dioxide (CO_2) at low temperatures (Williams 1949). On the other hand, just because cold water can hold more CO_2, this does not mean that it will contain more, since the production of CO_2 is largely a function of biological activity, which is reduced in high mountains.

Rock surfaces often present evidence of chemical weathering in their altered and weakened exteriors and in various deposits, crusts, and coatings. Chemical weathering may also be ascertained by measuring the quantity of dissolved minerals being trans-

Mean annual precipitation (Inches)

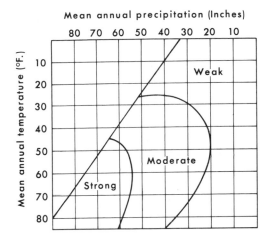

Mean annual precipitation (Inches)

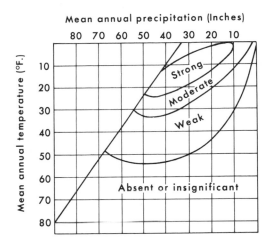

Fig. 6.5. Intensity of chemical (left) and mechanical (right) weathering in relation to temperature and precipitation. Note that the conditions favorable for one are unfavorable for the other. (After Peltier 1950, p. 219)

ported away by streams. A number of specific processes are involved in chemical weathering. Although a detailed discussion of these is beyond the present purpose, a few examples of the more obvious effects may be useful (Ollier 1969b; Birkeland 1974). One is the presence of a *weathering rind*, the chemically altered zone at the rock surface. The depth of weathering provides an index of the age of the surface and the rate of the process under varying conditions (Porter 1975b). Although it penetrates only a few millimeters, the weathered zone is usually easily distinguishable when the rock is broken open. The weathering rind commonly has a slightly reddish-brown color because of the oxidation of iron and manganese silicates. Two similar processes, *desert varnish* and *case-hardening*, produce shiny protective coatings or patinas. Desert varnish is a thin film of iron or manganese oxide; case-hardening involves the induration of porous rock surfaces by the evaporation of mineral-bearing solutions or the movement of ions to the surface from the inside. In either case, the exterior is strengthened at the expense of the interior, so that once the

surface is breached, the underlying rock deteriorates at a faster rate than the protective covering (Fig. 6.6). Wind abrasion may also be important in creating shiny and polished surfaces (Ollier 1969b, pp. 174–79).

Much of the effect of chemical weathering is not immediately visible, since it involves the removal of minerals through solution. When precipitation first falls it is relatively pure, but the water soon becomes loaded with dissolved salts which are subsequently transported away; a classic example is the solubility of limestone. These chemical reactions are fundamental and illustrate the nature of chemical weathering in general. The process begins when water absorbs carbon dioxide (CO_2) to form a weak solution of carbonic acid (H_2CO_3). This acid then reacts with the calcium carbonate ($CaCO_3$) in limestone and produces a soluble salt, calcium bicarbonate [$Ca(HCO_3)_2$], which is easily dissolved and transported away in solution. Other minerals are less susceptible to chemical reaction than the calcite in limestone, but all undergo some reaction with water that results in more soluble minerals. Consequently, the quantity

Fig. 6.6. The surface of this rock in the Ruby Mountains, Yukon Territory, displays greater resistance to weathering than the subsurface, apparently because of chemical induration. Sandblasting action by the wind may also be partly responsible for the selective weathering. (Author)

of dissolved solids in a stream draining a mountain area provides a good index of the rate of chemical weathering in that region (although some care must be taken to allow for the quantity of particulate matter dissolved out of the atmosphere and that due to the decomposition of organic material) (Livingston 1963; Meade 1969; Zeman and Slaymaker 1975). Mountains located in marine environments and those containing highly soluble rocks display the most rapid rates of dissolution (Reynolds 1971; Reynolds and Johnson 1972; Drake and Ford 1976). Studies of limestone regions in the Alps have indicated that the solution rate is on the order of 0.1 mm/yr. (0.0025 in./yr.) (see Caine 1974, p. 729). In dolomite (limestone containing magnesium) areas of the White Mountains in eastern California, the rate is only about 0.02 mm/yr. (0.00005 in./yr.), but of course the climate is much drier and the dolomite is somewhat less soluble (Marchand 1971, p. 125).

Rock types can vary considerably in their rate of chemical weathering. A study of chemical degradation on the northeast and southwest sides of the Wind River Range, Wyoming, indicates that solutional removal from granitic rocks on the southwest is about 7 tons/km^2/yr. (26 tons/$mi.^2$/yr.), while sedimentary rocks on the northeast dissolve at a rate of 19 tons/km^2/yr. (49 tons/$mi.^2$/yr.), even though stream runoff on the southwest is one and one-half times greater than on the northeast side (Hembree and Rainwater 1961). Similarly, in the Sangre de Cristo Range, New Mexico, average solute contents of stream waters draining quartzite, granite, and sandstone are in the proportion of 2 : 5 : 20, an index of the relative solubility of each of these rocks in this area (J. P. Miller 1961).

Physical Weathering

Although chemical weathering is probably a more significant process in mountains than has generally been recognized, physical forces account for the greater share of mountain rock disintegration. Rocks are subjected to rapid and unequal heating and cooling, to pressures exerted by ice-crystal growth, and to other sorts of internal strains. Many of the milder examples of physical weathering can be grouped under the heading of *insolation weathering*, since they involve the heating and cooling of rocks. Insolation is radiation from the sun, the intensity of which has already been discussed for high altitudes; rapid and extreme temperature changes are characteristic. Each heating and cooling causes unequal expansion between the surface and the interior of the rock, so that it may eventually become weakened and break apart. However, other lines of evidence suggest that heating and cooling alone is not sufficient to break rocks apart. For example, in the desert near Cairo, Egypt, ancient granite columns have fallen on their sides and lie half-buried in the sand. The sun-exposed surfaces are smooth but the sides in the sand, where some moisture is available, are pitted and disintegrated due to chemical alteration (Barton 1938). Laboratory experiments involving rapid heating-and-cooling cycles on rocks in dry air have also failed to produce any noticeable weakening of rocks, but when water is added there is a definite weakening (Blackwelder 1933; Griggs 1936). It is probable, therefore, that both physical and chemical processes are involved, each complementing and reinforcing the other.

One result of these combined processes is *granular disintegration*: grains are loosened around the periphery of a rock and crumble

Fig. 6.7. Granular disintegration taking place on a granodiorite boulder in a subarctic alpine environment, Ruby Range, Yukon Territory. The pea-sized rock particles collecting in a trail below the rock, burying the vegetation, provide an indication of the rapidity of the process. (Author)

away (Fig. 6.7). It is frequently possible to brush the surface of such rocks and have the particles crumble into your hands. Granular disintegration is most effective in rocks with large crystals—e.g., granite—particularly where light and dark minerals are involved, since the latter absorb more heat than the former (Blackwelder 1933; Washburn 1969). A related process is *exfoliation*: the rocks spall, or peel off, in concentric scales or layers much like the skin of an onion, creating rounded features (Fig. 6.8). Exfoliation may result from the chemical decay of minerals, as well as from the volumetric expansion and contraction of the rock surface through heating and cooling (Blackwelder 1925; Matthes 1937; Czeppe 1964). The

Fig. 6.8. Exfoliation of granodiorite in the Ruby Mountains, Yukon Territory. This process probably involves both chemical and physical weathering, and results in the outer part of the rock peeling away in concentric layers to create rounded boulders. (Author)

freezing and expansion of water in cracks and crevices are also undoubtedly important in cold climates. The spheroidal shape of many weathered boulders apparently results from the innate structure of the rock, or from chemical migration of elements and their redeposition in peripheral rings (LaMarche 1967).

A very interesting type of physical weathering, not necessarily related to the mountainous climate, but more to the past history and nature of the bedrock, is *unloading*. This is best displayed in intensely deformed rock created under great heat and pressure deep within the earth but now exposed to the surface under atmospheric conditions and very little pressure. Such rocks may have an innate energy-potential or tendency to expand, so that large slabs of rock 1 m (3.3 ft.) thick or more simply flex outward and break off by themselves (Fig. 6.9). This process is displayed in many young mountainous regions. Once the rocks have broken apart, the increased surface area is exposed to other weathering processes (Ollier 1969b).

The primary cause of rock breakdown in most high mountains, however, is frost action. When water freezes, it expands about 9 percent; and, if confined, it has the ability to exert considerable pressure. You have probably seen the effects of this when the liquid inside a capped pop-bottle freezes and, in expanding, forces off the cap or breaks the bottle. This process, the simple expansion of water to ice, was believed to be the main method in nature for breaking rocks apart. The theory was that water would freeze in the cracks of rocks, expand, and break them apart. However, in a series of classic experiments, Stephen Taber (1929, 1930) found that frozen rocks and soil expand much more than would be predicted from the changes in water volume alone. He concluded that the excessive heave experienced was due to the growth of ice crystals as additional water was attracted to the freezing plane through molecular cohesion. In this respect, freezing behaves like desiccation. Water is attracted to the freezing surface from the surrounding area and accumulates as ice crystals growing in the direction of cooling. Consequently, pressure is exerted in the direction of ice-crystal growth, not in the direction of least resistance, as was formerly believed (Taber 1929, pp. 460–61).

The fundamental process of rock breakdown under the general category of frost action is *frost-wedging*, the mechanical prying apart of rocks upon freezing. It results from the volumetric increase of water to ice as well as from the directional growth of ice crystals (Washburn 1973, p. 60). A recent paper seriously questions the role of frost action in rock breakdown, however, suggesting instead that the chief process is *hydration-shattering* (White 1976a). In this process molecular water is adsorbed in various thicknesses on the surface of silicate minerals, so that pressure is exerted on surrounding rock surfaces. Apparently, a force of over 2 tons per square centimeter can be generated. While hydration-shattering may be an important contributory process, frost-wedging is still considered to be the most important factor in rock fragmentation in mountain environments. Frost-wedging works in two ways: (1) by the deep penetration of ice into the cracks of rocks; and (2) by the growth of ice crystals around the surface

Fig. 6.9. Unloading taking place in medium-grained quartz monzonite, Sierra Nevada, California. (N. King Huber, U.S. Geological Survey)

particles of solid rock. The most important of several factors controlling the efficacy of these processes are the availability of water, the composition of the rock, and the rate and extent of cooling.

Since water must be present for changes in temperature to wreak their damage (Potts 1970), one of the areas of most intense frost-weathering in mountains is the moist zone immediately below late-lying snow patches (Thorn 1978a). The effects can also be seen at the moist bases of cliffs and rock walls, which are often notched by frost action (Gardner 1969). The structure and texture of the rocks helps to determine the amount of frost-shattering that takes place:

porous and multi-jointed rocks that allow ingress of water facilitate rock breakdown; dense and solid rocks are more nearly impervious. Sedimentary rocks are generally more susceptible to frost-shattering than are hard crystalline rocks, although much depends upon their exact characteristics. Crystalline rocks with deep cracks may be more susceptible to frost action than compact sedimentary rocks, and the surface crystals of large-grained rocks are often very vulnerable to dislodgment by frost. Frost-wedging is most effective on rocks with reticulate hairline fractures, where moisture is allowed to penetrate but does not drain away, as often occurs in larger cracks. The frozen moisture wedges each tiny fissure apart slightly, and this produces rock fatigue and eventual breakdown (Tricart 1969, p. 74) (Fig. 6.10). Coarse and angular debris is the typical product of frost-wedging. The exact size and shape depend upon the kind

Fig. 6.10. Frost-wedging of bedrock (granodiorite) in the Ruby Mountains, Yukon Territory. (Author)

of rock and the intensity of the frost action: rocks with stratification planes, such as slate or schist, typically break into flat slabs, while massive rocks, such as limestone or granite, shatter more randomly.

The rate and extent of freezing can produce different results within the same rock type. For example, the few but intense annual freeze-thaw cycles of middle- and high-latitude mountains may produce more frost debris than many freeze-thaw cycles of low intensity and short duration in tropical mountains. The reason for this is that a certain amount of crystal growth and expansion takes place upon initial freezing, but as the temperature lowers and the freezing continues, the remaining interstitial water is frozen and produces much greater internal disruption. Therefore, in those middle- and high-latitude areas where prolonged low temperatures allow deep frost penetration, frost-wedging produces large angular blocks and frost debris. High tropical mountains experience the greatest number of freeze-thaw cycles on earth (Fig. 4.18), but the temperatures are only moderately low and the frost periods last only a few hours (at night). Consequently, the frost penetrates only a few centimeters and the frost debris is small in size (Zeuner 1949; Troll 1958a; Hastenrath 1973).

Regardless of the size of rock fragmentation, once the bedrock has been broken the efficacy of frost comminution increases: more surface area is exposed to weathering and, as the material diminishes in size, its water-holding ability increases. The ultimate size to which material can be reduced by frost-wedging is generally thought to be that of silt, although a small amount of clay may result (Washburn 1973, p. 62). The production of clay-sized material is primarily a function of chemical weathering, however. For this reason, the absence of clays in most mountain environments is taken to be a reflection of the dominance of physical weathering over chemical weathering. The typical end result of frost reduction is an-

gular silt-sized particles that are very susceptible to wind transport and frequently accumulate as loess deposits to the lee of source regions or in locally wind-protected sites. Such deposits provide a much better basis for soil development in mountains than does the normal *in situ* weathering of bedrock.

FROST ACTION

Frost achieves its primary importance in the initial breakdown of rocks but it is also important afterward in the unconsolidated deposits which result. The general tendency of frost action is to cause flux and instability through frost-heaving, frost-thrusting, frost-cracking, and needle-ice growth. These processes give rise to distinctive geomorphic features and affect biological processes by stirring the soil, tearing plant roots apart, and creating an unstable environment for burrowing animals. They make a landscape more vulnerable to disturbance, since frost processes are opportunistic and often increase as vegetation is destroyed. Consequently, it may take a very long time for disturbed surfaces to be colonized or stabilized by vegetation. The efficacy of frost action is determined by its intensity and duration. Both of these factors are reflected by the presence of frozen ground.

Seasonally Frozen Ground

Seasonally frozen ground is ground which freezes and thaws every year. Seasonal freezing penetrates the surface most deeply in the subarctic; in the lower latitudes it is much shallower. The zone of freezing and thawing in mountains may be thought of as a ring or halo that moves up and down with the seasons. The vertical mobility and extent of this belt are largely determined by latitude and altitude. The zone of freeze and thaw on a tropical mountain occupies a relatively narrow vertical extent and remains fairly stationary. If the mountain is high enough, there may be an area at the top where thawing seldom occurs. On the other hand, freezing seldom takes place at the lower elevations. It is in the transitional zone that freezing and thawing take place. In the middle latitudes, however, this nicely storied effect does not hold. There may be a zone of continually low temperature at the top, but freezing and thawing extend to the lowlands in winter. The zone of freeze and thaw is narrowest in summer and widest in winter. It is compressed as it moves up the mountains in the spring and extended as it moves down in the fall; the width of this belt may also vary significantly with exposure.

Although the intensity and duration of low temperatures are the major factors controlling the depth of frost penetration, site conditions are also very important. Soil composition, moisture presence, vegetation, and snow cover all greatly affect the rate and depth of freezing (Hewitt 1968; Fahey 1973, 1974). For example, snow is an excellent insulator—mountain surfaces covered with deep snow are relatively protected from the vagaries of freeze and thaw as well as from deep frost penetration. This is well displayed in mountains under a marine influence, such as the Cascades, where frost penetration is relatively unimportant because the landscape above a certain elevation is muffled by a blanket of heavy snow in winter. In more continental mountains, where there is less snow and temperatures are lower, the depth of freezing increases. This can pose special problems for human settlements. In the mountain towns of Colorado, for example, water supply and garbage disposal are major engineering problems (Wright and Fricke 1966). Plants and animals also encounter difficulty with frozen ground: the soil is impenetrable, and the water is locked up as ice. For all intents and purposes, frozen ground transforms the alpine landscape into a cold desert (Cameron 1969).

Permafrost

Permafrost is defined as soil, bedrock, or any other material that has remained below 0° C. (32° F.) continuously for two or more years (Muller 1947, p. 3). According to this definition, permafrost is purely a temperature condition; the kind of material involved is not important to its definition. In the strict sense of the word, even a glacier is a kind of permafrost, since its temperatures are continually below freezing. Usually, however, permafrost is used to describe the state of the ground.

Although widespread in arctic and subarctic regions, permafrost is restricted to isolated sites in middle-latitude mountains. Nevertheless, it may have local significance through its effect on soil impermeability and as a reservoir of cold. High-mountain lakes and springs have great ecological significance and frequently result from melting *ground-ice* (ice within frozen ground). The presence of permafrost may adversely affect engineering projects, e.g., mining, road-building, well-drilling, and installation of structures such as ski lifts and powerline towers. If ground-ice is present, it may pose further problems because of differential melting and settling. For example, buildings installed near the summits of Pikes Peak and Mount Evans at 4,000 m (13,200 ft.) in the Colorado Rockies have experienced considerable settling because of melting ground-ice (Ives 1974a, p. 187).

The thermal relationships involved in the origin and maintenance of permafrost are complex. Ideally, permafrost should be expected to develop in any area where the mean annual temperature is 0° C. (32° F.) or less. It does not work out this way, however, because of variations in local site conditions. Mountainous sites that receive heavy snowfall usually do not have permafrost, regardless of the air temperature (Bay et al. 1952). On the other hand, permafrost may develop on a windswept, shaded ridge under only marginal temperature conditions. Permafrost in mountains includes both relict and modern occurrences. Much of the relict permafrost was formed during the Pleistocene refrigeration, when it achieved considerable depths and a much broader distribution. It has been preserved in only a few sites, e.g., windswept, bare ridges where the cold can penetrate with facility, and poorly drained peat bogs where the exchange of heat is minimal. The relict nature of such occurrences is proved by their location at depths well below the earth's surface. For example, if permafrost is encountered at a depth of 10 m (33 ft.) and the current depth of freezing is only 1 m (3.3 ft.), the permafrost is obviously not a result of present climatic conditions. Another example of relict permafrost occurs where glacial ice has been buried and preserved by morainal material (see p. 142). This tells a very different story about past conditions, however; formation of the glacial ice probably depended more on precipitation than on temperature. Also, its preservation may have largely been due to an insulating debris cover; present climatic conditions need be only marginally sufficient to allow its preservation.

Permafrost in the mountains of the continental United States is best developed in the Rocky Mountains, where it extends to southern Colorado (Ives 1974a, p. 184). It is usually restricted to elevations above 3,500 m (11,500 ft.) in Colorado but lowers to the north, in Montana and Wyoming (Pierce 1961). At the continental divide between Alberta and British Columbia, permafrost is common above 2,600 m (8,600 ft.) (Scotter 1975). Some of this may be a carry-over from the past, but present climatic conditions in the Rocky Mountains are certainly adequate to create and maintain permafrost in favorable sites. This is proved by the existence of frozen ground at the base of the thawed layer at summer's end (Ives 1973).

Along the east coast of North America,

permafrost occurs on Mount Washington, New Hampshire, and probably on other windswept peaks in the Presidential Range at elevations slightly below 1,800 m (6,000 ft.) (Thompson 1960–61; Goldthwait 1969). The permafrost in this area is at least partially relict; drill holes on Mount Washington have revealed the presence of permafrost at depths up to 45 m (150 ft.) (Howe 1971). Since permafrost penetrates the ground at a rate of only a few centimeters per year, its presence at these depths indicates an age of several thousand years. Permafrost is reported from Mount Jacques Cartier in the Shickshock Mountains of the Gaspé Peninsula at 1,200 m (4,000 ft.), and it becomes commonplace further north, in the mountains of Labrador (Ives 1974a, p. 183). On the west coast, isolated occurrences of permafrost are postulated for the White Mountains of California and the Sierra Nevada (Retzer 1965, p. 38), but its presence has not been definitely confirmed. There is also a good possibility that permafrost exists on the higher peaks of the Cascades and other mountains of Oregon and Washington, but this, also, has not been investigated. Permafrost has been observed just across the border, however, at an elevation of 1,800 m (6,000 ft.) in the Coast Range of southern British Columbia (Mathews 1955).

In the Alps, isolated occurrences of permafrost have been reported at elevations as low as 2,300 m (6,500 ft.), and by 2,700 m (9,000 ft.) it becomes common in favorable sites (Barsch 1969; Furrer and Fitze 1970). Permafrost is also reported from the high ranges of Eurasia, i.e., the Caucasus, Northern Urals, Pamirs, Tien Shan, Karakoram, and Himalayas (Gorbunov 1978). Permafrost has recently been reported from Mount Fujiyama and other high peaks in Japan (Higuchi and Fujii 1971). The most tropical occurrence yet reported is from Mount Mauna Loa, Hawaii (Woodcock et al. 1970; Woodcock 1974). In the southern hemisphere, permafrost is likely to occur on some of the higher peaks, especially in the Peruvian Andes and in the southern Alps of New Zealand but, with the exception of the south polar region, I know of no definite reports of permafrost from south of the equator.

Frost Heave and Thrust

When *ice lenses* (horizontal accumulations of ice crystals) build beneath the surface, they cause the ground to expand in the direction of the ice-crystal growth. The most common direction is vertical (*heave*), toward the soil surface, since this is the source of the cold, but expansion may also take place laterally (*thrust*) due to the variations in conductivity of heterogeneous materials (Washburn 1973, p. 65). Frost heave and thrust are the major causes of stirring and disruption of the soil. The exact mechanisms of operation have not yet been isolated, but it is known that these processes operate best in fine soils with ample moisture. As the soil freezes, water is attracted to the freezing plane, where it accumulates in the form of ice lenses that push up the soil. The displacement of the soil is particularly striking where local variations in soil texture, water availability, or the insulating effects of snow and vegetation bring about differential heaving. Under these conditions, disruption may take place in one area while adjacent surfaces are unaffected. This partially accounts for the "trouble spots" in paved roads in mountains and other areas where frost is a problem.

One conspicuous result of frost heave and thrust in natural environments is the upheaval and ejection of rocks from depth. The common phenomenon of upward movement of stones in cultivated fields apparently results from the same processes that operate in high mountains (except that the processes are greatly magnified in mountains). The upheaval of rocks can be deduced from the presence of newly exposed and unweathered rock surfaces, ab-

sence of lichens, and disrupted vegetation and soil surfaces. In some cases, rocks may be heaved 1–2 m (3–7 ft.) above the surface and stand like lonely tombstones amid the tundra (Price 1970) (Fig. 6.11). The exposed rock is then highly susceptible to weathering, and will eventually be transformed into a pile of rubble. The upheaval of blocks occurs in bedrock as well as in soil, with similar results.

The principal processes involved in the movement of stones through frost heave and thrust can be grouped into two groups, called *frost-pull* and *frost-push* (Washburn 1969, pp. 52–58). Frost-pull operates when the soil freezes and expands upward, pulling rocks with it, and upon thawing the rocks do not return all the way to their original positions. Thus, the stones migrate surfaceward by increments with each freeze and thaw. Frost-push, on the other hand, results from ice lenses growing underneath stones and pushing them upward. Because rocks have greater conductivity than soil, heat (or cold) can pass through them more quickly than through the soil; therefore, ice lenses accumulate at their bases and cause differential heaving. As with the frost-pull mechanism, finer material then seeps into the cavity and prevents the full return of the rock to its original position (Washburn 1969, pp. 55–56; 1973, pp. 71–80). Under natural conditions, the two mechanisms operate simultaneously and are difficult to separate. Frost-pull is probably more important for the overall migration of rocks to the surface and the upfreezing of posts in the ground. Frost-push is probably primarily responsible for the relatively rapid displacement of large blocks upward, owing to the potential for ice-lens growth at their bases.

It was formerly believed that much of the frost-stirring evident at the surface in mountain environments was caused by frequent freeze-thaw cycles. Recent investigations, however, have proven that diurnal freeze and thaw generally penetrates no more than about 10 cm (4 in.) even on bare

Fig. 6.11. Freshly upheaved block occurring amid tundra on a gentle south-facing slope at 1,800 m (6,000 ft.) in the Ruby Range, Yukon Territory. Hunting knife—20 cm (8 in.) long—provides scale. The uplift of this rock appears to be due to downslope movement as well as to upfreezing. (Author)

and exposed surfaces, let alone on sheltered or vegetated surfaces (Fahey 1973; Thorn 1979a). Frost heave and thrust depend upon relatively deep freezing, so their operation is essentially limited to once a year, on the annual freeze-thaw cycle. This in no way diminishes the efficacy of the process; it simply puts a different light on its disposition. It is the prolonged and intense cold of the alpine winter that is responsible for the major features of frost heave. Needle ice, however, does operate at the surface in response to diurnal freeze and thaw.

Needle Ice

Needle ice consists of small individual columns or filaments of ice 1–3 cm (0.4–1.1 in.) high, projecting perpendicular to the soil surface (Fig. 6.12). Each ice needle issues directly from the soil; its top is usually capped by a thin ice-layer on which dirt and small rocks can settle. The needles

Fig. 6.12. Needle-ice development in the Coast Range, Oregon. The four layers represent four different needle-ice events, probably over as many nights. (William G. Loy, University of Oregon)

may be densely packed like bristles in a brush or scattered like columns in an abandoned mine, depending upon variations in soil moisture and the extent of cooling. Needle ice typically forms at night and melts during the day. If it does not melt during the day, and new growth accumulates the following night, a tiered or storied effect may develop. Rarely, three to four layers may develop, each representing a separate needle-ice event.

The typical conditions for needle-ice occurrence are a calm clear night with freezing temperatures and a fine soil with a high moisture content. Under these conditions the ice begins to segregate and grow as the water migrates to the freezing plane (Outcalt 1971). The needles grow from their bases and push upward at a rate that may reach several centimeters per hour, although it is usually somewhat slower. One prime requirement for good needle-ice growth is a soil fine enough to hold ample water but one which will still allow rapid migration of the water to the freezing plane. A soil that is too coarse may not hold enough moisture, while a tight clay may inhibit the migration of water. A silty loam seems to be the ideal texture (Beskow 1947, p. 6).

Needle ice is the major frost process operating in tropical mountains and in middle-latitude mountains in marine climates. It becomes somewhat less important in continental mountains, because of the more severe winters and deep freezing there. It is also less important in high latitudes, since the number of freeze-thaw cycles decreases. Needle ice can uproot plant seedlings and disrupt plant establishment (Schramm 1958; Brink et al. 1967). It contributes to slope erosion, because each freeze lifts soil and rock particles at right angles to the slope, and upon thawing the particles settle more nearly vertically, resulting in a net downslope movement (Gradwell 1954; Soons 1968). Since surfaces affected by needle ice are often left in a fluffed or frothy state, soil particles are more easily transported by wind and meltwater (Beaty 1974a). The development of needle ice also contributes to sorting processes that produce patterned ground (Troll 1958a; Hastenrath 1973, 1977; Mackay and Mathews 1974).

Patterned Ground

Patterning of the rocks, soil, and vegetation into various geometric forms is a common feature of high-mountain landscapes. The patterns fall into three basic categories: polygons, circles, and lines or stripes (Fig. 6.13). These "surface markings" or "structure soils," as they have been called, range in size from tiny features measured in centimeters to large-scale forms several meters across. Because of their striking geometric arrangement and curious nature, they have attracted a great deal of attention; the literature dealing with patterned ground is extensive (Troll 1958a; Washburn 1956, 1973). In spite of this (or perhaps because of it), the exact mechanism of their origin is still controversial and little understood. Washburn (1956, p. 823) listed nineteen different theories that have been proposed to account for their development. One problem is that similar patterns can be caused by different processes. The polygon, for example, is one of the most ubiquitous forms in nature. It can be created by thermal contraction upon freezing, and by the drying and cracking of soil in a mud puddle or dry lakebed; it forms on age-cracked porcelain, and in the cooling of molten lava. I am reminded of the process every time I eat a baked potato! It is not surprising, then, that the process of freezing and thawing also creates polygons.

One most useful contribution to the study of patterned ground is the descriptive, and almost universally accepted, classification devised by A. L. Washburn in 1956. It is based on only two criteria—geometric form, and the presence or absence of sorting (the segregation of rocks and fines). The basic types of patterned

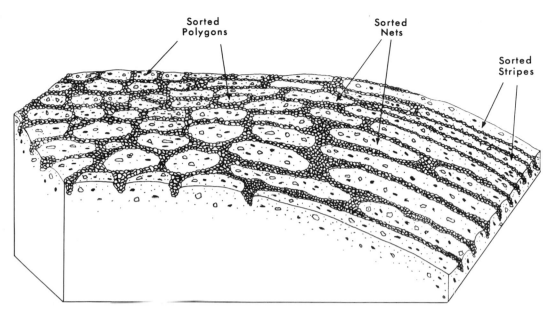

Fig. 6.13. Schematic view of patterned-ground development, showing how the patterns become elongated on slopes due to mass-wasting. (After Sharpe 1938, p. 37)

ground are sorted and non-sorted circles, polygons, nets, steps, and stripes. A pattern is sorted if particle size varies from one part of the feature to another. A sorted circle, for example, has finer material in the center and larger particles around the perimeter (Fig. 6.14a). A non-sorted circle displays no difference in particle size; its form is usually determined by the bordering vegetation (Fig. 6.14b). Similarly, sorted polygons contain rocks along the pattern lines with finer material between them, while non-sorted polygons are the result of a cracking matrix at the surface with no difference in the size of material (Fig. 6.14c). Sorted stripes (stone stripes) are marked by alternating zones of larger and finer particles (Fig. 6.15), while non-sorted stripes may be identified by ridges and furrows or by alternating bare and vegetated strips (Fig. 6.14d). Although both types of patterned ground present recognizable and conspicuous patterns, the sorted variety is the most intriguing, both because it has a

more striking appearance and because the segregation of rock sizes suggests a more complex origin. Moreover, the sorting occurs on a vertical as well as a horizontal basis. The larger particles that compose the borders characteristically accumulate in a wedge (when viewed in cross-section), with the widest part of the rocky material occurring at the soil surface and tapering downward. In addition, the largest rocks are near the surface; progressively smaller rocks are found with depth. In small-scale features the stony margins are typically composed of pea-sized particles extending to a depth of only a few centimeters, while in large-scale features the rocks may be sizable and extend to a depth of 1 m (3.3 ft.) or more.

Origin of Patterned Ground

Patterned ground can be created by a number of different processes, as is proven by the wide variety of environments and materials in which it occurs (Washburn

(a)

(b)

(c)

(d)

Fig. 6.14. An assortment of patterned-ground types. (a) Large-scale sorted circle. Note that the larger rocks at perimeter are heavily lichen-covered, suggesting that the feature has been inactive for some time. The bare area in middle is fresh, however, denoting recent renewal of activity. (b) Non-sorted circle. This is simply a bare area in a vegetated surface, with no distinction in particle size from one area to the other. Both of the above are situated at about 1,800 m (6,000 ft.) in the Ruby Range, Yukon Territory. (c) Small-scale non- sorted polygons at 2,575 m (8,500 ft.) in the Wallowa Mountains, Oregon. The soil is only a few centimeters deep above bedrock. The darker areas denote greater soil moisture. (d) Large-scale non-sorted stripes at 1,640 m (5,400 ft.) in the Old Man Range, New Zealand. These features appear to be fossil and inactive. Note that the vegetation is better-developed in the furrows than on the ridges. (Author and J. D. McCraw, University of Otago)

Fig. 6.15. Small-scale sorted stripes at 2,700 m (9,000 ft.) in the Wallowa Mountains, Oregon. Hunting knife, located below granite exposure, is 20 cm (8 in.) long and provides scale. The miniature ridges and troughs are probably a result of needle-ice activity and rill wash, although wind may also have contributed to their formation. The finer material exists on the ridges; the larger (pea-sized) particles occur in the furrows. This area at one time supported a fairly complete cover of vegetation but it has been badly denuded by overgrazing; consequently, much of this patterned ground is probably of recent origin. (Author, 1974)

1956, 1970, 1973). It is best displayed in mountains and in polar regions, however, so by looking more closely at the dominant processes in these environments, an approach can be made to understanding its origin. The initiating process in polygonal patterns is generally cracking of the surface due to desiccation or frost-cracking, while circular patterns are probably due to frost heave. Sorting of materials is caused by various processes, but in cold climates it is mainly due to frost action.

Frost heave and thrust and needle-ice growth all contribute to the segregation of rocks and fines. The precise mechanisms are still unknown, but the sorting can be explained in a general way. The surface of the ground typically consists of a heterogeneous mixture of coarse and fine particles. The fines hold more water than the coarse material, and will expand more when they freeze, and also cohere and contract more when they thaw, than will areas of predominantly coarse material. With each expansion, particles move outward from the freezing nucleus; when they settle back, they fail to return completely to their original positions. The fines tend to congregate in these cycles of expansion and contraction, leaving the coarser materials in the intervening areas. The process continues until the centers of fine material begin to impinge on each other, with the larger particles forming the perimeters of the polygons or circles. Although these statements refer primarily to level areas, they apply to slopes as well, except that the features will tend to elongate downslope (Fig. 6.13).

Surface sorting in small-scale micropatterned ground, as found in middle-latitude mountains with marine climates and in tropical mountains, is probably largely due to shallow freezing and needle-ice processes; deep freezing is not common in these environments. Needle ice only affects the uppermost 2–3 cm (1 in.) of the surface and cannot move rocks bigger than 5–10 cm (2–4 in.) in diameter. Consequently, the features that result are limited to a thin zone at the surface and are composed of small rocks (Fig. 6.15). Such small-scale features have all the characteristics of large-scale patterned ground, however, including the basic forms—polygons, circles, and stripes—and show sorting on both a horizontal and vertical basis (Troll 1958a; Corte 1968; Hastenrath 1973, 1977; Mackay and Mathews 1974).

Blockfields

When bedrock is shattered and broken apart by frost action, the result is frequently a jumble of angular stones accumulating at the surface. The bedrock becomes buried under its own detritus. Such *blockfields* are common in alpine landscapes (White 1976b) (Fig. 6.16). The German term *felsenmeer*, meaning "sea of rocks," is very descriptive of this phenomenon. Although blockfields have various origins, frost action is generally thought to be the prime factor (Washburn 1973, p. 192). The bedrock is broken apart by frost-wedging, and the rocks are slowly extruded by frost heave and thrust. No appreciable amount of transport is involved in blockfields except on slopes, where there may be movement due to gravity-settling and frost heave. Blockfields may also merge into or serve as source areas for *rock streams*;

Fig. 6.16. A blockfield situated at 2,700 m (9,000 ft.) in the Wallowa Mountains, northeastern Oregon. Rock type is granodiorite and the vegetation consists of low-lying clumps of Subalpine fir (*Abies lasiocarpa*) and Dwarf juniper (*Juniperus sibirica*). (Author)

as their name implies, these are narrow accumulations of rocks on slopes, resembling streams of rocks. These do exhibit movement and are similar to stone stripes except for their larger size and the fact that they may occur singly (Caine and Jennings 1969). The important point is that blockfields are basically sedentary features that develop in place and are not the result of rockfall from upslope.

The dimensions of blockfields, as well as those of their component blocks, vary depending upon the rock type, present and past climate, and local geomorphic history. In middle- and high-latitude mountains, blockfields may cover extensive areas, particularly on unglaciated upland surfaces (Perov 1969). The blocks range from fist-size up to 3 m (10 ft.) in diameter. In tropical mountains, blockfields are much less impressive, appearing as local rubble-strewn surfaces with rocks usually only a few centimeters in diameter.

Blockfields are inactive or relict in some mountains, but may be actively forming in others. Evidence of recent activity includes freshly shattered surfaces, the absence of soil and vegetation, and a general appearance of newness. Active blockfields are relatively unstable, with frequent teetery and unbalanced rocks. If you have ever crossed a blockfield, you know that it is safest to stick to the most heavily lichen-covered areas, since they exhibit greater stability (this advice may not hold when the rock surfaces are wet, since the lichens can be extremely slippery). Inactive or relict blockfields in areas where blockfields are not now actively forming may be good evidence of a more severe former climate. This is particularly true in middle latitudes around the margin of the continental ice-sheet (Smith 1953; Potter and Moss 1968), but it is also true of lower elevations in mountains. For example, during the Pleistocene, snowline and glaciers extended to lower elevations, as did colder climates; and the presence of inactive periglacial features like patterned ground

and blockfields in these areas can help establish the extent of past environmental conditions. In some mountain areas the same processes that formed these relict features at lower elevations may still be operating at higher elevations. If the higher surfaces were covered by ice during the Pleistocene so that they were protected from deep frost penetration, blockfields there have probably formed since deglaciation. Where peaks and ridges were not covered with ice but stood like islands (*nunataks*) amid the ice, they would have been susceptible to frost-shattering for a much longer period of time. Such areas offer critical information about past environments, but their identification and interpretation are difficult and controversial (Ives 1958, 1966, 1974b; Dahl 1966a, b).

MASS-WASTING

Mass-wasting is the downslope movement of material due to gravity without the aid of a specific transporting medium such as wind, streams, or glaciers. Many different processes are included, from slow imperceptible creep and solifluction, to more rapid mudflow and slumping, to spectacular rockfalls, debris avalanches, and landslides (Sharpe 1938). These processes achieve their greatest development in mountains because of the dominance of steep slopes, great local relief, and environmental variability. At high altitudes, frost action is the chief agent of rock disintegration and mass-wasting is the chief agent of transport. With the exception of glacial sculpture, frost action and mass-wasting account for most of the characteristic features of high mountain landscapes (Russell 1933; Bryan 1934).

The delineation of the forms of mass-wasting has long been a difficult problem, because most processes display more than one type of motion. A mass of rock breaking loose from a mountain may slide, fall, and flow during various segments of its journey and will result in very different forms depending upon where it comes to rest. Processes and forms are transitional, and so are their identification and classification. The literature is filled with different names applied to similar features (Sharpe 1938; Terzaghi 1950; Eckel 1958). Without becoming embroiled in this problem, we will discuss several of the more distinct processes. Some of these, such as creep and slumping, may occur anywhere that sufficient slope exists, while the more rapid forms, such as debris avalanches and landslides, are more or less restricted to mountains.

Creep

Creep, the slow downslope movement of surface material, is usually not detectable except through long-term observations (Sharpe 1938, p. 21). It is a process found in all environments and can be caused by wetting and drying, heating and cooling, freezing and thawing, disturbance of the soil by organisms, and simply the effect of shear stress on slopes (Carson and Kirby 1972, p. 272). The rate of creep is so slow in most lowland environments that its effect can only be seen over decades or centuries. In mountains, however, the effect of these processes is greatly intensified. This is especially true of *frost creep*, "the ratchet-like downslope movement of particles as the result of frost heaving of the ground and subsequent settling upon thawing, the heaving being predominantly normal to the slope and the settling more nearly vertical" (Washburn 1967, p. 10). Frost creep is primarily controlled by the number of freeze-thaw cycles and achieves its greatest importance in tropical and middle-latitude mountains (Troll 1958a; Corte 1968; Benedict 1970, 1976). Although it is a clearly distinguishable process, the measurement and isolation of frost creep are difficult because other processes are also involved, particularly when the soil is saturated and flowage occurs (Washburn

Fig. 6.17. Curved tree trunks such as these may indicate slow downslope soil movement due to creep. This is the Subalpine fir (*Abies lasiocarpa*) at 1,800 m (6,000 ft.) near Crater Lake in the Oregon Cascades. (Author)

1967; Benedict 1970, 1976). On drier slopes where flowage is not a factor, the effects of frost creep can often be seen. The downslope movement may result in small steps and terracettes. Below timberline, the downslope curvature of tree trunks may be good evidence of creep, although heavy snowfall, among other factors, may also be important (Sharpe 1938, p. 24; Parizek and Woodruff 1957; Phipps 1974) (Fig. 6.17).

Solifluction

Solifluction is a word derived from the Latin *solum*, "soil," and *fluere*, "to flow"

(Andersson 1906, p. 95). It is a process best developed beyond timberline in cold climates where permafrost or a subsurface frozen layer prevents the downward percolation of water. Under these conditions the soil becomes saturated, cohesion among soil particles is reduced, and the viscous mass begins to deform downslope as flowage (Williams 1957). Although more rapid than creep, solifluction is still one of

Fig. 6.18. Excavated soil pit in the Ruby Mountains, Yukon Territory, exposes polyethylene tube which was inserted (straight) into the ground five years earlier. The curvature of the tube represents the amount of surface movement due to solifluction. Plumb bob hanging from shovel handle indicates departure from the vertical. (Author)

the slower forms of mass-wasting. Average rates of movement range from 0.5–5.0 cm/yr. (0.2–2.0 in./yr.) (Washburn 1967; Benedict 1970, 1976; L. W. Price 1973) (Fig. 6.18).

The essential ingredient for solifluction is water. This generally comes from melting snow or ground-ice, with the affected area saturated for several weeks in the spring and early summer. Where the westerlies prevail in middle latitudes, the favored orientation of solifluction slopes is easterly, because snowdrifts tend to accumulate on the leeward slopes. Other important factors governing solifluction include soil texture, slope gradient, rock type, and vegetation. Slopes of only 2°–5° are sufficient to induce solifluction in the Arctic, where there is permafrost and the soil is continually saturated, but in most mountains it occurs on slope gradients of 5°–20°. If the slopes are steeper than this, the water tends to be lost through runoff. The soil is also eroded more quickly on steeper slopes, and the reservoir for holding water is reduced. In general, the finer the soil, the more likely solifluction is to occur, because there is greater water-holding ability, frost susceptibility, and potential for flowage. Rock type comes into play here: some rocks break down more rapidly and into finer particles than others (Jahn 1967). In some mountains solifluction is limited to slopes with glacial deposits, since they are the only sites with enough fine material.

Vegetation plays a major role in solifluction by increasing the moisture content through reduction of runoff, insulation of the surface, and decrease in evaporation. It also acts as a retarding or binding agent giving the downslope movement definition and form (Warren-Wilson 1952). Solifluction lobes and terraces often resemble huge soil tongues moving downslope, frequently coalescing and forming crenulate, lobate banks running for considerable distances along the slope (Fig. 6.19). Such features form a striking microrelief and

Fig. 6.19. Solifluction lobes on a gentle southeast-facing slope in the Ruby Range, Yukon Territory. Close-up inset shows size of lobe front. (Author)

have important ecological implications (Price 1971b, c).

In many middle-latitude mountains, solifluction features may be inactive, a carry-over from the past. Evidence of inactivity includes well-vegetated stabilized lobes with little sign of movement and lobes which are now being eroded. Elsewhere they may display evidence of movement, either actively forming or being reactivated. In any case, an understanding of their disposition can provide insight into past and present environmental conditions (Benedict 1966, 1976; Costin et al. 1967; Worsley and Harris 1974).

Mudflow

Mudflow is a major geomorphic process in mountains (not to be confused with mudslides, such as occur in California, involving the massive failure of large sections of slopes). Mudflow consists of the downslope flowage of water-saturated heterogeneous material, usually confined to a definite channel. Mudflow differs from solifluction in its much greater speed of movement (up to several meters per second), its characteristic confinement to a definite channel, and its composition. The name *mudflow* is actually a misnomer, because the material is composed largely of rocks; it resembles the aggregate of fresh concrete, although the rocks can sometimes be very large. Mud is the matrix and transporting medium, however, and the name has been widely adopted (Blackwelder 1928; Sharpe 1938).

The conditions most favorable for mudflow include: (1) abundant water to saturate the mass of mud and rocks; (2) lack of stabilizing vegetation; (3) unconsolidated material with enough fines to serve as lubrication; and (4) moderately steep slopes (Blackwelder 1928, p. 478; Sharpe 1938, p. 56). These conditions are best met in steep topography, and mudflows have in fact been documented from all major mountain ranges. They occur most often in the spring and summer, when there is ample melting snow and occasional periods of heavy downpour during thunderstorms (Fryxell and Horberg 1943; Curry 1966; Broscoe and Thomson 1969; Rapp and Strömquist 1976). Under these conditions, masses of unconsolidated material may become saturated, and where a slightly unstable situation already exists, the material may collapse and flow downslope.

The typical point of origin for a mudflow is high on the slope where there is a source of periodic moisture, i.e., confluence of runoff or below snow patches, and sufficient fine material exists. Mudflows also develop at breaks in slopes where the gradient increases abruptly. I have observed

mudflow development in the Ruby Mountains, Yukon Territory: solifluction lobes on a gentle slope above a glacial trough slowly migrate onto the steeper slope, where they become unable to maintain themselves and eventually collapse, moving downslope as mudflows (Price 1969) (Fig. 6.20). Whatever the local situation, once a mudflow channel has been established it is likely that future flows will follow the same path.

Mudflows are so sporadic and unpredictable that very few people have witnessed them, but if you are fortunate enough to observe one it will be a sight you will not soon forget. The saturated debris moves in a rapidly advancing snout of rocks, mud, and water. In its upper reaches, the mudflow is primarily an agent of erosion, scouring and removing debris in its path and frequently creating a steep-walled, canyon-like channel up to several meters wide and deep, plastered with mud but otherwise free of debris. As the mudflow progresses downslope, it may slow or stop temporarily when the slope gradient decreases or when the snout and other sections become too dry. The stationary

Fig. 6.20. Generalized cross-section showing the local collapse of solifluction lobes as they move onto lower but steeper valley slopes. This site can also be seen in the lower left of Figure 6.39. The longest mudflow is shown on that photo as an elongated white strip. (From Price 1969, p. 398)

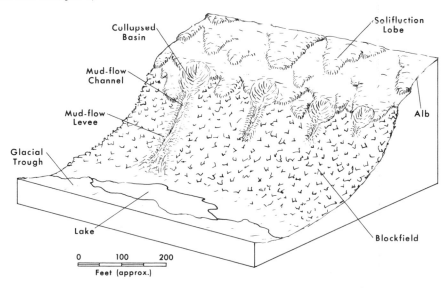

Fig. 6.21. Mudflow deposits at base of rocky slope in the St. Elias Mountains, Yukon Territory. Scale is provided by man in lower left. The lighter-colored material in center represents the most recent flow; the debris on either side is from older flows. Observe the mudflow channel and levees on narrow part of feature in upper center of picture. (Author)

sections serve as dams, pooling water behind them until the mass once again becomes saturated or the water breaks through and the material begins moving again. The movement of a mudflow, then, is often in a series of stops and starts, progressing down the slope like a giant

serpent. Along the edge of the mudflow channel, particularly in the middle and lower reaches of the slope, debris is piled on either side like natural levees along a stream (Sharp 1942). At the base, the material spreads laterally in lobate fashion to form a debris fan (Fig. 6.21). Although generally occupying only a few square meters, mudflows may occasionally move several kilometers onto the adjacent lowland and may transport boulders weighing several tons. Examples of this can be seen along the bases of many of the world's mountains.

Mudflows have caused considerable destruction of life and property (Sutton 1933). In the Andes of Peru, for instance, earthquakes and the melting of glacial ice during the past century have resulted in numerous major mudflows. Glacial meltwater collects in lakes behind morainal dams; if there is an earthquake or if the dam is breached, a huge mudflow may result. A long history of such catastrophic mudflows can be read in the geomorphology of the base of the Andes (Lliboutry et al. 1977).

Slumping

Slumping is the downslope slippage of unconsolidated material moving as a unit or as several subsidiary units along a concave surface of rupture (Fig. 6.22). Creep, solifluction, and mudflow usually display more rapid movement at the surface, but slumping moves more rapidly at depth, or at least it starts out that way (until or if the movement changes to mudflow or landslide). Slumping typically takes place along a zone of weakness where the area downslope has been disturbed and the basal support removed. Consequently, this process is important along road cuts and where lakes or streams have undercut their banks. The rate of movement by slumping is rapid enough to be observable but it is not as rapid or as destructive as mudflows or landslides.

Fig. 6.22. Slumping taking place on a disturbed
slope in the Madison Range, southwestern Montana.
(J. R. Stacy, U.S. Geological Survey)

Rockfall

Rockfall is simply the falling of rock downslope (Sharpe 1938, p. 78). Rocks may fall directly from a cliff or headwall or they may tumble downward in a series of leaps and bounds. They may be released directly from bedrock or they may be dislodged from a secondary resting place. In many mountain areas, rockfall is frequent enough to be of considerable geomorphic significance (Crandell and Fahnestock 1965; Gardner 1967, 1970a; Gray 1973; Luckman 1976).

By its very nature, rockfall is a localized and sporadic process. It achieves its greatest intensity above timberline in steep terrain where there is little vegetation and frost action operates to loosen rocks and make them unstable. Under these conditions, the slightest disturbance may dislodge rocks and send them plummeting. The triggering agent may be wind, water, melting snow, disturbance by an animal or man, or simply the differential contraction and expansion of the surface with heating and cooling from day to night. The sound of falling rock is a very common one in mountains. I will always remember my first mountain-sheep hunt in the Chugach Mountains, Alaska. Stalking a large Dall sheep from above, I was getting within close range when suddenly I dislodged a rock and it went tumbling downslope, sounding, to my sensitive ears, like thunder. I quickly dropped to the ground but was sure that the rock would frighten the mountain sheep. The huge ram did not even look up; the sound of falling rock was a natural part of his world. It is eloquent testimony to the inherent instability of the alpine environment.

A recent investigation of the importance of rockfall as a geomorphic agent achieved an approximation simply by listening for and recording the rockfalls in a small area of the Rocky Mountains of Alberta, Canada (Gardner 1970a). A total of 842 hours were spent in this activity over three summers, and 563 rockfalls were counted (0.7 per hour of observation). As might be expected, the greatest number of rockfalls occurred at mid-afternoon, when the temperature was highest, but a second period of high frequency was observed between 8 and 9 A.M., during the initial warming and thawing of the surface for the day (Table 6.1). In general, rockfalls were most frequent in the highest and steepest terrain on northeast and east-facing slopes, where frost processes were more active (Gardner 1970a).

The chief geomorphic significance of rockfall lies in its rapid and powerful transport of material downslope. When a rock falls, it may strike and dislodge other

Table 6.1. *Average rockfall frequency during summer in the Lake Louise area of the Canadian Rocky Mountains (Gardner 1970a, p. 17).*

Time of Day	Number of Rockfalls
01	—
02	—
03	—
04	—
05	0.0
06	0.0
07	0.1
08	0.5
09	0.8
10	0.2
11	0.3
12	0.7
13	1.2
14	1.1
15	1.0
16	0.7
17	0.5
18	0.3
19	0.5
20	0.2
21	0.1
22	0.3
23	0.0
24	—

rocks. Rocks move at high speeds and can cause considerable damage on impact, whether they strike another rock, a tree, or simply the ground. Of course, falling rocks hold very grave danger for man and his structures; this is why protective structures are often built next to mountain highways passing through precipitous terrain or large sections of netting are draped over critical sections of steep walls (Fig. 6.23). Preventing rocks from falling on railways is even more critical, since a single rock can cause a train to be derailed. An interesting method of dealing with fallen rocks is by the erection of closely spaced electrical wires to form a fence along the side of the track. The wires are connected to lights in control stations; when a rock falls and breaks a wire, a light goes on and the workman can go out and remove the rock from the rails. But all these methods are expensive, and the traveler on the highway usually must settle for a sign announcing "Falling Rock."

Landslide and Debris Avalanche

Landslides and *debris avalanches* have been identified as separate processes: landslides move predominantly by sliding, whereas debris avalanches exhibit flow in their distal parts (Sharpe 1938, pp. 61-78). The distinction is difficult to make in practice, however, since sliding, falling, and flowing are generally all involved to various degrees. For our purposes, they will be considered jointly and simply called landslides, but with the recognition that the movement is not restricted to sliding alone.

The landslide is the most spectacular form of mass movement known. It is best developed in mountains where there are steep slopes and great local relief to provide sufficient room for the cascading rock to develop its speed of fall and potential for transport. Some landslides reach velocities of over 100 m/sec. (200 mi./hr.), and the mass can move horizontally for several ki-

Fig. 6.23. Protective fences constructed along mountain highway in Alps to prevent falling rocks from reaching the roadway. (Author)

lometers, and even ascend neighboring slopes.

Landslides resemble snow avalanches in that air may become trapped under the falling debris and the mass tends to move rapidly on this cushion of compressed air (Shreve 1966, 1968). Controversy exists, however, since some believe that the movement is more a flow like that of a suspended mass of cohesionless grains (Kent 1966; Hsu 1975). Whatever the mechanism, there are many examples of landslides in mountains where huge masses of rock have collapsed and moved several kilometers, often resulting in catastrophe.

Fig. 6.24. Landslide on the Sherman Glacier, Alaska. Slide was released during the great Alaska earthquake of 1964. Rocky debris has since been transported to terminus. (Austin Post, 24 August 1964, U.S. Geological Survey)

Among the better-known are the great slide in 1881 at Elm, Switzerland (Sharpe 1938, p. 79), and the ancient Saidmarreh landslide in the Zagros mountains of southwestern Iran (Harrison and Falcon 1937, 1938; Watson and Wright 1969). The latter was apparently the single largest in

the world: the side of a mountain broke loose, descended 1,500 m (5,000 ft.), and traveled horizontally some 14 km (9 mi.), including an ascent of 500 m (1,600 ft.) over an intervening obstacle. The area of fallen rock covers 274 km² (64 mi.²) at an average thickness of over 100 m (330 ft.), with individual rock sizes ranging from dust up to huge blocks 18 m (60 ft.) in diameter (Harrison and Falcon 1937, 1938).

In North America, the most famous slides have been the Turtle Mountain landslide that destroyed the small mining town of Frank, Alberta, in 1903 (McConnell and Brock 1904; Daly et al. 1912), the Gros Ventre slide, Wyoming, in 1925 (Alden 1928), and the Sherman landslide, which came to rest atop the Sherman Glacier during the Alaska earthquake of 1964 (Shreve 1966; Cruden 1976) (Fig. 6.24). An ancient slide which temporarily blocked the Columbia River

midway through the Cascades and gave rise to the "Bridge of the Gods" of Indian legend is now the site of Bonneville Dam (Lawrence and Lawrence 1958; Waters 1973).

The most destructive landslide of this century took place in the Peruvian Andes during the great 1970 earthquake. Over 50,000 people were killed in this quake, 18,000 of whom were buried in a landslide originating on the slopes of Mount Hauscarán, a volcanic peak with an elevation of 6,768 m (22,334 ft.) located about 350 km (210 mi.) north of Lima. The earthquake caused a huge mass of overhanging snow

Fig. 6.25. Landslide that originated on Mount Huascarán during the 1970 earthquake in Peru. Slide moved a distance of over 16 km (10 mi.) and destroyed the towns of Yungay and Ranrahirca. (Servicio Aerofotografico Nacional, Lima)

and ice to break loose from the summit and fall 1,000 m (3,300 ft.), until it crashed into the mountain and pulverized. The impact dislodged the unconsolidated slope material at this point and caused massive slope failure. The frictional heat created by the snow and ice colliding with the slope also caused melting, so that vast amounts of water were available to saturate and lubricate the mass (Clapperton and Hamilton 1971; Browning 1973). The slide swiftly descended the mountain, going from an elevation of 5,500 m (18,150 ft.) down to 2,500 m (8,250 ft.) in less than 3 minutes, traveling at speeds of up to 480 km (300 mi.) per hour (Fig. 6.25). The survival of delicate morainal ridges and vegetation in its path suggests that the slide rode on a cushion of air for parts of its journey. The mass careened back and forth from one side of the valley to the other in its descent, like a great sloshing liquid (Fig. 6.26). Before the slide came to rest on the far flanks of the valley, it had traveled more than 16 km (10 mi.) and had utterly destroyed two villages in its path: Yungay and Ranrahirca. Ridges as high as 140 m (460 ft.)

Fig. 6.26. View upvalley toward Huascarán. Steep rockwall shows source of landslide. As the material came down it apparently trapped a cushion of air beneath it and literally flowed, sloshing from one side of the valley to the other. The varying heights of contact can be seen on valley slopes. (Chalmers M. Clapperton, University of Aberdeen)

were overridden and blocks up to 6 m (20 ft.) in diameter were scattered about like pebbles. The slide was preceded by a turbulent blast of air that demolished buildings even before the rock debris struck, and a dense dust cloud hung over the area like a pall for three days (Clapperton and Hamilton 1971).

The awe-inspiring power of such slides was graphically described by a Peruvian geophysicist who happened to be in Yungay taking a French couple on a tour of the area:

As we drove past the cemetery the car began to shake. It was not until I had stopped the car that I realized that we were experiencing an earthquake. We immediately got out of the car and observed the effects of the earthquake around us. I saw several homes as well as a small bridge crossing a creek near Cemetery Hill collapse. It was, I suppose, after about one-half to three quarters of a minute when the earthquake shaking began to subside. At that time I heard a great roar coming from Huascarán. Looking up, I saw what appeared to be a cloud of dust and it looked as though a large mass of rock and ice was breaking loose from the north peak. My immediate reaction was to run for the high ground of Cemetery Hill, situated about 150 to 200 m away. I began running and noticed that there were others in Yungay who were also running toward Cemetery Hill. About half to three-quarters of the way up the hill, the wife of my friend stumbled and fell and I turned to help her back to her feet.

The crest of the wave had a curl, like a huge breaker coming in from the ocean. I estimated the wave to be at least 80 m high. I observed hundreds of people in Yungay running in all directions and many of them towards Cemetery Hill. All the while, there was a continuous loud roar and rumble. I reached the upper level of the cemetery near the top just as the debris flow struck the base of the hill and I was probably only 10 seconds ahead of it.

At about the same time, I saw a man just a few meters down hill who was carrying two small children toward the hilltop. The debris flow caught him and he threw the two children towards the hilltop, out of the path of the flow, to safety, although the debris flow swept him down the valley, never to be seen again. I also remember two women who were no more than a few meters behind me and I never did see them again. Looking around, I counted 92 persons who had also saved themselves by running to the top of the hill. It was the most horrible thing I have ever experienced and I will never forget it. (Cited in Bolt et al. 1975, p. 39)

These landslides were exceptionally large and involved millions of cubic meters of material; most are smaller, but also of greater frequency. Their efficacy in transporting material downslope and in changing the face of the landscape is tremendous. It is difficult to spend much time in mountains without seeing landslide scars and deposits (Fig. 6.27). Like many other processes in mountains, the landslide is a low-frequency, high-energy event capable of accomplishing more geomorphic work in a few seconds than day-to-day processes accomplish in centuries (Tricart et al. 1961; Starkel 1976). It is important to realize, however, that although the landslide is a sudden and intense event, it depends in many ways upon the less spectacular processes which have been slowly preparing the way for its eventual release.

Specific causes of landslides are usually divided into two groups: internal condition of the rocks, and external factors affecting slopes. The first group includes such factors as weak rock formations, steeply dipping rock with bedding planes, joints, fault zones, and steep slopes; the second group includes climatic factors, erosion, and different kinds of disturbances such as earthquakes (Howe 1909, p. 49; Sharpe 1938, p. 84). It is difficult to point to any single factor responsible for a landslide. The Turtle Mountain slide at Frank, Alberta, is a good example of the interaction of several slide-causing factors. The mountain stood 940 m (3,100 ft.) above the valley and was composed of massive limestones overthrust across softer sandstones and shales, which formed a natural zone of weakness. This weakness was further exaggerated by coal-mining in an interlying seam, which decreased the cohesiveness of the material; finally, several

Fig. 6.27. Debris of landslide near Flimerstein, Switzerland, on April 10, 1939. It buried several houses and killed 11 people. (Swissair photo)

earthquakes had shaken the area within the previous two years. The precise trigger that caused the mountain to collapse is unknown, but this combination of factors surely led to its eventual release. Over 30,000,000 m³ (39,240,000 yd.³) of rock buried the town and railroad and killed 70 people. Only part of the mountain fell, however; the north shoulder still stands, an ever-present threat to the people of the now rebuilt town. The mountain may stand for centuries with no further problems; on the other hand, it may only require the slightest trigger to release another tremendous landslide.

Features of Mass-Wasting

Many surface forms result from the mass-wasting processes just described. Some of these occur as specific features, e.g., stone stripes or solifluction lobes. Other, less distinct features are simply identified as various sorts of deposits, e.g., mudflow or landslide deposits. Three features deserve special mention because of their distinctive character and importance in the alpine landscape; these are talus, protalus ramparts, and rock glaciers.

Talus

A *talus* is an accumulation of rocks at the base of a cliff, headwall, or slope. It results primarily from rocks breaking off and falling until they come to rest to form a ramp or rock apron (Fig. 6.28). Also known as *scree* or simply *rock-debris slopes*, talus accumulations are best developed above timberline, where there is little vegetation and frost action causes rapid breakdown and displacement of rocks (Behre 1933; Rapp 1960). Most active talus accumulations are bare and rocky with very little fine material visible, but where mudflows, avalanches, and landslides have contributed to the talus, fine material may be present (Gardner 1970b; Luckman 1971, 1972, 1978; Gray 1972). Because the larger rocks have more kinetic energy and hence travel farther, the rock debris will show a rough gradation in size,

with the larger rocks at the bottom of the slope (Rapp 1960, p. 97; Bones 1973, p. 32). The downslope sorting will not be perfect, however, since the rock size, shape, height of fall, nature of surface, and interference from other processes will affect this arrangement (Gardner 1971).

The status of a talus slope is determined by: (1) the supply of material; (2) the movement of material within the talus; and (3) the removal of material. The rate of talus accumulation provides a gross index of the rate of weathering and denudation in mountain environments. For example, in an area of glacial erosion where a bare bedrock surface was left after glacial melting, any talus which exists has obviously accumulated since that time (Fig. 6.39). Recent measurements based on the rate of cliff retreat in the Colorado Rockies reveal a rate of 0.76 mm/yr. (0.03 in./yr.), with a seasonal peak of activity in spring and early summer (Caine 1974, p. 728). Similar rates have been measured in the Canadian Rockies of Alberta (Gardner 1970c; Gray 1972). Movement within the talus may also be substantial because of rockfall, snow avalanches, mudflows, running water, creep, and the removal of material from below by stream action. The average rate of surface movement is probably about 20 cm/yr. (8 in./yr.) above timberline in the Rocky Mountains, although measurements of such features are circumstantial—individual rocks may move great distances while others remain motionless (Gardner 1973; Kirby and Statham 1975). There is also considerable regional variability depending on the local environment, slope orientation, gradient, and rock type.

In some areas the talus is now inactive. Evidence for this includes lack of new material from above, heavy presence of lichens, weathering rinds on rock surfaces, infilling of rock voids by fine material, and encroachment by vegetation. Inactive taluses may be seen at lower elevations in some mountainous areas; presumably, they were

Fig. 6.28. Talus accumulation along a glaciated valley in the Ruby Mountains, Yukon Territory. Material is composed of angular rocks which have broken off from above and tumbled downslope. Small mudflow channels can be seen cutting across the talus, suggesting that this process may make significant contributions to the total accumulation. Larger rocks are at the base, due to their greater momentum of fall. To provide sense of scale: the large white rock in center foreground is 1.5 m (5 ft.) in diameter. (Author)

created under more extreme conditions in the past, i.e., when glaciers extended to lower elevations. This is particularly likely where talus is actively forming at higher elevations in the same mountain region today. Although talus formation is best developed in cold climatic regimes, it may also form in other environments (Hack 1960), so its interpretation as evidence of a cold climate must be made with caution.

Protalus Ramparts

A *protalus rampart* is an accumulation of rocky debris found near the base of a slope but separated from it by a small trough or depression (Bryan 1934) (Fig. 6.29). Such features are usually oriented parallel to the slope. They are closely related to talus in that they are built from falling rocks, but they accumulate as isolated ridges, benches, or mounds because of snow (Richmond 1962, p. 20; Yeend 1972). A snowcovered surface or a late snow patch at the base of a slope provides an elevated surface on which the rocks move; after the snow melts, the rocky ridge is all that remains (Fig. 6.30).

Protalus ramparts are best developed above timberline in shaded spots near steep

Fig. 6.29. Protalus ramparts occurring at an elevation of 2,700 m (9,000 ft.) on the floor of a north-facing cirque in the Wallowa Mountains, Oregon. Rocks from above tumble onto snowcovered slopes and slide to the bottom, where they accumulate as small arcuate ridges. (Author, July 1973)

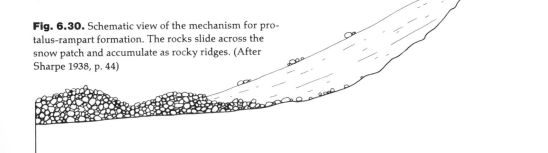

Fig. 6.30. Schematic view of the mechanism for pro-talus-rampart formation. The rocks slide across the snow patch and accumulate as rocky ridges. (After Sharpe 1938, p. 44)

Fig. 6.31. An active rock glacier in the St. Elias
Mountains, Yukon Territory. Both lateral and terminal
moraines can be seen. Vegetation grows around the
margins, where the material has been stabilized. Elevation at base is 1,200 m (3,800 ft.), which coincides with
the timberline for this region. (Author)

rock walls or in cirques where there is ample rock material and where abundant snow accumulates and melts slowly throughout the summer. Protalus ramparts resemble glacial moraines, in that they occur as arcuate sinuous ridges, but they are usually restricted to within 100 m (330 ft.) of the slope base and they consist of larger rocks with very little fine debris. The average height is 2–4 m (7–13 ft.), but they have been reported as high as 24 m (80 ft.) (Blagbrough and Breed 1967). Since their formation depends upon the existence of snow, protalus ramparts may be helpful in interpreting past environments. Their presence at lower elevations where snow does not now persist, for example, may indicate the former existence of a much lower snowline as well as that of a more severe frost climate (Blagbrough and Breed 1967; Washburn 1973, p. 199).

Rock Glaciers

Rock glaciers are accumulations of rocky debris with a form similar to that of true glaciers (Fig. 6.31). They head in cirques or steep-walled cliffs, have glacier-like features—including a lobate front or tongue, lateral and medial moraines, conical pits, crevasses, and lobes—and those that are active display movement throughout in much the same way a glacier does. Nevertheless, they are composed primarily of rocks, and as such, are among the most intriguing of all geomorphic forms.

Rock glaciers are commonly narrowest in their upper reaches, spreading outward in their distal parts, particularly after they pass through the confines of a narrow valley (Fig. 6.31). They vary from a few hundred meters to over a kilometer in length and average from 15–45 m (50–150 ft.) in thickness. Active rock glaciers are almost twice as thick as inactive ones (Wahrhaftig and Cox 1959, p. 383). They may be lichen-covered, with fine material and scattered vegetation on the surface; if they extend below treeline, trees may become established even though an

active rock glacier makes a very unstable environment (Fig. 6.32). Rock glaciers are best developed in areas where there is a continual supply of block material delivered from upslope. The rock size depends upon the rock type and structure as well as upon the nature of the local environment. I have seen rock glaciers in the mountains of Yu-

Fig. 6.32. A live spruce tree growing on a rock glacier tongue in the St. Elias Mountains, Yukon Territory. This section of the rock glacier is apparently being reactivated, since the fresh color of the wood and the presence of fresh sap indicate that the tree has been split apart only in the last year or so. (Author)

kon Territory, Canada, composed entirely
of walnut-sized rocks and others only a few
kilometers away composed of blocks which
average 2–3 m (7–10 ft.) in diameter.

Although not as abundant and ubiquitous
as talus, rock glaciers are well-developed in
many middle- and high-latitude mountains.
They are apparently not present in tropical
mountains, and are at best poorly developed
in middle-latitude mountains with marine
climates. They reach their finest development in continental mountains where there
is rather poor snow cover and where low
temperatures and frost action prevail. For
example, in North America they do not occur on the Pacific side of the Sierra Nevada,
the Cascades, the Olympics, or the Coast
ranges of Canada and Alaska (at least up
to Cook Inlet), but they do occur on the
leeward side of all these mountains (Thompson 1962a). There is an interesting relationship between true glaciers and rock
glaciers in western North America: true glaciers occur on the windward Pacific side of
the mountains, while rock glaciers occur on
the drier, more continental eastern side.
Nevertheless, the occurrence of rock glaciers
even on the leeward side of these maritime
ranges is sporadic and restricted to isolated
locations where conditions are ideal. They
generally do not achieve the level of development displayed in the more continental
mountains of the interior (except to the lee
of the Coast ranges in Canada and Alaska,
where they are very well-developed.)

Controversy surrounds the origin of rock
glaciers. Because of their similarity to true
glaciers, some investigators have believed
that rock glaciers are nothing more than ice
glaciers that have been covered by rocky
material (Kesseli 1941), while others have
maintained that they can form independently of pre-existing glaciers (Wahrhaftig
and Cox 1959). Still others have argued that
they are the result of landslides (Howe
1909). It is possible that each of these explanations correctly accounts for the formation of some rock glaciers. It has been clearly

established that rock glaciers can and do
develop without the presence of an ice glacier. This is proved by their development in
unglaciated alpine areas such as the San
Mateo Mountains of New Mexico (Blagbrough and Farkas 1968). It is also well-established that they move at a fairly constant
rate and are not dependent upon landslides
for their origin. In some cases, rock glaciers
may be former ice glaciers that have been
buried by rock debris; in others, rock glaciers may have formed simply from accumulations of rocks from above, achieving
their classic form through slow downslope
movement. Rock glaciers occur in all sorts of
transitional states between true glaciers,
morainal features, talus, protalus ramparts,
and even blockfields (Lliboutry 1953, 1977;
Thompson 1962a; Blagbrough and Farkas
1968; Caine and Jennings 1969; Barsch 1971,
1977; Östrem 1971; Benedict 1973; Smith
1973; White 1976b).

Rock glaciers are active in many alpine
environments but inactive in others. Evidence of activity includes freshly overturned
and exposed rocks, uplifted or depressed
zones, disrupted vegetation cover, and burial of material at the front. If the rock glacier
is active, ice of some sort, either an ice core
or interstitial ice, is usually present, which
accounts for its movement (Potter 1972).
From this point of view, then, active rock
glaciers may be considered as secondary
evidence for the presence of permafrost
(Barsch 1977). One very characteristic feature of active rock glaciers (as well as of
some that are inactive) is an ice-cold stream
issuing from the base throughout the summer.

Rates of rock-glacier movement vary
from a few centimeters per year in the
Rocky Mountains of Colorado and Wyoming (White 1971a, b, 1976b; Potter 1972),
to an average of about 0.5 m (1.7 ft.) per year
in the subarctic mountains of Yukon and
Alaska (Wahrhaftig and Cox 1959; Johnson
1973). It is estimated that, in the Alaska
Range, the material contributed to the

growth of rock glaciers represents a denudation rate on bedrock walls of 0.4–1 m (1.3–3.3 ft.) per century (Wahrhaftig and Cox 1959, p. 434). In the Swiss Alps, rock-glacier activity amounts to 20 percent of all mass-wasting (Barsch 1977).

NIVATION

The presence of late-lying snow patches on mountain slopes may contribute markedly to localized erosion through a number of related processes known collectively as *nivation*. Nivation includes frost action, mass-wasting, rill and sheet wash from melting snow, and movement within the snow itself (Embleton and King 1975b). Nivation and its effects have already been mentioned in passing, but it is an important and distinctive process in its own right. Nivation is restricted to the snowline area, and is essentially a transitional process occupying the narrow interface between the glacial and periglacial systems (Fig. 6.4).

Nivation works in a variety of ways. The presence of snow may increase the efficiency of chemical weathering, as is indicated by the greater thickness of weathering rinds in such sites (Thorn 1975, 1976). Snow lowers the temperature of the immediate surroundings and thereby increases the number of freeze-thaw cycles (Gardner 1969). Of course, snow may at the same time insulate and protect the surface it covers, but as the snow melts, more and more of the surface will be exposed, so that the freeze-and-thaw zone migrates with the retreating edge of the snow cover. The water released by melting provides the moisture necessary to allow the effective operation of frost-wedging and other frost-action processes. As a result, snow accumulation sites frequently display a greater abundance of frost rubble than do surrounding areas (Lewis 1939). Nivation also provides an effective means of transporting the frost-shattered· rock downslope. This may take place through melt-

water runoff and from increased rates of frost creep and solifluction (Ekblaw 1918; Thorn 1976, 1979b). Movement within the snow may also contribute to minor downslope movement of debris, as well as abrading rock surfaces (Costin et al. 1973).

The net effect of nivation is the creation of hollows and depressions in bedrock (St.-Onge 1969). In late-lying snow patches, the snow countersinks slowly into the slope. Once begun, this is a self-perpetuating process: the larger the depression, the more snow that will accumulate and the longer it will take to melt in summer, thereby increasing its erosive effect. The shape and orientation of the depressions depend upon the configuration of the land with respect to wind and sun, which, in turn, control the amount of snow accumulation and the rate of melting. Lewis (1939) identified three types of nivation hollow: transverse, longitudinal, and circular. The transverse hollow occurs when snow accumulates in horizontal bands along the contour, eventually resulting in benches or terraces (Fig. 6.33). The longitudinal hollow develops when snow accumulates in elongated stream valleys or gullies, widening and deepening the pre-established depressions. The circular type is an amphitheater-like depression resulting from snow gathered as a central mass. This occurs along ridge crests, where snow accumulates in pockets and creates circular notches or bowls resembling small cirques.

Nivation, with frost action and mass-wasting, is a powerful tool for rock sculpture and erosion in cold climates. In many areas, benches, terraces, and rounded or flattened summits are attributed to the combined workings of these processes. Such features, called *altiplanation* (*cryoplanation*) terraces, are well-documented in several middle- and high-latitude mountain regions (Demek 1969a, b, 1972; Pewe 1970; Pinczes 1974; Reger and Pewe 1976) (Fig. 6.34). Demek (1969a) has identified three main stages in the development of altiplanation terraces.

First, nivation hollows form where the snow accumulates in horizontal bands along the contour. The depressions are enlarged and a small bench or terrace is created, which increases the ability of the area to hold snow. The headwall or cliff of the terrace is slowly eaten headward by frost-shattering, and the debris is broken down and transported across the terrace by a combination of frost action, running water, and mass-wasting. Eventually the cliff is entirely consumed, and in the final stage a rounded or flattened summit is produced (Figs. 6.34, 6.39). The rate of altiplanation-terrace formation varies under different conditions but apparently one can develop in a few thousand years (Demek 1969a, p. 124). Relict forms are thought to be widespread but identification

and interpretation of them must be made with great care, because other processes operating in warm climates may produce similar features. Where their identity is confirmed, they provide excellent evidence for periglacial conditions (Washburn 1973, p. 208).

STREAM ACTION

Ever since very ancient times, mountains have been recognized as a source of water. Mountains are the starting-place for many of the world's major streams, and this water is more important to human populations now than ever before. Irrigation, power production, navigation, recreation,

Fig. 6.33. A late-lying snow patch near summer's end on a northeast-facing slope in the Ruby Range, Yukon Territory. Note the rock that has slid halfway across the snow from upslope. The fairly level surface below the snow is apparently a result of nivation processes eroding the hillside. (Author)

Fig. 6.34. Cryoplanation surfaces in the Old Man Range, Central Otago, New Zealand. Elevation is 1,640 m (5,400 ft.). This is largely a fossil landscape formed under more severe conditions. The rocky remnants above the general surface level are called *tors*. (J. D. McCraw, University of Otago)

and commercial and domestic consumption are but a few of the uses of mountain streams. One need only think of streams such as the Danube, which rises in the Alps and mountains of eastern Europe, the great Indo-Gangetic rivers that head in the Himalayas, or the Nile, which rises in the mountains of East Africa and Ethiopia, to appreciate their great significance to the areas through which they flow. The source of a stream and the direction of its flow are essential geographic facts. The hydrologic center of the continental United States is in the Rocky Mountains near Yellowstone National Park, where three great rivers —the Snake, the Colorado, and the Mis-souri—have their sources. The downstream components of each of these are vital to the regions through which they flow. If you have ever seen any of these rivers, or others like them, you know that they are typically laden with sediment, particularly during the spring runoff.

While running water is the most important denudational agent for the earth as a whole, in mountains it is probably less important than mass-wasting. The vast amounts of material transported downslope by creep and solifluction and the speed and size of mudflows, rockfalls, avalanches, and landslides bear this out. Nevertheless, precipitation does increase in mountains, at least up to a certain elevation, and this water has a high potential energy, owing to the presence of steep slopes and high local relief. In addition, the frequent bare areas, with abundant surface detritus and little protective vegetation, of mountain landscapes are vulnerable to erosion by running water (Soons and Rayner 1968; Dingwall 1972). Much of the sediment load of streams is probably obtained from slopes adjacent to small tributaries eating headward at the upper ends of drainage basins. In the Amazon Basin, for example, it is estimated that 85 percent of the total stream load is provided by just 12 percent of the drainage area where tributaries head in the high Andes (Bloom 1978, p. 287). Streams also reach far beyond the mountains, while mass-wasting is limited to specific slope regimes within the alpine system. Streams serve as linkages to the lowlands and, ultimately, to the sea. Mountains may be worn down primarily by frost action and mass-wasting; but if streams did not transport at least some of the material away, the valleys would eventually be buried by the detritus. The fact that this does not happen is evidence for the importance of streams.

Actually, mountain watersheds, especially those containing glaciers, have one of the greatest erosional rates on earth (Corbel 1959). The upper Indus and Kosi rivers draining the Himalayas reflect a regional denudational rate of 1.0 mm/yr. (0.04 in./yr.) (Hewitt 1972, p. 18). Other mountain ranges may also approach this rate. The Alps are estimated to be eroding at between 0.4–1.0 mm/yr. (0.01–0.04 in./yr.) (Clark and Jäger 1969). Mountains in humid tropical climates may display even more rapid rates of erosion (Ruxton and McDougall 1967) (Fig. 6.3). The Canadian Rockies and the mountains of Alaska are being denuded at a rate of up to 0.6 mm/yr. (0.02 in./yr.) (McPherson 1971a; Slaymaker 1972, 1974; Slaymaker and McPherson 1977), although the Rocky Mountains in Colorado and

Wyoming reflect the somewhat lower rate of 0.1 mm/yr. (0.004 in./yr.) (Caine 1974, p. 741).

Characteristics of Mountain Streams

Mountain streams are similar to other streams in most respects, but they do have special attributes. The water flows down steep slopes through highly varied terrain with great local relief; the moisture supply is highly variable, depending upon rainfall, melting snow, and ice; and the debris delivered to the streams is often too large to be transported effectively. The physical behavior of water in mountains, though, is no different from that in any other natural environment. When the gradient or volume increases, so do the velocity and the ability of the stream to transport material. Since all of these factors change rapidly in mountains on both a spatial and temporal basis, a flux or pulsation is frequently displayed within the system. This can be seen in the velocity of a stream between steep slopes and valley flats; between streams and interconnecting pools or lakes; between the melting rates of day and night; and with the sudden addition of thunderstorm rain, to note only a few circumstances.

The smaller streams in high mountains are ephemeral, flowing only at certain times of the year (Leopold and Miller 1956). Perennial streams are found at lower elevations, where there is a greater drainage network to feed them. The volume and velocity of streams also increase on lower mountain slopes, making these regions more liable to stream erosion (although this is counteracted somewhat by better-developed vegetation). The relationship of drainage area to stream volume can be understood by considering a single peak where mountain mass and area decrease with elevation; consequently, the surface available for the reception of precipitation is reduced. The slopes are steep and fre-

quently composed of bare, poorly vegetated bedrock surfaces, with little reservoir
capacity for holding or slowing the rate of
runoff. The peak is exposed to strong winds,
so snow accumulation is limited to a thin
carapace and to sheltered nooks. High peaks
are among the driest of environments; it is
often possible to observe from a distance,
e.g., across the valley, the level where rills
and gullies disappear, indicating the lack of
channel flow above this point. On the other
hand, snow may accumulate to the lee of
some peaks and result in the formation of
glaciers and cirque basins, producing a
steady and copious supply of meltwater
through the summer (although it may be
limited to a single stream-valley).

The typical mountain stream is steepest in
its upper reaches and gradually flattens
downstream to form a concave longitudinal
profile. Rocky ledges and other abrupt
changes in the local relief create waterfalls.
In semiarid mountains, the channels of
ephemeral streams often consist of a series
of steps composed of larger rocks interspersed with sand patches. This is apparently a response to intermittently heavy runoff
and flooding, which first scour and then
refill the bed (Wertz 1966; Heede 1975).
Downstream, channel width increases and
the bed material tends to become finer
(Miller 1958; Fahnestock 1963; McPherson
1971b).

High mountain streams typically have
small discharges and low velocities despite
their steep slopes. They are consequently
able to transport little of the larger material
delivered to them by mass-wasting. The
size-sorting downstream and the characteristic clearness of the water in high-mountain
streams even at full-bank flow are evidence
of this. The beds of mountain streams, originating from present or past weathering
and mass-wasting processes, consist of gravel or boulders. The water flows around and
between these boulders, which are really
more a part of the channel than of the bed-

load. Glacial meltstreams are an exception to
the typical clear rushing brooks found in
many mountains: they have a more continuous supply of fine sediment, particularly
during late summer afternoons when heavy
melting is taking place. I have crossed glacial
meltstreams late in the day when the water
was a raging torrent, and I could hear the
dull thud of rocks being bounced along the
stream and could feel them passing around
my boots while crossing.

A dominant characteristic of most lowland streams is the presence of alternating
deep and shallow areas. Typically, a deep
area exists on one side of the stream while a
gravel bar or shallow area exists on the
opposite side. These bars tend to alternate
from one side of the channel to the other.
Smooth-water pools often form over the
deeper areas and riffles (or rapids) over the
bars, features well-known to trout fishermen. There is evidence, however, that many
high mountain streams, especially those
under semiarid regimes, lack pools and
riffles (Miller 1958, p. 49). This is apparently
because of the dominance of coarse bed
material; the typically small discharges
are unable to move the larger material.
In more humid mountains, e.g., the Rockies,
streams do exhibit pools and riffles but their
spacing is much more variable than in lowland streams (Leopold et al. 1964, p. 207;
Heede 1975). Flood plains and natural levees
are less common in high mountains than
in lowlands, since the streams tend to be
confined to bedrock channels and tend not
to overflow their banks. There may be occasional valley flats but these are often
formed by other processes, e.g., morainic
dams, landslides, and avalanches, rather
than being strictly a result of stream action
(Hack and Goodlett 1960, p. 53). Mountain
streams with bedrock channels display little
meandering except in stretches of lower
gradient, such as mountain meadows, but
their channels are also not perfectly straight
(Miller 1958, p. 49).

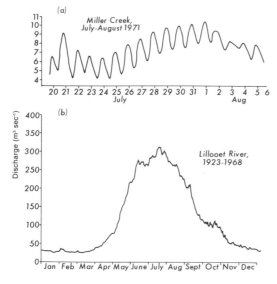

Fig. 6.35. The discharge hydrograph of two mountain streams in British Columbia on a daily (a) and annual (b) basis. Glacial meltwater contributes markedly to runoff in both cases. (After Slaymaker 1974, p. 148)

Discharge Regime

The dominant flow characteristic of mountain streams is their periodicity, on a daily as well as a seasonal basis. The tendency toward intermittent flow has already been mentioned. Snowmelt is reduced at night and increases during the day (the exact amount depends upon the weather and local site conditions). Consequently, streams supplied by meltwater carry their greatest volume during the afternoon and early evening and their lowest volume during the early morning. The resulting hydrograph displays a high daily fluctuation in flow during the summer (Fig. 6.35a) (Slaymaker 1974, p. 149). Much of the winter precipitation falls as snow and stays in the high country until temperatures rise in the spring. Many high mountain streams freeze and the flow decreases to a trickle (except in tropical or middle-latitude coastal mountains where temperatures are not as low and rainfall or wet snow is common throughout the winter). In the summer, however, water stored in the form of snow is

released by melting and the streams fill. This may result in near-flood conditions for short periods in the spring (Fig. 6.35b). In some years, great damage is done in the lower stream channels and to bridges and highways.

Where alpine glaciers exist, the normal spring runoff is augmented by glacial melting. Streams must also carry the normal seasonal increase in precipitation that most continental areas experience during summer. In summer, unlike winter, mountains cannot store much water, so thunderstorm rainfall surges quickly through the drainage network. In the San Juan Mountains of southern Colorado, erosional rates are three to four times greater in summer than in winter, owing to the intensity of summer thunderstorms (Caine 1976). Exceptionally heavy precipitation can set off flash floods, with an even greater potential for erosion (Beaty 1959). These are major environmental hazards to settlements in and near semi-arid mountains. For example, Salt Lake City, Utah, where over a million people live in a narrow belt along the Wasatch Front (Fig. 10.19), has had an average of three major cloudburst or flash floods every summer for the last century (Marsell 1972). The sparsely vegetated slopes allow rapid runoff and the water collects in the major drainage ways, quickly picking up velocity and becoming charged with mud and rocky debris. Upon reaching the base of the mountains, the streams overflow their banks, or if there is no defined streambed, the water and debris disperse in fans; the mud and rocky debris bury the surface and cause considerable damage. Until recently, the loss was principally of outbuildings, highways, and farmlands. With increasing pressure for land, however, housing developments are pushing higher and higher up the slopes and, in some cases, literally into the canyon mouths. The streets may even follow the streambed. This is foolhardy, but paradoxically, the people most affected are often those living in older established areas on lower slopes. The construction of paved streets and roads up the canyon mouths provides impermeable channels for flash-flood waters to move swiftly downslope, whereas large amounts of water used to sink into the rocky ground, lessening the potential for damage in lowlands and contributing to groundwater recharge. Now, however, much more of the water is directed to the foot slopes, with considerable potential for damage. This is a case in which strong and effective land-use planning is required.

There is disagreement about when streams accomplish the most work. It has long been believed that major floods and catastrophic events can accomplish more erosion in a short time than day-to-day flow can accomplish in centuries. Measurements of several streams, however, including some streams draining mountain areas, indicate that the bulk of the erosion is accomplished by normal flow and by modest floods occurring once or twice a year rather than by the rarer and more catastrophic floods (Wolman and Miller 1960; Leopold et al. 1964, p. 71). This evidence is countered by a number of other studies which indicate that much of the transport and erosion of streams, as well as mass-wasting, is accomplished in only a few days of a decade or century, rather than on a more regularly spaced annual basis (Beaty 1974b; Rapp 1974; Rapp et al. 1972; Rapp and Strömquist 1976; Starkel 1976). It will probably be a number of years before the controversy is resolved, but the argument for the efficacy of infrequent but larger events appears to have more validity in mountains than in lowlands because of the greater potential in mountains for intermittent and spectacular events. This is particularly true of mountain streams with a bedload of cobbles and boulders, since only peak or catastrophic events allow the movement of such material (Beaty 1959; Steward and LaMarche 1967; Nanson 1974). It is during these times that the truly awesome potential of running water is demonstrated.

Drainage Features

A number of drainage features reach their finest development in mountains. These include braided channels, alluvial fans, and asymmetric valleys. The basic drainage patterns, when viewed from the air or from a map, are also strikingly diagnostic of geomorphic processes and reflect the presence of certain types of rocks, structures, and past geologic events.

Braided Channels

Braided streams consist of shallow intertwined channels that divide and reunite within a sediment-choked streambed (Fig. 6.36). Braiding occurs when there is too much coarse bedload material for the stream to transport in a single deep channel. The excess sediment is deposited in bars or miniature islands and the water divides to flow around it. This raises the streambed, increasing the slope and downstream velocity. At the same time, the channel is made shallower, which increases the flow velocity along the streambed and allows a larger amount of bedload to be carried at the same discharge. Braided sections of streams display gradients several times steeper than sections with single channels. Consequently, the shallow but relatively steep channels of braided streams facilitate the transport of coarse particles along the stream bottom; deeper streams cannot do this because the highest velocities occur near the water surface, which is far removed from the streambed. Braiding, therefore, can be viewed as a natural response by streams to an increased bedload consisting of material too large for transport by a single channel.

Braided channels reach their finest development in arid mountain regions where runoff is rapid and periodic. Many glacial streams display excellent braiding because of the abundant debris contributed to the stream by glacial melting. Braiding is also found in intermediate-sized streams fed by smaller streams that originate on higher and

Fig. 6.36. A braided channel in the Wrangell Mountains, Alaska. Most of the bed material is too coarse for the small stream to carry, so it simply works its way through the material, dividing and reuniting. (Author)

steeper slopes. The small but turbulent streams often transport coarser material to the valley bottom than the intermediate stream can carry in a single normal channel. Non-braided channels may also become braided as a result of human disturbance in areas of steep slopes, e.g., logging, agriculture, or hydraulic mining.

Braided channels typically have fairly wide valleys without confining walls, and the water occupies only a small part of the total streambed. In many cases the braided stream has inherited a valley greatly widened and deepened by glacial action. Braided channels are composed of poorly sorted material varying from fine silt, sand, and gravel to cobbles and boulders. Mid-chan-

nel bars composed of this loosely consolidated material are subject to continuous erosion as the current impinges upon their flanks. During high stream discharges, erosion takes place on the upstream ends of the bars, with deposition occurring at their downstream ends. Thus, the bars are continually changing shape and migrating downstream, but their overall appearance remains similar. The channels themselves display much greater variations, since they are subject to rapid changes during periods of high runoff. This may happen within a matter of minutes or hours, or it may take much longer. The White River draining the Emmons Glacier on Mount Rainier, Washington, has moved laterally more than 100 m

(330 ft.) in eight days (Fahnestock 1963, p. 48). Large braided streams may display even greater lateral displacement. The extreme is demonstrated by the Kosi River which rises near Mount Everest in Nepal and eventually empties into the Ganges. At one point along its channel the Kosi has migrated westward a distance of 112 km (70 mi.) over the last 200 years. The river is also known to have shifted 19 km (12 mi.) in a single year (Leopold et al. 1964, p. 291).

Alluvial Fans

Alluvial fans are cone or fan-shaped deposits occurring at the mouths of mountain valleys or canyons where streams debouch onto the lowlands. The stream at this point loses velocity (and therefore drops some of its load) since the gradient is reduced. Moreover, the stream is no longer confined to a steep-walled valley with a bedrock channel, so it may spread laterally, transforming into a braided pattern, diffusing its energy, and meandering amid the deposited sediment. The resulting debris accumulation builds up in the form of a cone or fan with the apex at the valley mouth and an outward slope to a semicircular perimeter (Fig. 6.37). The larger material is dropped first; smaller-sized material is transported farther (McPherson and Hirst 1972). Alluvial fans are essentially composed of that portion of the bedload

Fig. 6.37. An alluvial fan in the St. Elias Mountains, Yukon Territory. The fan has been deposited onto the flood plain of the Slim's River, indicating a relatively young age. Note that the left side of the feature is forested, while the right side is largely bare, owing to recent activity in this area. The stream now appears to be moving to the left and encroaching on the forest. Alluvial fans serve as good indicators of the amount of erosion and other geomorphic activities taking place in mountains. (Author)

which mountain streams have been unable to transport farther. In general, the larger the upland watershed and source region, the larger the alluvial fan (Denny 1967).

Alluvial fans occur in all kinds of environments and present a multitude of forms, but they are best developed in arid and semiarid mountains where stream flow is intermittent and much of the deposition takes place during times of flood and heavy runoff (Beaty 1963, 1974b; Denny 1967; Cooke and Warren 1973). Mudflow may also contribute to the construction of alluvial fans, especially in semiarid and polar mountains (Blackwelder 1928; Beaty 1963, 1974b; Slaymaker and McPherson 1977). In some cases the streams may flow throughout the year, but the water does not usually reach far out onto the alluvial fan before it sinks into the coarse sediments and disappears. This results in the curious situation of increasing discharge and velocity downstream in mountains but decreasing discharge and velocity down the alluvial fan. Upon reaching the lowlands, the stream deposits part of its load, contributing to fan construction and infilling its channel in the mountains. This produces a smooth concave profile upward from the valley floor and well into the adjacent highlands (Denny 1967, p. 83). If stream flow is strong and continuous, it may cut a deeper channel near the fan head, making it difficult for the stream to escape, so fan deposition ceases and the feature becomes inactive (at least in its upper reaches). In actively building fans, the channel does not become fixed but, instead, weaves back and forth across the fan surface over the years like a huge serpent periodically visiting its domain (Fig. 6.37). Accordingly, one side of the fan may be gaining material from deposition while the other side is being gullied and eroded. Each stream valley opening onto the lowlands may have its own alluvial fan and adjacent fans may eventually coalesce to form a relatively large apron of debris at the base of the mountain front. Major examples include the Great Valley of California along the western margin of the Sierra Nevada, the Vale of Chile at the base of the Andes, the Tarim Basin of western China, and the Samarkand district of Russian Turkestan along the base of the Hindu Kush, Pamir, and Tien Shan.

Alluvial fans are key areas for agriculture and settlement in mountainous regions because of their relatively smooth surfaces, productive soils, and availability of water. Water is the primary factor, of course, particularly in the drier regions. Streams are sometimes dammed in the mountains and the water diverted for use, while in other areas wells are drilled into the fan. Alluvial fans provide excellent aquifers and are good sources of groundwater. A major contributing factor is the method of fan construction: the finer particles are carried to the perimeter, where they accumulate as fine and dense sediments with a relatively low permeability. There they help dam the groundwater, preventing outflow and maintaining a higher water table. In parts of Asia from China to Iran, and in North Africa along the Atlas Mountains, tunnels have been dug laterally into alluvial fans to tap groundwater located by exploratory wells sunk at the stops of the fans. These tunnels, known as *qanats* or *foggaras*, are specimens of an ancient technology practiced long before the birth of Christ (English 1968). Qanats often extend for several kilometers and reach depths of several hundred meters before reaching the water table. Vertical shafts are sunk to the tunnel at short intervals to allow removal of excavated material, to provide air for the workmen below, and to provide later access to the tunnel for maintenance (Fig. 6.38). When viewed from the air, these shafts and the excavated material piled around them look like a line of doughnuts. Although modern pumped wells are now becoming common in Central Asia, qanats are still the major source of water. Literally thousands of such features dot the surface of alluvial fans in this region, providing a continuous supply of water for

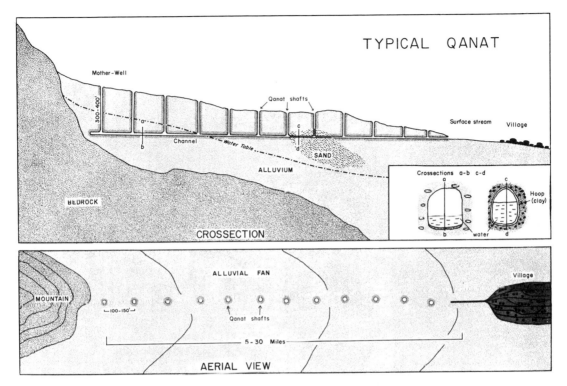

Fig. 6.38. Schematic representation of a typical qanat in central Asia, showing both cross-section and aerial view. The inset shows the tunnel and how clay hoops are used in soft areas to prevent collapse. (From English 1968, p. 171)

irrigation and the maintenance of fairly large populations (Cressey 1958; Wulff 1968; English 1968).

Valley Asymmetry

An *asymmetric valley* is one in which one side is steeper than the other (Fig. 6.39). Such features are common in mountains, and where a clear tendency toward valley asymmetry occurs, it may provide valuable information on stream-valley history. The most obvious cause of asymmetric slopes is geologic structure: the dip and strike or other characteristics of the rock control the orientation and relative gradients of slopes. In other cases, valley asymmetry may occur without any significant structural control, or even in opposition to the basic lithology.

This often happens where streams impinge against slopes and steepen them by erosion. Melton (1960) saw this as happening primarily when larger and more powerful tributaries on one side of the valley directed the force of the main stream against the opposite slope. An equally important factor is sediment production, since the deposition of excess bedload or the building of alluvial fans will also tend to force the main stream toward the opposite valley wall. In the Karakoram Himalayas, for example, the north-facing slopes have relatively large, clear streams which persist through the summer, while those on the drier, more poorly vegetated south-facing slopes are smaller and flow only intermittently, but carry a greater sediment load. Consequent-

Fig. 6.39. East-west asymmetric valley in a subarctic alpine environment (Ruby Range, Yukon Territory). The more gentle slope on the left is south-facing. This valley was recently glaciated; unconsolidated material has largely accumulated since melting of the ice. Solifluction is the primary process operating on the south-facing slope and accounts for the displacement of the lakes to the south side of the valley. The major processes operating on the bare and rocky north-facing slope are frost-wedging, nivation, rockfall, and mud-flow. Figure 6.28 provides a closer view of one of the talus cones. The upper surface of this region is relatively gentle, owing to cryoplanation (see also Figure 6.33). (Author)

ly, the main streams are forced against the north-facing slopes (Hewitt 1972, p. 31).

Valley asymmetry may occur in all orientations but there is a tendency for it to be best displayed in east-west valleys where one slope is more exposed to the sun than the other. This has led many geomorphologists to believe that the disproportionate valley sides have developed because of microclimatic and environmental factors (Kennedy 1976). In the northern hemi-sphere, for example, north-facing slopes are generally steeper than south-facing slopes (although many exceptions exist) (Beaty 1962). The basic pattern is apparently created by increased physical weathering, mass-wasting, and runoff from melting snow on the south-facing slopes. Much depends upon regional climatic conditions, of course (Karrasch 1972). In the tropics there is no great difference in sun exposure between north and south slopes; consequently, exposure to wind and rain is more important than exposure to the sun. Thus, in the tradewind belt the windward and leeward slopes (which are basically east- and west-facing) are asymmetric.

In the arid and semiarid regions of middle latitudes, north-facing slopes generally have greater moisture and better-developed vegetation than south-facing slopes, as in the Karakoram example; bare and poorly vegetated slopes are more susceptible to sheet wash and gully erosion and so acquire a longer profile. In polar and subpolar regions where permafrost exists, the depth of thawing is critical to surface processes. South-facing slopes generally display greater solifluction and gentler slopes, while at the same time north-facing slopes undergo greater nivation, resulting in steeper gradients (Currey 1964; Kennedy and Melton 1972). Where solifluction is a dominant process, the accumulation of transported material in the valley may tend to force the streams toward the opposite slopes, accentuating the asymmetry (Fig. 6.39). Conditions similar to this probably existed in middle latitudes during the Pleistocene, and many landscapes retain evidence of their inheritance of periglacial conditions (French 1972a).

Another factor in valley asymmetry is glaciation (Gilbert 1904; Tuck 1935; Evans 1972). Glacial ice may produce steeper north-facing slopes (in the northern hemisphere), because the ice in an east-west valley will tend to be deepest in the shadow of the north-facing slope and thinnest next to the south-facing slope, where greater melting takes place. Therefore, greater deepening and steepening of the south side of the valley ensues. Clearly, valley asymmetry is caused by a number of factors, but it does provide evidence of the operation of certain processes whose identification and proper interpretation can lead to valuable insights into the history and development of landscapes.

Drainage Patterns

The most common drainage pattern on earth is the *dendritic* pattern, which looks like the branches of a tree, with the top being the headwater tributaries and the trunk being the main stream. The dendritic stream pattern develops under homogeneous surface conditions and is generally accepted as evidence for lack of significant structural control. In mountains, however, where stream flow is more strongly controlled by slope and structure, other types of stream patterns develop (Fig. 6.40). The presence of any given type of stream pattern may aid in understanding the geomorphic history of the landscape. For example, a dome or volcanic peak will frequently display a *radial* stream pattern, in which the streams flow outward from the central mountain area like spokes on a wheel (Fig. 6.40a). If the mountain mass is domed upward but with a series of encircling ridges, as in the Black Hills of South Dakota, an *annular* drainage pattern may prevail—the streams follow the circular outcrops of erodible rocks until they find a path through the ridges of resistant rock (Fig. 6.40b). In folded mountains with parallel ridges and valleys such as the Appalachian or Jura mountains, the common pattern is for a main stream to occupy the center of the valley with many short tributary streams joining it at right angles, forming a *trellis* pattern (Fig. 6.40c). Faulting and jointing also greatly affect the direction of stream flow. Many parts of the Adirondack Mountains in New York display a *rectangular* pattern because the streams are forced to make right-angle bends in response to the regional joint system (Fig. 6.40d). Other types of stream patterns could be mentioned, but these are the principal kinds. In general, whenever a rigid or repetitive geometric pattern presents itself or a stream displays very straight segments, it is evidence for some kind of structural control (Howard 1967).

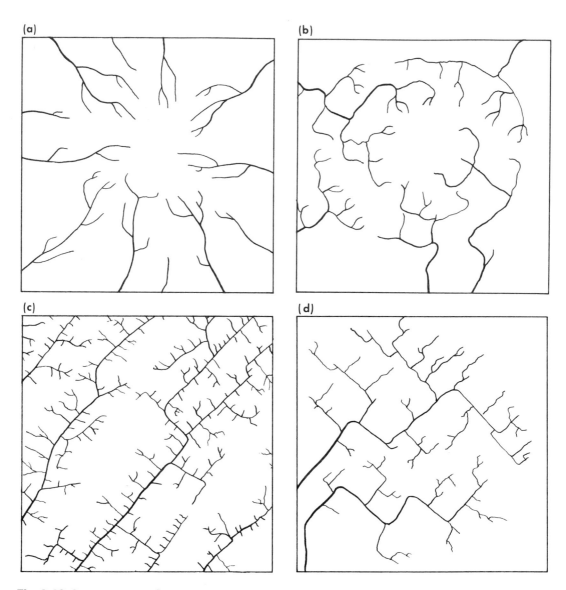

Fig. 6.40. Stream patterns reflecting structural control. (a) Radial. (b) Annular. (c) Trellis. (d) Rectangular. (From various sources)

Another very striking and diagnostic feature of stream drainage is streams cutting across the mountains. This is a curious and enigmatic phenomenon: the development of stream valleys running transverse to landforms seems to be opposed to the basic law of nature that water flows downhill. In fact, four different processes can bring about such features. In one, the lowest outlets of the stream are across the ridges, so the water simply backs up until it spills through a low place and eventually erodes a channel through it. In another, a stream erodes headward until it cuts across the apparent obstacle. The two other processes are known as antecedence and superimposition (Thornbury 1969, p. 116).

An *antecedent* stream is one which existed before the mountains were formed; when uplift took place, the stream kept pace in downcutting and maintained its channel through the mountains (Fig. 6.41). Antecedent streams have created some spectacular valleys. The Brahmaputra and Indus rivers originate on the Tibetan Plateau and flow across the highest mountains in the world to reach the sea. Another example is the Columbia River, which cuts through the Cascades and provides a major sea-level route across this barrier. *Superimposed* streams, on the other hand, develop where the former topography has been buried, e.g., by sediments, lava, or glacial deposits. New streams form on this surface and establish themselves; when they eventually reach the harder rocks and structures of the underlying topography, they simply continue eroding downward in their established channels. Later, when the overlying softer material is stripped away, the streams appear to have cut transversely through the topography,

when in reality the streams did not have any choice, since their pathways were established under different conditions. Many examples of superimposed streams in the Rockies have been cited and an even greater number have been proposed for the Appalachians (Johnson 1931; Atwood and Atwood 1938). The Hudson and Susquehanna rivers are among the better-known of these. The Rockies and Appalachians present very different situations, however; the cover mass remains in the Rockies, proving superimposition, while in the Appalachians there is no cover mass, and superimposition is more hypothetical. Since it is difficult to prove antecedence, and superimposition is probably a fairly local phenomenon, much more emphasis has been given in recent years to the efficacy of headward erosion by streams. Also, a stream may cut through beds of alternating resistance, eventually encountering and becoming entrenched in resistant strata composing structures running transverse to the direction of stream flow. This may produce stream patterns similar to those of antecedence or superimposition, but it does

Fig. 6.41. The origin of antecedent drainage running transverse to the structure. (a) Stream at an early stage before major uplift occurs. (b) Stream maintaining itself during uplift and deformation of mountains. This illustration may also represent superimposed drainage if it is assumed that (a) represents a newly deposited surface, e.g., lava flow or glacial deposit, that has buried the original landforms. Streams form in this new material, and as stream entrenchment and valley development

proceed, the buried structural features are eventually encountered. By now the drainage is established, so the stream has no choice but to maintain itself and continue downcutting. The depositional material, usually less resistant than the structural features, is removed by erosion and the structural features are eventually left standing in relief. In (b) the drainage has now been through the process of superimposition rather than antecedence. (From Oberlander 1965, p. 105)

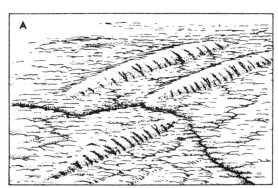

not involve either (Twidale 1971, p. 211). The whole topic of transverse drainage in mountains has become problematic. A study by Oberlander (1965) of the Zagros Mountains in Iran, for example, strongly challenges many classical ideas about antecedence and superimposition and their importance in stream development across the grain of mountains.

When streams do cut across mountains, by whatever means, they create what are known as *water gaps*. As might be expected, such features are valuable to man, since they provide easy passage across mountain barriers. The Columbia Gorge through the Cascade Mountains, for example, contains two highways and two railways and also serves as a major waterway and flightway for east-west air traffic; it is probable that more passengers and freight pass through the Columbia Gorge than through all the other Cascade passes combined. Many valleys have been left without a stream, either because the stream could not keep up with the rapid uplift or because the water was diverted to some other part of the drainage system. Such features, known as *wind gaps*, are also important as mountain passes (VerSteeg 1930; Meyerhoff and Olmsted 1934). One of these is the celebrated Cumberland Gap in the southern Appalachians, through which early settlers passed on their way to the interior. A highway (U.S. 25) passes through there today, but—thanks to the bulldozer, automobile, and the Interstate Highway System—travelers can choose other routes, and Cumberland Gap's importance as a focus of transportation has dwindled.

WIND ACTION

Elevated and exposed peaks and ridges in middle latitudes are among the windiest of environments (see pp. 107–108). The geomorphic effects of the wind in mountains are still not completely understood, however. The persistence of high winds on exposed slopes with relatively little snow, the lack of vegetation to bind the soil and reduce the wind velocity, and the presence of frost comminution processes all suggest considerable potential for erosion, but the effects of wind must be placed in their proper perspective. For example, wind was formerly believed to be the primary agent of erosion in many desert areas, but it is now known that running water, even though infrequent, is the major factor in landscape sculpture in most deserts (Cooke and Warren 1973, p. 39). Wind is certainly more important in desert environments than it is elsewhere, but its geomorphic effect is still less than that of water. A similar condition exists in mountains. Wind becomes more important with increasing elevation and exposure, but its role as a denudational agent is still less important than the other processes we have discussed.

Wind Erosion

Wind erodes by picking up small particles and transporting them, and by using these airborne particles to create a sandblast effect. The three principal sources of fine material in mountains are: braided streams; the deposits around glaciers, which contain large amounts of glacial flour; and the frost-rubble zone, where fine material is produced by active frost comminution. The size of the particles that can be picked up depends upon the wind velocity and the shape and density of the particles. The greatest work is accomplished during fierce gusts under turbulent conditions (Fig. 6.42). The largest particles normally lifted into the air are about the size of pea-gravel. Such material travels along the ground in a series of small hops. In high winds, sand grains can be lifted up to 1–2 m (3–7 ft.) and carried for much longer distances. Silt and clay-sized material can be lifted far into the atmosphere and carried for great distances; this is the stuff of which dust storms are made. Under certain circumstances, the wind can move

Fig. 6.42. A "dust devil," or whirlwind, moving along the lateral moraine of Collier Glacier in the Three Sisters Wilderness Area, Oregon Cascades. A large rock to immediate lower left of dust has been dislodged and is shown in mid-air. Numerous other rocks have accumulated on snow surface. (Author)

Fig. 6.43. Large wind-faceted rock (granite) in the Wind River Range, Wyoming. (W. H. Bradley, U.S. Geological Survey)

Fig. 6.44. Wind-eroded rocky surface (desert pavement) near the alpine timberline at 2,100 m (7,000 ft.) in the Three Sisters Wilderness Area, Oregon Cascades. The material under the rocky surface debris consists primarily of fine sand and silt. Many of the larger rocks have surfaces made smooth and shiny by sand and snowblast. (Author)

rocks along the ground. When rocks freeze in shallow water, for instance, the wind can move the ice and the embedded rocks may leave a trail in the bottom mud as they move. The wind can also push and slide rocks as large as walnuts across ice-glazed surfaces (Schumm 1956).

Several features result from wind erosion in mountains. Among the most distinctive are *ventifacts* (Whitney and Dietrich 1973). These are stones which have been polished and faceted by the abrasion of wind-carried particles. If a stone is partly buried, only one main surface can be sandblasted at a time; if the stone happens to be overturned or undercut, then another surface will be exposed to wind abrasion. Thus, ventifacts commonly have one or more flat faces or facets divided by sharp angles (Fig. 6.43). On larger stones that remain relatively stationary for long periods, one side may show considerable abrasion and cutting by the wind, providing evidence of the prevailing wind direction (Sharp 1949; Rudberg 1968). In order for abrasion to occur, the particles being carried by the wind must be harder than the rocks they are striking. Snow increases in hardness with lower temperatures; under certain conditions, blowing snow can abrade rock surfaces (Teichert 1939; Fristrup 1953).

Related to ventifacts are *lag deposits.* These consist of a veneer of pebbles and larger rocks overlying sand and silt. They are generally attributed to wind removal of the fines, leaving the larger particles as a stony surface layer. Although such features are common in mountains, they are best known from deserts, where they are called *desert pavement* because after the fine material is removed the larger particles tend to provide a protective covering for the underlying fine material (Fig. 6.44). Processes other than wind—including the removal of fines by water and the upward migration of stones by frost action—may also contribute to the development of lag deposits (Cooke and Warren 1973, pp. 124–29).

Fig. 6.45. Weathering pits on upper surface of Sentinel Dome, at 2,700 m (9,000 ft.) in Yosemite National Park, California. The rock type is a massive granite. Tree on left is a Bristlecone pine (*Pinus aristata*). The surface was glaciated during the Wisconsin Ice Age, which ended about 15,000 years ago. These unusually large and deep weathering pits have developed since that time, through a combination of weathering and wind removal. (Ted M. Oberlander, University of California)

Wind has been deemed responsible for the cavernously weathered, fluted, honeycombed, and deeply pitted rock walls displayed in some mountainous areas. Where there are ample tools for abrasion, wind erosion may partially account for these surfaces, but they are probably mostly the result of chemical weathering (Blackwelder 1929; Washburn 1969, p. 31). Wind is an accessory agent, however, since loose particles are continually whisked away, exposing fresh surfaces. Related features are *weathering pits*, circular depressions occurring on more or less horizontal rock surfaces (Roberts 1968) (Fig. 6.45). These are common in high mountains, and although principally formed by chemical and physical weathering, wind removes the fine debris from the depressions and is a necessary companion process in their origin.

Wind Deposition

What the wind picks up, it must put down. In some areas, particularly to the lee of rapidly weathering source rock and along glacial meltstreams, sand may accumulate, forming dunes. The finer material, predominantly of silt size (since clay production is not important in cold climates), may be carried much greater distances and result in deep deposits and good-quality soils. The mountain region itself is an area of loss rather than gain, but some of the fine material may accumulate in moist and sheltered sites, such as meadows, and produce some of the best soils and vegetation within the mountain region. The wind may also carry the fine material to higher altitudes, where it falls on the snow (Warren-Wilson 1958) and provides an airborne source of nutrients for organisms living far above the snowline (Mani 1962; Swan 1963a, b; Windom 1969).

Perhaps the single most important geomorphic (as well as ecologic) aspect of wind in mountains is its role in the distribution of snow (Thorn 1978a). Ridges and exposed slopes are typically blown free of snow, while lee slopes receive increased amounts. Thus, one slope will be virtually bare while another is heavily laden with snow. In some cases snow will even create and maintain small drift or pocket glaciers. Many of the glaciers of the Colorado Front Range in the Rocky Mountains are of this type. The accumulation of snow on lee slopes protects these surfaces from severe temperature fluctuations and high winds near the ground—both common on exposed slopes. However, such slopes are more prone to avalanches, and once the snow begins to melt it contributes to the development of nivation, frost action, solifluction, and mudflows. The availability of moisture on such lee slopes will generally encourage the growth of plants, except in those sites where the snow does not melt soon enough to allow the plants to complete their life cycle.

Because snow patches tend to countersink into the slope and to establish still larger areas for catching new snow, the various processes set in train by the accumulating snow can feed upon themselves and become magnified over the years. Wind and snowdrift thus influence the relative rates of frost action, surface runoff, and mass-wasting from slope to slope, which in turn have marked effects on the distribution of soil, vegetation, drainage patterns, and slope asymmetry (French 1972b).

LANDSCAPE DEVELOPMENT

If you were to stand on a high peak in almost any major mountain range and look out into the distance, you would see that the peaks and ridges are all roughly the

Fig. 6.46. Peaked plain in the rugged North Cascades, Washington. View is of the Picket Range, taken from the southwest at about 2,100 m (7,000 ft.). (Will F. Thompson, U.S. Army Natick Laboratories)

same height (Fig. 6.46). This is very curious: mountains constitute the most rugged landscape on earth, yet there is an astonishing similarity in the heights of individual peaks within a range. When viewed against the horizon and the peaks connected by an imaginary line, they look almost like a plain. In the Alps this is known as *gipfelflur* or "peaked plain" (Penck 1919).

The tendency toward accordance of summits at the upper levels in mountains was observed long ago. Its significance and origin in terms of landscape evolution have been variously interpreted. One theory is

that the peaked plain is a remnant of a *peneplain* (a land surface worn down by erosion to a nearly flat plain). According to this, the mountains were created by uplift and then allowed to stand more or less quiescent for several million years while erosion wore them down almost to a plain (Davis 1899, 1923); a second uplift was followed by another cycle of erosion. The upper surface of the peaks and ridges are thus all that survives of the peneplain surface. Although this theory was very popular after the turn of the century and still has some adherents (King 1967, 1976), it fails on at least two counts. It is unlikely that after the initial uplift the landmass would have stood still long enough for erosion to wear the mountains down to a peneplain; erosion and uplift seem to take place concurrently. And, given the relatively greater rates of erosion at higher elevations, it is doubtful that peneplain surfaces could have survived over such long periods of time.

Another school of thought on the origin of alpine-summit accordance was initiated from early work in the northern Cascades of Washington (Daly 1905). Although extremely rugged, the North Cascades display a remarkable accordance of summits at about the 2,500 m (8,000 ft.) level (Fig. 6.46). Daly did not believe that these were peneplain surfaces, but thought they were instead the result of similar types of rock structure being eroded in the presence of continuing uplift. "In both the architecture and the sculpture of her alpine temple, Nature decrees that its new domes and minarets shall not be indefinitely varied in height. Such accordance as they have among themselves will be preserved and accentuated as her chisels fashion new details on the building" (Daly 1905, p. 114). Major emphasis was placed on rapid rates of erosion occurring in the alpine zone, whereas below the timberline erosion would operate at a slower rate due to the protection afforded by the forest. In a recent extension of these ideas, Thompson (1962b, 1968) has claimed that timberline alone is the primary factor in the development of the gipfelflur, as well as of the lower gentle shoulders or *alp slopes* which frequently exist between the steep rocky ridge above and the glacial valley below. According to Thompson's observations, present alp slopes in western North America coincide fairly closely with the present location of the timberline. The gipfelflur, or upper summit accordance, occurs about 600 m (3,000 ft.) above the present-day timberline (Thompson 1969, p. 668). It has been pointed out, however, that accordance of summits and other levels occur in

widely separated areas, and in some cases—such as parts of the arid Puna de Atacama or in the high Himalayas—timberline is hardly a factor. In fact, some students view the timberline more as a function of surface morphology than as a cause of it (Hewitt 1972, p. 29). Yet another study questions the entire validity of ancient erosion surfaces, suggesting that they are instead (at least in granitic rocks) the result of more rapid weathering where the rocks are buried than where exposed (because of continuous contact with groundwater solutions and chemical weathering). The disintegrated rock debris would be removed by small streams and the underlying unweathered outcrops exposed by accelerated erosion would act as local base levels. It is these, according to the author, which often have been misinterpreted as ancient erosional surfaces (Wahrhaftig 1965).

The most recent idea of mountain-landscape evolution is tied to plate tectonics, with uplift active during denudation (Garner 1959, 1965, 1974; Oberlander 1965; Hewitt 1972, p. 29). The uplift may receive its motive power in several ways, e.g., continent/continent collision or island arc/continent collision, so that a variety of situations may be involved (see pp. 37–42). In addition, uplift occurs simultaneously with denudation because of isostatic readjustment. As material is transported away from the mountain region, the range itself becomes lighter and undergoes uplift in order to remain in equilibrium with rocks in the surrounding areas.

The other major part of the process involves erosion under different climatic regimes during uplift. In some areas the entire uplift may occur under similar conditions; the only differences are those caused by elevation. In other cases, the uplift may take place through different levels of humidity or aridity (Fig. 6.47). This is most striking in places like the western side of the Andes, where there are both low-altitude and high-altitude deserts, separated by more hu-

Fig. 6.47. Idealized scheme showing landform development under different climatic conditions—humid, arid, and sequential. The column on the left shows probable development under continuously humid conditions; middle column shows development under arid conditions. Note the different landforms that result. The column on the right demonstrates the probable development of landforms under a changing climate, where the mountains are uplifted through initially arid conditions, then humid ones, then back to arid at the highest levels. The effects of alpine glaciation are also shown, as is downwearing, with arid conditions existing in the lowlands and humid conditions occurring at the higher levels. (From Garner 1974, p. 611)

mid climatic zones. For example, in Peru (depending on the exact latitude) a landscape being uplifted would be subjected to arid conditions for the first few hundred meters, then would pass into a humid environment, and at the highest levels go into a cold desert. In its passage to the highest level it may or may not retain vestiges of former landscapes. The possibilities and combinations for landscape development under different conditions of latitude and continentality are diverse, but when the altitudinal changes are added to this mosaic, the complexity becomes awesome (Fig. 6.47). Here, again, the nature of mountain origin is important, since the presence of an ocean (continent/continent collision) may result in marine conditions initially but it will be altered to continental conditions as orogenesis proceeds (since the ocean is destroyed). Consequently, the climate may change from humid to arid. In addition, the uplift of the mountain itself may alter and intensify climatic differences between the windward and leeward sides. Evidence for a mountain range passing through different climatic regimes is present in parts of the Andes of Peru and Ecuador (Garner 1959; Myers 1976), although the exact interpretation may be disputed (Cotton 1960).

The attractiveness of this concept is that it is tied to modern theories of mountain-building and behavior, and it also takes into account the impact of climate and environment on rates of geomorphic processes. Diverse landscape assemblages containing evidence of their development under continual uplift and denudation, as well as under the control of different climatic regimes, result from these conditions. The prospects of this new, highly complex approach are satisfyingly challenging. Earlier ideas gave the impression that all the major questions had been answered, but it is now clear that we are only beginning to ask the right questions.

Not every soil can bear all things.

Virgil, *Georgic II* (30 B.C.)

7

Mountain Soils

oil is such a common phenomenon that most people take for granted that they know what it is, yet to formulate a scientific definition of *soil* is extremely difficult. Much depends upon who is using the term. To an engineer, soil is simply the unconsolidated material at the surface of the earth; to a biologist, soil is a living organism, limited only in its ability to reproduce and to migrate. Of the two definitions, the biological—that life is essential to the development of soil—is closer to our purposes. This definition must be interpreted liberally, however, since in high mountains the amount of biological activity may be minimal. For example, there are many unconsolidated surfaces that could support plants but do not, owing to other environmental factors. On the other hand, bare exposed bedrock may support plants (lichens and mosses) but it does not fit the usual view of soil. For our purposes, soil will simply be considered as the uppermost layer of the earth's surface in which organisms live.

Soils are created by weathering and the breakdown of rocks, in combination with the activity of plants and animals and the products of their decay. Since the biological component is lessened at high altitudes, the soil-forming process also weakens, until at the highest levels it is scarcely operative. The balance between physical and biological processes becomes increasingly disproportionate in the direction of environmental severity, until the physical component almost totally dominates the soil-forming process. (A similar trend may be seen as one progresses toward the hot deserts or polar regions.)

A typical soil consists of distinct layers or zones called *soil horizons*, which compose the *soil profile*. These layers are identified by characteristics such as color, texture, structure, organic matter, and pH (acidity). Water normally moves downward through the soil; in the process, some constituents are taken into solution and carried downward by leaching, and tiny solid particles may also be transported until redeposition takes place. Consequently, the upper layers continually lose material to the lower layers. The uppermost layers (A horizon) contain the largest quantity of organic material and are generally darkest in color, while the middle layers (B horizon) are composed of weathered and finer mineral matter. The lowest part of the soil profile (C horizon) consists of the partially weathered parent material. Well-defined horizons are the product of normal soil development under long-persisting, undisturbed, and favorable conditions; hence they are uncommon in mountain soils. Mountain soils are characteristically shallow, rocky, acidic, infertile, and immature. Diverse stages of soil development may, however, exist in close proximity to each other. Mountains stand at the opposite extreme from plains, where environmental variability is minimal and there are large contiguous units of similar soils. The diversity of mountain landscapes has the effect of creating a discontinuous and heterogeneous patchwork of microenvironments characterized by continually changing and contrasting site conditions. It is within this framework that mountain soils develop, and, accordingly, reflect the nature of their origin.

SOIL-FORMING FACTORS

The primary factors responsible for different kinds of soils are climate, biological factors, topography, parent material, and time (Jenny 1941). Each of these will be discussed briefly. It should be remembered that the factors affecting soil development are similar in all environments; it is simply their intensity and combination that are unique in mountains. In addition, it is difficult to isolate the effects of any single factor, since all are interrelated.

Climate

The primary climatic factors affecting soil development are temperature, precipitation, and wind. Climate, of course, has significance far beyond itself, since it controls the distribution of vegetation, which in turn has a fundamental influence on the kind of soil that develops in any given area. Separately, however, climate has special ramifications of its own. For example, temperature is important in controlling the rate and type of weathering that affect rock breakdown (see pp. 175–79). Physical weathering generally dominates in cold climates and results in coarse soil texture, but there is increasing evidence for more chemical weathering in mountains than was formerly thought, especially in marine climates (Bouma et al. 1969; Bouma and Van Der Plas 1971; Reynolds 1971; Reynolds and Johnson 1972; Buurman et al. 1976). Many factors are involved, including rock type, presence of organic acids, moisture availability, and the periodicity of temperature (Johnson et al. 1977). Although it may freeze every night in tropical mountains, the equal period of warmth during the day provides ample heat for chemical weathering to produce a moderate amount of clay. By contrast, in middle-latitude and polar mountains held in the grasp of winter for most of the year, chemical weathering is more restricted.

Low temperatures and frost action are

responsible for the formation of various types of structured soils or patterned ground (see pp. 184–86). The daily frost of high tropical mountains penetrates only a few centimeters below the surface, whereas the seasonal frost in middle and high latitudes is of much greater intensity (Figs. 4.17, 4.18). Consequently, the rocks in tropical mountains are quickly reduced to small aggregates and the resulting patterns are of small dimension, while in middle and high latitudes patterned ground occurs on a large scale and is composed of much larger rocks (Figs. 6.14, 6.15). Related slope processes operating in low-temperature regimes include frost creep, solifluction, and other types of mass-wasting. These tend to cause movement and intermixing of surface layers, subjecting the soil profile to more or less continual disruption.

A major significance of low temperature is its role in limiting biological activity, both plant and animal. Consequently, less organic material is added to the soil, what does accumulate decomposes very slowly, and soil fauna are rarer (Rall 1965; Faust and Nimlos 1968; Edwards 1972; Shulls 1976; Tolbert et al. 1977). Although not precisely established, a soil temperature of 5° C. (41° F.) is commonly accepted as the temperature below which biological activity in the soil becomes very slow or is prohibited. Therefore, the length of time the temperature is above this figure gives a rough approximation of the level of biological activity in any given soil area (Retzer 1974, p. 781). Several years of data are available from an alpine tundra station in the Colorado Rockies (Niwot Ridge) at 3,750 m (12,375 ft.). The soil temperatures at varying depths in this area are above 5° C. (41° F.) for the following lengths of time:

5 cm (2 in.)	110 days
15 cm (6 in.)	93 days
30 cm (12 in.)	45 days
60 cm (24 in.)	21 days

The details of soil temperature will vary with exposure, snow cover, and other microsite conditions, but these figures provide a gross index (Marr et al. 1968b). In the extreme situation of permafrost, where the earth below certain depths remains frozen all year round, biological activity is restricted to the active layer. Soil temperatures are lowered by the reservoir of cold and the length of the frost-free period is reduced. Drainage is restricted, producing waterlogged soils (Retzer 1965).

The effect of decreasing moisture and precipitation on soil development is in many ways similar to that of low temperature. There is less biological activity, the amount of organic material decreases, and decomposition takes place at a lower rate as available moisture diminishes. Physical weathering becomes relatively more important than chemical weathering. Excess moisture, on the other hand, results in waterlogging, poor aeration, and increased soil acidity. Nevertheless, wet soils do generally support more vegetation than dry soils and are considered to be somewhat more productive (Webber 1974, p. 461). The best soils develop in the intermediate, well-watered but adequately drained sites. Unfortunately, such sites are usually in the minority compared to those with either too little or too much moisture, e.g., exposed slopes and ridges, or poorly drained meadows and bogs.

Many factors control the distribution of moisture in mountains. The general trend of precipitation increasing with altitude is well-known, although beyond a certain point (the zone of maximum precipitation) precipitation may again decrease. This is especially well-marked in the tropics. Thus, while the intermediate slopes of Kilimanjaro and Kenya are clothed in luxuriant vegetation, the summit areas have a desert-like appearance (Hedberg 1964; Coe 1967) (Fig. 4.28). In addition, there is a strong contrast in precipitation between the leeward and windward sides of mountains, as well as in the effects of solar intensity and the distribution of sunlight on slopes, with its major implications for heating and drying of soil surfaces. Regardless of the general context, precipitation that falls as rain is quickly lost as runoff. Snow may be retained longer, but it is highly susceptible to further transport by wind; some slopes are blown free while others receive more than their share. Exposed ridges and slopes are often snow-free and dry while lee slopes contain snow patches that provide meltwater for the areas immediately downslope.

Wind as a climatic factor achieves its major importance in causing evaporative stress on vegetated and bare surfaces, either by direct application of wind or indirectly through transport and unequal redistribution of snow. Wind also erodes and removes fine material from exposed surfaces, especially where frost action has left the soil in a "frothy" condition highly susceptible to transport. Wind erosion is important around glacial and stream deposits, where ample fine material is available.

The corollary to erosion is deposition, and although much of the fine material is transported out of the mountain system, some is deposited locally and contributes to soil development. Volcanic ash is also important in this regard. In addition, some fine material from the surrounding lowlands may be transported by the wind into the mountain region. The local distribution of wind-deposited material is similar to that of snow patches (which are themselves highly efficient in catching atmospheric dust), and the combined presence of fine material and moisture is favorable to vegetational development. This is particularly true since wind-blown deposits are often alkaline in reaction and help to counteract the natural acidity of alpine soils (Windom 1969). Many mountain soils seem too good to have developed completely from the breakdown of bedrock through normal weathering processes, particularly where the area has been glaciated and the surfaces are young. These soils have apparently been built up from

deposition rather than developing in place through normal breakdown of bedrock (Retzer 1965; Marchand 1970).

It is important to keep in mind that climates have not always remained the same. The most recent geologic epoch, the Pleistocene, had at least four glacial and four interglacial periods. Mid-latitude and polar mountains experienced the effects of these major climatic incursions even more acutely than lowlands, as is evidenced by intensive glacial erosion. Consequently, most soil surfaces in mountains such as the Alps or Rockies are younger than Late Wisconsin (10,000–15,000 years ago) (Retzer 1974, p. 773). The climate since then has gradually warmed, although marked fluctuations have occurred within this framework (see p. 137). Those surfaces that escaped the direct effects of glaciation may still provide evidence of the soil-forming and geomorphic effects of these climatic events (Fig. 7.1). In some cases, even older soils may persist and retain the characteristics gained under very different climatic regimes. In the Coast Range of northern Oregon there are ancient reddish lateritic soils formed during the Miocene (20 million years ago). As the climate changed, its effect on soil development also changed, and the older soils served as parent material for the modern soils. A similar situation exists in the Transcaucasus of southern Russia (Romashkevich 1964).

It is also possible for the soils to develop under a climatic regime existing in the lowlands and then to be uplifted to higher elevations in the course of mountain-building. This probably happened in the Oregon Coast Range, since the major uplift of this area took place during the Pliocene (10 million years ago). Similarly, in the limestone Alps of northern Austria, tropical soils were formed during the late Tertiary (20–30 million years ago) and later uplifted. These now exist as soil relicts at an altitude of about 2,100 m (7,000 ft.) (Kubiena 1970, p. 45). In such cases, the complexity of environmental conditions can be very great indeed, since

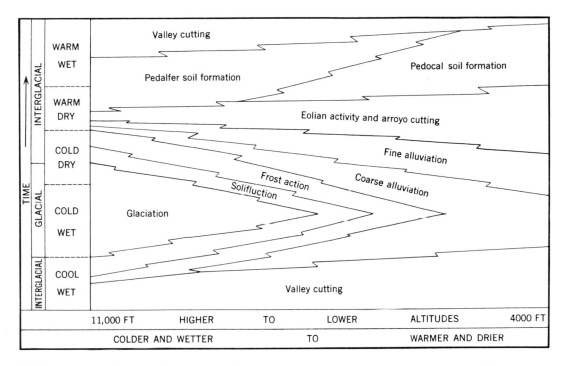

Fig. 7.1. Climatic effects on soil development during glacial and interglacial periods. The illustration was constructed to show the combined effects of altitude, temperature, moisture, and time for the La Sal Mountains, Utah. (From Richmond 1962, p. 18)

the soils are exposed to a variety of environmental systems during uplift. This is a matter not only of changes in temperature but of moisture regimes as well. The uplift of the Peruvian Andes resulted in landscapes passing from arid conditions in the lowlands through humid conditions at intermediate altitudes and eventually into a cold desert environment at the highest levels (see pp. 230–32). Such variable conditions have the potential for creating polygenetic soils and landscapes (Fig. 6.47) (Garner 1959, 1974).

Biological Factors

Vegetation, more than any other factor, gives the soil its distinctive character (Jenny 1958). In particular, vegetation controls the amount and kind of organic material added to the soil. Generally, annual grasses and herbaceous plants add more organic matter than do shrubs or trees. In grasslands, the aerial part of the plant dies each year, adding organic matter to the soil, while trees only lose their leaves. If the trees are evergreens, even this annual increment is reduced. Evergreen needles and leaves are often rich in silica, making the soil more acidic, while grasses and herbs are more basic in reaction. Moreover, certain kinds of evergreen plants have tough leathery leaves that are inherently slow to decay, especially under the lower temperature regimes of high altitudes (Edwards 1977).

One of the sharpest soil boundaries to be found anywhere is that occurring between forest and grasslands. This is somewhat less true at the alpine timberline because of the weakening of the soil-forming process, but even there, ample evidence of this major vegetation zone is still reflected in the soils. In many areas the timberline has advanced or retreated, indicating climatic change or some other modification—e.g., fire, disease, or human intervention (see p. 284). Evidence for this may be contained in the fabric of the soils, making it possible to reconstruct the former distribution of the timberline (Nimlos and McConnell 1962; Molloy 1964; Retzer 1965; Zimina 1973; Olgeirson 1974; Miles and Singleton 1975; Reider and Uhl 1977; Van Ryswyk and Okazaki 1979).

Little is known of the effects of animals and other organisms on mountain soils. Microfauna are generally thought to be less abundant at higher altitudes (Rall 1965; Faust and Nimlos 1968; Edwards 1972; Shulls 1976; Tolbert et al. 1977), although in the tropics this may not hold true: micro-

fauna do very well under the conditions of increased moisture and cooler temperatures in tropical mountains, where prolonged freezing does not occur. On the upper slopes of Mount Kinabalu, Borneo, and Mount Kosciusko, Australia, large earthworms and microorganisms continually incorporate surface litter into the soil (Costin et al. 1952; Askew 1964). Consequently, organic material decomposes rapidly—at least in Australia, more rapidly than in the surrounding lowlands (Wood 1970, 1974).

Small burrowing animals are important to the alpine tundra. The Pocket gopher (*Thomomys spp.*) is a common occupant of meadows where there is good vegetation and a fairly complete winter snowcover. These little creatures create complex networks of shallow tunnels under the soil in search of plant roots. The excavated material is taken

Fig. 7.2. Soil casings resulting from Pocket gopher (*Thomomys spp.*) activity during winter in subalpine meadows at 2,600 m (8,500 ft.) in the Wallowa Mountains, Oregon. Photo was taken soon after the snow melted in late June, so the excavated material still retains its original shape; by summer's end it will have been scattered across the surface. (Author)

above the surface and stuffed into similar tunnels in the overlying snow. The following spring, the soil in these snow tunnels is deposited on the ground as interwoven soil casings (Fig. 7.2). The mixing and overturning of the soil by burrowing animals increase its vulnerability to erosion (Ellison 1946; Turner et al. 1973). This is even more true on slopes, since the excavated material is invariably moved downslope (Jonca 1972; Imeson 1976; Thorn 1978b). I have found the amount of material moved downslope by the Arctic ground squirrel (*Citellus undulatus*) on certain slopes in the Ruby Mountains, Yukon Territory, to be on the order of 145 kg per 0.4 hectare (320 lbs./acre) per year (Price 1971c). Many years ago, Grinnell (1923, p. 143) estimated that Pocket gophers in Yosemite Park, in the Sierra Nevada in California, were excavating 6.5 metric tons of soil per 1.6 sq. km (7.2 tons/sq. mi.).

Topography

Topography affects soil formation largely through its control of exposure to sun and wind, slope steepness, and drainage. Exposure to the sun controls biological activity and greatly affects physical and chemical processes. Exposure to wind is also important: soils formed on a windy ridge are very different from those in a sheltered valley flat. Slope gradient has many implications. The potential for soil development is obviously different for a steep rock face than a level surface. Upper slopes are susceptible to erosion, while lower slopes are recipients of deposition. There is a continual transfer of mass downslope. Probably, more slope soils in mountains develop out of transported materials than directly from the underlying bedrock (Parsons 1978). Slope soils are also subject to continual disturbance in their development. Soils on elevated and steeper slopes are generally well-drained, and surface water is quickly lost as runoff. On lower slopes and in valleys, soils are moister because of the greater precipitation collection area above

them, a higher water table, and more persistent shade climates (the sun is blocked by surrounding slopes).

Various schemes have been devised to analyze soils based on their topographic position, e.g., soil catenas or toposequences, but none has been universally accepted (Bushnell 1942; Jenny 1946; Ollier 1976). These approaches are based on the observation that similar soils commonly develop under similar topographic situations in a given area, especially when one or more additional factors, such as parent material or time, are the same. The exact contribution of topography is difficult to assess, however, since changes in topography also involve changes in the other soil-forming factors. For example, soil quality changes with elevation and exposure, but is this because of topography or because of changing climate and vegetation? Topography is generally viewed as being a relatively passive soil-forming factor, while climate and vegetation occupy active roles in soil development. In any event, surface morphology is critical—gradient and drainage make direct contributions to soil quality.

Parent Material

The inorganic stuff from which soils are made has a major impact on soil character. It may be solid bedrock or unconsolidated material such as glacial deposits, talus, blockfields, mudflows, alluvial fans, or windblown deposits. Soils generally develop more rapidly on unconsolidated material than on solid bedrock, but much depends upon the nature of the rock and site conditions. Volcanic ash weathers very rapidly; it consists of finely divided material containing an abundance of silicate minerals that readily break down into clay. For this reason, in many regions volcanic soils are highly productive. Within bedrock itself, soft and weak rocks (sedimentary) usually weather more rapidly than hard and resistant rocks (igneous or metamorphic). Hard crystalline rocks predominate in mountains, however, owing to the great heat and pressure associated with the orogenic process. Fine-grained rocks, such as shale or sandstone, typically break into fine particles; coarse-grained rocks such as granite break into coarse particles. Some rocks weather fairly rapidly into clays; others do not. Thus, the type of parent material affects soil texture, soil structure, moisture-holding ability, and base-exchange capacity (a measure of fertility.)

The type of parent material also plays a considerable part in soil chemistry. Many igneous and metamorphic rocks are acidic, while sedimentary rocks tend to be basic in reaction. Some rocks undergo such strong reactions that they form distinctive soils in almost all climates. Limestone, for example, is famous for forming the *rendzina*, a humus-rich carbonate soil that occurs in several mountain regions (Jenny 1930; Ugolini and Tedrow 1963; Kubiena 1970). Other rock types with unusual chemical properties—e.g., serpentine, gypsum, and calamite (an ore of zinc)—limit soil development by inhibiting plant growth and metabolism (Domin 1928; Billings 1950; Whittaker 1954; Kruckeberg 1954, 1969; Komarkova 1974). The effect of these rock types may be so strong that it is possible to plot their distribution simply by mapping the vegetation.

The effect of parent material is generally strongest in the early stages of soil development and diminishes with age. For this reason, parent material plays a somewhat disproportionate role in the distribution of soil types in mountains, as compared with the surrounding lowlands. Mountains are relatively young geologically; glacial advances have exposed and created extensive new surfaces, and other erosional processes continue to expose and create fresh rock surfaces.

Time

Time, like topography, is often considered a passive factor in soil formation,

since it makes no direct contribution to soil characteristics; nevertheless, it is only through time that a soil can develop. The longer the duration, the more complete the soil formation will be. If a lava flow has buried a mountain slope, soil formation has to begin anew. The former soil may remain, but it is now buried and part of the geologic record. Similarly, if a mountain has been severely glaciated, the eroded areas will most likely be bare rock: the soil that existed before has been removed and destroyed. Time starts at zero again as far as soil and vegetation are concerned. The same is true in the lower valley areas where glacial deposition has taken place. The only compensation there is that the material is aggregated and the environment somewhat more favorable, so soil development typically proceeds at a faster rate than on the ice-scoured uplands.

A number of studies have documented the relative rate of soil development on more recent features such as glacial moraines and mudflows in mountains (Dickson and Crocker 1953, 1954; Retzer 1954; Richmond 1962; Birkeland 1967; Crandell 1967; Reider 1975). While the rate of soil formation is variable, some positive evidence of soil development is usually displayed within a century or so (Fig. 7.3). In the moist tropics, the rate is greatly telescoped, particularly on volcanic parent material, so that a soil may develop within only a few years, while in mid-latitude and polar mountains it may take thousands of years. The eruption of Krakatoa in the South Pacific in 1883 totally inundated the island with lava and volcanic debris and destroyed all forms of life. Today, however, there exists a lush tropical vegetation with a relatively well-developed soil. By contrast, in many areas in middle- and high-latitude mountains, several millennia of exposure to the elements have failed to result in anything approaching a soil. A recent investigation of glacial deposits in the subalpine zone of the Indian Peaks region, Colorado Rockies, indicates that it takes about 2,750 years for the soil to devel-

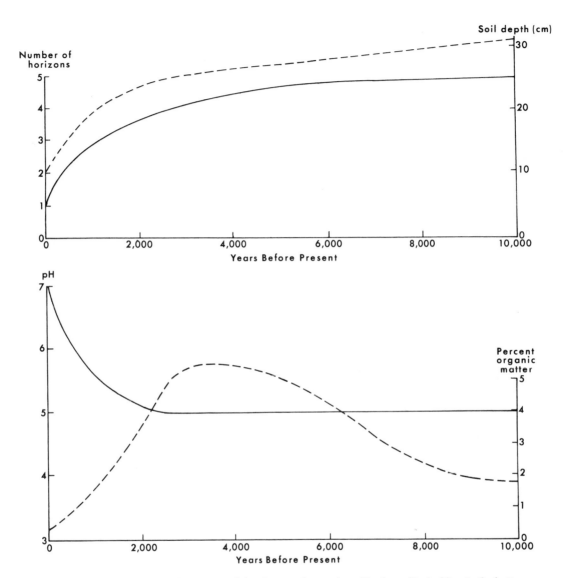

Fig. 7.3. Generalized pattern of changes in soil development through time on glacial deposits in the Indian Peaks region, Colorado Rockies. Dashed line in the top illustration represents soil depth; solid line represents the number of horizons. Dashed line in the bottom illustration represents percent of organic matter; solid line represents pH. (After Retzer 1974, p. 783)

op distinctive horizons and to achieve a steady pH; complete development of soil horizons requires much longer. Soil development is limited by low moisture as well as by low temperatures: in maritime mountains the rates of soil development are probably slightly faster than in arid mountains (Retzer 1974, p. 784).

MAJOR KINDS OF MOUNTAIN SOILS

It is difficult to discuss the nature of mountain soils in detail, both because of the great diversity displayed within individual regions and because of the diverse positions mountains occupy with respect to the earth's environmental matrix. What is true of a moist, protected meadow does not hold for an exposed ridge. Similarly, the changes that take place with altitude in one environment may not apply in another. The effect of increasing altitude on soil development differs somewhat from a desert to a marine location and from a middle-latitude to a tropical area. Soil development is clearly hindered with increasing altitude in most humid mid-latitude areas, but the soils may actually improve with altitude in arid and tropical mountains (within certain limits). In mid-latitude humid mountains temperature is the primary limiting factor, while in desert mountains the increase in precipitation with altitude may more than compensate for the decreasing temperature, and conditions for soil development become more favorable than at lower altitudes (Shreve 1915; Martin and Fletcher 1943; Whittaker et al. 1968; Messerli 1973; Hanawalt and Whittaker 1976). In the humid tropics the decreasing temperatures with altitude tend to slow the rate of decomposition and leaching, so at high elevations more organic material accumulates at the surface and more nutrients are retained in the soil (Jenny 1948; Thorp and Bellis 1960; Askew 1964; Frei 1964; Haantjens 1970).

Added to the problem of great diversity within mountain soils is the fragmented nature of our knowledge about them. Much of what we know comes from isolated research carried out in widely separated areas through individual efforts rather than through a systematic and unified approach. Generally much less is known about desert and tropical mountain soils than about mid-latitude humid mountain soils, and there are very few cases of detailed soil mapping even in middle-latitude mountains (Retzer 1962, 1974, p. 785). Consequently, on most world-soil maps mountain areas are provisionally labeled "undifferentiated." In spite of the heterogeneity of mountain soils and our lack of detailed information about them, their

general nature under similar environmental systems can be predicted with a fair degree of assurance. Before moving into this discussion, it is necessary to describe some of the basic concepts on which the study of soil development is based.

Soil Classification

A number of schemes for the identification, classification, and mapping of soils have been suggested over the years, but none has achieved universal acceptance. Even today many countries have their own systems of soil classification and mapping (Kubiena 1953; Soil Survey Staff 1960, 1974; Bunting 1965). Many of the earlier ideas about soil development came from Russia—the so-called "dynamic soil classification" and "great soil groups." The Russian system was based on the fundamental assumption that soil development accompanies vegetational development as controlled by climate. Therefore, given enough time, similar climatic (vegetational) regions should support similar soils regardless of differences in parent material or topography. The early stages of soil development were viewed as following a progression similar to the initial stages of vegetative succession. Vegetation and soil develop contemporaneously, each reflecting greater complexity through time, until eventually a dynamic equilibrium between themselves and the climate is achieved. This stage of development is represented by the "climax vegetation type" (see p. 258) and the "mature soil profile." Theoretically, no major changes take place beyond this point, and those changes that do occur are considered to be fluctuations around a point within the context of a steady state, rather than directional.

Mature or *zonal* soil types are usually considered to coincide with the major climax vegetative regions of the world. Most soil maps reflect this approach: thus, we have "prairie soils" in areas supporting prairie grasses, "brown forest soils" in areas supporting broadleaf deciduous trees, "podzol soils" in the boreal forest, etc. In mountain regions, mapping of soils usually shows a series of zones or belts following the climax vegetation zones with increasing altitude (Thorp 1931; Martin and Fletcher 1943; Marr 1961; McCraw 1962; Haantjens and Rutherford 1965; Johnson and Cline 1965; Whittaker et al. 1968; Hanawalt and Whittaker 1976). These are considered to be mature soil types created by the long-term presence of similar vegetation and climate. Such zonal soils theoretically occupy average or typical sites under good drainage and gentle slope. Many areas within these broad regions do not match the zonal soil types, however, because of various local conditions. Those soils that differ because of local factors such as drainage, rock type, and topography are called *intrazonal* and those that are developing on surfaces too young for full soil development are called *azonal* (Jenny 1941). In many mountainous landscapes intrazonal and azonal soils occupy more territory than do the zonal soils.

Although still in broad use, this system has come under increasing criticism in recent years because the terminology is imprecise and the soil characteristics are difficult to quantify. In addition, the system has a strong genetic bias that many specialists find limiting. As a result, a new system of soil classification, popularly known as the "7th approximation," has been developed in the United States. It is based entirely on soil morphology, with no consideration given to soil origin. Only those soil properties that can be determined by human senses or by instrumentation are included (Soil Survey Staff 1960, 1974). The new system has many advantages over other approaches, but it is complex and the terminology is like a foreign language, consisting of such exotic combinations of Greek and Latin as *Cryaquents*,

Ustochrepts, and *Psammaquents*. Nevertheless, most people are slowly adopting this system (Birkeland 1974).

Humid Mid-Latitude Mountain Soils

There are five major types of humid mid-latitude mountain soils (new soil-taxonomy equivalents in parentheses):

Lithosols, regosols (entisols)
Bog, peat soils (histosols)
Alpine turf, alpine meadow soils (inceptisols)
Subalpine and alpine grassland soils (mollisols)
Subalpine forest soils (spodosols)

Each of these is described briefly below. For a more detailed breakdown and discussion of soil types in the Rocky Mountains see Retzer (1974).

Lithosols, Regosols (Entisols)

Lithosols are thin, poorly developed soils found on bare rock surfaces, e.g., slopes and exposed ridges. Owing to their shallow depth and exposure, they are usually dry and support a scanty cover of lichens, mosses, and cushion plants. Some darkening of the surface may be present because of organic material, but there is usually little other evidence of soil horizons. Lithosols are highly susceptible to erosion and are often simply accumulations of fine or rocky material rather than true soils. In any case, they are classified as being azonal or intrazonal because of their relative youthfulness and/or inherent slowness to develop into normal soils.

Regosols differ from lithosols in that they develop from unconsolidated rocky material—e.g., moraines, talus, or mudflows—rather than from bedrock. They are located in more protected sites and show more rapid development because the parent material is initially subdivided. Regosols may be slightly deeper but are in other regards similar to lithosols. All gradations can be found, from fresh, unstable rock slides with no soil to stabilized glacial deposits several thousand years old with evidence of slow soil development. Lithosols and regosols occur in all mountains and are generally quite common, especially in the higher altitudes of desert and glaciated regions.

Bog, Peat Soils (Histosols)

Bog or peat soils form where drainage is poor—typically, in depressions and other areas where water from seeps or springs accumulates. The predominant characteristic is an abundance of mosses and partially decomposed plant remains at the surface; these vary in thickness from a few centimeters up to a meter (3.3 ft.) or more. The mineral soil is generally composed of material eroded from upland slopes, and there is an abrupt transition from the mineral to the organic material. The mineral soil is frequently mottled with orange-ish and bluish-grey, reflecting the lack of soil aeration. Bog soils are strongly acid, with a pH of 4.0 to 5.0. Permafrost is often present and probably reaches its most nearly equatorial position under bog conditions because of the insulating ability of the mosses and the cool and damp nature of shaded topographic depressions. If permafrost is present, it contributes in turn to poor drainage and the accumulation of sedges and mosses. Bog soils are classified as intrazonal, since they develop under locally restrictive conditions. They are found in all mountain areas except in extreme deserts, but reach their greatest importance in humid glaciated mountains where former drainage patterns have been destroyed and ample rock basins collect water. Bog and peaty soils are particularly abundant in the oceanic mountains of Europe (Pearsall 1960).

Alpine-Turf, Alpine-Meadow Soils (Inceptisols)

These are the classic zonal soil groups of humid mid-latitude mountains. They comprise most of the soils found above timberline in the Pyrenees, Caucasus, Rockies, and Alps (Jenny 1930; Kubiena 1953; Retzer 1956, 1965, 1974; Agri. Exp. Sta. 1964). The alpine-turf subgroup (cryumbrepts) is well-drained; the alpine meadow (cryaquent) is less well-drained. Alpine-turf soils occur on upper slopes and exposed areas; alpine-meadow soil develops in valleys and on lower slopes, where water is more plentiful. Both soils support a fairly complete cover of herbs and grasses that form a tight, interlocking, and highly organic root zone. The turf layer provides a good degree of stability for these surfaces. Once the turf is destroyed, however, the soils become highly susceptible to erosion and depletion (Bouma 1974). Consequently, protection of these surfaces is essential to the preservation of alpine landscapes.

Alpine-turf and alpine-meadow soils are both relatively deep, extending 30–80 cm (12–32 in.); they show distinct horizon development; and they are weakly to strongly acid (pH generally increases with depth). These characteristics reflect at least some downward movement of water through the profile, resulting in weak leaching and removal of bases (Sneddon et al. 1972, p. 109). The finest material occurs at the surface and increases in size with depth, reflecting greater weathering and biological activity near the surface. Aeolian (wind) deposition may also contribute to the finer surface texture. The "A" horizon is dark brown to black with a high organic content, but nutrient status is still fairly low. Alpine-meadow soil stays moist almost continually. Alpine-turf soil, however, usually dries out completely during the summer; the moisture trapped beneath flat-lying stones attracts plant roots, often resulting in black organic deposits immediately under such rocks (Retzer 1956, p. 25). The "B" horizon of both soils is brownish to greyish-brown and is distinguished largely on the basis of color, since there is little translocation of clay and soil structure is weakly developed. Texture is typically coarse and gravelly.

Subalpine and Alpine Grassland Soils
(*Mollisols*)

These are similar to the alpine-turf and alpine-meadow soils (inceptisols) in that they are relatively deep and good soils with distinct horizons, but they have neutral to slightly alkaline pH's with a higher presence of bases and, therefore, a better nutrient status. This may partially be because they are somewhat drier and less leached than alpine-turf and alpine-meadow soils, but in many cases they have been derived from calcareous sedimentary rock or other bedrock types high in bases. Subalpine and alpine grassland soils include the Great Soil types of prairie, chernozem, brown forest, and rendzinas (Retzer 1974, p. 796). These soil types are of limited extent in the Rockies, Sierra Nevada, and Cascades, but are somewhat more common in European mountains such as the Pyrenees, Alps, and Caucasus (Buurman et al. 1976).

Subalpine Forest Soils (Spodosols)

Subalpine-forest soils are moderately deep, well-drained, acid soils with well-developed and distinct horizons. They form under a complete cover of coniferous forest on many types of parent material, although crystalline rocks predominate. The primary soil-forming process is *podzolization*, which consists of the selective leaching of the "A" horizon and the translocation of bases and clays to the "B" horizon (Johnson and Cline 1965; Bouma et al. 1969; Brooke et al. 1970; Singer and Ugolini 1974). Rates of decomposition and incorporation of organic matter into the soil are slow, owing to the low temperatures and the heavy snowpack found in many high mountain forests. Under these conditions, a layer of litter and partially decomposed organic material typically accumulates above the mineral soil; the water moving down through the profile becomes impregnated with humic acid from the decomposing humus, and the oxides of iron and aluminum are dissolved and transported

Fig. 7.4. Podzol-soil profile under subalpine forest in the Canadian Rockies (Jasper National Park). The whitish-grey layer in the upper part of the profile represents the bottom of the "A" horizon. Underlying this is an orangish-yellow "B" horizon. The "C" horizon and parent material consist of boulder till, but the soil has developed largely within volcanic ash-enriched aeolian deposits. This profile has taken at least 7,000 years to develop. The hand trowel, 30 cm (12 in.) long, gives scale. Forest at this site consists of Engelmann spruce (*Picea engelmannii*) and Lodgepole pine (*Pinus contorta*). (Roger King, University of Western Ontario)

downward. This causes severe leaching of the lower part of the "A" horizon, which becomes a greyish bleached siliceous zone, the trademark of the true podzol (Fig. 7.4). The oxides of iron and aluminum accumulate in the "B" horizon, giving it a reddish-yellow color. The translocation of clays and bases to the "B" horizon often results in a blocky or prismatic soil structure that may inhibit drainage. Podzols are strongly to very strongly acid, have a low base status, and are not very productive.

At the upper limit of the forest, in the krummholz and tundra zone (see pp. 289–93), podzols grade into alpine turf and/or alpine-meadow soils. The very low temperatures at these altitudes inhibit the rate of organic-matter breakdown, and the leaching of the "A" horizon weakens; but, depending on the exact climatic regime, a weak level of podzolization may continue to operate into the tundra (Molloy 1964; Bliss and Woodwell 1965; Johnson and Cline 1965; Bouma et al. 1969; Sneddon et al. 1972; King and Brewster 1976).

Below the subalpine forests and the zone of true podzols, in the direction of increasing temperatures and decreasing snowfall, the organic material tends to become better incorporated into the mineral soil, resulting in a black or dark-brownish "A" horizon that grades into a lighter-brown "B" horizon. This is the grey-brown podzolic soil. Depending on the climate, forests may continue into the lowlands or they may give way to grasses and desert shrubs. If forests persist, the soils continue as grey-brown podzolic or variations of it, while under grasses and shrublands they merge into prairie, chernozem, and chestnut-brown soils (Agri. Exp. Sta. 1964; Johnson and Cline 1965).

Arid Mountain Soils

The environmental changes that take place with increasing altitude in arid regions frequently present the paradox of deeper soils, increasing numbers of plant and animal species, increasing biomass, and greater productivity than in the lowlands. This is because in arid places moisture is the primary limiting factor, so as precipitation increases and evaporation decreases with altitude, conditions become more favorable for life in spite of the lower temperatures (up to a certain point). Forests often occupy the intermediate elevations in semiarid mountains and display both upper and lower timberlines. The lower timberline is generally due to lack of moisture, while the upper timberline is due to low temperatures (see pp. 286–89) (Daubenmire 1943). This situation can be observed in many places where mountains in dry areas provide "islands" of greater moisture. Tropical examples include mounts Kilimanjaro and Kenya in East Africa and the west slope of the Andes in South America. Middle-latitude examples include the Australian Alps, the Caucasus, various ranges of the Trans-Himalayas, the Rockies, Great Basin ranges, and the east slopes of the Cascades and Sierra Nevada in North America. Such intermediate-altitude forests do not occur in the drier regions of subpolar regions because temperatures are too low to allow favorable development with elevation.

The fundamental reason for better soil development with increasing altitude in arid and semiarid regions is the increasing moisture, which results in more complete plant cover and greater production of organic material. It also intensifies chemical and physical weathering processes and thus hastens breakdown in parent material and creates deeper soils and finer particles. The greater leaching and an increased population of soil microorganisms speed up the decomposition and incorporation of organic matter; hence, arid soils tend to be darker in color with increasing altitude. Arid soils are generally alkaline but become less so as moisture increases with elevation (Fig. 7.5). Lastly, nitrogen content and the base-exchange capacity of soils increase with increasing elevation in arid mountains (Whittaker et al. 1968; Hanawalt and Whittaker 1976, 1977).

Exposure to the sun is especially critical in dry areas, and marked differences may occur in soil and vegetation development between north and south-facing slopes

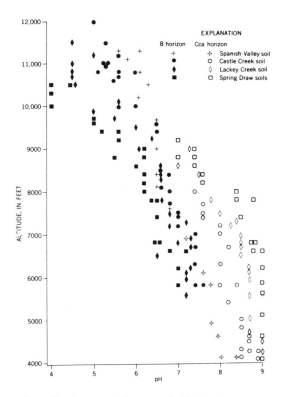

Fig. 7.5. The general decrease of pH of soil with altitude in the La Sal Mountains, Utah, a semiarid region. (From Richmond 1962, p. 89)

of steep slopes and narrow ridges, the area favorable to soil development will be relatively small; if the landscape in the zone is composed of broad and gentle upland slopes, the area of favorable soil development will be considerably larger (Costin 1955). Examples of broad, gently sloped areas situated within favorable climatic zones at higher altitudes include the Altiplano of Bolivia and Peru and the Tibetan Plateau. To a lesser degree, similar conditions occur on the gentle dip slopes of fault blocks in the Basin and Range mountains of the western United States.

The optimum climate area may occasionally occur in the subalpine zone— e.g., the Australian Alps. This area has a maximum elevation of 2,220 m (7,328 ft.) on Mount Kosciusko and coincides with the broad, gentle upland surfaces. The timberline is located at about 1,800 m (6,000 ft.). Lack of extensive glaciation, with the presence of adequate moisture in the subalpine zone, has favored soil devel-

(Shreve 1915; Whittaker et al. 1968). There is frequently a vertical displacement of tens of meters or more within a given vegetation or soil zone from one exposure to another (Fig. 7.6). In hot and dry areas the more favorable plant sites usually extend to higher elevations on poleward-facing slopes and shaded areas, while in wet or cold areas they extend higher on sunny slopes. If the terrain is steep and rugged, particularly if it is glaciated or erosion is continuously active, soil development is greatly limited. In addition, in arid mountains optimum conditions for plant and soil development prevail only in a narrow vertical zone between the low-temperature high altitudes and the arid low altitudes. If the mountainous topography within this zone of optimum conditions is composed

Fig. 7.6. Idealized cross-section of plant-community patterns from north- to south-facing slopes in the Santa Catalina Mountains, Arizona, a desert environment. Elevations above 2,700 (9,000 ft.) are extrapolated from the nearby Pinaleno Mountains. (Adapted from Whittaker et al. 1968, p. 441)

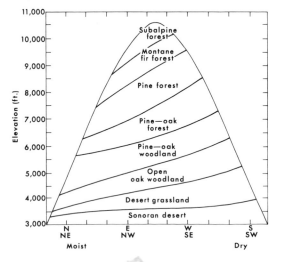

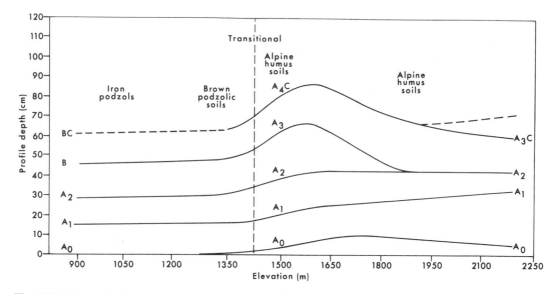

Fig. 7.7. Relationship between soil development and altitude in the Australian Alps. While the profile terminology is complex, the important point is that soil depth is greater at intermediate altitudes in the transition to the alpine zone (dashed line) than at either lower or higher levels: there is insufficient moisture for good soil development at lower levels, while at the highest levels temperatures become limiting. (After Costin et al. 1952, p. 203)

opment to an unusual degree (Fig. 7.7). In fact, Costin (1955, p. 35) has called the Australian Alps "soil mountains" to distinguish them from others such as the European Alps that are predominantly peat or rock.

The soil types of dry mountains have not been well-documented. Of the major soil groups listed for middle-latitude humid mountains in the previous section, the lithosols and regosols (entisols) are probably most common, followed by subalpine and alpine grassland soils (mollisols). The other major soil groups of humid mountains are represented sparingly, if at all. Shrubs, open forests, and dryland grasses are the dominant types of vegetation in semiarid areas, with the amount of bare land increasing with aridity. Soil development should follow accordingly, with the driest areas supporting lithosols and regosols (entisols) or grey or red desert soils (aridisols), and in the direction of increasing moisture grading into grey or brown wooded soils (alfisols), or chestnut-brown, chernozem, and prairie soils (mollisols).

Humid Tropical-Mountain Soils

Mountains of the humid tropics characteristically rise from lowlands supporting dense tropical forests. With increasing elevation, the lowland forests are replaced by montane forests that become lower in stature and density until the trees eventually give way to shrubs, grasses, and herbaceous plants at the highest levels (see pp. 263–69). Thus, the environment becomes less productive with altitude, but this may reflect the interplay between temperature and moisture, and their combined effects on a highly selective flora, rather than soil productivity. Indeed, soils in the humid tropics, like those of deserts, generally improve with elevation (up to a certain point). The soils of most tropical lowlands are notoriously poor; they exist in a hot and humid environment with excessive rainfall, rapid decomposition of organic material, and heavy leaching of nutrients. Whereas most soils serve as a storehouse of nutrients to be tapped by plants, lowland tropical soils are so depleted that the living biomass of the forest, rather than the soils, holds the available nutrients. As long as the forest remains, so do the nutrient reserves; they are continuously recycled through leaf fall, decomposition, leaching, and uptake by tree roots. If the forest is destroyed, the source of nutrients is removed and the soils quickly become leached of their nutrients. For this reason, most attempts to grow annual crops on a large scale in the tropics, as is done in middle latitudes, have failed. In the higher altitudes of the tropics, where soils are more fertile but where temperatures are still favorable, annual crops are much more successful. In fact, corn, potatoes, beans, and squash, among others, were first domesticated and grown in the tropical highlands (Sauer 1936). The presence of agriculturally suitable soils, plus a moderate climate at intermediate altitudes, often results in greater population densities in tropical highlands than in the lowlands (see pp. 393–400).

One striking characteristic of humid tropical-mountain soils is the increase of organic matter with increasing altitude (Thorp and Bellis 1960; Askew 1964; Frei 1964; Rutherford 1964). This is due to the lower rates of decomposition under lower temperature regimes. In the lower montane forests of New Guinea, at 2,500 m (8,250 ft.), the ratio of organic matter in the soil is 4 : 1, compared to 0.5 : 1 in adjacent lowland tropical forests (Edwards and Grubb 1977, p. 943). Leaching also decreases and nutrients are depleted less rapidly. As a consequence, tropical mountain soils commonly have a higher nutrient status than those in the lowlands (but see Grubb and Tanner 1976; Grubb 1977; Edwards and Grubb 1977). The accumulated organic material provides a ready source of nu-

trients, especially of phosphorus and nitrogen (Jenny 1941; Haantjens 1970, p. 102). Another reason for the greater nutrient content of humid tropical-mountain soils is that they have been less severely weathered than in the lowlands (Burnham 1974). This is because of the reduced rates of weathering that occur with altitude, as well as the relative youthfulness of the mountain landforms. Many tropical mountains were created only during the late Tertiary period. In New Guinea, for example, strongly weathered soils are restricted to elevations below 2,100 m (7,000 ft.). On the other hand, weathering is almost always sufficiently rapid in the tropics, even at higher altitudes, to create adequate soil profiles. Consequently, lithosols (entisols) are relatively scarce except on the highest summits and ridges. Considerable contrasts are found between mountains, however (Smith 1977b). Owing to the relatively rapid rates of soil weathering, rock type generally has less significance for soil formation in humid tropical mountains than in middle- and high-latitude mountains.

The primary soil-forming process in the humid tropics is *laterization*: the selective leaching of silica from the upper layers of the soil, leaving the iron and aluminum (iron and aluminum are largely responsible for the red-and-yellow color of tropical lowland soils). Optimum conditions for laterization are high rainfall, high temperature, and the absence of organic material. The oxides of iron and aluminum are relatively insoluble in the absence of humic acids, so they are retained, while silica is soluble under these conditions and is easily transported downward. With increasing elevation, however, temperatures become lower, organic matter accumulates, and laterization weakens. Podzolization is the reverse of laterization: it involves the selective leaching of iron and aluminum and leaves the silica behind in the upper layers of the soil. Therefore, as the organic matter increases (creating humic acids), and temperatures become lower, podzolization becomes more prevalent. Although most characteristic of the coniferous forests of middle-latitude and subpolar mountains, podzolization also operates at higher altitudes in the humid tropics (Hardon 1936; Askew 1964; Harris 1971; Burnham 1974). Podzolization results in increasing acidity, more distinct soil horizons, and darker soil colors with increasing altitude. These tendencies only hold true up to the timberline; beyond this point the climate becomes markedly drier, and diurnal frost-action means that the vegetation and soils, under a system of continual disturbance, show only limited development (Zeuner 1949; Coe 1967; Agnew and Hedberg 1969).

POTENTIAL AND LIMITATIONS OF MOUNTAIN SOILS

With the exception of intermediate elevations in arid and humid tropical mountains, soils generally deteriorate with increasing elevation. They become thinner, coarse and rocky, acidic, unstable, infertile, and immature. In spite of these limitations, mountains support a fairly complete vegetation cover and display moderate productivity (see pp. 298–300). Compared to lowland environments, however, the potential of high mountain soils is limited.

Soil productivity is a function of the totality of processes operating at any location. If soils remain frozen or snowcovered for long periods, the operational level of physical, chemical, and biological processes is greatly reduced no matter what the soil quality. Low temperatures during the growing season effectively limit the number and kinds of species which exist in that environment, and lack of moisture sets similar limits. Therefore, the most obvious way to increase the productivity of mountain soils is to increase the temperature and provide adequate moisture; under these conditions, the biological component should improve and this will soon be reflected

in the soils. Unfortunately, such environmental alterations are impractical in most cases.

The character of mountain soil itself helps to explain why these soils are relatively unproductive. Their shallow depth restricts the penetration of biological activity. Their coarse texture and lack of structure reduce their base-exchange capacity and water-holding ability. Their low pH (high acidity) restricts plants and soil organisms. Their deficiency of nutrients, especially nitrogen, is also limiting. The more luxuriant growth of plants around animal burrows and bird roosts in alpine areas reflects the high nitrogen content of animal droppings. It would seem that soil productivity could be increased simply by adding fertilizers. Experiments have demonstrated this to be true, but plants are apparently inefficient users of nitrogen at low temperatures (Scott and Billings 1964; Bliss 1966).

An additional factor in the nutrient status of mountain soil is the relatively high presence of organic matter. Most exchangeable bases are found near the surface and decrease with depth, just as organic material does. There is a clear trend toward increasing organic matter with altitude in many mountains, but this does not always connote a similar increase in fertility. In fact, the reverse may be true. The increased accumulation of organic matter is commonly caused by decreased rates of decomposition and assimilation under lower temperatures rather than by an increase in organic-matter production. The build-up of organic material through decomposition actually takes nutrient material out of circulation. This is an important factor affecting productivity in high altitudes, where nutrient capital is already small (Smith 1969, p. 9; Edwards and Grubb 1977; Edwards 1977; Grubb 1977).

Organic material is also important to mountain soils in its capacity as an efficient water-absorbing medium, reducing runoff

Fig. 7.8. Soil erosion in subalpine grassland, Wallowa Mountains, Oregon. Top view, taken in August 1938, shows the effects of trailing and heavy grazing by sheep during the early part of the century. Turf-defended soil pedestals demonstrate extent of erosion. Bottom view, taken in August 1968, shows the situation thirty years later, after grazing has been greatly curtailed. The area had not been grazed at time of taking the photograph. Aside from the general expansion and recolonization of grasses, the most spectacular development is the establishment of numerous tree seedlings, mainly Whitebark pine (*Pinus albicaulis*). (E. H. Reid, courtesy of G. S. Strickler, U.S. Forest Service)

and buffering the mineral soil from erosion. The stability of soils beyond timberline is largely due to the presence of a fairly complete cover of herbs and grasses that forms a tight matrix of organic material and interwoven roots. Once the vegetation is destroyed, the soil becomes much more susceptible to erosion. Herein lies one of the greatest limiting factors to the use of mountain soils for agricultural purposes.

Agricultural land-use in mountains varies greatly, depending on the cultural and physical context of the local mountain area. In North America we have scarcely begun to use our mountain areas for agricultural purposes, while in other parts of the world— e.g., the Alps, Andes, and Himalayas— settlement and intensive agriculture have been practiced for centuries. The highest altitudes are used primarily for grazing, and the intermediate altitudes are used for cultivation of cereals and tuber plants.

Most high mountain areas can withstand some grazing, but animals that graze in herds, especially sheep and goats, can rapidly damage an area (see pp. 421–26). Many examples of the effects of overgrazing in mountains could be given. Perhaps the classic area is in the Mediterranean and Middle East, where several thousand years

of grazing have so stripped the surrounding hills that scarcely any natural vegetation remains and soils have been severely eroded. At the same time, there has been large-scale destruction of forests. The Cedars of Lebanon, those formerly widespread and choice timbers used in Solomon's temple, have been so reduced in extent that only a few small enclaves of original growth remain (Mikesell 1969) (Fig. 12.1). Even in the mountains of the western United States, where grazing is not much more than a century old, the clearly evident effects are a cause for concern (Fig. 7.8) (Strickler 1961; Marr 1964; Johnson 1965). Fortunately, steps have been and are being taken to counter this danger. Many higher areas of public lands that were once freely grazed are now either declared off-limits, or their use is carefully regulated.

Cultivation of mountain lands is limited not only by steep surfaces and thin soils, but also by climate (Fig. 7.9; Table 11.1). If the climate is adequate and the need is great, even the steepest slopes may be cultivated. If steep slopes are to be brought under cultivation, terracing is the single best method, but it is an extremely expensive endeavor. In most cases terracing has been accomplished by highly organized and sophisticated cul-

Fig. 7.9. Climatic ecological zones in the high Andes of southern Peru and northern Bolivia. (From Troll 1968, p. 33)

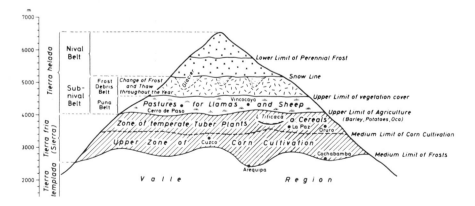

tures which have settled permanently in an area and have continued to maintain the fields and terraces (see pp. 393–400) (Figs. 2.2, 11.1, 11.3). Such an approach is in the minority, however; most mountain agriculture is much less ecologically sound and leads to rapid erosion. An intermediate situation is that in the Alps, which have a long history of settlement and agriculture. This landscape has been remarkably preserved, considering the length of time it has been used; nevertheless, the replacement of natural vegetation by other crops has led inevitably to soil depletion (Bouma 1974; Lichtenberger 1975).

Mountain land-use in the more advanced countries of western Europe or North America is now fairly strictly regulated, but in many other areas, such as parts of the Andes, Himalayas, and the mountains of Australasia, unrestricted use of marginal lands continues. Population densities are increasing, and in some cases great damage is being done to the mountain environments (Eckholm 1975). So great is the concern for mountain environments that they have become a major focus for investigation by the recently established UNESCO Man and the Biosphere Program (Man and Biosphere 1973a, 1974a, 1975; Ives 1974c, d, 1975, 1979). Mountain soils have a limited capacity to support life, but the increasing pressure on these lands requires us to learn a great deal more about them and about the consequences of our actions. The Man and the Biosphere Program is a big step in the right direction.

8

Mountain Vegetation

So call not waste that barren cone
Above the floral zone,
Where forests starve.

Ralph Waldo Emerson,
Monadnoc (1845)

Because they extend vertically into different environmental regimes within small horizontal distances, mountains display the most rapid and striking changes in vegetation of any region on earth. The recognition of different vegetation zones on mountain slopes was one of the earliest activities of plant geographers. Albrecht Von Haller, author of *Die Alpen*, published a paper on vegetation in the Alps in 1742 (in Braun-Blanquet 1932, p. 348), and the number of studies has grown steadily since that time. One important study was Alexander Von Humboldt's investigation at the end of the eighteenth century in the new-world tropics, for which he established the terms *tierra caliente, tierra templada,* and *tierra fria* to describe climatic zones (hot, temperate, and cool) identified and delineated on the basis of vegetation. He also tacitly assumed that the vertically arranged climatic and vegetative sequence in tropical mountains—from lush tropical rainforest in the lowlands to perpetual frost and snow at the highest levels—was a microcosm of similar zones with changing latitude from the tropics to the poles. This analogy between altitudinal and latitudinal changes in climate has caused a great deal of misunderstanding, because its truth depends upon how literally it is taken. At a very broad and simple level the patterns of climate and vegetation are similar, but in important details they are not at all alike. Unfortunately, this distinction is not usually made in elementary texts, and the uncritical acceptance of the concept by even some leading plant geographers (Good 1953) has perpetuated the problem.

The only climatic similarity between a high tropical-mountain climate and a polar climate is that of the average annual temperature. Except for purposes of gross generalization, this is meaningless, because the distribution of temperature in time and space differs so greatly (Troll 1948, 1959, 1968). The polar climate is one of seasonal extremes, with short summers with very long days and long winters with very long nights. The change in temperature between day and night is small, however, since the sun is either always shining (hence "land of the midnight sun") or almost totally absent. The situation in the tropical highlands is just the opposite, with essentially no seasonal variations in temperature through the year (unless there is a wet and dry season) (Figs. 4.17, 4.18). There is no winter or summer, and the length of day and night remains about the same. The sun is high overhead every day, with great capacity to warm the surface, but it is absent an equal number of hours at night, allowing rapid loss of heat to the cold darkness of space. Consequently, the temperature range in the tropics is usually greater between day and night than between the winter and summer periods.

The climate of middle-latitude mountains is, predictably, somewhere between that of tropical mountains and that of polar regions. In contrast to tropical mountains, middle-latitude mountains have a definite seasonal development with accompanying environmental extremes, but at the same time, the daily fluctuations exceed those of polar climates. The proof of the essential difference

among these three environmental systems is the fact that plants from one environment usually have difficulty growing in another. This can be seen even within the same species, e.g., the Alpine sorrel (*Oxyria digyna*) from the Sierra Nevada of California and from the Arctic tundra. While both areas have cold climates, the length of day during the growing season is very different, so plant populations in the two regions display slightly different characteristics. If an individual is taken from one environment and planted in the other, it usually fails to survive, and even if it survives, it will not reproduce (Mooney and Billings 1961).

The distribution of vegetation and climate on a global scale varies not only with respect to altitude and latitude, but also from the northern to the southern hemisphere. This is primarily because of the unequal distribution of land and water. The northern hemisphere contains two-thirds of the land area of the earth, with most of the land mass located between 30°–70° north latitude (Fig. 8.1). This produces a much greater degree of continentality in the northern hemisphere, and this, in turn, has favored the development of the boreal forest (northern coniferous forest) and Arctic tundra, neither of which has any real counterpart in the southern hemisphere. The basic asymmetry of global vegetation between the two hemispheres is nicely displayed in a vertical cross-section (Troll 1959, 1968) (Fig. 8.2). Vegetation types are unequally distributed on either side of the equator, with a sharp transition between the northerly high altitudes and tropical mountains. Mid-latitude southern-hemisphere mountains are climatically and vegetatively more similar to tropical mountains, owing to the stronger ocean presence which moderates the seasonal extremes (Troll 1960).

In addition to the normal changes that occur with altitude and latitude, the presence of mountains profoundly influences the biogeography of the earth through their effects on global climate as well as their

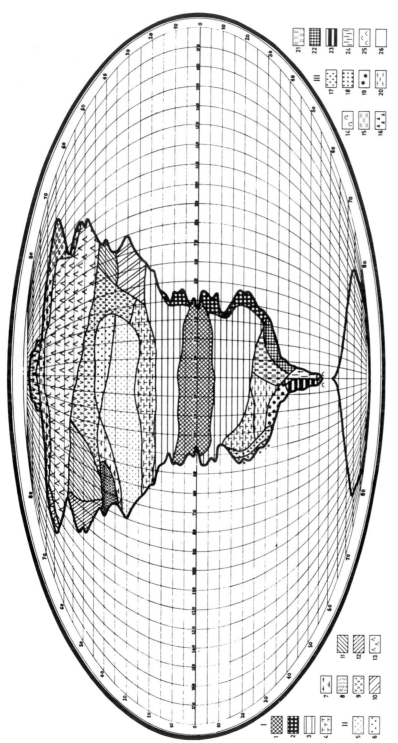

Fig. 8.1. Asymmetrical distribution of land and climatic vegetation zones in the northern and southern hemispheres, as displayed on a "summarized continent."

I. *Tropical climates:* 1. Equatorial rainforests; 2. Tropical rainforests based on orographic rainfall in winter; 3. Tropical moist savanna belt; 4. Tropical dry and thorn savanna belt.

II. *Extratropical climates of the northern hemisphere:* 5. Hot deserts; 6. Temperate continental deserts with cold winters; 7. Subtropical winter-humid steppes; 8. Warm-temperate shrubland of Mediterranean type; 9. Continental grass-steppes with cold winters; 10. Subtropical summer hot monsoon-climates with evergreen broadleaf woodlands; 11. Suboceanic cold-temperate deciduous woodlands; 12. Oceanic cold-temperate deciduous and evergreen woodlands; 13. Boreal coniferous forests; 14. Boreal birch woodland; 15. Subarctic tundra; 16. Arctic frost debris desert.

III. *Extratropical climates of the southern hemisphere:* 17. Coastal deserts with moderately warm summers; 18. Coastal deserts; 19. Warm temperate evergreen woodland with summer dryness; 20. Subtropical thorn and succulent shrubland; 21. Subtropical grasslands; 22. Subtropical rainforests; 23. Cool-temperate rainforests; 24. Cold-temperate steppes with mild winters; 25. Subantarctic tussock grasslands; 26. Antarctic ice-cap and frost deserts. (After Troll 1968, p. 31)

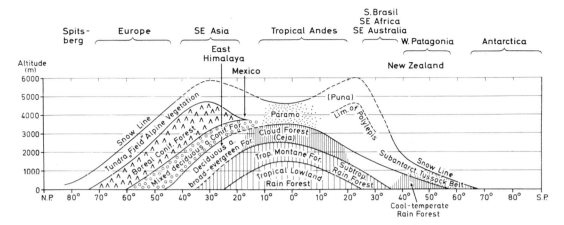

Fig. 8.2. Vertical cross-section of the major humid-vegetation types, showing general altitudinal and latitudinal relationships. Note the presence of several vegetation types in the northern hemisphere that have no counterparts in the southern hemisphere. This is largely due to the unequal distribution of land and water. (After Troll 1968, p. 30)

stricter biological role of serving as pathways, barriers, and islands with respect to the migration and evolution of species. Mountains serve as pathways for plant migration because they extend into areas of lower temperature and provide an environment more like that found nearer the poles. Plants that have evolved in cold climates and are adapted to these conditions may move freely in either direction along the mountain crests, especially when the mountains are oriented north-south, as they are in the Americas. Here the cordilleras—e.g., the Andes and Rockies—have facilitated interchange of species (Weber 1965; Van der Hammen 1968; Troll 1968; Lauer 1973). Much less interchange has taken place between Europe and tropical Africa, although many Afroalpine plants are related to temperate-latitude species (Engler 1904; Good 1953, p. 185; Hedberg 1961, 1969, 1971). The east-west orientation of European mountains with no interconnecting range, plus the presence of the Mediterranean Sea and the Saharan barrier, have interfered with the free interchange of species. Although the Himalayas are also oriented east-west, they are much more massive and have interconnecting ranges through Malaysia and Indonesia, so extensive interchange of species has occurred in the high mountains of Australasia (Van Steenis 1934, 1935, 1962, 1964; Raven 1973).

Mountains also act as barriers to the migration of species. When a mountain range blocks the direction of migration, species which cannot survive in the hostile environments at high altitudes will not be able to cross the mountains (Janzen 1967). The unlike conditions which typically develop on the windward and leeward sides of ranges also present an obstacle. Even if a species does manage to pass across the mountains (perhaps through a transecting valley), it may still be unable to establish itself, because of the unsuitable environment on the other side and because of competition from other species which are better adapted to these conditions.

Mountains, particularly isolated peaks and mountain masses separated from each other by many kilometers of lowlands, often serve as mainland islands, with many of the biogeographic characteristics of oceanic islands (MacArthur 1972; Carlquist 1974). Migration to or from a mountain is hindered

by a "sea" of unlike environment and vegetation. The smaller the size of mountain
masses at different altitudes and the farther
apart they are, the greater the difficulty of
species interchange. Some of the best examples of mainland islands are the high
tropical mountains of Africa, surrounded as
they are by savannas, and the Basin and
Range mountains of the western United
States, which are separated from each other
by many kilometers of desert shrubs (Figs.
9.2, 9.3). An important consequence of this
isolation is that each species has a limited
gene pool that receives little infusion from
outside. Consequently, adaptation becomes
adjusted primarily to local environmental
conditions, and evolution frequently results
in the creation of species found only on that
mountain (endemics). The implications of
the island-like distribution of mountains for
animals are discussed at greater length in the
next chapter (pp. 310–13).

A number of typical plant-community
characteristics occur with increasing altitude. Foremost among them is decrease in
number of species. Changes also take place
in the form and structure of plants and in the
assemblages of species that grow in any
given area: the tendency is toward smaller
and less elaborate plants with slower growth
rates, decreased productivity, decreased
plant diversity, and less interspecies competition. Of course, there are exceptions,
e.g., the increased diversity in some tropical
cloud-forests and the increase in species
with altitude in some desert mountains
(Myers 1969; Pearson and Ralph 1978), but
these are special circumstances and do not
negate the general tendencies.

The primary characteristic of mountain
vegetation is the presence of sequential
plant communities with increasing altitude.
Whether there exist clear and recognizable
vegetation zones or belts is another question
(Beals 1969). In the tropics, such zones may
be quite distinct and obvious, while in latitudes nearer the poles, zones are often more
difficult to identify. In addition, the status of

the vegetation is important: disturbed sites
typically support plant communities different from those which have remained undisturbed for long periods. The most frequently used approach in classifying and
mapping vegetation is based on the recognition of a plant association or community
being at *climax* (Oosting 1956; Daubenmire
1968). A climax community is the culminating stage in natural plant succession, wherein a complex of species is so well-adjusted
to each other that they are able to reproduce
and maintain themselves for long periods of
time (at least for centuries) (Churchill and
Hanson 1958). For example, if tree seedlings
on the forest floor are of the same species as
the oldest trees of the forest, the plant community is apparently maintaining itself
and is therefore at climax. Similarly, if a
plant community partially destroyed by fire
eventually replaces itself through a succession of intermediate vegetation types and
then becomes relatively stable with no
further directional change, it can be considered as the climax for that region. Much
controversy surrounds the concept of climax; for our purposes, it will be assumed
that the climax vegetation type is controlled
by climate, even though other local factors
(e.g., rock type, topography, continual disturbance of various sorts) may overrule or
substitute for the general control of climate.

Several different approaches to the study
of altitudinal zones have been proposed
(Merriam 1898; Daubenmire 1943, 1946;
Troll 1958b, 1972a, 1973b; Holdridge 1957;
Love 1970). Each of these approaches may
work well for one region or another, but
their application on a global scale becomes
difficult. Nevertheless, most mountains display a sequence of forest vegetation of some
sort on their upper slopes and, if they are
high enough, they display a treeless zone.
The lower mountain forest is generally
known as the *submontane* or *montane zone* (often divided into upper and lower areas); the
higher forest composes the *subalpine zone*.
The treeless area above is known as the

alpine zone (Daubenmire 1943, 1946; Marr 1961; Love 1970).

MOUNTAIN FORESTS

Forests consist of three dominant life forms: needleleaf evergreen conifers (pine, spruce), broadleaf evergreen trees (banyon, magnolia), and broadleaf deciduous trees (oak, maple). The needleleaf conifer grows primarily in middle and higher latitudes of the northern hemisphere and presents a very different appearance from conifers found in the montane forests of the southern hemisphere, where they are much less important and occur mainly as associated species with broadleaf evergreen trees. The conifers of the southern hemisphere belong to different genera and have different life forms from the pines, spruces, and firs of the northern hemisphere. A good example is the Araucaria pine, or Monkey-puzzle tree (*Araucaria spp.*), from South America, which has been widely planted in the northern hemisphere as a garden ornamental. Broadleaf evergreen trees tend to be dominant in warm and humid regions with small temperature ranges. Such conditions are exemplified in the tropics and in the middle latitudes of the southern hemisphere, where the presence of the ocean reduces seasonal temperature extremes. In the northern hemisphere, with its much greater continentality and seasonal contrasts, the dominant broadleaf trees are deciduous rather than evergreen.

Northern-Hemisphere Mountain Forests

The needleleaf evergreen conifer dominates the higher reaches of northern-hemisphere mountain forests. The species of these forests are closely related to those of the boreal forest (the great north woods), which stretches in an almost unbroken band across North America and Eurasia immediately south of the Arctic tundra. The climate of widespread mountain-ous areas is obviously different from that of the subarctic, but the general temperature decrease with elevation and the resultant brevity of the growing season are similar enough that boreal species have extended even into the subtropics. In some cases they have persisted as the same species; in others there are different but related species in the two areas. There is no question about their common ancestry, however. This is demonstrated by the remarkable fact that 90 percent of the coniferous species dominating the mountains of the northern hemisphere belong to only three genera: pine (*Pinus spp.*), spruce (*Picea spp.*), and fir (*Abies spp.*) (Eyre 1968, p. 59).

Broadleaf deciduous forests are also a dominant life form in mountains of the northern hemisphere, especially on the lower and intermediate slopes of humid regions in the middle and lower-middle latitudes. The major concentrations of these forests are in western Europe, eastern Asia, and the eastern United States. These broadleaf deciduous forests display great similarity in appearance and structure. Although the species are distinct, the genera are similar, suggesting former connections between the now widely separated plant formations. The major genera in common are oak (*Quercus spp.*), maple (*Acer spp.*), beech (*Fagus spp.*), elm (*Ulmus spp.*), hickory (*Carya spp.*), chestnut (*Castanea spp.*), ash (*Fraxinus spp.*), hornbeam (*Carpinus spp.*), and birch (*Betula spp.*) (Eyre 1968, p. 78). At high altitudes, broadleaf deciduous trees generally give way to conifers, which persist on the upper slopes until conditions become so unfavorable that trees can no longer grow. In a few areas broadleaf deciduous trees (mainly birches) form the upper timberline, but these are the exception rather than the rule (Troll 1973a).

While broadleaf deciduous trees cover large areas of the middle latitudes and have been very successful in post-glacial times, needleleaf conifers display an amazing range of adaptability and have been particularly successful in occupying marginal habitats. Thus, coniferous forests dominate such disparate mountain environments as the cloudy, rainsoaked climate of the Cascades, the sunparched slopes of the Atlas Mountains in North Africa, and the cold and windy slopes at the upper timberlines in mountains throughout the northern hemisphere. In all these environments conifers have proven to be well-suited to cold winters and short growing seasons, as well as to a variety of other adverse conditions. Their form is usually compact, with a streamlined crown that tapers to a point and exposes a minimum of surface to the environment. This has the advantage of shedding snow quickly and being less vulnerable to the wind. Needleshaped leaves also have an advantage over broad leaves in that less area is exposed to wind damage and to loss of moisture through transpiration. This is critical in summer under the desiccating high-altitude sun, and in winter when the roots are frozen and unable to replenish the tree's moisture supply.

Most coniferous species require fewer nutrients from the soil than do broadleaf trees, so they are in a better position to take advantage of the diverse and rocky substrates found in high mountains. By the same token, conifers return fewer nutrients to the soil through leaf fall and litter accumulation, so the soils formed under coniferous forests are relatively acid and infertile compared to those that develop under broadleaf deciduous forests (Hoff 1957). Another advantage of evergreen conifers is their ability to begin photosynthesis as soon as conditions permit in the spring, while broadleaf deciduous trees have to spend valuable time growing new leaves before they can begin photosynthesis. This is especially critical in areas with a very short growing season. Of course, if conditions become too severe, as in parts of northern Siberia and some high mountain areas, the evergreen conifer may be eliminated simply because it is evergreen. The

trees cannot maintain live leaves during the extremely cold winter. If trees grow at all in such environments, the evergreen conifer is replaced by the deciduous conifer, larch (*Larix spp.*) or by broadleaf deciduous trees such as birch (*Betula spp.*) or aspen (*Populus spp.*) (Troll 1973a, p. 7).

Plants respond not only to the physical environment but also to competition with other species. Conifers dominate in some areas because they are better adapted to the environment, but they may also dominate because the broadleaf trees growing in that area are relatively short-lived species that require high sunlight for germination and do not reproduce well under the shade of the forest. This hastens the rate of change and species turnover. In many areas, broadleaf deciduous trees are the first to occupy disturbed sites, but they are eventually replaced by conifers. The broadleaf species are not eliminated by the rigors of the environment, however, but by competition. This is nicely demonstrated by the distribution of Quaking aspen (*Populus tremuloides*) in the Rocky Mountains, where it grows primarily in disturbed sites, e.g., landslides, mudflow, or fire-devastated areas. One can fly over the Rockies in autumn when the aspen leaves are turning and easily plot the areas that have undergone recent disturbance (Ives 1941). In some cases, the aspen is eventually replaced by more shade-tolerant coniferous species such as the Subalpine fir (*Abies lasiocarpa*) and Engelmann spruce (*Picea engelmannii*) (Marr 1961, p. 65). It is interesting to conjecture what would happen in the absence of conifers. Would the aspen then be the climax species? This seems to be the case in several of the Basin and Range mountains in Nevada and southeast Oregon. These mountains stand like elevated islands amid a sea of desert shrubs and are separated by considerable distance from other forested areas (Fig. 9.3). Their vegetational histories are complex, but the important point here is that their upper slopes largely lack coniferous trees, so

Fig. 8.3. The Quaking aspen (*Populus tremuloides*) forming the upper timberline at 2,700 m (9,000 ft.) on Steens Mountain, Oregon. Note the wind-shaped and stunted appearance of the tree. (Author)

the aspen ipso facto becomes the dominant species and forms the treeline (Faegri 1966) (Fig. 8.3).

In mountains where broadleaf deciduous trees form the climax vegetation type, e.g., at lower and intermediate altitudes in western Europe, eastern Asia, and the eastern United States, they are normally replaced by their own kind after disturbance. But in the higher reaches of these same mountains, and at all levels in other mountains, such as those of the western United States, broadleaf trees are usually replaced by conifers. Consequently, the existence of broadleaf deciduous trees in areas where coniferous forests form the climax vegetation type provides evidence of recent disturbance. Since most mountain surfaces are highly

Betula in Himalayas

unstable in both time and space, what typically results is a mosaic of vegetative communities of different ages and composition occupying a mosaic of contrasting habitats. If an area passes for long periods of time without substantial disturbance, and especially without a fire, diversity decreases and the community becomes more and more exclusive. There are many good examples of this in the mountain forests of the western United States, where stringent fire-control measures have been in effect since the turn of the century.

This brings up important philosophical and practical questions of environmental policy. There has been great pressure in the United States to preserve mountain areas in their natural state. The Wilderness Act of

1964 requires that the management of such areas aim at retaining their natural qualities with a minimum of human intervention. The philosophy of this act comes into direct conflict with long-standing policies of forest-fire prevention. Although fire may seem to be a destructive and unnatural force, it is very much a natural part of most ecosystems. This is especially true of mountain forests, where lightning fires are a common phenomenon. If we truly plan to retain pristine and natural "wilderness" areas, fires must be allowed to burn (albeit under a watchful eye) (Heinselman 1970; Habeck 1972a; Wright 1974).

Major ecological changes have come about in the mountain forests of the western United States in the last fifty years as a result of stringent forest-fire control. In general, the dominant species have taken over at the expense of habitat diversity. Without frequent small fires, the broadleaf successional species which would otherwise grow in the burnt-over areas have become much less important. This, in turn, reduces the number of potential ecological niches that plants and animals can occupy (Loucks 1970). A good illustration is what happens to large browsing animals, such as deer, elk, and moose, that feed on the young and tender leaves of successional species like birch, aspen, alder, and willow. If the forest is allowed to develop without any major sort of disturbance, these tree species are eventually eliminated and replaced, greatly reducing the food sources for those animals, with the result that their populations decrease. In recognition of this factor, as well as for other ecological considerations, many forests once carefully protected from fire are now being selectively burned (Kilgore and Briggs 1972; Wright and Heinselman 1973).

The decision to allow forests to burn has not been arrived at easily. It has required a major reversal in our way of thinking. This is poignantly illustrated by the comments of an enlightened forester working in the Selway-Bitterroot Wilderness of western Montana and northern Idaho:

Early Tuesday we contoured east to the old Bell Point Trail and from the first vista overlooking East Moose Creek we spotted a small fire burning on a steep slope west of Footstool Point. Started by lightning, that little smoke was an obvious part of the natural scene. Since its opportunity to spawn a giant conflagration is small, as we live—it should burn. And that certain life chains may thrive in this wilderness—it should burn. Our pre- and post-season policy, if applied, would let it burn under surveillance. But I wonder, once discovered, if the adrenalin generated in men born of fire suppression will let that life-giving spark over there on the mountain give life. (Quoted in Habeck 1972a, p. i)

Mountain meadows present another interesting example of the kinds of conflicts that can arise between natural processes operating in forested areas and the will of man. These grassy, treeless openings in the forest are usually due to poor drainage, excess snow, or fire. Meadows offer a visual and ecological contrast with the forest and, like the spaces between notes of a song, account for much of the beauty of the subalpine landscape. A recent massive invasion of conifers into the mountain meadows of the Cascades and Sierra Nevada has therefore been observed with some alarm (Brink 1959; Franklin et al. 1971). The period of greatest invasion was in the 1930s, so that a well-developed stand of fairly evenly aged trees is now beginning to overtake parts of the meadows (Fig. 8.4). This development is apparently due to the warming and drying trend, especially the decreased snowfall, experienced between the late 1800s and the mid-1940s (Franklin et al. 1971). The invasion was short-lived—very few seedlings have been established since; but as those that have become established mature, block out the light, and drop their own seed, they threaten the existence of the meadows. Since the meadows are key recreational attractions and provide forage for game and livestock, this raises interesting management questions. If tree encroachment is allowed to proceed naturally, the meadows may very well pass into forest within a few

Fig. 8.4. Meadow invasion taking place at an elevation of 1,800 m (6,000 ft.) in the subalpine zone, Three Sisters Wilderness Area, Oregon Cascades. The young trees, all about 25–35 years old, consist primarily of Mountain hemlock (*Tsuga mertensiana*). (Jay Marcotte, Portland State University)

decades. On the other hand, if the meadows are to be preserved, it may be necessary to cut the young trees and saplings (Franklin et al. 1971). These are characteristic of the kinds of problems that are increasingly presenting themselves in mountain areas. They require careful consideration and difficult decisions, but they must be faced and acted upon (wisely, it is to be hoped) by man in his role as steward of the earth.

Tropical Mountain Forests

The forests of tropical mountains are very different from those in the northern hemisphere. They consist of broadleaf evergreen and coniferous trees with rounded, umbrella-shaped crowns and relatively luxuriant foliage. A great variety of species occur, flowering more or less continuously throughout the year. There are no seasons in the moist tropics, only the rhythmic changes from day to night. The old clichés of "winter every night, summer every day" or "eternal spring" are not inappropriate in many cases. One day is much like another; seasonal manifestations, if present, usually result from variations in moisture rather than in temperature. Some tropical areas have a wet season and a dry season; if the seasonal differences are extreme enough, the trees may display adaptations similar to those found in mid-

Table 8.1. *Changes in the character of tropical forest with altitude on Mount Maquiling, Philippine Islands (after Brown 1919, p. 110, in Richards 1966, p. 355).*

	Dipterocarp Forest (450 m)	Mid-Mountain Forest (700 m)	Mossy (Cloud) Forest (1,020 m)
Number of tree stories	3	2	1
Height of tallest tree on plot (m)	36	22	13
Average height of stories (m)	27, 16, 10	17, 4	6
Number of individuals of woody plants over 2 m high	353	539	610
Number of species of woody plants over 2 m high	92	70	21

dle latitudes, e.g., they become deciduous and drop their leaves during the dry season. Variations in moisture also produce temperature differences—it is cooler when cloudy and moist than when sunny and dry; however, distinct thermic seasons do not generally exist until a latitude of 15°–20° is reached.

The most obvious vegetational changes from place to place in tropical forests are those that occur with altitude. The lush rainforests of the lowlands gradually decrease in height and complexity on upper slopes, being replaced by communities that are poorer in species and simpler in structure. The typical three-storied effect so

Fig. 8.5. Generalized scheme showing the vertical zonation of vegetation in tropical-mountain regions. (After Troll 1968, p. 35)

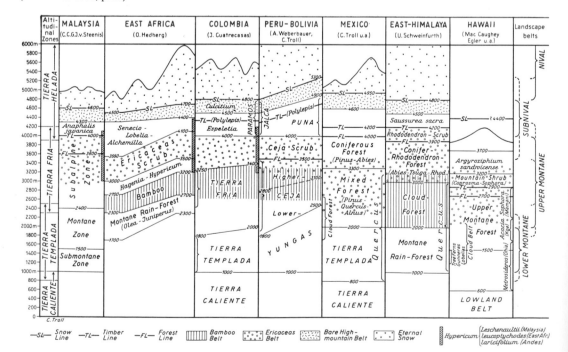

Fig. 8.6. The mossy forest on Cerro Pando at 2,290 m (7,500 ft.), near the border between Costa Rica and Panama. (Charles W. Myers, American Museum of Natural History)

common in the lowlands is replaced by a two- and then a one-storied forest (Table 8.1). Leaves decrease in size, lose their drip tips, and show other adaptations to drier and sunnier conditions. The buttressing of tree trunks becomes less frequent and eventually disappears, while the bark becomes thicker. The abundance of lianes (hanging vines) and the profusion of elaborate flowering plants decrease, while lichens and mosses increase on the upper slopes (Richards 1966, p. 373; Grubb 1977, p. 84). A number of temperate genera make their appearance above 1,000 m (3,300 ft.). Although these, are generally represented by only a few species in the temperate latitudes, some have proliferated into a great number of distinct species in the tropics. For example, there are over 40 species of pine (*Pinus spp.*) and 200 species of oak (*Quercus spp.*) in Mexico; a similar development can be observed in Malaysia (Troll 1960, p. 532). There is nevertheless a decrease in the total number of species with elevation (Table 8.1).

Tropical forests generally show a well-developed zonation in the major plant communities with altitude (Fig. 8.5). The typical progress is from lowland tropical, to submontane, to montane, to subalpine forest, and eventually into the alpine zone of grasses and shrubs. The most distinctive and characteristic of these is the so-called *mossy forest* or *elfin woodland* found in the montane and/or subalpine zone between 1,000–3,000 m (3,300–10,000 ft.). This is essentially a cloud forest adapted to the shade and damp of the clouds which persist at this level (see pp. 100–101). The trees consist of a single layer of stunted and gnarled individuals about 6 m (20 ft.) in height, with an almost overwhelming abundance of epiphytic mosses and liverworts that literally cover every trunk and branch, giving the forest a dank and somber lushness (Fig. 8.6). These forests, characteristic of tropical mountains, can be found at approximately the same elevations in Malaysia, Africa, and South America (Fig. 8.5). In the tropical Andes the cloud forest is called *ceja de la montaña* ("eyebrow of the mountain"). Although species differ in the widely separated regions, the general appearance of the forests is similar (Grubb 1974). Above the cloud

forest, the trees may increase in height for a short distance due to sunnier and drier conditions, but their height is soon reduced again as the severity of the environment increases. The forest ceases to be continuous and breaks into patches interspersed with grasses. Lower temperatures become increasingly important in limiting trees, and by 3,500–4,000 m (11,500–13,200 ft.) the trees disappear altogether and are replaced by grasses, shrubs, and bare rocky ground. A long history of man-set fires often makes it difficult to interpret the interaction of vegetation and climate in high tropical mountains. In many places, such fires have been responsible for pushing the timberline well below its climatic limits (Gillison 1969, 1970; Hope 1976; J. M. B. Smith 1975, 1977a).

The sequence of vegetation zones from lowland tropical forest to alpine shrubs and grasses is extrapolated from observations on tropical mountains that are high enough to reach the climatic timberline. Most moun-

Fig. 8.7. The effect of mountain mass on the height of different vegetation zones in the humid tropics of Indo-Malaysia. (Adapted from Eyre 1968, p. 267)

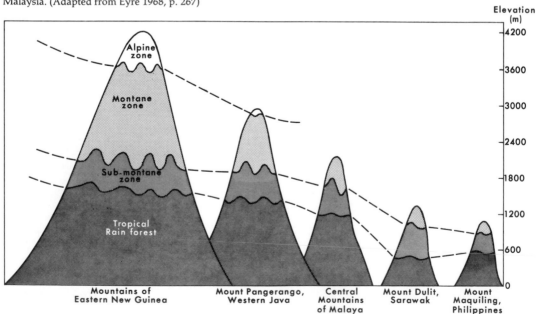

Mountains of Eastern New Guinea
Mount Pangerango, Western Java
Central Mountains of Malaya
Mount Dulit, Sarawak
Mount Maquiling, Philippines

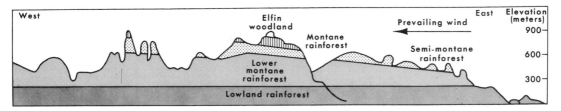

Fig. 8.8. Vegetation cross-section of the Northern Range, Trinidad, West Indies. Total horizontal distance is 29 km (18 mi.). There is a distinct zonation of vegetation in spite of the small elevational differences; the zones are depressed toward the eastern end of the island owing to the effect of the prevailing trade winds. (Adapted from Beard 1946, p. 41)

tains do not extend to this height, but a few in each of the three tropical regions do, and the representative vegetation zones are usually present. This is not a simple matter, however, since the larger a mountain is, the higher in elevation any given plant community goes and, conversely, lower mountains may have the same vegetation communities but at lower elevations (Fig. 8.7). This has historically been interpreted as being a reflection of the "mountain-mass effect," on the supposition that the larger a mountain is, the more it modifies its own climate (see pp. 77–81). While this concept is valid and is still broadly adhered to, it is not entirely satisfactory as an explanation for vegetation distribution in the wet tropics because of the uniform tropical climate, absence of seasons, and dominance of marine conditions there, all of which tend to override the mountain-mass effect (Van Steenis 1961; Grubb 1971). A recent explanation suggests that the altitude of vegetation zones in the tropics is controlled by the persistence of clouds. The depressed levels of vegetation zones on smaller mountains are a result of the lower cloud levels, which tend to raise the water content of the soil and slow the rate of decomposition of organic matter. These conditions, in turn, reduce the supply of nutrients to the plants, so that each plant community adjusts downward (Grubb 1971, 1974, 1977). Whatever the exact reason or reasons, a distinctive "mountain vegetation" may be found on many tropical mountains whose elevation does not exceed 1,000 m (3,300 ft.) (Beard 1946; Richards 1966; Howard 1971; Grubb 1974) (Table 8.1).

A similar pattern of forest-zone depression can be seen on windward and coastal mountains, as compared to leeward or more continental mountains. The depression of vegetation zones is demonstrated by the distribution of forests on the low mountains of Trinidad, an island off the coast of Venezuela at about 10° N. latitude (Fig. 8.8). Submontane, montane, and elfin-woodland zones are represented even at these low elevations. The zones are also depressed toward the eastern side of the island, which faces the prevailing trade winds (Beard 1946, p. 41).

In association with latitude and altitude, lack of moisture is also a major factor in controlling the distribution of mountain vegetation in the tropics. Not all areas support lush forests. Some regions are so dry that trees will not grow; others support trees only in certain areas. This is demonstrated in East Africa on the isolated peaks of Kilimanjaro, Kenya, Ruwenzori, etc., which rise from relatively dry plateaus supporting scattered forest and savanna grasses. The mossy forest occurs at an elevation of about 2,400 m (8,000 ft.). Although it does not develop from the wet rainforest sequence just discussed, it is similar in appearance to those in other tropical areas and the vegetational zones above this level are similar to those found in Malaysia and on the eastern side of

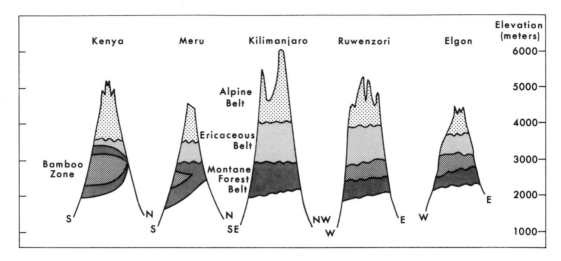

Fig. 8.9. Vegetation zones in the mountains of East Africa. The wettest side of each mountain is turned to the left. Savanna or steppe vegetation dominates below the montane forest belt, although in some areas there is lowland tropical forest. Only the vertical distances are drawn to scale. (Adapted from Hedberg 1951, p. 165)

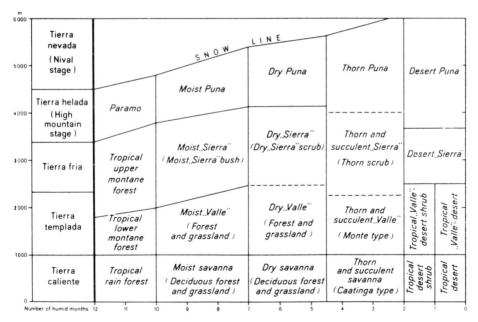

Fig. 8.10. The relationship of vegetation to temperature and precipitation in the tropical Andes. Altitudinal changes controlling temperature are shown along the lefthand column and moisture gradients, largely controlled by latitude, are shown along the bottom. Where it is continually moist (left side), forests dominate throughout, but with decreasing moisture trees become less important, until they disappear entirely in the driest sequence (right side). (From Troll 1968, p. 44)

the Andes (Figs. 8.5, 8.9). Bamboo forests are a distinctive plant community on the mountains of East Africa. These forests occur in other tropical mountains but not to the same extent. Even in East Africa, bamboo forests are found only in certain mountain areas and are not found at all on Kilimanjaro. Some authors feel that the bamboo should be considered only a transitional phase of montane forests because of the great fluctuations it displays in its peculiar life cycle (Hedberg 1951, p. 165).

The most extreme examples of lack of moisture occur where highlands rise from tropical deserts. The mountains of the Sahara, such as the Ahaggar and Tibesti, exceed 3,000 m (10,000 ft.) but they are fairly dry and do not support a forest, although scattered *xerophytic* (adapted to drought) shrubs and trees occur above 1,500 m (5,000 ft.) (Messerli 1973). The western side of the Andes is so arid in some areas that trees do not grow anywhere, from the valleys to the peaks. The Andes, which display the entire gamut of environmental extremes, are an ideal place to study the interplay among latitude, altitude, and moisture availability in montane forests (Figs. 8.10, 8.11). Near the equator in northern Ecuador and Colombia, the rainforest ascends to similar elevations on both sides (Fig. 8.11, top). Convectional processes operate on both slopes and precipitation is equally heavy. Within a few degrees to the north or south, however, these areas come under the influence of the northeast and southeast trade winds; the east side of the Andes is wet, while on the west side, in the rain shadow, desert conditions prevail. This produces a strongly asymmetrical distribution of vegetation across the range (Fig. 8.11, bottom) (Troll 1968, p. 46).

Despite the negative effects of lack of moisture on tree growth, trees nevertheless attain their highest altitudes in the drier zones. This paradoxical situation is apparently a result of the greater build-up of heat in areas where there is less cloudiness: the sun, allowed to reach the ground more of the time, raises the surface temperature above that of the surrounding air. The snowline reaches its highest elevation in the same areas. Pine forests (*Pinus hartwegii*) grow up to 4,000 m (13,200 ft.) in central Mexico at 20° N. latitude (Lauer 1973). In western Bolivia at 18° S. latitude, a stunted Polylepis forest (*Polylepis tomentella*) exists at 4,800 m (15,800 ft.) in the dry Puna belt (Fig. 8.14). This is thought to be the highest forest limit in the world (Troll 1968, p. 44).

Southern-Hemisphere Mountain Forests

Southern-hemisphere mountain forests are composed primarily of broadleaf evergreen trees. These forests display considerable diversity and luxuriance, with more species of trees, shrubs, lianes, epiphytes, and herbs than those of the northern hemisphere. There are elaborate tree-ferns in the understory of many southern-hemisphere temperate mountain forests, even near the timberline. Although some species interchange has taken place between the northern and southern hemispheres, the floras on either side of the equator have evolved more or less separately and are, therefore, relatively distinct.

In the humid tropics, there is little difference in species composition north and south of the equator, but by 15°–20° latitude, where seasonal contrasts begin to be expressed, the differences become apparent, particularly at the higher elevations. The montane forests extending from Bolivia to Mexico have very similar genera, with *Weinmannia*, *Podocarpus*, and *Fuchsia* occurring throughout, but by an elevation of 2,000 m (6,600 ft.) the forest composition in the north becomes distinctly boreal, while the forests to the south become dominated by southern-hemisphere species. This pattern probably results primarily from geological history and plant evolution rather than from differences in the present climate, since the mountain environments this close to the equator are similar. The

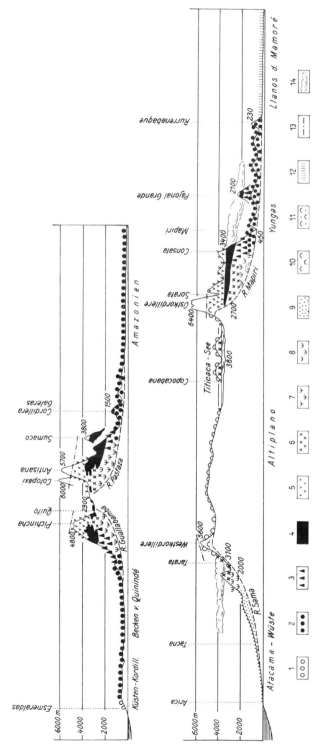

Fig. 8.11. Cross-section of major plant communities in the equatorial Andes (top) and subtropical Andes at the latitude of Lake Titicaca, 16° S. (bottom). West is to the left. Symbols for vegetation types are as follows: 1. Semideciduous lowland forest; 2. Tropical lowland forest; 3. Tropical lower-montane forest; 4. Tropical upper-montane forest (cloud forest); 5. Humid alpine communities (páramos); 6. Evergreen shrub and *Polylepis* woodland; 7. Thorn and succulent woodlands; 8. Thorn and succulent shrubs; 9. Desert; 10. Moist grass Puna; 11. Dry thorn Puna; 12. Moist lowland savanna; 13. Snowline; 14. Cloud belt. (From Troll 1968, p. 45)

situation changes rapidly beyond the Tropics of Cancer and Capricorn, however, because of the contrasting size of land masses in the northern and southern hemispheres at higher latitudes (Fig. 8.1). As a result, a much greater marine influence is displayed in the southern hemisphere, and this tends to produce typically cool and damp climates.

The cool lowland temperate forests of Patagonia and New Zealand very much resemble the upper-montane forests of tropical Malaysia, East Africa, and the Andes (Fig. 8.2). The analogy between altitudinal and latitudinal changes in vegetation is more or less applicable to the southern hemisphere. Many tree genera and species found in middle latitudes of the southern hemisphere are also found in tropical mountains (Troll 1960, p. 532). A good comparison can be made between the mountain forests of New Guinea just below the equator, and New Zealand, which is 40° farther south. In both the forests consist of evergreen beeches (*Nothofagus spp.*) and conifers such as *Podocarpus spp.* and *Papuacedrus spp.*, although New Guinea has a much greater profusion and mixture of species, while New Zealand forests tend to be pure stands of the evergreen beech (*Nothofagus spp.*) (Wardle 1973a). A similar situation is found in Australia, where the upper forests are dominated by evergreen gums, especially the Snow gum (*Eucalyptus niphophila*) (Costin 1957, 1959). In southern Chile the evergreen beech (*Nothofagus spp.*) is again important, as are the Araucaria pine (*Araucaria spp.*) and the southern Cypress (*Fitzroya spp.*). Just as in the northern hemisphere, however, there is still a distinct decrease in timberline elevations and a marked decrease in species with distance from the equator.

TIMBERLINE

The transition from forest to tundra on a mountain slope is one of the most dramatic ecotones on earth. Here, within a vertical distance of a few tens of meters, trees disappear as a life form and are replaced by low shrubs, herbs, and grasses. Although the exact nature of the timberline varies from place to place, the general pattern is sufficiently similar throughout the world that it can be discussed as a single phenomenon. For some reason or combination of reasons, trees grow only up to a certain elevation. This fact has major implications to all forms of life. For example, beyond the timberline there are no tree squirrels or bark beetles; birds must look elsewhere for a song perch or a place to build a nest. The shaded and quiet stillness of the forest floor gives way to the exposed and rapidly fluctuating environment of the open tundra. It is truly another world.

Ecologists have long been fascinated by the upper timberline, and their studies in this zone have introduced a wide array of terms, some of which need defining here. *Timberline* is an all-inclusive word connoting the entire transition from closed forest to open treeless tundra. *Forestline* is the upper limit of contiguous forest. Where the transition is very abrupt, the forestline essentially coincides with timberline; where there is a gradual transition from forest to tundra, the forestline may be relatively indistinct. *Treeline* is the upper limit of erect arborescent growth and is usually represented by scattered clumps of trees or isolated individuals beyond the forestline. It is sometimes difficult to decide exactly what constitutes a tree, however, so that an arbitrary height is normally assigned, usually 2–3 m (6–10 ft.). This is done to differentiate between the treeline and the *scrubline* or *krummholz line*, which is the upper limit of stunted scrublike trees (Arno 1967). In some areas, e.g., the grassy balds of the southern Appalachians or of the Great Basin of Nevada, there are anomalously low timberlines that exist below the climatic limit because of various local factors (Billings and Mark 1957; Gersmehl 1971, 1973). There is also a lower timberline in many semiarid mountain areas where the forest passes into desert shrubs or grasses at its lower edge, usually because of lack of moisture (Daubenmire 1943). Our concern, however, is with the upper timberline at its climatic limits.

Characteristics of Timberline

In general, the upper timberline is highest in the tropics and lowest in the polar regions (Fig. 8.12). However, the absolute highest timberlines occur between 20°–30° latitude in the dry Puna de Atacama of Peru and the high plateau of Tibet, rather than in the moist tropics. The timberline ranges from sea level in the polar regions to 3,500–4,000 m (11,500–13,200 ft.) in the moist tropics and up to 4,500 m (14,900 ft.) or even slightly higher at its extreme upper limits in the dry subtropics. Timberline in the middle latitudes rises an average of 110 m (360 ft.) per degree of latitude until it reaches the subtropics, at about 30°, where the line abruptly levels out or descends

slightly toward the equator (Daubenmire 1954). As a general rule, timberlines are lower in marine locations and higher in continental areas. In the United States, for example, timberline occurs at 1,500 m (5,000 ft.) on Mount Washington in New Hampshire, rises to over 3,000 m (10,000 ft.) in the Rockies of Wyoming and southern Montana, and descends again to 1,800 m (6,000 ft.) in the Oregon Cascades. In addition, timberline tends to reach higher altitudes on larger mountains than on smaller mountains, because of the mountain-mass effect (see pp. 77–81). This well-established relationship can be observed in all climatic regions. We have already noted it in tropical mountains (although the precise mechanism may be somewhat different in the tropics) (Figs. 8.7, 8.8), and it is equally well, if not better, displayed in middle-latitude continental mountains. Thus, trees grow higher in the central Alps than they do in the marginal ranges, and a similar pattern can be seen in the Rockies (Brockmann-Jerosch 1919; Griggs 1938).

Another major characteristic of timberline on a global scale is the dominance of evergreen species. Although broadleaf de-

Fig. 8.12. Schematic north-south view of the highest summits (top solid line) and the upper limit of vascular plants (dotted line). Timberline altitudes are shown both for the drier continental situations (lower solid line) and for the wetter marine situations (dashed line). (After Swan 1967, p. 32)

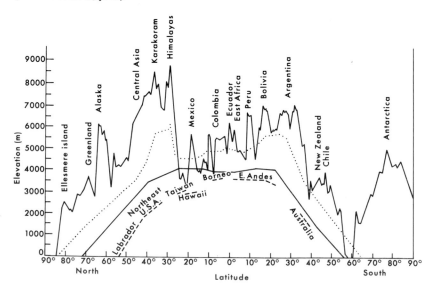

ciduous species do form the timberline in some areas, the preponderance is of evergreens. This can be seen with the evergreen conifers and beeches of the southern hemisphere and tropics, as well as with the needleleaf conifers of the northern hemisphere. The conclusion is that there must be some advantage to evergreen over deciduous trees in the extreme environments of the upper timberline (see pp. 260–61) (Daubenmire 1954, p. 122).

Floristics

The timberline trees of northern-hemisphere mountains are all closely related to the boreal forest with the pine family being most dominant, especially pine (*Pinus spp.*), spruce (*Picea spp.*) and fir (*Abies spp.*). These genera are represented by similar species in mountains throughout the northern hemisphere; in many cases they occupy similar ecological niches. This is strikingly illustrated by the Whitebark pine (*Pinus albicaulis*), which occupies the upper timberline in the Cascades, Sierra Nevada, and parts of the Rockies. The large, wingless seeds of this tree cannot be wind-transported. Instead, they are dispersed by the Clark's nutcracker (*Nucifraga columbiana*), a large grey jay that eats some of the seeds but caches the rest. Although the nutcracker invariably finds the cache, even through a meter (3.3 ft.) of snow, it usually misses a few seeds, and these may sprout and grow the following season. Thus the relationship between tree and bird works to the advantage of both. An identical relationship between pines and nutcrackers is found in western Europe from the Alps to the Caucasus between *Pinus cembra* and *Nucifraga caryocatactes*, and in the mountains of eastern Asia between *Pinus pumila* and *Nucifraga caryocatactes* var. *japonicus* (Holtmeier 1972, p. 95; Franklin and Dyrness 1973, p. 273).

Other members of the pine family (*Pinaceae*) found at timberline include hemlocks (*Tsuga spp.*) and larches (*Larix spp.*). The hemlock is represented only by the Moun-

tain and Western hemlocks (*Tsuga mertensiana* and *T. heterophylla*) in the Cascades and Coast ranges of western North America. The larch (*Larix spp.*), a deciduous conifer, is represented by a handful of species in North America and Eurasia. The juniper (*Juniperus spp.*) is also found in most northern-hemisphere mountains but usually grows as a scattered and low shrub (Wardle 1974, p. 372) (Fig. 6.16).

Broadleaf deciduous trees form the timberline in some areas, especially Scandinavia, eastern Asia, and parts of the Himalayas (Troll 1973a, p. 7). The dominant genus is birch (*Betula spp.*), but others such as aspen (*Populus spp.*), alder (*Alnus spp.*), and beech (*Fagus spp.*) also occur (Fig. 8.3). Although these broadleaf genera grow at the timberline in some areas, it is usually in the absence of any serious competition from conifers. Even where conifers dominate, broadleaf deciduous trees may still exist as associated species, especially in areas of instability. For example, broadleaf trees frequently dominate in avalanche tracks, since they can regenerate from underground organs and their stems are flexible and can withstand deformation by moving snow (Fig. 8.13).

Timberline areas in tropical and southern-hemisphere mountains are much more limited and floristically more diverse than in the north (Wardle 1974, p. 373). Mountains high enough for timberline to occur form a meridianal ridge through South America, but are limited to the tropics in Africa and exist only as scattered enclaves in Australasia, where New Zealand has the most extensive timberline area. Broadleaf evergreen species dominate throughout the southern hemisphere, with the evergreen beech (*Nothofagus spp.*) being by far the most prominent. The distribution of this genus is especially noteworthy because it is ill-adapted to long-distance dispersal, yet is found in such widely separated areas as South America, Tasmania, Australia, New Zealand, New Caledonia, and New Guinea.

Fig. 8.13. Avalanche path in the northern Caucasus near Dombai, U.S.S.R. Note the dominance of broadleaf deciduous trees (aspen) in the active avalanching zone. This is because the broadleaf trees are successionary after disturbance and, more resilient than the conifers, can stand the stress better. Consequently, as long as active avalanching continues in this zone, the broadleaf trees will continue to dominate. The prostrate trees in foreground are a result of avalanching during the preceding winter. (Author)

On the basis of this and other curious plant and animal distributions, many southern-hemisphere biogeographers were led to becoming early staunch supporters of continental drift (Darlington 1965). Although *Nothofagus* is generally evergreen, in the slightly drier and more continental areas of Patagonia, Australia, Tasmania, and New Zealand it becomes deciduous. Coniferous species of *Araucaria*, *Podocarpus*, *Libocedrus*, and *Papuacedrus* grow in association with the *Nothofagus*. In Australia, however, the upper timberline is dominated almost entirely by the Snow gum (*Eucalyptus niphophila*) (Costin 1959).

The timberline vegetation of tropical mountains is dominated by the heath family, *Ericaceae*. The many species in this family grow as evergreen shrubs and trees with characteristically tough and leathery leaves. Dominant genera include *Gaultheria*, *Vaccinium*, *Rhododendron*, *Befaria*, *Pernettya*, *Erica*, and *Philippia*, to name only a few. The exact significance of *Ericaceae* in tropical mountains has not been determined, although many species are resistant to fire and instability and reproduce quickly after an area has been burned or otherwise disturbed (Sleumer 1965). Troll (1959, 1968) has identified an "Ericaceous belt" in all the tropical mountains (Fig. 8.5). In the tropical Andes, an ericaceous genus, *Polylepis*, grows as shrubby trees on steep rocky slopes above the cloud forest. One of these, *Polylepis tomentella*, reaches almost 4,800 m (15,800 ft.), the highest elevation of tree growth in the world (Troll 1973a, p. 11) (Fig. 8.14).

In the high mountains of tropical Africa, an ericaceous woodland of *Erica* and *Philippia* grows up to 3,500–4,000 m (11,500–13,200 ft.). Tussock grasslands occur above this, along with the very curious giant *Senecios* and *Lobelias* (Fig. 8.15). Equivalent plant forms grow in the high mountain grasslands of the tropical Andes (*Espeletia spp.*) (Fig. 8.16), as well as at the timberline in Java (*Anaphalis spp.*). The presence of similar life forms in these widely separated areas is generally interpreted as representing convergent evolution under similar conditions. These huge plants are extremely bizarre. Although they grow to heights of several meters and are tree-like, they are in fact tall, massive, unbranched columnar herbs. The confusion as to whether to call them trees has made the delimitation of timberline in these areas somewhat problematic (Hedberg 1951; Troll 1960, 1973a).

Fig. 8.14. Small patch of *Polylepis* woodland (*Polylepis tomentella*) at an elevation of 4,600 m (15,100 ft.) in the Puna belt of northern Chile. This is near the absolute upper limit of tree growth for the world. (Carl Troll, 1927, University of Bonn)

Fig. 8.15. View of Mount Kenya, 5,199 m (17,157 ft.), from the head of the Teleki Valley at 4,200 m (13,860 ft.). This mountain, which stands almost exactly on the equator, still has glaciers: Tyndall Glacier is on the left and Lewis Glacier is on the right. The tall columnar plants on valley floor are *Senecios spp.*, and the tree(?) in the lower right corner and others like it are *Lobelias spp.* (Å. Holm, courtesy of Olov Hedberg, University of Uppsala)

Fig. 8.16. Páramo vegetation at 4,200 m (13,860 ft.) near the foot of Tolima Volcano (not shown) in the Colombian Andes. This is an *Espeletia spp.* community with a groundcover of grasses. Note the similarity between these curious plant forms and the *Senecios* and *Lobelias* (Fig. 8.15) from the mountains of East Africa. (Jose Cuatrecasas, 1932, Smithsonian Institution)

Timberline Patterns

The pattern of timberline varies a great deal from the tropics to the poles: it is represented by different species and life forms, as well as by different environmental regimes and infinite variations in local conditions. Nevertheless, in all latitudes the general timberline pattern is for the forest to decrease gradually in density and height, eventually breaking into scattered clumps of trees separated by meadow or park-like openings dominated by shrubs and other low-lying vegetation. In the northern hemisphere, trees beyond the forestline are commonly stunted and their branches flagged from the force of the wind (Figs. 8.17, 8.18).

The trees frequently grow in small clumps or islands with the tallest trees in the center, decreasing in height outward to the margins. Such tree islands are a characteristic feature of the forest-tundra ecotone in the northern hemisphere (Fig. 8.18). They usually become established around a single tree which has found a small niche or favorable site on the open tundra. As this tree grows, it modifies the environment around it slightly, i.e., the snow melts sooner because of the darker color and greater heat absorption of the tree, thereby providing a better habitat for tree seedlings in its immediate vicinity. In addition, many trees at timberline have the ability to reproduce by layering: a branch touches the ground, takes

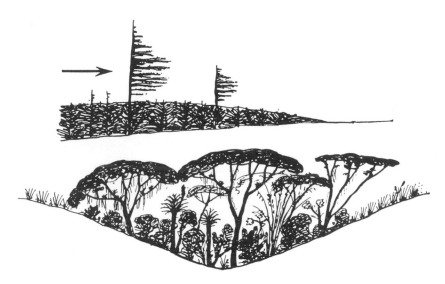

Fig. 8.17. Characteristic flagged tree-form at timber-line in the northern hemisphere (top), contrasted with umbrella-canopy form of the humid tropics (bottom). (From Troll 1968, p. 28)

Fig. 8.18. A well-developed tree island near the upper timberline, at 2,700 m (9,000 ft.) in the Wallowa Mountains, Oregon. Large trees in middle are White-bark pine (*Pinus albicaulis*), smaller surrounding trees are Subalpine fir (*Abies lasiocarpa*) and Engelmann spruce (*Picea engelmannii*). (Author)

Fig. 8.19. Windswept and prostrate tree growth (krummholz) on a ridge at 1,800 m (6,000 ft.) in the Olympic Mountains, Washington. View is to the northwest and prevailing winter wind is southwesterly (from the left). Species are Subalpine fir (*Abies lasiocarpa*), Whitebark pine (*Pinus albicaulis*), and Mountain hemlock (*Tsuga mertensiana*). (Author)

root, and eventually becomes a separate tree. In this way tree clumps originate and expand. They may eventually merge with one another to form forest if long-term climatic trends are favorable, but it is a slow process.

Trees at timberline also begin to display *krummholz*, a German term used to describe the stunted, gnarled, and misshapen tree forms of the high mountains (Fig. 8.19). With increasing altitude, trees become more and more prostrate and deformed. Characteristically, the small tree clumps have one or two trees in the center with trunks surrounded by a dense skirt of limbs and shoots extending horizontally around the base (Fig.

8.20). The height of this skirt reflects the depth of winter snow: below the snow, the scrubby tree growth is protected, but any buds or shoots protruding above the snow are killed by the cold, desiccating winter wind (Figs. 8.19 and 8.20). In the most exposed sites, the trees exist only as low-lying mats of contorted shrubby growth a few centimeters high. This is perhaps the classic image of the treeline: lonely, bowed, and twisted trees clinging tenaciously to a cold and windswept mountain slope. For northern-hemisphere mountains, this is a fairly accurate impression but in tropical and southern-hemisphere mountains krummholz, although present, is generally not

Fig. 8.20. Summer and winter photos of the same small tree island, located near the upper timberline at 500 m (1,650 ft.) in northern Finland (68° N. lat.). Species is spruce (*Picea abies*). The snow clearly protects and insulates the lower shrubby growth, whose height is almost exactly limited by the depth of the winter snow. Above this, the trees bear the full brunt of exposure to the wind and cold. (F. K. Holtmeier, University of Münster)

well-developed. In New Zealand, where the timberline is formed by the evergreen beech (*Nothofagus spp.*), the forestline is usually quite sharp, passing abruptly from erect trees to a zone of low-lying shrubs. These shrubs consist of different species from those of the forest, however, and are naturally (genetically) low-growing, not reduced in stature by environmental factors. This is in fundamental contrast to northern-hemisphere timberlines (Wardle 1965). A few northern-hemisphere species have become genetically stunted—e.g., the Dwarf mountain pine (*Pinus mugo*) in the European Alps—but most are deformed and stunted in response to environmental stress. The relative contributions of internal (genetic) and external (environmental) factors in producing krummholz are still little-understood (Clausen 1963; Wardle 1974; Grant and Mitton 1977).

The reason for the abrupt forestline in New Zealand is that the evergreen beech seedlings are apparently very delicate and need shade, so they do not form outposts beyond the closed forest (Wardle 1973b). A similar pattern exists in the moist tropics. On Mount Wilhelm in New Guinea, the treeline occurs at about 4,000 m (13,200 ft.) (Wade and McVean 1969). There is some stunting of the trees but they maintain their umbrella-shaped crowns and the canopy is still 3–6 m (10–20 ft.) high (Fig. 8.17). The forest passes rather abruptly into grasses or shrubs at this elevation with no marked tendency toward krummholz, reflecting the relative lack of strong prevailing winds. The abruptness of the forestline may also be due to a history of fire (Gillison 1969, 1970; Hope 1976; J. M. B. Smith 1975, 1977a).

Another basic difference between the distributional patterns of timberline in the tropics and in the northern hemisphere is that trees grow to higher altitudes on the ridges in the northern hemisphere, while in the tropics trees reach their highest point in the valleys (Troll 1968) (Fig. 8.21). Northern-hemisphere timberlines are strongly in-

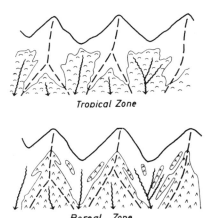

Fig. 8.21. Generalized timberline pattern on tropical and middle-latitude mountains. Trees normally reach their highest altitudes in valleys (wavy arrows) in the humid tropics, while they reach their highest altitudes on ridges (dashed lines) in the middle latitudes. (From Troll 1968, p. 29)

fluenced by the depth and duration of the snow cover, especially where the snow does not melt soon enough for new trees to become established or to allow mature trees to complete the metabolic processes necessary for successful reproduction. Since valleys and depressions are loci of greater snow accumulation, trees normally grow higher on the ridges in middle-latitude northern-hemisphere mountains even though they are more exposed to the desiccating wind and the soils are thin and poorly developed.

In the tropics, where snow is relatively unimportant, valleys offer a more favorable habitat than the more exposed ridges. Under the strongly diurnal climatic regime, the valleys experience smaller temperature ranges than the ridges and there is less danger of frost. Valleys also have deeper soils and are less exposed to the full sun, so more moisture is available to the plants (Troll 1968, p. 28). Elevated valley flats surrounded by higher slopes are an exception: they frequently support alpine vegetation rather than trees. This results in an *inverted timberline*, and, although poorly drained soils

Fig. 8.22. Ribbon forest separated by snow glades at 1,950 m (6,435 ft.) in Glacier National Park, Montana. Forest strips are 10–50 m (33–165 ft.) across and are oriented north-south, at right angles to the prevailing wind, which tends to pile the snow up in drifts in the immediate lee of the forest strips. The deep snow accumulation inhibits forest encroachment. At increasing elevations and wind exposure, ribbon forests give way to smaller patches of trees and eventually to krummholz. (Ernest Hartley, courtesy W. D. Billings, Duke University)

or fire may also contribute, is generally thought to be caused by cold air moving into the valley flat, forming ponds and creating frost pockets. A similar development of mountain meadows occurring below the

timberline exists in middle-latitude mountains, and for much the same reasons (see pp. 262–63), although increased snow accumulation and poorly drained soils are probably more important than air drainage in these areas (Wardle 1974, p. 388).

A last example of the variety of timberline patterns is provided by the *ribbon forests* and *glades* of the central Rocky Mountains (Billings 1969) (Fig. 8.22). These occur on gentle upper slopes exposed to heavy snowfall, strong winter winds, and cool summers. Under these conditions, tree ribbons develop at right angles to the prevailing wind and serve as natural snow fences, so that snow accumulates to their lee and persists late into the summer, preventing the expansion of the forest and maintaining the pattern of tree ribbons separated by glades (Billings 1969).

Causes of Timberline

The ultimate explanation for the cessation of tree growth on a mountainside is still unknown. A number of theories have been proposed, but the cause of timberline remains disputed. In any specific region or site, we can account for the timberline by such factors as excessive snow, strong winds, poor or excessive drainage, lack of soil, and recent disturbance by fire, disease, or volcanic eruptions. On Mount St. Helens in the southern Washington Cascades, for example, the timberline is at 1,340 m (4,400 ft.)—more than 300 m (1,000 ft.) lower than on Mount Rainier or Mount Hood a few kilometers to the north or south—because the volcanic cone is very recent (less than 2,000 years old) (Lawrence 1938). On a global scale, however, the overall similarity in the occurrence of timberlines (Fig. 8.12) has persuaded most investigators that some overriding ecologic principle must be at work transcending the local variations and fundamentally accounting for tree behavior at timberline (Boysen-Jensen 1949; Daubenmire 1954, p. 122; Wardle 1971, 1974, p. 379). Before discussing this, however, we must review the major environmental factors known to limit tree growth.

Snow

Snow is favorable to life in many ways: it provides excellent protection from the cold and wind and becomes a source of moisture when it melts in the spring. Too much snow, however, can smother trees, and avalanches or snow creep can damage and destroy them. Late-lying snow harbors molds and fungi which attack the trees (Cooke 1955). More importantly, late-lying snow reduces the effective growing season to the point that seedlings cannot establish themselves. This is chiefly why trees grow at higher altitudes along ridges than in valleys in most middle-latitude mountains (Shaw 1909) (Fig. 8.21). Of course, if conditions become too severe, as they do in some high-latitude mountains, then the trees again reach their greatest altitude in the valleys. In such cases, the valley, even with persistent snow, is preferable to exposed slopes where conditions are too severe for trees to exist. In spite of its obvious effects on the position of timberline, however, snow cannot be an ultimate controlling factor on a global basis, since it is insignificant in many tropical and arid mountains. Even in middle-latitude areas where heavy snow is important, it is probably best viewed as one of a complex of factors operating at timberline.

Wind

Wind velocity increases with altitude and may be a serious stress factor in high mountains, especially for trees, since they extend well above the ground. Wind can fell trees or break limbs and branches, particularly when they are coated with rime or glazed with ice and snow. Wind also serves as an abrasive agent, blasting trees with sand, soil, and snow particles; the bark may be worn smooth and limbs and branches broken on the windward side, giving rise to flagged trees (Figs. 8.17, 8.18).

Most important, however, is the damage the winter wind does to the young shoots and buds of evergreens by carrying off their moisture faster than the tree roots can replace it from the cold or frozen ground (Griggs 1938; Sakai 1970; Tranquillini 1979). The desiccating wind acts like a gardener trimming shrubs: shearing of the primary shoots encourages lateral growth. The results are plain to see in flagged branches, krummholz tree-forms, flat tree-canopies, and the characteristically streamlined appearance of tree clumps with their outer dwarfed trees and higher, more protected individuals toward the center. In very high, exposed sites, any branch sticking above the snow is killed by the wind (Figs. 8.19, 8.20).

Of course, if sites are too wind-exposed, trees may not even be able to establish themselves, let alone survive (Wardle 1968; Caldwell 1970). Most tree seeds are wind-transported from the forest at lower elevations, since trees at timberline frequently do not produce viable seeds. A study of the European spruce (*Picea abies*) in the Alps revealed that this tree produces cones at favorable sites every 3–5 years, at higher altitudes every 6–8 years, and at timberline only every 9–11 years. In addition, cones at timberline usually contain underdeveloped seeds or none at all (Tranquillini 1979, p. 11). Whether or not seeds produced lower down reach the higher elevations depends upon local conditions of wind and topography. Even if viable seeds do arrive at higher sites, their chances of survival are relatively small, because the steep and rocky surfaces are not favorable growing sites. On the other hand, neither are broad and level upland areas which are wind-swept and snow-free and provide no winter protection or summer moisture to the seedlings.

The importance of wind notwithstanding, it cannot be considered the ultimate factor in controlling timberline. This is demonstrated by the fact that wind is relatively unimportant in many areas, e.g., the tropics, where timberline is reached. There is also no correlation between latitude or continentality and wind velocity, as there is with the distribution of timberline (Fig. 8.12). Wind is certainly a major factor in the control of local timberlines, as is demonstrated by the absence of trees in such windy places as the Aleutian Islands, where the temperatures are not nearly as low as they are in the interior of Alaska, but trees still grow much nearer the poles in the interior. The importance of wind is also demonstrated by the marked depression of countless local timberlines on the windward side of mountain ranges (Fig. 8.8).

Sunshine

Several theories argue that the location of timberline is a consequence of either too much or too little sunshine (see Daubenmire 1954). Sunlight intensity increases with elevation because of rarification of the air; the relatively high component of ultraviolet light may impair the photosynthetic process and thereby limit the altitude to which trees can ascend (Collaer 1934). It has also been suggested that the excessive heat build-up at soil surfaces may be limiting to tree growth (Aulitzky 1967). Although ultraviolet light has been proven to have some deleterious effects in plants, their extent remains unknown (Caldwell 1968) (see pp. 70–73). A major objection to light intensity and heat build-up as overall limiting factors in the distribution of timberline is that trees grow highest in the dry subtropics of Tibet and Peru, where sunlight intensity is as great as any place on earth.

Cloudiness has similarly been invoked to explain the upper limit of forests. There is a correlation between cloudiness and low timberlines, since timberlines are invariably lower in marine than continental regions, but in areas other than the tropics it is difficult to separate the effects of clouds from those of wind, precipitation (especially snow), and temperature. For example, the timberline averages 500 m (1,650 ft.) higher on the east side of the Cascades (leeward) than on the west side (windward), but the

percentage of cloud cover is only one of the environmental differences to be considered. Associated with heavy cloud cover on the west are stronger winds, heavy precipitation (snow), and ameliorated temperatures.

Biotic Factors

Porcupines eating the bark of trees, mice or rabbits nibbling on young seedlings, and larger browsing animals eating leaves and shoots are all examples of the importance of biotic factors in controlling the growth of trees. The ibex (*Capra ibex*), which was exterminated in the Alps over 300 years ago by heavy hunting, was reintroduced in the 1920s; under protection, their numbers have increased to the point that they are now doing considerable damage to the timberline in parts of Switzerland (Holtmeier 1972, p. 96) (Fig. 8.23). Insects and diseases can cause considerable destruction of trees at timberline. The bark beetle (*Dendrocotonus engelmannii*) and spruce budworm (*Choristoneura occidentalis*) are both serious pests at timberline in the Rocky Mountains (Johnson and Denton 1975; Schmid and Frye 1977). In the Alps and Scandinavian mountains, the *Oporinia autumnata* and *Zeiraphera grisena* moths periodically damage the high-altitude forests (Holtmeier 1973). Insects greatly suppress the growth rates of eucalyptus in the subalpine forests of the Snowy Mountains, Australia (Morrow and LaMarche 1978). The various blights, rusts, and other pathogens that live in snow also cause considerable damage to timberline species (Cooke 1955).

Man, too, can greatly alter the location of the upper timberline. Since prehistoric times, humans have used fire for hunting and to clear land for agriculture. In the tropics, where these activities have been practiced longest, it is likely that few, if any, tropical timberlines are truly "natural." The heath family, Ericaceae, abounds near timberline in this environment precisely because of its ability to regenerate after fire (Sleumer 1965; Janzen 1973). The *Ericaceae*

Fig. 8.23. Several male ibex (*Capra ibex*) in the Swiss Alps. This wild goat was exterminated from the mountains of western Europe over 300 years ago, but was reintroduced during the 1920s. Under protection, their numbers have grown so much that they are now causing damage to the timberline in some areas. (Nicholas Shoumatoff)

are also well-represented in the subalpine and alpine zones of northern-hemisphere mountains. In the Pacific Northwest, Indians regularly set fires in the upper forest to maintain and increase their huckleberry (*Vaccinium spp.*) picking grounds. Fire (both man-set and natural) has been so important in some areas that a few trees have become fire-adapted. For example, in the mountains of the western United States, the Western larch (*Larix occidentalis*), Lodgepole pine (*Pinus contorta*), and Quaking aspen (*Populus tremuloides*) all regenerate quickly after a fire. These are successional species, but their replacement by other timberline species is frequently a very slow process. In Australia, the Snow gum (*Eucalyptus niphophila*) can regenerate from underground organs after its crown has been destroyed by fire (Costin 1959). Most timberline species are not adapted to fire, however, and recapture lost ground only slowly. For this reason, the effects of fire in timberline regions may persist for centuries.

Man has also greatly altered the location of timberline by cutting trees for lumber, for agricultural land, and for firewood (especially charcoal), and the intensive grazing of livestock has destroyed young trees and prevented seedlings from reestablishing themselves. In many areas the original level of timberline has been lowered by tens to hundreds of meters (Costin 1959; Molloy et al. 1963; Budowski 1968; Pears 1968; Holtmeier 1972; Eckholm 1975; Plesnik 1973, 1978) (Fig. 8.24). This is particularly true in parts of the Andes, Alps, and Himalayas which have supported large populations for millennia. The result has been increased erosion and flooding through more rapid runoff, less snow-storage capacity and, importantly, a greatly increased danger from ava-

Fig. 8.24. Remnants of a formerly much more extensive forest near Fluela Pass at 2,300 m (7,500 ft.) in the Swiss Alps, just east of Davos. Evidence that this is an anthropomorphic and not a climatic timberline is the upright growth form and the lack of flagging or other evidence of environmental stress on the trees. Centuries of timber-cutting and grazing have taken their toll on such regions. (Author)

lanches. There is now a concerted effort in the Alps to reforest the mountain slopes back to their natural limit (Douguedroit 1978). This has very practical implications, especially in those areas that depend heavily upon winter tourists, because of the role of the forest in reducing avalanche danger (Fig. 8.25). Vast amounts of money and time have been spent in establishing avalanche protection, but it is now realized that the ultimate protection lies in reestablishing the forest. This will be a slow and difficult process because of the severity of the local environment (Aulitzky 1967), but perhaps the biggest hurdle has already been cleared in the recognition of the need and importance of the task (Fig. 8.26). We are fortunate in North America to have relatively pristine alpine timberlines. This heritage is of great value and should be maintained at all costs.

Temperature

The ultimate cause of timberline has long been considered to be low temperature. This conclusion is based on the simple and logical observation that arctic and alpine tundras are very cold places and that a point is eventually reached along a continuum of decreasing temperatures where trees can no longer grow. The severity of the winter is far

Fig. 8.25. Pontresina, a famous health resort in the Upper Engadin Valley, Switzerland. Owing to past deforestation of slopes, this town is in considerable danger from avalanches. Extensive protective structures have been installed above the timberline, but avalanches still occur, as can be seen by the treeless avalanche chutes. The only satisfactory answer to this problem is reforestation. In the meantime, stringent land-use regulations must be invoked to protect life and property in the critical runout zones. (Lochau, courtesy of F. K. Holtmeier, University of Münster)

Fig. 8.26. Reforestation project being carried out by Swiss Avalanche Institute on steep, deforested slopes near Davos, Switzerland. (Author)

less critical than the warmth of the summer, however, since the primary metabolic and growth processes occur in summertime. Observations in both arctic and alpine areas have established the fact that timberlines correlate closely with the 10° C. (50° F.) isotherm for the warmest month (Brockmann-Jerosch 1919). Although there are insufficient weather stations in these areas to substantiate this observation fully, it seems to be fairly accurate and is widely accepted as fact.

The exact mechanism whereby low temperatures stop tree growth is still unknown, however. Boysen-Jensen (1949, p. 10) has suggested that it is a function of the amount of energy allocated to maintain normal metabolic processes and the amount left over for the production of new wood. If all the available energy is needed just to maintain normal metabolic processes, tree growth ceases. Under this theory, we would expect adaptations in tree growth which would reduce the amount of energy locked up in the non-productive tissues of the trunk and roots; in fact, it is not unusual to find dwarfed trees at timberline—less than 1 m (3.3 ft.) tall and 2.5 cm (1 in.) in diameter—that are over a hundred years old. Their annual growth rings may be so tiny that a microscope must be used to count them. However, slow growth need not in itself be the limiting factor for timberline. One of the oldest living trees (up to 8,000 years old), the

Bristle-cone pine (*Pinus aristata*), grows at timberline in the mountains of the southwestern United States (Ferguson 1970; LaMarche and Mooney 1972). Some researchers feel that very slow growth rates may actually be a positive adaptation to a short growing season, since they allow the shoot tissues to ripen whereas more rapid growth rates might not permit this (Wardle 1974, p. 383).

Wardle (1971, 1974) hypothesizes that the ultimate explanation for the cessation of trees is the inability of shoots to ripen (mature) their tissues. This can happen when the shoots freeze or dry out because they are losing more water to the atmosphere than can be replaced by the roots. Shoots are considered to be *ripened* when they have completed their seasonal growth and have lost the succulent appearance imparted by high water-content. The ripened shoots of timberline trees possess impermeable surfaces and can withstand low temperatures and desiccation, and their cells are not damaged by the growth of ice crystals (Wardle 1971, p. 373). The upper timberline, therefore, represents the highest altitude at which woody shoots can grow and mature under the environmental conditions that exist at the height of the tree canopy. The critical factor is protection against winter desiccation. As the growing season decreases with altitude, the time for maturation of needles and buds is reduced. Consequently, they have thinner cuticles (protective coverings) and lower drought-resistance, while at the same time the environmental stresses become intensified (Tranquillini 1979, pp. 109–10). However, as long as there is time for ripening of shoots in the summer, the trees can withstand severe winter conditions. This explains the apparent anomaly of trees reaching higher altitudes in extreme continental areas with more severe winters than in milder marine areas. Of course, different species have different inherited tolerances to various climatic extremes (Clausen 1963). "Thus, whereas

there are some 13 species at tree limit on Mount Wilhelm (New Guinea) alone, there are only 4 or 5 species in the whole of the Colorado Rockies" (Wardle 1974, p. 381).

Whatever the cause of timberline, it affects tall and short plants differently; krummholz trees and other woody plants extend far above the forestline by benefiting from warmer daytime temperatures close to the ground. In addition, the wind stress is less near the ground and there is protection from snow during winter. As a counterbalance to the attractiveness of near-surface habitats in high mountains, the summer heat build-up may be so excessive in some cases that greater stress is put on plants at this time than during winter (Aulitzky 1967).

Nevertheless, trees reach their highest altitudes by taking advantage of the warmer conditions near the surface; they almost always grow higher on sunny slopes than on shaded slopes, and they grow higher in sunny continental climates than in cloudy marine climates. All of these observations underscore the importance of temperature in establishing the altitude of the upper timberline. Still, several decades of research into the energy relationships of plants and their net assimilation rates at the timberline have not produced conclusive results. The concept of the ripening of shoot tissues offers a fresh alternative and opens up new avenues of approach. Even so, the explanation for the upper timberline at the ultimate level remains elusive.

ALPINE TUNDRA

Tundra is a Russian word meaning "treeless plain." It was originally used for Arctic areas north of the timberline and was later applied to areas above timberline in mountainous regions farther south, since the plant communities are similar. A number of studies have been made comparing and contrasting arctic tundra and alpine tundra (Bliss 1956, 1962, 1971, 1975; Billings and Mooney 1968; Billings 1973,

Fig. 8.27. Low alpine tundra immediately above timberline at 1,800 m (6,000 ft.) in the Olympic Mountains, Washington. Abundant flowering plant is the Glacier lily (*Erythronium grandiflorum*). (Author)

1974a). The vegetation of areas above timberline in high-latitude mountains is essentially the same as that of the arctic tundra. By the middle latitudes, however, less than half of the species in the alpine tundra are also found in the Arctic, and the total flora of middle-latitude mountain tundras is much richer and more diverse than that of the Arctic. This is because of the diversity of mountain environments,

their scattered distribution and isolation, and their various developmental histories. The differences continue to increase to the tropics, where the use of the word *tundra* becomes inappropriate—the flora and life forms are almost entirely different, with few arctic representatives present (Van Steenis 1935, 1962; Hedberg 1951, 1961, 1964; Troll 1958b, 1959; Cuatrecasas 1968). In the southern hemisphere, tundra is much more limited than in the north: Antarctica is largely ice-covered, and the only places which support tundra are small subantarctic islands and mountain areas. The flora is entirely different from that of the northern hemisphere (except for a few bipolar plants), but they are similar in function and structure, so the use of the word *tundra* is justified (Ward and Dimitri 1966; Billings 1974a, p. 403). Nevertheless, most writers have preferred to use the term *alpine vegetation* to refer to the low-lying plant communities growing above the climatic timberline in southern-hemisphere and tropical mountains (Van Steenis 1935; Hedberg 1964; Costin 1967; Mark and Bliss 1970, p. 382).

The alpine tundra is commonly divided into low, middle, and high tundra, just as in the Arctic (Polunin 1960; Swan 1967). The low alpine tundra is the zone immediately adjacent to the timberline, and consists of a fairly complete cover of low-lying shrubs, herbs, and grasses (Fig. 8.27). The greatest number and diversity of species are found in this zone and it is generally the most productive area within the tundra. Most grazing above timberline, for example, takes place in the low alpine tundra (Bliss 1975). At the opposite end of the spectrum is the high alpine zone, which is equivalent to the high Arctic or polar desert. The highest vegetated area in mountains, it is characterized by bare and rocky ground with occasional mosses, lichens, and dwarfed vascular plants. The number of species is greatly reduced and eventually there is one last species, like a lonely sentinel, which grows higher than any other.

The highest altitudes reached by *vascular plants* (advanced plants having strands of conducting tissue) are located not in the tropics, as one might suspect, but at latitudes of 20°–30° in the Himalayas and Andes, where they extend to a height of 5,800–6,100 m (19,100–20,100 ft.) (Zimmermann 1953; Webster 1961; Swan 1967). In the equatorial tropics, vascular plants only extend up to about 5,200 m (17,100 ft.), because the cloudiness in this region tends to depress the temperatures. Another factor is the simple fact that the highest mountains—the Himalayas and Andes—are located in subtropical latitudes. In addition, these ranges are much more massive than most tropical mountains, and the interior ranges are somewhat protected from moisture laden air: drier conditions there mean a higher snowline and a longer growing season (Swan 1967, p. 36).

Beyond the level of flowering plants exists another biotic region, called the *aeolian zone* (Swan 1961, 1963a, b, 1967; Mani 1962; Papp 1978; Spalding 1979). This was first recognized in the high Himalayas by mountain climbers and scientists who observed insects, algae, fungi, crustaceans, and birds far above the level of the last green plants. Since most forms of life depend on energy derived from resident plants, the question arose: How do these forms of life exist? What is their source of food? It was first believed that the insects simply lived on each other (Hingston 1925, p. 194). If this were true, what a depraved state of affairs! The absurdity of this was soon proved (Glennie 1941) and we now know that they live on a variety of organic materials—pollen, spores, seeds, dead insects, and plant fragments—carried to high altitudes by the wind. A similar life zone is thought to exist in the extreme deserts and polar regions.

Environmental Gradients in Alpine Tundra

A person visiting the alpine tundra for the first time may be struck by the appar-

ent monotony of the vegetation, but upon closer inspection he will discover a variety of plant communities responding to different landscape features. Most alpine plants are generalists, however, with a broad tolerance range and the ability to occupy a wide number of habitats. Many are, in fact, closely related to middle-latitude weeds (Griggs 1934). Tundra plants are very different in this regard from the highly specialized plants of tropical lowlands, which have narrow tolerance ranges and occupy narrow ecological niches. However, even alpine species do vary in their sensitivity to environmental extremes, and distinctive patterns emerge in response to the sharp environmental gradients that occur within short distances.

Assuming suitable substrates, i.e., something other than bare rock or vertical headwalls, the harshest environments in the alpine tundra result from the interaction of wind and snow (Billings and Mooney 1968, p. 496). An exposed ridge is usually blown free of snow and offers little moisture or protection from the wind. Only lichens, mosses, and a few prostrate cushion plants are able to grow in such sites. At the other extreme are areas where snow accumulates and persists late into the season. In some cases, the last snow melts only a few days before new snow begins to fall; the growing season is simply too brief for plants to survive. On the other hand, where the snow melts soon enough, snow-accumulation areas may be among the most favorable and productive sites, affording the vegetation both winter protection and summer moisture. Thus, the pattern of snow accumulation and snow melt is a primary factor in the establishment of alpine vegetative patterns (Billings and Bliss 1959; Canaday and Fonda 1974; Webber et al. 1976). In the extremes of the alpine environment, the presence of microhabitats may make all the difference between life and death, success and failure. A plant may be able to live in the shelter of a small rock where it is provided some protection, while it could not exist a few centimeters to either side. It is a tribute to the tenacity and resilience of alpine plants that they grow at all in such extreme environments. They succeed in part because they can take advantage of sites where conditions are most favorable. If a seed falls on a spot and the plant grows, it can usually continue to survive there (barring catastrophes).

Some plants even grow into the zone of permanent snow. This happens on rocky peaks where fine material has accumulated in small crevices, providing a sufficient stronghold for roots. Miniature snowbeds protect the dwarfed plants during winter and provide life-giving moisture the following

summer. By taking advantage of such micro-habitats, these snow-cranny plants reach exceptionally high elevations. A tiny buttercup (*Ranunculus glacialis*) reaches the highest elevation of any vascular plant in the Alps, at 4,270 m (14,100 ft.) on the Finsteraarhorn; another buttercup (*Ranunculus grahami*) occurs above the permanent snowline in the New Zealand Alps on Malte Brun at 2,900 m (9,600 ft.) (Billings and Mooney 1968, p. 497). The highest plants in the world, at approximately 6,100 m (20,100 ft.) on Makalu in the Himalayas, are ecological equivalents to these buttercups (Fig. 8.28). They grow where rocks, warmed by the sun, melt small snowdrifts. The

Fig. 8.28. Rock-base or snow-cranny plants (*Stellaria decumbens*) growing near the absolute upper limit for plant growth, at 5,900 m (18,000 ft.) on Makalu in the Himalayas. This same species grows at least 610 m (2,000 ft.) higher on the same mountain, becoming ever more dwarfed and scarce. (L. W. Swan, San Francisco State College)

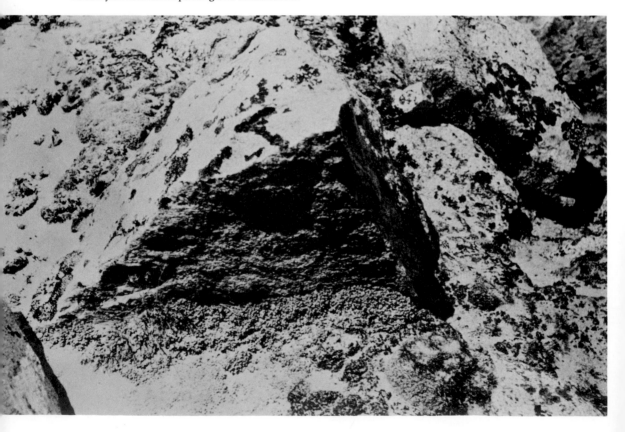

meltwater provides enough moisture and warmth for the plants to live at altitudes where the air temperature itself seldom rises above freezing and would not otherwise allow melting of the snow.

Characteristics and Adaptations of Alpine Plants

The primary adaptations of alpine plants are those that allow them to live in an extreme and variable environment characterized by low temperatures, a short growing season, lack of nutrients, and general instability. Their main concern is with the environment, not with other organisms. Although there may be some competition between species, especially in the more favorable sites, interspecies competition is relatively unimportant compared to most other environments. Alpine plants show many kinds of morphological, physiological, and ecological adaptations; we will touch here only on the most important of these. For more information, the reader should see the excellent papers of Bliss (1956, 1962, 1971, 1975), Tranquillini (1964), Billings and Mooney (1968), and Billings (1974a, b).

Floristics

The size and composition of widely scattered mountain floras depend upon many factors, including latitude, general climatic regime, size of mountain mass, continuity or isolation with respect to other mountains or the Arctic, age of the tundra surface (especially since last glaciation), and local or regional vegetative history. Alpine floras generally become less arctic-like with decreasing latitude. There are approximately 1,000 arctic tundra species, about 500 of which reach middle latitudes in the northern hemisphere. A handful of the genera found in the Arctic also extend into the highest levels in the tropics—e.g., *Poa, Draba, Arenaria, Potentilla*—and two or three are truly bipolar, reaching from the·Arctic to the sub-Antarctic. The grass *Trisetum spicatum* is

one of these. A slightly larger number of lichens and mosses are bipolar (Billings and Mooney 1968, p. 482).

In some cases the flora of middle-latitude mountains may consist mainly of arctic species, as it does on Mount Washington in the Presidential Range of New Hampshire. There are about 75 alpine species in this area, nearly all of which occur in the Arctic (Bliss 1963). On the other hand, the alpine flora of the Sierra Nevada in California contains over 600 species, but only about 20 percent have arctic affinities; most are either related to the surrounding desert or to the Rockies and Cascades (Went 1948; Chabot and Billings 1972). The Rocky Mountains occupy an intermediate position with respect to arctic and alpine species. The Beartooth Mountains on the Montana-Wyoming border contain 192 species, 50 percent of which also occur in the Arctic (Billings 1974b, p. 138). Farther south in Colorado, the number of alpine species increases to about 300, while the proportion of arctic species decreases to 40 percent or less (Bliss 1962, p. 118).

A similar pattern is present in Eurasia: the Scandinavian and Siberian mountains have the highest number of arctic-related species, owing to the mountains' proximity and continuity with the Arctic. There are 180 alpine species in Scandinavia, 63 percent of which are circumpolar, while in the Swiss Alps there are 420 alpine species with about 35 percent arctic affinity. Similarly, in the Altai Mountains of Central Asia there are 300 alpine species with 40 percent arctic affinity; progressing north, this figure increases to 50 percent in the Sayan Mountains and to 60 percent in the Stanovoi Ranges (Major and Bamberg 1967, p. 99). The alpine flora of the Central Asian mountains—Pamirs, Tien Shan, Altai, Himalayas, Karakoram, Hindukush, and Caucasus—is markedly larger and more distinctive than that of any other northern-hemisphere mountain region, because these mountains were not inundated by glacial ice as most other middle-latitude mountains were. Consequently, the vegetation has had a longer time for development and differentiation. The Himalayan region is believed to have served as a refugium for both plants and animals throughout the Pleistocene, and many species of the alpine tundra may have originated there (Hoffmann and Taber 1967). Although no exact figures are available, the number of alpine plants in these high central Asian ranges probably exceeds 1,000, with about 25–30 percent also occurring in the Arctic (Major and Bamberg 1967, p. 98).

In the tropics, the mountain floras become increasingly insular and disjunct. There are approximately 300 alpine species on the high volcanoes of East Africa and 80 percent are endemic (found only locally). These Afroalpine plants have evolved largely through speciation from the surrounding lowland vegetation and are very unlike anything in middle latitudes (Hedberg 1965, 1969, 1971). A similar developmental process is evident in the floras of the Andes and of the mountains of Malaysia, Indonesia, and New Guinea (Van Steenis 1934, 1935, 1962, 1972; Troll 1958b, 1959; Cuatrecasas 1968).

Low Growth Form

Perhaps the most striking characteristic of alpine plants is their low growth form, which allows them to take advantage of the more favorable environment near the ground and to escape the markedly harsher conditions at 1–2 m (3–7 ft.) above the surface. The wind is greatly diminished near the ground, so there is less physical and transpirational stress. It is much warmer near the surface, since this is where the sun's energy is absorbed and the heat is not transported away so quickly by the wind. Plant leaves and foliage may warm up much more than the air does. A study in the Colorado Rockies revealed plant temperatures as much as 22° C. (40° F.) higher than that of the air during sunny periods (Salisbury and Spomer 1964). In an area where low temperature is limiting to life, the importance of this additional heat near the surface cannot be overemphasized. Finally, the low growth form can take advantage of the insulative qualities of the snow cover in winter. Thus, the near-surface environment of many areas in high mountains is not as severe as one might think, at least from the point of view of alpine tundra plants. They experience relatively warm conditions near the surface during the summer and often escape the harshness of winter under a protective cover of snow.

An exception to the dominance of low growth forms in the alpine environment is the giant rosette form characteristic of some plants in tropical mountains (Figs. 8.15, 8.16). These strange plants with their peculiar candle-like forms reach heights of several meters; they include the giant *Senecios* and *Lobelias* of the East African volcanoes and convergent growth forms of *Espeletia* and *Lupinus* in the paramos of South America. A closely related form is the Silversword (*Argyroxiphium sandwicense*), which grows at high altitudes in Hawaii (Troll 1958b, 1959). Since the environment of tropical mountains allows metabolic processes to be carried out throughout the year, the principal adaptations of these large columnar plants are various mechanisms to protect the buds from nightly frost: large woolly leaves that curve inward at night and cover the buds; the presence of corky coverings; and the secretion of liquid over the buds at critical times. The sheathing of the stem by the woolly and hairy leaves also helps protect them against intense sunlight during the day (Hedberg 1964, pp. 41-64).

Perennials

Most plants in the alpine tundra are perennials. Only one to two percent of the flora are annuals (Billings and Mooney 1968, p. 493). This suggests that there is survival value in permanence. Alpine plants have to be able to metabolize quickly, once condi-

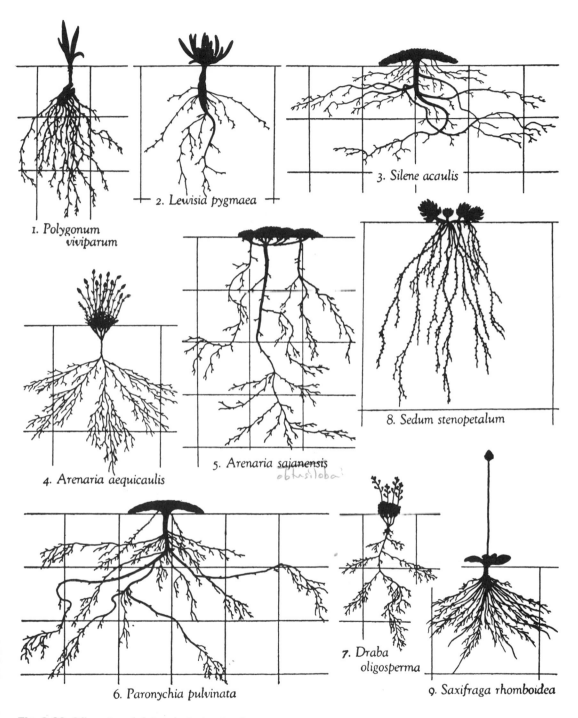

1. *Polygonum
    viviparum*

2. *Lewisia pygmaea*

3. *Silene acaulis*

4. *Arenaria aequicaulis*

5. *Arenaria sajanensis*
   obtusiloba

6. *Paronychia pulvinata*

7. *Draba
   oligosperma*

8. *Sedum stenopetalum*

9. *Saxifraga rhomboidea*

Fig. 8.29. Silhouettes of alpine plants showing the
relative size of their root systems compared to above-
ground shoot areas. (From Daubenmire 1941, p. 372)

tions permit, so that their life cycles can be completed within the short time allowed. The cool and brief growing season in middle- and high-latitude mountains does not favor annuals: it is difficult for seeds to germinate, flower, and fruit in such a short period. Perennials, on the other hand, do not have to spend valuable time and energy in germination and initial growth processes. Tundra perennials have several other adaptations to allow them to complete their life cycle more rapidly. For example, they commonly develop a pre-formed shoot and flower bud for more speedy shoot elongation and flowering once conditions permit (Billings 1974a, p. 412). Many tundra plants are evergreen, eliminating the need to grow new leaves before photosynthesis can begin, and at the same time allowing storage of food reserves in the old leaves.

Tundra plants develop relatively large and extensive root systems that provide vital life support for the small aerial part of the plant and help to tide it over lean periods. Most tundra plants have two to six times more biomass below the ground than above it (Daubenmire 1941; Webber and May 1977) (Fig. 8.29). Food reserves in the form of carbohydrates and starches are stored in the roots, and the plant draws on this stored energy for rapid initial growth in the spring. A large root system is also useful in the summer when droughty conditions prevail. The importance of moisture stress in high mountains is reflected by such adaptations to dry conditions as thick waxy leaves, corky bark, succulence, and high osmotic pressures which enable the roots to take up any available ground moisture (Tranquillini 1964). A final advantage of perennials over annuals is the simple fact that mature plants are usually more hardy and resistant to the vagaries of the environment than young and immature plants. This is true with almost all forms of life; mature individuals can withstand more adverse conditions and stress than the young.

Reproduction

The fitness of any organism to survive and maintain continuity over long periods of time ultimately depends on its ability to reproduce successfully. This becomes especially critical in the harsh environments above timberline. During many years conditions are so unfavorable that flowering and fruiting are seriously hampered and few or no viable seeds are produced; those seeds that are produced have difficulty in germinating under the adverse conditions present in some years. There is also the distinct likelihood of "the seeds falling on stony ground," as in the biblical parable. If tundra plants depended entirely on seeds for the production of progeny, the ensuing vegetation patterns would be highly sporadic from year to year. This is not the case, however, due to the dominance of perennials and the existence of other mechanisms of reproduction.

Pollination is a major problem for alpine plants, since low temperatures confine insect activities to a brief period during the summer (Billings 1974a, p. 452). In some cases it is limited just to sunny days. Bees, for example, usually fly only when the air temperature is 10° C. (50° F.) or higher (Macior 1970). Therefore, at altitudes above 4,000 m (13,200 ft.) in the Himalayas, bee-pollinated flowers disappear, to be replaced by those pollinated by other insects (Mani 1962, p. 181). Hummingbirds are important in tropical mountains (Cruden 1972; Carpenter 1976) and to a limited extent in middle latitudes where there is still adequate heat during the day, e.g., the southern Rockies or Sierra Nevada of California, but they do not live in polar mountains. The most important pollinators in middle and high-latitude mountains are bees, flies, butterflies, and moths.

The size and beauty of alpine plant-blossoms, relative to their tiny stems, are legendary (Fig. 8.30). Almost everybody has

Fig. 8.30. Close-up of *Erigeron pinnatisectus* at 3,300 m (10,800 ft.) on Libby Flat in the ~~Wind River~~ Mountains, *Medicine Bow* southeastern Wyoming. Observe the large size of the blossoms compared to the rest of the plant. (L. C. Bliss, University of Washington)

heard the story of some young man in the Alps risking his neck climbing a high rocky precipice to pick an Edelweiss blossom for a lady friend (apparently, many have done so, for now the Edelweiss, threatened by extinction, is protected by law). The biological value of large and showy blossoms may have several explanations, but it is at least partially a function of their ability to attract insects. This is a two-way street, since the presence of flowers provides nectar that helps to support the insect population. An exception to the presence of large and colorful blossoms is found in the mountains of New Zealand, where the alpine flowers are small and flat with relatively monotonous white and yellow colors. This has been explained as being due to the absence of

long-tongued bees in New Zealand, so the plants have evolved to attract flies and other small insects as pollinators (Heine 1937).

Although most alpine plants are insect-pollinated, as environmental conditions become more severe, wind and self-pollination become relatively more important. There is less energy available in the system to support the more elaborate and involved process of insect pollination, which depends upon adaptations in both plant and insect (Hocking 1968; Macior 1970; Heinrich and Raven 1972; Hickman 1974). In addition, as conditions become more limiting, it is not good survival strategy to leave such an important task to chance. It should be pointed out, however, that while wind and self-pollination provide assurance of continued procreation, they result in less genetic diversity than cross-pollination, and diversity may, in the long run, also be important for survival (Bliss 1962, p. 129).

The production of viable seeds may or may not follow pollination; much depends upon environmental conditions. A severe freeze or snowstorm at the time of blooming can eliminate seed set for that year. Even if viable seeds are produced, they may be forced to wait to germinate until some later year when conditions are more favorable. Consequently, most alpine tundra plants have alternative methods of reproduction, the most common being through *rhizomes*. These are root-like stems running out from the plant with the ability to send up new shoots. It is not uncommon to find a single plant occupying an area of several meters; the surface shoots may give the appearance of many individual plants, but they are all tied together through an interconnecting system of rhizomes. This is a particularly useful adaptation in mountain environments with frost activity and mass-wasting, because if part of the plant is destroyed, the remaining part can reproduce and spread. Several other methods of vegetative reproduction (layering, stolons, apomixis, vivipary) are prevalent in the alpine tundra. Suffice it to say that as seed production and germination become less reliable in high mountains, these methods become more important (Billings and Mooney 1968, p. 519). Plants may still produce seeds, but they do not depend on them entirely. This demonstrates the survival value in extreme environments of not "putting all your eggs in one basket."

Productivity

Although the alpine environment is one of the harshest on earth and the vegetation growing there is greatly reduced in stature and diversity, alpine plants display an amazingly high level of productivity during the growing season. The production of dry matter in middle-latitude alpine tundra has been measured to average 0.20 to 0.60 gr/m^2/day over the entire year; when the production rates are calculated just for the growing season (30–70 days), the values range from 1 to 3 gr/m^2/day (Bliss 1962, p. 138). This is only the above-ground production. Since root biomass exceeds shoot biomass by two to six times, these figures should be multiplied by a factor of about 3 for total productivity (Billings and Mooney 1968, p. 521; Webber and May 1977). On a yearly basis, these rates are similar to those of deserts and are far less than those for temperate environments, but on a day-to-day basis for the growing season, the productivity of alpine tundra compares favorably with (and may even exceed) many temperate environments (Bliss 1962, 1966; Scott and Billings 1964; Bliss and Mark 1974; Webber 1974).

The explanation for the relatively high productivity rates of alpine plants lies in the fact that they are well-adapted to low temperatures and can metabolize at subfreezing temperatures (Fig. 8.31). They can, therefore, begin growing very early in the spring and grow until the last possible date in the fall. Some alpine plants can carry on photosynthesis at temperatures as low as –6° C. (21° F.) (Billings 1974a, p. 424). Most alpine plants can withstand being frozen while blooming. I have observed this in the mountains of Yukon Territory, where blossoms of the Mountain aven (*Dryas octopetela*) and Snow buttercup (*Ranunculus nivalis*) were encased in ice in the early morning, and after the ice melted at midday the plants continued blooming with no apparent damage. Another factor is the ability of alpine plants to carry on rapid rates of metabolism. They have high caloric values and during the initial period rely heavily on food reserves stored in old leaves and in large root systems. These reserves are then replenished later in the season. The rate of growth is determined by both the length of the growing season and day-to-day conditions. In areas where the snow melts early, plants may develop relatively slowly, taking the full time for the various phenological processes; but where the snow melts late, the processes are greatly compressed and the entire life cycle is completed within a few short weeks (Billings and Bliss 1959; Rochow 1969). Various other physiological details could be mentioned about photosynthesis and respiration but enough has been said to demonstrate the considerable efficiency of alpine plants within the context of their environment.

The plant geography and ecology of mountain forests and alpine tundra present a study in contrasts. On an overall basis there is an amazing similarity in the form and function of the vegetation. This is displayed in the major vegetation zones or belts, and in the predictable changes in character that take place with increasing altitude. Locally, however, the species composition and floristic structure differ vastly. The plant species in any mountain region are products of migration, adaptation, and evolution. In some cases–e.g., in most middle-latitude mountains—they are recent arrivals following the melting of extensive Pleistocene glaciers, pre-adapted species moving from one like environment to another. They are essentially recapturing and recolonizing land that they formerly occupied (Fig. 9.4). In other cases, the plants have evolved from very ancient stock that has remained in one area. The plants have adapted slowly over the millennia as the mountains themselves were created and uplifted. In still other cases, the mountain vegetation is composed of surrounding lowland species that have been able to adapt to the conditions at altitude and have moved slowly, step by step, up the mountain slopes. These have generally become isolated and no longer interact with their distant relatives in the lowlands (especially in the tropics). Many alpine tundra species are closely related to plants that occur as middle-latitude lowland weeds. Extreme hardiness, ability to live under conditions of instability, and

Fig. 8.31. The Glacier lily (*Erythronium grandiflorum*) growing through a late-lying snowbank at 1,800 m (6,000 ft.) in the North Cascades, Washington. This plant is able to grow in very cold and wet sites. (Author)

ability to pioneer new sites are a few of the qualities that allow weed-like species to survive and dominate in the tundra. Although local adaptations have occurred and some plants are limited in their distribution, others have developed a very wide amplitude, ranging successfully from the lowlands to the highlands.

The current status of mountain vegetation is (as it has perhaps always been) one of dynamism and flux. Changes are continually taking place in response to environmental, genetic, biotic, and human pressures. Because of rapid changes in technology, population increase, and land use, man has become the critical factor. This is a matter of great concern and requires careful consideration of our actions in mountains, but it is not cause for undue alarm; the entire history of mountain vegetation has been one of coping with instability and alteration. The current status and presence of similar plant communities in mountains around the world testify to its success in this regard.

Close to the western summit [of Kilimanjaro] there is the dried and frozen carcass of a leopard. No one has explained what the leopard was seeking at that altitude.

> Ernest Hemingway,
> *The Snows of Kilimanjaro* (1927)

Wildlife

The study of the nature and distribution of animals in mountains is somewhat more difficult than the study of vegetation, because animals arc more mobile and secretive. The firmly rooted individuals of a plant community can easily be observed and their distribution mapped. This is usually possible with animals only through extended sampling techniques. Animal distribution is also complicated by daily or seasonal migration: their winter range, summer range, breeding area, and migration route must all be taken into account (Udvardy 1969). Some animals have large and dispersed ranges; others are restricted. Some are full-time residents; others are part-time residents, temporary visitors, or even unintentional migrants, e.g., the occasional swarms of lowland insects drawn up to high altitudes and deposited on snowfields by ascending air currents.

Most animals at high altitudes are summer residents that spend most of the year at lower altitudes or latitudes. These include many of the larger and more mobile species. Birds are the most mobile, of course, and some species, such as eagles and hawks, commute daily to the alpine tundra. They frequently nest in the subalpine or montane zone and ride the slope breezes up the mountain to spend their summer days foraging for small mammals above the timberline. On the other hand, those species that live permanently, or at least reproduce, in high mountains are of greatest significance for our purposes, for they reveal most clearly the characteristics and adaptations necessary to survive in the mountain milieu.

In spite of the dynamic and multifaceted nature of animal populations, they share with mountain vegetation many characteristics and patterns. One of the most pronounced of these is the decrease in number of species with altitude (except in some desert mountains). This can be observed in virtually every order and family in the animal kingdom. Thus, there are 96 species of butterflies in the coniferous forests of the Swiss Alps but only 27 in the shrub and meadow zone, while 8 species range into the high tundra (Hesse et al. 1951, p. 592). There are 61 species of grasshoppers at the base of the Front Range in Colorado at 1,650 m (5,000 ft.). At an altitude of 3,300 m (10,000 ft.) this number is decreased to 17, and at 4,300 m (13,000 ft.) there are only 2 (Alexander 1964, p. 79). In New Guinea 320 species of birds live in the lowlands, while at 2,000 m (6,600 ft.) this number is reduced to 128, and only 8 species are found above 4,000 m (13,200 ft.) (Kikkawa and Williams 1971). The entire fauna of the upper part of Mount Kilimanjaro—birds, mammals, reptiles, amphibia, and insects—has been estimated as follows by Salt (1954, p. 409):

Life Zone	Elevation (m)	Number of Species
Cloud forest	2,000–2,800	600
Lower moorlands	2,800–3,500	300
Upper moorlands	3,500–4,200	150
Alpine desert	4,200 +	43

The decrease in number of species with altitude results in decreased species diversity and, potentially, less interspecies competition. The primary adaptations are those that allow the organism to survive the rigors of the physical environment. As with vegetation, the lower number of species may be counterbalanced somewhat by an increase in the numbers of individuals within any given species, but the total biomass and biomass productivity nevertheless decreases. This is particularly true above timberline, since the number of large mammals able to cope year-round with the extremes of the alpine tundra, where there is neither shelter nor sufficient food, is relatively low. Consequently, the composition of the animal community shifts toward smaller creatures that can find shelter and food near the ground, amid stones, and beneath snow.

High mountain environments are relatively undeveloped ecosystems, and the majority of inhabitants are pioneers. They may be viewed as colonizers, opportunists, a rough-and-ready lot taking advantage of a new and unpopulated land. Being pioneers, most species are generalists able to cope with a broad range of environmental conditions, rather than specialists highly skilled in a narrow spectrum of circumstances. Versatility and flexibility are the qualities of highest survival value. For this reason, the bulk of high-altitude faunas are rodents, scavengers, and unspecialized insects, just as the flora is primarily weedy species.

It may be instructive at this point to look at the components of a typical alpine animal population. The Beartooth Mountains are located about 50 km (31 mi.) east of Yellowstone National Park. This is an area of roughly 160 km^2 (100 sq. mi.) with elevations of 3,300–3,800 m (10,900–12,500 ft.). The birds and mammals of this alpine zone have been studied by Pattie and Verbeek (1966, 1967).

Thirteen species of herbivorous mammals are more or less permanent residents of the alpine zone. These provide the base of the food chain and include one species of Pocket gopher (*Thomomys talpoides*), one species of ground squirrel (*Sperophilus lateralis*), four voles (*Arvicola, Clethrionomys, Microtus,* and

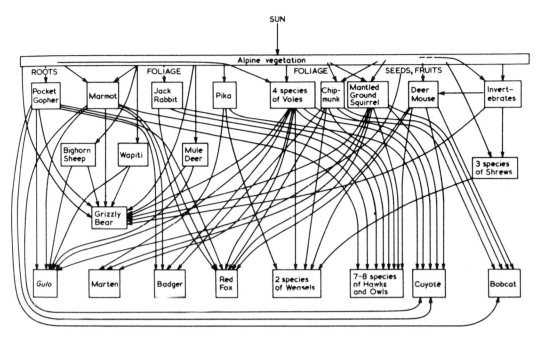

Fig. 9.1. Schematic representation of the trophic web established among the warm-blooded mammals living for at least part of the year (summer) above timberline in the Beartooth Mountains, Montana. (From Hoffmann 1974, p. 515)

Phenacomys spp.), one pika (*Ochotona princeps*), one jackrabbit (*Lepus townsendii*), one chipmunk (*Eutamias minimus*), one marmot (*Marmota flaviventris*), the Deer mouse (*Peromyscus maniculatus*), the Bighorn sheep (*Ovis canudensis*), and the Mountain goat (*Oreamnos americanus*) (this last was introduced by man) (Fig. 9.1). Six species of herbivorous and insectivorous birds regularly breed above timberline in the area—e.g., the horned lark (*Eremophila alpestris*), rosy finch (*Leucosticte atrata*), and water pipit (*Anthus spinoletta*)—but all abandon the land of their birth and migrate to warmer climates during winter. Carnivores include the weasel (*Mustela spp.*), the pine marten (*Martes americana*), badger (*Taxidea taxus*), grizzly bear (*Ursus arctos*), red fox (*Vulpes vulpes*), coyote (*Canis latrans*), and bobcat (*Lynx rufus*). With the exception of the weasels and the martens, these are also primarily sum-

mer animals, because the smaller mammals on which they depend retreat into subterranean and undersnow habitats during winter. There are 7 or 8 species of predatory hawks and owls, including the golden eagle (*Aquila chrysaetos*), but most of these, too, abandon the area during winter (Hoffmann 1974, p. 515).

In addition to those species which are truly alpine in nature, there are others that occasionally wander up beyond timberline. These include about 10 mammals, e.g., the snowshoe rabbit (*Lepus americanus*), porcupine (*Erethizon dorsatum*), mule deer (*Odocoileus hemionus*), and elk (*Cervus canadensis*)—and 15–20 species of vagrant birds—e.g., the robin (*Turdus migratorius*), Clark's nutcracker (*Nucifraga columbiana*), raven (*Corvus corax*), mountain bluebird (*Sialia currucoides*), and pine siskin (*Spinus pinus*). Domestic sheep should also be added to this list, since several hundred are still driven annually to the high country (Pattie and Verbeek 1967, p. 114). Thus, about 30 species of mammals and 30 species of birds may be present at one time or another during the summer above timberline in the Beartooth Mountains, Wyoming. The relationships among these mammals and the trophic web they form is presented in Figure 9.1. (This picture is altered considerably during winter when the total number of species present is reduced to 15–20.)

The exact number and composition of species will vary for different mountain regions, depending on environmental conditions and the size, age (history), and relationship to other mountain areas. Generally, the larger the mountain area, the greater the number of species. Thus, the largest number of mountain species exists in the Himalayan region. There are no accurate surveys for this area, but species number in the hundreds (Hoffmann 1974, p. 516). The opposite is also true: small, isolated mountains display the least diversity. A good example is the Big Snowy Mountains, a small isolated range on the Great Plains of central Montana; there are only 7 species of mammals and 4 species of birds known to breed in this alpine area (Hoffmann 1974, p. 515). A number of other species visit in the summer, just as on the Beartooth Plateau, but the contrast in numbers is considerable.

Although alpine and arctic zones have much in common, the islandlike, patchy distribution of mountains and the large, nearly continuous circumpolar belt of the Arctic constitutes a fundamental difference between them. Arctic animals are able to maintain relatively large populations and there is a good degree of continuity and interchange, with the same species occurring throughout. This is impossible in disjunct and widely scattered mountains, because of the difficulty in dispersal and colonization. Therefore, the flora and fauna become increasingly diverse away from the polar re-

gions. Mammals are the most exclusive—to the point that "not a single tundra species is common to both the alpine [tundra] in temperate latitude mountains and the arctic tundra" (Hoffmann 1974, p. 475). This is true, however, for those species which live *only* in arctic or alpine tundra; a number of more widely ranging species—i.e., subarctic and subalpine—occasionally occupy both environments. Birds, insects, and vegetation are less exclusive; a number of species are shared by arctic and alpine tundra. Amphibians and reptiles are notably rare in both areas (Hock 1964a, b).

LIMITING FACTORS

In spite of differences in distribution, arctic and alpine animals have similar approaches to life. One early observation in biogeography was that of convergent tendencies in the environment, as expressed in the flora and fauna, with increase in latitude and altitude. We now know that there are a great many exceptions to this simple rule, but at the broadest level it is still useful (see pp. 254–55).

Because it gets colder as altitude and latitude increase, it has also long been assumed that low temperature is one of the major limiting factors to life. Modern ecology still operates on this basis, although the idea has recently been challenged. Dunbar (1968) contends that, while low temperature may be the immediate or proximate cause for the decrease in numbers of species, it is not the ultimate reason. The ultimate limiting factors are, rather, large environmental oscillations, lack of nutrients, lack of habitat diversity, and youthfulness of the ecosystem (Dunbar 1968). Alpine environments have all of these problems, plus two other limiting characteristics of their own—the disjunct islandlike distribution of mountain areas, and reduced oxygen with altitude. Whether or not temperature is the ultimate limiting factor, each of the above-mentioned factors takes its toll and helps to establish the environmental framework in which mountain life exists.

Temperature

Although temperature has been singled out as being fundamental in controlling the distribution of organisms in mountains, all climatic factors are interrelated. The alteration of one factor alters all others, and any one of these may in specific cases exceed the effect of temperature. This is implicit, but there is something compelling about narrowing the explanation for any given phenomenon to a single cause. A classic example is C. Hart Merriam's life-zone concept, in which he attempted to show that the flora and fauna of North America are distributed into distinct life zones based on temperature (Merriam 1890, 1894, 1898). This concept had a profound impact on North American ecology, but it has fallen into disrepute specifically because of its singular dependence on temperature (Daubenmire 1938, 1946; Kendeigh 1932, 1954). Such an approach may be useful in a small area where the mesh of factors is kept fairly constant, but when the fundamental relationships change, so will the relative importance of each. Alexander Von Humboldt's climatic zones *tierra caliente, tierra templada,* and *tierra fria* work reasonably well in the humid tropics, but not elsewhere. Likewise, Merriam's life zones—Arctic-alpine, Hudsonian, Canadian, etc.—can be applied fairly usefully in the region of his original study, the San Francisco Mountains, Arizona (although the assumed convertibility of latitude and altitude is questionable), but not necessarily in other areas.

Another major problem with temperature as a limiting factor is in ascertaining its effect on organisms. Humboldt's and Merriam's life zones, and those of many other studies, have been based on correlations between temperature and the distribution of plants and animals. A certain species will reach a particular elevation but go no higher: the temperatures at that elevation are presumed to be responsible for this point of maximum distribution, but it is hard to identify the specific processes involved. For example, it is well-established that the upper timberline coincides closely with the 10° C. (50° F.) isotherm for the warmest month. The reason for this relationship remains elusive, however (see pp. 286–89). A number of animals reach their altitudinal limits at timberline, but it would be dangerous to say that these creatures are limited by temperature, when in fact they may simply be limited by the absence of trees. In this case, then, temperature may be more or less directly responsible for the location of timberline, but only indirectly responsible for the distribution of the associated animal species. In spite of all that has been said, however, temperature is still the major environmental factor in cold climates, just as moisture is in dry climates.

Temperature operates in several ways to limit life. The first and most obvious is where it exceeds the tolerance limits of organisms. All species have an upper and lower threshold of temperature that they can withstand, and within this range there is an optimum or preferred level. The same can be said of any environmental factor, and animals with different potentials, tolerances, and abilities seek out, as near as possible, their own preferred range. This is one of the basic reasons for the distributions of species on the earth. All life exists within the fairly narrow temperature range of 0° C. to 50° C. (32° F. to 122° F.). Temperatures on the earth far exceed these limits, but most organisms escape the extremes by one means or another. The absolute low-temperature limit is reached when body fluids begin to freeze, usually within a few degrees below the freezing point of pure water. The upper limit is reached when body fluids begin to undergo destructive chemical change. The two effects are not equal, however. There is much greater flexibility at the lower end of the spectrum than at the higher: high temperatures usually result in irreversible damage and death, but cells can freeze in some animals without irreversible damage, and activity may be resumed when temperatures rise (Hesse et al. 1951, p. 18). The length of exposure and extremity of the temperature are important, of course, but a number of creatures, especially insects, do survive winters of subfreezing temperatures. During Sir John Ross's second voyage to the Canadian Arctic in 1829 to 1833, the larvae of butterflies were found frozen to the point of brittleness. Specimens were taken inside and allowed to thaw. The larvae became active within two hours. They were then taken back outside into the –40° C.(–40° F.) weather and allowed to refreeze. The process was repeated three times, and although there was considerable mortality, some of the larvae still pupated in the spring (in Downes 1964, p. 283).

This is an extreme case, since insects are the most versatile and adaptable of all animals. Most of the animal kingdom has more rigidly controlled tolerance limits, and each species is distributed along a given segment of the temperature spectrum. Compared to the total number of species in the world, only a handful have adapted to extreme cold. One primary reason for the reduction in number of species in cold climates is that organisms must use a larger portion of their energies in adapting to the cold and coping with the harsh environment, so there is less energy available for diversification than is true of more propitious environments.

Temperature limits life through slowing the rate of development. It reduces the level of metabolism and the rates of activity, fecundity, and reproduction (Andrewartha and Birch 1954). The deer mouse (*Peromyscus maniculatus*) in the Sierra Nevada of California produces three times as many young at 1,360 m (4,500 ft.) as at 3,760 m (12,400 ft.) (Dunmire 1960), primarily because low temperatures at high altitudes shorten the breeding season. The same is true with birds: alpine species are generally limited to one nesting a year, whereas birds at lower elevations may nest two or three times (Lack 1954, p. 53). Insects at high altitudes frequently take two or three years to complete their life cycle (Fig. 9.12). They may hibernate at different stages of development in succeeding years—egg, larvae, pupae, and adult—until complete metamorphosis is achieved (Mani 1962, p. 112). This lower level of productivity in turn reduces opportunities for diversification and speciation. Temperature also has a number of indirect effects on animal distributions through its influence on landform, vegetation, and soil development, which contribute to environmental stability, habitat diversity, and food supply.

Environmental Oscillation

Fluctuation of environmental conditions increases with latitude and altitude; it is greatest in the polar regions and least in the tropics. Consequently, organisms must adapt to wide ranges of conditions. Latitude controls the length of day and the seasons, while altitude combines with latitude to accentuate these effects. For example, the growing season at any given latitude is generally shorter in mountains. Even in the humid tropics, where there is no marked seasonality, the range of daily environmental extremes is increased with altitude; a species may have to cope with intense sunlight every afternoon and freezing temperatures every night. The number of species that can survive these conditions decreases with elevation, and each loss brings about concurrent changes in community structure and environment. The most striking change occurs at timberline, since the forest provides a buffered habitat. Beyond timberline, species that depend on trees must either adapt to the open habitat or be eliminated. The environment itself changes; the soil becomes exposed to the full brunt of sun, rain, wind, and extremes of temperature. This may lead to other developments such as increased frost creep and solifluction, which in turn lead to greater erosion, stream infiltration, and habitat instability. Consequently, with the loss of trees, community structure becomes much less complex; there are less food, fewer ecological niches, and greater environmental extremes.

Longer winters work to several ends; primarily, they reduce the food supply, since the length of the growing season is abbreviated. While there may be ample food during the summer, very little is available during the winter. Organisms must either leave the area in search of more favorable conditions (migrate), reduce their need for food physiologically (hibernate), or circumvent the need for food in some other way. For example, the Pocket gopher (*Thomomys spp.*) stays active throughout the winter by burrowing and by harvesting plant roots in snow-protected areas. The strategy of many animals for dealing with the lack of food also solves the problem of dealing with great environmental extremes—i.e., migration, hibernation, or escaping under snow. All of these procedures, however, require energy that could be spent in diversification, niche specialization, or reproduction. With increasing environmental oscillation there is increasing fluctuation of nutrients and of population numbers, and energy flow through the system is interrupted (Dunbar 1968, p. 66). The opposite is true in humid tropical lowlands, where there is great environmental stability, complexity of species, and a maximum flow of energy through the system. Environmental oscillation clearly disrupts the stability of ecosystems and limits life.

Lack of Nutrients

The abundance of nutrients in any system is ultimately a function of the total energy capital available—i.e., heat and light energy from the sun, chemical and organic energy locked up in the rocks, soils, and organic substances, and kinetic energy depending upon movement of water, wind, etc. The availability of nutrients and amount of productivity generally decrease with elevation. This is largely a function of temperature and length of the growing season, coupled with the poor quality of mountain soils and lack of suitable sites. The long dark winter of high latitudes has a counterpart in the higher reaches of middle-latitude mountains, where the surface is cut off from the sun by a heavy snow cover. Most high mountain plants are well-adapted to the growing season and other adverse conditions so that their daily productivity during summer is fully equivalent to most lowland environments (Bliss 1962; Webber 1974). The problem is that the process is abbreviated and annual productivity is quite low (see pp. 298–99). It is a matter of feast or famine. On a relative basis, there is abundant food during the short growing season, and a surprising variety of animals spend their summers in high mountains; they might stay during the winter if there were sufficient food, but there is not. The lack of nutrients is an almost insurmountable problem to year-round occupancy of alpine tundra, and in this respect limits the utilization and efficiency of the ecosystem.

Lack of Habitat Diversity

The fundamental characteristic of high mountain landscapes is the openness of the habitat—the low-lying alpine vegetation and bare rocks. I will always remember my first extended experience with this landscape. It was during dissertation research in the Ruby Mountains of southwest Yukon Territory. Timberline in this area occurs at 1,150 m (3,800 ft.) and my research area, where we were spending the summer, was located at 1,800 m (6,000 ft.), so the nearest trees were about 3 km (2 mi.) away. We were flown in by helicopter early in June. I went in with the first load, and after the initial excitement of unloading the helicopter and watching it depart, I stood quietly and looked around. What I saw was somewhat disconcerting. For one who had spent much of his life surrounded by trees, the sensation of suddenly being without them was a little frightening. I felt naked and exposed and very susceptible to the elements (and totally dependent on the Primus stove). It did not take long to become accustomed to the landscape and to feel comfortable in it, but my initial reaction underscores one of the fundamental characteristics and limiting factors of the alpine tundra—lack of habitat diversity.

The tundra is essentially a two-dimensional habitat. The absence of trees eliminates the vertical component and reduces the number and diversity of ecological niches. Species that depend upon the forest for food or shelter are eliminated unless they can adapt to the open country. There birds must build their nests on the ground and hover in the air to give their mating calls. The vegetation above timberline consists of grasses and herbaceous species with a simple community structure and little variety from place to place. Rocks usually abound, and these become increasingly important as habitats (Hoffmann 1974, p. 497). Some creatures are found almost exclusively in rocky areas—e.g., pikas (*Ochotona spp.*) and marmots (*Marmota spp.*) (Fig. 9.7). Snow cover is also a prime consideration: a number of species depend upon it for insulation and protection during winter. Patterns of population distribution for many small creatures are directly related to the distribution of snow (Pruitt 1960, 1970; Sleeper et al. 1976; Stoecker 1976).

The most important source of habitat diversity in the alpine zone is the lay of the land itself. Topography largely controls the distribution of rocks and snow. Rocky crags, cliffs, valleys, and differences in slope gradient and exposure provide a variety of surfaces for the interplay of climatic, geomorphic, edaphic, and biologic factors, resulting in a mosaic of microhabitats. In general, areas of the least topographic diversity, e.g., smooth slopes, have fewest ecological niches and least species diversity, while areas of maximum topographic diversity support the greatest number of ecological niches and maximum species diversity. Minimum complexity is found on small and simple mountains that slope directly to the summit, e.g., volcanic cones, while maximum complexity is found on large and diverse folded mountains such as the Alps or Himalayas. Topographic diversity is a major reason why there are more species in alpine environments than in the arctic tundra (Hoffmann 1974, p. 526). Nevertheless, compared to lowland environments, habitat diversity is considerably decreased in alpine areas.

Youthfulness of the Ecosystem

Most mountains are young landscapes, both because they are relatively recent geological creations and because they have experienced severe glaciation. The Tertiary, which extended over 65 million years, was a period of major mountain-building, while the Pleistocene—the last 2 or 3 million years—was a period of major climatic fluctuation. Although mountain-building during the Tertiary was the initial event and life had to adapt to the changing conditions of increasing altitude and relief with uplift, the Pleistocene has been by far the most important in terms of the present distribution of life in mountains. At least four major glacial periods occurred during the Pleistocene, the most recent of which ended only about 10,000 years ago. Owing to its larger land masses and resulting continental climate, the northern hemisphere was most affected; huge lowland ice sheets extended from the north into the middle latitudes and wrought great destruction to the surfaces covered. Mountains also served as centers of increased snow and ice accumulation; local ice-caps developed, and valley glaciers moved downward and away in all directions. The result was removal of soil and loose material, leaving bare and polished rock in its place.

Glacial movement has a devastating effect on living creatures. Only nival (snow) insects, algae, and a few migrant birds can survive on glaciers; other organisms must either migrate or be destroyed. In some cases this may simply involve movement to lower elevations; in others it may involve translocations of hundreds of kilometers. Mountain species may not fare well in other environments. They must find different sources of food and shelter, and they face increasing competition and predation. Those species that survive have to expend considerable effort and energy just to stay alive and to maintain viable populations. There is little opportunity for diversification. They can reoccupy the highland environment only after the ice has melted, but this is analogous to returning home after a catastrophe has struck. The home must be totally rebuilt. The glacier destroys everything, leaving only barren rock and rubble in its wake. It will be a long time before the environment can again support a full spectrum of life.

The evidence of the most recent ice age (Wisconsin) is still relatively fresh, and the pattern of glacial development can be easily reconstructed. Although the lowland ice retreated 10,000–15,000 years ago, mountain glaciers melted more slowly; the largest present-day glaciers may be remnants of the Pleistocene ice. Most smaller mountain glaciers are believed to have melted entirely, however, and to have reformed just after the warm hypsithermal that ended about 5,000 years ago. Numerous small advances and retreats have occurred within the last 10,000 years; there is considerable evidence for widespread glacial retreat during the last century, for example. Many studies have shown the slow rate of soil and vegetation development in

areas abandoned by these retreating glaciers (see pp. 240–41). Some of the first animal inhabitants are primitive species of springtails and mites, followed by arthropods such as beetles and spiders. Most early occupants are carnivores; there is not enough primary productivity to support herbivores (Brinck 1966, 1974). These predatory insects live on algae, larvae, and other insects. Eventually, as the ecosystem develops, the various components and niches are filled with a variety of life forms, but it is a slow process.

Clearly, age of surface is a major factor in ecosystem development. This is demonstrated on a macroscale by the great floral and faunal richness of the Central Asian highlands (Sushkin 1925; Meinertzhagen 1928; Swan and Leviton 1962; Zimina and Panfilov 1978). This area escaped extensive glaciation during the Pleistocene owing to its aridity, so it served as a refugium for numerous species. In fact, it is believed that many present arctic and alpine species originated here and later spread to the Arctic and to the mountains of Europe and North America (Hoffmann and Taber 1967; Hoffmann 1974).

The immaturity of mountain ecosystems can perhaps best be seen by comparing mountains with lowland tropical environments. The humid tropics are the oldest and most stable of all environments and contain the greatest number of species and organic complexity. The major problem for life in the tropics is competition with other species. Consequently, organisms use their energies primarily for diversification and specialization. The result is a complex network of species occupying a maze of ecological niches for fairly complete utilization of available resources (Dobzhansky 1950). Just the opposite is true in mountains, where the bulk of energy is devoted to coping with physical conditions and there is little diversification or specialization. The result is only partial use of the available resources. This will probably always be true in mountains, at least those in middle and high latitudes, because of the environmental stress imposed by the seasons and the even greater environmental oscillations imposed by the ice ages.

Island-Like Distribution

Mountains have been likened to true islands, since they provide habitats unlike those of surrounding lowlands and support different floras and faunas. The analogy is only approximate, however. The surrounding lowlands present a less hostile environment to terrestrial alpine organisms than does the sea. An alpine bird tiring from flight between mountain areas can stop to rest in the lowlands, but one who tires over the sea is almost certainly doomed. Another difference is that the zone of transition between environments for oceanic islands takes place abruptly at the shoreline and always at the same elevation, that of sea level. The mountain equivalent of a shoreline, though, occurs at various absolute elevations, depending on the climate, and the transition from the adjoining environment is more gradual.

Nevertheless, mountains and oceanic islands share a number of ecological characteristics (Diamond 1972, 1973, 1975, 1976; MacArthur 1972; Carlquist 1974; Mayr and Diamond 1976). In particular, the number of species and their diversity are closely related to the size of the island (mountain) and its distance from the mainland or other islands (mountains). The larger the island the greater its resource base and carrying capacity and the greater its variety and availability of habitats. The greater the distance from other islands, the fewer species that are likely to be found. Both of these characteristics are demonstrated by the size and distance between enclaves of alpine vegetation (páramos) in the northern Andes and the number of bird species they support (Fig. 9.2).

Another characteristic of islands is their increasing taxonomic specificity with insu-

larity. The more isolated and remote an island, the more nearly unique its flora and fauna, since evolution has operated under local conditions to create endemic taxa. One has only to think of the exotic species on islands such as New Zealand or the Galapagos for confirmation. For high mountains, the greatest insularity exists in the tropics. This is well shown in the curious and bizarre giant *Senecios* and *Lobelias* that are found nowhere else (Fig. 8.15). Fully 80 percent of the plants occurring in the alpine areas of East Africa are endemic (Hedberg 1969). Similar trends occur among the animals (Salt 1954; Coe 1967; Coe and Foster 1972).

The opposite situation exists in arctic and subarctic mountains: because there is free

Fig. 9.2. Islands of páramo vegetation in the northern Andes. These areas, shown in black, have base altitudes of 3,000–3,500 m (10,000–11,500 ft.), depending upon size and local climatic regime. The 1,000 m (3,300 ft.) contour line is represented by a dashed line. The numbers indicate the total number of bird species present in each area. As can be seen, there is a positive correlation between the number of species and the size of the alpine "islands." (Adapted from Vuilleumier 1970, p. 374)

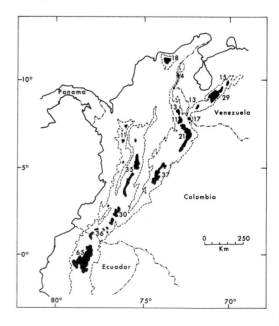

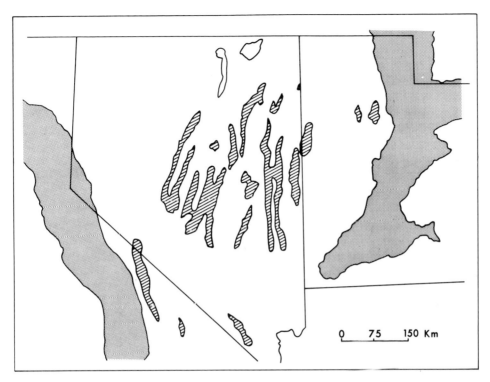

Fig. 9.3. Mountain "islands" in the Great Basin between the Sierra Nevada (left) and Rockies (right). Each of these islands is at least 3,000 m (10,000 ft.) high, surrounded by lower-lying country supporting desert shrubs. During the Pleistocene, there was relatively easy access from one mountain area to the other, but as the climate became warmer and drier, the species became isolated on individual mountain regions. The two top islands are unshaded because their faunas are poorly known and were not used in the original investigation. (After Brown 1971, p. 468)

interchange with lowland tundra species, virtually no endemic species occur (Brinck 1974). Middle-latitude mountains are intermediate in this regard; their insularity is determined by their age and the nature of the surrounding habitats. For example, the alpine zone in the Rocky Mountains is surrounded by subalpine forests, and there is a direct connection to the north. The plants and animals thus have fairly easy access from arctic and subarctic to alpine and subalpine settings. Differences between the two tundras increase southward; in Colorado more than half the plant species are non-arctic in origin, and the percentage for animals is even higher. Some endemic species exist, but they are relatively unimportant. On the other hand, the Caucasus

Mountains between the Black and Caspian seas, separated from the Arctic by vast expanses of semiarid steppe, are much more isolated; consequently, more than half the species found there are endemic (Zimina 1967, 1978). Another striking example is provided by the Basin and Range mountains of the American West. These mountains exist as isolated alpine tracts surrounded by desert shrublands; as such, they are extremely insular (Fig. 9.3). The alpine populations are totally isolated and each peak has its own set of endemic species (Faegri 1966; Brown 1971; Johnson 1975).

Theoretically, the number of species an island supports is set by the establishment of an equilibrium between rates of colonization of new species and extinction of other species. This principle also operates in mountains (Vuilleumier 1970; Brinck 1974; Simpson 1974). While true islands can only be colonized by immigration from the mainland or other islands, mountains may be colonized by several other methods. One of these is by species from adjacent lowlands adapting to the habitats of higher elevations (Fig. 9.4a). This is particularly important where the vegetation is similar enough that the degree of adaptation required is not drastic (Janzen 1967). Specia-

tion commonly occurs by stages—there may be a series of species up a mountain slope each belonging to the same genus and fundamentally related, but isolated through morphology or behavior so that they may no longer interbreed, or at the very least, have little interaction with each other; the most famous examples of this on oceanic islands are Darwin's finches from the Galapagos Islands. The giant *Senecios* and *Lobelias* from tropical African mountains have distant cousins in the surrounding montane forest

Fig. 9.4. Schematic representation of different methods of colonizing mountains. (a) Slow adaptation of lowland species to successively higher levels. (b) Direct migration from one mountain area to another. (c) Slow

adaptation of lowland species to changing conditions with mountain uplift. (d) Direct migration during times of climatic change, especially glacial periods. (Author)

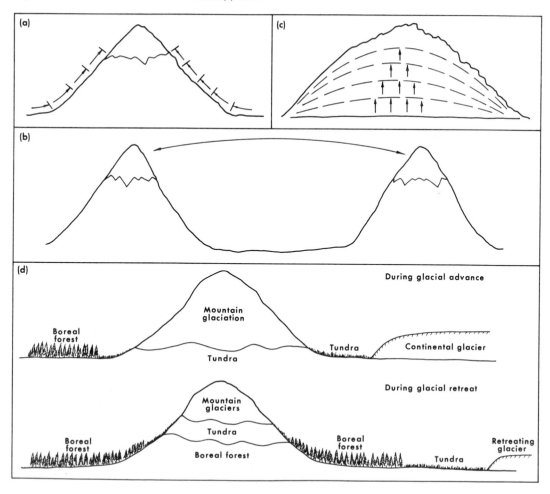

(Hedberg 1969, 1971). Another good example from the mountains of East Africa is the hyrax, a small rabbit-like rodent related to the coney of the Bible. Several species live on the mountain slopes. The lowland species is poorly insulated, has different food preferences, and lives entirely in trees; the hyrax of the alpine zone has a heavy fur coat, burrows under the ground, and makes its home in rocky areas (Fig. 9.9). The species living at different altitudes have become so differentiated that they no longer interbreed (Coe 1967, p. 120).

In general, however, the alpine areas of the tropics have been colonized primarily through direct immigration from other alpine areas, not from the surrounding lowlands (Fig. 9.4b). This is because the lowland organisms have evolved from very ancient stock in a specific and relatively stable environment and very few have the ability to pioneer a new habitat, especially one which requires the ability to withstand freezing, a phenomenon unknown in the tropical lowlands. Consequently, most high-altitude species in the tropics have been derived from species in the middle latitudes and are fundamentally different from anything found in tropical lowlands. Recent investigations in the Andes, however, indicate that climatic change in the tropics may have been considerably greater than is generally believed. In some cases this may have lowered the vegetation zones by as much as 1,500 m (5,000 ft.) (F. Vuilleumier 1969, 1970; B. S. Vuilleumier 1971; Simpson 1974, 1975). Under these circumstances the islands of alpine vegetation would have been greatly expanded, and in some areas they may have overlapped, allowing free interchange of species. Similar changes probably occurred in Africa but the isolated nature of the volcanic peaks precluded direct contact (Hedberg 1969, 1971, 1975).

Another method responsible for the isolation of high-altitude species is the process of mountain uplift (Fig. 9.4c). Some plants and animals appear to have originally been lowland species, but as the land was uplifted they were able to adapt to the slowly changing conditions. In this way they became isolated from the lowland forms. A bird of the genus *Tinamous* in the páramos of the tropical Andes lives near and on the snow, breeding only above the timberline, while all other species of the genus live in the tropical lowlands. The bird resembles a northern-hemisphere ptarmigan (*Lagopus spp.*) in appearance and behavior, but it is far removed in terms of structure and taxonomy. It is apparently an example of convergent evolution (Brown 1942, p. 13).

A final method of colonization is through direct immigration during periods of climatic change (Fig. 9.4d). This has happened chiefly in the middle and high latitudes, where major migrations took place during the glacial and interglacial periods. Species moved in advance of the ice and established themselves in belts or zones around the ice in much the same way as happens today in arctic and alpine areas—tundra first, then coniferous forest. As the climate warmed and the ice melted, these plants and animals began to reoccupy their former sites. Some moved northward, while others moved upward into mountains where suitable habitats existed. In some cases, as in the Rockies, the potential for exchange of species and colonization has continued, whereas in other smaller, isolated ranges, the alpine communities were cut off and became relict populations. Examples are the alpine species in the Basin and Range mountains (Fig. 9.3). For this reason they do not follow the equilibrium theory mentioned above: there have been extinctions but no new colonizations (Brown 1971).

Lack of Oxygen

Free oxygen is essential for life, and so far as we know it is unique to the planet earth. This is because it is entirely a product of the life process of photosynthesis. The composition of the atmosphere is relatively constant, containing about 21 percent

Table 9.1. *The natural decrease in atmospheric pressure with altitude and its effect on the partial pressure of O_2 (Houston 1964, p. 471).*

Altitude		Barometric Pressure (mm of Hg)	Partial Pressure of O_2 (mm of Hg)
(m)	(ft.)		
0		760	159
610	(2,000)	707	148
1,220	(4,000)	656	137
1,830	(6,000)	609	127
2,440	(8,000)	564	118
3,050	(10,000)	523	109
3,660	(12,000)	483	101
4,270	(14,000)	446	93
4,880	(16,000)	412	86
5,490	(18,000)	379	79
6,100	(20,000)	349	73
6,710	(22,000)	321	67
7,320	(24,000)	294	62
7,930	(26,000)	270	56
8,540	(28,000)	247	52
9,150	(30,000)	226	47

free O_2 both at sea level and in the upper part of the atmosphere. Nevertheless, there is less oxygen in the air at higher altitudes because air is compressible and has greater density and more molecules of oxygen per unit volume at lower elevations than at greater heights. The availability of oxygen is expressed as the partial pressure of oxygen (pO_2), which is derived by multiplying the total atmospheric pressure by 21 percent. Thus, normal atmospheric pressure at sea level is 760 mm, so the pO_2 is 159 mm. With increasing elevation and decreasing atmospheric pressure, the pO_2 decreases proportionately (Table 9.1).

The lack of oxygen at high altitudes does not affect all organisms equally. In general, the smaller the animal, the less restrictive its requirements for internal regulation and, therefore, the greater its altitude tolerance. Oxygen deficiency apparently has no noticeable effect on vegetation, insects, or reptiles and amphibians (Bliss 1962; Mani 1962; Hock 1964a). Very little is known about its effects on birds, but indications are that they are little affected by it. The South

American condor (*Sarcorhamphus gryphus*) nests in the high Andes but migrates daily to and from sea level, where it feeds on dead fish along the Pacific coast (Lettau 1967, p. 64). The Bar-headed goose (*Anser indicus*) winters in the lowlands of India but flies over the summit of Everest on its way to nesting grounds in the high lakes of Tibet (Swan 1970). Many mammals have similarly overcome the effects of oxygen deficiency so that they can occupy almost any environment where there is sufficient food. The yak (*Bos grunniens*) lives up to 6,000 m (19,800 ft.) in the Himalayas and llamas (*Lama spp.*) live at over 5,000 m (16,500 ft.) in the Andes. For this reason some scientists believe that lack of oxygen (*hypoxia*) is not really a limiting factor to life. "The higher reaches are sterile because of infertility rather than the physiological inadequacy of the fauna" (Morrison 1964, p. 49).

If an animal lives and reproduces in an environment, that is clear evidence that it can survive there. Organisms can escape the full brunt of most kinds of environmental stress by retreating into microhabitats, but this is not possible with oxygen deficiency. Nevertheless, the fact that some organisms have adapted to hypoxic conditions does not mean that these conditions do not limit other organisms. This is proven by the pronounced symptoms experienced when certain low-altitude mammals (including man) go to high altitudes. If these mammals move to high altitudes rapidly, acute mountain sickness (see p. 354) or other maladies may develop, possibly resulting in death. If they go up slowly, acclimatization to the changing conditions takes place, but there are limits beyond which lowland mammals cannot go. For lowland cattle this is approximately 3,000 m (10,000 ft.) (Alexander and Jensen 1959). For man it is about 5,450 m (18,000 ft.); beyond this altitude progressive deterioration sets in. The famous mountaineer George Mallory put it aptly when he said that being above this elevation is like "a sick man walking in a dream" (in Houston 1972, p. 87). Even when occupancy extends over long periods (millennia), as it has in native high-altitude populations, and the people have become adapted to hypoxic conditions, the limit still appears to be about 5,450 m (18,000 ft.). This is demonstrated by a mining community located at 5,400 m (17,500 ft.) in the Peruvian Andes, purported to be the highest inhabited settlement in the world. The mine is located at 5,750 m (19,000 ft.) and the native miners climb the 450 m (1,500 ft.) to the mine daily. A new camp was constructed at 5,600 m (18,500 ft.) but the miners rebelled, saying they had no appetite, lost weight, and could not sleep (Hock 1970, p. 53).

Although beyond a certain altitude the lack of oxygen becomes a limiting factor to some mammals, other environmental stresses are likely to prevent them from living at such heights in the first place. Absence of sufficient land surfaces at altitudes beyond 5,450 m (18,000 ft.), low plant productivity and lack of food, as well as general environmental stress from cold, wind, aridity, and solar intensity, limit the altitudinal

extent of most mammals. It remains true, however, that lack of oxygen is a major stress factor—one to which organisms can adapt, just as they can to low temperatures, but one which takes its toll (Bullard 1972).

SURVIVAL STRATEGIES

Organisms respond to environmental stresses by morphological adaptations, physiological adjustments, behavior patterns, and community relations and interaction. Plants, being relatively immobile, respond primarily through morphological and physiological adaptations, while animals respond primarily through behavior (Kendeigh 1961). Animals often deal with environmental extremes by escaping them—through migration, hibernation, burrowing, or the use of microhabitats. The nature and timing of growth and reproduction also comprise an important part of survival strategy in extreme environments. Only a few species expose themselves to the full brunt of the climate throughout the year; those that do, however, display the broad range of adaptations necessary for existence under such conditions. Escaping environmental extremes is primarily a function of behavior (although some metabolic adjustments are also involved), but for an animal to withstand extreme conditions, it must, like the plants, rely on morphological and physiological adaptations.

Migration

Migration allows those species that are strong and mobile enough a way of utilizing the high mountain environment during favorable periods and lowland or other mountain environments during more stressful periods. Strictly speaking, migration is the "large scale shift of the population twice each year between a restricted breeding area and a restricted wintering area" (Lack 1954, p. 243). The twice-yearly movement is important in mountains, but other lesser movements are of equal or greater importance. These include seasonal migrations up and down a mountain, as well as irregular movements in response to the sporadic occurrence of severe weather or poor food years. The essence of migration is that it is a cyclical movement rather than being simple emigration (leaving never to return).

Migration in middle and high latitudes generally coincides with the seasons, although some birds migrate daily during summer. In lower latitudes, migration is less important but occurs to a certain extent (Moreau 1951, 1966). The island-like nature of mountains greatly facilitates part-time occupancy, since animals can reach the area above timberline or escape it by relatively short vertical migrations. This is one fundamental difference between alpine and arctic environments: daily occupancy is not possible in the Arctic, and migration is almost totally limited to birds for, with the exception of the caribou, mammals make no attempt to move the great distances required (Irving 1972). By contrast, mammals move relatively easily to and from the alpine tundra, although few migrant mammals breed there. A number of herbivores—e.g., rabbit, porcupine, deer, and elk—and a variety of predators—e.g., weasel, badger, fox, wolf, and bear—wander above timberline during summer but retreat to lower altitudes during winter. The number of birds in the alpine tundra rises exponentially as they arrive like a floodtide for the brief summer season. Many are returning from overwintering in lower latitudes, while others are simply migrating upward from the surrounding lowlands. In the passing parade from early spring to autumn, the first birds in the high country are usually herbivores (which also harvest dead insects on the snow). As conditions improve and insects become plentiful, insectivores become dominant. A fairly high percentage of these herbivores and insectivores breed in the alpine tundra. Later in the summer, *raptors* (birds of prey) move in to harvest the newborn crop of small ro-

dents. The raptors seldom breed above timberline but are mobile enough to migrate daily to and from the alpine area. In the Beartooth Mountains of Wyoming, raptors usually do not appear before the last of July but are plentiful from then on (Pattie and Verbeek 1966, p. 175).

Migration is primarily restricted to birds and mammals. Reptiles and amphibians are not mobile enough, and such barriers as waterfalls and beaver dams generally prevent mountain fishes from migrating. Although there are some remarkable movements of insects in mountains, true insect migration is rare and takes place primarily among lowland species. For example, insects exhibit a curious tendency to seek out the summits of mountains, known as *summit swarming* or *hilltopping* (Hudson 1905; Van Dyke 1919; Chapman 1954; Edwards 1956, 1957; Shields 1967). This has been observed by many people in many parts of the world, but the exact reasons for such behavior remain elusive. Some consider the insects to be victims of the winds, blown there against their will, while others maintain that the wind may aid them but they move primarily of their own volition. Both explanations appear to be true. A variety of lowland insects are occasionally drawn up to high altitudes by ascending air currents, and if sufficient heights are reached, they are frozen by low temperatures. The dead and stunned insects are then deposited in vast quantities on glaciers and snowfields, where they serve as an important source of food for resident birds and nival insects (Swan 1961; Mani 1962; Papp 1978; Spalding 1979). Such movement is unintentional, however, and it is clearly a one-way trip.

The case of insects moving upward under their own volition is much closer to true migration. The principal insect groups displaying this behavior are the Coleoptera (beetles, weevils), Diptera (mosquitoes, flies), Hymenoptera (bees, ants), and Lepidoptera (butterflies, moths) (Shields 1967, p. 73). Explanations include: an innate urge to ascend the highest point; the search for food; attraction to the heat and light; and the use of the highest point as a meetingplace for mating. There is no reason to choose among these, since they may all operate at one time or another, but the last explanation seems best borne out by the known facts. The tendency among many insects to seek out the highest available point in order to mate has a selective advantage among sparse and isolated populations, for it insures the meeting of males and unmated females and helps to stabilize the gene pool (Shields 1967, p. 72).

A specialized example of insect migration is that of ladybird beetles (Coccinellidae). Vast swarms of these colorful little creatures have been observed on mountain peaks around the world (Edwards 1956, 1957; Mani 1962). They apparently swarm up from the

lowlands to certain peaks in summer and congregate in assemblages numbering up to thousands of individuals per square meter (11 sq. ft.). One author tells of encountering large numbers of them while climbing Mount Rainier, Washington. "They swarmed over my body and face, they violated my lunch, and they tried to crawl into the lens of my camera—For months thereafter I found squashed ladybug remnants in odd places in my equipment" (Edwards 1957, p. 41). The largest single mass assemblage ever documented was in the western Himalayas at an elevation of 4,200 m (13,850 ft.). Discovered on a snowfield, where they covered a solid patch 10 m (33 ft.) in diameter, they were estimated to number about 200,000 individuals per square meter (11 sq. ft.). This was in May, and most of the beetles were alive but inac-

Fig. 9.5. Mass assemblage of Ladybird beetles (*Coccinella septempunctata*) at 4,260 m (14,000 ft.) on Lakka Pass Glacier in the Dhauladar Range, western Himalayas. (M. S. Mani, St. John's College, India)

tive. It was possible to scoop up handfuls of the creatures and they would stir only slightly (Mani 1962, p. 138) (Fig. 9.5).

The exact purpose of ladybird-beetle migration to mountain peaks is unclear, since they apparently do not mate or feed there. Some scientists believe that they go there to hibernate (Mani 1962, p. 137), while others do not believe that they overwinter on the high peaks intentionally, but think that they simply get caught by cold weather and have no other choice (Edwards 1957, p. 45). Whatever the case, it is not uncommon to find large numbers of dead beetles under rocks and in crevices in the spring, while others are alive and preparing to move into the lowlands (as is demonstrated by the example in the Himalayas, cited above). Such mass assemblages serve as food for other high-altitude creatures—mainly birds and predatory insects, but also large mammals. The Himalayan bear (*Ursus thibetanus*) is known to overturn stones in search of ladybird beetles, and the grizzly bear (*Ursus arctos*) also feeds on them whenever it can (Chapman et al. 1955; Mani 1962, p. 139).

Another cause of migration among mountain animals is outbreaks of bad weather or poor food years. Migrations for these reasons are well-known for the Arctic— e.g., the fluctuating populations of lemmings and voles and their predators, the Arctic fox (*Alopex lagopus*) and Snowy owl (*Nyctea scandiaca*)—but such cyclical fluctuations are not usual in alpine environments (Hoffmann 1974, p. 541). Nevertheless, the downward migration of species is frequently observed when especially bad conditions exist (Verbeek 1970, p. 427; Ehrlich et al. 1972). A specialized illustration of this is provided by the Clark's nutcracker (*Nucifraga spp.*), a large jay that lives in the subalpine zone of many northern-hemisphere mountains and feeds through the winter on pine seeds it has cached in the ground. During years of poor seed production, lack of food may force the jay to leave

the high country. In the Sierra Nevada of California, seven major invasions of these birds into the lowlands have taken place since 1898 (Davis and Williams 1957, 1964). These movements are apparently the result of poor seed-production. With the arrival of spring some of the birds return to the high country, but doubtless not all do so.

Hibernation

Another method of effectively escaping the winter cold and lack of food is hibernation. In this amazing adaptation, an organism becomes inactive and passes the stressful period in a state of dormancy. Hibernation is essentially a deep and prolonged sleep. The metabolic rate in warm-blooded mammals may be reduced by up to two-thirds and the internal temperature may be lowered to within a few degrees above freezing. Many cold-blooded mammals and insects survive internal temperatures below 0° C. (32° F.) (Hesse et al. 1951; Mani 1962). This results in vast energy savings for the organism. Hibernation is an extremely efficient survival mechanism for those species not mobile enough to migrate or unable or disinclined to remain active all winter feeding themselves. This includes members of almost all divisions of animal life except for the birds, which, owing to their mobility, find it much more expedient to migrate (but see Carpenter 1974, 1976). Hibernation is principally a phenomenon of the middle latitudes, since there are no marked seasons in the humid tropics and the polar regions are simply too cold; permafrost eliminates the possibility of frost-free refuges.

Among alpine mammals, hibernation is best-developed in ground squirrels and marmots. Of these, the ground squirrel (*Citellus spp.*) is perhaps the most remarkable: its hibernation period may last over eight months. The behavior of this creature has been described from Glacier National Park, Montana:

Long before winter seems imminent the squirrels disappear into their hibernation dens, which may be part of a larger system of burrows or may be separate and remote. At any one locality the old males disappear first, then the old females, and finally the young of the year, perhaps several weeks later. The sleeping chamber itself is effectively sealed off by a plug of earth some 2 feet long. Here the squirrel curls up tightly, lying vertically on its back with head tucked into its belly and partly covered by the tail, and sleeps without eating and, apparently, without awakening for many months. It is in a torpid condition; its temperature drops from the normal 98° to about 40° F. At the proper time in spring it emerges by digging straight up at the entrance. Often, at the higher elevations, it is also necessary to tunnel up through packed snow several feet deep. The males emerge in spring a week or two before the females. (Manville 1959, p. 40)

The timing of hibernation is greatly affected by environmental conditions, especially the length of the growing season. In the Montana Rockies, ground squirrels in mountain valleys emerge in late April or early May, while those above timberline emerge in mid-June. Similarly, valley populations disappear into their dens by mid-August, while those in alpine meadows may stay active until the last of September, when snow is beginning to fall (Manville 1959, p. 40). The higher populations apparently need this extra time in the fall to provide for the sufficient maturation of the young, the accumulation of body fat to see them through the winter, and the storage of enough food for the spring. Similar behavior patterns have been observed among marmots (Pattie 1967; Hoffmann 1974, p. 505).

Cold-blooded animals—insects, reptiles, amphibians, and fish—all hibernate. Only warm-blooded animals are able to remain active during winter. Some invertebrates overwinter as eggs, while others hibernate as larvae, pupae, or adults. Species that normally complete their development in one season in the lowlands may take two or more seasons at higher elevations (Alexander and Hilliard 1969; Coulson et al. 1976). Butterflies in the Alps are known to overwinter as eggs in one generation and as pupae in the next. Carabid beetles in the western Himalayas were found hibernating as adults one year and as larvae the next (Mani 1962, p. 112). A similar situation exists among the moths, flies, and spiders. On the other hand, high-altitude flies and mosquitoes complete their development in one season (Smith 1966). The exact behavior depends upon the insect type and environmental conditions, but since the growing season decreases at higher altitudes, overwintering in intermediate forms becomes increasingly characteristic (Fig. 9.12).

Insects hibernate by shallow burrowing or by crawling under rocks and into crevices. Snowfall must be adequate to cover the hibernation site during winter. Since the temperature under the snow remains fairly constantly at or near freezing, hibernating insects need not endure extreme and fluctuating air temperatures. Insects usually do not emerge from hibernation in summer until the snow has melted. Thus, patterns of emergence depend on local conditions more than on altitude. Similarly, because hibernation is prolonged, development must be very rapid once conditions permit, in order for the insect to complete its life cycle or at least a segment of it. Since conditions are highly variable from year to year and from place to place, organisms must maintain considerable flexibility in the timing of their activities. Nature is not very precise or predictable in mountain environments; variability is the rule rather than the exception. Many animal forms show a kind of opportunism in their capacity to take advantage of favorable conditions when they appear and, equally, are able to withstand and persist through unfavorable periods (Downes 1964, p. 294). For example, many high-altitude insects have the ability to begin hibernation at almost any stage of development and to remain dormant for prolonged periods. A case in point is when an avalanche traps insects under the snow for several years; they are usually not killed, but simply remain dormant until the snow melts and they are freed (Mani 1962, p. 112).

Reptiles and amphibians do not generally inhabit the highest elevations but some do range into the lower alpine zone (Hesse et al. 1951; Pearson 1954; Swan 1952, 1967; Karlstrom 1962; Campbell 1970; Bury 1973; Pearson and Bradford 1976). Being cold-blooded, their internal temperature is dependent upon the surrounding environment. They are largely limited to periods of activity when the sun is shining, and there is simply not enough heat or food during winter to maintain activity. Hibernation in cold-blooded animals is very different from that in warm-blooded animals. Warm-blooded animals experience a profound and controlled drop in internal temperature, but in cold-blooded animals it is difficult to detect any physiological difference between hibernating and non-hibernating individuals. Nevertheless, apparently the heart rate and blood pressure do drop, and other subtle metabolic changes occur (Aleksiuk 1976).

In preparation for hibernation, snakes and lizards crawl under rocks or into animal burrows. They have a tendency to gather in groups and it is not uncommon to find a variety of life forms, including insects, all congregated under one rock. This leads to very mixed bedfellows, with predator and prey gathering under the same roof, snuggled together for the duration (Fig. 9.6). Snails, frogs, and salamanders bury themselves in mud at the bottom of ponds or in boggy areas, where they fall into a death-like sleep that lasts until the snow and ice melt in the spring. As with other life forms, the development of amphibians may be delayed at higher altitudes. Thus, frogs in the Alps commonly pass the winter as tadpoles and require an extra year for full development (Hesse et al. 1951, p. 602). Many

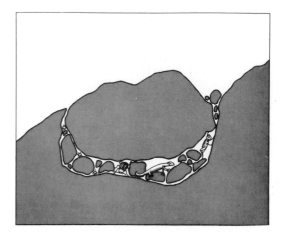

Fig. 9.6. Various cold-blooded animals using the area underneath a rock as a microhabitat. The greatly tempered environmental conditions in such locations allow the survival of species in areas where surface conditions may be prohibitive. (After Mani 1962, p. 60)

high-mountain fish hibernate once the ice forms over their heads and cuts off both their oxygen and food supply. They commonly gather in small schools at the bottom of the lake or stream and emit a protective ooze that enshrouds them all like a cloud. Fish living in shallow lakes or streams which freeze down to the bottom may actually be encased in ice without suffering damage.

Burrowing and Use of Microhabitats

Those species that cannot withstand full exposure to the alpine climate, but are unable to migrate or hibernate, escape climatic extremes by burrowing or by taking advantage of microenvironments under snow, rocks, and vegetation. During middle and high-latitude winters such activity is restricted to small mammals that remain more or less active, whereas during summer (year-round in the tropics) it includes the reptiles, amphibians, insects, and those mammals that have come out of hibernation. The small mammals that remain active exhibit one of two basic types of behavior. In one group, the animal stores up food for use during winter; in the other, foraging continues much as usual. The first group includes pikas (*Ochotona spp.*), deer mice (*Peromyscus spp.*), wood rats (*Neotoma spp.*), various Eurasian hamsters (*Cricetinae*), and certain of the voles (*Microtus spp.*). These are all herbivores that gather bits of vegetation for their winter food. They construct nests in well-drained ground or amid rocks, and depend heavily on the presence of snow for insulation. Some species, e.g., lemmings, huddle together in subterranean nests and share body heat while others, e.g., pikas, are strictly solitary. Chipmunks and hamsters have the ability to become torpid for intermittent periods. This intermediate level of hibernation is a very useful adaptation, but they must occasionally awake and feed between periods of slumber. Other species such as the Pocket gopher, deer mice, and pikas do not have this ability and must remain active throughout the winter (Hoffmann 1974, p. 493).

The pika is a particularly interesting little creature (Fig. 9.7). It is steel-grey in color, about the size of a baby rabbit, has small rounded ears, and produces a distinctive call that sounds like a shrill-pitched "ank" (Broadbooks 1965, p. 309). Pikas live in

Fig. 9.7. A pika (*Ochotona princeps*) in a typical rocky habitat at 3,760 m (12,400 ft.), Rocky Mountain National Park, Colorado. (L. C. Bliss, University of Washington)

rocky habitats such as talus slopes and blockfields located near or above timberline. They are strongly territorial, with a definite spacing between their dens (Barash 1973; Smith 1974, 1978). Much of their summer activity consists of gathering twigs, which they deposit into a central "hay pile," for winter food. The exact winter behavior of pikas is unknown. They apparently do not build up stores of body fat or become torpid, so they depend heavily on their hay piles. Their dens are separated from the hay piles so they must come up to the surface to feed, while other animals such as chipmunks use their winter supply of seeds as a bed and have only to turn their heads to feed. Another curious dietary characteristic of the pika is its tendency to reingest its own fecal matter. Like other members of the rabbit family, pikas excrete two kinds of feces. One is the familiar pellets, which are not reingested; the other is an elongated dark mass called "night" or "soft" feces, which is thought to come from excavation of a pouch in the large intestine. This material contains a high concentration of proteins and nitrogen and its ingestion adds significantly to the pika's caloric intake (Johnson and Maxwell 1966, p. 1060).

The small mammals that continue foraging during the winter include the Pocket gopher (*Thomomys spp.*), some voles (*Microtus spp.*), shrews (*Sorex spp.*), and weasels (*Mustela spp.*). With the exception of the shrews and weasels, these all depend on seeds, roots, and other vegetable matter for their food supply. The critical factor for their survival is the presence of snow, since they do not have adequate insulation to protect themselves from extremely low temperatures (Fig. 9.8). Even when snow is present, temperatures remain near the freezing mark and conditions are suboptimal. The animals compensate by constructing warm nests, clustering together to share body heat, or, in the case of the weasel, by maintaining a high level of metabolism (Brown and Lasiewski 1972).

The Pocket gopher is a good example of a small mammal that continues foraging during the winter. These little creatures have well-developed front claws for digging and spend most of their time below ground or under snow. They are solitary: during summer, each maintains its own underground burrow system, where it harvests the plant roots that extend into the tunnels (Aldous 1951). During winter, however, the Pocket gopher moves freely above the ground, under the protection of a deep snow cover, and harvests the surface vegetation. While most animals deposit their excavated material in mounds, the Pocket gopher carries its refuse upward and stuffs it into snow tunnels. These are frequently quite extensive, and after the snow melts in spring the material is deposited on the ground surface in a curious pattern of interwoven soil ropes (Fig. 7.2). There has been considerable concern over the question of whether the Pocket gopher increases erosion through his

Fig. 9.8. Generalized temperature gradient above and below a snowcovered surface in the sub-arctic. High mountain environments are similar. Note that the lowest temperatures occur at the snow-air interface, and temperatures increase rapidly within the snow down to the ground surface. This demonstrates the excellent insulative qualities of snow. (After Pruitt 1970, p. 86)

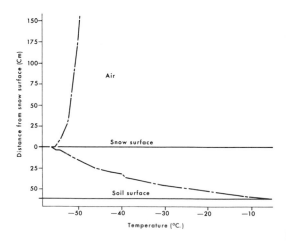

burrowing activities. It is true that the close browsing of grasses and sedges under the snow may do temporary damage, but it does not kill the plants. The annual deposition of fresh, loose soil on the surface may also result in some loss, but there is no evidence of major erosion (Ellison 1946; Stoecker 1976). In fact, it is generally believed that the fecal droppings and the continual mixing of soil have a beneficial effect on soil and vegetation development in mountain meadows (see pp. 238–39) (Ingles 1952; Turner et al. 1973; Laycock and Richardson 1975).

These examples have come from middle- and high-latitude mountains where strong seasonal contrasts exist. There, the chief problem for survival is posed by winter. No similar prolonged period of stress exists in tropical mountains; here the environmental extremes occur on a daily basis (see pp. 85–87). In tropical mountains there is very little migration or hibernation; instead, animals are heavily dependent on burrowing and use of microhabitats. Most animals are diurnal, and are most active in early morning and late afternoon, between the periods of high sun intensity. At night they retreat to sheltered sites amid rocks and vegetation or in shallow burrows. Most tropical mountain animals are not well-adapted to cold and find alpine conditions only marginal. This is demonstrated by the fact that if small animals are live-trapped at night and left without bedding, they cannot survive freezing temperatures for more than an hour or two (Coe 1969, p. 111). These animals capitalize on the fairly constant temperatures found in cavities under rocks or shallow burrows, however, and their own body heat raises the temperature of the confined space. The huddling together of certain species, as in middle latitudes, also aids in heat conservation.

A good example of a high mountain mammal in the tropics is the Mount Kenya hyrax (*Procavia johnstoni mackinderi*), which lives above timberline on Mount Kenya in East Africa (Coe 1967, p. 98; Roderick and

Fig. 9.9. The Mount Kenya hyrax (*Procavia johnstoni mackinderi*), living among rocks at 4,100 m (13,500 ft.) on Mount Kenya, East Africa. It is about 15 cm (6 in.) high and 35 cm (14 in.) long. Hyraxes are found only in Africa and western Asia; the species pictured is found only on Mount Kenya and is now protected by law. (David Roderick, Nature Expeditions International)

Roderick 1973) (Fig. 9.9). The hyrax occupies rocky habitats below cliffs and in glacial moraines. Like many tropical mountain animals, it emerges early in the morning and basks in the sun by stretching out on its side so as to expose maximum body area to the sun; this compensates for the night chill. It then feeds for several hours, seeks cover during the hottest time of day, and appears again toward late afternoon to finish feeding (Coe 1969, p. 109). Another animal on the same mountain, the Groove-toothed rat (*Otomys orestes orestes*), finds shelter from night frosts and the intense sun by crawling underneath the drooping basal leaves of the giant *Senecios*. It frequently spends its resting hours in a cavity it has excavated in the trunk (Coe 1967, p. 99).

Reptiles, being cold-blooded, are even more strongly controlled by the diurnal climatic regime in tropical mountains. The low night temperatures force them to be inactive and immobile. In early morning they are barely able to crawl into the sunlight that will raise their internal temperatures and allow them to operate efficiently. When they emerge in the morning, they orient themselves to receive the maximum sunlight and bask on rocks or dark surfaces so they are also heated from the underlying surface. Unlike warm-blooded mammals, they remain in the sun as much as possible. In fact, their periods of activity are almost entirely limited to sunshine; even a passing cloud will send them scurrying for cover. As a result, their feeding periods are generally limited to four hours or less per day. At night they seek shelter under rocks, in shallow burrows, and in vegetation to escape the full extent of the cold (Pearson 1954; Pearson and Bradford 1976). Most reptiles select rocks at least 20 cm (8 in.) thick—a size large enough to moderate the temperature extremes (Swan 1952, 1967; Coe 1969).

Invertebrates in tropical mountains also escape the daily extremes through timing of activities and clever use of microhabitats. In contrast to the highly active and visible insects of lowlands, those above timberline are sedentary and secretive. Consequently, there are very few insects visible at any given time. Insect collectors in tropical mountains have found most of their specimens beneath rocks and amid vegetation. This reclusiveness is viewed as a major adaptation to the rigors of the environment. Like mammals, insects largely restrict their activities to early morning and late afternoon. They are forced to this behavior because the low night temperatures make them lethargic and comatose (Salt 1954, p. 413).

An excellent example of vegetation serving as a microhabitat for insects is provided by the giant *Senecios* and *Lobelias* (Fig. 8.15). These plants open their leaves each day and close them at night, and a number of insects take advantage of this habit to escape the nightly frosts. Temperature measurements on a giant lobelia revealed that, while the surrounding air cooled to –2.4° C. (27.7° F.), the base of the flower remained at 3.3° C. (37.9° F.) and the center of the hollow stem was 4.0° C. (39.2° F.) (Coe 1969, p. 120). Some insects live their entire lives without ever leaving the plant. This is true for a bibionid fly which lives within the flowers of the giant *Lobelia keniensis* on Mount Kenya. It feeds and reproduces in the flowers, where it may be found in all stages—adult, egg, larvae, and pupae. These flies form the primary food source for the Scarlet-tufted malachite sunbird (*Nectarinia johnstoni johnstoni*), which hovers in front of the plant or moves up and down the trunk feeding on the insects (Coe 1969, p. 121).

Another excellent plant shelter is provided by the large grass tussocks on Mount Kenya. Measurements within these tussocks reveal that temperatures fluctuate violently on the outer perimeter, less so halfway down the leaves, and remain fairly constant at the leaf base (Fig. 9.10). Temperatures on the outer leaf area during the measurement period showed a range of 13.3° C. (44.9° F.), while those at the leaf base revealed a range of only 2.1° C. (6.9° F.) (Coe 1969, p. 114). A variety of insects live in these tussocks, regulating their temperature by moving up or down the blades of grass. One of the most interesting is a moth whose larva constructs silken tubes between the base and the outer leaves. The pupa has small spines on its side, these allow it to move up and down the tube to select the optimal temperature depending on the time of day. Similarly, several species of flies living in the tussocks display distinct diurnal movements:

At sunset large numbers of flies can be seen sitting on the ends of the tussock leaves, and if the temperature does not fall below freezing they will remain in this situation until sunrise the next morning. If the temperature falls to below freezing they are too cold to actively seek shelter, so

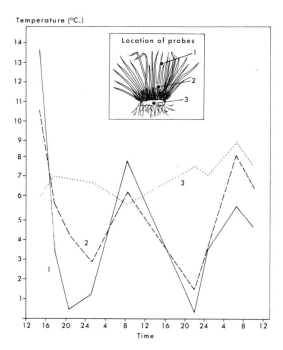

Temperature (°C.)

Location of probes

Time

Fig. 9.10. Temperature differences within a grassy tussock (*Festuca pilgeri*) in the alpine zone at 4,000 m (13,200 ft.) on Mount Kenya, East Africa. Measurements were made on 19–21 March 1966. Temperatures at the periphery of the tussock display much greater fluctuations than those within, indicating the more favorable microhabitat conditions within the tussock. (After Coe 1969, p. 115)

release their grip on the grass stem and fall down into interstices of the tussock. They will remain here until the next day when they can be seen slowly climbing the grass stems to reach the tip; after a short period of basking they fly off. (Coe 1969, p. 116)

Timing of Activities

A major survival strategy for organisms in high mountains is the timing of critical activities to coincide with the most favorable periods. This has already been discussed in connection with migration, hibernation, and escape into microhabitats; most small animals avoid the extremes of the seasons by employing one of these methods. Even during the favorable season, most activity is confined to the daylight hours. For this rea-

son, predators such as the ermine, fox, and badger (which normally hunt at night in lowlands) hunt during the day in mountains (Zimina 1967). Restriction of activity to daylight hours is even more common in the tropics (Hingston 1925; Brown 1942; Pearson 1951; Salt 1954; Coe 1967, 1969).

The period of reproduction is of greatest interest and importance, since it is critical to the continuation of the species and is also a period of great vulnerability. The major problems for reproduction in high mountains are the same as those for other functions: brevity of the growing season, lack of food, and severity of the environment. A number of adjustments are made in order to cope with these conditions. Migratory birds often arrive already paired, eliminating the need to spend time in courtship; others reduce the period of courtship (Hoffmann 1974, p. 501). They arrive as early as possible in the spring (usually about the time the snow is beginning to melt), and occupy temporary roosts until appropriate nest-building areas are bare (Pattie and Verbeek 1966, p. 167). In the short alpine summer of middle- and high-latitude mountains only one nesting attempt can be made. Because of the overwhelming urgency to complete the necessary functions within the brief time allowed, the baby birds mature exceedingly quickly. I have been greatly impressed by this among the birds that nest in the Ruby and St. Elias mountains of Yukon Territory. The young hatch one day in middle or late summer, looking like little balls of fluff; within three or four days they are walking around, and by the time they are a week or so old they are flying. Within two weeks they are essentially independent of their parents, feeding and fending for themselves. A week or two later they are gone, en route to the winter migration ground.

A wide variety of behaviors are displayed by different species of birds in relation to local environmental conditions. Often either the male or the female does not stay and care for the young, but one or the other leaves as soon as the young are hatched. This is apparently an attempt to reduce competition for food, thereby increasing the chances of their offspring's survival (Hoffmann 1974, p. 502). The timing of brood arrival in many species is closely synchronized with the seasonal peak in insect supply. This provides abundant and accessible food for the young at a time when they are poorly equipped to forage for themselves. From the insect's point of view, this approach also has survival value, since their avian predators are so swamped with insects that the survival of adequate numbers is insured (Maclean and Pitelka 1971; Hoffmann 1974, p. 502).

Another carefully timed function is the molt (replacing feathers). It is usually coordinated with the breeding cycle and migration so that these energy-expensive functions do not overlap. In some cases molting may be compressed and take place before hatching occurs (Holmes 1966; Verbeek 1970), but more commonly it is delayed until after the breeding cycle has been completed (French 1959; A. H. Miller 1961). Long-distance migratory birds may leave the high country relatively early in the season and molt after arriving at their winter grounds, whereas short-distance migrants usually molt after the young arrive and remain as long as possible before abandoning the alpine tundra (Hoffmann 1974, p. 502).

Mammals show similar adjustments in their breeding cycles. The reproductive organs of many small animals enlarge and mature while the snow still covers the ground, so that breeding can take place during or immediately after snowmelt (Vaughan 1969, p. 69). This is analogous to the tendency among alpine plants to begin growth under the snow in order to complete their life cycle in the short growing season (see pp. 298–99). Another characteristic among mammals, as among birds, is that birth usually takes place when food is most readily available. Thus, animals living at

higher altitudes breed later in the season than those in the lowlands. This is partly because of the delayed snowmelt, but it is also because there would not be adequate food if they gave birth earlier (Pearson 1948, 1951; Geist 1971; Sweeney and Steinhoff 1976). The Mule deer (*Odocoileus hemionus*) living at high altitudes in the Sierra Nevada of California fawn about the middle of July, while those at lower elevations fawn by the middle of May or earlier (Hoffmann 1974, p. 504). Animals in tropical mountains do not have the problem of timing their breeding cycles, since food is available throughout the year. Consequently, reproduction can and does take place at any time (Coe 1967, 1969). It should be pointed out, however, that the tendency of middle- and high-latitude animals to reproduce in the favorable season of the year greatly reduces the environmental stress on them during this most vulnerable of periods. This is not true in tropical mountains, where climatic extremes occur on a daily basis; there, even newborn animals have to be capable of withstanding the entire range of environmental conditions present during the day and the night (Salt 1954).

Like birds, most mammals in middle- and high-latitude mountains are restricted to a single breeding attempt each year. Thus, while deer mice at lower elevations in the White Mountains, California, have two breeding seasons, those at high elevations have only one (Dunmire 1960). Similar behavior occurs among the reptiles and amphibians (Saint Girons and Duguy 1970; Goldberg 1974). In addition, the few reptiles that extend into the alpine zone (only three in the Alps) characteristically carry their young inside them and give birth to live young rather than laying eggs as lowland forms do. The reason for this is that there is simply not enough heat for cold-blooded animals to bring eggs to complete development and hatching in high mountains (Hesse et al. 1951, p. 602). By carrying the young inside her and by keeping in the sun, the mother can put the heat she absorbs to maximum use. The ability to bear living young, therefore, is fundamental to the entrance of reptiles into cold environments.

The reduction in number of breeding attempts is offset somewhat by a tendency for litter size to increase with altitude and latitude (Lack 1948, 1954; Lord 1960; Spencer and Steinhoff 1968). The strategy behind this has been interpreted in different ways, but the most generally accepted explanation is that the shorter seasons at high altitudes limit the number of times an animal can reproduce in its lifetime compared to lowland environments, so it is advantageous to invest in a few large litters. This is true in spite of the fact that doing so reduces the life expectancy of the parents and that it is not as efficient as the production of several small litters (it is harder to care for a larger number of offspring). The production of a few large litters can be viewed as an all-or-nothing approach adopted because nothing is gained in being conservative (except in poor years, when they may not reproduce at all) (Spencer and Steinhoff 1968, p. 282).

The timing of reproduction in relation to environmental severity is demonstrated by a comparative study of the woodchuck (*Marmota monax*) in southern Pennsylvania, the yellow-bellied marmot (*M. flaviventris*) in Yellowstone National Park, Wyoming, and the Olympic marmot (*M. olympus*) from Olympic National Park, Washington (Barash 1974). The lowland woodchuck, with the longest growing season, reproduces annually; the yellow-bellied marmot, with an intermediate growing season, also bears young annually but occasionally skips a year, while the alpine Olympic marmot has the shortest growing season and reproduces only in alternate years (Fig. 9.11). This is

Fig. 9.11. Correlation among length of growing season, age of dispersal, and sexual maturity in three species of marmots in different environments. (Protruding vertical lines at top represent separate years from January 1 to January 1.) The woodchuck, living in an area with a long growing season, disperses and breeds at the end of the first year, whereas the Olympic marmot, living under harsher conditions with a very short growing season, waits two years to disperse and another year before breeding. (After Barash 1974, p. 418)

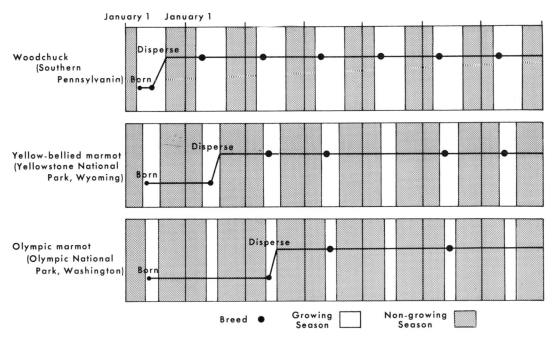

Woodchuck
(Southern
Pennsylvania)

Yellow-bellied marmot
(Yellowstone National
Park, Wyoming)

Olympic marmot
(Olympic National
Park, Washington)

January 1 January 1

Disperse   Born

Breed ●   Growing Season □   Non-growing Season ▨

interpreted as being an adaptation to the limited capacity of more extreme environments to support life.

The timing of reproduction is also tied to social behavior, which in some marmots increases with environmental severity. Thus, the woodchuck is solitary, aggressive, and non-social, while the Olympic marmot lives in tightly knit colonies and is highly social. The yellow-bellied marmot in Wyoming and Montana is intermediate in sociability. This is a critical factor in determining when the young marmots disperse and form new colonies. If the young are forced to leave too early, their chances for survival decrease. Accordingly, woodchucks disperse the year they are born and become sexually mature as yearlings; yellow-bellied marmots remain with the parents for the first year and disperse the next, becoming sexually mature as two-year-olds. The Olympic marmot, however, remains with the parents for two full years and becomes sexually mature only in the third year. This is apparently because of the time required in each environment for the animals to develop sufficient size and maturity to be able to disperse and reproduce successfully. For example, woodchucks achieve 80 percent of adult weight as yearlings, yellow-bellied marmots 60 percent, and Olympic marmots only 30 percent (Barash 1974, p. 416). At the same time, increased sociability with increased environmental severity (which allows the young to remain with their parents longer) and the reduced number of reproductive cycles efficiently control the population levels in keeping with the ability of the environment to support them. It should be mentioned, however, that a recent investigation of the yellow-bellied marmot in the Colorado Rockies indicates that growth rates at high altitudes are actually faster than those at lower altitudes (Andersen et al. 1976). These investigators also believe that the degree of sociability may be more a function of the extent and density of satisfactory hibernating sites than a function of environmental severity.

As with the larger animals, insects at higher altitudes increasingly limit their activities to the daytime hours. Those species that are predominantly nocturnal in lowlands, e.g., moths, become less common at higher altitudes, and those that do persist often alter their habits, becoming active during the day rather than at night (Mani 1962, p. 106). Feeding is limited to brief periods in early morning and late afternoon, perhaps only two or three hours daily. They spend much of the rest of the time hidden under rocks and vegetation (but see Schmoller 1971). The proportion of plant-eating species decreases above the timberline (as might be expected, since plants also decrease) until near the snowline predators dominate, living on other insects or on organic material transported upward by rising air currents. In the aeolian zone (see p. 291) utilization of the snow as a storehouse of food becomes an increasingly important part of adaptation for life (Swan 1961, 1967; Mani 1962; Papp 1978; Spalding 1979).

Reproduction in insects is synchronized to match environmental conditions. They develop very rapidly within the brief growing season and the velocity of development increases through the summer, so that later stages in the life cycle are more accelerated than earlier ones. This is particularly marked at higher altitudes and around the margins of melting snow. Even though development during the summer is fast, the season is frequently so short that the insect must overwinter at intermediate stages of its life cycle, taking two or three years for complete maturation (Mani 1962, p. 117). Like other animals, insects display a tendency to become single-brooded at greater heights. A species that is double-brooded at lower elevations may become single-brooded at higher elevations. This is expressed differently in various insects, but

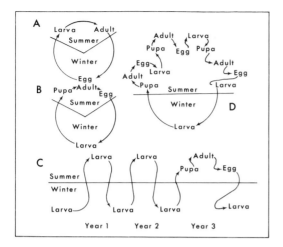

Fig. 9.12. Diagrammatic representation of reproductive cycles displayed among mountain insects. (a) A normal one-year cycle with hibernation in the egg stage and adults emerging late in summer. (b) A one-year cycle with hibernation in the larval stage and adults emerging in mid-summer. (c) A two-year cycle displayed among beetles at higher altitudes, with larval development taking place in summer, relapsing into dormancy in winter, and final development occurring in the third year. (d) An example of multiple-cycle reproduction in flies and mosquitoes, where up to three or four generations develop within the brief summer. (After Mani 1962, p. 118)

the adaptive strategy is similar (Fig. 9.12a, b, c). A few insects, such as the Diptera (mosquitoes, flies), can reproduce several times in spite of the brevity of the growing season (Fig. 9.12d). The ability to do so is one reason for their abundance in high-altitude and high-latitude environments compared to such species as butterflies, which take two or more seasons for the completion of a single generation.

Withstanding

Although most animals living in high mountains escape the full brunt of the environment by one means or another, a few hardy souls expose themselves to the elements throughout the year. These are mainly the larger mammals such as the yak (*Bos grunniens*), mountain sheep (*Ovis spp.*),

mountain goat (*Oreamnos spp.*), ibex (*Capra spp.*), and chamois (*Rupicapra rupicapra*) of the northern hemisphere (Clark 1964; Geist 1971), and the camelid mammals, e.g., the llama (*Lama glama*), guanaco (*L. guanaco*), alpaca (*L. pacos*), vicuna (*Vicugna vicugna*), of the southern hemisphere (Pearson 1948, 1951). In addition, there are predators such as the bear (*Ursus spp.*), wolf (*Canis spp.*), fox (*Vulpes spp.*), and a few felines (Seidensticker et al. 1973). Among the birds only a handful remain, the most characteristic of which is the ptarmigan (*Lagopus spp.*) (Choate 1963; Braun and Rogers 1971). All of these animals are physically, metabolically, and behaviorally well-adapted to the environment and are able to eke out a meager existence during the winter.

Large animals that live in snowy, rocky areas—e.g., the chamois, ibex, sheep, and goats—are remarkably surefooted and have features such as large front feet, pincer-like toes, and hooves with elastic soles (Hoffmann 1974, p. 497). Animals that cannot move around easily in heavy snow—e.g., deer, moose, and elk—are forced to migrate to lower elevations during winter (Pruitt 1960, 1970; Kelsall and Telfer 1971; Strickland and Diem 1975; Ward et al. 1975). Sight and smell are exceptionally keen in many mountain animals. Mountain sheep have binocular-like eyes and can see long distances. If several sheep are together, they usually face in different directions so that all approaches are covered; very little escapes their attention that happens below them. They also use the wind to good advantage: during the day, they typically bed down on cliff ledges to be cooled by upslope breezes and to catch scents from below. Hearing is less important because sound does not travel well in windy and rugged topography. This may be one reason for the high shrill calls characteristic of many mountain animals, e.g., marmot, pika, ground squirrel, and chamois. Since these loud, piercing sounds travel farther and are more easily distinguished from that of the wind or of falling rocks, they enhance communication and aid in reducing predation (Hoffmann 1974, p. 497).

Behavior modifies environmental extremes in other ways. Mountain sheep and goats seek out sunny or wind-protected slopes, feed in areas blown free of snow rather than struggling in areas of deep snow, and become very familiar with their home range. Tendencies toward gregariousness, intricate and exact social behavior, and aggressiveness also contribute to survival; the young are forced to learn and adapt quickly. In this way familiar and predictable social and physical environments are maintained, helping to minimize energy waste and exposure to danger (Geist 1971). The exact approach varies in different animals, but the extremes are usually buffered somewhat; nevertheless, as long as they remain exposed, it is impossible to escape them altogether.

MORPHOLOGICAL AND PHYSIOLOGICAL ADAPTATIONS

The fundamental ingredient for survival is the ability to withstand climatic extremes and to find adequate food in winter. This is achieved through morphological and physiological adaptations, a few of which —concerning snow, rocks, and wind—have already been mentioned. The major adaptations, however, are those in response to temperature and low oxygen pressure.

Temperature

Warm-Blooded Animals

Early observations on the effect of altitude and latitude on the nature and distribution of animals established several correlates or climatic rules about the response of warm-blooded animals to low temperature. One of these, Bergmann's Rule, states that the body size of similar species tends to increase in colder climates (Bergmann 1847). The phys-

iological basis for this is that heat production is proportional to mass, whereas heat loss is proportional to surface area: the larger an animal, the less area (proportionately) is exposed to the atmosphere. Another long-standing maxim in animal ecology is Allen's Rule, which states that extremities such as tails and ears tend to become shorter and more compact with increasing cold (Allen 1877). Again, this reduces the exposed surface area, heat loss, and the energy required to heat the distal parts. A last rule of note is Gloger's Rule, which maintains that warm-blooded animals living in cold climates tend to be white or light-colored so that they lose less heat through radiation (Hock 1965).

Although these empirical rules are based on simple observation and correlation, a number of species obey them (see Hesse et al. 1951, pp. 462–66), but many do not. In recent years the validity of these rules has become the source of considerable controversy. Scholander (1955) strongly criticized them, maintaining that surface area is of little importance in the conservation of heat compared to insulation:

The hopeless inadequacy of cold adaptation via Bergmann's Rule may be seen by the following consideration. Take a body-to-air gradient in the tropics of 7° and in the arctic of 70°, i.e., a tenfold increase. A tenfold greater cooling in the arctic animal is prevented by covering the surface with fur a few centimeters thick. A relative surface reduction of ten times would require a weight increase of the animal of one thousand times. . . . There is no physiological evidence, in beast or man, that the minor and erratic subspecific trends expressed in Bergmann's and Allen's Rules reflect phylogenetic pathways of heat-conserving adaptation. (Scholander 1955, p. 22)

Other scholars have responded that Bergmann's and Allen's Rules are only empirical observations and that physiological interpretation is another matter; and they have offered other interpretations for the significance of body size (Mayr 1956; Newman 1956, 1958; Rensch 1959; Kendeigh

(a)

(b)

(c)

(d)

Fig. 9.13. The White-tailed ptarmigan (*Lagopus leu-curus*) in the alpine zone of the Colorado Rockies. (a) In winter, their white plumage blends beautifully with the snow. (b) In summer, they are again almost indistinguishable from their surroundings. (c and d) In spring and fall, they stick either to the snow or bare areas, depending upon the condition of their plumage. (Clait Braun, Don Domenick, and Mario Martinelli, courtesy of Clait Braun, Colorado Division of Game, Fish, and Parks)

1969; Brown and Lee 1969; McNab 1971).

With respect to Gloger's Rule, several studies have shown that radiative heat loss is actually no less from white than from black pelage (Hammel 1956; Svihla 1956). The raven (*Corvus corax*) is coal-black, but it is one of the few animals that remain in arctic and alpine areas throughout the winter. A number of animals do become white seasonally—e.g., ermine, fox, ptarmigan, caribou, collared lemming, and arctic hare —but the survival value of this is probably higher as camouflage than as insulation (Green 1936; Hock 1965). This is illustrated by the ptarmigan, which blends imperceptibly into the winter landscape (Fig. 9.13a) but is equally well color-adapted to the summer substrate (Fig. 9.13b). During the spring and autumn, the ptarmigan carefully keeps either to the snow patches or to the bare areas, depending on the stage of development of its winter plumage (Figs. 9.13c, 9.13d). There is apparently no marked difference in insulative value between winter and summer plumage (Irving et al. 1955; Johnson 1968). In general, then, a tendency toward larger size, reduced extremities, and/or white coloration is observed in many species, but the physiological importance of these characteristics is questionable, and there is no question that there are more effective ways of reducing heat loss.

The fundamental problem for animals living in cold climates, aside from getting enough food, is that of maintaining their internal temperature. It has long been known that the body temperature of warm-blooded mountain and polar animals is essentially the same as that of tropical species; therefore, the contrast between internal temperature and environment is much greater in cold than in warm climates. At times there may be a difference of as much as 100° C. (180° F.) between the interior of the body and the surrounding environment. Since internal temperature is relatively inflexible and must be maintained within narrow limits, the question is: How is this accomplished in animals that must live exposed to such conditions for weeks or months at a time? There are two main approaches: to reduce heat dissipation, or to increase heat production.

Reducing Heat Dissipation. Heat dissipation is reduced by increasing insulation, and by reducing the temperature of extremities. In-

creased insulation is fundamental and is a typical response of cold-climate animals. It is shown in the tropics by the Mount Kenya hyrax, which lives at 3,490 m (13,000 ft.) and has thick luxurious fur, quite unlike the very thin-furred hyrax in the surrounding lowlands (Coe 1967). Perhaps the best example of insulation found anywhere is that of the arctic fox, which is so well-protected that it can rest comfortably on the snow at temperatures down to –40° C. (–40° F.) before it has to raise its metabolism (Scholander et al. 1950b, p. 251). Similar abilities exist in larger animals such as mountain sheep and goats, wolves, bear, and caribou, but fur depth does not continue to increase on larger animals in proportion to their size; it appears to reach its maximum efficiency at about the size of the fox (Fig. 9.14). On animals smaller than the fox the fur becomes thinner; if it did not, these animals would not be able to move about. This is particularly true for the smallest forms, e.g., shrews, lemmings, and weasels. The insulative value of the fur on these small animals is little more than that of tropical forms. Consequently, the only way they can survive is to escape into burrows and under snow. Bird species display no marked difference in plumage between warm and cold environments. This is apparently because of the restrictions imposed by flight requirements. However, the feathers of arctic and alpine birds are frequently structured in such a way that more air is trapped for insulative purposes than in the feathers of birds in warm climates (Irving 1972).

The amount of insulation on an animal is variable in space and time, owing to the need for both heat dissipation and heat conservation. Thus, certain areas of the body, especially the head, legs, and underbelly, may have thinner insulation than the rest. The guanaco (*Lama guanicoe*) of the high Andes has densely matted fur on parts of its body, while other areas are almost bare (Fig. 9.15). This animal lives in a dry environment with intense sun and heat during the day but

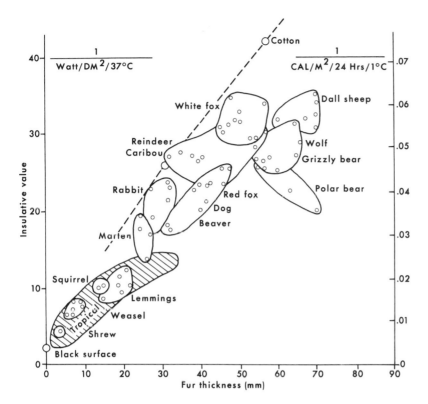

Fig. 9.14. Insulation in relation to winter fur-thickness in arctic and tropical animals. The insulative value of fur is roughly proportional to its thickness. Lemmings, squirrels, weasels, and shrews have a low degree of insulation, comparable to that of tropical animals (denoted by crosshatched area). Consequently, they can only survive the cold by burrowing and sharing body heat. Heat transmission through the fur was measured in a room at 0° C. (32° F.), by stretching the fur over a ring and heating one side of it to 37° C. (98.6° F.) with a hot plate. Thermisters were used to ascertain the temperature on the other side of the skin. (After Scholander et al. 1950c, p. 230)

rapid cooling and freezing at night. The variable insulation of the guanaco is designed to allow maximum flexibility (Morrison 1966). When the animal is hot, it can expose the more thinly insulated areas, but when cold, it can curl up and protect itself. This behavior is common in all animals. The mountain sheep rests with its legs extended during warm weather, but when it is cold, it tucks them under its body. Similarly, the fox or the wolf coils into a tight ball and wraps his long bushy tail across his face. Birds tuck their heads under their wings. The insulative ability of fur or feathers may also be controlled to a certain extent by flexing the fur or fluffing feathers to create more dead air spaces. Alternatively, the hair may be wetted or sleeked against the body, allowing greater heat loss. This is frequently associated with evaporative cooling through sweating and panting.

On a seasonal basis, animals commonly vary their insulation by molting or shedding fur or feathers. The mountain sheep's coat consists of a layer of dense woolly underhair and an outer layer of long brittle guard hairs. Most of the guard hairs are rubbed off in spring during the major molt (Geist 1971, p. 257). Similar behavior is observed in many

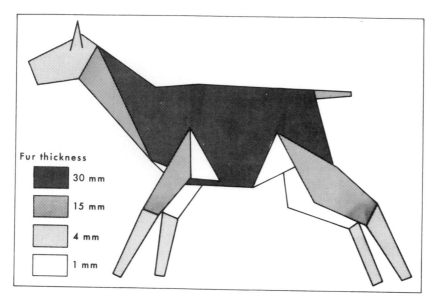

Fig. 9.15. Diagrammatic representation of fur thickness on the guanaco (*Lama guanicoe*). The large variations in insulative quality from its back to underbelly allow the animal to adjust to a wide range of temperatures (After Morrison 1966, p. 20)

cold-climate animals, and measurements made of the insulative ability of fur show marked differences between winter and summer (Hart 1956). The insulative value of the feathers of birds may be slightly less in summer, but the differences are not so marked as with animal fur (Johnson 1968). One of the most complex molts of any kind is that of the ptarmigan, which displays a continuously changing plumage from spring through autumn (Hoffmann 1974, p. 487) (Fig. 9.13).

The other major method of reducing heat dissipation is to lower the temperature of the extremities. This decreases the thermal gradient between the body and the surrounding environment so that less heat is lost from these less insulated areas, and it saves the energy that would be required to maintain the extremities at a higher temperature. Examples are the bare legs and feet of birds, and the legs, feet, and noses of animals such as the fox, wolf, caribou, or mountain sheep

(Fig. 9.16). The bare feet of birds and mammals standing in icy water or on cold snow are maintained just above the freezing temperature of the tissue, which may be as low as –1° C. (30.2° F.) (Irving and Krog 1955; Irving 1964, 1966, 1972; Henshaw et al. 1972). This is accomplished by controlling the temperature and volume of the blood circulating to these areas. Many cold-climate animals have a circulatory system in which the bood coming from the extremities through the veins, and the blood leaving the heart through the arteries, passes through a series of vascular heat exchangers (Scholander 1957) (Fig. 9.17). This lowers the temperature of the blood moving toward the extremities and raises the temperature of the blood returning to the heart, thus conserving heat within the body (Scholander 1955, p. 19). If the animal suddenly has to increase its metabolism, e.g., to escape predation, it then has to dissipate heat. To accomplish this, it increases the flow of blood to the extrem-

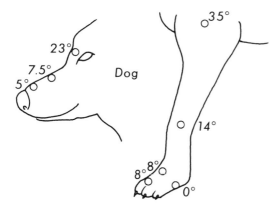

Fig. 9.16. The skin temperature of an arctic sled dog at –30°C. (–22° F.). Note the lower temperatures of the extremities. This results in considerable energy being saved by the animal. The body-to-air temperature gradient is reduced, as is heat loss. (After Irving 1972, p. 142)

ities, raising their temperature and therefore the air-to-body gradient.

Increasing Heat Production. The internal temperature of warm-blooded animals is about 37° C. (98.6° F.), no matter what climate they live in, and their heat production (metabolism) is primarily a function of body size. Larger animals produce more heat than small animals, but they also have more mass to maintain, so their internal temperatures are similar. Additional heat is produced through bodily exercise and muscular activity. This may help to compensate for cold but it is only a temporary measure; it cannot be maintained indefinitely. Increased activity requires increased food, and an animal cannot and does not spend all of its time eating (especially when food is limited). Most cold-climate animals spend as much of their time resting and playing as they do eating. Consequently, producing additional heat through increased metabolism is effective but expensive, and can only be maintained for short periods of time (Irving 1972, p. 121).

Insulation, by contrast, is efficient and flexible. This is demonstrated in Figure 9.18,

which shows the temperature sensitivity of selected tropical and cold-climate animals. Tropical animals increase their metabolic rate sharply when the external temperature drops only slightly, while the arctic fox and mountain sheep are so well-insulated that they do not have to increase their metabolic rate at all until a temperature of –40° C. (–40° F.) is reached, and then their metabolic rate increases only slightly (Scholander et al. 1950b, p. 254). The weasel does not have much better insulation than tropical animals but it is less temperature-sensitive, and has an unusually high metabolic

Fig. 9.17. Schematic representation of a vascular heat-exchange system. The warm blood from the heart moves toward the extremities and is cooled by transfer of heat to the returning venous blood, which in turn is warmed. This results in the saving of considerable energy, since the temperature of both core and extremities is maintained at an appropriate level with little effort. (Adapted from Scholander 1955, p. 19)

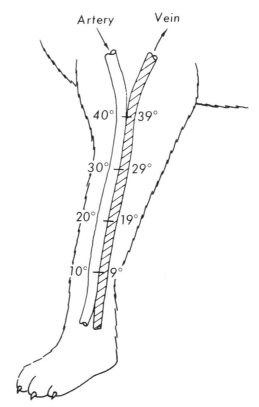

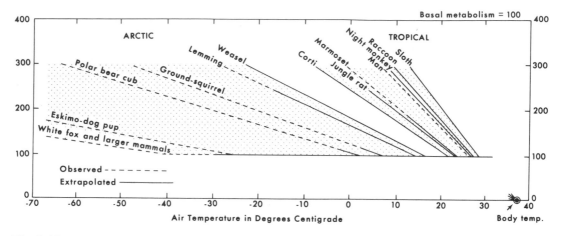

Fig. 9.18. Heat regulation and temperature sensitivity of cold-climate and tropical mammals. All warm-blooded animals have similar internal temperatures, but owing to differing amounts of insulation and sensitivity to cold, some must increase their metabolism more rapidly than others when the external temperature decreases. This is seen in the steepness of the gradient for the various animals. The basal metabolic rate is the temperature where heat loss begins to exceed heat production in a relaxed, resting animal. Note that man is a tropical animal and increases his metabolism immediately upon a decrease in external temperature, whereas the arctic fox is so well-insulated that it does not have to increase its metabolism until a temperature of –4° C. (24° F.) is reached. (After Scholander et al. 1950b, p. 254)

rate maintained by a voracious appetite and continual activity. This is metabolically expensive, however, "the cost of being long and thin" (Brown and Lasiewski 1972).

Man is a tropical animal, highly temperature-sensitive, and, when naked and resting, begins to shiver at about 27° C. (80.6° F.) (Fig. 9.18). Humans may become acclimatized to cold to a certain degree: some primitive peoples sleep with little cover in freezing weather or expose their extremities for prolonged periods with no adverse effects. This is accomplished largely through nerve insensitivity and increased metabolism. The Andeans also chew coca leaves, which apparently act as an anaesthetic, reducing the discomfort associated with cold and hunger (Little 1970; Hanna 1974, 1976). It has long been known that the hands of the natives are warmer than those of newcomers to the Arctic (Brown et al. 1954). Similar conditions exist among North Atlantic fishermen who handle cold nets. If you have ever spent an extended period camping during winter (or in high mountains during summer) you may have noticed that you gradually become accustomed to the cold.

Perhaps the most impressive example of human tolerance to cold yet reported is that of a Nepalese pilgrim encountered at an elevation of 4,650 m (15,300 ft.) in the Himalayas by the 1960–1961 American expedition (Bishop 1962; Pugh 1963). He was dressed only in thin cotton trousers and shirt and an old khaki overcoat. He had no shoes, gloves, or sleeping bag. When first encountered, he was told to return to lower elevations where he could find shelter, but he refused and followed the expedition for the next four days, walking on the snow in his bare feet and sleeping outside at temperatures down to –13° C. (8° F.). By this time the curiosity of the expedition physiologist was aroused and he invited the man to join the camp, provided that he allow a few physiological observations. Even the Sherpa guides were amazed at his feat. Briefly, the observations indicated a substantial increase in metabolism (up to 2.7 times normal) with only slight shivering (not enough to disturb his sleep). While sleeping outside at 0° C. (32° F.) in light clothes his rectal temperature and skin temperature over the trunk showed only minor changes, and his hand and foot temperatures did not fall below 10°–13° C. (50°–55° F.) (Pugh 1963). There were no signs of frostbite and he did not feel any pain or numbness from walking barefooted on the snow (Fig. 9.19). This may be due to local tissue adaptation as is found in some animals and birds (Irving 1960). It clearly shows that, if forced to it, humans can display considerable flexibility in adjusting to climatic extremes. Nevertheless, maintaining such a high level of metabolism is expensive and eventually takes its toll. Man, like other large animals, must have insulation (clothing, shelter) in order to live in the cold climates of the earth.

Cold-Blooded Animals

Smaller size. Among cold-blooded animals and insects at high altitudes the tendency is for body size to decrease rather than increase. This is the opposite of Bergmann's Rule. The tendency toward smaller body size with altitude can be seen in almost all cold-blooded vertebrates and invertebrates (Fig. 9.20) (Schmidt 1938; Darlington 1943; Park 1949; Martof and Humphries 1959; Mani 1962, 1968). There is also a tendency for orders composed of smaller-sized individuals to dominate. Thus, among the insects, the Diptera (flies, mosquitoes) and Collembola (springtails) become more important than any others at the highest alti-

Fig. 9.19. The hard and cracked feet of Man Bahadur, the Nepalese pilgrim who was found walking barefoot in the snow near the base camp of the 1960–1961 American expedition on Mount Everest at 4,650 m (15,300 ft.). He had no shoes, wore only a khaki overcoat, and slept in the snow at subfreezing temperatures without suffering from frostbite. (Barry Bishop, National Geographic Society)

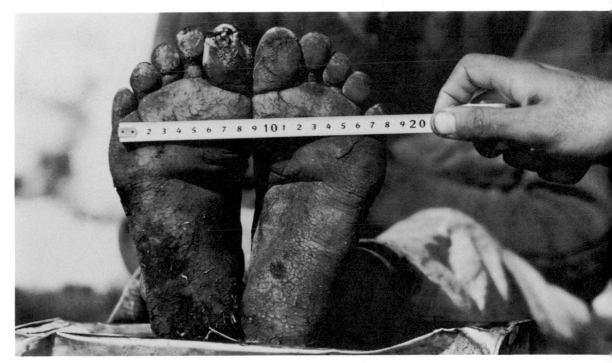

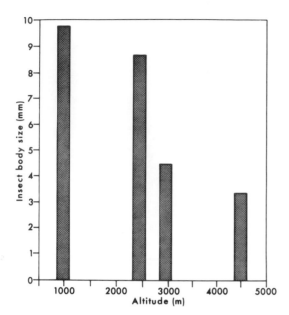

Fig. 9.20. Decrease in beetle (*Carabidae*) body-size with elevation in the Himalayas. (After Mani 1962, p. 97)

into microhabitats. These factors are important to warm-blooded animals as well, but not to the same degree, since their level of metabolism is considerably higher.

Winglessness and flightlessness. A corollary of smaller size in insects is a tendency toward winglessness or reduced wing-size. This is a dominant characteristic of high-altitude insects, observed in many mountain areas (Darlington 1943; Janetschek 1956; Salt 1954; Mani 1962, 1968; Hackman 1964). In the Himalayas 50 percent of the insects above timberline have no wings, and at the snowline the proportion is 60 percent (Mani 1962, p. 92). Wingless species are 25 times more abundant above the snowline than in the surrounding subalpine forests. Even those species with wings rarely fly; they are essentially ground-dwelling organisms, some with the ability to fly but seldom availing themselves of the opportunity, others with only partial or abbreviated wings incapable of keeping them aloft. Thus, at the highest levels it is a common sight to see butterflies, moths, and flies crawling around on the ground. They flatten themselves against the surface into the wind, flying only when the air is relatively calm.

The reasons for winglessness and abbreviated wings are not immediately obvious. Darlington (1943) believed it to be a response to the insular character of mountains and to the limitation of habitats, so that the survival value of flight would be reduced. An analogy to this would be the flightless birds—e.g., kiwi and dodo—found on oceanic islands. The flightlessness of insects on high mountains, however, must also be due to environmental extremes, especially that of low temperature. Insects require a certain critical temperature—usually about 10° C. (50° F.)—to be able to function, and since the highest temperatures occur at ground level, there is an advantage in remaining close to the ground. Those insects with the ability to fly must preheat their flying muscles by vibrating or by pumping

tudes (Mani 1968, p. 60). This must be due in part to the lack of food at the highest levels, since food is largely restricted to airborne nutrients. The main reason for the difference in size between warm- and cold-blooded animals, however, is that the warm-blooded animals maintain a high internal temperature that is essentially independent of environmental conditions, so that large body size allows efficient heat conservation. Cold-blooded animals, on the other hand, are totally dependent on environmental temperature, so a smaller size works to their advantage. There is less mass to heat, so response is more rapid, and the smaller size means a relatively greater surface area to capture external heat (Pearson 1954; Pearson and Bradford 1976). Of course, temperature is only one component of the environmental complex. Other factors that encourage small size in cold-blooded animals include the short time available for maturation, the lack of nutrients, and the advantage small size provides in escaping them before taking off (Heinrich 1974). Once aloft, muscular activity generates enough heat to maintain flight under the lower temperature conditions. Another problem for flying insects is the low atmospheric pressure and thin air of high altitudes. The major factor, however, is the wind, which is too strong for effective and sustained flight by insects. For this reason Darwin thought that flying insects tended to be blown away from mountaintops, leaving the wingless stock to occupy the area (in Hesse et al. 1951, p. 598). Whatever the explanation, winglessness and flightlessness are common traits of high-altitude insects.

Darker coloration. A well-known characteristic of cold-blooded animals and invertebrates in mountains is a tendency toward darker coloration. This is the reverse of the coloration of many warm-blooded animals. Thus, salamanders, frogs, lizards, and snakes are almost universally dark-colored in mountains (Hesse et al. 1951; Swan 1952; Pearson 1954; Swan and Leviton 1962; Hafeli 1968–69). Similar conditions are seen among the arthropods. Species that are light-colored below timberline become darker above timberline: beetles which are pale brown, green, or metallic blue at lower elevations become dark brown or black at higher elevations; butterflies also display darker coloration with altitude (Walshingham 1885; Downes 1964). In addition, body markings, such as spots and stripes, tend to enlarge and coalesce at higher altitudes. For example, the spots on ladybird beetles become larger, darker, and coalescent above timberline in the Himalayas (Mani 1962, p. 90).

The tendency toward darker coloration among cold-blooded animals at higher elevations apparently contributes to heat absorption and helps to protect against the greater ultraviolet radiation. Body temperatures of cold-blooded animals basking in the sun may exceed that of the surrounding air by 20°–30° C. (36°–54° F.). The temperature of the Andean lizard, *Liolaemus multiformis*, was measured by radiotelemetry. Over a three-day period its internal temperature cycled between 3° C. to 34° C. (37.4° F. to 93.2° F.), while temperatures in the shade ranged from –2° C. to 15° C. (28.4° F. to 59° F.) (Fig. 9.21) (Pearson and Bradford 1976, p. 155). An equally great thermal capacity is presumed for dark-colored invertebrates at high altitudes (Mani 1962, p. 91).

Cold-Hardiness. It may seem redundant at this point to say that organisms living in cold

Fig. 9.21. Body temperature of a free-living lizard, *Liolaemus multiformis*, at an altitude of 4,300 m (14, 200 ft.) in the Peruvian Andes. This lizard is able to achieve and maintain a higher temperature (dashed line) than that of the surrounding air (solid line) by its behavior, e.g., basking or seeking shelter according to weather conditions. (After Pearson and Bradford 1976, p. 157)

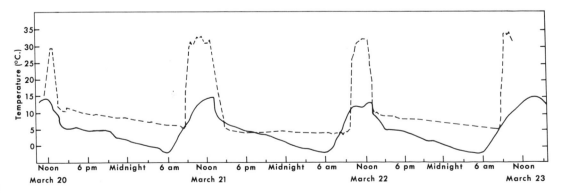

climates must have the ability to survive low temperatures, but cold-hardiness is itself a major adaptation, especially in cold-blooded animals and invertebrates, which have no way to maintain their internal temperature. We have seen something similar in plants: a sudden freeze may encase the delicate blossoms of alpine flowers in ice, but they are seldom harmed by it. Despite the efforts that reptiles, amphibians, fish, and invertebrates make to escape extreme cold through the use of microhabitats and timing of activities, there are inevitably times when these organisms are subjected to subfreezing temperatures. Consequently, they must have the ability to withstand at least partial freezing. The frog *Rana temporaria* lives at higher altitudes than any other in the Alps—2,600 m (8,580 ft.)—and can withstand freezing as long as its heart is not frozen (Hesse et al. 1951, p. 602). Fish in shallow lakes that freeze to the bottom may be encased in ice with no apparent damage, owing to plasma-protein concentrations which act as antifreeze, protecting their cells from disruption (Hargens 1972). Lizards and snakes are less well-adapted to freezing and for this reason are less common in middle- and high-latitude mountains.

Arthropods have the ability to supercool and retard ice nucleation, in some cases down to –40° C. (–40° F.). A few insects can withstand being frozen solid, mainly in the intermediate stages, i.e., eggs, larvae, or pupae, but the major adaptation to subfreezing temperatures in insects is supercooling, which is achieved through the presence of glycerol, a natural antifreeze ingredient (Smith 1958; Salt 1961, 1969). Resistance to freezing is also related to moisture content and atmospheric pressure; the less body fluid an insect has and the lower the air pressure, the more supercooling the insect displays (Salt 1956; Crawford and Riddle 1974). This is particularly important in the highly arid environments of many alpine areas.

Adaptation to cold has become so complete in a few organisms that they are limited to environments with low temperatures. In the humid páramos of the Andes, frogs of the genus *Telmatobius* are found up to the snowline, 4,550 m (15,000 ft.), but they seldom come below 1,500 m (6,000 ft.) and then only along cold meltwater streams (Hesse et al. 1951, p. 601). A cave beetle (*Silphidae*) lives in ice grottoes on glaciers at temperatures ranging from –1.7° C. to 1.0° C. (30.7° F. to 33.8° F.) (Hesse et al. 1951, p. 19). Almost everyone who has hiked in mountains in the spring has observed *watermelon snow*, the result of reddish-colored snow algae that accumulate in melt depressions in the snow (Fig. 9.22) (Pollock 1970; Hardy and Curl 1972; Thomas 1972). The optimal growth temperature of most snow algae ranges from 0° C. to 10° C. (32° F. to 50° F.) (Hoham 1975). Mention should also be made of snow worms, springtails, glacier fleas, and mites, all of which live in a constantly cold milieu (Marchand 1917; Scott 1962; Swan 1967) (Fig. 9.23). These are so cold-limited that they can be killed by the warmth of the human hand (Mani 1962, p. 102).

Of course, most organisms live at lower altitudes than snowline and can withstand much larger ranges of temperature. In arid mountains, moisture may be more important than temperature. Thus, frogs, snails, slugs, and many water-born insects are limited to areas with adequate moisture and are not found in areas such as the Puna de Atacama, the inner ranges of the trans-Himalayas, or desert mountains.

Lack of Oxygen

The decrease in oxygen with altitude is more or less constant, so all mountain animals are subjected to oxygen-deficient conditions. Surprisingly little research has been done concerning effects of lack of oxygen on naturally high-altitude animals; some of the very earliest work was carried out in the mid-1930s (Hall et al. 1936; Kalabukov 1937). By contrast, there has long

Fig. 9.22. Snow algae in the high Cascades, Oregon. These algae accumulate in large numbers in the spring as the snow melts, turning pockets and depressions a deep red color. This is known as "watermelon snow" because of its distinctive color and odor. (Author)

Fig. 9.23. Snow worms (*Mesenchytraeus solifugus*) from the Coast Range, British Columbia, Canada. These creatures, resembling small black earthworms, are found on glaciers and perennial snowbanks, where they feed on aeolian debris. They are active during the day, especially when the sun is shining, and hundreds may often be seen. (Gretchen T. Bettler, University of Nevada)

been interest in the effects of high altitude on humans. The early Spaniards, in their conquest of South America during the sixteenth century, were well aware of the negative effects of high altitude (Monge 1948). One of the major chroniclers of the period, the Jesuit priest Jose de Acosta, vividly described the effects of high altitude: "And thereupon I was seized with such retchings and vomitings that I thought I should give up my soul, for after the food and phlegm came bile and more bile, this one yellow and the other green, until I came to spit up blood." Father Acosta is also regarded as one of the first to realize the cause of these symptoms:

Because the air is so thin and penetrating that it goes through one's bowels, and not only men feel this anguish but also the animals, which sometimes get so out of breath that there are no spurs sufficient to budge them . . . so I am persuaded that the element of air there is so thin and delicate that it does not provide for human respiration which needs it to be thicker and more tempered. (In Monge 1948, p. 3)

Alexander von Humboldt is generally considered the first to observe scientifically the effects of oxygen deficiency in humans. In 1837, after unsuccessfully trying to reach the summit of Mount Chimborazo in Ecuador—6,231 m (20,561 ft.)—he suggested that future expeditions to such elevations should carry a supply of "special air" enriched with oxygen (Luft 1972). Since that time countless expeditions to high altitudes have been made, and many observations have been carried out on the physiological reactions of the climbers. By the turn of the century high-altitude research stations had been established in Europe and South America to study the effects of high altitude on both native high-altitude and sea-level man (Von Muralt 1964).

The era of exploration of Mount Everest and the high Himalayan peaks added another dimension to high-altitude research, as did the advent of the air and space age. The primary focus throughout has been on human acclimatization and adaptation, although considerable work has been performed by taking low-altitude animals to high altitudes and observing their physiological reactions. This has shed some light on natural acclimatization, but it appears that the short-term adjustments made by sea-level animals to high altitudes is somewhat different from that observed in natural high-altitude species.

When low-altitude animals (including man) are taken to high altitudes, they respond to oxygen deficiency in several ways. The breathing rate increases to provide more oxygen, the heart beats faster in order to increase the flow of blood to the tissues, the production of red blood cells and hemoglobin is increased to improve the oxygen-carrying capacity of the blood, and there

are changes in the hemoglobin itself to allow more rapid absorption of oxygen by the cells. Other adjustments include opening of muscle capillaries to create a finer matrix for increased blood circulation, and numerous other physicochemical changes that aid in oxygen diffusion and utilization by the tissues (Hock 1970; Frisancho 1975).

These changes are involuntary physiological adjustments to lack of oxygen. The primary features—increased breathing rate, faster heartbeat, and increased production of red blood cells and hemoglobin—may be viewed as emergency measures by the body to maintain its proper functioning under changing conditions, that is, acclimatization. These adjustments do not continue at increased rates indefinitely, however, but gradually decrease and level out. Thus, if residence at high altitudes is prolonged, the breathing rate lowers after about one month, although it is still maintained at a higher rate than at sea level. The heartbeat may actually decrease to below what it was at low altitudes. The production of red blood cells and the quantity of hemoglobin in the blood continue to increase for the first two or three months and then level off (Hurtado 1964; Hock 1970).

The native highlander reacts to oxygen deficiency similarly, although there are key differences. One characteristic of high mountain dwellers is an exceptionally large chest and lung volume, allowing them to take in and retain a greater amount of air with each breath. The larger chest and lungs are apparently developed during the first few years of life. Persons acclimatized to high altitudes as adults do not increase their lung volume markedly (Frisancho et al. 1973). The breathing rate of high-altitude dwellers is about 20 percent faster than that of lowlanders, but native highlanders do not have to hyperventilate, as do newcomers upon going to high altitudes (Hurtado 1964). The blood of native highlanders contains more red cells and hemoglobin and is able to diffuse oxygen into the tissues rapidly. The heart is considerably larger than in low-land natives but the heartbeat is similar or slightly slower. Heart enlargement occurs primarily during the first few years of life, although some heart enlargement is found in adults who have lived at high altitudes for several years (Penaloza et al. 1963). The blood pressure of mountain dwellers is lower than that of sea-level residents, and this partially accounts for the reduced frequency of heart attacks among highland people (Marticorena et al. 1969).

As can be seen, both native highlanders and sea-level dwellers use a combination of coordinated processes to adjust to the lack of oxygen, but the paths they follow are somewhat different. The primary difference is that lowland people rely on rapid breathing to supply adequate oxygen, whereas highland natives do not have to hyperventilate because of their much larger lung capacity and a totally coordinated system of supplying oxygen to the tissues (Fig. 9.24). Consequently, the chemical and physiological characteristics related to energy production and utilization in highlanders are different from those of lowland natives (Frisancho 1975).

The contrast in ability to provide oxygen to the body can best be seen by comparing the relative ability of high and low-altitude natives to carry out physical activities at high elevations. The physiological adjustments made by sea-level man to high altitudes over a few days or weeks may provide him with sufficient oxygen to rest comfortably, but it does not allow the expenditure of much physical energy. At 4,500 m (14,850

Fig. 9.24. Graphic representation of adaptive pathways in high-altitude and low-altitude people. Low-altitude natives depend almost entirely on an increased breathing rate to supply needed oxygen, whereas high-altitude natives are able to depend on the blood carrying more oxygen and the opening of capillaries for better diffusion of oxygen throughout the body. (After Frisancho 1975, p. 317)

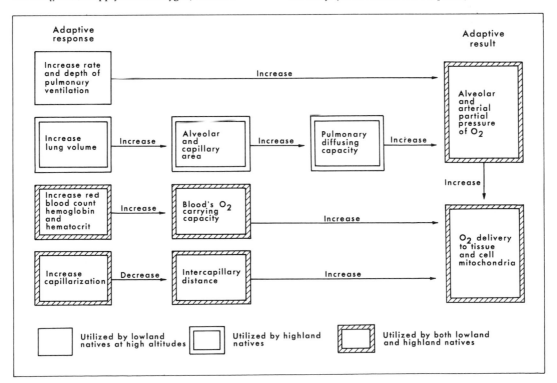

ft.), sea-level man's capacity for performing exercise without creating oxygen deficiency in the body is only 70 percent of that at sea level, and by 5,500 m (18,000 ft.) it is only 50 percent (Mazess 1968; Horvath 1972; Buskirk 1976). Work capacity is measured by the maximum amount of oxygen intake per unit of body weight. This reflects the capacity of the muscles and tissues to assimilate and utilize oxygen. An investigation of sea-level athletes indicates an average decrease in maximum oxygen intake of 3.2 percent per 300 m (1,000 ft.) (Buskirk et al. 1967). By contrast, the ability of highland natives to take in oxygen at high elevations is fully comparable to that of lowland natives at sea level (Grover et al. 1967; Kollias et al. 1968; Grover 1974). It is well-known that native Andeans and Sherpas can do heavy work at high altitudes with little effort (Pugh 1964; Lahiri et al. 1967; Baker 1976), and a favorite sport in the high Andes is the very taxing game of soccer. Similarly, high-altitude animals such as the yak and llama can carry heavy loads for long distances without tiring. Hall (1937) tells of two cars going at 48 km (30 mi.) per hour chasing a herd of vicuna in Bolivia at 4,550 m (15,000 ft.), without gaining on them.

The response of most lowland wild animals to altitude is basically similar to that observed in humans (Chiodi 1964; Timiras 1964; Hock 1964c, 1970). Curiously, however, some of the animals best adapted to high altitudes—e.g., rodents, the Camelidae (llama, alpaca, vicuna, guanaco), and the yak, sheep, and goats—do not display these characteristics. The physiological characteristics of these high-altitude animals are often the opposite of those observed in sea-level animals exposed to high altitudes. The primary contrast is that they do not show an increase in red blood cells or hemoglobin (Hall et al. 1936; Morrison et al. 1963a, b). They tend to have a larger blood-plasma volume, but there is less oxygen in the blood and they are able to function at a very low

partial-pressure of oxygen (Morrison and Elsner 1962; Bullard 1972). They do have larger hearts and lung volumes as well as higher heart and breathing rates, just like animals transported to high altitudes, but the increase in number of red blood cells and quantity of hemoglobin is missing. Since this is one of the most conspicuous responses by lowland species when taken to high elevations, its absence in native highland animals is striking. Although the increase in production of red blood cells and hemoglobin appears to be the simplest means of improving oxygen transport, it must also present some disadvantage—perhaps that of the increased viscosity of cell-rich blood (Morrison 1964, p. 52).

These differences in approach may be accounted for by two distinct processes, *acclimatization* and *adaptation*. Both meet the requirements of high altitudes, but the former is an adjustment or distortion of an existing pattern, whereas the latter is achieved through long-term selection and development. Acclimatization operates at the individual level on a short-term basis, whereas adaptation operates at the species or population level through time. A few wild mountain animals do display an increase in production of red blood cells and hemoglobin (Kalabukov 1937; Hock 1964c), but these occur in mountains where there is direct contact between valleys and peaks, facilitating intermixture. The Andes and trans-Himalayas, however, present broad areas at high altitudes which support a stable population separated from lowland habitats by barriers (Morrison 1964). The animal populations in smaller dissected mountains are apparently displaying acclimatizations to altitude rather than adaptations, while those populations native to the higher and more massive uplands have developed their abilities through isolation and evolution, and their characteristics are viewed as adaptations (Morrison 1964). It has been suggested that even these mammals probably increased production of red cells and hemoglobin upon first inhabiting the mountain area, but through time this response was replaced by increased blood-plasma volume (Bullard 1972, p. 219). It is unfortunate that the native highland animals most thoroughly studied are the rodents and Camelids, since the rodents are essentially pre-adapted to lack of oxygen because of their ability to live underground, and the Camelids possess a number of unusual adaptations as a family even at sea level (Chiodi 1970–71).

The question of acclimatization versus adaptation also arises with respect to native high-altitude peoples. Some investigators have believed that the unique abilities of native highlanders are inherited and reflect continuous residence at high altitudes since prehistoric times (Monge 1948). According to this theory, children born and raised at high altitudes, but not of ancient native stock, would not be as well equipped to live at high altitudes. This view has become increasingly less tenable with findings that the major adjustments to hypoxia take place in the first few years of life (Frisancho et al. 1973; Frisancho 1976). There do seem to be some innate physiological differences between native highlanders and lowlanders, but not enough to separate them genetically; certainly, mountain people intermarry freely with lowlanders. It is likely that highland natives have derived most of their special attributes from acclimatization to environ-

ment rather than through genetic adaptation (Hock 1970).

Based on present knowledge, mammals appear to fall into two categories. One is represented by those species, such as mice, rats, and man, which show an increase in the number of red blood cells and the quantity of hemoglobin at high altitudes. These are primarily low-altitude animals with the ability to acclimatize and live successfully at high altitudes. The other group consists of those species which have been native high-altitude animals through geologic time, e.g., certain rodents, the Camelidae, and other hoofed animals such as the yak, sheep, and goats; these do not display an increase in number of red cells or quantity of hemoglobin in their blood (Bullard 1972). This approach has apparently been favored by long-term selection and is viewed as adaptive. Although both approaches appear to achieve the same end, they are not equally efficient: the former, based on the need for greater oxygen in the system, is metabolically more expensive (Morrison 1964).

Clearly, animals cope with the stressful conditions of high altitudes in a number of ways. Some display elaborate adaptations to reduce the effects of low temperature, brevity of growing season, and lack of food, but most modify and escape these negative factors through behavior. Human populations also extend into the high mountains primarily through modification and amelioration of the environment.

10

Implications for Man

What is the significance of mountains for man? How does the presence of mountains affect the human experience? Some answers come immediately to mind: it is colder at higher altitudes, the air is thinner, slopes are steep, and the soil is generally poor and less productive. Mountains serve as barriers to human activity, and environmental conditions often differ from one side of a range to the other. Some mountain regions remain virtually unpeopled, while others have been settled for millennia. Clearly, mountain landscapes require different approaches for successful occupancy and land use than plains. The foregoing chapters have discussed the basic environmental components of mountain systems and have attempted to define the major processes operative in each. It is within this framework that human activities in mountains take place.

While the physical realities of the environment are paramount for those who live in mountains, it is unsafe to attribute cultural features solely to the environment. Human activities take place within the context of social and historical conditions as well as within the constraints and potentials of the physical landscape. The inscrutability of human nature must also be considered. People frequently do things "simply because they feel like it" rather than in response to a specific stimulus. Therefore, to discuss the consequences of the presence of mountains for man is to walk a very thin line between the interpretation of natural and cultural patterns, on the one hand, and their interrelationships with respect to cause and effect, on the other.

This chapter discusses the importance of mountains in establishing natural environments and the significance these environments have for human populations. Chapter 11 examines the human-cultural landscape and the ways in which it reveals the intricate ties between man and the land. The final chapter discusses the impact of human populations on mountain environments.

WEATHER AND CLIMATE

The overriding significance of mountains is their effect on the control and distribution of natural phenomena on the earth. Mountains join with the other climatic controls to govern the basic patterns of weather and climate, which, in turn, influence landscape processes. This is accomplished primarily through the effects of altitude and climatic barriers that create strikingly different environments within a short distance of one another. Coupled with the climatic effects are the topographic: increased local relief and steep slopes bring gravity into play, with its considerable potential for the transfer of energy through the system. Mountain climate and topography, together with associated biological processes, combine to produce patterns and environments distinct from those in surrounding lowlands. The result is a diversity in space and time that greatly enriches the human experience.

Climatic Divides

The effects of mountains on natural systems may be considered on several different levels. At the highest level, they exert control over planetary circulation patterns, influencing and modifying climatic conditions halfway around the world (Bolin 1950; Kasahara 1967). Although this clearly affects man greatly, our primary interest here is on the more local level—the mountains themselves and the countryside surrounding them.

Perhaps most important is the role that mountains play in serving as climatic divides, especially where they lie athwart the prevailing winds and divide marine from continental conditions. The windward side generally receives greater precipitation and experiences more moderate temperatures than the leeward side. For example, the western side of the Cascades in the western United States receives abundant precipitation and enjoys moderate temperatures; the eastern side receives only one-fourth to one-third as much precipitation and the temperature extremes between winter and summer are considerably greater. The western side supports one of the world's most productive coniferous forests, of Western hemlock and Douglas fir, and the lower slopes and valleys are well settled and intensively used for agriculture. The Ponderosa pine forests on the eastern slopes of the Cascades are considerably less dense and less productive. The adjoining plateau is a sparsely cultivated, semiarid steppe, mainly used for growing dryland wheat or for grazing (except in locally irrigated areas). The basic structure of the Cascades also plays a role: the range is asymmetrical, with a relatively broad and gentle west-facing slope and a narrow and steep eastern slope. This effectively increases the amount of mountain surface exposed to moisture-laden winds on the west and results in much more area there that can produce high-yield timber. That the western side is a far more productive and valuable environment is reflected by population distribution; 80 percent of the people in Oregon and Washington live on the windward side of the Cascades, although two-thirds of the land area is located on the leeward side.

Stream Development

The climatic contrasts between one side of a range and the other give rise to a multiplicity of indirect effects. One is the pattern and development of streams. Those slopes receiving the heaviest precipitation have the greatest potential for runoff and for groundwater recharge. Therefore, depending on the geologic character of rock types and slope surfaces, areas that receive the heaviest precipitation usually display the densest perennial stream patterns. The results for the hinterlands range from the purely ecological (greater fish population, abundant riparian habitats, diversity of species), to the economic (water for recreation, transportation, hydroelectric power, domestic, agricultural, and industrial uses). The beauty of mountain streams also has economic importance: building lots near streams make attractive homesites and raise the value of the land.

The broad western slopes of the Cascades with their abundant precipitation display all of these conditions, since the number of streams and the volume of water carried by the streams there are greatly in excess of the number and volume on the eastern slopes. The Sierra Nevada of California is an even more striking example (Fig. 10.1). This range, consisting of a series of fault blocks tilted toward the west, with steep and abrupt east-facing scarps, is even more strongly asymmetrical than the Cascades; eastern slopes receive less precipitation than do the eastern slopes of the Cascades and extremely arid conditions exist in, for example, parts of Nevada, Owens Valley, and the Mojave Desert. The stream patterns in the

Sierra reflect both topography and climate: they originate in the high mountains along the climatic divide, and most flow westward into the Central Valley; there is very little flow to the east.

The streams flowing from the Sierra Nevada are the very life-blood of California. California is now the most populous state in the United States, but without the Sierra's water it would not have been possible to support a fraction of this population. As it is, many people believe that California is overpopulated, considering its natural ability to support life. In recent years California has begun to look enviously at the water supply of other areas, especially the Pacific Northwest and Canada. These facts considered, the value of mountain streams becomes ever more critical. It is estimated that runoff from the Sierra Nevada into the Central Valley amounts to 48 percent of the total state runoff. If these streams and this water, or even some of it, were altered or eliminated, it would have serious repercussions for the development of the region. Therefore, it is fair to say that much of what California has become, it owes to the presence of the Sierra Nevada and the effect of these mountains in controlling the distribution of climate and the direction of stream flow.

Snowpack

An associated attribute of mountains which also has far-reaching implications is the snowpack. Much of the precipitation above a certain elevation falls as snow. Since precipitation increases with elevation, the zone of maximum precipitation commonly occurs in the snow zone (at least in middle latitudes) (see pp. 102–107). Much of this snow is preserved through the winter, melting during the summer. Consequently, there is not only increased precipitation, but also a time-lag between snowfall and runoff; the snow performs a storage function. Such a system permits the most advantageous use of the water, especially in those middle-lati-

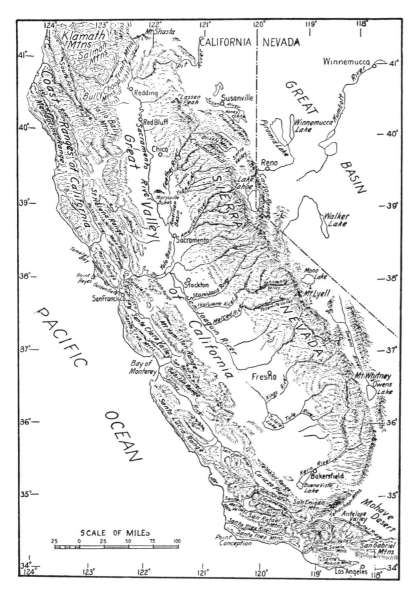

Fig. 10.1. Stream patterns in the Sierra Nevada demonstrate the importance of the mountain range in providing water for runoff as well as in controlling its direction of flow. (Drawn by G. H. Smith, in Fenneman 1931, p. 317)

tude areas where summer precipitation is insufficient for good agricultural production (as in much of the American West). With increasing population in the semiarid regions of the western United States, assessment, management, and improvement of

this resource has become a major enterprise (see p. 128).

The mountain snowpack is of great significance to recreation (Rooney 1969). Mountains have become increasingly important as winter playgrounds because of improved access to remote regions, increased leisure time, the attractiveness of mountain landscapes, and a more or less guaranteed supply of snow, which allows long-range planning of activities and justifies the construction of permanent facilities. The appeal of snow differs for different people: some may simply come to enjoy the winter scenery, the quiet and vast solitude, while others arrive in search of various types of athletic challenge, with skiing as the overwhelming focus of attention. Whatever the attraction, the contrast in environment from that in which most of us live serves as a tonic from the work-a-day world of the city.

The presence of snow and snow-related activities also contributes greatly to local economies. The population of many mountain areas is appreciably higher during winter than in summer. Anyone who has visited one of the more popular ski areas, such as Davos or St. Moritz in the Alps, or Aspen or Sun Valley in the western United States, has a good idea of what this means. Ski resorts take in money from direct spending which increases the economic base of mountain communities, and money is also spent along the way for transportation, lodging, food, and the purchase of ski equipment and clothing (Rooney 1969).

Snow-covered peaks are one of nature's most awesome and beautiful sights. They have been a central theme in art, literature, and music in the Western world principally since the Renaissance, but artistic appreciation of mountain peaks has much more ancient roots in the Orient and Middle East. In addition to serving as a major motif for expressions of creativity, the purity and aloofness of snowcovered peaks have made them natural foci of religious inspiration. Monasteries and temples are common in the Himalayas and the mountains of the Far East. Many areas have been maintained as natural preserves or otherwise protected for religious reasons. Snowcovered moun-

tains do not in themselves have such religious connotations for the Western world, although the Judeo-Christian tradition includes mountains in many of its writings and "the highest mountain" is a popular symbol of aspiration and striving in the West.

Clearly, mountains provide a dimension of shared sensual and intellectual experience. For those people fortunate enough to live within view of high mountains, the towering snowcovered peaks are a constant source of enjoyment. Others must travel greater distances to experience the beauty and grandeur of this landscape. That they do so, and in increasingly large numbers, is evidence of the attraction that mountains hold for all mankind.

In spite of its beauty and many positive attributes, snow has a number of drawbacks. Consider, for example, the problems of travel in the snow zone. Snowcovered mountains were once regarded as impassable barriers and their passage was attempted only when absolutely necessary. With the development of modern transportation and the construction of highways and railroads across mountains wherever access is reasonable, many of these routes are now traveled almost as heavily in winter as in summer. However, this means that road maintenance must be vastly increased. The task of keeping mountain passes open in winter is truly monumental. Huge mechanized snow augers and blowers make the job easier, but it is nonetheless expensive. The cost of snow removal in the Cascades alone amounts to over a million dollars a year. Some of the most difficult roads to keep open are those leading to ski areas, because of the heavy snowfall there. The non-skiing sector has complained that this expense should be borne by the people who ski rather than by the general public. Accordingly, in 1977 the state of Oregon began placing much of the financial burden for access-road and parking-lot clearance directly on the skiers, by implementing a $1.00 per day snow-parking fee. This is still not totally equitable, however, because the economic advantages of such recreational activities reach far beyond the immediate community.

Heavy snowpack poses problems for man-made structures. Steep slopes, high winds, and heavy snow put considerable stress on power and communication lines, which thus become more expensive to build and maintain (Grauer 1962). The steep-roofed architecture of mountain chateaus is apparently an attempt to escape the effects of heavy snow. Interestingly, however, this type of architecture is not typical of traditional mountain villages (except for churches). In fact, the tendency is just the reverse. Many of the dwellings in the Alps and Himalayas have low-angled roofs that allow the snow to accumulate and provide insulation against the winter cold. Such

roofs are sturdily constructed to support the weight of the snow and the heavy roofing material—often local slate or schist (Fig. 10.2) (Peattie 1936; Karan 1960a, 1967).

Heavy snow on slopes has a tendency to undergo downslope deformation (snow creep) and to apply pressure against structures, particularly those presenting a broad upslope surface to the snow. If not properly constructed, such buildings may be dislodged from their foundations and eventually destroyed. The most destructive situation is total failure of the snow, with avalanching (Fig. 5.22). Although avalanche zones have usually been avoided, increasing development and population pressures in mountain areas have resulted in construction of new buildings in potentially dangerous sites (Fig. 8.25). Stringent land-use planning and zoning are essential in popu-

Fig. 10.2. A small village in the Alps displaying both traditional slate roofs and modern composition roofs. The gentle pitch of these roofs is typical throughout the Alps. (Author)

lated mountain areas (Man and Biosphere 1973a, 1974a, 1975; Ives et al. 1976; Ives and Bovis 1978).

Besides problems of road maintenance and stress on engineering structures, snow poses other difficulties for those who live in mountains. The presence of deep snow means that a greater effort is necessary to accomplish normal activities such as clearing access to living quarters, feeding livestock, and transporting children to school. Before the development of modern transportation, small mountain communities were frequently cut off from the outside world during the winter and suffered from lack of fresh produce, mail delivery, fire protection, and adequate medical care. Consider the dilemma of a winter death in an isolated village; in the Alps, in times past it was common simply to freeze the body and wait until spring for burial (Peattie 1936, p. 50).

Although snow is an obstacle to highway or rail transportation, it may facilitate local travel by skis or sled. Streams become covered by thick snowbridges and rocky terrain is smoothed. In the Alps, the hay from high isolated meadows is traditionally stored near the fields in small sheds and transported to the village during the winter by sled. The major problem with this method is not in transporting the hay, but in holding the sled speed down! Alternatively, stall-barns to store hay are built near the high meadows where cattle are kept. The hay can be fed directly to the cattle and the manure collected on the site (Friedl 1973). Still, someone has to feed and care for the livestock; this requires daily travel under difficult and dangerous conditions (or long periods alone with the cattle). When the hay is depleted, the cattle have to be brought down to a lower barn. Cattle cannot walk in deep snow, so a path must be cleared for them, which entails long and arduous work and is usually a communal project.

Although outside chores become more difficult in the deep snows of winter, there is generally much less to do, especially for the men. Before the introduction of electricity, mountain dwellings were poorly lighted and ventilated; this, coupled with lack of fresh food and exercise, often led to unhealthy conditions. In fact, the combination of isolation and poor health has been cited as one of the reasons for the relatively large number of insane and mentally retarded people in some of the more remote villages of the Alps (Peattie 1936, p. 51). Another unfortunate aspect, from some points of view, of village life during winter was the large amount of time spent in the local tavern.

The long snowy winter has been cited as an important factor in the development of cottage industries, e.g., carving toys, constructing clocks, and assembling optical and scientific instruments. Switzerland, the Jura, and the Black Forest are most famous for such products, but mountain people all over the world are known for their weaving and handicrafts. These are usually made from local raw materials, e.g., wood, metal, stone, or wool, and are commonly articles of small bulk, making their transport easy. Mountain dwellers of the Middle East are famous for their woven articles. In the Andes, natives have traditionally woven the fleece of alpacas and guanaco. Manufacture of gold and silver jewelry, woodcarving, weaving, and embroidery have all been practiced for centuries in Tibet and the Himalayas (Karan and Mather 1976). Needlepoint, embroidery, and lace were produced in the Swiss, Austrian, and Italian Alps. Some of the finest violin strings in the world, made of goat gut, were manufactured in the central Apennines (Semple 1911, p. 578).

Modern technology has brought an end to much of the winter isolation of mountain dwellers. Even the most remote villages of the Alps now have electricity, telephones, and snowmobiles. Switzerland has become one of the most modern and sophisticated countries of Europe; to think of it as a land of wood-carving and cuckoo clocks is anachronistic (most of these are now imported to supply tourist demands). Nevertheless, cottage industries remain an important source of income in many mountain societies, supplementing a limited economic base.

Reduced Atmospheric Pressure and Lack of Oxygen

The lower atmospheric pressure and reduced oxygen availability of high altitudes create a more stressful environment for humans. People newly arrived in the mountains may suffer from dizziness, headache, nausea, nose-bleeds, and a general feeling of malaise, and those long resident at high altitudes are subject to such long-term effects as reduced fertility and growth/maturation rates. Activities such as the preparation of food and the operation of machinery and equipment take more effort and require special precautions. Unlike most other environmental stresses, it is impossible, or at least impractical, to escape the effects of low oxygen through cultural modification; with respect to lack of oxygen, technologically advanced societies experience the same conditions as primitive societies.

Physiology

The short-term physiological effects of reduced oxygen are experienced by those who reside at low elevations but occasionally go to high altitudes, e.g., mountain climbers, and tourists. Some individuals may begin to feel the effects of altitude at elevations as low as 2,000 m (6,600 ft.); by 4,000 m (13,200 ft.) almost all sea-level dwellers will experience some altitudinal effects even though they may not actually become ill. The best defense is to make the ascent slowly, to be in good physical condition, and not to smoke, drink, or take drugs. Climbers attempting high peaks in the Himalayas characteristically spend several weeks trekking into the mountains. Through this process of slow acclimatization and physical conditioning they can reach heights

of over 8,000 m (26,400 ft.) without supplementary oxygen and usually without severe repercussions other than headache, loss of appetite, and diminution of mental and physical ability. By contrast, a person going immediately from sea level to 8,000 m (26,400 ft.) would probably lose consciousness within five minutes, and death would occur within 20 to 30 minutes (Houston 1972, p. 85).

Modern transportation makes it possible to go to high elevations quickly. Yearly, thousands go from sea level to high altitudes to ski or climb. In Nepal, which has become a major attraction in recent years, tourists are flown in from sea-level cities of India to Kathmandu, where they take jeeps to higher villages. Invariably, some are afflicted with altitude sickness. Similar reactions may be experienced in Peru by those taking the train from Lima to Huancayo. This is the highest passenger railway in the world, going from sea level to an elevation of 4,754 m (15,688 ft.) in less than a day. One of the special duties of the conductor is to administer oxygen to those who need it. Most people experience only mild discomfort, but occasionally severe symptoms develop which can be fatal if not treated properly.

The effects of rapid movement to high altitudes are well demonstrated by modern military operations. A group of 120 soldiers was recently transported from sea level to 4,000 m (13,200 ft.) for maneuvers in the Colorado Rockies. Within twenty-four hours more than half of the men experienced shortness of breath, nausea, and headaches, and a third of these became so ill that they had to be returned to a lower elevation. During the first three days the stamina and performance of the entire group were poor and they were generally ineffective in carrying out their duties (Moyer 1976, p. 20). Perhaps the most spectacular effects of high altitude on military operations in this century were displayed during the 1962 border conflict between India and China in the Himalayas. Indian soldiers were airlifted from sea level to elevations of 3,300–5,500 m (11,000–18,000 ft.) and were immediately deployed. As might be expected, there was widespread sickness and the Indian troops suffered disastrous losses compared to the better-acclimatized Chinese soldiers, who had been stationed in Tibet and were accustomed to high-altitude conditions (U.S. Dept. Army 1972).

Unfortunately, it is impossible to prepare troops physiologically for hypoxia. Even if they spend time at high altitudes, they quickly lose acclimatization when they return to sea level. Therefore, efforts in mountain warfare are best aimed at providing troops with an understanding of the problems involved in dealing with the terrain and other peculiarities of the mountain environment (Thompson 1967). Parenthetically, it is interesting to observe that the Inca overcame the problem of high altitudes by having two armies—one for fighting in the lowlands and one for fighting in the highlands (Monge 1948).

There are two forms of severe high-altitude sickness, acute and chronic. *Acute mountain sickness* is a sudden and violent reaction of the body against lack of oxygen, whereas chronic mountain sickness (see p. 359) generally develops over a period of months or years. The most common form of acute mountain sickness is *pulmonary edema*, an affliction resulting from the accumulation of fluid in the lungs. It usually takes two or three days to strike and is most common among those who have gone rapidly to 3,000 m (10,000 ft.) or higher and have then engaged in strenuous activity without pausing for acclimatization. Symptoms include "increasing weakness, shortness of breath greater than expected, irritative cough frequently with bloody sputum, and bubbling noises in the chest often audible to the victim and his companions. Breathing becomes more labored, the frothy sputum increases, pulse rate and temperature usually rise, the victim becomes unconscious, and may die within hours unless vigorously treated"

(Houston 1972, p. 87). The best treatment is to remove the person to a lower elevation as quickly as possible. Early climbers and explorers were doubtless afflicted with pulmonary edema, but it was not specifically identified as a major risk until the mid-1950s. Much of what we know about it was learned from the 1962 Chinese-Indian dispute. During this conflict, over 2,000 Indian soldiers suffered from acute mountain sickness. The incidence of occurrence ranged from 1 up to 83 cases per 1,000 troops (Roy and Singh 1969; Singh et al. 1969).

Although individuals may suffer a variety of symptoms when first going to high altitudes, if they ascend slowly and remain at high altitudes for a prolonged period most symptoms will pass as the body becomes acclimatized. There are lingering effects, however, that have important implications to the population in general. These include reduced fertility levels, reduced growth and maturation rates, and increased morbidity (sickness) and mortality (death) rates. Although genetic background, diet, and various social-cultural factors are obviously involved, there seems to be strong evidence that increasing elevation imposes a special and pervasive stress on human populations (Monge 1948; Monge and Monge 1966; Baker and Little 1976; Baker 1978).

Fertility. When the Spanish conquistadors conquered the South American highlands, it was a bitter disappointment to them that they could not sire children. During the seventeenth century over 20,000 Spaniards were reported to be living in Potosi, Peru, at an elevation of 4,000 m (13,200 ft.), but it was 53 years before a Spanish child was conceived, born, and raised in this city (Calancha 1639, in Monge 1948, p. 36). During the same period the natives gave birth at a normal rate. It was only after several generations of living at high altitudes and gradual interbreeding with highland natives that the Spanish birthrate began to approach that of the Andeans. The Spanish also discovered that lowland animals (horses, chickens, and pigs) were unable to reproduce when taken to high altitudes. These were among the reasons that in 1639 the Spanish moved their capital from Jauja, at 3,300 (11,000 ft.), to Lima, which is on the coast (Monge 1948, p. 34).

The effects of high altitude on the Spanish were apparently much more drastic than anything reported subsequently; information from other regions suggests a moderate birthrate among low-altitude women living at high altitudes (Harrison et al. 1969). The reduced partial pressure of oxygen may affect all stages of the reproductive process, from conception to delivery. Observations of men taken from sea level to high altitude show temporary reductions in sperm counts and increased production of abnormal sperm. Women often display disturbance in menstrual cycle and ovulation (Clegg 1978). These are usually short-term impairments,

however; the functions return to normal in a few days or weeks (Donayre et al. 1968; Hoff and Abelson 1976, p. 130).

The major problem after conception is in supplying sufficient oxygen and nutrients to the foetus. Pregnancy increases the energy requirements of the mother, and these requirements are magnified at high altitudes. The breathing rate changes and hyperventilation is necessary, especially during the final three months, when the position of the foetus restricts expansion of the diaphragm. Consequently, the risk of miscarriage is much greater at high altitudes. Among native highlanders there is a tendency toward a larger placental size. This is viewed as adaptive, since it increases the capacity to deliver oxygen and nutrients to the foetus (Hoff and Abelson 1976, p. 131). Babies born at high altitudes—whether of native or non-native mothers—weigh less, on the average, than babies born at low altitudes (McClung 1969; Krüger and Arias-

Table 10.1. *Percentage of live but immature births (weighing 2,500 grams or less) at various altitudes in the United States: 1952–1957, white population only (Utah not included) (Grahn and Kratchman 1963, p. 341).*

Mean Altitude (m)	Atmospheric Pressure (mm Hg)	Number of Live Births	Percentage of Births Weighing 2,500 Grams or Less
79	753	35,166	6.57
192	743	7,147	6.66
339	729	73,318	6.17
541	713	13,809	7.97
693	699	56,570	7.78
868	684	12,207	7.14
986	674	50,933	8.24
1,138	662	60,226	8.46
1,299	649	63,160	8.67
1,462	636	100,420	9.47
1,586	627	133,617	10.37
1,715	217	28,011	9.80
1,863	205	53,899	10.74
2,051	591	26,619	11.54
2,186	582	10,712	11.17
2,340	570	9,427	13.04
2,582	553	2,474	12.93
2,899	532	887	16.57
3,155	513	1,697	23.70

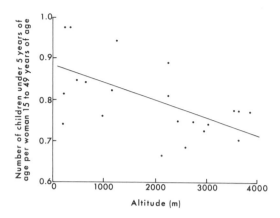

Fig. 10.3. The relationship between altitude and number of children under 5 years of age per woman of reproductive age in 21 provinces of Peru. (After Hoff and Abelson 1976, p. 134)

Stella 1970; Hoff and Abelson 1976). This has been documented for several mountainous regions, including the western United States (Table 10.1). In Lake County, Colorado, at 3,000 m (10,000 ft.) the highest county in the continental United States, infant weight averages 380 grams less at birth than in Denver, at 1,500 m (5,000 ft.), and birth weight in Denver is still lower than in sea-level cities (Lichty et al. 1957). The exact reasons for the lighter weight at birth at higher elevations are unknown, but probably include a shortened gestation period, fetal malnutrition, and/or a decrease in fetal growth rate (McClung 1969, p. 76). Among high-altitude Indians in Peru, the birth weight is more nearly that of sea level regions than that of other high-altitude regions. This may be due to racial differences or it may reflect the Peruvians' adaptation to the high-altitude environment over millennia of occupancy (McClung 1969, p. 60).

When viewed on a broader basis, i.e., between populations living in elevated and sea-level regions, the general relationship between reduced fertility and altitude may still be seen (James 1966; Heer 1967) (Fig. 10.3). Factors other than lack of oxygen—

e.g., cultural, social, economic, and behavioral considerations—could account for the reduced number of children per mother (Whitehead 1968; DeJong 1970), but hypoxia seems to be the most significant factor. For example, a study in Peru compared the reproductive performances of sea-level and high-altitude natives before and after migration to high and low elevations. The results indicate that women born in lowland regions become less fertile upon going to high altitudes and that native-born high-altitude women become more fertile upon going to low altitudes (Abelson et al. 1974; Hoff and Abelson 1976).

Growth and Maturation. Growth and maturation rates tend to be reduced at high altitudes. Exceptions occur in the humid tropics, where the extremely high rate of infectious diseases in the lowlands makes the high and intermediate altitudes more healthful than the hot, humid lowlands (Harrison et al. 1969; Clegg et al. 1970; Clegg et al. 1972). But in most other regions, e.g., the Andes and Himalayas, high-altitude dwellers are smaller in stature than equivalent populations living in the surrounding lowlands (Frisancho and Baker 1970; Pawson 1972; Frisancho 1978). This has generally been attributed to the effects of oxygen deficiency at high altitudes, although nutrition and genetic factors are doubtless also important. The lower weight at birth for infants born at high altitudes has just been mentioned. Thus, the child typically begins life at a disadvantage; it is thrust from a warm and secure intrauterine environment into a cold and hypoxic environment with which it is not yet physiologically equipped to cope. Infant growth at high altitudes is characterized by smaller body size, lower weight, less fat, and slower skeletal development than lowland infants.

Studies from Peru show that the physical growth of high-altitude natives is slow in general. This can be seen by comparing growth-rate figures from high, intermediate,

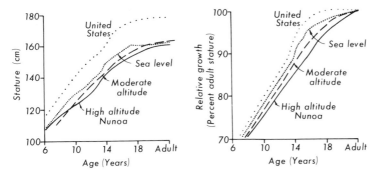

Fig. 10.4 Growth rates for boys living at various altitudes in Peru compared with the rates at sea level in the United States. Graph on left shows absolute growth rates; graph on right shows percentage of full adult stature reached at different ages. In every case, the higher-altitude boys are smaller and exhibit slower growth. (After Frisancho and Baker 1970, p. 290)

and sea-level elevations in Peru as well as those from the United States (Fig. 10.4a). High-altitude boys are both absolutely and relatively smaller than sea-level boys from the United States and Peru, and their rate of development is slower (Fig. 10.4b). Skeletal maturation is delayed and sexual differences in stature between boys and girls—e.g.,

body size, disposition of fat, and muscle size—does not occur until after 16 years of age. The adolescent growth spurt is less pronounced in high-altitude people and growth is prolonged past the age of 20 (Frisancho 1976, p. 195). Puberty is reached at a later age. High-altitude girls reach menarche (begin to menstruate) about one and one-half years later than sea-level girls, and many do not reach menarche until the ages of 16 to 18 (Fig. 10.5). Similar findings have been reported for the Himalayas (Clegg et al. 1970, p. 502; Frisancho 1978).

Fig. 10.5. Percentage of girls in various age groups who have begun to menstruate in high-altitude and low-altitude Indian populations in Chile. High-altitude girls reach menarche about one-and-one-half years later than lowland girls. (After Cruz-Coke 1968, in Clegg et al. 1970, p. 502)

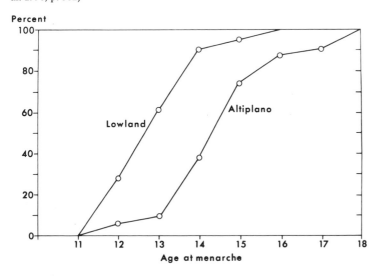

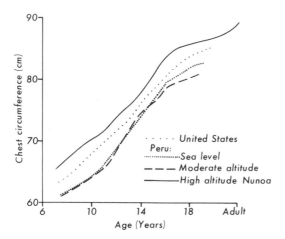

Fig. 10.6. Comparison of chest size of boys living at various altitudes in Peru and at sea level in the United States. Moderate altitude is 2,300 m (7,600 ft.); Nunoa is situated at 4,000 m (13,100 ft.). High-altitude Peruvian boys have larger chests than boys from the United States. (After Frisancho and Baker 1970, p. 290)

Although the preponderance of evidence points to reduced growth among high-altitude natives, in two ways their growth exceeds that of sea-level natives: chest size, and production of bone marrow. Natives of the high Andes and the Himalayas are renowned for their "barrel chests"; chest circumferences average 8 to 10 percent larger than those of Americans or of natives in the surrounding lowlands (Fig. 10.6). The larger chest size is interpreted as a corollary of accelerated and expanded development of the heart and lungs. Consequently, chest size is not adaptive in itself but is a by-product of the increased development of heart and lungs. Bone marrow produces red blood cells, which carry oxygen to all parts of the body (see p. 342). The increased production of bone marrow and marrow space is believed to be a response to the need for more red blood cells under the hypoxic conditions of high altitude (Frisancho 1976, p. 198).

Morbidity and Mortality. The number of infant deaths increases markedly with increasing elevation. This is shown for the United States by Figure 10.7. The rate is

even higher in areas such as the Andes or Himalayas, with higher altitudes and poorer health-care. In Peru, prenatal and infant death rates in the highlands are 40–45 percent greater than in the lowlands (Mazess 1965, p. 211). Total loss of life occurring below the age of five years is about 30 percent, compared to a world average of 13 percent (Way 1976, p. 153). Lack of oxygen and its effect on initial growth and development are apparently primary factors responsible for this increased infant death-rate.

The mortality rate decreases after five years of age and is not markedly different from the lowlands from then on, in spite of poorer health-care facilities. There are only half as many hospital beds and one-fourth as many physicians per person in the Andes as on the coast in Peru (Little and Baker 1976, p. 410), but high-altitude populations

Fig. 10.7. Relationship between altitude and infant death-rate in the United States. Open circles represent statistics from Utah, where data do not follow the norm. Atmospheric pressure of 620 mm of Hg is that of an altitude of 1,700 m (5,600 ft.). (After Grahn and Kratchman 1963, p. 338)

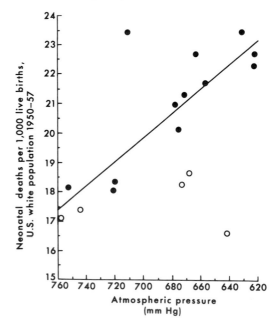

seem to be able to maintain themselves under these conditions. They offset the greater infant mortality rate simply by having more children. The average number of births per woman in the Nunoa district of Peru at elevations above 4,000 m (13,200 ft.) is 6.7 (Hoff and Abelson 1976, p. 38). Large families are desired and achieved, in spite of the stress of hypoxia, by maximizing the reproductive capacity of women. Almost all women have babies, and most continue to do so throughout their reproductive lives.

There is evidence for a difference in patterns of disease and sickness at high altitudes. Some afflictions, of course, are unique to high altitudes, e.g., acute and chronic mountain sickness. As we have seen, acute mountain sickness is caused by rapid ascent without proper acclimatization; *chronic mountain sickness*, however, is loss of acclimatization by those accustomed to living at high altitudes. Chronic mountain sickness seems to be a true disease; it results in gradual physical and mental deterioration. The disease may occur at any age but is most common in young adults. It may strike persons who have lived at high altitudes for only a few months or it may affect natives born and raised at high altitudes. Symptoms include increased hyperventilation and a breakdown in the efficiency of oxygen diffusion through the system. The bone marrow becomes hyperactive, the number of red blood cells and blood volume increase, and the right ventricle of the heart enlarges abnormally. The only cure for it is for the victim to go to a lower elevation; to stay at the high altitude means certain death. Upon reaching sea level all functions soon return to normal, although it is rare that such a person will ever be able to live at high altitudes again (Monge and Monge 1966).

A number of diseases are relatively more prevalent at high altitudes than at sea level. These include tuberculosis, bronchitis, pneumonia and other respiratory problems, gastric ulcers, tumor formation, a bleeding tendency, inflammation of the kidneys, and

gall-bladder disease (Hurtado 1955, 1960; Monge and Monge 1966; Hellriegel 1967; Way 1976). Respiratory diseases are the major cause of death at high altitudes. This is apparently connected with the cold and lack of oxygen, although the exact relationship is unknown. On the other hand, infectious diseases and parasitic infections such as measles, chicken pox, various "fevers," malaria, hookworm, and schistosomiasis afflict highlanders less than lowlanders (Buck et al. 1968; Roundy 1976). This is apparently because the high-altitude environment is less favorable to bacteria and to certain vectors, e.g., the mosquito (Highman and Altland 1964; Clegg et al. 1970, p. 510). However, with the lower incidence of infectious diseases goes a lower natural immunity, so highlanders are often unwilling to go to the lowlands during the wet season, when they will be exposed to malaria and other diseases. This has important implications for the human ecology and economics of certain mountain regions; in the Himalayas and Andes, travel to the lowlands is usually timed to concide with the dry season (travel is also easiest at this time, since snow and stream flooding present less of a problem) (Roundy 1976).

One major difference in disease-related phenomena between high and low-altitude populations is the decrease in heart problems at high elevations. Chronic symptoms such as leukemia, hypertension, arteriosclerosis, and heart attacks are greatly reduced among highlanders. There is also a tendency toward a lower blood-sugar count, lower blood-pressure, and lower cholesterol level (Buck et al. 1968; Marticorena et al. 1969; Way 1976, p. 148). To what extent these characteristics are the effect of diet and life style rather than of altitude is unknown.

This brings up the very interesting topic of the great longevity of certain mountain peoples. There are three regions of the world in which individuals are reported to live to ages of 120 to 160 years, all located in mountains—the village of Vilcabamba in the Ecuadorian Andes; Hunza, Kashmir, a small protectorate of Pakistan in the western Himalayas; and the Caucasus Mountains of southern Russia (Leaf 1973; Benet 1974, 1976; Davies 1975). What is it about the mountain environment in these areas or about these particular groups of people that results in such extreme longevity? Unfortunately, the secret has not been discovered. In fact, some scientists doubt that these people actually live that long (Clark 1963; McKain 1967; Medvedev 1974). The problem is that the village of Vilcabamba in the Andes (which, because it is Catholic, has church records of births and baptisms) is the only one of these regions which can produce records to substantiate their claims of great age. The oldsters simply say they are a certain age; they support their claims only by the number of generations in their offspring and by their recollections of historical events that took place within their lifetimes. Although the debate will doubtless continue, some of the oldest people on earth do seem to live in these areas. Vilcabamba in the Andes has a population of 819, and the 1971 census found that nine of these were above the age of 100. By comparison, in the United States the figure is about three centenarians per 100,000 population (Leaf 1973, p. 96).

A number of reasons have been suggested for the great ages reached in these areas but none is applicable to all three and to no other region. Diet is characterized by low caloric intake in all these areas (less than 2,000 calories per day, compared to over 3,000 for the U.S.) and includes very little sugar, fats, or artificially prepared foods. The people are physically active, engaging in manual labor throughout their lives; there are no provisions for retirement. They are not faced with the pressures of the competitive job market and their lives are slower-paced, so they do not experience the anxieties of the city dweller. These statements, however, are equally applicable to much of the developing world, which does not share the rewards of exceptionally long life.

What, then, is the special contribution of the mountain environment to longevity? One conjecture is that there are trace elements in the water, soil, and food which may be beneficial in some way (Davies 1975). A related factor is the relative absence of industrial contaminants and pollution in most mountain environments. Another possible explanation is that in these areas, where the gene pool has been isolated, selection has favored great longevity. This may be true in some areas but it certainly does not apply to the Caucasus, which is renowned for a diverse mixture of peoples. Finally, the adaptations for providing more oxygen to the system (large heart and lungs and increased red blood cell production) may counteract the aging process. The provision of oxygen in an integrated way is thought to prevent the cell and tissue deterioration that typically occurs with senescence (McFarland 1972). Of course, the related characteristics of low blood-pressure, low cholesterol levels, and the relative absence of chronic diseases like cancer and heart attacks are also a major boon. None of these explanations, however, applies only to the three areas mentioned. The contribution of the mountain environment per se to great longevity must therefore be viewed as questionable but, on the other hand, so are all of the other factors mentioned.

Food Preparation

An entirely different topic, but one still intimately associated with atmospheric pressure, is that of the problems associated with food preparation in mountains. Food generally takes longer to cook with increasing altitude. If a cake is baked using a standard sea-level recipe the batter generally rises too high and overflows the pan, but when it is taken out of the oven the cake may collapse to half its original size (Fig. 10.8). Even microwave ovens operate less efficiently at high altitudes (Bowman et al. 1971; Lorenz 1975a, p. 437). The effects of

Fig. 10.8. Angel-food cakes baked at 1,500 m (5,000 ft.). The cake on the left was baked using a recipe adjusted for altitude, while the one on right was baked using a standard sea-level recipe. (Klaus Lorenz, Colorado State University)

altitude on food preparation begin to be seen at elevations above 900 m (3,000 ft.).

Three major types of problems are involved in cooking at high altitudes: the greater expansion of leavening gases, the lower boiling temperature of water, and the increased evaporation of moisture from foods (Kulas 1950; Lorenz 1975a, b). The main gases involved in cooking are air, steam, and carbon dioxide. Air is incorporated when the raw ingredients are mixed together, steam is a product of vaporization while cooking, and carbon dioxide results from the chemical reaction of baking soda or baking powder. The volume of these gases depends upon the temperature and pressure, i.e., it is directly proportional to temperature and inversely proportional to pressure. Since air pressure is lower at high altitudes, it follows that less leavening gas is required to perform the same task. This applies to all baked products, whether, like cakes and bread, they are leavened with carbon dioxide, or, like angel-food and

sponge cakes, with air, or, like popovers and cream puffs, with steam (Kulas 1950; Lorenz 1975b, p. 282).

A liquid is said to boil when vapor bubbles form within it, rise to the surface, and burst. This occurs when the saturated vapor pressure of the liquid is equal to the atmospheric pressure. Since the atmospheric pressure is less at higher altitudes, the pressure of the vapor necessary for the liquid to boil is less and will be reached at a lower temperature. The average decrease in boiling temperature is about 1° C. (1.8° F.) per 300 m (1,000 ft.) (Table 10.2). Tests have shown that it takes between 4 and 11 percent longer to cook food with each 300 m (1,000 ft.) of elevation. Much depends upon the cooking conditions, however; food cooks much more quickly and efficiently at high temperatures. Cooking times increase at an increasing rate with lower temperatures. Even at sea level, hard-boiling an egg at 91° C. (196° F.) requires 12 hours, while at 100° C. (212° F.) it takes less than 10 min-

Table 10.2. *The boiling temperature of water at various altitudes (Lorenz 1975a, p. 406).*

Altitude (m)	Atmospheric Pressure (mm Hg)	Boiling Point of Water (° C.)
0	760.0	100.0
300	734.0	99.0
600	700.6	98.1
900	683.2	97.0
1,200	657.8	96.0
1,500	632.4	95.0
1,800	607.0	93.9
2,100	511.6	92.7
2,500	556.2	91.5
2,900	530.5	90.3
3,300	505.4	89.0
3,600	480.0	87.8
4,200	454.0	86.3
4,600	429.2	84.0

utes. These differences are further accentuated at higher altitudes (Lorenz 1975a, p. 407). At high altitudes it is best to cook at as high a temperature as possible, and to remember to cook for a longer time than would be necessary at sea level. This is particularly true in canning, where undercooking may result in incomplete denaturization of bacteria and possible food poisoning.

Evaporation takes place more rapidly in cooking at higher altitudes, because the air molecules under lower atmospheric pressure offer less resistance to the transfer of water from the liquid to the gaseous state. If the temperature remains constant, evaporation will increase as atmospheric pressure decreases. The faster rate of evaporation tends to dry out food and to lower the cooking temperature (since relatively more heat is used in the evaporation process). Therefore, the cook needs to use more heat than at sea level to achieve the desired results. Cakes baked at 3,000 m (10,000 ft.) do not brown as much or as quickly at the same temperature as at sea level because the sugar in the cake fails to caramelize completely.

Caramelization (changing of sugar to caramel) is temperature-dependent, and the heat used by evaporation prevents the crust from reaching the temperature of the oven (Lorenz et al. 1971; Lorenz 1975a, b).

There is evidence that high elevations may affect the flavor of foods, as well as the taste threshold of those eating it. Flavor is closely associated with odor and the volatility of the gases emitted by the food. Volatility is increased at lower atmospheric pressure, so there is a loss of flavor with increasing altitude. Some loss of flavor probably takes place in foods eaten raw, but the major loss occurs in foods that require cooking or baking (Lorenz 1975a, p. 409). Taste is a function of solubility rather than volatility. Therefore, a lessening of taste sensitivity would not be expected with changes in altitude. However, a test for salty, sour, bitter, and sweet tastes showed that people were less and less able to perceive these tastes (bitter tastes in particular) as altitude increased (Maga and Lorenz 1972). Apparently, taste depends not only on solubility but also on some unexplained physiological response that varies with altitude (Maga and Lorenz 1972, p. 670).

Most problems associated with food preparation at high altitudes can be surmounted by minor adjustments in the ingredients or the preparation. A number of U.S. food companies prepare special baking mixes for high-altitude cooking, or give high-altitude-cooking instructions on the package. Agricultural experiment stations in mountain states (especially in Colorado) have published much information on high-altitude cooking, ranging from methods of canning to candy-making.

Operation of Motorized Equipment

Not only is man less efficient at high altitudes, but so are most of his machines. The internal-combustion engine is a case in point. Because of lower atmospheric pressure and lack of oxygen, the combustion process becomes less complete with altitude and results in the production of less heat and more carbon monoxide (thus increasing the amount of air pollution for a given period of motor operation). Internal-combustion engines lose power at an average rate of about 3 percent per 300 m (1,000 ft.). If you have ever driven a car or operated machinery at a high altitude, you have experienced this reduction in engine performance. The fuel-to-air mixture in the carburetor becomes increasingly rich with elevation, until the engine begins to cough and sputter or cuts out altogether. This can usually be corrected by adjusting the carburetor to increase the flow of air. It is essential to make this adjustment if the vehicle is to be operated for any length of time at a high altitude; otherwise, there is danger of internal damage, e.g., burning of valves.

Beginning in 1977, all U.S. automobile manufacturers were required by law to provide a specially designed carburetor on any car or truck sold in regions having elevations of over 1,200 m (4,000 ft.). There are various designs: the basic idea is to allow more air into the carburetor once a certain atmospheric pressure is reached. The modification, necessary in order to meet new air-pollution standards set by the Environmental Protection Agency, will also result in increased engine efficiency.

The problem of operating motorized equipment at high altitudes is perhaps best demonstrated by aircraft. Not only is engine power lost at increasing elevations, but flight control and efficiency also decrease. The higher an aircraft flies, the faster it must travel in order to have good maneuverability and control in the thin air. The rate of loss of power with altitude is given in Figure 10.9. For practical purposes, most small single-engine airplanes have an altitudinal ceiling of about 3,600 m (12,000 ft.). The larger and more powerful the engine, of course, the higher the aircraft can go. Rockets and turbojets are not limited by these constraints, since they operate at such high speeds that the decreased density of the air works to

Fig. 10.9. Generalized illustration showing loss of power with altitude in conventional aircraft engines. (Adapted from several sources)

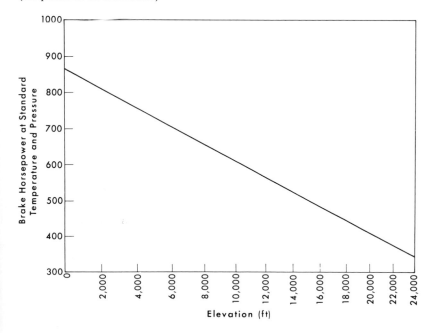

their advantage. Turbojet engines do lose power with altitude, but the drag of the aircraft decreases at an even greater rate, so that higher speed and better economy are achieved by flying at high altitudes (Gill et al. 1954, pp. 17–29). It should also be mentioned that flying above an elevation of 9,000 m (30,000 ft.) is relatively smooth, with little weather disturbance.

The supercharger is a successful answer to the problem of reduced atmospheric pressure on conventional engines. This device is essentially a blower or compressor which helps to maintain pressure within the intake manifold, forcing enough air into the cylinders for complete combustion. Superchargers are used on many kinds of engines operated at high altitudes, e.g., generators and heavy equipment, and are best known for their use in aircraft. The Icefield Ranges Research Project (with which I was associated in Yukon Territory) had such an airplane (a Heliocourier). This single-engine aircraft was equipped with ski landing-gear and regularly made takeoffs and landings with cargo at an elevation of 5,300 m (17,500 ft.) on Mount Logan (see Fig. 5.5). Helicopters equipped with superchargers have landed at altitudes exceeding 5,450 m (18,000 ft.) on both Mount Logan and Mount McKinley in search-and-rescue missions. Although the ceiling for helicopter flight is much lower than that for fixed-wing aircraft, recent developments have greatly increased their payload and efficiency at high altitudes. Consequently, helicopters are being used more and more in mountain operations, e.g., the installation of power-lines and ski-lift towers. Helicopters are also being used increasingly in forestry operations; this eliminates the necessity for building roads and reduces environmental damage.

A major application of the newly developed ability of helicopters is in mountain warfare. While small, scattered, highly mobile groups of local troops in mountains have traditionally been effective against much larger, better-equipped, but therefore less mobile armies, the helicopter has swung the balance of power to the side with the better technology. Troops and fire-power can be transported rapidly by helicopter to even the most nearly inaccessible spot. The military significance of this has not yet been fully demonstrated: helicopters were not used in the 1962 skirmish between India and China in the Himalayas, for example, but they will almost certainly be used in any future military operations in high mountains. Their effectiveness in this respect has been amply demonstrated in the low but rugged mountains of Viet Nam, where the relatively low altitudes did not limit the usefulness of the helicopters then available (Thompson 1970).

LANDFORMS AND GEOLOGY
Topography

Dominant characteristics of mountain topography include steep slopes, high relief, and lack of level land. Such landscapes have long challenged man's imagination and ingenuity, serving both as refuges and obstacles. The disposition and nature of mountainous terrain affects not only those who dwell within the mountains and in the surrounding country but even those who live far from mountains.

The significance of steep and rugged terrain to those who live within mountains is manifold and on every hand. Consider the energy it takes to accomplish normal tasks or just to go from place to place. The consequences of this become clear when it is realized that most traditional mountain economies are agriculturally based; in their attempt to maximize use of the land they are forced to shift activities on an altitudinal basis. For example, livestock are taken to high pastures during summer while other activities are carried out in intermediate zones. An additional factor that increases the energy outlay in mountainous terrain is the relative absence of modern technological devices; most fields are too small and steep to allow use of tractors or motorized equipment. It is reported that some fields in the Alps are so steep that farmers secure themselves with ropes in order to harvest the hay. This extreme situation underscores both the scarcity of resources and the great demand for energy expenditure in steep terrain.

The amount of level or gently sloping land and its distribution are critical for human occupancy in mountains. The epigraph at the head of this chapter, "Man feels the pull of gravity," smacks strongly of environmental determinism, but it is nevertheless true that population density generally decreases with increasing elevation. If one were to take a topographic map of most mountainous regions of the world and overlay it with a population map, the relationship between density and level areas would be clear. The blank areas on the map would generally coincide with the higher elevations and areas of rugged topography. For example, 90 percent of the population of Switzerland is situated in a narrow belt at the base of the Alps stretching from Lake Geneva to Lake Constance, and a similar pattern can be seen in many other areas with mountainous topography (Fig. 10.10).

Those who settle within mountainous regions require suitable land for the construction of homesites and sufficient arable land to grow crops. Depending upon the mountain structure and geomorphic history, these areas may be concentrated in the uplands, in the lowlands, or at intermediate elevations. Whatever their disposition, level and gently sloping areas usually support the most productive soils and are least susceptible to erosion. There are also climatic ramifications: the larger the level area, the greater the mountain-mass effect, resulting in higher summer temperatures than occur in smaller and more isolated tracts at the same altitude (see pp. 77–81). Therefore, the more level

land there is within any given mountain area, the greater its potential for human settlement. The high-altitude plateaus— e.g., the Altiplano of Bolivia and Peru, the highlands of Ethiopia, and the Tibetan Plateau—together support 70 percent of the world's population dwelling at elevations above 3,000 m (12,000 ft.) (De-Jong 1970). By contrast, many of the high narrow valleys of the Himalayas have so little level land that villages are usually situated on slopes and ridges, and the land's carrying capacity is very low. Of course, mountain dwellers in many areas have purposely built their houses on the slopes in order to preserve the best land for farming. Other environmental factors, including flash floods and spring melt-floods, make valley bottoms undesirable and encourage building on slopes. Air drainage is a negative factor: colder air moves into the valley, causing frost and persistent fog. Another major consideration is the location of the valley or slope with respect to the sun. North-south valleys may receive ample sun, but east-west valley bottoms may remain shaded for much of the day, making higher slopes preferable for homesites (Garnett 1935, 1937).

The operation of all these factors is illustrated in the settlement patterns in the Alps. Many villages are located in the valleys, and many are preferentially situated on the broad gentle shoulders (*alps*) immediately above steep glacial troughs (Fig. 11.7). In most mountain areas, however, the population is concentrated in the valleys and on alluvial fans. In Old-World mountains, all suitable land has long been settled. Land-holdings are traditionally passed down from generation to generation, and this has often led to fragmentation of the land into such small parcels that efficient land-use is difficult (Friedl 1973). The modern demands of tourism for hotels and recreational facilities have also reduced the amount of land that can be used for agriculture (Lichtenberger 1975). This is a curious situation: the small

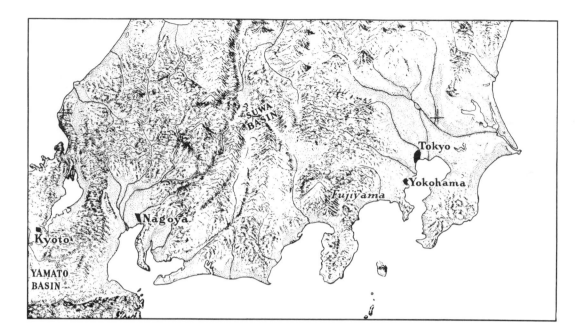

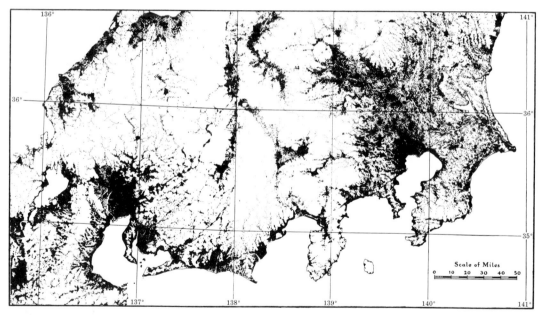

Fig. 10.10. Landform map and population distribution of Central Honshu, Japan. Each dot represents 200 people. Although based on older population data, the relationship between settlement and topography is still the same. (From James 1959, pp. 442–43)

alp pastures and quaint villages are one of the major tourist attractions of the Alps, and yet they are being destroyed by the demands of the very people who seek to admire them (see pp. 415–18).

Isolation

Steep mountainous topography hinders transportation and communication. Under traditional conditions, people living in separate mountain valleys were isolated from each other as well as from the lowland populations. Like mountain plants and animals, human populations may occur as islands of settlement, and although much more complex in their relationships, they may display similar tendencies. Much depends upon the disposition of the landscape and the cultural history of the region. In extensive mountain regions with deep and narrow valleys separated by precipitous alpine ridges, people tend to settle in individual valleys and to have little or no contact with neighboring valleys. The effects of topography are reinforced by history; many mountain settlements were established by minority groups in search of refuge or escape from conditions of their past. This built-in individuality or distinctiveness of groups contributes to the heterogeneity of population often encountered in mountains. Large and complex mountain systems such as the Caucasus, Himalayas, and Alps are the homes of very diverse cultures, nationalities, and languages.

Modern technology has eliminated much of the isolation experienced in former times, but many mountain settlements are still relatively removed from the mainstream of activity; the effects of past isolation are still evident. Mountain people's conservative philosophy, clannishness, and distrust of outsiders are proverbial. Traditional customs and attitudes are preserved under these conditions; education and modern innovations make headway slowly. The Appalachian region of the southeastern United States is a good example of this. When pop-

ulations have little interchange with other groups, the gene pool may be limited and result in inbreeding. The oft-cited but seldom documented prevalence of mentally retarded and insane individuals in remote villages of the Alps has been attributed to this factor. Genetic isolation has, in fact, been documented in remote districts of the Alps (Cavalli-Sforza 1963; Morton et al. 1968). The case for genetic adaptations among native Andeans is even stronger than in the Alps, since they have been isolated in the highlands for a much longer period (Monge 1948). Still, caution should be used when considering genetic adaptations in such a complex system as a human population. In addition, continuous human occupancy in most high-altitude regions has been limited to post-glacial times, i.e., the last 15,000 years, and many believe that this is too brief a time-span to allow the development of adaptive genes establishing distinctive genotypes for high altitudes (Cruz-Coke 1978).

The effects of isolation due to topography are evident in the diversity of spoken languages and dialects encountered in the major mountain ranges. In Switzerland alone over 35 different dialects of German, French, Italian, and Latin (Romansh) are spoken (Delgado de Carvalho 1962, p. 82). Such developments are less common in plains, owing to greater ease of interaction. Of course, the development of modern communication and transportation systems has disrupted traditional conditions in most mountain areas, providing increased mobility and freer exchange of people and ideas.

Unlike deeply dissected mountains composed of narrow valleys and ridges, those that contain large areas of relatively level land, whether in uplands or in high valleys, facilitate local communications and transportation. Depending upon the elevation and environmental conditions, such regions may support relatively large populations with a common bond or cohesiveness. These areas become centers of population and government, as they are (or have been) in some tropical and subtropical regions, e.g., Ethiopia, Bolivia, and Ecuador. Most centers of government are located in the lowlands, however, so mountain dwellers are politically and culturally isolated. Highland populations usually pay more allegiance to their own inclinations than to those of the distant government.

In some cases a strong local consciousness develops and leads to the creation of mountain communes, cantons, or independent states. A classic example is the small independent state of Andorra, located along the crest of the Pyrenees between Spain and France. Andorra is united by extensive upland pastures that have historically been the focus of a summer grazing economy (Fig. 10.11). Mountain pastoralists of both Spanish and French ancestry have met and mixed peacefully in these uplands since ancient times and there has always been a stronger bond and allegiance to the local region than to either of the larger powers (Peattie 1929). Consequently, Andorra has maintained itself as an independent state since feudal times, and although the local economy has now changed, with many people moving to the cities, the region retains its independent status. Numerous other mountain states and regions have various degrees of local autonomy or at least a strong sense of self-identity: for example, the region of the Montagnards of Viet Nam; Montenegro in the Balkans; and the Himalayan kingdoms of Sikkim, Bhutan, and Nepal, as well as La-

Fig. 10.11. Distribution of pasture, tilled land, forest, and areas of steep slope in Andorra (as of 1929). The tilled land is largely restricted to the valley bottoms, and grassy pastures occupy the uplands. (From Peattie 1929, p. 224)

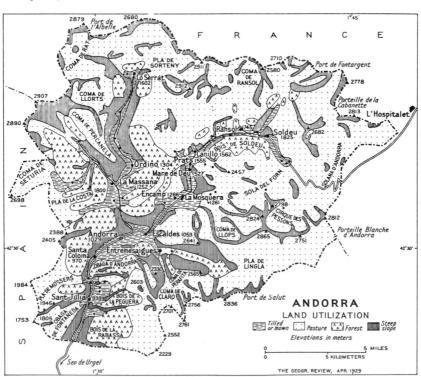

dakh, Kashmir, and Tibet. Switzerland itself is a confederation of mountain states born and nurtured by a common cause and identity.

Barriers

Steep mountainous terrain imposes restrictions on travel and communication from one side to the other. Mountains tend to separate and impede, while level areas facilitate, exchange and interaction. Nevertheless, the relationships between cultural and physical phenomena, even those as striking as mountain barriers, are seldom simple and direct. Mountains have served (and continue to serve) as obstacles to human activities, but not in the same absolute way that they establish climatic divides or control the distribution of vegetation.

The extent to which mountains serve as barriers to human activity depends upon ecological conditions, e.g., the presence of forests and the altitude of the snowline, as well as their height, breadth, length, and general ruggedness and the presence or absence of transecting valleys. Elongated fold or fault mountains with no major transecting valleys are the most formidable obstacles. The Pyrenees between France and Spain are one of the most effective mountain barriers in Europe. North-south travel in this area has historically passed around rather than across the mountains, although the Pyrenees are now transected by several roads. Another major barrier is the great east-west rampart of the Himalayas. Travel across this range is so exceedingly difficult that transportation between India and China has traditionally been by sea rather than overland. There is still no highway or railway across the Himalayas, although this has become a political rather than a logistical problem. Several new roads have been built from India to Nepal, Sikkim, and Bhutan (Karan 1960a, 1967). Similarly, China has constructed an all-weather road from the north into Lhasa, Tibet, and beyond (Karan 1976). It will probably be only a matter of

time before it is possible for tourists to drive all the way across the Himalayas. The role as barrier that both these mountain systems have played throughout history is clear from the contrast in cultures found on the two sides: Indo-Malayan peoples live to the south of the Himalayas, and the Chinese dominate to the north. Similarly, the Alps, Carpathians, Balkans, and Pyrenees have long separated the Mediterranean cultures from those of northern Europe (Semple 1915). Of course, human decisions and activities have established and maintained these patterns, but their close coincidence with the mountain ranges suggests the importance that such barriers can have.

In the United States, the varying effectiveness of mountain barriers can be seen by comparing the Appalachians and the Rockies. The elongated fold system of the Appalachians is breached by numerous valleys, simplifying travel (Semple 1897). The Rockies, on the other hand, with very few low passes, form a much less passable barrier (Lackey 1949). The Cascades and Sierra Nevada served as major obstacles to east-west travel during pioneer days. The problem of crossing such formidable barriers in covered wagons filled with family and belongings seems remote to us now, but it produced an extremely challenging segment of our history. The hardships and heartaches were countless and the trail took a great and heavy toll. This is poignantly demonstrated by the trials encountered by the ill-fated Donner Party (Stewart 1960).

The barrier effect has been greatly diminished during the last century; we now communicate readily across mountains through use of radio, television, and telephone, and to travel across most mountains is scarcely more difficult. Nevertheless, man can never totally escape his physical setting. Modern aircraft easily fly over mountains, yet a large percentage of airplane crashes occur in mountains. Railroads, highways, and communication networks have now been constructed across most mountain

Fig. 10.12. Tight hairpin turns or switchbacks on a steep mountain slope in the northern Caucasus, U.S.S.R. This road leads up to the Klukhor Pass at 2,782 m (9,125 ft.), which is snowcovered and impassable for most of the year. Across the mountains 60 km (38 mi.) to the southwest lies the Black Sea. This pass was an important military location during World War II. Several battles took place here, and it is a matter of great local pride that the Caucasians successfully defended the pass against the Germans on their march to the Black Sea. (Author)

ranges but the expense in building, using, and maintaining such systems is vastly greater than it would be in the lowlands. Problems increase with steepness of slope and narrowness of valleys. Roads must be engineered so as not to exceed a critical gradient and this usually involves the construction of switchbacks (Fig. 10.12). Often expensive blasting and construction techniques are required, and in any case it takes several times more roadway in mountains to go an equal distance! The costs of using mountain roads are also high: driving takes more time and fuel, vehicles suffer extra wear and tear, and road maintenance is more expensive. In winter, only major roads are kept open, and even then the snow and ice make driving hazardous and tire chains are often required. If the road is situated in an avalanche zone, expensive protective devices must be installed, either upslope in the snow accumulation area or as shelters over the highway. Such structures have been built by the hundreds in the Alps (Figs. 5.29, 5.30).

A tendency in recent years has been to construct tunnels through mountains. Although the sightseer misses the spectacular views from the road, tunnels are a boon for commerce and for those who want to go from one place to another in a hurry. Tunnel construction has been especially important for railroads since trains cannot negotiate steep roads and sharp switchbacks as easily as automobiles. The famous Swiss railway running through the Rhaetian Alps has 376 bridges and 76 tunnels in 240 km (150 mi.)! Many of the major tunnels in the Alps follow the ancient routes and passes of foot travelers—e.g., the St. Gotthard tunnel, the Simplon tunnel on the road between Lausanne and Milan, or the tunnel under the Grand St. Bernard between Switzerland and Italy. In some cases, however, the tunnels have pierced huge mountain masses which have heretofore served as impassable barriers. One such is the highway tunnel completed in 1965 under the Mont Blanc massif between Italy and France, a distance of 12 km (7.5 mi.). The world's longest tunnel as of this writing (1979) has just been completed under the mountainous spine of Central Honshu, Japan. This tunnel, which is 21.3 km (13.3 mi.) long, was built to carry one of Japan's 240 km (150 mph) "bullet trains." It is now possible to go from Tokyo to Niigata on the opposite coast in one and a half hours; before construction of the tunnel the trip took four hours.

Mountain Passes

Travel across mountains is generally directed along the passes. These are transecting valleys, natural depressions, gaps, or places where the mountains narrow, allowing somewhat easier passage. In general, the higher and more massive the range, the fewer and more difficult the passes. Linear ranges that have few gaps, such as the Pyrenees, Caucasus, Himalayas, and Andes, pose truly formidable barriers. On the other hand, the Alps are arranged in a series of radiating valley systems which have long allowed travel. The much lower parallel ridges of the Appalachians are likewise cut by streams, creating numerous, though circuitous, routes. The most famous of these is

Cumberland Gap, the "Wilderness Road" through which pioneers moved westward to Kentucky and beyond. The imposing Hindu Kush and other ranges of Afghanistan have a number of passes, e.g., the Khyber, so that these mountains have never offered a serious obstacle to travel from the northwest to India. It is through these routes that the Greeks, Assyrians, Persians, Turks, Tartars, and Mongols swept on their way to the rich Indus Valley (Semple 1911, p. 536).

Mountain passes have played a major role in military engagements throughout history. Passes are at once the easiest places to cross and the easiest to defend. Troops confined to a narrow valley are much more susceptible to attack than when they are dispersed, and if they are forced to move single-file through a narrow path or along a ledge, their passage is slowed immensely. For example, if movement through a difficult defile takes each soldier one minute, a patrol of 10 men will be delayed 10 minutes, and if there are 1,000 men the delay will be over 16 1/2 hours! During this period they will be strung out and more vulnerable than usual. This is one of the circumstances under which a few well-trained men can hold off a large army. Perhaps the most famous holding action in history took place during the invasion of Greece by Persia in 480 B.C. The Persian fleet landed to the north and in their march southward had to pass through the narrow pass of Thermopylae. A Greek commander and 300 men held up the entire Persian army at this pass for a day and a night before eventually being overcome. The delay was critical because it gave the Greek navy time to rally and to end the invasion by destroying the Persian fleet. The problems of ground troops in mountains will probably always remain similar but the availability of airplanes and helicopters eliminates many of the traditional problems of mountain warfare (Thompson 1970).

A curious fact about mountain passes is that they are generally more important to those living in surrounding areas, or even far distant, than they are to the mountain dwellers themselves. This is because the value and use of the pass depend upon the demand for a route across the mountains at that point, which, in turn, is created and controlled by factors outside the mountains, rather than by local resources. Passes do take on local economic value when the inhabitants exploit their strategic location. Historically, this has been done by levying tolls or fees for passage; more recently, hotels, restaurants, and other service facilities have captured transient dollars.

The importance of a pass depends on the difficulty of access imposed by the surrounding landscape and on the cultural demand for access at that point. In some cases there may be easy access across a barrier but only minimal use of the pass, as in the southern Andes, where there are only trails because of insufficient demand for better facilities. In other cases heavy demand causes transportation or communication routes to cross very difficult obstacles. The recently completed tunnels under Mount Blanc and the mountains of central Honshu, Japan, are illustrations of this. Vast monies are sometimes spent to build transportation facilities across difficult terrain in order to tap the mineral resources in mountains. In most cases, however, major transportation routes follow the easiest route. The Panama Canal takes advantage of the Isthmus of Panama, a natural break in the mountains of Central America. South Pass in the Rockies of southern Wyoming provided the most favorable passage for westward-bound pioneers on the Oregon Trail. Here was not only passable terrain for their wagons but also an adequate supply of water and grass for their animals. A few years later the Union Pacific Railway, less dependent on grass and water than on terrain, was located 80 km (50 mi.) to the south through a more barren and arid but shorter and more gentle corridor across the mountains (Vance 1961). The transcontinental highway (and eventually the Interstate Highway System) fol-

lowed the railway route. The major highway and railway routes across the Cascades follow the two sea-level valleys that transect them—the Columbia Gorge between Oregon and Washington, and the Fraser River Valley in southern British Columbia. The Alaska pipeline, with all its environmental debate, follows the mountain passes through the Brooks Range and the Kenai-Chugach Mountains.

The physical presence of a pass and the demand for access at that point are often interrelated historically. This is because communication and interaction between the two sides of a range are commonly established and maintained by reason of the pass. Travel on a plain is easy in all directions, but in mountains travel is usually funneled or channeled into narrow zones. For this reason, towns and other service facilities spring up along the pass routes, and major cities often develop at either end. Thus, the presence of a pass may establish the initial lines of travel, but subsequent developments, such as the location of principal towns, reinforce the pass function and engender continued activity across the mountains at this point. The cities of Portland, Oregon, and Vancouver, British Columbia, both owe their location and commercial greatness at least partially to the presence of the low-level mountain passes.

Perhaps the classic example of a mountain route being instrumental in regional development is the Brenner Pass in the central Alps. This is one of the easiest passes across the Alps and has long been a principal route from Italy to the countries of western Europe—Roman armies traveled along this route on their way to the Danube. Early trade across this pass was based on the amber of Germany and the fabric and wine of Italy. During the Middle Ages the German emperors invaded Italy by way of the Brenner. Later, people from the north used it on their way to the cultural attractions of Venice. Thus, Brenner Pass has been a key factor in the location and growth of northern centers like Augsburg, Nurenberg, and Leipzig, as well as Venice and Verona to the south (Semple 1911, p. 544). The first carriage road and, later, the first railroad across the Alps followed the Brenner. It remains one of the important passes in the Alps.

The Dariel Pass in the Caucasus is another case in which the easiest natural crossing through a range assumed major historical importance. The Caucasus averages 200 km (125 mi.) in width and provides a formidable 1,200 km (750 mi.) barrier between the Black and Caspian seas. About midway, however, the range narrows to a distance of only 96 km (60 mi.) and elevations are slightly lower. Here the Dariel Pass crosses, at an elevation of 2,379 m (7,503 ft.). It is through this corridor that travel between Russia

and the Turkish Republics has historically funneled. Today it remains the only year-round pass through the Caucasus. All the other passes are higher, snowbound, and generally more difficult to cross (the railways go around the range on either end rather than across). During Russian expansion to the south in the middle of the nineteenth century, the famous Georgian Military Highway was constructed across the Dariel Pass, from what is now Ordzhonikidze to Tiblisi, in order to control South Georgia and the Transcaucasus. Consequently, the development of these two cities has been greatly influenced by the presence of the pass. Interestingly, the Ossetes, who occupy the pass region, are the only group which has traditionally occupied

Fig. 10.13. View to the east along the famous Khyber Pass in Pakistan near the Afghanistan border. The upper road is for motor traffic; the lower one is a caravan route for pack animals. (Clarke Brooke, Portland State University)

both sides of the range. All other tribes and languages are confined to one side or the other. Like many other pass peoples, the Ossetes were not above preying on unwary travelers. This largely ceased, however, once the Russians established the military road (Semple 1911, p. 539).

Another famous mountain transit area is Khyber Pass at 2,068 m (6,825 ft.) in the Hindu Kush mountains between West Pakistan and Afghanistan (Fig. 10.13). The topography of this range is extremely complex and the passage takes a circuitous route with a number of ascents and descents. Nevertheless, it is the main route from central Asia to India and caravans have passed this way since before the birth of Christ, coming from Tashkent and Bukhara in Turkestan through Kabul across the Khyber Pass to Peshawar and the Indus Valley. It is also across this pass that the numerous invasions from the northwest, which have so markedly contributed to the heterogeneous character of India's population, have come. The cities of Kabul and Peshawar are trading and service centers on either side of the pass. Khyber Pass is notorious for the ruthless local tribesmen who have long exploited their strategic location by imposing tolls upon caravans and travelers, robbing, killing, and plundering at will: Genghis Khan decided that it was better to pay a toll to insure safe passage of his armies than to struggle against these local tribesmen, and the British, too, paid the tribesmen an annual sum to keep the road open (Holdich 1901, p. 48). Even today the highway is closed at night out of concern for traveler safety.

Boundaries

A logical extension of the barrier function of mountains is their role as boundaries. Wherever mountains exist they have been important in the evolution of states and in the establishment of national borders. Mountains make ideal boundaries because they are prominent, permanent, and periph-

eral. The value of prominence and permanence is obvious: mountains are easy to recognize and identify and they are long-enduring. Mountains are peripheral in that most human activity takes place in the lowlands. As states evolved, they naturally tended to claim and protect these richer, populous regions at the expense of peripheral highlands. Mountains were also strategic for defense, serving as easily defended natural bulwarks, and by waging war in the mountains, the disruption and damage of war could be diverted from the more productive and valuable central regions.

Mountains have been more important in the location of boundaries in Europe than anywhere else. The Pyrenees divide France from Spain; the Carpathians set off Poland from Czechoslovakia; the border between Norway and Sweden follows the Scandinavian mountains; and no fewer than five countries abut upon the Alps. Other major mountain boundaries include the Andes, which divide Chile from Argentina, and the Himalayas, which divide India from China (although there are also several small border states). It is important to remember, however, that political boundaries are cultural phenomena, determined by the interrelationships of nations, and in many cases other factors may be more important than that of the physical landscape. For example, although the Urals divide Russia from Siberia, they have never been an effective political barrier. Similarly, the great mountain systems of North America have never posed serious obstacles to political unity.

In some cases, mountain states have evolved as buffers between larger and more aggressive lowland states on either side: medieval Burgundy and modern Savoy (between Italy and France) are examples. Andorra is situated astride the Pyrenees between France and Spain. Switzerland may be considered a buffer state, since it has long controlled the passes of the central Alps and maintained its independence and neutrality, even during World War II when all its larger neighbors waged war around it. The small Himalayan kingdoms of Bhutan, Sikkim, and Kashmir all serve as buffer states between India and China, although this is now more in a symbolic than a physical sense (Levi 1959); nuclear missiles and warheads make the traditional role of mountains and buffer states during warfare almost meaningless. The preservation of these kingdoms is nevertheless of real concern to India, particularly now that China has extended her sovereignty over Tibet and is pushing for parts of Bhutan and Kashmir (Karan 1960b, 1973, 1976).

The presence of a mountain border does not guarantee an indisputable boundary, as the many conflicts in these regions amply demonstrate. Consider, for example, the Andean boundary between Chile and Argentina. The 1881 treaty states: "The frontier line shall run . . . along the highest crests . . . which may divide the waters, and shall pass between the slopes which descend on either side" (quoted in Boggs 1940, p. 86). Watersheds seldom correspond exactly with the highest crests, however, particularly in the southern part of the Andes, where west-flowing rivers have eaten headward and drain areas well to the east of the line connecting the highest crests. This was the crux of the problem. Chile claimed that the term "highest crests" should be interpreted to mean only those crests which acted as water divides and that the boundary should follow these watershed divides. Argentina, on the other hand, maintained that the line should be drawn strictly on the basis of the highest crests without taking into account the drainage divides. The bitter and prolonged dispute over this boundary was finally settled in 1902 by arbitration through the offices of the Queen of England (Boggs 1940, p. 89). The famous *Christ of the Andes* statue erected at the boundary in Uspallata Pass along the main road between Buenos Aires and central Chile commemorates that agreement (Fig. 10.14).

The more recent and on-going dispute

Fig. 10.14. Statue, *Christ of the Andes*, stands at Uspallata Pass at the mountain boundary between Chile and Argentina, and commemorates the border treaty of 1902. (Grace Lines)

between India and China over their boundary line in the Himalayas is another interesting case. The boundary, known as the McMahon Line, was established in a 1914 treaty to which Tibet, Great Britain, and China were parties. The boundary line was never physically demarcated, owing to the difficulty of the terrain, but it was assumed to follow the crest of the Himalayas (Karan

1960b, p. 20). Again, however, the interpretation of exactly where this line runs is in dispute, especially since China has been aggressively pursuing an expansionist policy in this area (Woodman 1969). The critical locations are in Bhutan and Kashmir, where Chinese maps show the boundary far to the south of the original agreement (Karan 1960b, p. 17). There have already been several military conflicts between India and China and more will probably occur before the matter is settled. It is somewhat ironic that the most formidable mountain range in the world should be the focus of one of the most bitterly contested boundary disputes.

The establishment of boundaries on the basis of purely physical features may be justified from a strategic point of view, but it is usually less than satisfactory to the people living within the region. This is especially true of pastoral societies who have traditionally driven their flocks and herds from one valley to the next or to distant high pastures long held as communal property. These are sometimes called "straddle economies" because the way of life and economic interests are similar on either side of the crest. The close integration of the Andorrans in the upland pastures of the Pyrenees is a case in which cohesiveness and common interests have resulted in the establishment of a separate state in the summit region (Peattie 1929, 1936). Andorra is the exception, however; more commonly, boundaries serve only to disrupt and complicate local activities. The border between France and Italy in the western Alps has had a long and involved history. The boundary now basically follows the crest line; in 1951 the two countries signed a convention designating a frontier zone for 10 km (6 mi.) on either side of the boundary "within which freedom of circulation of persons and of movement of livestock, vehicles, seeds, tools, and fertilizers would be stimulated" (House 1959, p. 129). This approach is much more humanistic and logical than its more arbitrary predecessors, since it allows practical activ-

ities to continue uninterruptedly. Such a boundary concept has the potential for integration and cooperation rather than separation.

One of the most unfortunate cases of the establishment of a mountain boundary on a strictly physical basis is that of the South Tyrol between Austria and Italy (Freshfield 1916). Tyrol was originally a pass country like Switzerland, and extended across the crest on both sides. The people of Tyrol were German-speaking and practiced a very similar way of life in the high alpine valleys and meadows. After World War I, however, Italy wanted a strategic border to exclude Austria from the southern slope of the Alps. President Wilson of the United States saw the crest line as a logical boundary and lent his support to the Italian claim. He was later to regret his decision because the people of the South Tyrol were fundamentally related to the North, not to Italy; in language, culture, and economy they were completely different from the vine-growers farther to the south (Peattie 1936, p. 213). The establishment of the boundary at the crest line may have made good sense strategically, but it caused great human disruption. The·South Tyrol became the Italian Trentino. The German-speaking peoples were forced to adjust themselves to the Italian regime and to adopt Italian as their official language. It was even forbidden to sing German songs in public. The pressure continued, and during World War II, under Mussolini, an order was given to destroy everything with German associations in the region. Even gravestones with German inscriptions were destroyed. The wounds of disruption brought about by this ill-conceived boundary line have perhaps now healed, but the scars will remain for generations (Rusinow 1969).

Environmental Hazards

Every region is exposed to some degree of risk from natural disasters of one sort or another—tornadoes in the American Midwest, earthquakes in California, hurricanes along the Gulf Coast—but mountains, with their volcanic eruptions, earthquakes, landslides, mudflows, snow avalanches, and flash floods, are particularly dangerous places. The environmental hazards associated with the rapid transport of material downslope were discussed in Chapter 6 (see pp. 197–203). The focus here will be on volcanoes and earthquakes.

Volcanoes

The distribution of volcanic activity is centered around the margins of the tectonic plates, for example, the "ring of fire" around the Pacific Ocean: Indonesia, Japan, Kamchatka, the Alaska Peninsula, the Cascades, and the Andes (Fig. 3.15). In other cases, like the Hawaiian Islands, there are thought to be "hot spots" within the earth over which the crust is slowly moving (see pp. 44–45) (Burke and Wilson 1976). Volcanic activity is usually sporadic and intermittent. An active volcano may lie quiescent for tens, hundreds, or thousands of years, its calm beauty belying the violence in its depths. This very quiescence adds to the hazard by lulling people into ignoring or forgetting the dangers. Many volcanic regions are indeed tempting for settlement: they are typically located in coastal areas with moderate climates, and the volcanic soils are usually quite productive. Consequently, large agricultural populations and major cities are to be found near active volcanoes in spite of the potential hazards.

The odds are small that any specific place will be destroyed this year, but they are high that some place will be. Living close to an active volcano (or any other natural hazard) is like playing Russian roulette with nature. Apparently, many people feel it is worth the gamble. The populations occupying the slopes of Vesuvius have been decimated time and time again, but after each disaster others move back to take their place. Similarly, Mount Etna in Sicily has experienced a continuous series of eruptions during the last few centuries, with a major one occur-

ring every 10–20 years, yet over one million people live on its slopes, returning after each eruption with the persistence of moths hovering about a flame (Clapperton 1972). If the eruptions are more remote in time, the concern is even less. A study of the perception of the volcanic hazards in the Pacific Northwest, for example, found that the occupants of the region gave very little, if any, thought to the danger of living near such potentially active volcanoes as Mounts Rainier, Baker, St. Helens, Hood, or Shasta (Folsom 1970). Yet, each of these peaks has erupted within the last few hundred years. Mount Rainier contains a major thermal anomaly (Lange and Avent 1973) and Mount Baker has been showing increased fumarolic activity (Rosenfeld and Schlicker 1976). Mount St. Helens erupted on Sunday morning, 18 May 1980, in the most disastrous eruption ever observed in the coterminous United States. The north side of the formerly symmetric cone now has a huge crater, and the summit has been reduced in elevation by 460 m (1,500 ft.). Approximately eighty people lost their lives in the initial eruption. During the summer and fall of 1980, further eruptions spewed ash and lava. In some parts of Washington and Oregon, falling ash so reduced visibility that speed limits of 8 to 48 km. (5–30 miles) per hour were temporarily imposed, and ash removal became a major problem. As of late October 1980, the mountain continues to show signs of activity.

During the last 400 years there have been about 500 major volcanic eruptions and these have taken the lives of nearly 200,000 people (Williams 1951). Not surprisingly, a rich and varied volcano folklore has developed among inhabitants living near active volcanoes (Vitaliano 1973), especially among primitive societies seeking a way to comprehend and rationalize volcanoes' awe-inspiring and devastative power. Volcanoes have been almost universally regarded as either the abode or the embodiment of deities and demons, and sacrifices are made to satiate or appease the gods (Bandelier 1906; Gade 1970). The Hawaiian goddess Pele, said to dwell in Kilauea Crater, is considered responsible for its great activity. Numerous legends exist concerning Pele, and belief in her existence is still widespread in the Islands (Westervelt 1963; Herbert and Bardossi 1968). During the 1960 eruption of Kilauea, special ceremonies were held and sacrifices made to appease Pele. Western influence has contributed an interesting touch: the sacrifices were wrapped in Christmas paper and green ribbon (Lachman and Bonk 1960). Another example of modern folklore is the story of St. Januarius, whose blood is supposedly kept in vials in a cathedral in Naples. The blood is said to liquify several times a year, notably on December 16, the anniversary of the 1631 eruption of Mount Vesuvius. According to local legends, St. Januarius protects the people from the eruptions of Mount Vesuvius and is considered their patron saint (Crandell and Waldron 1969).

Lava Flows. The greatest danger from volcanic eruptions comes from lava flows, volcanic ash eruptions, volcanic mudflows, and glowing avalanches (*nuées ardentes*). Lava flows, although perhaps the most publicized features, are seldom directly responsible for loss of life, since the molten material usually moves so slowly that people can escape; an average speed is 5 km (3 mi.) per hour, with larger flows reaching a distance of 40–50 km (24–30 mi.). The encroaching lava destroys everything in its path, burying farmland and towns. Very little can ordinarily be done to deter it, although some success has been achieved by diversion walls and by bombing the flow to alter its direction of movement (Mason and Foster 1953; Macdonald 1972). In Iceland, they have had considerable success by pumping seawater onto potentially damaging flows near the coast; this causes the lava to harden and stop. The solidified material then itself helps to dam and deflect later flows. The indirect effects of lava flows

can also be destructive: the molten lava may start forest fires and cause rapid melting of snow and ice, setting off floods or mudflows.

Volcanic Ash. Volcanic ash can spread great distances. The eruption of Mount Katmai on the Alaska Peninsula caused the deposition of a layer of ash 30 cm (1 ft.) thick on the town of Kodiak, 160 km (100 mi.) distant (Wilcox 1959). An even more spectacular occurrence was the cataclysmic eruption of Mount Mazama (Crater Lake) in the Oregon Cascades about 6,600 years ago. Over 16 cubic km (10 cu. mi.) of debris was ejected from its subterranean feeding chamber, eventually causing collapse of the peak and leaving a *caldera* 9.6 km (6 mi.) wide and 1,200 m (4,000 ft.) deep (Williams 1942). This displaced material covers several hundred thousand square kilometers in the Northwest states (Fig. 10.15). Areas immediately adjacent were smothered under 30 m (100 ft.) of pumice and ash; at the other

Fig. 10.15. Distribution of volcanic ash from the eruption of Mount Mazama (Crater Lake), Oregon. Stippled area, extending 240 km (150 mi.), indicates area where ash is more than 15 cm (6 in.) thick. Total distance of contiguous ash-fall exceeds 1,100 km (700 mi.). (After Williams and Goles 1968, p. 38)

Fig. 10.16. Volcanic ash burying houses during the 1914 eruption of Sakurajima Volcano in southern Kyushu, Japan. (Courtesy Gordon Macdonald, University of Hawaii)

extreme, measurable amounts have been traced well into Canada (Williams and Goles 1968).

The environmental hazard from volcanic ash depends upon the severity of the eruption, the direction and velocity of the wind, and the distance from the source. The wind was southwesterly during the eruption of Mount Mazama, so areas to the east and northeast received heavy amounts while areas upwind were scarcely affected (Fig. 10.15). Volcanic ash seldom results directly in loss of life, although damage to property may be severe. Plants and soil are buried, and the dense dust clouds of ash, pumice, and poisonous gases may damage the eyes and the respiratory system. During the 1943

eruption of Parícutin in Mexico, for example, several thousand cattle and horses in the immediate vicinity died from eating and breathing the volcanic ash, as well as from the lack of food. The heavy deposition of volcanic ash may contaminate water supplies (both by sediment and acidity) and bury or overload roofs and other structures (Fig. 10.16). If there are heavy rains after the eruption, roofs may cave in under the weight of the water-saturated ash, and—a particularly great peril—the slopes may collapse and move rapidly downward as huge mudflows.

Volcanic Mudflows. Volcanic mudflows, known as *lahars,* are like normal mudflows

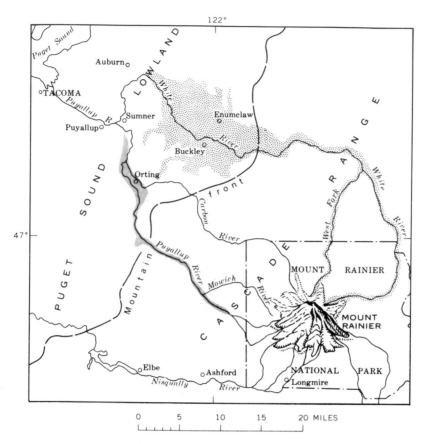

Fig. 10.17. The distribution of two major mudflows on Mount Rainier. The coarse-dot pattern represents the largest, which occurred 5,000 years ago. The fine-dot pattern shows the extent of another major mudflow, which occurred 500 years ago. (From Crandell and Mullineaux 1967, p. 2)

(see pp. 192–94) except that they are composed of volcanic debris. Such material is especially unstable once it becomes saturated, because the ash is easily and rapidly altered to clay by the action of steam and acids in volcanic gases. Although this may seem surprising, volcanic mudflows are one of the most destructive features of volcanism. They have probably taken more lives during the last few centuries than any other single form of volcanic action (Macdonald 1972, p. 170). Mudflows typically start high on the volcano and move downward along stream channels or depressions, flowing at

speeds averaging 32–48 km (20–30 mi.) per hour. Most volcanic mudflows travel only a few kilometers, but large ones may extend up to 160 km (100 mi.).

Mount Rainier has had a long history of mudflows: evidence exists for at least 55 major flows in the last 10,000 years (Crandell and Mullineaux 1967). The largest occurred about 5,000 years ago, originating high on the peak in steam-altered material, and traveled 64 km (40 mi.) down the White River Valley before it spread out into a lobate mass covering 104 square km (65 sq. mi.) in the Puget Sound lowlands. The site of the present town of Enumclaw was buried to a depth of 21 m (70 ft.) (Fig. 10.17) (Crandell and Waldron 1956). As far as is known, there was no loss of human life in that flow; but if it should ever be repeated, it is doubtful if the same could be said, for over 30,000 people now reside there.

The water necessary to create mudflows usually comes from precipitation, but another source with disastrous potential is crater lakes. The most famous example is the eruption in 1919 of Kelut Volcano in Java, which drained its crater lake and created mudflows that buried 130 square km (81 sq. mi.) of farmland and resulted in 5,000 deaths. After this disaster Dutch engineers constructed a series of tunnels to keep the lake drained so that future eruptions would do less damage. The value of the project was proven in 1951, when there was a major eruption but no major mudflows. Unfortunately, this eruption clogged the tunnels, and the lake refilled. The situation was not corrected, and in 1966 the volcano erupted and mudflows killed several hundred people. Since then, new tunnels have been drilled to keep the lake drained (Macdonald 1972, p. 173).

Where lakes and reservoirs are located in stream valleys near the base of the volcano, mudflows may cause rapid infilling of the lakes, resulting in overflow and massive flooding downstream. This is one of the great potential hazards in the Pacific Northwest (Crandell and Waldron 1969; Crandell and Mullineaux 1974, 1975). Near the base of Mount Baker are two reservoirs with a combined length of 29 km (18 mi.). Immediately downstream several small communities, with 15,000 inhabitants, are vulnerable to flooding. Similar situations exist near several of the other major peaks; the one with the greatest threat to human life is Mount St. Helens near the city of Portland. Mount St. Helens is the youngest of the Cascade volcanoes (Crandell et al. 1975). Three large hydroelectric reservoirs are situated at its base and a sizable mudflow down its slopes could have a chain reaction producing flooding downstream into the Columbia River Valley, where over one million people live. It has all the makings of a classic disaster scene (Crandell and Waldron 1969). The 18 May 1980 eruption resulted in massive mudflows and floods, but they moved to the north, so that Portland was not directly affected.

Glowing Avalanches. The last major volcanic hazard to consider is by far the most concentrated and violent: the so-called glowing avalanche (*nuée ardente*). This is a highly heated mass of gas-charged rock fragments expelled as a dense fire cloud which behaves much like a fluid. It moves rapidly down the mountain—generally following the topography—trapping air underneath and using it as a cushion. The molten rock fragments emit gases that release energy and lubricate the movement. These glowing clouds may travel at speeds of up to 160 km (100 mi.) per hour, with internal temperatures approaching 1,000° C. (1,832° F.). It is a totally destructive phenomenon that consumes everything in its path.

The most famous and best-documented occurrence of a glowing avalanche took place in 1902 on Mount Pelee, Martinique, a small island in the West Indies. The mountain is situated about 8 km (5 mi.) away from the coastal town of St. Pierre, a beautiful little Caribbean town where life is peaceful and uncomplicated. Mount Pelee was known to be a volcano, but it had done nothing more than smoulder for centuries. About two weeks before the fateful eruption, it began to show renewed activity, rumbling and spewing steam. There was considerable concern among the citizenry but the mayor enjoined them to stay, because an election was scheduled. Early on the morning of May 8, 1902, a deafening explosion was heard and the city was engulfed in a swiftly moving incandescent cloud of such high heat that it melted glass. The destruction was total; over 30,000 people lost their lives in that brief encounter with the volcano (Fig. 10.18). Two people survived the holocaust: one in the hull of a ship anchored off the shore and the other a prisoner in an underground dungeon with

Fig. 10.18. St. Pierre, Martinique, after the eruption of Mount Pelee in 1902. (Courtesy of American Museum of Natural History)

only one small window facing away from the mountain (Macdonald 1972, p. 145).

In counterbalance to the destructive aspects of volcanoes, it should be stressed that they also provide benefits for man. Some scientists believe that the origins of life itself depended upon volcanism; water and carbon dioxide, both prerequisites for evolution, were originally liberated from the interior of earth by volcanoes (Rubey 1951). Volcanism is responsible for the creation of new land: associated with the margins of the plates, volcanoes contribute to the building of continents. Many islands are nothing more than volcanoes rising from the ocean floor with their summits protruding above the water. I think that you would agree that the world would be a poorer place without jewels of the Pacific like Fiji, Pago Pago, and Tahiti.

Volcanic areas contain great energy reserves with the potential for the production of geothermal power. Steam, hot water, and vast amounts of heat are just waiting to be tapped. Only a fractional amount of this energy is now being utilized. As fossil fuels are depleted, volcanic sources of energy look more and more attractive. Geothermal energy is cheap and renewable, with few pollution problems.

Volcanic material, especially volcanic ash, decomposes rapidly and develops into excellent soils. In the humid tropics where most soils are so heavily leached, volcanic soils contain a relatively high nutrient and mineral content. Consequently, there is often a correlation between population and soil type; by far the densest agricultural populations in areas like Indonesia live near active volcanoes (Mohr 1945).

Volcanic rock itself has a number of practical uses. Pumice is used in scouring compounds and soaps. Volcanic ash weathers into bentonite, a clay that is used in oil-well drilling. Volcanic rocks are put to a number of constructive and decorative uses. A last major benefit is the beauty and grandeur of volcanic peaks. Their unique shapes and characteristics set them apart from other mountains. In this respect alone they are a priceless resource for the enjoyment and enrichment of mankind.

Earthquakes

Earthquakes and volcanic activity are closely related; they often develop simultaneously, and both are fundamentally related to the margins of continental plates and to mountain-building. Most earthquakes occur in a narrow band around the Pacific Ocean and in an east-west belt stretching from southeast Asia along the Himalayas to the Mediterranean (Fig. 3.8). The continental interiors are relatively free of earthquakes, although they do occasionally occur there. Approximately 80 percent of all earthquakes take place in coastal areas around the Pacific Ocean, 17 percent occur in the east-west extension through the Himalayas and the Mediterranean, and the remaining 3 percent take place along the mid-ocean ridges and elsewhere (Oakeshott 1976, p. 23).

Earthquakes are truly great destroyers of life. Unlike volcanoes, which usually give at least some indication of impending disaster, earthquakes occur suddenly and without warning. There may be pre-shocks and tremors, but these are often so common in earthquake country that they are unreliable as indicators of anything more serious to follow. Once a major earthquake begins, it typically builds to a peak of intensity within 10 or 15 seconds and there is little chance to escape or to prepare adequately. Approximately 10,000 people die each year from earthquakes. A review of some of the major earthquakes over the last few centuries and their toll in human lives will illustrate the stark reality of this danger (Table 10.3).

Earthquakes are causally connected to mountainous regions, but their most disastrous effects take place in the surrounding lowlands (Hewitt 1976). This is because of greater population density, especially where cities are located in close proximity to the mountains. It has long been known that it is safer to be out in the open than in or near buildings during an earthquake (Lomnitz 1970). The almost unbelievable toll of 830,000 deaths in the great Chinese earthquakes of 1556 in Shensi province (Table 10.3) was due to a very dense population living in hillside caves cut into *loess* (windblown silt deposits). The earthquake took place at 5:00 A.M., while the inhabitants were sleeping; the caves collapsed, creating instant graves (Bolt et al. 1975, p. 19).

The environmental hazards of earthquakes are those of ground-shaking, fault rupture, the creation of *tsunamis* (tidal waves), and the dislodgment of landslides, mudflows, and avalanches. Secondary effects include falling debris from buildings and the ignition of fires caused by the disruption of fuel and electrical systems. The discussion here will be limited to ground-shaking and fault rupture—tsunamis do not affect mountains, and landslides and the other features of mass-wasting were discussed earlier (pp. 192–203).

Ground-Shaking. I will always remember my first encounter with an earthquake. It was in 1959 in the Talkeetna Mountains of Alaska.

Table 10.3. *Some of the world's most disastrous earthquakes* (*from Hill 1965, p. 58, and* Earthquake Information Bulletin, *1970–1979*).

Year	Place	Deaths (rounded estimate)
856	Corinth, Greece	45,000
1038	Shemisi, China	23,000
1057	Chihli, China	25,000
1170	Sicily	15,000
1268	Silicia, Asia Minor	60,000
1290	Chihli, China	100,000
1293	Kamakura, Japan	30,000
1456	Naples, Italy	60,000
1531	Lisbon, Portugal	30,000
1556	Shenshi, China	830,000
1667	Shemaka, Caucasia	80,000
1693	Catania, Italy	60,000
1693	Naples, Italy	93,000
1731	Peking, China	100,000
1737	Calcutta, India	300,000
1755	Northern Persia	40,000
1783	Calabria, Italy	50,000
1797	Quito, Ecuador	41,000
1822	Aleppo, Asia Minor	22,000
1828	Echigo (Honshu) Japan	30,000
1847	Zenkoji, Japan	34,000
1868	Peru and Ecuador	25,000
1875	Venezuela and Colombia	16,000
1896	Sanriku, Japan	27,000
1898	Japan	22,000
1906	Valparaiso, Chile	1,500
1906	San Francisco, California	500
1907	Kingston, Jamaica	1,400
1908	Messina, Italy	160,000
1915	Avezzano, Italy	30,000
1920	Kansu, China	180,000
1923	Tokyo, Japan	143,000
1930	Apennine Mountains, Italy	1,500
1932	Kansu, China	70,000
1935	Quetta, Baluchistan (Pakistan)	60,000
1939	Chile	30,000
1939	Erzincan, Turkey	40,000
1948	Fuki, Japan	5,000
1949	Ecuador	6,000
1950	Assam, India	1,500
1954	Northern Algeria	1,600
1956	Kabul, Afghanistan	2,000
1957	Northern Iran	2,500
1960	Southern Chile	5,700
1960	Agadir, Morocco	12,000
1962	Northwestern Iran	12,000
1964	Anchorage, Alaska	100
1966	Eastern Turkey	2,500
1970	Chimbote, Peru	66,000
1971	San Fernando, California	65
1972	Managua, Nicaragua	5,000
1974	West Pakistan	5,200
1975	Eastern Turkey	2,400
1976	Guatemala	23,000
1976	Northeast Italy	1,000

Table 10.3. *Continued*

Year	Place	Deaths (rounded estimate)
1976	Western New Guinea	9,000
1976	Northeast China	Many thousands (probably greatest death toll in last 400 years and second greatest in recorded history)
1976	Mindanao, Philippines	5,000
1976	Northwest Iran	5,000
1977	Bucharest, Romania	1,500
1978	Northeast Iran	15,000
1979	Northeast Iran	200
1979	Southern Yugoslavia	121

I had camped in a narrow glacial valley rimmed by high rocky slopes. The weather was bad; visibility had been zero for several days and I was almost constantly confined to my tent. On this day I was suddenly awakened before dawn by the violent shaking of the ground under me. My first thought was of falling rocks or landslides; my second was a feeling of complete helplessness—there was nothing I could do. I suspect that the reaction of helplessness and awe at the violence and energy being released is fairly common among persons caught in an earthquake.

The shaking during earthquakes is caused by seismic waves created by the sudden displacement of the earth along a fault. This displacement may result in both vertical and horizontal movement of the ground, with intense vibrations. Shaking of the ground is the single greatest hazard associated with earthquakes. The major danger in heavily populated areas, however, comes from debris falling from damaged buildings; those constructed from rigid and unreinforced material such as concrete, masonry, or adobe are particularly susceptible to earthquake damage. Wooden structures have the greatest resiliency. In Chile and Peru, where earthquakes have taken such a devastating toll in recent years, the typical house has a tile roof and adobe block walls veneered with plaster. Similarly, houses in Iran are of adobe mud with domed roofs, while in northern Turkey the roofs are commonly overlaid with large rocks to prevent wind damage. Such structures are very likely to collapse with heavy ground-shaking. In more developed areas, like California, the greatest loss of life has been associated with the failure and collapse of unreinforced masonry structures. California has enacted strict building codes in recent years, however, and is beginning to alleviate many of these risks (Cal. Div. Mines and Geol. 1973).

Earthquake vibrations can increase the shear stress and pore pressure between particles in unconsolidated or saturated sediments (especially in recently deposited or back-filled areas composed of fine sand), so that the material behaves like a dense fluid. When this happens on slopes, landslides or mudflows are apt to occur. This process was responsible for the destruction of many expensive homes in Anchorage during the 1964 Alaska earthquake (Hansen and Eckel 1966). Similarly, during the 1971 San Fernando, California, earthquake, "liquidification" of the earth in the San Fernando Dam caused several small landslides in that structure (although the dam held and was repaired). If the liquified material is located on level land, buildings may sink or tilt into the earth as if they were in quicksand. This happened during the 1964 earthquake in Niigata, Japan, in which over 13,000 houses and buildings were damaged or destroyed (Bolt et al. 1975, p. 37).

Fault Rupture. Perhaps the most striking of all earthquake phenomena, although it is generally less important as an environmental hazard than ground-shaking, is that of breakage, rupture, and displacement of the earth's surface along fault zones. Any structure located on or near an active fault is vulnerable to disruption. The critical factors are the kind of fault involved and the intensity and duration of the earthquake (Fig. 3.19). In some cases the damage may be restricted to within a few meters of the rupture zone; in others the effects may be widespread. Most earthquake movements in California displace the ground sideways (slip-strike). As much as 6 m (20 ft.) of horizontal displacement occurred along the San Andreas Fault during the 1906 San Francisco earthquake. Thrust-faulting and vertical displacement have also occurred, however, as the east face of California's Sierra Nevada magnificently attests (Fig. 3.20). In fact, during the 1971 San Fernando earthquake thrust-faulting dominated, and ground disruption from this source caused more structural damage than did the shaking. Seismological studies made afterward indicate that the thrusting uplifted and moved the San Gabriel Mountains southward into the San Fernando valley by as much as 2 m (6.6 ft.) (Bolt et al. 1975, p. 40).

The most spectacular display of surface deformation in modern history took place during the 1964 Alaska earthquake. Vertical displacements of up to 11 m (36 ft.) occurred along 1,000 km (600 mi.) of the Alaska coast adjacent to the Kenai, Chugach, and Wrangell mountains. Curiously, the coastal region was uplifted while the mountains appear to have subsided about 2 m (6.6 ft.) (Plafker 1965).

The central fact to remember about fault zones is that they are, by their very nature,

areas of stress where fracturing and displacement take place. This is usually not simply a one-time occurrence but a continuing process caused by the operation of more fundamental mechanisms, i.e., plate movement and mountain-building. Stresses and strains that build within the earth must eventually be released, and this release generally takes place along fault zones. In California, for example, studies of strain build-up along the San Andreas Fault indicate that relative movement takes place at the rate of 3.2 cm (1.3 in.) per year (Bolt et al. 1975, p. 24). It is critical, therefore, to know the location of faults, the prime sites for continued movement. This is especially true when active faults pass through heavily populated areas or across dams or utility conduits carrying water, gas, and electricity.

In many areas, population growth and demand for land have brought about development on or near active fault zones with little concern for the potential hazards. California has been one of the worst offenders in this regard. In some cases urban sprawl and housing developments have extended directly onto active faults. In other circumstances, the local setting may be such that development has historically taken place near active faults. Salt Lake City, Utah, is a classic example. When the Mormon pioneers first settled this area they located near the base of the Wasatch Mountains, where they found adequate level, fertile land, with streams issuing out of the mountains to provide water for irrigation. It was the most attractive and desirable place to live in the region (Fig. 10.19). The fact that the settlement was located virtually on top of one of the most active faults in North America was beside the point. The earthquake hazard was soon realized, but the advantages of living there outweighed the disadvantages. The same could be said today: there are now over one million people living along the Wasatch Front, and the environmental hazards from earthquakes and related phenomena along this zone have never been

Fig. 10.19. The Wasatch Mountains rise abruptly along a fault scarp and provide a spectacular backdrop for Salt Lake City, Utah. View is toward the southeast. (Hal Rumel)

greater (Cook 1972). With increasing demand for land, people are moving up the slopes of the Wasatch, building on and near faults and in places subject to landslides, mudflows, snow avalanches, and flash floods (Utah Geol. Assoc. 1972; Henrie and Ridd 1977).

The beneficial aspects of earthquakes are fewer than those of volcanoes, but seismic activity does provide some benefits for man. Earthquakes are fundamentally related to

the creation of initial relief and mountain-building, with all its ramifications. In addition, the vertical displacement of rock along fault zones exposes the rock, providing a view of what lies underground. This is particularly useful for the discovery and extraction of mineral deposits. The Rift Valley of East Africa consists of a series of blocks which have dropped down, creating a deep and steep walled valley (graben). It was in the cliffs of this valley, the Olduvai Gorge, that the famous anthropologists Louis and Mary Leakey discovered what appears to be the oldest evidence of early man that has yet been found. The area was buried by lava flows and volcanic debris; these preserved the remains until they were re-exposed by subsequent faulting after several million years of interment.

Mineral Deposits

Mountains are the loci of many of the world's mineral deposits. Every major industrial country must either have mineral deposits within its borders or have access to them through some other means. The highly sporadic distribution of mineral deposits, however, has led to unequal development, often involving unrest and aggression. Those who control the minerals control the power. Consequently, the distribution of mountains, both past and present, takes on considerable importance in the economic development of countries and in international affairs.

Since prehistoric times, such metals as gold, silver, copper, and iron have been indispensable to technology and to expressions of art, religion, and economic status. Ore deposits have often been the coveted spoils of war. The search for minerals has stimulated exploration and development of unknown regions. Such searches in mountain terrain had much to do with the opening of the American West. Colorado, California, and Alaska owe much of their early development to this activity; mining was followed by frontier settlement and the need for better transportation facilities. In many cases, roads or railroads were constructed into or across mountain regions primarily to extract mineral deposits. The narrow-gauge railways across the White Pass from Skagway, Alaska, to Whitehorse, Yukon Territory, and into the San Juan Mountains, Colorado, are examples.

The occurrence of mineral deposits creates a node of economic activity, trans-portation, and population growth. There is a two-way flow of merchandise, and economic benefits accrue both to the mountain region and to the hinterlands. Mining may be more exploitative than developmental, but generally the benefits provided by minerals far overshadow locally negative circumstances, and the demand for new sources is ever-increasing.

The origin of metalliferous ores is complex. Considerable controversy exists as to the processes involved, but their close association with igneous activity and mountain-building has long been recognized (Spurr 1923). Mineral deposits are found in all of the major mountain ranges of the world. In some cases they are associated with the thick accumulations of sedimentary rocks that have been uplifted and deformed into fold mountains; in others they are located near volcanic peaks or in conjunction with fault-block mountains. The fundamental requirement in all cases is the presence of great heat and pressure to create and localize the deposits. Their genetic relationship in this respect is often proven by the presence of radial zones outward from the area of most intense heat. Predictable types of ores are found nearest the center—usually an igneous contact zone—and other minerals are located in halos surrounding the core area. Even in regions where mountains do not now exist, mineral deposits can often be explained as occurring in association with the roots of ancient mountains that have been eroded away. Good examples of this are around Lake Superior and in Newfoundland and Labrador.

Metalliferous ores are associated with mountains in time as well as in space. Minerals are created during periods of major mountain-building. Thus, the Precambrian geologic era (700 million years ago or more) is characterized by widespread deposits of iron, copper, zinc, gold, silver, and other metals. Most of these mountains are so ancient that they have been destroyed by erosion, leaving only their roots to testify to their former existence. They coincide very nearly with the continental shields (Fig. 3.1). Another notable metallogenic era was during the late Mesozoic or early Tertiary (100 million years ago), when great igneous intrusions occurred in the Rocky Mountains and along the Pacific Coast from Mexico to Alaska, as well as in Siberia and southeast Asia. The last major mountain-building epoch occurred during the late Tertiary (30 million years ago), when vast mineral deposits were again created. Most of today's spectacular ranges—the Himalayas, Alps, Andes, and Cascades–Sierra Nevada—were built at this time. Igneous intrusions associated with these ranges produced rich deposits of copper, silver, gold, molybdenum, and other metals (Bateman 1951, p. 34).

The theory of plate tectonics offers new ideas about the formation and location of mineral deposits. Although not confirmed in detail, we are discovering that the origin of many of the world's mineral deposits are closely associated with plate tectonics (Sawkins 1972; Rona 1973; Hammond 1975;

Strong 1976; Wright 1977). Minerals are created along convergent plate boundaries when two adjacent plates move toward each other, collide, and result in uplift and deformation of crustal material as one plate descends under the other (Fig. 10.20). Convergent plate boundaries are the loci of molten rock, hot metal-bearing liquids, and gases created by the heat and pressure of plate consumption in the subduction zone (Figs. 3.7, 3.9). The major mineral deposits resulting from these processes include gold, silver, copper, lead, zinc, and iron (Fig. 10.21).

Minerals are also formed at divergent plate boundaries, that is, where two plates are pulling apart, disrupting the surface and allowing the emplacement of molten material from depth (Fig. 3.7). Metallic minerals are created at the mid-ocean ridges or in rift zones such as the Red Sea. Iron, manganese, copper, lead, zinc, and other metals are produced through the interaction of seawater with the molten material and gases being emitted by the volcanic process. In addition, high concentrations of numerous

Fig. 10.20. The creation of mineral deposits at plate boundaries through subduction, melting of oceanic crust, and recombination into minerals. The mountains on the right (with mineral sequence noted above) are analogous to the Andes; those on the left are representative of an island arc like Japan. Mineral formation is associated with both situations, as well as with the mid-ocean ridge where two plates are diverging. (Adapted from Rona 1973, p. 94, and Hammond 1975, p. 779)

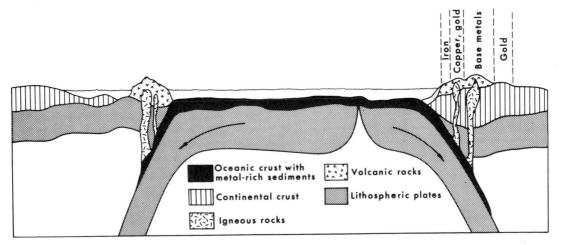

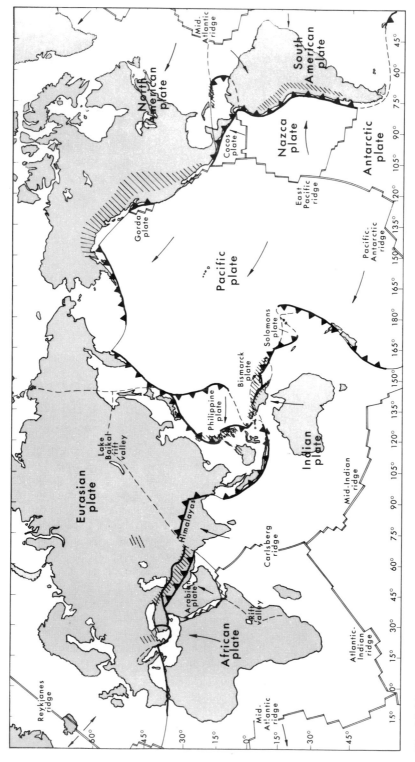

Fig. 10.21. Distribution of porphyry copper (usually low-grade and associated with igneous intrusions, as compared to sedimentary copper deposits). The rela-tionship between the occurrence of this mineral (diag-onal lines), plate tectonics, and mountain-building is evident from map. (After Sillitoe 1972, p. 187)

minerals are found in hot brine pools in the Red Sea. Although these are presently underwater and therefore not accessible, in at least one case a portion of oceanic crust, formed at a divergent plate boundary, has been uplifted and exposed at the earth's surface. This is the Troodos Massif on Cyprus in the Mediterranean, an island that has long been famous for its copper. Mining was an important industry there in Roman and Phoenician times. These ore bodies are now thought to provide the first firm evidence of the kinds of mineral deposits to be expected in sea-floor rocks generated from mid-oceanic ridges along divergent plate boundaries (Moores and Vine 1971).

The origins of ore deposits located in the stable interiors of continents are more problematic. In some cases they may be attributable to ancient plate boundaries where mountains were once created but have long since been destroyed by erosion. Old mountain ranges such as the Appalachians or Urals, which have been considerably subdued by erosion, represent intermediate stages in this process. In other cases, such as

the nickel deposits near Sudbury, Ontario, or the platinum deposits of Bushveld, South Africa, ore formation is associated with igneous intrusions emplaced in the center of plates. The exact connection with plate tectonics, however, is unclear. They may be related to the "hot spots" within the earth causing the local mobilization of crustal rock and the creation of metallic ores (Hammond 1975, p. 781). In still other cases, such as the lead-zinc deposits of the Mississippi Valley which occur primarily in sedimentary rocks, no connections have yet been found between their formation and plate tectonics (Sawkins 1972). Nevertheless, in much the same way that discovery of the connection between oil and anticlines greatly expedited the search for petroleum, the recognition that many ore deposits are directly related to the origin of mountains and to plate tectonics opens up vast prospects for the discovery of new minerals (Rona 1973). We now know where to begin looking for mineral deposits hidden far below the surface. The cry will no longer be "There's gold in them thar hills," but "There's gold *under* them thar hills."

Along their track lay the villages of the hill-folk—mud and earth huts, timbers now and then rudely carved with an axe—clinging like swallows' nests against the steeps.

Rudyard Kipling, *Kim* (1919)

Agricultural Settlement and Land Use

Mountains pose special problems to settlement and land use. Although the mountains of North America remain relatively unpeopled, most Old-World mountains have long supported substantial populations. The ways in which various cultures have overcome the limitations of these rugged landscapes are illuminating and provide insight into the nature of mountains themselves. Highland settlement has traditionally been based on agriculture. In some cases this may consist entirely of sedentary cultivation, while at the other extreme are nomadic folk who depend largely upon livestock and a pastoral way of life. The most prevalent condition is a combination of cultivated crops and animal husbandry. Circumstances have changed greatly in the last century, at least in the more advanced middle-latitude areas, e.g., the Alps, where there has been widespread migration to cities with a de-emphasis on mountain agriculture. Nevertheless, the basic settlement patterns remain and agricultural activities are carried out much as before, although to a lesser degree. By contrast, most tropical and subtropical mountains have continued to gain population, increasing pressure on the available land (De Planhol 1970; Eckholm 1975).

The fundamental factors affecting agricultural land use in mountains are the vertical distribution of different environments and, in extratropical areas, the different seasonal conditions at each level. The result is a stratification of resources and the need for a staggered schedule for their exploitation. One notable response is the annual movement of livestock to high pastures in spring and summer and back to the lowlands in the fall. Other aspects of middle-latitude mountain agriculture include different uses for various altitudes, e.g., cultivated fields, hay fields, and pasture lands. This allows effective scheduling of labor throughout the growing season since planting, ripening, and harvesting take place at different levels at different times. It also provides some protection against disasters or bad years, since efforts are dispersed over a variety of microenvironments.

SEDENTARY AGRICULTURE

Sedentary agriculture in mountains reaches its finest development and is most widely practiced within the tropics. Here occurs the anomaly of soils and climate at intermediate to high altitudes often being more productive and favorable for cultivation than are those in the lowlands. In addition, the higher elevations are healthier places to live; malaria and other infectious diseases are less common there than in the lowlands. As a result, highland areas in the humid tropics characteristically support denser populations than do the lowlands. Weather conditions at any given altitude are much the same throughout the year, so there is no reason for the migration or movement within the system that occurs in middle-latitude mountains. Consequently, greater efforts can be applied to sedentary and intensive use of the land; this is epitomized by the terracing and irrigation

of mountain slopes. Unlike the middle latitudes, where the lowlands are the focus of intensive sedentary agriculture and mountains are characterized by comparatively sporadic land-use, the poor soils and low productivity of the humid tropical lowlands result in a land-use pattern of shifting, slash-and-burn (*swidden*) agriculture, while the predominant agricultural activities and permanent settlements are located in the uplands.

The form of agriculture in tropical mountains depends on environmental conditions and on cultural and technological history. In some cases, such as in the highlands of New Guinea, cultures are just emerging from a Stone Age technology (Brass 1941; Brookfield 1964, 1966), while elsewhere ancient agricultural landscapes reflect a relatively high level of technology. Best-known of these are the beautifully terraced mountains of the Ifugao people in northern Luzon in the Philippines and those of the Inca in the Peruvian Andes (Fig. 11.1; cf. Fig. 2.2). The similarity among these cultures is their tendency to settle within circumscribed areas and to find support through fixed agriculture. Where there are animals, they are secondary to the cultivation of crops and are usually allowed to fend for themselves (exceptions to this are found in the highlands of East Africa). Most tropical-mountain agriculture is at a subsistence level, but intensive utilization of the land supports relatively large populations. Permanent homes are typically constructed in compact agglomerations, and the people go out from the village to work the fields. Such an arrangement gives better protection from enemies, preserves the best land for cultivation, and facilitates communal activities.

One basic characteristic of tropical-highland agriculture is the year-round growth of crops (except at very high altitudes). More or less continuous cropping is essential in areas where there are no provisions for preservation or storage of food.

Fig. 11.1. Steep <u>stone-walled</u> agricultural terraces near Banaue, northern Luzon, the Philippines. These are irrigated terraces used for growing rice and some taro. Sweet potatoes are cultivated in less permanent clearings on the higher slopes. Villages may be seen in middle and upper left of photo. (Harold C. Conklin, Yale University)

Of course, different crops have different requirements, growing better at one level than at another. In most areas, settlement concentrates in the middle highlands (*tierra templada*), where the moderate temperatures and precipitation permit a variety of crops (Townsend 1926). Crop variety is important, since it allows alternate food sources in case of disease, drought, or other disasters (Gade 1969). Accordingly, most mountain peoples have incorporated a number of different crops into their economies, although emphasis is usually placed on one or two main crops. Throughout much of southeast Asia and Indonesia, for example, the chief crop is rice; in the Ethiopian highlands the emphasis is on other cereals and pulses, and in the Andes it is on tubers, especially the potato.

Where people rely on a restricted diet, the ecological requirements of the crop can impose limits on human settlement. The people of the highlands of New Guinea, for example, depend almost completely on the sweet potato (*Ipomoea batatas*). Over 100 language groups occupy the high altitudes of this region, with population densities reaching 500–1,300 people per square km (200–500 per sq. mi.). This is in great contrast to the sparsely populated lowlands. These highland people practice a primitive hoe culture and support themselves through intensive cultivation, using a system of active and fallow plots. Fences around the plots keep out the pigs, which are otherwise allowed to roam free. In the easily accessible areas a cash crop, coffee, has recently been introduced, resulting in a money economy (Brookfield 1966; Hayano 1973); nevertheless, in most areas the sweet potato is still the staple, accounting for 90 percent of the food consumed. The dependence on a single crop and the absence of food storage mean that food is normally harvested the day it is to be consumed. It is obvious, therefore, that conditions for the growth of this crop must be continuously favorable; disruption of production would result in hardships and possible starvation (Brown and Powell 1974; Waddel 1975).

The sweet potato apparently originated in the Andes of South America and was brought to southeast Asia either by Polynesian voyagers or by Spaniards (Yen 1974). It can grow in a variety of conditions in New Guinea, from sea level to 3,000 m (10,000 ft.). Ideal conditions for its production, however, are found in middle altitudes, and this is mirrored by a pattern of settlement sharply delimited in a zone between 1,800–2,700 m (6,000–9,000 ft.) (Fig. 11.2). The danger of frost, the presence of cloud forests, and excessive moisture establish the upper limits of settlement. The lower limits are set by the presence of malaria (against which the highland people have little immunity), warfare with lowland tribes, soils made nonproductive by past cultivation and burning, and occasional drought (Brookfield 1964, p. 34). To insure an unfailing supply of their single crop, these people have come to restrict themselves to a narrow spectrum of the landscape.

This pattern of land use contrasts with that found in most tropical mountains. For example, the mountains of northern Luzon in the Philippines support a much higher total population than that of New Guinea, and the people employ a broader range of habitats, involving both irrigated and dryland rice and a variety of other crops (Scott 1958). In the Ethiopian highlands, crops are grown from the lowlands up to the limit of agriculture—3,600 m (12,000 ft.). Sorghum and maize are the main crops below 1,500 m (5,000 ft.); wheat, barley, peas, beans, lentils, and the tiny seeded grass *t'eff* are grown at intermediate altitudes. Above 3,300 m (11,000 ft.), wheat, barley, rye, and flax are cultivated (Simoons 1960, p. 66). A similar range of environments is under cultivation in the Andes of Colombia and Peru, from the arid margins of the Atacama Desert within 660 m (2,000 ft.) of sea level to the cold heights above 3,600 m (12,000 ft.) (Dillehay 1979). Principal crops include maize,

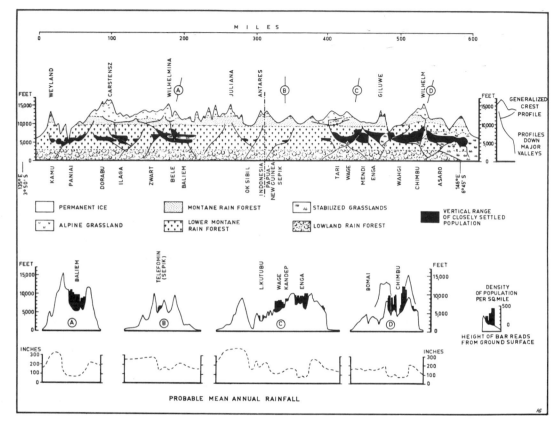

Fig. 11.2. The distribution of vegetation, precipitation, and population in the highlands of New Guinea. Note the confined location of the densely populated areas—between 1,500–3,000 m (5,000–10,000 ft.) in the lower montane rainforest, mainly in higher valleys receiving somewhat lower amounts of rainfall. The people have settled here because sweet potatoes, on which they depend for 90 percent of their food, grow best under these conditions. (From Brookfield 1964, p. 23)

manioc, wheat, barley, rye, and a variety of tubers (Gade 1975; Mitchell 1976).

Traditional farmers in tropical highlands have generally shown a sensitivity to soil erosion and soil fertility. They have piled stones and logs along the contour, dug furrows, built fences, planted and preserved trees, and otherwise attempted to prevent erosion and to distribute water along slopes. They have improved crop lands with animal fertilizers and mulch. Permanent cropping and conservation techniques like these represent an advanced stage in land use and are generally thought to have evolved from shifting, slash-and-burn agriculture once

the population became too great to support itself through this method (Boserup 1965). Some disagreement exists on this point: it is argued that the lowlands have a low carrying capacity and it was only in the highlands that intensive agricultural techniques were appropriate or effective (Street 1969; Turner 1977). In any case, permanent cropping in the mountains required its own technology and attitudes toward the land: farmers could not let the soil lie fallow for long periods, as they had done in the lowlands. The soil now had to support intensive agriculture in order to feed large numbers of people on a sustained basis. This required new land-use tactics, especially for the prevention of erosion and the continued maintenance of productivity. As a result, many high-altitude agricultural areas have long supported relatively large populations while at the same time maintaining their productivity. The unprecedentedly severe erosion that now afflicts agricultural land in many mountain regions is a consequence both of rapidly increasing populations and of the abandonment of traditional patterns of use (Eckholm 1975).

The most elaborate and intensive use of mountain slopes involves terracing. Terraces have been constructed in almost all Old-World mountains, although they vary greatly in their dimensions, their distribution, their purpose, and the methods and quality of their construction. The terraces may simply consist of shallow corrugations along the contour, or they may involve construction of elaborate stone walls several meters high, carefully engineered to support broad, level areas on their treads. They may cover entire slopes, adhering to the mountainsides and fitting into the topography like giant stairways (Fig. 11.1). In some cases they have been built primarily to allow irrigation, in others chiefly to prevent erosion or to create more usable level land; in the end, all these functions are served to a certain extent (Cook 1916; Perry 1916; Lewis 1953; Beyer 1955; Swanson 1955; Spencer and Hale 1961). Terracing can also take advantage of and improve microclimates; slopes facing the sun are preferred, and the terraced levels receive the sun at a higher angle than the unterraced slopes and thus have warmer soil. Thanks to the moderating effect of water on low temperatures, irrigated fields commonly go up to higher elevations than do dry fields. Thus, terracing vastly improves productivity by transforming steep slopes into segmented level areas that can be irrigated, fertilized, cultivated, and maintained on a sustained basis.

The origin of terracing is uncertain. Some believe that it is simply a logical adaptation to local terrain, and therefore originated in many places; others consider it to have started in one or two main centers, perhaps the Near East or China, and then to have spread outward (Spencer and Hale 1961). Whatever its origin, the construction and maintenance of terraces take great time, effort, and expertise. If constructed of stones, these must be transported to the proper location; and, if the terrace is to be used soon, soil must be brought in to fill the reservoir created by the terrace wall. Often people must carry these materials on their backs up from the valley. The enterprise has aptly been called "desperate agriculture" (Semple 1911, p. 569). Such great investments of energy are only recaptured through careful, intensive, and long-term use of the land, and, indeed, terraces in some areas have been in use for millennia with no diminution in their productivity. The best-developed terraces are those in tropical mountains, because it is here that large populations have settled in fixed areas and have supported themselves through sedentary agriculture.

The building of terraces, and particularly the distribution of irrigation water, requires a high degree of cooperation and organization. Some scholars have felt that these techniques are themselves important instruments in social and political evolution (Steward 1955; Wittfogel 1955). It is certainly true that many traditional societies which practice terracing and irrigation display a high level of technology and an advanced social order and political structure. Examples that come immediately to mind include the Inca of South America, the Igorots of Northern Luzon, the Hunza in the Himalayas, and many cultures of the Orient, especially in Japan and in the mountains of Szechuan, China (Fig. 11.3).

It is instructive to look more closely at an example of terracing and irrigation as a method of land use in tropical mountains. In the district of Quinua in the central Peruvian highlands at 13° S. latitude, there is a dis-

Fig. 11.3. Artist's view of a rural Japanese landscape (circa 1800), with its many cultivated terraces. Fujiyama is visible in middle background. (From Hokusai, *The Thirty-Six Views of Mt. Fuji*)

tinct wet and dry season, while desert conditions exist in the coastal lowlands. The various ecological zones and their uses are shown in Table 11.1. Cultivation occurs from 2,500 to 4,100 m (8,250–13,500 ft.), with the most productive zone from 2,850 to 3,400 m (9,300–11,200 ft.). The amount of irrigation water is limited but its judicious use results in a remarkably high level of productivity from this terrain.

Interestingly, irrigation is used in different ways at high and low altitudes, and its net effect is to double the usable area for certain crops. In the drier, lower reaches of the district, dry-season crops are restricted to the upper slopes near the source of the irrigation system, since areas farther down lose too much water to evaporation and seepage (Mitchell 1976, p. 33). The main

period of cultivation in the lower regions is during the wet season. Irrigation water is used at this time only in the lower two more arid zones, since the upper areas do well without it.

Irrigation at the higher levels is used primarily at the beginning of the planting season in order to extend the growing period, since it takes crops longer to mature at higher altitudes. Wheat, barley, potatoes, and other tubers can grow fairly well without added water but maize, beans, and squash require the extra time that early germination provides. Irrigation at the higher levels also expedites drainage of areas which would normally remain waterlogged and rot the plant roots. According to local farmers, drainage of these areas is the single most important function of this irrigation system (Mitchell 1976, p. 34). It can be seen, therefore, that water is made available to successive levels at different times for different purposes, with the result that each zone benefits and more land can be cultivated (Mitchell 1976, p. 35).

In order to make such systems work, however, the terraces must be maintained efficiently and the irrigation channels must be kept clean. This is achieved only through cooperative community efforts. Generally, each family is responsible for a certain segment and contributes a given amount of labor to these activities. If a person does not do his share, he is assessed accordingly so that somebody else can be paid to do the work. If a person refuses to pay the fine, he is denied use of irrigation water. Other problems that arise, such as people using water out of turn or diverting more water than their share, are dealt with individually

(by arguments and fights), as well as at the community level. Various cultures have different methods of dealing with such problems but some kind of political structure and authority is necessary, or the entire system would break down (Bacdayan 1974; Mitchell 1976). For this reason, traditional societies which depend on terracing and irrigation typically display a fairly high level of organization and political structure.

An integral part of the continuity and maintenance of most intensive agricultural systems is an arrangement for the transfer of land down through the family. Because the amount of the more productive land is limited and can support only a limited number of people, fields are usually passed on to the oldest son or daughter, while younger children may or may not receive land, depending upon how wealthy the parents are. Each child must be given enough

Table 11.1 *Altitudinal (ecological) zones in the Quinua district of the central Peruvian highlands, 13° S. lat. (Mitchell 1976, p. 30).*

Ecological Zone	Elevation (m)	General Characteristics	Irrigation Use	Climate
Alpine tundra and subalpine páramo	4,100+	High puna grasslands; grazing	Source of irrigation water	Cold, moist, cloudy
Montane prairie	4,000–4,100	Grassland; grazing and tuber cultivation	Source of irrigation water	
Montane moist forest	3,400–4,000	Dense underbrush of small trees and shrubs	Beginning of irrigation canals	
		Cultivation of tubers and frost-resistant, quick-maturing crops		
Lower montane savannah	2,850–3,400	Town of Quinua and major population zone; manor cultivation zone	Zone of irrigated fields	
Lower montane	2,500–2,850	Xerophytic vegetation; non-irrigated cultivation of short-growth plants with low water needs	Valley-bottom irrigation	Warm, dry, sunny

land to support himself and his family; anything less would be self-defeating. Consequently, if no land is left by the time it is the younger children's turn, they must move elsewhere. In this way the population is maintained at a level that the land can support under a given level of technology. Some such system exists in almost all tropical areas of intense mountain agriculture (Drucker 1977).

More exclusive systems exist in middle-latitude mountains, where the land's ability to support population is considerably more limited. In some areas of the Alps, for example, land can be inherited only by a single male heir, usually the oldest son; all other children must eventually leave (Burns 1963). Again, the rationale is that an equal distribution of land among all the heirs (partible inheritance) would result in such small parcels of land for each that no one would be able to support his family on a sustained basis. This would ultimately lead to disaster. Partible inheritance for all heirs is practiced in other areas of the Alps (especially the western part) but even here there are built-in mechanisms for limiting the degree of fragmentation (Wolf 1970; Weinberg 1972, 1975). It can be seen, therefore, that controlling the method of inheritance and land transmission is fundamental to the maintenance of a traditional agricultural system in mountains.

PASTORALISM

Little grazing of livestock generally takes place in tropical mountains, but it becomes increasingly prevalent in middle and high latitudes, where agriculture becomes more and more difficult at high elevations. Grazing serves as an indirect method of cropping marginal environments. Pastoralism has traditionally utilized mountain areas that would otherwise go unused.

There are three approaches to the use of mountain landscapes through grazing of livestock: nomadic pastoralism, transhumance, and mixed grazing and farming. All are found primarily in middle and high latitudes and are cultural adaptations to the annual cycle and the seasonal changes in mountain and lowland grasslands. Nomadic pastoralism is a highly fluid way of life in which small bands of people and their animals have no permanent home base but simply migrate between winter and summer pastures. Transhumance also requires migration between winter and summer pastures, but most of the community stays in permanent settlements and raises crops while shepherds or a few families accompany the animals to the high pastures some distance away. The last approach, that of mixed grazing and farming, is still more localized: vertical migrations of livestock within the same valley or mountain slope are an adjunct to cultivation. Between these major types, of course, is found every transitional form.

Various versions of pastoral and cultivation systems can exist side by side—even within a single valley system—since one type seldom exploits all the habitats; each approach occupies its own ecological niche. In the major longitudinal valleys of the western Himalayas, several different cultural groups have developed distinct strategies to accommodate the contrasting environments with altitude (Barth 1956; Uhlig 1969). For example, in the Swat Valley of North Pakistan, located just east of the famous Khyber Pass, the Swat River rises among 5,500 m (18,000 ft.) peaks in the Hindu Kush and flows southward through the Swat Valley, which gradually widens in its lower reaches until by 1,500 m (5,000 ft.) it consists of broad alluvial flats. This lower area is occupied by sedentary agriculturalists who depend upon irrigation and plowing of the land. Principal crops include wheat, maize, and rice. These agriculturalists have settled the valley only up to the elevation where they can raise two crops per year, however. Their economic and social systems include profuse political and social activities which divert manpower from agricultural pursuits, and they need the surplus that two crops per year gives them in order to engage in these extra-agricultural activities.

Directly above this group in the valley is another group of agriculturalists. In these more marginal areas, the slopes have been terraced and irrigated. The climate allows only one crop per year. Principal crops include maize and millet, although wheat and rice are grown in a few of the lower areas. Here the political-social system puts all available manpower into subsistence activities. In addition to intensive cultivation of the slopes, this group practices transhumance. Sheep, goats, cattle, and water buffalo are kept for wool, meat, and milk. The herds are taken up to summer pastures at 4,200 m (14,000 ft.) and in some cases the whole population goes along, passing through a series of seasonal camps. The fields are planted and then left with only a small contingent to watch over them. By having two strings to their bow, they are able to wrest a satisfactory living from the higher and less productive environment (Barth 1956, p. 1082).

The last group occupying the valley consists of a floating population of nomadic pastoralists. These herdsmen depend primarily upon their livestock, although they acquire some grain and necessities through trade with the other groups. In the lowest region they are allowed to graze their livestock on surrounding hills which the sedentary agriculturalists use only for gathering firewood. The nomadic pastoralists are charged a small grazing fee and are tolerated because they provide milk, meat, and other animal products (including manure) necessary to the village economy. They also serve as caretakers for village animals and as laborers during the peak agricultural season (Barth 1956, p. 1083). There is less interdependence between the nomads and the transhumants of the higher valleys, but the basic pattern is similar. The nomads are tol-

erated in this area because they use different pastures. Here, then, is a case of three traditional groups of people practicing different ways of life within the same valley system, whose approaches to using the land have insured that each exploits a different ecological niche: the result is a fairly complete utilization of the available resources. Let us now look more closely at the different forms of pastoralism in mountains.

Nomadic Pastoralism

Nomadic pastoralism is largely a phenomenon of arid and semiarid regions. Small groups of people and animals make use of large areas of land which have a low carrying capacity. A fair proportion of the earth's population has practiced this way of life; until recently nomadic pastoralists numbered five million (or about 10 percent of the population) in southwest Asia alone (Barth 1960a, p. 341). Each year, the nomads migrate to high altitudes during spring and early summer, after the snow has melted and relatively lush grasses develop in the mountains, while the lowland grasses are withering in the extreme dry heat. When winter approaches in the high country, autumn rains and clouds turn the lowland grasses green, and the nomads and their animals return to the low country. It is this seasonal rhythm and complementarity of conditions between high and low-altitude grasslands that provides the ecologic basis for nomadic pastoralism. It should be stressed, however, that nomadism is a cultural decision, not one forced on the people by conditions of the environment. Other approaches may be equally successful, as is demonstrated by the many groups that support themselves through sedentary agriculture in the same areas used by the nomads. If one looks to history this fact becomes even more striking. For example, before the twelfth century A.D., Iran, Anatolia, and much of Afghanistan supported an ancient population of sedentary agriculturalists. It was only after the Turkish-

Mongolian invasions of the Middle Ages, when the land was ravaged and a nomadic way of life forced on the sedentary inhabitants, that nomadism became important in these areas (De Planhol 1966).

This is not to deny that nomadic pastoralism is a solidly based ecologic and economic endeavor taking advantage of mountain areas that might not otherwise be used. Nomadic pastoralism is found primarily in the Old World but it has also long been practiced in the Andes with llamas and alpacas (Murra 1965; Webster 1973; Browman 1974). Sheep, goats, and cattle are the animals most commonly herded in the Old World although in some areas camels, reindeer, horses, and yaks are also kept. Principal areas of nomadic pastoralism include the highlands of East Africa, the Atlas Mountains of North Africa, the Balkans in the Mediterranean, the Zagros, the Central Afghan massif and the western Himalayas in southwest Asia, and the Pamirs, Tien Shan, and Altai mountains of central Asia (Arbos 1923; Krader 1955; Kaushic 1959; Barth 1960a, b, 1961; Bose 1960; Jacobs 1965; Downs and Ekvall 1965; Ekvall 1968). Pastoralism is not generally found in China or Japan, owing to the traditional emphasis on intensive cultivation and the Buddhists' reluctance to exploit animals.

The people who practice nomadism are generally ethnically and culturally distinct from those who practice sedentary agriculture. This is especially true in Asia, where nomadism as a way of life has been passed down from parent to child for centuries. The family is the unit of social organization and the group remains relatively isolated from other people, since it is constantly on the move. The contrast in life style between herder and farmer often leads to conflicts, but their interdependence also makes for close relationships. The nomadic herds provide milk, meat, wool, and skins, which are used either directly or are traded for other necessities. Wheat, rather than meat or milk, is the staple food for most nomads

in southwest Asia, and they get it by trading with sedentary agriculturalists. In turn, the farmers receive animal products as well as indirect benefits like manure for fertilizer and abundant labor at certain times of the year (Barth 1960a). There is a similar heavy dependence upon trade and reciprocity among herders and farmers in the Andes. While milk and blood are both important foods throughout the Old World, neither is used by the Andeans. They make up for the absence of these nutritious foods in their diets by eating vegetable products, especially tubers, which they get in trade (Webster 1973, p. 117). The reindeer herders of the sub-Arctic and the classic nomadic cultures of central Asia, however, do depend almost entirely on the products of their animals (Krader 1955).

The distance between the nomads' winter and summer pastures vary greatly from region to region. In the Himalayas and the Andes, for example, they may move only a few tens of kilometers up and down a major valley system (Barth 1956; Webster 1973). In other areas, such as Iran, the annual round trip may involve distances of over 1,000 km (600 mi.). These long migrations are necessary if the lower reaches of the mountain valleys are occupied by sedentary agriculturalists, forcing the nomads to travel farther out onto the arid lowlands for their winter grazing. Migration routes are often circuitous; the numerous side trips are an attempt to use the landscape as effectively as possible. In southwest and central Asia, nomadic groups have developed elaborate systems to coordinate their use of grazing and water resources, particularly along migration routes where grazing pressure on the land is heavier. Specific groups usually have rights to distinct regions for the summer but they must plan their migrations carefully, since one group is typically allowed use of an area for a few days, while another takes its place the following week. Such movements and rights to the land are based on both spatial and temporal factors but are probably best expressed as a schedule rather than as exclusive proprietorship (Barth 1960b).

Overgrazing and erosion are serious problems which are very difficult to control under nomadic pastoralism. They become particularly critical in exceptionally dry years or when livestock numbers swell. Nomadic herds are highly susceptible to the vicissitudes of weather and to epidemic diseases which can decimate herds within a few days and leave the herdsmen with barely enough animals to survive. As in other biological systems in mountains, this kind of boom-or-bust behavior is due to the vagaries of the elements. Unlike those who practice cultivation in conjunction with pastoralism, the nomads have nothing to fall back on for security. Consequently, herdsmen usually try to build up their herds—and unabashedly overgraze them—as insurance against such catastrophes.

Pastoral nomadism as a way of life is now passing rather quickly from the scene, a victim of increasing population pressure, technological advances, and political restrictions that make it increasingly difficult to wander at will from place to place. Population increase and settlement ended true nomadism in Europe centuries ago; in 1900 it still existed only in the Balkan Mountains of Bulgaria (Arbos 1923). Pastoral nomadism requires vast open spaces for the unrestricted movement of people and animals. The amount of land is finite, however, and has become steadily less and less available. In much of southwest Asia, nomads have traditionally had the right to draw water from public wells and irrigation channels and to graze within a reasonable distance of cultivated fields. The land is not reserved for the nomads. It is available for their use as long as it is not cultivated, but there is nothing to stop the farmer from expanding his cultivated fields and nothing to prevent the establishment of new farms. With increasing pressure on the land, such reclaiming of uncultivated land is more and more frequent and invariably occurs on the better sites

where water is available. Consequently, less land remains for the nomad, and what is available is less valuable. Even more serious, free passage between traditional pastures may be restricted or blocked. This often leads to conflicts as the nomad struggles to maintain his way of life.

A last major problem arises with governments. Nomads are transients, following an ancient way of life with little regard for state boundaries or political controls like taxation, court orders, and military conscription. Throughout history, nomads have been renowned as ruthless fighters, and their fierce resistance to limits on their freedom poses a further threat to governmental authority. On the other hand, governments have had a difficult time in providing nomads with social services such as health care and education. For these and other reasons, governments have made a concerted effort to force permanent settlement. This is reflected in a statement published in 1934: "For the unity of Persia—for the development of the spirit of solidarity and social life in the country—finally, in order that public order and stability . . . be secured, it is indispensable that one terminate—once and for all—the wandering existence of the nomadic tribes" (quoted in Stauffer 1965, p. 295).

One problem in forcing nomads to settle, under present economic conditions, is that as nomads they may actually be more prosperous than many of the sedentary farmers. Both lead essentially subsistence existences, but the nomads own their livestock and have a better diet and more money for luxuries. A cultural stigma is also associated with settlement: in many traditional societies nomadism has high status, while working the soil is considered demeaning. This is particularly true in Tibet and the Himalayas (Ekvall 1968; Palmieri 1976). Even if all these other factors were equal, a nomad who decided to settle would probably be less prosperous than he was as a nomad: lacking capital to buy a farm of his own and the agricultural skills to run it, he could only fit in at the bottom of the scale, as a day laborer (Stauffer 1965).

Nevertheless, most governments feel that nomadism is an anachronism and its abolition is essential to modernization. Although even massive efforts to force the settlement of nomads have failed (except for some under the Soviet regime), nomadism is steadily decreasing by attrition as other options become more attractive. Many experts believe that governments should relax their opposition and allow nomadic pastoralism at least on a limited basis, since it does provide a mechanism for using marginal landscapes (Krader 1959; Barth 1960a; Stauffer 1965). It is argued that nomads occupy a distinct ecological niche in these semiarid areas, and thus increase productivity and diversity—desirable attributes in a world steadily becoming more hungry and homogeneous.

Transhumance

Transhumance is based on many of the same ecological principles as nomadic pastoralism, but it also provides for the concurrent cultivation of valley fields. The bulk of the population typically remains in the permanent settlement to work the fields during summer while a small group accompanies the flocks to the mountains. This system is more productive than sole reliance on either cultivation or pastoralism would be. Consequently, transhumance as a basic land-use strategy in mountains has been much more widely adopted than pastoral nomadism; it is found throughout the Old and New Worlds, including western North and South America, New Zealand, Australia, Africa, and Eurasia (Arbos 1923; Carrier 1932; Sömme 1949; Barth 1956, 1960a; Kaushic 1959; De Planhol 1966, 1970; Matley 1968; Webster 1973; Langtvet 1974; Gómez-Ibáñez 1975, 1977; Stewart et al. 1976). China and Japan, again, are the major exceptions.

A major contrast between transhumance

and nomadic pastoralism is the nature of winter activity in the two systems. Nomadic pastoralism simply involves movement to other pastures, while in transhumance there is movement to lowland pastures but these are commonly smaller, include protective shelters, and normally require supplemental feed to carry the animals through the winter. This includes hay and grains produced in the fields while the livestock are absent in summer. The amount of feed that can be raised limits the number of livestock that can be maintained by the group (or at least this was true until the advent of modern technology and transportation). Although overgrazing on mountain pastures during summer is also limiting, this has apparently had less to do with controlling the size of the herd. Livestock which could not be maintained through the winter was traditionally sold at special fairs held several times each year, with the largest held in the fall. These also served as social occasions and were a cherished part of the pastoral way of life (Allix 1922; Valcarcel 1946). Like most other features of pastoralism, these fairs have diminished in importance with modern developments.

Perhaps the classic region for transhumance is around the Mediterranean Sea. There, winter rains and summer drought with moderate temperatures throughout the year allow winter pasturage; temperatures are moderate in the lowlands and grasses are at their prime in winter. During summer, when the grasses begin to dry, the livestock are taken to the mountains. This provides a succession of good pastures for the herds and also allows cultivation of the fields after they have been vacated. Not all fields are cultivated, but the presence of irrigation plus fertilizer from the animals insures a fairly high return from those that are tilled.

Those practicing transhumance in most areas of the world usually travel only a few tens of kilometers between winter and summer pastures, but in the Mediterranean they may go up to 300 km (180 mi.) each way. The migrations of huge flocks on their way to the mountains must have been a magnificent sight. The flocks were divided into bands of 500 to 2,000 each, led by old, large-horned billy goats carrying bells, trailed by a pack train and big dogs with spiked collars (Arbos 1923). Special trails existed as rights-of-way to the mountains. At first these were numerous and broad, but as the land became settled and cultivated, the trails shrank both in number and in size. Conflicts between the transhumants and the people across whose land they traversed became increasingly more common. In Italy, Spain, and Portugal, the transhumants were favored because of the influence of powerful sheep-owner organizations and the taxes that these countries derived from them, but in the French Alps the story was different. Here agriculture was more intensive, with a denser rural population, and legal disputes with the shepherds invariably ended in the shepherds coming out second-best. Pressure mounted against the transhumants until, by the end of the nineteenth century, the huge and colorful migrations were essentially a thing of the past. Travel was now limited to public roads and the transhumants had to purchase grazing rights from individual farmers along the way. The construction of the railroads in the mid-nineteenth century provided a timely alternative; by 1920, 80 percent of the sheep being transported from the Mediterranean to mountain pastures went by rail.

Coinciding with difficulties in moving the sheep was a growing reaction against the transhumants by conservation groups who claimed that the alpine grasslands were being severely damaged. These changing attitudes toward the land, coupled with rapid developments in agricultural technology, brought about a continuing decline in the importance of transhumance. In Spain alone the number of transhumant sheep decreased

from 3,000,000 in the sixteenth century to less than 1,400,000 at the end of the nineteenth century (Arbos 1923, p. 566). Transhumance is now only a local phenomenon. It is estimated that grazing pressure in the Pyrenees and western Alps is less than half what it was even in 1850 (Gómez-Ibáñez 1977, p. 292). More intensive cropping techniques in the lowlands, recreational facilities and summer homes in the mountains, and more intensive types of animal husbandry, especially the production of dairy cattle, have taken the place of grazing as uses of the land.

In North America, the mountains have remained relatively untouched, although transhumance has been practiced here. The practice began just when it began declining in Europe in the mid-1800s and expanded until the early 1900s, when it began to decline here, too (Fig. 11.4). Transhumance was common throughout the western mountains, many of which rise above semiarid lowlands, providing an ecological basis similar to that found elsewhere. Cattle and sheep were driven to the higher altitudes during summer and back to the lowlands during winter. A number of Basques were brought to this country from the Pyrenees to serve as shepherds in the lonely high country. Grazing during the winter initially depended on the availability of extensive lowland areas but, as the population increased, crops and fenced pastures were used to feed and contain the livestock in the lowlands. The high mountain grazing areas were largely on governmental land, and a small fee was charged for their use. By the early 1900s, however, it became apparent that the sheep and cattle were badly damaging the alpine grasslands, and the U.S. Forest Service began to impose restrictions on the number of livestock that could be grazed (Fig. 7.8). Eventually the economics of the operation began to swing in favor of year-round fenced pastures at lower elevations: it no longer paid to drive the livestock back and forth from the mountain pastures.

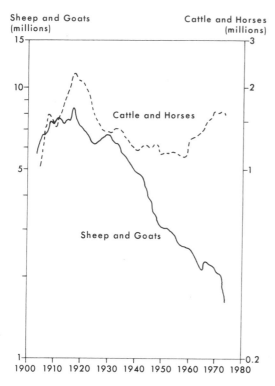

Fig. 11.4. Grazing on National Forest lands in the United States. These grazing amounts closely approximate those of transhumance, since almost all high-altitude range lands lie within the National Forests. The scale for sheep and goats is different from that of cattle and horses because cattle and horses require about five times more forage than do sheep. The disparity in decline of numbers is due to the fact that sheep are the primary users of the highest pastures, while cattle are generally grazed at lower elevations. (Adapted from Gómez-Ibáñez 1977, p. 288)

Consequently, transhumance, although still practiced in the United States, is no longer economically significant (Fig. 11.4) (Gómez-Ibáñez 1977). Variations on this theme, such as ranching in the high mountain parks, are still practiced in the Rockies and other western ranges, but these too seem destined to give way in the near future to recreation, summer homes, and other types of land use (Crowley 1975).

As with nomadic pastoralism, the decline of transhumance has been lamented by some on the grounds that the disuse of

mountain pastures eliminates valuable productivity. It is also argued that, in an increasingly energy-conscious world, transhumance is more energy-efficient than the pasture-feedlot system in which animals consume feed that has been produced at a much higher energy cost. Therefore, as energy becomes more scarce and more expensive, transhumance may again rise in importance (Gómez-Ibáñez 1977, p. 296). However, it is unlikely that the extensive use of mountainscapes for grazing will ever again be permitted in the United States, given present pressures on mountains for direct human uses as well as a pervading concern to maintain at least some mountain areas in a relatively wild and natural condition.

In Eurasia, where various forms of land use in mountains have been practiced for centuries, the continued use of transhumance depends upon historical and political factors, as well as upon population pressures and the ability of certain ecological agricultural systems to support life on a sustained basis. Current patterns of land use in mountains differ markedly from Norway to India (Fig. 11.5). Population pressures have greatly decreased in the mountains of Western Europe, while they have greatly increased in parts of North Africa and in the Middle East. Under these circumstances, transhumance could increase without much harm in Europe, but not in the Middle East, where environmental damage and the demand for intensive cultivation are greater (De Planhol 1970, p. 245). In practice, however, changing economic and land-use patterns make it doubtful that transhumance will ever again be very important in Europe.

MIXED AGRICULTURE

Land use and settlement in middle-latitude mountains have traditionally been based on mixed agriculture characterized by a dual dependence on grazing and cultivation: the animals are taken to high pastures during the summer while an intensive cropping program is carried out in the valleys and on lower slopes. In fall the cattle are brought back to the village, where they are sheltered and fed through the winter on hay and grains harvested during summer. Thus, although much of the work and effort goes into cultivation and harvesting of crops, the center of attention is still the livestock, upon which the inhabitants depend for a large proportion of their foodstuffs. This approach to mountain agriculture has been called the "pastoral life of the mountains" (Arbos 1923) and is found throughout the Alps, Pyrenees, Caucasus, Himalayas, and associated ranges of Eurasia, as well as the Andes, the Atlas Mountains of North Africa, the New Zealand Alps, and the mountains of Scan-

dinavia. Mixed farming and grazing has never been important in the mountains of the Far East, where societies have depended heavily on intensive cultivation, nor in North America, where recent settlement, low population density, and abundant land have made mixed agriculture unnecessary.

The fundamental characteristic of the pastoral life of the mountains is permanent occupancy. The highest areas are used seasonally, of course, but movement of livestock is much more restricted, usually taking place only between the upper and lower slopes of a mountain area, rather than between the mountains and the surrounding plains (although again, every gradation may be found within this larger framework). Mixed farming and grazing are highly structured and intense, with the emphasis on agriculture, since the production of supplemental feed becomes essential in areas without winter pasture. Accordingly, it should be pointed out that the reason for sending the livestock to high pastures during summer is not that lowland grasses dry up, as it usually is for nomadic pastoralism and transhumance, but is in-

Fig. 11.5. Population pressure in highland regions of western Eurasia. (1) Highland life in decline. (2) Transitional. (3) Low population pressure, in process of recolonization. (4) Overpopulated areas and regions of low population pressure being recolonized. (5) Mountain refuge areas with very high population pressure. (6) Appreciable population pressure. (7) Low population pressure. (8) Low population pressure. (From De Planhol 1970, p. 239)

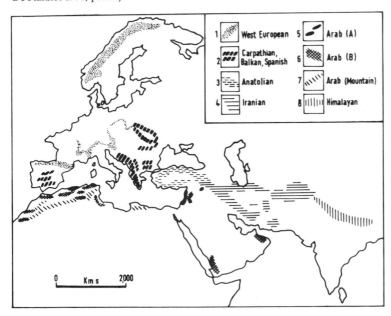

stead a matter of expediency. The lush grasses typical of most mid-latitude mountain valleys could easily support the livestock during the summer, but if the livestock were allowed to remain, it would not be possible to cultivate the fields or to reap the hay without which there would not be enough feed to carry the livestock through the long cold winters (Carrier 1932).

The importance of mixed farming varies considerably from one mountain region to the next. In some areas it is only a sporadic and localized phenomenon; in others it is a dominant feature. Without question its best development occurs in the Alps, and much of the following discussion is based on this region. The details of land use and settlement vary for other areas—e.g., llamas and yaks become relatively more important than cattle in the Andes and Himalayas, respectively—but the ecological principles are similar. The fundamental limitations to agricultural land-use in mid-latitude mountains are low temperature, short growing season, lack of level land, poor soil, lack of adequate moisture, and low productivity. Cultural modifications of these conditions include irrigation, terracing, manuring, the construction of buildings, the introduction of cultigens, and the indirect cropping of marginal areas through animal husbandry. These activities, along with a variety of accompanying social and behavioral adaptations, divert and capture a good portion of the energy flowing through the system and allow human populations to support themselves on a subsistence basis at moderate to high elevations in extratropical mountains (Thomas 1976).

Permanent settlement in these areas requires the storage and preservation of food through the non-productive season of the year. Inhabitants of Eurasian mountains rely heavily on milk and milk products, for if the dairy animals are well-fed and well-cared-for, they will provide milk through the

winter. In the Andes, however, milk has never been an important food item, because llamas and alpacas are relatively inefficient at lactation (Webster 1973). For millennia the altiplano of Bolivia and Peru was used seasonally for cultivation, but permanent settlement became possible at these altitudes only after a method of preserving the crops—the potato in particular—was devised (Troll 1968, p. 32). This is accomplished by freeze-drying the tubers to create a product called *chuño*. The process takes advantage of the dry climate and nightly freezing in this region. The potatoes are spread out on the ground in the open air and allowed to freeze, and in the morning they are put into water (Fig. 11.6). This process is repeated daily for several weeks, until the tubers become hard and black. Then they are either stored intact or are mashed and the white pulp removed for later use. In either case, they will keep indefinitely (Hodge 1949; Gade 1975). Since their introduction from the Andes in the sixteenth century, potatoes have also become a major food source throughout the mountains of Eurasia. They are not freeze-dried in these more poleward mountains, but instead are stored in underground cellars. The popularity of the potato rests on the fact that it is one of the few dependable and productive crops under the marginal conditions of high altitudes, and it is also nutritious, versatile, and tasty. As such, it forms an important part (in many cases, the major part) of the diet of traditional societies in mountains throughout the world.

The origins of mixed farming and permanent settlement in mid-latitude mountains are unknown. To be sure, certain fundamental developments such as agricultural technology and the storage and preservation of crops (worked out by trial and error as land-use strategies evolved) were necessary, but an initial impetus was also required. Seasonal pastoralism in the mountains is a much more ancient endeavor, and the eventual decision to turn to permanent

Fig. 11.6. Chuño manufacture at 3,700 m (12,200 ft.) on the altiplano of Bolivia. The potatoes are spread on the ground at night and allowed to freeze; in the morning they are put into water. The daily repetition of this process for several weeks produces a hard, black, and shriveled product that, if handled properly, will last for a long time. (Carl Troll, 1928, University of Bonn)

settlement must have hinged on a number of environmental and human factors, especially that of population pressure (De Planhol 1970, p. 236). There is evidence for seasonal pastoral occupancy in the Alps during the Neolithic, with agriculture first making its appearance during the late Bronze or early Iron Age. Permanent settlement came somewhat later: the present pattern of land use was well-established by the second century B.C. (Burns 1961). The classic cultural landscape of the Alps still consists of small villages nestled amid mosaics of tiny, odd-shaped fields on valley slopes surrounded by towering and jagged snowcovered peaks. The combination of the subdued and peaceful quality of fields and buildings in the wild and rugged topography presents an almost storybook appearance (Fig. 11.7). It is one of the most charming landscapes on earth.

The basic strategy of the pastoral life of the mountains is one of intensive use of the land and all its habitats through the vertical deployment of activities at different times of the year. The highest elevations are used for the collection of hay from natural grasses or are grazed directly by livestock; conditions there are simply too marginal for cultivation. Herding activities center around dairy cattle, although sheep and goats are also important, especially toward the eastern sector of the Alps. Cattle typically graze upon the more gentle and accessible sites, while sheep and goats reach the highest and most barren sites. Montane forests were at one time extensive in the Alps, but they have been depleted by cutting for timber, the

Fig. 11.7. Storybook appearance of settlement in the Swiss Alps. The village of Lauterbrunnen is situated in the deep glacial valley, while scattered farmhouses are located on the alp slopes. The jagged and snowcovered peaks include the Jungfrau at 4,150 m (13,688 ft.). (Bob and Ira Spring, Free Lance Photographers Guild, Inc., New York)

making of charcoal, and the expansion of upland pastures. The destruction of the forests has now been reversed in the Alps, but it continues to be a problem in other areas, especially in the Middle East and the Himalayas. At lower elevations, near the villages, the land is used as permanent meadows for the cropping of hay or as plowed fields for the production of potatoes and bread grains. Small gardens produce a variety of hardy vegetables, such as beans, cabbage, and beets, for local consumption. In the southern Alps, where the climate is warmer and drier, the lowest slopes are often planted in vineyards and the grapes are used for making wine (Netting 1972). Thus, the landscape is broadly zoned according to altitude and its most suitable use (Fig. 11.8).

This zoning by altitude and habitat also explains the patchwork pattern of tiny unfenced fields so characteristic of the cultural landscape in the Alps. This pattern has often been regarded as a consequence of a partible inheritance system, which favors division of the land into smaller and smaller parcels. Although this is true to a certain extent, fragmentation of the land also has a firm ecological basis and would probably happen without partible inheritance (Burns 1963; Friedl 1973). In order to be successful, each household must have access to land in several different ecological zones: high pastures (alps), forest, meadows, and cultivated fields. The first two are usually under communal control, while the meadows and cultivated fields are privately owned (Netting 1976). In some cases, a single family may own up to 200 different plots at various elevations and under various site conditions, although the number is usually less than this. In the area of Torbel in southern Switzerland (Fig. 11.8) the average household

in 1920 owned 8.5 meadows, 4 pastures, 5 grain fields, 2.5 gardens, and a few small vineyard parcels (Netting 1972, p. 134). The size of parcels varied greatly but averaged about 24 square m (80 sq. ft.). Such a combination of holdings, plus access to the community forest and pastures, was sufficient to provide a satisfactory level of subsistence.

The fragmentation and dispersed ownership of fields entails the maintenance of a rhythm of activities. Fields situated at different exposures and altitudes are ready for planting and harvesting at different times. By far the most time-consuming job during the short summer is haying; large quantities of hay are required to carry the animals through the winter. It is important, therefore, that the farmer be able to use his time efficiently, and the diverse local settings of

Fig. 11.8. Generalized scheme of traditional land-use and types of buildings at various altitudes near Torbel, a village in the Swiss Alps 26 km (16 mi.) north of Zermatt. (From Netting 1972, p. 143)

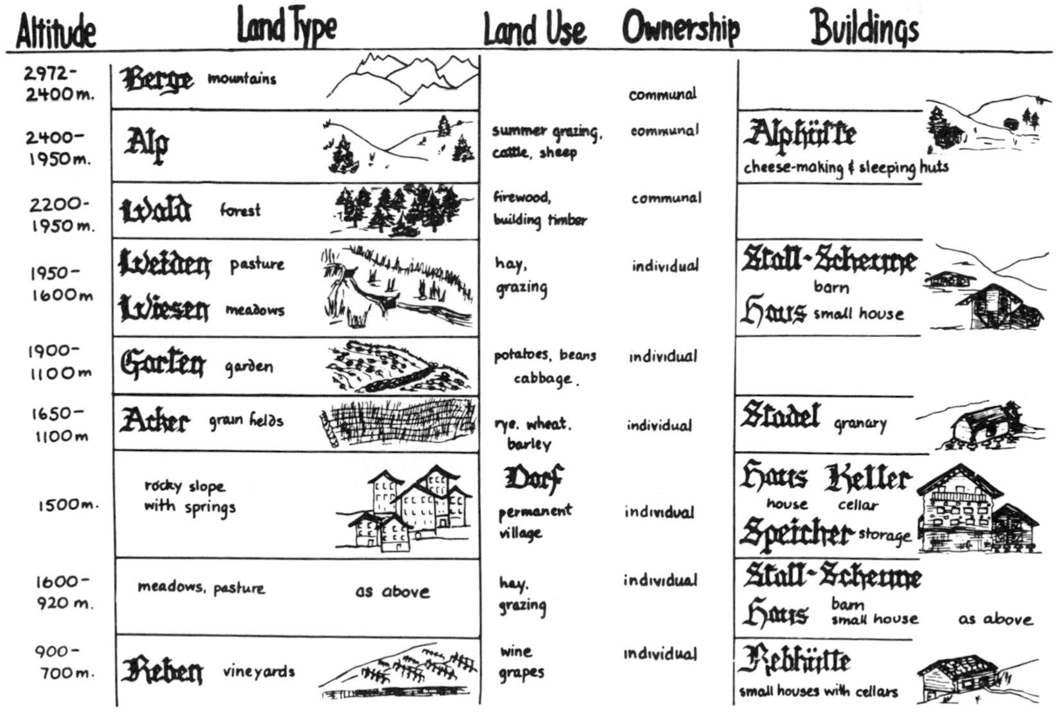

Altitude	Land Type		Land Use	Ownership	Buildings	
2972–2400 m.	𝕭𝖊𝖗𝖌𝖊 mountains			communal		
2400–1950 m.	𝕬𝖑𝖕		summer grazing, cattle, sheep	communal	𝕬𝖑𝖕𝖍ü𝖙𝖙𝖊 cheese-making & sleeping huts	
2200–1950 m.	𝖂𝖆𝖑𝖉 forest		firewood, building timber	communal		
1950–1600 m.	𝖂𝖊𝖎𝖉𝖊𝖓 pasture 𝖂𝖎𝖊𝖘𝖊𝖓 meadows		hay, grazing	individual	𝕾𝖙𝖆𝖑𝖑-𝕾𝖈𝖍𝖊𝖚𝖓𝖊 barn 𝕳𝖆𝖚𝖘 small house	
1900–1100 m.	𝕲𝖆𝖗𝖙𝖊𝖓 garden		potatoes, beans cabbage.	individual		
1650–1100 m.	𝕬𝖈𝖐𝖊𝖗 grain fields		rye, wheat, barley	individual	𝕾𝖙𝖔𝖉𝖊𝖑 granary	
1500 m.	rocky slope with springs		𝕯𝖔𝖗𝖋 permanent village	individual	𝕳𝖆𝖚𝖘 𝕶𝖊𝖑𝖑𝖊𝖗 house cellar 𝕾𝖕𝖊𝖎𝖈𝖍𝖊𝖗 storage	
1600–920 m.	meadows, pasture	as above	hay, grazing	individual	𝕾𝖙𝖆𝖑𝖑-𝕾𝖈𝖍𝖊𝖚𝖓𝖊 𝕳𝖆𝖚𝖘 barn small house	as above
900–700 m.	𝕽𝖊𝖇𝖊𝖓 vineyards		wine grapes	individual	𝕽𝖊𝖇𝖍ü𝖙𝖙𝖊 small houses with cellars	

mountain environments make this possible. Grassy meadows located on elevated but gentle south-facing slopes with good soil may yield abundant hay by July; fields in poor and shaded sites may yield only pitifully by late August. Fragmentation of the land into small parcels also allows more people a chance at subsistence and provides a measure of protection against natural disasters. There are negative aspects, of course, including the time required for travel to widely scattered fields and the impracticability of using modern machinery in such small plots (Friedl 1973, p. 33).

Although land-use patterns have changed greatly in the Alps over the last century, it will be worthwhile to trace the activities of a typical Alpine household through the busy summer under traditional conditions to gain a sense of the nature of this endeavor. The snow begins to melt in March or April and the cattle are let out of their stalls to graze near the village. One of the first big jobs in the spring is to clean the manure from the stalls and to spread it on the fields. This is also the time for maintenance activities: removing avalanche debris from fields, tending to vineyards, repairing barns, and servicing terrace and irrigation systems. As the snowline retreats, livestock are taken higher but grazing is still complemented with stall-feeding, especially for milk cattle and draft animals, which are kept near the village. Fields are usually tilled and planted into grains and potatoes from late April to early June. By late June the snow has melted sufficiently in the alpine zone for the livestock to be taken to the high pastures. Depending upon local circumstances, the entire family may accompany the animals to the alp pastures, where they stay in small huts and engage in butter and cheese making. After a few days the women and children carry on these tasks while the men tend to duties at other levels on the mountain. In this way, family resources are distributed through several different ecological zones

and permit complete utilization and higher returns from the land.

The arduous task of harvesting the hay begins in July. The lowest south-facing slopes are cut first, then harvesters progress to higher and higher meadows; then the process is repeated on the shaded slopes. The hay is stored in small barns near the fields; during winter, cattle are taken up to certain of the barns and fed until the hay is consumed. Although someone must feed the livestock during winter, storing the hay near the meadows where it is cut reduces the total workload and also eliminates the need to carry manure up to the fields.

By late August or September, the rye and barley fields are ready for harvest, and shortly thereafter the livestock are brought down from the alp pastures and allowed to feed on stubble and grass around the village. Careful analysis is made at this time of the natural increase in livestock, as well as the status of the hay supply, to judge the household's ability to carry the animals through the winter—the ultimate limiting factor in determining how many animals can be maintained. Excess livestock is either reserved for butchering or is taken to the annual livestock fair and traded for other commodities (Allix 1922). The last major activity in the fall is the potato harvest, which is usually completed by late September. By the middle of October, all crops are securely stored and the household is prepared for winter. With the return of snow and cold weather, the long process of stall-feeding begins and continues until the following spring, when the routine begins again (Friedl 1973, p. 32).

This program of activities is accomplished through movement of some or all of the members of the household to different altitudinal zones on a synchronized schedule through the season. Each region has its own pattern of movement. In some areas the family may all move together up to the high pastures in the spring and return to the village in the fall; in other areas movement may be extremely complex, with various members of the household working at several different levels with circulation between them (Fig. 11.9). Whatever the pattern, these are not sporadic or impulsive movements but are part of a carefully planned strategy, adapted to the local setting, for what is perceived to be the most efficient use of the landscape (Arbos 1923; Peattie 1936; De Planhol 1970). The variety of the movements demonstrates the extreme lengths to which traditional mountain economies go in their efforts to support moderate to high population densities under circumscribed and limiting conditions.

Although the pastoral life of the mountains continues today on a limited basis in the Alps, it has greatly diminished over the past century. Like other traditional approaches to land use in mid-latitude mountains, it has fallen prey to progress. The spread of industrialization and mechanization in the nineteenth century increased the productivity of lowland agriculture, but mechanization did not particularly help the mountain areas. Relatively high-paying non-agricultural jobs began to attract people from the rural areas. The development of transportation networks into the mountains during the 1850s allowed better access to outside markets, but since the mountain economy was self-sufficient, this was, at least initially, no great boon. On the contrary, its main effect was to provide better interchange between the urban and rural areas and to allow the mountain folk to see the disparity between their standard of living and that of the cities. So the exodus began, consisting at first of younger people accepting employment during the winter, but later including people of all ages and on a full-time basis. The result was rapid depopulation of the mountains, a process that has continued, although there has been some resurgence of population in recent years based on recreation and tourism.

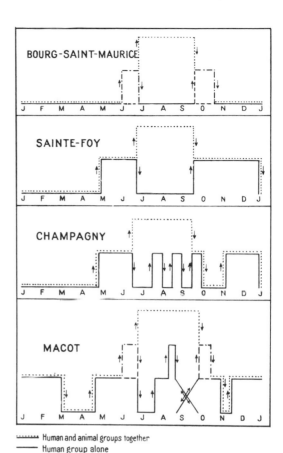

········· Human and animal groups together
———— Human group alone
········· Animal group with herders only
— · — · Part of human group with animal group
- - - -   "   "   "   " without   "   "
X Back and forth between stages

Fig. 11.9. Diagrams of some annual migration patterns in the French Alps under traditional agriculture. Examples are from various villages in the Tarentaise. (From Arbos 1923, p. 572)

The loss of household members from the traditional agricultural system required an alteration of strategies. It was no longer possible (or necessary) to maintain such intensive programs of land use. First the highest, least accessible, and least productive areas were abandoned, and the most difficult and least productive activities, such as the raising of bread grains, were gradually discontinued, since these commodities could now be purchased at relatively low cost from lowland areas. Reduced cultivation made more fields available for pasturage and hay land near the village, so the annual trek to the high alp pastures was discontinued in many areas. The emphasis moved from mixed farming to specialized meat and dairy products. Where the system had once been self-sufficient, it now turned into a cash economy based on the sale of dairy and beef products to lowland markets and the purchase of necessities from the village store.

The major turning point in the status of mixed farming and grazing in the Alps occurred just after World War II. Depopulation and decline in mountain agriculture had been widespread since the mid-1800s, but many of the traditional patterns had continued. After the war, however, the economy of the mountain areas began to change drastically. New construction projects and industries came into the mountain valleys. These attracted more and more people to salaried jobs; farms were either left unused or were operated by the women and old men.

The three patterns of agricultural land-use that have emerged since the war depend to a large extent upon the altitude and accessibility of the land. First, in the lower valleys and accessible areas, where it is possible to use mechanized equipment, there has been an almost total commitment to commercial production of specialized foodstuffs for market. In the outer periphery of the Alps the focus is on grains; interior valleys are devoted to stock-raising and dairying. In the southern Alps, vineyards and orchards predominate and a number of people find employment in the local processing and marketing of wine, fresh fruit, and preserves (Cole 1972, p. 170).

Second, in the mid-elevation valleys, the climate is less favorable for cultivation, and fragmented land-patterns and steep slopes discourage extensive use of tractors and modern equipment, so mixed agriculture

remains important. The major difference between the traditional and modern approaches is that production is now aimed at regional markets rather than for home consumption alone. However, the inhabitants of these areas do grow much of their own produce—they have found that a combination of subsistence and market farming results in a better standard of living than does selling their total output. Finally, in the highest areas many traditional patterns of land use remain. They differ from the middle range not in what is grown but in how it is used. Environmental conditions are marginal and productivity low, so little surplus is left for sale to lowland markets. In addition, access to many of these areas has remained relatively poor. All-weather roads have been constructed to most middle-altitude valleys, but they have only occasionally been extended to the highest communities, whose economy retains a distinctly archaic flavor (Cole 1972, p. 171).

A development concomitant with depopulation and changes in traditional patterns of land use and settlement is that of recreation and tourism. Tourism in the Alps has gone through several phases. First, wealthy noblemen acquired mountain farms and forest reserves for hunting estates, then came the development of hot mineral baths and spas. A number of elaborate hotels served as health resorts and catered to the well-to-do who came to spend a month or two at such places as St. Moritz or Davos in Switzerland (Bernard 1978). Another early tourist activity was mountaineering. This was originally the domain of rich Englishmen, but others from the continent soon joined in attempts to conquer the high peaks. By 1900 the British Alpine Club had built over 1,000 refuges and mountain shelters in the Alps (Lichtenberger 1975, p. 31). The construction of the railroads at mid-century permitted increased penetration and use of the mountains but it was still mainly the well-to-do who visited the Alps.

Not until after World War II did average citizens take advantage of the alpine scenery. The construction of new roads and ownership of automobiles brought the Alps within reach of far more tourists, and automobiles could travel to areas the railroads had been unable to reach. The increasing affluence of the working class and their increasing amounts of leisure time have continued this trend toward car tourism. Even as late as 1954 only 19 percent of the tourists in Austria used their own cars, but in 1966 the proportion was 57 percent and in 1975 it was 63 percent (Lichtenberger 1975, p. 31). Traffic on major highways in the Alps on holidays and weekends during summer is now often bumper-to-bumper, more like rush hour in the city than the wild and primitive landscape most of us expect in mountains.

This massive influx of tourists has changed the landscape in many ways. Foremost among these is a demand for hotels and other service facilities. Many agricultural villages have been converted to tourist resorts. Land that was formerly used for farming now supports ski areas, hotels, restaurants, and summer cottages. This development has been a great boon to the economy of the mountain areas, but there are also a number of drawbacks, one of which is inflation. The demand for land has forced the prices up to such a level that it has become increasingly difficult for younger families to own their own home. This is aggravated by the traditional pattern of fragmented land-holdings. Although much of the rationale for fragmentation has disappeared under present land-usage, the pattern of small, odd-shaped parcels persists. In order to get enough land to build on, it is often necessary to purchase parcels from several different people, which means a higher total price than if they were purchased as a single unit. The result can be staggering. For example, in the small village of Kippel, located on an alpine tributary of

the Rhone River in the canton of Valais, Switzerland, land recently sold for 200 Swiss francs per square meter, or over $186,000 per acre (Friedl 1972, p. 156).

Fragmented holdings are only part of the problem. The basis for judging the value of land has also changed. Land is no longer valued primarily for agriculture but as potential building sites for tourist facilities. In Kippel, a British investment company recently spent over one million dollars for a sunny but poor and rocky area high above the village. This had always been considered one of the poorest sites in the village. Land with an exceptionally good view, even though rocky and of little agricultural value, has risen in value much more than other areas owing to its potential as a building site. Such developments have forced local inhabitants to alter their way of thinking about the land (Friedl 1972, 1974).

Although many aspects of traditional agriculture persist in the Alps, very few people now live solely from the proceeds of farming and livestock. Most households have members who hold jobs in nearby tourist facilities or in one of the many small industries that have located in the mountain villages. In Kippel, a knitting factory employs several people full-time and also hires housewives to do detailed finishing work in their own homes. Another important source of income is the renting of rooms to tourists. When the children of a household have grown and moved to the city, their rooms are let, and the income from this source often exceeds that of agricultural output. So lucrative is the renting of rooms that many rural households have added extra rooms or are building new houses with additional rooms for this purpose. While in the Alps, my wife and I always tried to spend the night in private homes such as these, because it was usually less expensive and provided more insight into local life (Fig. 11.10).

The decline of mountain farming has not only resulted in changed land-use patterns,

Fig. 11.10. Swiss farmhouse near Grindelwald where my wife (on right) and I spent one night during the summer of 1976. This house was built in the 1700s and the original stone oven is still in use. For breakfast we were served homemade bread, butter, cheese, strawberry jam, and goat's milk. (Author)

but it has also made life more difficult for those who have remained in agriculture. Farming has become more and more an individual pursuit. Formerly there were strong traditions of cooperation and communal reciprocity, pooling efforts to overcome extreme environmental conditions and disasters and to accomplish tasks that were too difficult for an individual. For example, building an alp hut was a private responsibility, but transporting the wood to the alp was too much for a single household, so the entire village would pitch in. For this help the owner would typically pay a small fee to the village treasury and provide wine for all the workers. The clearing of paths in the snow along which to take the cattle to high stall barns was also a communal effort, as was transportation of hay to the village from the scattered storage buildings during winter. With everybody joining in, the danger and difficulties of these tasks were reduced, and at the same time an air of camaraderie and merriment transformed the activities into pleasant social functions. The entire village was happy to be involved (Friedl 1972, p. 151).

As more and more people left the villages for outside jobs, however, the tradition of communal labor dwindled. Technological advances and motorized equipment partly compensate for this impact: where in the past an individual depended upon communal help to carry lumber up the alp, he can now do it himself with a tractor. If he needs further help, he hires somebody for wages. The communal task of clearing a path through the snow for the cattle has all but disappeared, but hay is still brought down to the village during winter, although now the job is largely handled by tracked snow vehicles. The capital expenditure for these machines, however, is difficult to afford on a farmer's income. In addition, the rugged topography and fragmented fields pose major obstacles to the use of motorized equipment. Even if tractors could be used, there is often no access to the fields since, under traditional conditions, all the land was required for productivity. If every field had been served by a road little land would have been left for farming! Consequently, special arrangements must be worked out for permission to cross other people's land.

The continuing and overriding problem with mountain farming, however, is the disparity in income between rural and urban ways of life (Fig. 11.11). In the past, mountain populations were willing to accept a

lower standard of living because of their love for the land and a general ignorance about or lack of interest in alternatives, but this has now changed. More and more young people are choosing jobs and leaving the farms. If a son inherits a farm, he is usually more interested in selling or renting it than in working it himself. Under traditional conditions, a young married couple would pool their inheritances to create a minimal amount of land for subsistence, but this is no longer necessary if they both earn cash incomes. This eliminates the pressures to marry within the village, and more and more often the young choose a mate from outside (Friedl 1972, p. 154). Those young men who do decide to stay in farming are finding it more difficult to find wives; fewer girls are willing to marry farmers and undertake the hardships of rural mountain life (Lichtenberger 1975, p. 7).

Without question, the economic future of the Alps is in recreation and tourism. Paradoxically, however, the continuation of mountain agriculture is much desired for that very reason: a major attraction is the picturesque rural landscape. Realizing this, virtually every Alpine country has implemented programs to aid mountain agriculture. They provide crop subsidies, invest-

Fig. 11.11. Disparity of income between mountain peasants and industrial workers in Austria, 1958–1969. Note that lowland peasants earned more than those living in the mountains. (After Lichtenberger 1975, p. 12)

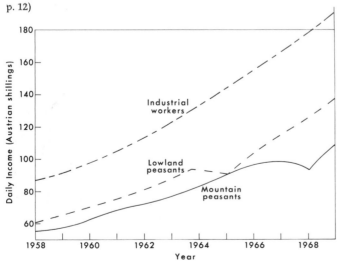

ment credits for capital improvements, and direct supplementation of income to encourage people to remain in mountain farming. Some programs have been in effect for a number of years to help offset the greater expense of producing crops in the mountains. Now, however, the emphasis has changed from one of concern with production itself to one of concern with conservation of the cultural landscape (Lichtenberger 1975, p. 26). Mountain farmers can buy lowland hay and grains more cheaply than they can produce them, but in order to receive the subsidies, they must plant and harvest crops and cut the meadows. The yields from these activities are valuable, but the primary reason for carrying them out is the visual effect they produce. Mixed farming and grazing in the Alps, therefore, is essentially an artifact, preserved under modern conditions by strong infusions of money as in maintenance of a public reserve or museum. It is a far cry from the days when mixed farming and grazing in the mountains ruled supreme as the chosen way of life for a proud and resourceful people under conditions that were marginal, but exhilarating.

Topsoil washing down into India and Bangladesh is now Nepal's most precious export, but one for which it receives no compensation.

Erik P. Eckholm,
The Deterioration of Mountain Environments (1975)

12

Human Impact on Mountain Environments

Mountain environments are fragile, highly susceptible to disturbance, with a low ability to rebound and to heal themselves after damage. The degree to which this is true varies according to regional and local conditions, but the general vulnerability of mountains to outside disturbance is well-established (Man and Biosphere 1973a, 1974a, 1975; Billings 1973; Ives and Barry 1974; Eckholm 1975). Many traditional mountain cultures, too, are very fragile and vulnerable to disruptions from technology and urbanization; apparently well-adapted cultures have been brought to near-collapse after only a few years of increasing population pressure, migration to lowland cities, and the adoption of new, untried tools and practices.

It may be hard for some people to believe that mountain environments are fragile, since mountains are the most rugged of landforms and display the greatest extremes of any environment on earth. Similarly, the flora and fauna of mountain ecosystems are composed of the most rugged and hardy species, well-adapted to cope with the environmental extremes, low productivity, and fluctuations within the system. Why, then, the fragility? The answer lies in the very nature of the environment. Climatic extremes, brevity of the growing season, lack of nutrients, low biological activity, low productivity, youthfulness, island-like character, steepness of slopes, and the basic conservatism of the dominant life forms all make the rate of restoration to original conditions after disturbance slow; in some cases, the original conditions may never return. This is particularly true of small ecosystems, such as isolated peaks or ranges with small mountain mass and limited diversity of habitats. Under these conditions the gene pool is small, many species may be endemic, and the extinction rate may be high (see pp. 310–13). Restoration is hampered by the marginal conditions of exposed, steep slopes with their thin and poorly developed soil. The type and intensity of disturbance is also critical: disruption from outside the system is usually more difficult to assimilate than that from within. Most mountain ecosystems evolved in the absence of human activities and have no ready response to some kinds of disturbances. For example, environmental pollution can move quickly through the system, with possibly irreversible results, as witnessed by the recent rapid build-up of trace and heavy metal concentrations as well as radioactive substances in mountain ecosystems (Osburn 1963, 1967, 1974; Likens and Bormann 1974; Schlesinger et al. 1974; Hirao and Patterson 1974; Jaworowski et al. 1975; Reiners et al. 1975).

Granted that mountains are less resilient with respect to man's use and abuse than many other environments, the question still remains: why the concern? Why is it so critical to maintain and preserve mountain habitats? A number of reasons have already been discussed. Mountains are water reservoirs; they are a source of habitat diversity; they have a splendor and beauty unmatched by any other environment; they provide recreational, research, and educational oppor-

tunities; and they are the loci of numerous resources. Here our concern is not with the usefulness of mountains, but with the importance of continued maintenance and preservation of their ecosystems. The two topics are related, however; the deterioration of mountain environments leads to the deterioration of their other functions; and the use of mountains for some purposes is not compatible with other purposes.

One of the chief reasons for maintaining mountain ecosystems is the simple fact that damage in the uplands will eventually find its way to the lowlands. Avalanches, masswasting, and erosion all have a way of making themselves felt through the linkages in the system. Pollution by heavy metals and radioactive contaminants serves to illustrate the principle. Mountains intercept windladen materials both directly from the atmosphere and from precipitation. Snowfall is a particularly effective means of concentrating air pollutants. As a result, mountains often display a more rapid build-up of pollutants than do the lowlands, especially when the mountains are located downwind from major industrial areas, as are those of western Europe and the eastern United States. Recent studies indicate that these mountains are "pollution sinks," receiving locally heavy amounts of acid rain and radioactive contaminants (Elgmork et al. 1973; Likens and Bormann 1974; Hirao and Patterson 1974; Schlesinger et al. 1974; Jaworowski et al. 1975; Man and Biosphere 1975; Reiners et al. 1975; Vitousek 1977; Grant 1980). The build-up of pollutants not only has serious local effects (many of which are still unknown) but it will eventually harm the lowlands, too, as the pollutants move downward through snowmelt, groundwater, and stream flow, and through animal foodchains.

The preservation of at least some mountain environments in their natural state is an equally if not more important concern. Mountains are unique; they stand at one end of the continuum of terrestrial environments and their extent is limited, especially in the higher reaches. Because mountains, at least those in middle and high latitudes, have traditionally been among the last regions to be settled, they are among the last relatively pristine and wild landscapes. Damage to these environments reduces the variety and quality of habitats on the earth, and by the same measure, the richness and variety of their biota. In many cases, mountains serve as the final retreat for formerly much more widely distributed plants and animals; thus, they are valuable reservoirs of genetic material (Man and Biosphere 1973b; Billings 1978). The loss of these landscapes means, too, that people now and in the future will not have the chance to experience such environments. We should continue to use mountains for the variety of purposes that they now accommodate, but we should carefully evaluate our priorities for those mountain areas which still remain relatively untouched. Like endangered species, once these mountain habitats are destroyed, they are gone forever.

MAJOR SOURCES OF IMPACT

Historically, people have damaged mountain environments in their traditional activities of hunting, grazing, cutting or burning forests, and by modifying the landscape through building terraces, irrigation systems, and other functional structures. These activities have had a definite impact, but small populations and limited technology insured that they were carried out on a relatively small scale; so while the effects may have been negative, they have not generally been devastating. People in many traditional cultures, in fact, found ways to adjust themselves to environmental conditions and to live within the potentials and limitations of the natural environment rather than making major modifications to it. It was to the advantage of these people to cause as little disruption as possible,

since their livelihood depended upon continued maintenance of the system.

The types of activities and their potential impacts have changed with changing technology, however. Human activities have become increasingly disruptive and their effects much further-reaching. New transportation networks and mechanically powered vehicles now give people greater access to mountain areas. Ambitious landscape-modification projects such as the construction of large-scale dams with huge reservoir impoundments and hydroelectric systems, as well as mining, forestry, agriculture, and recreation projects, irreversibly alter the character of mountain valleys. It is estimated that modern erosion rates exceed those before the industrial revolution by an order of magnitude (Trimble 1977).

The major thrust of encroachment into mountains came after World War II; rapid technological developments changed the economic status and increased the mobility of middle-latitude populations. The industrialization of mountain valleys, the production and use of off-the-road vehicles, and the uncontrolled boom in building for recreation and tourism were the most obvious signs of this encroachment. More subtle but perhaps more important in the long run are air, water, and soil pollution, including the build-up of radioactive materials. In addition, there have been both intentional and unintentional introduction of new species and control of animal and plant populations with herbicides, pesticides, and the selective killing of pests and predators. The most recent developments have implications that reach even further: man is now beginning to tinker with the weather and climate.

Overgrazing and Deforestation

Overgrazing of mountain grasses and cutting or burning forests were among the earliest destructive activities. The negative effects of such activities depend upon the intensity and scale of the impact and the resilience of the local environmental regime. For example, agricultural settlement in tropical mountains has always involved clearing and burning forest, but it was traditionally carried out in a restricted way. Disturbed areas were allowed to revert to forest after a few years, so that both the forest and the soil could regenerate. Due to the environmental conditions at intermediate altitudes in the tropics and the generally low level of use, this method of clearing land has not led to irreversible damage. On the other hand, the large-scale burning of forests near the timberline in tropical mountains has greatly expanded the area of grasses and other low-lying and fire-resistant plants at the expense of woody vegetation (Gillison 1969, 1970; Janzen 1973; J. M. B. Smith 1975, 1977a; Hope 1976). This has led to major changes in vegetation patterns, and in many areas the forest is not returning.

Perhaps nowhere is the impact of grazing and deforestation more severe than in the arid and semiarid mountains of the Middle East and the Mediterranean. These areas have supported pastoral populations since long before the birth of Christ, and many mountain slopes have been so badly denuded that little soil remains. The sheep and goats disrupt the vegetation and soil with their sharp hoofs, they crop the vegetation so closely that plants cannot grow back, and they tenaciously seek out every bit of living vegetation until there is nothing left. Goats even climb trees and eat the leaves! In an area where rates of plant growth and soil development are already exceedingly slow, the uncontrolled grazing of such animals can have a profound effect. Many early nomadic tribes had arrangements which spread out the consequences of grazing over large areas and over long periods of time. Where the population pressure and land use were more concentrated, however, overgrazing and erosion have taken a heavy toll. In much of Iran, Afghanistan, Pakistan and Turkey,

as well as Lebanon, Syria, Algeria, Tunisia, and Morocco, the forests are much smaller than they once were.

It is estimated that the oak forests of the Zagros Mountains now cover only ten percent of the area over which they were originally distributed, and similar estimates can be made for other areas of the Middle East. The famous cedars of Mount Lebanon, used by the ancient pharaohs, by Solomon and David in the construction of their temples, and later by the Greeks and Romans in ship-building, are no more. All that remain are a few remnant groves preserved as sanctuaries or because of their inaccessibility (Fig. 12.1). Scrub vegetation and bare slopes now dominate where the once proud cedars stood (Mikesell 1969). Only five percent of the cedars of the interior slopes of the Elburz Mountains remain, and the pistachio-almond forests of the hills of interior Iran have been almost totally destroyed (De Planhol 1970, p. 243).

Deforestation is a continuing problem in arid and semiarid areas. In Pakistan and Afghanistan, forests have never covered more than five percent of the land, and that mainly in the mountains, but activities within the last century have reduced their extent even further. Reckless cutting by shifting cultivators, uncontrolled grazing by sheep and goats, and cutting for firewood have been ruinous. A German forester who spent eight years working in the area recently stated: "In Afghanistan the last forest is dying—and with it the basis of life for the entire region" (cited in Eckholm 1975, p. 766).

Vegetation removal is especially critical in arid regions since once the surface of the dry soil is exposed to the elements, it becomes very vulnerable to disturbance. The infrequent precipitation usually occurs as sudden thunderstorms. The water does not soak into the soil, but flows off as sheetwash or as rivulets, carrying with it a goodly amount of fine material. Strong winds, too, pick up the fine surface material, leaving behind the

Fig. 12.1. One of the few remaining groves of the cedars of Lebanon (*Cedrus libani*). This stand is located near Bsharri at 1,900 m (6,300 ft.) and is now a recreation/tourist site, especially for winter skiing. (Clarke Brooke, Portland State University)

larger particles as a rocky lag deposit (desert pavement). The overall result is a high rate of erosion. Recent studies of sediment transport of the Indus River and its tributaries (the drainage system for Pakistan and Afghanistan) indicate a denudational rate of 1 mm/yr. (0.04 in./yr.), one of the highest erosional rates on earth (Hewitt 1972, p. 18). The long-term effects are difficult to assess, but they certainly include a reduction in the region's potential productivity. The most immediate effect is the infilling of reservoirs only recently built. The realization that

these expensive reservoirs are quickly becoming useless has spurred the governments to action; they are now implementing stringent land-use regulations and are starting a number of reforestation projects (Eckholm 1975, p. 766).

Deforestation and erosion are major problems in the Himalayas as well (Kaith 1960). As population pressures increase, people settle in progressively more marginal areas on steeper slopes. Trees and woody shrubs are being cut for firewood and animal feed at a rate that greatly exceeds the

Fig. 12.2. Himalayan woman (in tree) lops off new growth for animal feed (near the ground the trees have already been picked clean). The practice is common throughout the region. Many trees die from the continual lopping; erosion and environmental deterior- ation result. (Pictured is the Sal tree, *Shorea robusta*, a dominant species in low-elevation forests in the Hima- layas.) (Barry C. Bishop; copyright National Geographic Society)

rate of replacement (Fig. 12.2). The demand for firewood by tourists, trekkers, and mountain climbers has exacerbated the problem in Nepal in recent years. Wood-cutting provides employment for many people, but they find they must chop down smaller and smaller trees at higher and higher altitudes (Bishop 1978). Even before this demand for wood by outsiders, it was common to find a treeless zone surrounding a village. There had probably been plenty of trees when the land was first settled, but as intensive cutting continued, the inhabitants have had to go farther and farther for wood. At this point, going after wood is no longer worth the effort, and the villagers have begun to rely on animal dung for heating and cooking. This may seem to be a godsend, since it reduces the pressure on the forest, but it is actually another step in the direction of environmental degradation; fertilizer is essential for the maintenance of soil fertility under a cropping program. Once mountain agriculturalists begin to withhold the fertilizers that were traditionally added to the soil, productivity declines and the land is less able to sustain the population. The typical reaction to this situation is expansion of agricultural activities to even more marginal areas, which results in renewed soil instability and erosion (Eckholm 1975, p. 765).

In the Himalayas, the burning of dung has apparently not been widely practiced traditionally (Pant 1935, p. 129), but the use of dung for fuel has long been common in the Andes. At altitudes above 3,700 m (12,200 ft.) on the altiplano of Bolivia and Peru, there are only single, stunted, and widely scattered trees; hence it was never possible to rely solely on these for fuel. Dung, the traditional fuel for heating and cooking, is an essential resource for the local way of life (Winterhalder et al. 1974). Llama and cattle dung is used for fuel; sheep dung is used for fertilizer. This practice has a solid basis: laboratory analysis indicates that sheep dung is more concentrated and causes more rapid

bacterial action and the formation of humus. It is also higher in nitrogen, calcium, and potassium. On the other hand, cattle and llama dung has a higher caloric content and is preferred for fuel: a dung fire provides only seven percent fewer kilocalories than a comparable amount of wood (Winterhalder et al. 1974, p. 101). Estimates indicate that an average family in the area of Nunoa in Peru at 4,000 m (13,200 ft.) uses about 11,000 kg (24,200 lbs.) of dung for fuel and 1,000 kg (2,200 lbs.) for fertilizer annually. Thus, for a satisfactory existence, a family requires a minimum of 25 sheep and 75 llamas (Thomas 1976, p. 394). The result is a self-sustaining system, however, rather than the degrading one which has emerged recently in the Himalayas in response to increased population and outside pressures.

On the other hand, major land-use changes have taken place on the altiplano since land reforms were instituted in Bolivia and Peru during the 1950s and 1960s. These reforms have led to new freedom and access to the land for the peasants, since areas that were formerly held in large haciendas by wealthy landlords have now become available directly to the people. Although the humanitarian changes are strongly positive, the initial physical effects on the landscape appear to be negative. The peasants have had no experience in the nature of conservation because they have never had personal responsibility for the land. Consequently, the reforms, coupled with greatly increased population pressures, have led in many areas to overgrazing, clearing and cultivation of marginal areas, and cutting of trees for firewood—causing, in short, a general depletion of resources (Preston 1969, p. 12).

Tropical and subtropical mountains currently suffer the most severe environmental degradation because their populations have been growing especially rapidly and the associated land-use pressures, particularly for agriculture, have been heavy. This means that traditional, ecologically sound practices have been abandoned in favor of more exploitative approaches (Eckholm 1975). These problems are exceedingly difficult to solve, because most of the countries involved are poor and have few alternatives to offer to their highland populations. Yet, it is essential that something be done to halt this downward spiral. Before too much damage is done, these countries must find ways to develop their resources for the future while at the same time arresting environmental degradation. Unfortunately, although the future of many tropical countries appears to lie in the successful management of mountain ecosystems, they are instead being drawn to a middle-latitude urban and industrialized model of development that is inappropriate to their needs. The result is the agglomeration of populations and the adoption of economic and social goals and technologies for which mountains serve as obstacles rather than resources. A new model stressing self-awareness and the nature of local resources is needed (Man and Biosphere 1973a, p. 23).

Humid middle-latitude mountains are not exempt from the problems of overgrazing and deforestation. Forests can grow on surprisingly steep slopes with thin soil and provide maximum slope stability and habitat diversity. Once these marginal forests are destroyed, however, as untold areas of them have been, a progression of environmental degradation is initiated that is difficult to halt. The removal of trees alters the microenvironment so that temperature, precipitation, sunshine, and wind conditions near the ground are markedly changed from what they were under the forest cover. Wind, water, and frost processes increase erosion. Without the binding effect of tree roots, the soil is easily disturbed and transported; and without the forest, snow avalanches become common. These processes perpetuate themselves: erosion, avalanching, and slope instability inhibit the natural return of the forest. In the end, only bare and rocky slopes remain where green and productive forests once stood. This situation is found today in many areas of the Alps where the upper forests were destroyed during the centuries of agricultural expansion (Fig. 8.24). Most of the alpine countries are now involved in reforestation projects, but they are finding it a long, difficult, and expensive task (Hampel et al. 1960; Aulitzky 1967; Douguedroit 1978) (Fig. 8.26).

Dams and Reservoirs

Firewood from mountain forests can perhaps supply enough energy for human activities in villages, but cities and industries require much larger and more reliable sources of power. Damming mountain streams is an obvious, efficient way to make electricity. Snowmelt provides ample water, and the narrow deep valleys can be easily spanned by dams. Historically, most mountain areas were sparsely populated and the land was publicly owned (at least in the United States and Canada), so it was not hard to acquire the necessary land. However, the direct modifications of the landscape and the subsequent economic developments associated with hydroelectric projects can affect mountain environments on a large scale.

Dam construction and the creation of large reservoirs are largely irreversible acts; valleys are permanently inundated and their terrestrial ecosystems are lost forever. A lake stands where a stream once flowed. In some cases, man-made lakes are large enough to alter local climates, and wave action erodes the shoreline. Industry commonly locates nearby to use the low-cost energy, and this means more jobs and demand for housing and services. If access to the lake is good, the construction of summer homes and recreation and tourist facilities usually follows. Finally, a node of intensive development is created, with all its potential for environmental damage.

The building of dams has traditionally been generally acceptable: not only do they generate clean, cheap electricity, but they also provide flood protection, water storage, and recreational opportunities. As more and more have been built, however, they have come to be viewed less and less favorably. Valley habitats and free-flowing streams are increasingly being recognized as special habitats deserving of preservation. Consequently, the builders of dams have encountered resistance to additional construction.

For example, the Soca Valley in the Julian Alps, Yugoslavia (made famous by Ernest Hemingway's *A Farewell to Arms*), has some particularly beautiful mountain scenery. The region is economically depressed, however, and the population has shrunk from 6,000 in the 1860s to less than 3,000 today. Light industry and tourism provide some employment, but economic opportunities are few (Wilbanks et al. 1973, p. 22). Into this situation came a proposal in the mid-1960s to build several dams to generate hydroelectric power and to attract industry. Although the dams would lead to additional employment, they would also destroy the valley as it now exists. A national debate developed in Yugoslavia centered around the choice between economic and cultural/aesthetic factors. The essential question became: "Is the Soca landscape important enough to Slovenia so that any plan which substantially modifies it is unacceptable?" The final answer was an emphatic yes (Wilbanks et al. 1973, p. 29). An alternative long-range plan to develop the area as a tourist center is now being carried out and should provide jobs for many of the inhabitants. There will doubtless be undesirable results from this as well, but at least the valley will remain more or less what it has always been, and future generations will still be able to enjoy it.

Mining

The processes of extracting, concentrating, refining, and transporting minerals have great potential for disrupting mountain environments. Surface mining totally destroys the overlying ecosystems; shaft mining is less damaging but still takes its toll. In either case, the severity of damage increases with elevation, becoming greatest above timberline in the alpine zone (Berg et al. 1974).

Acids and heavy metals are common by-products of mining. The acids are typically produced by the oxidation of pyrites and other minerals when geologic strata are exposed and disrupted. At the same time, unusually high quantities of heavy metals such as copper and iron become soluble for absorption by plants. Such compounds accumulate through the food chains and are toxic beyond certain concentrations. All these processes occur under natural conditions as well, but at much lower rates. The artificial disturbance of ore-bearing bodies accelerates the release of toxic materials because the materials are exposed to direct oxidation and to increased infiltration and percolation of water. As a result, the acid content of water, air, and soil increases and the environment deteriorates. The water draining from mine works becomes charged with acids and heavy metals, so that streams may become sterile and display coatings of metal-oxidation products on the rocks and the streambed (Johnston et al. 1975, p. 71).

The unsightly tailings and spoil piles from mining operations add to slope instability, erosion, and stream sedimentation. The loose, unstable piles hold water poorly and revegetation is slow (Berg et al. 1974; Brown and Johnston 1976; Brown et al. 1976). In the past, worked-out mines were simply abandoned, leaving behind a variety of hazards and an ugly and persistent scar on the landscape often visible for long distances. Most companies are now much more aware of the environmental problems caused by mining and recognize their responsibilities. It requires more than concern, however, to rehabilitate high-altitude sites. Problems associated with acid production and acid drainage are much more difficult to rectify under low-temperature regimes; revegetation and soil stabilization are also hard to achieve (Brown et al. 1978). These factors must be taken into account when the decision is made to begin operations in potentially vulnerable areas. It is obviously impossible to stop all extraction of minerals in mountain areas, but more precautions can be taken to preserve the environment. In some cases, it may be necessary to forego mining deposits because of the unique, irreplaceable, or delicate nature of the particular mountain area.

Forestry

Like mining, forestry is a major industry in mountain areas. Forests are the dominant vegetation type of humid-climate mountains, and upland forests have tended to persist more or less intact, since the focus of most human activities is in the lowlands where agriculture is more favorable. With ever-increasing demand for lumber and timber products, however, mountain forests have become steadily more valuable as natural resources. The primary difference between modern forestry and the kinds of mountain deforestation described earlier is that deforestation takes place in areas marginal for tree growth, e.g., arid regions or near the timberline. Trees return only very slowly, and where there is continuing disturbance, they cannot return at all. Most modern forestry, though, takes place in the lower mountain forests where tree growth is more rapid; and the principle of sustained yield dictates selective cutting of older and larger trees, replanting of trees, fertilization, thinning, and spraying for insects so that the forest continually regenerates. Whether the ideal of sustained yield will ever be reached remains to be seen; in many areas of the American West, forestry continues to depend heavily upon natural tree stands.

The environmental impact of forestry has many facets. Tree removal increases slope instability and erosion. It eliminates the binding power of the roots and changes the basic soil/water relationships. There is less vegetation to absorb the water and less surface roughness to slow the rate of runoff (Hewlett and Helvey 1970; Patric and Reinhart 1971; Harr et al. 1975). The removal of forests may also lead to less retention of snowpack during winter. The volume and rate of runoff are nevertheless greater, since nonforested slopes are less efficient at absorbing water, and this often leads to flooding in the lowlands (Anderson and Hobba 1959). At the same time, logging debris may obstruct drainage channels; water is temporarily impounded, altering the local ecology and eventually resulting in the erosion of new channels. The increase in stream sedimentation and nutrient discharge generally hurts aquatic life (Chapman 1962; Leaf 1966; Platts 1970). The clearing of forests changes climatic conditions near the ground: there is now greater frost penetration, especially needle-ice activity, and, in turn, greater mass-wasting and sedimentation. This is particularly true when the forests are *clear-cut*, with no trees left standing within the cut areas, as they are in some of the forests of the western United States. All these effects are increased at high elevations and with steep slopes. In addition, some rock and soil types make certain areas especially prone to erosion—e.g., granites with coarse and sandy soils with little cohesion, owing to low silt and clay content (Anderson 1954; Andre and Anderson 1961).

Aside from the cutting of trees, perhaps the single greatest impact of logging on the landscape is road-building. Roads become primary sites for slumps and landslides and are major contributors to sedimentation (Megahan 1972; Megahan and Kidd 1972; Swanston 1974; Swanson and Dyrness 1975). Roads give people and vehicles greater freedom of access and result in more pollution and littering, a greater incidence of forest fires, and increased pressure on game animals from hunting. (More will be said about this in the following section.) Finally, logging roads and cut forests are blemishes on the land. Some attempt has been made to cushion these effects, at least at ground level, by retaining the trees for a few tens of meters along major highways, as a visual-shelter belt. In mountain forestry, as in mining, we are confronted with a dilemma; this valuable resource is needed but many environmental problems attend its extraction. There is no perfect solution, but a partial answer lies in a better understanding of the effect of certain types of actions under different environmental conditions (Ovington 1978). We may then modify our methods and approaches to accommodate these facts and strive to achieve a more harmonious relationship with nature while at the same time reaping its bounty.

Recreation and Tourism

One of the most insidious impacts on mountain landscapes stems from the large numbers of people coming to enjoy them. This began in earnest after World War II, due to rapid development of highways and increasing numbers of automobiles, a rising level of affluence, and increasing amounts of leisure time. Recreation is largely non-consumptive compared to agriculture, mining, or forestry, and would seem to be an ideal use of mountainscapes (as indeed it is). Unfortunately, however, as more and more people have come and facilities have been constructed to accommodate them, mountain areas have begun to resemble the very places their visitors are trying to escape, with overcrowding, high-rise buildings, noise, pollution, and neon lights.

The kinds of impact tourists and those seeking recreation in mountains have are as varied as the activities in which they engage, but the ability of mountains to absorb and assimilate any of these activities decreases with altitude: as elevation increases, a given intensity of environmental stress will have a much greater effect and it will make itself evident sooner and persist longer than a similar level of activity in lowlands. Consider, for example, what happens when people trample alpine vegetation. Of course, the environmental response to this simple stress depends upon the intensity and degree of disturbance as well as upon local site conditions. Studies in the alpine tundra of the Rocky Mountains indicate that occasional light human trampling in dry upland areas has little effect, but the same amount of traffic in wet areas produces significant damage. Trampling by hundreds of people can totally destroy the vegetation of either area within a few weeks, and it may take centuries or even millennia to return (Willard and Marr 1970, 1971). Consequently, "vista points" and other roadside attractions in the alpine zone should have paths and fences to limit the area of impact. This may seem harsh and restrictive, but if it is not done the entire site may be destroyed. As a general rule, extremely fragile areas should not be subjected to large concentrations of people at all (Habeck 1972b).

Back-country travel by hikers, climbers, and backpackers is more dispersed, so the impact is less. In addition, people who engage in these activities are usually more sensitive to the nature of the environment, so fewer problems are involved. Nevertheless, the number of hikers, climbers, and backpackers has increased so rapidly in recent years that it has been considered necessary to limit their numbers in certain areas. The nature of the impact has also changed with developments in technology. Shopping in a modern, well-stocked, outdoor sporting-goods store can be a fascinating experience. There has been a virtual explosion in the amount and diversity of camping supplies and equipment in recent years. So many kinds of hooks, chocks, nuts, wedges, slings, and swivels are now available for mountain climbing that people are able to scale walls and make ascents that were virtually impossible in free-climbing. This has resulted in ethical as well as environmental problems. For example, the line between legitimate use of pitons for protection and using them as a crutch to climb beyond one's ability is often very thin (Zimmerman 1976, p. 9). The use of these devices may also lessen the enjoyment of those who follow: how would you feel if you had spent a great deal of time and effort free-climbing a particularly difficult route, only to be greeted at every turn by scarred bolt holes and chipped piton placements? Mountain slopes are often marred by paraphernalia left behind by exhausted climbers retreating from a summit conquest or from storms. In other cases it seems, strangely, that climbers and backpackers are strong enough to carry in full containers of food and equipment but too weak to carry them out empty. Abandoned polypropylene rope, aluminum cans, oxygen bottles, plastic wrappers, and nylon fabric become an almost permanent kind of defacement. In 1974 and 1975 over three tons of rubbish were removed from the upper slopes of Mount McKinley by the Park Service (Zimmerman 1976, p. 9).

Many National Parks and Wilderness Areas in the United States now require climbing and hiking permits that involve restrictions, reservations, and waiting lists. It is a depressing development for anyone who has always enjoyed the "freedom of the hills," and yet it is necessary to preserve both the environment and the quality of the experience (Wagar 1964; Hendee and Lucas 1973; Stankey et al. 1976). The authorities have been forced to this position by sheer pressure on these resources. In 1976 there were 52 separate expeditions requesting permission to climb Mount McKinley. On a holiday weekend more people now climb Mount Rainier, Washington, than climbed it during a whole season in the 1950s. It is estimated that over 5,000 climb Mount Hood, Oregon, every year. At some of the more popular camps on climbing routes it is

difficult to obtain clean snow to melt. "Figuratively, we are all standing in a widening circle of yellow snow" (Zimmerman 1976, p. 10).

For mountain walkers and hikers, most back-country travel is done on trails. Although this causes greater impact on narrow corridors, the overall impact is reduced (Bell and Bliss 1973; Coleman 1977). On the other hand, in some areas hikers are urged to spread out. For example, concentration of foot travel on a trail across a poorly drained meadow is far more disruptive than it would be on a well-drained upland. Trails across wet meadows can quickly sink into the turf, disrupt drainage, and fill with standing water. Consequently, hikers using these trails tend to select the drier surfaces on either side, and the erosive process is repeated (Fig. 12.3). Trails cutting across meadows can also serve as pseudo-stream-beds; by facilitating drainage, they lead to other ecological changes such as the encroachment of trees and the eventual demise of the meadows (see pp. 262–63). Recreational man has a further idiosyncrasy, compared to wild animals or even to native mountain people, in often choosing direct ascent paths rather than more gentle zigzag and oblique routes up a mountainside. These vertically oriented trails maximize the rate of runoff and often become deep erosion gullies (Huxley 1978, p. 201). Even where well-constructed zigzag trails exist, it is not uncommon to find numerous places where people have cut corners or have bounded down precipitous inclines with generally negative results.

The contribution of foot travel and individual back-country users to environmental deterioration in mountains counts as nothing compared to the construction and use of highways, however. The building of roads disturbs the slope and changes local drainage patterns. It also involves construction of structures to protect travelers from avalanches or falling rock. The net result is a profound alteration of the environment and in the appearance of the landscape (Figs. 5.29, 5.30).

The greatest harm done by road-building, however, is that it allows ingress of large numbers of people into formerly isolated areas which may be extremely susceptible to disturbance. Animals are subjected to more hunting and harassment (Dourojeanni 1978). Uncontrolled shooting almost doomed the Marco Polo sheep (*Ovis poli*) in the Karakoram region of the Himalayas after it was opened by roads in the early 1960s (Ricciuti 1976, p. 32). The profusion of logging roads throughout the mountains of the American West has spawned an entire generation of "road hunters." Roads intrude into the sanctuary of wild animals, penetrating their winter feeding-grounds and interrupting traditional migration routes (Edwards and Ritcey 1959; Johnson 1976). Animals in preserves and parks often become dependent upon hand-feeding or upon garbage; they may develop such a taste for human foods that they begin to invade the human domain in search for it, thus becoming pests. If the pest is a large carnivore, this may lead to terrifying experiences—e.g., several recent incidents with grizzly bears in National Parks (Marsh 1969, p. 318; Houston 1971, p. 650; Cole 1974).

Roads also serve as avenues of access and provide specialized habitats for the introduction of alien species. Pets are released or escape; insects, plant spores, and seeds are carried in by vehicles and clothing. The success of introduced species decreases with altitude, but roadways still tend to harbor higher percentages of alien species (Frenkel 1974; Veblen 1975). Some animals have been deliberately introduced to mountain areas but have subsequently become pests or have proliferated to the point of causing environmental damage (Holtmeier 1972; Bratton 1974; Salmon 1975). A good case in point is the introduction of goats to the volcanoes of the Hawaiian Islands. The goats were apparently released there by Captain Cook in the 1770s to provide a source of

Fig. 12.3. Trails cut through poorly drained meadow at 2,575 m (8,500 ft.) in the Wallowa Mountains, Oregon. These are made by both pack horses and hikers. The trails often become drainage channels and are even further entrenched. (Author)

fresh meat for future explorations. The goats had no natural enemies, save man, and they multiplied rapidly and soon began seriously to damage the native biota. The nature of the problem has been described by two biologists from Hawaii Volcanoes National Park:

In less than 200 years, goats chewed their way from the seashore to the tops of island peaks and back down again, by which time they numbered in the tens of thousands, had eaten some species into extinction, and threatened the existence of many more. Moreover, the resultant forest destruction has been one of the major causes for declines in populations of native, endemic, nectar-feeding birds of the remarkable and unique family, Drepanididae, and perhaps birds of other families as well. Some of these endangered birds, the Hawaiian hawk, neene, creeper, akepa, akiapolaau, and ou, are very rare but important indigenous species of park habitats. When extinct elsewhere in Hawaii, some of these species may survive only because of suitable habitat which can be preserved under the protection of Hawaii Volcanoes National Park, providing that the goats can be controlled. (Baker and Reeser 1972, pp. 2–3)

The control of goats, as you may have surmised, is no easy task. Many thousands have been killed by hunters, but the goats are so prolific and reclusive that complete elimination is almost impossible. Also, the mountain areas are so extensive that fencing has not been effective. All that can be hoped for is that their numbers can be controlled, especially in high-altitude areas where the ecosystem is most susceptible to outside disturbance.

Goats are not the only exotic species that pose problems for the Hawaiian Volcanoes. Feral pigs, non-native rats, introduced mongooses, exotic birds, and a number of alien plants all compete with the native biota for space and dominance. It is a constant struggle to maintain these communities in a relatively natural state, but one, I think, well worth the effort. As the famous ecologist Aldo Leopold said after having studied the area: "A visitor who climbs a volcano in Hawaii ought to see mamane trees and silverswords, not goats" (Leopold et al. 1963, p. 34).

Lifts, cable cars, gondolas, and trams often transport people from road level to high and otherwise inaccessible spots for vistas or for access to the high country. The Alps have a greater number of such installations than any other mountain range. Besides subjecting alpine areas to greatly increased use, they pose inherent dangers for the in-

experienced and unwary who do not know about the possible consequences of sudden exertion at high altitudes, especially for those not in good physical condition. Typically, users of such facilities are not prepared for or knowledgeable concerning alpine conditions. When the weather is good, they are apt to overestimate their ability and underestimate distances and the potential of conditions to change abruptly; they hike distances that are too long for them or attempt climbs that are too difficult and for which they are unprepared. If the weather changes suddenly and drastically, as it is wont to do in mountains, it can convert a delightful outing into a grueling or perhaps fatal experience. Climbing and hiking accidents caused 329 deaths in the Alps alone during the summer of 1977 (*The Oregonian*, 6 Sept. 1977).

Like lifts and trams, off-the-road vehicles—trail bikes, four-wheel-drive vehicles, rubber-tracked vehicles, and snowmobiles—make it possible for people to reach otherwise inaccessible places, and increase the potential for environmental damage. They destroy the vegetation, make it easy to disturb and hunt animals, create noise and other kinds of pollution, compact the snow (which has numerous ecological ramifications), and irritate those traveling on foot (Schmid 1971; Hogan 1972; Greller et al. 1974; Ives 1974d).

Automobiles in mountains have a considerable impact in their own right. They take up space, require service facilities, and contribute substantially to atmospheric pollution. Space becomes a major consideration in steep mountainous topography, especially where people are concentrated in narrow valleys or where there is only one road into an area and bottlenecks develop. This frequently results in traffic jams as bad or worse than rush hour in the city. The problem has been circumvented to a certain extent in the Alps by building railways to the more popular places. Zermatt, the town at the base of the Matterhorn, can be reached only by rail; visitors must park their cars in the lower valley. But it is still possible to drive to such popular tourist spots as Lauterbrunnen or Grindelwald in Switzerland, which become so crowded on weekends that traffic jams and parking problems are common.

Mass transit is increasingly being used in North American National Parks as the pressures of tourism mount. I drove an automobile to the base of Mount McKinley in Alaska during the early 1960s; now the trip is restricted to buses provided by the Park Service. It is probable that other delicate and congested parks such as Glacier, Yellowstone, and Yosemite may turn to this approach in the future (Burford and Jones 1975). Aspen, Colorado, which has grown from a sleepy little town in 1946 to one of the largest and busiest ski resorts in the world, was deluged with problems of congestion, traffic jams, and air pollution until the citizens finally decided in 1972 to install a mass-transit system. It consists of 1920-vintage buses built to modern specifications; passage is free, supported by revenues from a sales tax on ski-lift tickets. The plan has worked so well that a light-rail system between Aspen and the nearby town of Snowmass is now being considered, in order to restrict automobiles even more (Standley 1975, p. 18). Vail, Colorado, has undergone similar patterns of growth in recent years, but it has not yet come to grips with the influx of automobiles, although the urgency of the problem has been recognized (Minger 1975). The ski areas of Alta and Snowbird located in the Wasatch Range near Salt Lake City, Utah, desperately need a mass-transit system. These resorts are situated at the head of a deep and narrow glaciated valley whose oversteepened slopes are extremely vulnerable to avalanches, but the valley is the primary access route and it has increasingly become the site of traffic jams and automobile-associated pollution. The completion of Snowbird in 1972 intensified these problems. Traffic increased

62 percent in that one year and it continues to grow. A variety of mass-transit alternatives are under consideration to provide access to the valley. The best option appears to be a narrow-gauge cog railway of the sort found in the Swiss Alps (Klein 1974, p. 18). The expense is staggering, however, and when or if it will be constructed is another matter.

The contribution of automobiles to air pollution is especially great at high altitudes because combustion processes are inefficient in the low-oxygen atmosphere. The relatively greater emissions of carbon monoxide (CO) and particulate matter that result become concentrated when there are large numbers of cars, especially in valleys where temperature inversions develop (see pp. 81–83). Air pollution under these conditions may actually exceed, on a temporary basis, that found in major industrial areas. Carbon monoxide is the most abundant and dangerous component of automobile exhausts. In the Rocky Mountain region of Colorado, CO constitutes 67 percent by weight of all air pollutants. Statewide, it is estimated that 928,000 tons of CO are emitted annually, of which 93 percent is due to transportation sources (Fox 1975, p. 260).

Particulate matter is produced by furnaces, fireplaces, and dust from roads, and hydrocarbons are emitted from engine exhausts. The tiny hydrocarbons are considered the most detrimental to health. Such suspended particulates serve as hydroscopic nuclei for condensation, and they also undergo chemical reactions to produce smog. This is probably responsible for the haze over the Smoky Mountains in Virginia and North Carolina. The gas in smog that is most damaging to life is ozone (O_3); although smog is not common in mountains, the intense solar radiation and decreased atmospheric pressure may lead to photochemical reactions favoring ozone production. For example, the high ozone levels found in the Sierra Nevada and Appalachians raise the question of whether the compound was transported there or was generated at the site (Fox 1975, p. 262). In any case, ozone is known to increase in concentration with altitude, particularly near urban centers, and mountains surrounding these areas already display various degrees of ecological damage (Miller et al. 1963); in particular, ozone impairs reproduction in certain species of plants and thus affects the structure of the plant community (Harwood and Treshow 1975). Ozone is also responsible for increasing eye, nose, and throat irritations suffered by airline passengers and crew members on high-altitude long-range flights (U.S. Dept. Transportation 1977).

Associated with automobiles are the gaseous pollutants, such as sulfur and nitrogen oxides, which can be converted chemically in the atmosphere to strong acids. These are responsible for the so-called acid rain received by mountains downwind of urban-industrial areas (Likens and Bormann 1974). The ecological implications are serious: the pH of solutes is lowered, which increases the rates of corrosion and weathering of rocks, leaching of salts from the soil, and leaching of nutrients from plant foliage. It leads to acidification of streams and lakes (Cronan and Schofield 1979). Some streams in remote mountain regions of Norway already have a pH so low that they cannot support life (Fox 1975, p. 262).

A corollary of road development and ease of access is the number of facilities required to accommodate the influx of tourists and other recreation demands—ski lifts, hotels, restaurants, gift shops, sports outfitters, service stations, parking lots, vacation homes, etc. (Huxley 1978). All require space and affect the environment. The development of ski resorts epitomizes the nature of the problem. Ski areas must of course be located above the winter snowline to assure continued snow cover. Cutting of timber to create ski runs increases slope instability, erosion rates, and the potential for snow avalanches and, if the cutting is improperly done, the resorts may display bare and ugly slopes

during summer (Klock 1973; Welin 1974). Ski areas offer an attractive sort of recreation and most people view them as being basically desirable, but the number of such facilities and their locations should be governed by more than simple demand and economics. Those slopes which are highly avalanche-prone or susceptible to instability or are ecologically delicate or valuable for other reasons should not be developed.

A successful ski area and its associated developments can affect an entire region: for example, Vail, Colorado, has grown from a few buildings in 1960 to a community handling over 11,000 skiers a day in the wintertime. There are now 15,000 beds available for visitors, and facilities are still being expanded (Minger 1975, p. 32). Vail, along with its sprawling suburbs in neighboring valleys, is a boom town with an annual growth rate of about 20 percent in skier visits, population, retail sales, vehicle registration, and real-estate values. Unfortunately, the quality of life is not increasing concurrently; Vail's problems have grown in proportion to its population. Crowding, traffic jams, smog, poorly planned developments, visual pollution, strain on county budgets, loss of small-town intimacy, and run-away inflation have all taken their toll: the cost of living there has become one of the highest in Colorado.

Where will it all end? If present growth trends continue, the population of Vail will double every four years. At what point will this beautiful mountain valley be so blighted by development that it will become unappealing and the crowds upon which it depends will no longer come? What makes the difference between a highly desirable resort area, more or less in equilibrium with its environment and providing high-quality recreational experiences, and a tourist trap? The criteria vary, of course, but it appears that Vail has reached the critical stage. Something must be done, and there is evidence that the community is moving in the right direction by beginning a program of aggressive land-use planning (Minger 1975).

Such planning is difficult when outside corporations and development firms build large resort facilities, condominiums, and subdivisions. Since the money comes from outside rather than from within, the developers have no particular reason to consider the support capacity of the local system. These outside-funded developers often withdraw after selling the facilities they have built. The local populace is left to deal with any problems that arise. Communities are placed in a dilemma when such developments are proposed: they are attracted by the prospect of new jobs and an increased tax base, but they must also take into account the inevitable increase in demands for schools, water supply, sewerage, road development, and expanded fire and police protection that are bound to follow.

It is interesting to observe that a recent proposal for a large ski resort involving over 1,200 hectares (3,000 acres) of government land at Beaver Creek near Vail was turned down by the governor of Colorado after it had been approved by the U.S. Forest Service (Brown 1975; Ohi 1975). Although there were critical environmental considerations, apparently the major factor was that in the governor's opinion, Colorado did not need another Vail in this region. The concern for both quality of environment and quality of life evident in this decision augurs well for the future. Large-scale developments are not inherently bad, but the larger they are, the greater their impact will be and the greater the caution that must be used in their planning and execution. A large development that was apparently carried out in excellent fashion is the Big Sky Ski Resort located near Bozeman, Montana. When plans for this resort were first announced, they were met with suspicion and opposition, but as the planning proceeded, concerns were allayed, and the project was accomplished in good taste and in an ecologically responsible way (Stuart 1975).

In another setting such a development might have been inappropriate, even if done with care. This is demonstrated by the highly controversial proposal for a ski resort at Mineral King in the Sierra Nevada, California, along the southern border of Sequoia National Park on U.S. Forest Service land (Hope 1968; Anderson 1970; Nienaber 1972; A. W. Smith 1975). Mineral King, an important mining locale during the nineteenth century, was not incorporated as part of Sequoia National Park; mining has long since ceased, however, and the area has reverted to semi-wilderness and serves as a game refuge.

In 1965 the Forest Service offered the area as a prospective ski resort to several large developers. Walt Disney Enterprises, which submitted the winning bid, proposed to spend 35 million dollars to build an elaborate system of ski lifts, lodges, restaurants, skating rinks, swimming pools, retail shops, theaters, and other facilities. The operation was expected to handle about one million people a year and gradually to build up to two or three million a year (Hope 1968, p. 53). The project was wholeheartedly approved by the governor of California, who agreed to build a 40 km (25 mi.) road into the area with state and federal funds. At this juncture a number of conservation groups entered the picture, appalled at the prospect of the area being transformed into a Sierran version of Disneyland. A variety of tactics were employed; the fight was eventually carried all the way to the U.S. Supreme Court. Now, after a decade of dispute, the Disney Corporation has apparently withdrawn, no longer interested. Whatever the eventual fate of this specific area, it is certain that it is going to become increasingly difficult to obtain approval to build very large-scale facilities like this. The potential for ecological disruption is too great and at the same time, the importance of preserving what remains of our steadily diminishing wilderness has become increasingly more evident.

PRESERVATION OF
MOUNTAIN ENVIRONMENTS

The quality of the landscape is a legacy passed down from generation to generation. Some mountain areas have been occupied for millennia, while others remain relatively untouched and pristine. Some have experienced deterioration from exploitation and overuse; others have been enhanced by the presence of man. For example, the Alps have suffered misuse and have been greatly modified by long human occupancy, but they have also been mellowed and preserved to a remarkable degree by a responsive set of cultural adaptations. It is the chemistry of the combination of man and the land that is the real beauty of the Alps. For many other areas, however, our appraisal of the effects of human occupancy cannot be so kind. Whatever their status, mountain landscapes form part of our heritage, and as we have received them from our forefathers, so we must pass them on to our grandchildren.

Conditions have changed a great deal over the years. In the past, mountain societies operated as isolated, closed systems. Technology was limited and the productivity and ability of any given environment to support life was similarly limited. Accordingly, if a satisfactory level of existence was to be maintained, the size of the population had to be controlled. This was achieved in numerous ways. The example of primogeniture, with its effects on land inheritance, was discussed earlier (see pp. 399–400). It was also pointed out that migration to the lowlands, especially during the winter, was standard. This relieved the pressure on limited resources during the less productive season. A variety of social responses existed as well: marriage took place at a relatively late age, quite large numbers of young people took vows of celibacy, and polyandry was a common practice (Semple 1911, p. 582; Goldstein

1976). In some villages of the Alps, local ordinances were passed prohibiting marriage when the population became too large.

With the rapid advances in technology and increases in population that have taken place during the last century, however, many traditional approaches to land use have been upset. Human populations have increased more within the last few decades than in the entire history of the earth. We have become increasingly concentrated in cities, and technology has given us unprecedented ability to alter and modify landscapes. The effects of these developments have been felt differentially in mountain environments. Some mountain areas—in the tropics and the Middle East—have steadily gained in population, while others—in Western Europe—have lost (Fig. 11.5). At the same time, people have tended to move from an agricultural economy to one based on industry or recreation. Even where agriculture has continued to be the major focus, as in the tropics, its impact on the environment has changed as people have become urbanized and have adopted new technologies. While the population of many tropical-mountain regions is growing at an excessive rate, migration to lowland cities is a problem in other areas. New technologies are often preferred because they are perceived as being more advanced and modern, when in fact they may not suit the needs of the region as well as more traditional approaches do. Such developments require the establishment of a new equilibrium between the mountain culture and the environment.

Curiously, it is not necessarily good for mountain regions to lose population. Under long-term settlement, human populations tend to arrive at a balance with nature and to become an integral part of the system. Consequently, if the human component is removed, the system may lose its stability, at least for the short term. For example, there is evidence from the Pyrenees and

Alps that the decline in grazing on the uplands has in some cases led to increased erosion, not less: grazing animals eat the shoots of new trees and woody shrubs, retarding their growth and allowing the grasses to dominate; the grasses apparently protect the soil against erosion more effectively than the early stages of forest return do (De Planhol 1970, p. 238; Gómez-Ibáñez 1977, p. 295). People tend to maintain an occupied area by repairing terraces, unclogging drainage ways, reinforcing unstable slopes, and building structures to prevent avalanches. Thus, although humans alter the environment in many ways, their presence may also provide a stabilizing influence.

The abandonment of mountain environments often does not benefit the people, either. Drawn to lowland cities by the attraction of high-paying jobs and a better way of life, they often find the transition extremely difficult. This poses many social and economic problems both for them and for the communities into which they move. In addition, the abandonment of mountain environments eliminates these areas from the productive realm and reduces the resource base of the regions involved. In poor and developing countries, especially where much of the land is mountainous, this is a major concern. The full solution is difficult to see, but these people must be made aware of their own worth rather than being degraded. They have accumulated a great deal of knowledge about the environment over the centuries; if this is lost, it will not be easily duplicated or reacquired by a few seasons of scientific research. Especially important is an understanding of local land-use and adaptive strategies, since modern methods developed for use under lowland conditions are usually unsuccessful when transferred to upland environments. Mountain cultures should have access to the advantages of modern technology, but that technology must be integrated with land-use techniques that are appropriate for the

situation. In this regard, mountain societies are in themselves valuable resources critically important to the future of many mountain environments (Man and Biosphere 1974a, p. 110).

The changes in population, technology, and basic approaches to mountain land-use over the past century have drastically altered the types and intensity of environmental impact. These now increasingly come from outside the mountain system and are in response to outside stimuli and conditions, so that the old constraints and controls are no longer effective. The formerly closed, self-limiting systems of traditional societies have become open systems heavily dependent on external factors. As a result, they are much more susceptible to uncontrolled development and environmental disruption, but the fundamental problem is the same: How can people use these environments and yet insure the land's ability to sustain continued use in the future (I.U.C.N. 1978)? A new equilibrium must be established. For those areas still relatively unpeopled and wild, the task is even more difficult because they are a finite and vanishing resource that is increasingly besieged from every side.

As pressures on mountain environments mount and detrimental activities accelerate, it is ever more evident that strong and positive action must be taken. Around the world, concern with protecting and preserving these environments is growing, although different countries take different approaches (Man and Biosphere 1973a, 1974a, 1975; Ives 1979). Programs include the establishment of various types of parks, nature preserves, wilderness areas, and other restrictions on use by human populations. Also involved are more aggressive land-use planning and a stronger degree of management than ever before (Lynch 1974; North Carolina Dept. Admin. 1974). This has resulted in conflicts and disputes between the various factions interested in mountain environments, since the more commercial and industrial uses are often incompatible with nature research, recreation, and the establishment of "wild" areas.

Although most countries share similar goals concerning environmental protection, their individual problems are different. In Old-World areas where man has long been an occupant, the landscape bears full witness to his environmental modifications and artifacts. There is also an historical ontogeny of land use: where people have used the land in certain ways for centuries, they tend to continue to do so. By contrast, the mountains of North America have scarcely been touched. Many areas still retain their pristine character, showing comparatively little evidence of disturbance. Consequently, actions that may be appropriate for one region are inappropriate for another. For example, in North America, mountain preservation efforts generally strive for the preservation of wilderness by keeping out man and his works (except for brief visits). But this is not an option in most areas of Europe and Asia, where very little true wilderness remains. The cultural element has become so much a part of these landscapes that it is neither possible nor desirable to eliminate it. Efforts there have aimed at the preservation of complete visual landscapes, since the cultural components are themselves valuable aspects of the mountain heritage (Newcomb 1972; Mesinger 1973). In many cases attempts are made to persuade the people who are part of these "living landscapes" to stay and continue their traditional way of life (see p. 418).

The United States and Canada have been leaders in establishing large nature preserves and parks in mountain areas, a task that has been relatively easy for these countries because of their vast size, brief history, and low population densities in the mountainous environments of the West (Nash 1973). The first major step was the establishment of the National Parks. This status was reserved for areas of exceptional scenic and natural beauty. The first was Yellowstone, designated a National Park in 1872; by 1916 over 30 National Parks had been established in the United States. These were largely in mountain areas and included Mount McKinley, Hawaiian Volcanoes, Glacier, Yosemite, Great Smoky Mountains, Crater Lake, the Olympics, Mount Rainier, Rocky Mountain, and the Grand Tetons. These were envisioned as being reserved for the protection and preservation of the natural environment, to insure their continued existence for the enjoyment of all. Their use and the facilities constructed to accommodate this use were to be minimal in order not to impair the natural beauty of the area.

The number of visitors to the National Parks during the first fifty years of their establishment was relatively low, but with the improvement of transportation facilities, population increase, and the rising level of affluence and mobility, their use has grown prodigiously (Fig. 12.4). By the 1940s use had increased to the point that concern was voiced for the preservation of the most pristine regions. Accordingly, a more stringent category, that of National Primeval Parks, was established, with the intention of limiting the development that could take place within these areas (Butcher 1947). Other large, relatively untouched areas were protected under new categories: wilderness, primitive, and wild areas. By 1961 over 5.9 million hectares (14.5 million acres) were in these categories, most of them located in mountainous regions of the West.

The crowning act was the 1964 Wilderness Act, whose basic purpose was "to assure that an increasing population, accompanied by expanding settlement and growing mechanization, does not occupy and modify all areas within the United States." The act placed the natural environment at the center of attention, while man was considered to be the intruder. Wilderness "is an area where the earth and its community of life are untrammeled by man, where man himself is a visitor who does not remain." Accordingly, no modern conveniences or mechanized equipment are allowed into

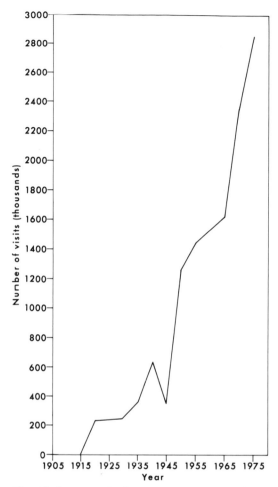

Fig. 12.4. Visits to Rocky Mountain National Park, Colorado, since records were begun in 1915. This demonstrates the situation facing park administrators—use clearly cannot be allowed to increase at the present rate indefinitely if the high mountain environment is to be maintained. (U.S. Dept. Interior 1904–1970)

wilderness areas. Even the landing of a rescue helicopter is questionable. The spirit of the act is caught in the motto placed at the entrance of some wilderness-area trails: "Take only photographs, leave only footprints."

Although establishment of the National Parks and primitive and wilderness areas was originally based on a philosophy of

protection and preservation, as pressures on their use have grown, the approach has shifted somewhat to one of management (Lucas 1973; Hendee 1974; Hendee et al. 1978). This trend alarms purist conservation groups, who view it as an attempt to allow greater use of these areas. They contend that "management" must be kept to the bare minimum needed to maintain true wilderness. The extent and type of use allowable is a matter of interpretation and philosophy. Some believe that wilderness exists for human use and should be used, while others believe that wilderness should be left free of any human imprint. These are both extreme views. Most people would probably agree that some management is desirable, at least to control fire, wildlife, pests, pollution, and disease. Controls should be minimal, but there must be watchful and responsible supervision in order to guarantee the continued integrity of these last remaining wild landscapes. This is so because they are no longer truly natural, but are only remnants of much larger units, now surrounded and affected by man-altered and occupied environments. Yet, they should remain as unmodified and natural as possible. The greatest single threat in this respect is the growing demand for recreation. Mountains are in danger of being "loved" to death. The number of people entering the mountain wildernesses of the western United States has been increasing on the order of 10 to 25 percent per year (Hendee and Stankey 1973, p. 538). In some of the National Parks the rate of increase is much greater. From 1967 to 1972, back-country camping in Yosemite National Park, California, went from 78,000 to 221,000 overnight visits—an increase of 184 percent. During the same period, overnight stays in the back country of Shenandoah National Park, Virginia, quadrupled, reaching 120,000. Back-country use of Rocky Mountain National Park, Colorado, increased an incredible 730 percent from 1965 to 1975 (Hendee et al. 1978, p. 308). Such growth cannot continue indefinitely or these natural systems will be hopelessly overloaded. But how much is too much? At what point do we draw the line? There is ample evidence that the critical mark has already been reached in some areas, and mandatory wilderness permits can be only part of the answer (Hendee and Lucas 1973).

A guiding principle behind landscape management is that of *carrying capacity*, i.e., use up to the level where environmental deterioration begins, or, in other words, use on a sustained basis (Wagar 1964; Stankey 1971, 1973). The application of this is a complex matter, however. Some effects, such as the impact of grazing on the environment, can be fairly accurately observed, but in the matter of recreation, where the quality of the experience depends not only upon interaction with the environment but also upon interaction (or lack of it) with other humans, the principle becomes much more difficult to apply. It is somewhat like defining how many people one pie will serve: it all depends upon how small you cut the pieces (Wagar 1964, p. 3).

For a person expecting or desiring a wilderness experience, meeting one or two other people a day may be acceptable, but meeting twenty people may not be. Much depends upon the perceptions and expectations of the individuals involved. If you go to a park for a picnic, you expect to have people using other tables around you; this is acceptable. But if you hike several kilometers to a high mountain lake, the presence of other groups camped every few meters around the shore can spoil the experience for you (and for them). The picnic area in the park is operating within its carrying capacity, but the carrying capacity of the high mountain lake has been exceeded. Both are desirable kinds of activities for which there should be opportunities. The wilderness experience, however, requires much more severe limitations than a picnic in the park. This is an important point, since it means that the opportunities to partake of wilderness must also be restricted. To make wil-

derness more available is to make it less so. By its very nature, wilderness cannot be multiplied and will stand very little subdivision. This is apparently a difficult concept for some to understand: consider this comment in the *Toronto Financial Post* about proposed improvements to a National Park: "During 1968 and early 1969, campsites will be expanded and roads paved to enable the visitor to enjoy the wilderness atmosphere that was nearly inaccessible only a few years ago" (cited in Hardin 1969, p. 20). This is a curious way of thinking—obviously, once the area has roads, people, and campsites, it is no longer a wilderness.

If wilderness use is limited but demand is steadily growing, how do we decide who and how many can enter these areas? If you are crippled or elderly, will you be able to experience wilderness? You have as much right as the next person and yet you may not be physically able to accomplish the task. Some would argue that roads should be built or other means of transportation allowed to facilitate use by such individuals. But if this step is taken, what is the next demand, the next request for equal treatment, and where does it end? Surely at least some wilderness areas should always remain free of modifications of any sort, should remain areas into which you must go on your own two feet and from which you return the same way. What is the experience of wilderness? The quiet, the solitude, the rugged grandeur, the experience of feeling yourself as an animal in the forest, communing, responding, and delighting in its different moods and situations, being one with nature. And just being there is only part of the experience. The challenge and effort of getting there adds to the pleasure, as does the knowledge that you are on your own and must depend upon your own devices and ability. This in itself is a powerful tonic which must be experienced to be appreciated (Hardin 1969).

Even if this elitist approach is taken, use must still be limited. Various methods have been suggested to accomplish this: queuing (first come, first served), selling to the highest bidder, deciding on the basis of merit, and running a lottery. These are unhappy choices, but not to limit the use of the truly wild areas would lead to an even more unhappy event—the loss of these environments for everybody (Stankey and Baden 1977).

Although mountain wildernesses are highly desirable and every effort must be made to preserve them, their preservation is a fairly restricted problem. The much larger and more pressing concern is how to maintain and preserve mountain environments in general. Part of the solution lies in putting stringent limitations and restrictions on the use of selected areas in every major climatic region, as has been suggested by the International Biosphere Reserve Program, to conserve the diversity and integrity of these natural ecosystems as last retreats for wild animals and as havens for endangered species. These areas would also serve as standards for comparison with more disturbed areas, and for research and education (Dasmann 1972; Man and Biosphere 1973b, 1974b; Franklin 1977). Another part of the solution lies in being more responsive to the problems of increasing population pressure and demand on the limited resources of mountain ecosystems. This involves conscientious land-use planning founded on the knowledge of the ability of different regions to accommodate certain kinds of stress. Lastly, it must be recognized that human use of mountainscapes is not necessarily bad. In areas where people have lived for generations, there is no value in suddenly insisting on discontinuation of human uses. On the contrary, mountain areas should continue to be occupied and developed in creative and responsive ways within the limitations of the environment. The great problem with much recent settlement and use of land in mountains is that it is based largely on outside resources and supplies and operates without regard for limitations within the system. Such processes will doubtless continue, but they must be thoughtfully adjusted to the carrying capacity of the mountain system and not merely be a response to outside stimuli. This should result not only in the maintenance of the environment and its continuing ability to sustain itself, but in new and creative relationships between man and the land, working to the advantage of both.

Bibliography

Abelson, A. E., Baker, T. S., and Baker, P. T. 1974. Altitude, migration and fertility in the Andes. *Soc. Biol.* 21(1):12–27.

Agnew, A. D. Q., and Hedberg, O. 1969. Geocarpy as an adaptation to Afroalpine solifluction soils. *J. E. Africa Nat. Hist. Soc.* 27(33):215–16.

Agri. Exp. Sta. 1964. *Soils of the western United States*. Wash. State Univ., Pullman, Wash.: Soil Cons. Serv., U.S. Dept. Agri. 69 pp.

Alaka, M. A. 1958. *Aviation aspects of mountain waves*. World Meteor. Org. no. 68, Tech. Paper no. 26.

Alden, W. C. 1928. Landslide and flood at Gros Ventre, Wyoming. *Amer. Inst. Min. Met. Eng. Trans.* 76:347–60.

Aldous, C. M. 1951. The feeding habits of Pocket gophers (*Thomomys Talpoides moorei*) in the high mountain ranges of central Utah. *J. Mammal.* 32(1):84–87.

Aleksiuk, M. 1976. Reptilian hibernation: Evidence of adaptive strategies in *Thamnoplis sirtalis parietalis. Copeia* 1:170–78.

Alexander, A. F., and Jensen, R. 1959. Gross cardiac changes in cattle with high mountain (Brisket) disease and in experimental cattle maintained at high altitudes. *Amer. J. Veterinary Res.* 20:680–89.

Alexander, G. 1951. The occurrence of Orthoptera at high altitudes, with special reference to the Colorado Acrididae. *Ecol.* 32:104–12.

——. 1964. Occurrence of grasshoppers as accidentals in the Rocky Mountains of northern Colorado. *Ecol.* 45(1):77–86.

Alexander, G., and Hilliard, J. R., Jr. 1969. Altitudinal and seasonal distribution of Orthoptera in the Rocky Mountains of northern Colorado. *Ecol. Monogr.* 39:385–431.

Alford, D. 1974. Snow. Pp. 85–110 in *Arctic and alpine environments*, ed. J. D. Ives and R. G. Barry. London: Methuen. 999 pp.

Allen, J. A. 1877. The influence of physical conditions in the genesis of species. *Radical Rev.* 1:108–40.

Allix, A. 1922. The geography of fairs, illustrated by Old-World examples. *Geog. Rev.* 12:532–69.

———. 1924. Avalanches. *Geog. Rev.* 14(4):519–60.

Alpine Journal. 1871. The Alps and consumption. *Alpine J.* 5(34):271–72.

Alt, D. D., and Hyndman, D. W. 1972. *Roadside geology of the northern Rockies*. Missoula, Mont.: Mountain Press Pub. 280 pp.

Anati, E. 1960. Prehistoric art in the Alps. *Sci. Amer.* 202:52–59.

Andersen, D. C., Armitage, K. B., and Hoffmann, R. S. 1976. Socioecology of marmots: Female reproductive strategies. *Ecol.* 57(3):552–60.

Anderson, D. 1970. Mineral King—a fresh look. *Nat. Parks and Consv. Mag.* 44(272):8–10. ρ·435

Anderson, D. L. 1962. The plastic layer of the earth's mantle. *Sci. Amer.* 207(1):52–59.

———. 1971. The San Andreas Fault. *Sci. Amer.* 225(5):52–68.

Anderson, H. W. 1954. Suspended sediment discharge as related to streamflow, topography, soil, and use. *Trans. Amer. Geophys. Union* 35:268–81.

———. 1972. Water yield as an index of lee and windward topographic effects on precipitation. Pp. 341–58 in *Distribution of precipitation in mountainous areas*, Vol. II. Geilo, Norway: Proc. Int. Symp. World Meteor. Organ. 587 pp. ρ·103

Anderson, H. W., and Hobba, R. L. 1959. Forests and floods in the northwestern United States. *Int. Assoc. Sci. Hydrol. Pub.* 48:30–39.

Andersson, J. G. 1906. Solifluction, a component of subaerial denudation. *J. Geol.* 14:91–112.

Andre, J. E., and Anderson, H. W. 1961. Variation of soil erodibility with geology, geographic zone, elevation, and vegetation type in northern California wildlands. *J. Geophys. Res.* 66:3351–58.

Andrewartha, H. G., and Birch, L. C. 1954. *The distribution and abundance of animals*. Chicago: Univ. Chicago Press. 782 pp.

Andrews, J. T. 1970. *A geomorphological study of post-glacial uplift with particular reference to arctic Canada*. British Inst. of British Geog. Spec. Pub. 2. 156 pp.

———. 1975. *Glacial systems: An approach to gla-*

ciers and their environments. North Scituate, Mass.: Duxbury Press. 191 pp.

Angstrom, A. K., and Drummond, A. J. 1966. Note on solar radiation in mountain regions at high altitudes. *Tellus* 18:801. ρ·70

Arbos, P. 1923. The geography of pastoral life. *Geog. Rev.* 13:559–75.

Arno, S. F. 1967. *Interpreting the timberline: An aid to help Park naturalists to acquaint visitors with the subalpine-alpine ecotone of western North America*. M. F. thesis, 1966, Univ. Montana, Missoula, Mont. San Francisco: Western Regional Off., Natl. Park Service. 206 pp.

Ashwell, I. Y. 1971. Warm blast across the snow-covered prairie. *Geog. Mag.* 43(12):858–63.

Ashwell, I. Y., and Marsh, J. S. 1967. Moisture loss under chinook conditions. Pp. 307–10 in *Proc. 1st Canadian conf. micrometeorology*, Toronto, Ontario.

Askew, G. P. 1964. The mountain soils of the east ridge of Mt. Kinabalu. *Royal Soc. Proc. Ser. B., Biol. Ser.* 161:65–74.

Asp, M. O. 1956. Geographical distribution of tornadoes in Arkansas. *Mon. Wea. Rev.* 84:143–45.

Atwater, M. M. 1954. Snow avalanches. *Sci. Amer.* 190(1):26–31. ρ·155

Atwood, W. W., Sr., and Atwood, W. W., Jr. 1938. Working hypothesis for the physiographic history of the Rocky Mountain region. *Geol. Soc. Amer. Bull.* 49:957–80.

Aulitzky, H. 1967. Significance of small climatic differences for the proper afforestation of highlands in Austria. Pp. 639–53 in *Int. symp. on forest hydrology*, ed. W. E. Sopper and H. W. Lull. Oxford: Pergamon. 813 pp.

Aung, M. H. 1962. *Folk elements in Burmese Buddhism*. London: Oxford. 140 pp.

Bacdayan, A. S. 1974. Securing water for drying rice terraces: Irrigation, community organization, and expanding social relationships in a western Bontok group, Philippines. *Ethnol.* 13:247–60.

Bader, H., and Kuroiwa, D. 1962. *The physics and mechanics of snow as a material*. Cold Regions Sci. and Eng. Monogr. II-B. Hanover: U.S. Army CRREL. 79 pp.

Bailey, E. B. 1935. *Tectonic essays, mainly alpine*. London: Oxford. 200 pp.

Baker, F. S. 1944. Mountain climates of the western United States. *Ecol. Monogr.* 14:223–54.

Baker, J. K., and Reeser, D. W. 1972. *Goat management problems in Hawaii Volcanoes National Park.* Washington, D.C.: U.S. Dept. Int., Natl. Park Service, Natl. Resources Rep. 2. 21 pp.

Baker, P. T. 1976. Work performance of highland natives. Pp. 300–314 in *Man in the Andes: A multidisciplinary study of high-altitude Quechua*, ed. P. T. Baker and M. A. Little. Stroudsburg, Pa.: Dowden, Hutchinson and Ross. 482 pp.

———, ed. 1978. *The biology of high altitude peoples.* Cambridge: Cambridge Univ. Press. 357 pp.

Baker, P. T., and Little, M. A., eds. 1976. *Man in the Andes: A multidisciplinary study of high-altitude Quechua.* Stroudsburg, Pa.: Dowden, Hutchinson and Ross. 482 pp.

Bandelier, A. F. 1906. Traditions of Pre-Colombian earthquakes and volcanic eruptions in western South America. *Amer. Anthrop.* 8:47–81.

Barash, D. P. 1973. Territorial and foraging behavior of pika (*Ochotona princeps*) in Montana. *Amer. Midl. Nat.* 89:202–7.

———. 1974. The evolution of marmot societies: A general theory. *Science* 185(4149):415–20.

———. 1976. Social behaviour and individual differences in free-living alpine marmots (*Marmota Marmota*). *Animal Behav.* 24:27–35.

Barazangi, M., and Dorman, J. 1969. World seismicity maps compiled from ESSA, Coast and Geodetic Survey, Epicenter Data, 1961–1967. *Bull. Seismol. Soc. Amer.* 59:369–80.

Barry, R. G. 1973. A climatological transect along the east slope of the Front Range, Colorado. *Arctic and Alpine Res.* 5(2):89–110.

Barsch, D. 1969. Permafrost in the upper subnival step of the Alps. *Geograph. Helv.* 24(1):10–12. (Trans. 1973 by D. A. Sinclair, Nat. Res. Council Canada Tech. Trans. 1657.)

———. 1971. Rock glaciers and ice-cored moraines. *Geog. Ann.* 53A(3–4):203–6.

———. 1977. Nature and importance of mass-wasting by rock glaciers in alpine permafrost environments. *Earth Surface Processes.* 2(2, 3): 231–46.

Barth, F. 1956. Ecologic relationships of ethnic groups in Swat, North Pakistan. *Amer. Anthrop.* 58(6):1079–89.

———. 1960a. Nomadism in the mountain and plateau areas of southwest Asia. Pp. 341–55 in *Proc. Paris symp. on the problems of arid zones.*

———. 1960b. The landuse patterns of migratory tribes of South Persia. *Norsk Geografisk Tidsskrift* 17.

———. 1961. *Nomads of South Persia.* Oslo: Oslo Univ. Press. 159 pp.

Barton, D. C. 1938. Discussion: The disintegration and exfoliation of granite in Egypt. *J. Geol.* 46:109–11.

Basak, R. 1953. The Hindu concept of the natural world. Pp. 83–116 in *The religion of the Hindus*, ed. K. W. Morgan. New York: Ronald Press. 434 pp.

Bateman, A.M. 1951. *The formation of mineral deposits.* New York: John Wiley. 371 pp.

Baughman, R. G., and Fuguay, D. M. 1970. Hail and lightning occurrences in mountain thunderstorms. *J. Appl. Meteor.* 9(4):657–60.

Bay, C. E., Wunnecke, G. W., and Hays, O. E. 1952. Frost penetration into soils as influenced by depth of snow, vegetation cover, and air temperatures. *Amer. Geophys. Union Trans.* 33(4):541–46.

Beals, E. 1969. Vegetational change along altitudinal gradients. *Science* 165:981–85.

Beard, J. S. 1946. *The natural vegetation of Trinidad.* Oxford For. Mem. 20. 152 pp.

Beaty, C. B. 1959. Slope retreat by gullying. *Geol. Soc. Amer. Bull.* 70:1479–82.

———. 1962. Asymmetry of stream patterns and topography in the Bitterroot Range, Montana. *J. Geol.* 70:347–54.

———. 1963. Origin of alluvial fans, White Mountains, California and Nevada. *Annals Assoc. Amer. Geog.* 53:516–35.

———. 1974a. Needle ice and wind in the White Mountains of California. *Geology* 2(11):565–67.

———. 1974b. Debris flows, alluvial fans, and a revitalized catastrophism. *Zeits. für. Geomorph.* Suppl. 21:39–51.

———. 1975. Sublimation or melting: observations from the White Mountains, California and Nevada, U.S.A. *J. Glaciol.* 14(71):275–86.

Beckwith, W. B. 1957. Characteristics of Denver hailstorms. *Bull. Amer. Meteor. Soc.* 38(1):20–30.

Behre, C. H., Jr. 1933. Talus behavior above timber in the Rocky Mountains. *J. Geol.* 41: 622–35.

Bell, K. L., and Bliss, L. C. 1973. Alpine disturbance studies: Olympic National Park, U.S.A. *Biol. Conserv.* 5(1):25–32.

Benedict, J. B. 1966. Radiocarbon dates from a stonebanked terrace in the Colorado Rocky Mountains, U.S.A. *Geog. Ann.* 48A:24–31.

———. 1970. Downslope soil movement in a Colorado alpine region: Rates, processes, and climatic significance. *Arctic and Alpine Res.* 2(3):165–221.

———. 1973. Origin of rock glaciers. *J. Glaciol.* 12(66):520–22.

———. 1975. Prehistoric man and climate: The view from timberline. Pp. 67–74 in *Quaternary studies*, ed. R. P. Suggate and M. M. Cresswell. Wellington: Royal Soc. New Zealand.

———. 1976. Frost creep and gelifluction features: A review. *Quat. Res.* 6(1):55–76.

Benedict, J. B., and Olson, B. L. 1973. Origin of the McKean Complex: Evidence from timberline. *Plains Anthrop.* 18(62):323–27.

———. 1978. *The Mount Albion Complex: A study of prehistoric man and the altithermal.* Research Rep. 1. Ward, Colorado: Center for Mountain Archaeology. 213 pp.

Benet, S. 1974. *Abkhasians, the long-living people of the Caucasus.* New York: Holt, Rinehart and Winston. 112 pp.

———. 1976. *How to live to be 100: The life-style of the people of the Caucasus.* New York: Dial Press. 201 pp.

Benevent, E. 1926. *Le climat des Alpes françaises.* Paris: Office National Météorologique de France. 435 pp.

Bent, A. H. 1913. The Indians and the mountains. *Appalachia* 13(3):257–71.

Beran, D. W. 1967. Large amplitude lee waves and chinook winds. *J. Appl. Meteor.* 6(2): 865–77.

Berg, H. 1950. Der Einfluss des Föhns auf den Menschen. *Geofisica Pura e Applicata* 17(3, 4): 104–11.

Berg, W. A., Brown, J. A., and Cuany, R., eds. 1974. *Proceedings of a workshop on revegetation of high-altitude disturbed lands.* Envir. Resources Center Info. Ser. 10. Ft. Collins, Colo.: Colorado State Univ. 88 pp.

Bergen, J. D. 1969. Cold air drainage on a forested mountain slope. *J. Appl. Meteor.* 8:884–95.

Bergeron, T. 1965. *On the low-level redistribution of atmospheric water caused by orography.* Pp. 96–100 (Rep. 5) in Proc. Int. Conf. on Cloud Physics. Tokyo and Sapporo.

Bergmann, C. 1847. Ueber die Verhältnisse der Wärmeökonomie der Thiere zu Ihrer Grösse. *Gottinger Studien* 3:595–708.

Bernard, P. P. 1978. *Rush to the Alps: The evolution of vacationing in Switzerland.* East European Monogr. 37. Dist. New York: Columbia Univ. Press. 228 pp.

Berndt, H. W., and Fowler, W. B. 1969. Rime and hoarfrost in upper-slope forests of eastern Washington. *J. Forestry* 67(2):92–95.

Beskow, G. 1947. *Soil freezing and frost heaving with special application to roads and railroads.* Trans. J. O. Osterberg. Evanston, Ill.: Northwestern Univ. Tech. Inst. 145 pp.

Beyer, H. O. 1955. The origin and history of the Philippine rice terraces. *Proc. Eighth Pac. Sci. Cong. 1951* 1:387–98.

Billings, M. P. 1956. Diastrophism and mountain building. *Geol. Soc. Amer. Bull.* 71:363–98.

Billings, W. D. 1950. Vegetation and plant growth as affected by chemically altered rocks in the western Great Basin. *Ecol.* 31(1):62–74.

———. 1954. Temperature inversions in the pinyon-juniper zone of a Nevada mountain range. *Butler Univ. Bot. Stud.* 11:112–18.

———. 1969. Vegetational pattern near alpine timberline as affected by fire-snowdrift interactions. *Vegetatio* 19:192–207.

———. 1973. Arctic and alpine vegetations: Similarities, differences, and susceptibility to disturbance. *BioScience* 23(12):697–704.

———. 1974a. Arctic and alpine vegetation: Plant adaptations to cold summer climates. Pp. 403–43 in *Arctic and alpine environments*, ed. J. D. Ives and R. G. Barry. London: Methuen. 999 pp.

———. 1974b. Adaptations and origins of alpine plants. *Arctic and Alpine Res.* 6(2):129–42.

———. 1978. The rational use of high mountain resources in the preservation of biota and the maintenance of natural life systems. Pp. 209–223 in *The use of high mountains of the world.* Wellington, N.Z.: Dept. Lands and Survey Head Office, Private Bag (in assoc. with Tussock Grasslands and Mountain Lands Inst., P.O. Box 56, Lincoln College, Canterbury, N.Z., for Int. Union Cons. Nature). 223 pp.

Billings, W. D., and Bliss, L. C. 1959. An alpine snowbank environment and its effect on vegetation, plant development and productivity. *Ecol.* 40:388–97.

Billings, W. D., and Mark, A. F. 1957. Factors involved in the persistence of montane treeless balds. *Ecol.* 38:140–42.

Billings, W. D., and Mooney, H. A. 1968. The ecology of arctic and alpine plants. *Biol. Rev. Cambridge Phil. Soc.* 43:481–529.

Birkeland, P. W. 1967. Correlation of soils of stratigraphic importance in western Nevada and California and their relative rates of profile development. Pp. 71–91 in *Quaternary soils*, ed. R. B. Morrison and H. E. Wright, Jr. Boulder, Colo.: Int. Assoc. Quaternary Res., VII Cong., Proc. 9.

———. 1974. *Pedology, weathering, and geomorphological research*. New York: Oxford Univ. Press. 285 pp.

Bishop, B. C. 1962. Wintering on the roof of the world. *Nat. Geog. Mag.* 122(4):503–47.

———. 1978. The changing geoecology of Karnali Zone, Western Nepal, Himalaya: A case of stress. *Arctic and Alpine Res.* 10(2):531–43.

Bishop, B. C., Angstrom, A. K., Drummond, A. J., and Roche, J. J. 1966. Solar radiation measurements in the high Himalayas (Everest region). *J. Appl. Meteor.* 5:94–104.

Black, J. F., and Tarmy, B. L. 1963. The use of asphalt coatings to increase rainfall. *J. Appl. Meteor.* 2:557–64.

Blackadar, A. K. 1957. Boundary layer wind maxima and their significance for the growth of nocturnal inversions. *Bull. Amer. Meteor. Soc.* 38:283–90.

Blackwelder, E. 1925. Exfoliation as a phase of rock weathering. *J. Geol.* 33:793–806.

———. 1928. Mudflow as a geological agent in semi-arid mountains. *Geol. Soc. Amer. Bull.* 39:465–83.

———. 1929. Cavernous rock surfaces of the desert. *Amer. J. Sci.* (Ser. 5) 17:393–99.

———. 1933. The insolation theory of rock weathering. *Amer. J. Sci.* (Ser. 5) 26:97–113.

Blagbrough, J. W., and Breed, W. J. 1967. Protalus ramparts on Navajo Mountain, Southern Utah. *Amer. J. Sci.* 265:759–72.

Blagbrough, J. M., and Farkas, S. E. 1968. Rock glaciers in the San Mateo Mountains, south central New Mexico. *Amer. J. Sci.* 266:812–23.

Blaney, H. H. 1958. Evaporation from free water surfaces at high altitudes. *Trans. Amer. Soc. Civ. Engr.* 123 (Pap. 2925):385–404.

Bleeker, W., and Andre, M. 1951. On the diurnal variation of precipitation intensity particularly over central U.S. and its relation to large-scale orographic circulation systems. *Quart. J. Royal Meteor. Soc.* 77:260–71.

Bliss, L. C. 1956. A comparison of plant development in microenvironments of arctic and alpine tundras. *Ecol. Monogr.* 26:303–37.

———. 1962. Adaptations of arctic and alpine plants to environmental conditions. *Arctic* 15:117–44.

———. 1963. Alpine plant communities of the Presidential Range, New Hampshire. *Ecol.* 44(4):678–97.

———. 1966. Plant productivity in alpine microenvironments. *Ecol. Monogr.* 36(2):125–55.

———. 1969. Alpine community patterns in relation to environmental parameters. Pp. 167–84 in *Essays in plant geography and ecology*, ed. K. N. H. Greenridge. Halifax: Nova Scotia Museum. 184 pp.

———. 1971. Arctic and alpine plant life cycles. *Ann. Rev. Ecol. System* 2:405–38.

———. 1975. Tundra grasslands, herblands, and shrublands and the role of herbivores. *Geoscience and Man* 10:51–79.

Bliss, L. C., and Woodwell, G. M. 1965. An alpine podzol on Mount Katahdin, Maine. *Soil Sci.* 100:274–79.

Bliss, L. C., and Mark, A. F. 1974. High-alpine environments and primary production on the Rock and Pillar Range, Central Otago, New Zealand. *New Zealand J. Bot.* 12:445–83.

Bloom, A. L. 1978. *Geomorphology: A systematic analysis of Late Cenozoic landforms*. Englewood Cliffs, N.J.: Prentice-Hall. 510 pp.

Blum, H. F. 1959. *Carcinogenesis by ultraviolet light*. Princeton, N.J.: Princeton Univ. Press. 340 pp.

Blumenstock, D. I., and Price, S. 1967. The climate of Hawaii. Pp. 481–975 in *Climates of the States*. Vol. 2: *Western states*. Port Washington, N.Y.: Water Information Center, Inc., 1974.

Blumer, J. C. 1910. A comparison between two mountain sides. *Plant World* 13:134–40.

Boellstorff, J. 1978. North American Pleistocene stages reconsidered in light of probable Pliocene-Pleistocene continental glaciation. *Science* 202(4365):305–7.

Boggs, S. 1940. *International boundaries: A study of boundary functions and problems*. New York: Columbia Univ. Press. 272 pp.

Bolin, B. 1950. On the influence of the earth's orography on the general character of the westerlies. *Tellus* 2(3):184–95.

Bolt, B. A., Horn, W. L., Macdonald, G. A., and Scott, R. F. 1975. *Geological hazards*. Berlin: Springer-Verlag. 328 pp.

Bonacina, L. C. W. 1945. Orographic rainfall and its place in the hydrology of the globe. *Quart. J. Royal Meteor. Soc.* 71(307–8):41–55.

Bones, J. G. 1973. Process and sediment size arrangement on high arctic talus, Southwest Devon Island, N.W.T., Canada. *Arctic and Alpine Res.* 5(1):29–40.

Bose, S. C. 1960. Nomadism in high valleys of Uttara Khand and Kumaon. *Geog. Rev. India* 23(3):34–39.

Boserup, E. 1965. *The conditions of agricultural growth.* Chicago: Aldine. 124 pp.

Bouma, J. 1974. Soil dynamics in an alpine environment. *Soil Sur. Horizons* 15(3):3–7.

Bouma, J., Hoeks, L., and Van Scherrenburg, B. 1969. Genesis and morphology of some alpine podzol profiles. *J. Soil Sci.* 20:383–98.

Bouma, J., and Van Der Plas, L. 1971. Genesis and morphology of some alpine pseudogley profiles. *J. Soil Sci.* 22:81–93.

Bowman, R., Page, E., Remmenga, E. E., and Trump, D. 1971. Microwave vs. conventional cooking of vegetables at high altitude. *J. Amer. Diet. Assoc.* 58:427–33.

Boysen-Jensen, P. 1949. Causal plant-geography. *Det. kgl. Danske Videnskabernes Selskab biologiske Meddelelser* 21(3):1–19.

Braham, R. R., and Draginis, M. 1960. Roots of orographic cumuli. Pp. 1–3 in *Cumulus dynamics*, ed. C. E. Anderson. New York: Pergamon Press. 211 pp.

Brass, L. J. 1941. Stone Age agriculture in New Guinea. *Geog. Rev.* 31(4):555–69.

Bratton, S. P. 1974. The effect of the European wild boar (*Sus scrofa*) on the high-elevation vernal flora in Great Smoky Mountains National Parks. *Bull. Torrey Bot. Club* 101(4):198–206.

Braun, C. E., and Rogers, G. E. 1971. *The white-tailed ptarmigan in Colorado.* Colo. Div. Game, Fish and Parks Tech. Publ. 27. Fort Collins, Colo. 80 pp.

Braun-Blanquet, J. 1932. *Plant sociology: The study of plant communities.* Trans. G. D. Fuller and H. S. Conrad. New York: McGraw-Hill. 439 pp.

Brinck, P. 1966. Animal invasion of glacial and late glacial terrestrial environments in Scandinavia. *Oikos* 17:250–66.

––––––. 1974. Strategy and dynamics of high altitude faunas. *Arctic and Alpine Res.* 6(2):107–16.

Brink, V. C. 1959. A directional change in the subalpine forest-heath ecotone in Garabaldi Park, British Columbia. *Ecol.* 40(1):10–11.

Brink, V. C., Mackay, J. R., Freyman, S., and Pearce, D. G. 1967. Needle ice and seedling establishment in southwestern British Columbia. *Can. J. Plant Sci.* 47:135–39.

Brinkman, W. A. R. 1971. What is a foehn? *Weather* 26(6):230–39.

Broadbooks, H. E. 1965. Ecology and distribution of the pikas of Washington and Alaska. *Amer. Midl. Nat.* 73:299–335.

Brockmann-Jerosch, H. 1919. Baumgrenze und Klimacharakter. *Ber. d. Schweiz. Bot. Gesellsch.* 26; reviewed in *J. Ecol.* 8:63–65.

Brooke, R. C., Peterson, E. B., and Krajina, V. J. 1970. The subalpine mountain hemlock zone. Pp. 147–348 in *Ecology of western North America,* Vol. 2, ed. V. J. Krajina and R. C. Brooke. Vancouver, B.C., Dept. Botany, University British Columbia. 348 pp.

Brookfield, H. C. 1964. The ecology of highland settlement: Some suggestions. *Amer. Anthrop.* 66(4):20–38.

––––––. 1966. The Chimbu: A highland people in New Guinea. Pp. 174–98 in *Geography as human ecology,* ed. S. R. Eyre and G. R. J. Jones. London: Edward Arnold. 308 pp.

Brooks, C. F. 1940. The worst weather in the world. *Appalachia* 23:194–202.

Broscoe, A. J., and Thomson, S. 1969. Observations on an alpine mudflow, Steele Creek, Yukon. *Can. J. Earth Sci.* 6(2):219–29.

Browman, D. L. 1974. Pastoral nomadism in the Andes. *Current Anthrop.* 15:188–96.

Brown, D. R. C. 1975. The developers' view of ski area development. Pp. 23–24 in *Man, leisure and wildlands: A complex interaction.* Proc. 1st Eisenhower Consortium Res. Symp., Vail, Colo. 286 pp.

Brown, F. M. 1942. *Animals above timberline.* Colorado Coll. Publ. Stud. Ser. 33. Colorado Springs, Colo. 29 pp.

Brown, G. M., Bird, G. S., Boag, T. J., Boag, L. M., Delahaye, J. D., Green, J., Hatcher, J. D., and Page, J. 1954. The circulation in cold acclimatization. *Circulation* 9:813–22.

Brown, J. H. 1971. Mammals on mountaintops: Nonequilibrium insular biogeography. *Amer. Nat.* 105(945):467–78.

Brown, J. H., and Lasiewiski, R. C. 1972. Metabolism of weasels: The cost of being long and thin. *Ecol.* 53(5):939–43.

Brown, J. H., and Lee, A. K. 1969. Bergmann's rule and climatic adaptation in wood rats (*Neotoma*). *Evolution* 23:329–38.

Brown, M., and Powell, J. M. 1974. Frost and

drought in the highlands of Papua New Guinea. *J. Trop. Geog.* 38:1–6.

Brown, M. J., and Peck, E. L. 1962. Reliability of precipitation measurements as related to exposure. *J. Appl. Meteor.* 1:203–7.

Brown, R. W., and Johnston, R. S. 1976. *Revegetation of an alpine mine disturbance: Beartooth Plateau, Montana.* U.S. Dept. Agri. For. Serv. Res. Note INT-206. Ogden, Utah. 8 pp.

Brown, R. W., Johnston, R. S., Richardson, B., and Farmer, E. 1976. Rehabilitation of alpine disturbances: Beartooth Plateau, Montana. Pp. 58–73 in *High-altitude revegetation workshop no. 2,* ed. R. H. Zuck and L. F. Brown. Fort Collins, Colo.: Colorado State University.

Brown, R. W., Johnston, R. S., and Johnson, D. A. 1978. Rehabilitation of alpine tundra disturbances. *J. Soil and Water Conserv.* 33(4):154–60.

Brown, W. H. 1919. *Vegetation of Philippine mountains.* Bureau of Sci. Pub. 13. Manila: Dept. Agri. and Nat. Resources. 440 pp.

Browning, J. M. 1973. Catastrophic rock slides, Mount Huascaran, northcentral Peru, May 31, 1970. *Amer. Assoc. Petrol. Geol. Bull.* 57:1335–41.

Brunhes, J. 1920. *Human geography.* Chicago: Rand McNally. 648 pp.

Bryan, K. 1934. Geomorphic processes at high altitudes. *Geog. Rev.* 24:655–56.

Bryan, M. L. 1974a. Water masses in Southern Kluane Lake. Pp. 163–69 in *Icefield Ranges Res. Proj. sci. results,* Vol. 4, ed. V. C. Bushnell and M. G. Marcus. Amer. Geog. Soc. and Arctic Inst. of N.A. Washington, D.C. 384 pp.

————. 1974b. Sublacustrine morphology and deposition, Kluane Lake, Yukon Territory. Pp. 171–88 in *Icefield Ranges Res. Proj. sci. results,* Vol. 4, ed. V. C. Bushnell and M. G. Marcus. Amer. Geog. Soc. and Arctic Inst. of N.A. Washington, D.C. 384 pp.

Bucher, W. H. 1956. Role of gravity in orogenesis. *Geol. Soc. Amer. Bull.* 67(10):1295–1318.

Buck, A. A., Sasak, T. T., and Anderson, R. I. 1968. *Health and disease in four Peruvian villages: Contrasts in epidemiology.* Baltimore: Johns Hopkins. 142 pp.

Budowski, G. 1968. La influencia humana en la vegetación natural de montañas tropicales americanas. Pp. 157–62 in *Geoecology of the mountainous regions of the tropical Americas,* ed. C. Troll. Proc. UNESCO Mexico Symp., Aug. 1966. Bonn: Ferd. Dümmlers Verlag. 223 pp.

Buettner, K. J. K., and Thyer, N. 1962. Valley winds in Mt. Rainier National Park. *Weatherwise* 15(2):63–67.

————. 1965. Valley winds in the Mt. Rainier area. *Archiv. Meteor. Geophys. Biokl.* (Ser. B) 14:9–148.

Bullard, E. 1969. The origin of the oceans. *Sci. Amer.* 221(3):66–75.

Bullard, E., Everett, J. E., and Smith, A. G. 1965. The fit of the continents around the Atlantic. Pp. 41–51 in A symposium on continental drift, ed. P. M. S. Blackett, E. Bullard, and S. K. Runcorn. *Phil. Trans. Roy. Soc. London* (Ser. A) 258(1088). 323 pp.

Bullard, F. M. 1962. *Volcanoes in history, in theory, in eruption.* Austin: Univ. of Texas Press. 441 pp.

Bullard, R. W. 1972. Vertebrates at altitudes. Pp. 209–26 in *Physiological adaptations, desert and mountain,* ed. M. K. Yousef, S. M. Horvath, and R. W. Bullard. New York: Academic Press. 258 pp.

Bunting, B. T. 1965. *The geography of soil.* Chicago: Aldine. 213 pp.

Burford, C. L., and Jones, T. W. 1975. Transportation system planning for wildland areas. Pp. 157–63 in *Man, leisure, and wildlands: A complex interaction.* Proc. 1st Eisenhower Consortium Res. Symp., Vail, Colo. 286 pp.

Burke, K. C., and Wilson, J. T. 1976. Hot spots on the earth's surface. *Sci. Amer.* 235(2):46–59.

Burnham, C. P. 1974. The role of the soil forming factors in controlling altitudinal zonation on granite in Malaysia. Pp. 59–74 in *Altitudinal zonation in Malesia,* ed. R. Flenley, Jr. Misc. Ser. 16. Univ. Hull Dept. Geog. Hull, Eng.: Univ. Hull. 109 pp.

Burns, R. K. 1961. The ecological basis of French alpine peasant communities in the Dauphine. *Anthrop. Quart.* 34:19–35.

————. 1963. The circum-Alpine culture area: A preliminary view. *Anthrop. Quart.* 36:130–55.

Bury, B. R. 1973. The Cascade frog, *Rana cascadae,* in the North Cascade Range of Washington. *Northwest Sci.* 47(4):228–29.

Bushnell, T. M. 1942. Some aspects of the soil catena concept. *Soil Sci. Soc. Amer. Proc.* 7: 466–76.

Buskirk, E. R. 1976. Work performance of newcomers to the Peruvian highlands. Pp. 283–99 in *Man in the Andes: A multidisciplinary study of high-altitude Quechua,* ed. P. T. Baker and M. A. Little. Stroudsburg, Pa.: Dowden, Hutchinson and Ross. 482 pp.

Buskirk, E. R., Kollias, J., Akers, R. F., Prokop, E. K., and Picon-Reategui, E. 1967. Maximal performance at altitude and on return from altitude in conditioned runners. *J. Appl. Physiol.* 23:259–66.

Butcher, D. 1947. *Exploring our National Parks and Monuments.* New York: Oxford Univ. Press. 160 pp.

Buurman, P., Van Der Plas, L., and Slager, S. 1976. A toposequence of alpine soils on calcareous micaschists, Northern Adula Region, Switzerland. *J. Soil Sci.* 27(3):395–410.

Caine, N. 1974. The geomorphic processes of the alpine environment. Pp. 721–48 in *Arctic and alpine environments*, ed. J. D. Ives and R. G. Barry. London: Methuen. 999 pp.

———. 1976. Summer rainstorms in an alpine environment and their influence on soil erosion, San Juan Mountains, Colorado. *Arctic and Alpine Res.* 8(2):183–96.

Caine, N., and Jennings, J. N. 1969. Some blockstreams of the Toolong Range, Kosciusko State Park, New South Wales. *J. and Proc. Roy. Soc. New S. Wales* 101:93–103.

Caldwell, M. M. 1968. Solar ultraviolet radiation as an ecological factor for alpine plants. *Ecol. Monogr.* 38:243–68.

———. 1970. The wind regime at the surface of the vegetative layer above timberline in the central Alps. *Zentralblatt fuer die gestamte forst- und Holzwirteschaft* 87:193–201.

Cal. Div. Mines and Geol. 1973. *Urban geology master plan for California.* Calif. Div. Mines and Geol. Bull. 198. 112 pp.

Cameron, R. E. 1969. Cold desert characteristics and problems relevant to other arid lands. Pp. 167–206 in *Arid lands in perspective*, ed. W. G. McGinnies and B. J. Goldman. Washington, D.C.: Amer. Assoc. Advancement Sci.; Tucson: Univ. Arizona Press. 421 pp.

Campbell, J. B. 1970. New elevational records for the Boreal toad (*Bufo boreas boreas*). *Arctic and Alpine Res.* 2(2):157–59.

Canaday, B. B., and Fonda, R. W. 1974. The influence of subalpine snowbanks on vegetation pattern, production, and phenology. *Bull. Torrey Bot. Club* 101(6):340–50.

Carey, S. W. 1958. A tectonic approach to continental drift. Pp. 117–355 in *Continental drift: A symposium.* Hobart: Univ. of Tasmania.

———. 1976. *The expanding earth.* Amsterdam: Elsevier. 488 pp.

Carlquist, S. 1974. *Island biology.* New York: Columbia Univ. Press. 660 pp.

Carpenter, F. L. 1974. Torpor in an Andean hummingbird: Its ecological significance. *Science* 183:545–47.

———. 1976. *Ecology and evolution of an Andean hummingbird* (*Oreotrochilus estella*). Univ. Calif Pub. Zoology 106. Berkeley: Univ. Calif. Press. 74 pp.

Carrier, E. H. 1932. *Water and grass: A study in the pastoral economy of Southern Europe.* London: Christophers. 434 pp.

Carson, M. A., and Kirby, M. J. 1972. *Hillslope form and process.* London: Cambridge Univ. Press. 475 pp.

Cavalli-Sforza, L. L. 1963. Genetic drift for blood groups. Pp. 34–39 in *The genetics of migrant and isolate populations*, ed. E. Goldschmidt. Baltimore: Williams and Wilkins.

Chabot, B. F., and Billings, W. D. 1972. Origins and ecology of the Sierran alpine flora and vegetation. *Ecol. Monogr.* 42:163–99.

Chapman, D. W. 1962. Effects of logging upon fish resources of the West Coast. *J. Forestry* 60:533–37.

Chapman, J. A. 1954. Studies on summit-frequenting insects in western Montana. *Ecol.* 35:41–49.

———. 1957. A further consideration of summit ant swarms. *Can. Ent.* 89:389–95.

Chapman, J. A., Romer, J. I., and Stark, J. 1955. Ladybird beetles and army cutworm adults as food for grizzly bears in Montana. *Ecol.* 36(1): 156–58.

Chappell, C. F., Grant, C. O., and Mielke, P. W., Jr. 1971. Cloud seeding effects on precipitation intensity and duration of wintertime orographic clouds. *J. Appl. Meteor.* 10:1006–10.

Charlesworth, J. K. 1957. *The quaternary era.* London: Edward Arnold. 1700 pp.

Chavannes, E. 1910. *Le Tai Chan.* Grimet: Annales du Musée Vol. 21.

Chiodi, H. 1964. Action of high altitude chronic hypoxia on newborn animals. Pp. 97–114 in *The physiological effects of high altitude*, ed. W. H. Weihe. New York: Macmillan. 351 pp.

———. 1970–71. Comparative study of the blood gas transport in high altitude and sea level Camelidae and goats. *Resp. Physiol.* 11: 84–93.

Choate, T. S. 1963. Habitat and population dynamics of white-tailed ptarmigan in Montana. *J. Wildlife Mgt.* 27:684–99.

Church, J. E. 1934. Evaporation at high altitudes and latitudes. *Trans. Amer. Geophys. Union* Part II:326–51.

Church, P. E., and Stephens, T. E. 1941. Influence of the Cascade and Rocky Mountains on the temperature during the westward spread of polar air. *Bull. Amer. Meteor. Soc.* 22:25–30.

Churchill, E. D., and Hanson, H. C. 1958. The concept of climax in arctic and alpine vegetation. *Bot. Rev.* 24:127–91.

Clapperton, C. M. 1972. Patterns of physical and human activity on Mt. Etna. *Scottish Geog. Mag.* 88(3):160–67.

Clapperton, C. M., and Hamilton, P. 1971. Peru beneath its external threat. *Geog. Mag.* 43(9):632–39.

Clark, E. E. 1953. *Indian legends of the Pacific Northwest.* Berkeley: Univ. of Calif. Press. 225 pp.

Clark, J. 1963. Hunza in the Himalayas: Storied Shangri-La undergoes scrutiny. *Nat. Hist.* 73(8):39–41.

Clark, J. L. 1964. *The great arc of the wild sheep.* Norman: Univ. Oklahoma Press. 247 pp.

Clark, S. P., Jr., and Jäger, E. 1969. Denudation rate in the Alps from geochronologic and heat flow data. *Amer. J. Sci.* 267:1143–60.

Clausen, J. 1963. Treelines and germ plasm: A study in evolutionary limitations. *Proc. Natl. Acad. Sci.* 50(5):860–68.

Clegg, E. J. 1978. Fertility and early growth. Pp. 65–116 in *The biology of high altitude peoples*, ed. P. T. Baker. Int. Biol. Prog. 14. Cambridge: Cambridge Univ. Press. 357 pp.

Clegg, E. J., and Harrison, G. A. 1971. Reproduction in human high altitude populations. *Hormones* 2:13–25.

Clegg, E. J., Harrison, G. A., and Baker, P. T. 1970. The impact of high altitude on human populations. *Human Biol.* 42:486–518.

Clegg, E. J., Pawson, I. G., Ashton, E. J., and Flinn, R. M. 1972. The growth of children at different altitudes in Ethiopia. *Phil. Trans. Roy. Soc. London* 264:403–37.

Clifford, R. J. 1972. *The cosmic mountain in Canaan and the Old Testament.* Cambridge, Mass.: Harvard Univ. Press. 221 pp.

Clyde, G. D. 1931. Relationship between precipitation in valleys and on adjoining mountains in northern Utah. *Mon. Wea. Rev.* 59:113–17. *p. 95*

Coe, M. J. 1967. *The ecology of the alpine zone of Mount Kenya.* Monographiae Biologicae 17. The Hague: Junk. 136 pp.

_____. 1969. Microclimate and animal life in the equatorial mountains. *Zoologica Africana* 4(2):101–28.

Coe, M. J., and Foster, J. B. 1972. The mammals of the northern slopes of Mt. Kenya. *J. East Africa Nat. Hist. Soc. and Nat. Museum* 131:1–18.

Cole, G. F. 1974. Management involving grizzly bears and humans in Yellowstone National Park. *BioScience* 24(1):1–11.

Cole, J. W. 1972. Cultural adaptation in the Eastern Alps. *Anthrop. Quart.* 45(3):158–76.

Coleman, R. A. 1977. Sample techniques for monitoring footpath erosion in mountain areas of north-west England. *Envir. Consv.* 4(2):145–48. *p. 430*

Collaer, P. 1934. La rôle de la lumière dans l'établissement de la limite supérieure des forêts. *Ber. d. Schweiz. Bot. Gesellsch.* 43:90–125.

Colson, D. 1950. Effect of a mountain range on quasi-stationary waves. *J. Meteor.* 7(4):279–82.

_____. 1963. Analysis of clear air turbulence data for March, 1962. *Mon. Wea. Rev.* 91(2):73–82.

_____. 1969. Detection and forecasting of clear-air turbulence and mountain waves. Pp. 236–55 in World Meteor. Org. Tech. Note 95. Geneva, Switzerland.

Conrad, V. 1939. The frequency of various wind velocities on a high and isolated summit. *Bull. Amer. Meteor. Soc.* 20:373–76.

Cook, A. W., and Topil, A. 1952. Some examples of chinooks east of the mountains in Colorado. *Bull. Amer. Meteor. Soc.* 33:42–47.

Cook, K. L. 1972. Earthquakes along the Wasatch Front, Utah: The record and the outlook. Pp. H1–29 in *Environmental geology of the Wasatch Front.* Salt Lake City, Utah: Utah Geol. Assoc.

Cook, O. F. 1916. Staircase farms of the ancients. *Nat. Geog. Mag.* 29(5):474–76, 493–534.

Cooke, R. V., and Warren, A. 1973. *Geomorphology in deserts.* Berkeley and Los Angeles: Univ. of Calif. Press. 374 pp. *p. 224*

Cooke, W. B. 1955. Subalpine fungi and snowbanks. *Ecol.* 36:124–30.

Coolidge, W. A. B. 1889. *Swiss travel and Swiss guide books.* London: Longmans, Green. 336 pp.

Corbel, J. 1959. Vitesse de l'érosion. *Zeits. für Geomorph.* 3:1–28. *p. 212*

Corte, A. E. 1968. Frost action and soil sorting processes: Their influence in the surface features of the tropical and sub-tropical high Andes. Pp. 213–320 in *Geoecology of the mountainous regions of the tropical Americas*, ed. C. Troll. Proc. UNESCO Mexico Symp., Aug.

1966. Bonn: Ferd. Dümmers Verlag. 223 pp.

Costin, A. B. 1955. Alpine soils in Australia with reference to conditions in Europe and New Zealand. *J. Soil Sci.* 6:35–50.

———. 1957. The high mountain vegetation of Australia. *Australian J. Bot.* 5:173–89.

———. 1959. Vegetation of high mountains in relation to land use. Pp. 427–51 in *Biogeography and ecology in Australia,* ed. A. Keast, R. L. Crocker, and C. S. Christian. Monographiae Biologicae 8. The Hague: Junk. 640 pp.

———. 1967. Alpine ecosystems of the Australasian Region. Pp. 55–58 in *Arctic and alpine environments,* ed. W. H. Osburn and H. E. Wright, Jr. Bloomington, Ind.: Indiana Univ. Press. 308 pp.

Costin, A. B., Hallsworth, E. G., and Woof, M. 1952. Studies in pedogenesis in New South Wales. III: The alpine humus soils. *J. Soil Sci.* 3:197–218.

Costin, A. B., Jennings, J. N., Bautovich, B. C., and Wimbush, D. J. 1973. Forces developed by snowpatch action, Mount Twynam, Snowy Mountains, Australia. *Arctic and Alpine Res.* 5(2):121–26.

Costin, A. B., Thom, B. G., Wimbush, D. J., and Stuiver, M. 1967. Non-sorted steps in the Mount Kosciusko area, Australia. *Geol. Soc. Amer. Bull.* 78:979–92.

Costin, A. B., and Wimbush, D. J. 1961. *Studies in catchment hydrology in the Australian Alps.* IV: *Interception by trees of rain, cloud and fog.* Div. of Plant Ind. Tech. Pap. no. 16. Commonwealth Sci. and Ind. Res. Organ., Melbourne, Australia. 16 pp.

Cotton, C. A. 1942. *Climatic accidents in landscape making.* New York: John Wiley and Sons. 354 pp.

———. 1960. The origin and history of central Andean relief: Divergent views. *Geog. J.* 125: 476–78.

———. 1968. Mountain glacier landscapes. Pp. 739–45 in *Encyclopedia of geomorphology,* ed. R. W. Fairbridge. New York: Reinhold. 1295 pp.

Coulson, J. C., Horobin, J. C., Butterfield, J., and Smith, G. R. J. 1976. The maintenance of annual life-cycles in two species of Tipulidae (Diptera): A field study relating development, temperature, and altitude. *J. Animal Ecol.* 45(1): 215–34.

Coulter, J. D. 1967. Mountain climate. *New Zealand Ecol. Soc. Proc.* 14:40–57.

Court, A. 1960. Reliability of precipitation data. *J. Geophys. Res.* 65(12):4017–24.

Cox, H. J. 1920. Weather conditions and thermal belts in the North Carolina mountain region and their relation to fruit growing. *Annals Assoc. Amer. Geog.* 10:57–68.

———. 1923. *Thermal belts and fruit growing in North Carolina. Mon. Wea. Rev.* Suppl. no. 19. 98 pp.

Crandell, D. R. 1967. Glaciation at Wallowa Lake, Oregon. Pp. C145–53 in *U.S. Geol. Surv. Prof. Pap.* 575–C.

Crandell, D. R., and Fahnestock, R. K. 1965. *Rockfalls and avalanches from Little Tahoma Peak on Mount Rainier.* U.S. Geol. Surv. Bull. 1221-A. 30 pp.

Crandell, D. R., and Mullineaux, D. R. 1967. *Volcanic hazards at Mount Rainier, Washington.* U.S. Geol. Surv. Bull. 1238. 26 pp.

———. 1974. Appraising volcanic hazards of the Cascade Range of the northwestern United States. *Earthquake Info. Bull. (USGS)* 6(5):3–10.

———. 1975. Technique and rationale of volcanic hazards. *Envir. Geol.* 1(1):23–32.

Crandell, D. R., Mullineaux, D. R., and Rubin, M. 1975. Mount St. Helens Volcano: Recent and future behavior. *Science* 187(4175):438–41.

Crandell, D. R., and Waldron, H. H. 1956. A recent volcanic mudflow of exceptional dimensions from Mt. Rainier, Washington. *Amer. J. Sci.* 254:349–62.

———. 1969. Volcanic hazards in the Cascade Range: Conference on geologic hazards and public problems. Pp. 5–18 in *Off. of emergency preparedness, May 27–28, 1969 Proc.,* ed. R. A. Olson and M. M. Wallace. Washington, D.C.: U.S. Govt. Printing Office.

Crawford, C. S., and Riddle, W. H. 1974. Cold hardiness in centipedes and scorpions in New Mexico. *Oikos* 25(1):86–92.

Cressey, G. G. 1958. Qanats, karez, and foggaras. *Geog. Rev.* 38(1):27–44.

Cronan, C. S., and Schofield, C. L. 1979. Aluminum leaching response to acid precipitation: Effects on high-elevation watersheds in the Northeast. *Science* 204(4390):304–6.

Crooke, W. 1896. *The popular religion and folklore of northern India.* Vol. 1. 2nd ed. New Delhi: Munshiram Manoharlal. 294 pp.

Crowley, J. M. 1975. Ranching in the mountain parks of Colorado. *Geog. Rev.* 65(4):445–60.

Cruden, D. M. 1976. Major rock slides in the Rockies. *Can. Geotech. J.* 13:8–20.

Cruden, R. W. 1972. Pollinators in high-elevations ecosystems: Relative effectiveness of birds and bees. *Science* 176(4042):1439–40.

Cruz-Coke, R. 1978. A genetic description of high-altitude populations. Pp. 47–64 in *The biology of high-altitude peoples*, ed. P. T. Baker. Int. Biol. Prog. 14. Cambridge: Cambridge Univ. Press. 357 pp.

Cuatrecasas, J. 1968. Páramo vegetation and its life forms. Pp. 163–86 in *Geoecology of the mountainous regions of the tropical Americas*, ed. C. Troll. Proc. UNESCO Mexico Symp., Aug. 1966. Bonn: Ferd. Dümmlers Verlag. 223 pp.

Currey, D. R. 1964. A preliminary study of valley asymmetry in the Ogotoruk Creek area, northwestern Alaska. *Arctic* 17:84–98.

Curry, R. R. 1966. Observation of alpine mudflows in the Tenmile Range, central Colorado. *Geol. Soc. Amer. Bull.* 77:771–76.

Czeppe, Z. 1964. Exfoliation in a periglacial climate. *Geog. Polonica* 2:5–10.

Dahl, E. 1951. On the relation between summer temperature and the distribution of alpine vascular plants in the lowlands of Fennoscandia. *Oikos* 3:22–52.

Dahl, R. 1966a. Blockfields, weathering pits and tor-like forms in the Narvik Mountains, Nordland, Norway. *Geog. Ann.* 48A:55–85.

———. 1966b. Blockfields and other weathering forms in the Narvik Mountains. *Geog. Ann.* 48A:224–27.

Dalrymple, P. C., Everett, K. R., Wollostron, S., Hastings, H. D., and Robison, W. D. 1970. *Environment of the central Asian highlands*. U.S. Army Laboratory Tech. Rep. 71-19-ES. Natick, Mass. 58 pp.

Daly, R. A. 1905. The accordance of summit levels among alpine mountains: The fact and its significance. *J. Geol.* 13:105–25.

Daly, R. A., Miller, W. G., and Rice, G. S. 1912. *Report of the commission appointed to investigate Turtle Mountain, Frank, Alberta*. Canada Geol. Surv. Mem. 27. 34 pp.

Darlington, P. J. 1943. Carabidae of mountains and islands. *Ecol.* 13:37–61.

———. 1965. *Biogeography of the southern end of the world*. New York: McGraw-Hill. 236 pp.

Dasmann, R. F. 1972. Towards a system of classifying natural regions of the world and their representation by National Parks and reserves. *Biol. Conserv.* 4:247–55.

Daubenmire, R. F. 1938. Merriam's life zones of North America. *Quart. Rev. Biol.* 13:327–32.

———. 1941. Some ecological features of the subterranean organs of alpine plants. *Ecol.* 22:370–78.

———. 1943. Vegetational zonation in the Rocky Mountains. *Bot. Rev.* 9:325–93.

———. 1946. The life zone problem in the northern intermountain region. *Northwest Sci.* 20:28–38.

———. 1954. Alpine timberlines in the Americas and their interpretation. *Butler Univ. Bot. Stud.* 11:119–36.

———. 1968. *Plant communities*. New York: Harper and Row. 300 pp.

Davies, D. 1975. *The centenarians of the Andes*. Garden City, N.Y.: Anchor Press, Doubleday. 150 pp.

Davies, J. L. 1969. *Landforms of cold climates*. Cambridge, Mass.: M.I.T. Press. 200 pp.

Davis, J., and Williams, L. 1957. Irruptions of the Clark nutcracker in California. *Condor* 59:297–307.

———. 1964. The 1961 irruption of the Clark nutcracker in California. *Wilson Bull.* 76:10–18.

Davis, R. T. 1965. *Snow surveys*. U.S. Dept. Agri. Soil Cons. Serv. Agr. Info. Bull. 302. Washington, D.C. 13 pp.

Davis, W. M. 1899. The peneplain. *Amer. Geol.* 23(4):207–39.

———. 1906. The sculpture of mountains by glaciers. *Scottish Geog. Mag.* 22:80–83.

———. 1911. The Colorado Front Range. *Annals Assoc. Amer. Geog.* 1:57.

———. 1923. The cycle of erosion and the summit level of the Alps. *J. Geol.* 31(1):1–41.

DeBeer, G. R. 1930. *Early travellers in the Alps*. London: Sidgwick and Jackson. 204 pp.

———. 1946. Puzzles. *Alpine J.* 55(273):405–13.

———. 1955. *Alps and elephants: Hannibal's march*. London: Geoffrey Bles. 123 pp.

Deevey, E. S., and Flint, R. F. 1957. Postglacial hypsithermal internal. *Science* 125:182–84.

Defant, F. 1951. Local winds. Pp. 655–72 in *Compendium of meteorology*, ed. T. F. Malone. Boston: Amer. Meteor. Soc. 1334 pp.

Deiss, C. F. 1943. Structure of the central part of the Sawtooth Range, Montana. *Geol. Soc. Amer. Bull.* 54:1123–68.

DeJong, G. F. 1970. Demography and research with high altitude populations. *Soc. Biol.* 17:114–19.

De La Rue, E. A. 1955. *Man and the winds*. New York: Philosophical Library. 206 pp.

Delgado de Carvalho, C. H. 1962. Geography of languages. Pp. 75–93 in *Readings in cultural geography*, ed. P. L. Wagner and M. W. Mikesell. Chicago: Univ. Chicago Press. 589 pp.

Demek, J. 1969a. Cryogene processes and the

development of cryoplanation terraces. *Biuletyn Peryglacjalny* 18:115–26.

———. 1969b. *Cryoplanation terraces: Their geographical distribution, genesis and development.* Ceskoslovenske Akademie Ved Rozpravy, Rada Matematickych a Prirodnich Ved 79(4). Praha: Academia. 80 pp.

———. 1972. Cryopedimentation: An important type of slope development in cold environments. Pp. 15–17 in *International geography 1972,* Vol. 1, ed. W. P. Adams and F. M. Helleiner. 22nd Int. Geog. Cong. Toronto: Univ. of Toronto Press. 694 pp.

Denny, C. S. 1967. Fans and pediments. *Amer. J. Sci.* 265:81–105.

Denton, G. H., and Karlén, W. 1973. Holocene climatic variations—their pattern and possible cause. *Quat. Res.* 3(2):155–205.

De Planhol, X. 1966. Aspects of mountain life in Anatolia and Iran. Pp. 291–308 in *Geography as human ecology,* ed. S. R. Eyre and G. R. J. Jones. London: Edward Arnold. 308 pp.

———. 1970. Demographic pressure and mountain life, with special reference to the Alpine-Himalaya belt. Pp. 235–48 in *Geography and a crowding world,* ed. W. Kosinski, L. A. Zelinsky, and R. M. Prothero. New York: Oxford Univ. Press. 601 pp.

de Quervain, M. R. 1963. On the metamorphism of snow. Pp. 377–90 in *Ice and snow properties, processes, and applications,* ed. W. D. Kingery. Cambridge, Mass.: M.I.T. Press. 684 pp.

Derbyshire, E. and Evans, I. S. 1976. The climatic factor in cirque variations. Pp. 447–94 in *Geomorphology and climate,* ed. E. Derbyshire. London: John Wiley and Sons.

DeSilva, A. 1967. *The art of Chinese landscape painting.* New York: Crown. 240 pp.

DeSonnerville-Bordes, D. 1963. Upper Paleolithic cultures in Western Europe. *Science* 142(3590):347–55.

Dewey, J. F. 1972. Plate tectonics. *Sci. Amer.* 226(5):56–68.

Dewey, J. F., and Bird, J. M. 1970. Mountain belts and the new global tectonics. *J. Geophys. Res.* 75(14):2625–47.

Dewey, J. F., and Horsfield, B. 1970. Plate tectonics, orogeny and continental growth. *Nature* 225(5232):521–25.

Dhar, O. N., and Narayanan, J. 1965. A study of precipitation distribution in the neighborhood of Mount Everest. *Indian J. Meteor. Geophys.* 16(2):229–40.

Diamond, J. M. 1970. Ecological consequences of island colonization by southwest Pacific birds. I: Types of niche shifts. *Nat. Acad. Sci. Proc.* 67:529–36.

———. 1972. *The avifauna of the eastern highlands of New Guinea.* Cambridge, Mass.: Nuttall Ornith. Club. 438 pp.

———. 1973. Distributional ecology of New Guinea birds. *Science* 179:759–69.

———. 1975. The island dilemma: Lessons of modern biogeographic studies for the design of natural reserves. *Biol. Conserv.* 7:129–46.

———. 1976. Island biogeography and conservation: Strategy and limitations. *Science* 193:1027–29.

Dickson, B. A., and Crocker, R. L. 1953, 1954. A chronosequence of soil and vegetation near Mt. Shasta, California. Parts I and II. *J. Soil Sci.* 4:123–54; 5:173–91.

Dickson, R. R. 1959. Some climate-altitude relationships in the southern Appalachian Mountain region. *Bull. Amer. Meteor. Soc.* 40:352–59.

Dickson, R. R., and Posey, J. 1967. Maps of snow cover probability for the northern hemisphere. *Mon. Wea. Rev.* 95:347–53.

Dietz, R. S. 1972. Geosynclines, mountains and continent-building. *Sci. Amer.* 226(3):30–38.

Dietz, R. S., and Holden, J. C. 1970. The breakup of Pangea. *Sci. Amer.* 223(4):30–41.

Dillehay, T. D. 1979. Pre-Hispanic resource sharing in the central Andes. *Science* 204(4388):24–31.

Dingwall, P. R. 1972. Erosion by overland flow on an alpine debris slope. Pp. 113–20 in *Mountain geomorphology,* ed. O. Slaymaker and H. J. McPherson. Vancouver, B.C.: Tantalus Research. 274 pp.

Dirks, R. A., Mahlman, J. D., and Reiter, E. R. 1967. *Evidence of a mesoscale wave phenomenon in the lee of the Rocky Mountains.* Atmosph. Sci. Paper 130. Ft. Collins, Colo.: Dept. Atmosph. Sci., Colorado State Univ. 50 pp.

Dobzhansky, T. 1950. Evolution in the tropics. *Amer. Sci.* 38:209–21.

Domin, K. 1928. The relations of the Tatra Mountain vegetation to the edaphic factors of the habitat. *Acta Botanica Bohemica* 6–7:133–63.

Domrös, M. 1968. Über die Beziehung zwischen aguatorialen konvektionsregen und der Meereshöhe auf Ceylon. *Archiv. Meteor. Geophys. Biokl.* (Ser. B) 16:164–73.

Donayre, J., Guerra-Garcia, R., Moncloa, F., and Sobrevilla, L. A. 1968. Endocrine studies at altitude. IV: Changes in the semen of men. *J. Reprod. Fert.* 16:55–58.

Douguedroit, A. 1978. Timberline reconstruction in Alpes de Haute Provence and Alpes Maritimes, southern French Alps. *Arctic and Alpine Res.* 10(2):505–17.

Dourojeanni, M. J. 1978. The rational use of wildlife in high mountains in relation to sport and tourism. Pp. 191–98 in *The use of high mountains of the world.* Wellington, N.Z.: Dept. Lands and Survey Head Office, Private Bag (in assoc. with Tussock Grasslands and Mountain Lands Inst., P.O. Box 56, Lincoln College, Canterbury, N.Z., for Int. Union Cons. Nature). 223 pp.

Downes, J. A. 1964. Arctic insects and their environment. *Can. Entomol.* 96:279–307.

Downs, J. F., and Ekvall, R. B. 1965. Animals and social types in the exploitation of the Tibetan plateau. Pp. 169–84 in *Man, culture, and animals: The role of animals in human ecological adjustments,* ed. A. Leeds and A. P. Vayda. Pub. 78. Washington, D.C.: American Assoc. Adv. Sci. 304 pp.

Drake, J. J., and Ford, D. C. 1976. Solutional erosion in the southern Canadian Rockies. *Can. Geog.* 20(2):158–70.

Drucker, C. B. 1977. To inherit the land: Descent and decision in northern Luzon. *Ethnol.* 16(1): 1–20.

Dubos, R. J. 1973. Humanizing the earth. *Science* 179(4075):769–72.

Dunbar, G. S. 1966. Thermal belts in North Carolina. *Geog. Rev.* 56(4):516–26.

Dunbar, M. J. 1968. *Ecological development in polar regions.* Englewood Cliffs, N.J.: Prentice-Hall. 119 pp.

Dunmire, W. W. 1960. An altitudinal survey of reproduction in *Peromyscus maniculatus. Ecol.* 41:174–82.

Eckel, E. B., ed. 1958. *Landslides and engineering practice.* Pub. 544. (Highway Res. Bd. Spec. Rep. 29.) Washington, D.C.: Natl. Acad. Sci., Natl. Res. Council. 232 pp.

Eckholm, E. P. 1975. The deterioration of mountain environments. *Science* 189(4205):764–70.

Eddy, J. A. 1974. Astronomical alignment of the Big Horn medicine wheel. *Science* 184(4141): 1035–43.

Edwards, J. G. 1956. Entomology above timberline. *Mazama Club Annual* 38(13):13–17. (Portland, Oregon.)

———. 1957. Entomology above timberline. II:

The attraction of ladybird beetles to mountain tops. *Coleopterists Bull.* 11:41–46.

Edwards, J. S. 1972. Soil invertebrates in North American alpine tundra. Pp. 93–143 in *Proc. 1972 tundra biome symposium,* ed. S. Bowen. Lake Wilderness Center, U.S. Tundra Biome Program. Seattle: Univ. Wash.

Edwards, P. J. 1977. Aspects of mineral cycling in a New Guinean montane forest. II: The production and disappearance of litter. *J. Ecol.* 65:971–92.

Edwards, P. J., and Grubb, P. J. 1977. Studies of mineral cycling in a montane rainforest in New Guinea. I: The distribution of organic matter in the vegetation and soil. *J. Ecol.* 65:943–69.

Edwards, R. Y., and Ritcey, R. W. 1959. Migrations of caribou in a mountainous area in Wells Gray Park, British Columbia. *Can. Field Nat.* 73:21–25.

Ehleringer, J. R., and Miller, P. C. 1975. Water relations of selected plant species in the alpine tundra, Colorado. *Ecol.* 56:370–80.

Ehrlich, P. R., Breedlove, D. E., Brussard, P. F., and Sharp, M. A. 1972. Weather and the "regulation" of subalpine populations. *Ecol.* 53(2): 243–47.

Eide, O. 1945. On the temperature differences between mountain peak and free atmosphere at the same level. II: Gaustatoppen-Kjeller. *Meteor. Ann.* 2(3):183–206.

Ekblaw, W. E. 1918. The importance of nivation as an erosive factor, and of soil flow as a transporting agency, in northern Greenland. *Natl. Acad. Sci. Proc.* 4:288–93.

Ekhart, E. 1948. De la structure de l'atmosphère dans la montagne. *La Météorologie* 3–26.

Ekvall, R. B. 1964. *Religious observances in Tibet: Pattern and function.* Chicago: Univ. Chicago Press. 313 pp.

———. 1968. *Fields on the hoof: Nexus of Tibetan pastoral nomadism.* New York: Holt, Rinehart and Winston. 100 pp.

Elgmork, K., Hagen, A., and Langeland, A. 1973. Polluted snow in southern Norway during the winters 1968–1971. *Envir. Pollut.* 4:41–52.

Ellison, L. 1946. The Pocket gopher in relation to soil erosion on mountain range. *Ecol.* 27:101–14.

Ellison, M. A. 1968. *The sun and its influence: An introduction to the study of solar terrestrial relations.* 2nd ed. London: Routledge and Kegan Paul. 235 pp.

Embleton, C., and King, C. A. M. 1975a. *Glacial geomorphology.* New York: Halsted Press. 573 pp.

_____. 1975b. *Periglacial geomorphology*. New York: Halsted Press. 203 pp.

Emiliani, C. 1972. Quaternary hypsithermals. *Quat. Res.* 2(2):270–73.

Engel, A. E. J. 1963. Geological evolution of North America. *Science* 140:143–52.

Engler, A. 1904. Plants of the northern temperate zone in their transition to the higher mountains of tropical Africa. *Ann. Bot.* 18:523–40.

English, P. W. 1968. The origin and spread of qanats in the Old World. *Proc. Amer. Phil. Soc.* 112(3):170–80. *p.218–7*

Evans, I. S. 1972. Inferring process from form: The asymmetry of glaciated mountains. Pp. 17–19 in *International geography*, Vol. 1, ed. W. P. Adams and F. M. Helleiner. Montreal: 22nd Int. Geog. Cong.

Eyre, S. R. 1968. *Vegetation and soils*. 2nd ed. Chicago: Aldine. 328 pp.

Faegri, K. 1966. A botanical excursion to Steens Mountain, S. E. Oregon, U.S.A. *Blyttia* 24: 173–81. *p.261*

Fagan, J. L. 1973. Altithermal occupation of spring sites in the northern Great Basin. Unpublished Ph.D. dissertation, Univ. of Oregon, Eugene. 309 pp.

Fahey, B. D. 1973. An analysis of diurnal freeze-thaw and frost heave cycles in the Indian Peaks Region of the Colorado Front Range. *Arctic and Alpine Res.* 5(3):(Pt. 1)269–82. *p.180*

_____. 1974. Seasonal frost heave and frost penetration measurements in the Indian Peaks region of the Colorado Front Range. *Arctic and Alpine Res.* 6(1):63–70. *p.180*

Fahnestock, R. K. 1963. *Morphology and hydrology of a glacial stream, White River, Mt. Rainier, Washington*. U.S. Geol. Surv. Prof. Pap. 422-A. 70 pp.

Faust, R. A., and Nimlos, T. J. 1968. Soil microorganisms and soil nitrogen of the Montana alpine. *Northwest Sci.* 42:101–7.

Fay, C. E. 1905. The mountain as an influence in modern life. *Appalachia* 11(1):27–40.

Fenneman, N. M. 1931. *Physiography of western United States*. New York: McGraw-Hill. 534 pp.

Ferguson, C. W. 1970. Dendrochronology of bristlecone pine, *Pinus aristata*: Establishment of a 7484-year chronology in the White Mountains of east-central California, U.S.A. Pp. 237–59 in *Radiocarbon variations and absolute chronology*, ed. I. U. Olsson. New York: John Wiley and Sons.

Fickeler, P. 1962. Fundamental questions in the geography of religions. Pp. 94–117 in *Readings in cultural geography*, ed. P. L. Wagner and M. W. Mikesell. Chicago: Univ. Chicago Press. 589 pp. *p.19*

Fisher, R. L., and Revelle, R. 1955. The trenches of the Pacific. *Sci. Amer.* 193(11):36–41.

Flint, R. F. 1971. *Glacial and Quaternary geology*. New York: John Wiley and Sons. 892 pp.

Flohn, H. 1968. *Contributions to a meteorology of the Tibetan highlands*. Atmosph. Sci. Pap. 130. Fort Collins, Colo.: Dept. Atmos. Sci., Colorado State Univ. 120 pp. *p.105*

_____. 1969a. Zum klima und wasserhaushalt des Hindukushs und der benachbarten Gebirge. *Erdkunde* 23:205–15. *p.105*

_____. 1969b. Local wind systems. Pp. 139–71 in *World survey of climatology*, Vol. 2, ed. H. E. Landsberg. New York: Elsevier. 266 pp.

_____. 1970. Comments on water budget investigations, especially in tropical and subtropical mountain regions. Pp. 251–62 in *Symposium on world water balance*. Int. Ass. Sci. Hydrol. Pub. 93, Vol. 2. Brussels: UNESCO. *p.105*

_____. 1974. Contribution to a comparative meteorology of mountain areas. Pp. 55–72 in *Arctic and alpine environments*, ed. J. D. Ives and R. G. Barry. London: Methuen. 999 pp. *p.103,107*

Folsom, M. M. 1970. Volcanic eruptions: The pioneers' attitude on the Pacific Coast from 1800 to 1875. *Ore Bin* 32(4):61–71. (Pub. by Ore. Dept. Geol. Min. Ind., Portland.)

Fox, D. G. 1975. The impact of concentrated recreational development on air quality. Pp. 259–73 in *Man, leisure, and wildlands: A complex interaction*. Proc. 1st Eisenhower Consortium Res. Symp., Vail, Colo. 286 pp.

Franklin, J. F. 1977. The biosphere reserve program in the United States. *Science* 195(4275): 262–67.

Franklin, J. F., and Dyrness, C. T. 1973. *Natural vegetation of Oregon and Washington*. U.S. Dept. Agri. For. Serv. Gen. Tech. Rep. PNW-8. Portland, Or. 417 pp.

Franklin, J. F., Muir, W. H., Douglas, G. W., and Wiberg, C. 1971. Invasions of subalpine meadows by trees in the Cascade Range, Washington and Oregon. *Arctic and Alpine Res.* 13:215–24.

Frei, E. 1964. Micromorphology of some tropical

mountain soils. Pp. 307–11 in *Soil micromorphology*, ed. A. Jongerius. Amsterdam: Elsevier. 540 pp.

French, H. M. 1972a. Asymmetrical slope development in the Chiltern Hills. *Biuletyn Peryglacjalny* 21:51–73.

————. 1972b. The role of wind in periglacial environments, with special reference to Northwest Banks Island, Western Canadian Arctic. Pp. 82–84 in *International geography*, Vol. 9, ed. W. P. Adams and F. M. Helleiner. 22nd Int. Geog. Cong. Toronto: Univ. of Toronto Press. 694 pp. *p.228*

French, N. R. 1959. Life history of the black rosy finch. *Auk* 76:158–80.

Frenkel, R. E. 1974. Floristic changes along Everitt Memorial Highway, Mount Shasta, California. *Wasmann J. Biol.* 32(1):105–36.

Freshfield, D. W. 1881. Notes on old tracts. IV: The mountains of Dante. *Alpine J.* 10:400–405.

————. 1883. The Pass of Hannibal. *Alpine J.* 11(81):267–300.

————. 1886. Further notes on the Pass of Hannibal. *Alpine J.* 13(93):29–38.

————. 1904. On mountains and mankind. *Alpine J.* 22(166):269–90.

————. 1914. *Hannibal once more*. London: E. Arnold, ed. 120 pp.

————. 1916. The southern frontiers of Austria. *Alpine J.* 30(211):1–24.

Friedl, J. 1972. Changing economic emphasis in an alpine village. *Anthrop. Quart.* 45(3):145–57. *p.415*

————. 1973. Benefits of fragmentation in a traditional society: Case from the Swiss Alps. *Human Org.* 32(1):29–36.

————. 1974. *Kippel: A changing village in the Alps*. New York: Holt, Rinehart and Winston. 129 pp. *p.415*

Frisancho, A. R. 1975. Functional adaptation to high altitude hypoxia. *Science* 187(4174):313–19.

————. 1976. Growth and morphology at high altitude. Pp. 180–207 in *Man in the Andes: A multidisciplinary study of high-altitude Quechua*, ed. P. T. Baker and M. A. Little. Stroudsburg, Pa.: Dowden, Hutchinson and Ross. 482 pp.

————. 1978. Human growth and development among high-altitude populations. Pp. 117–72 in *The biology of high altitude peoples*, ed. P. T. Baker. Int. Biol. Prog. 14. Cambridge: Cambridge Univ. Press. 357 pp.

Frisancho, A. R., and Baker, P. T. 1970. Altitude and growth: A study of the patterns of physical growth of a high altitude Peruvian Quechua population. *Amer J. Phys. Anthrop.* 32:279–92.

Frisancho, A. R., Martinez, C., Velasquez, T., Sanchoz, J., and Montoye, H. 1973. Influence of developmental adaptation on aerobic capacity at high altitude. *J. Appl. Physiol.* 34:176–80.

Fristrup, B. 1953. Wind erosion within the arctic deserts. *Geog. Tidsskr.* 52:51–65. *p.226*

Fritz, S. 1965. The significance of mountain lee waves as seen from satellite pictures. *J. Appl. Meteor.* 4(1):31–37.

Frutiger, H. 1964. *Snow avalanches along Colorado Mountains highways*. U.S. Dept. Agri. For. Serv. Res. Pap. RM-7. Fort Collins, Colo. 85 pp.

————. 1975. Historical background of Swiss avalanche control projects. Pp. 38–44 in *U.S. Dept. Agri. For. Serv. Gen. Tech. Rep.* RM-9, Fort Collins, Colo. 168 pp. *p.154*

Fryxell, F. M., and Horberg, L. 1943. Alpine mud flows in Grand Teton National Park, Wyoming. *Geol. Soc. Amer. Bull.* 54:457–72. *p.193*

Fuguay, D. M. 1962. Mountain thunderstorms and forest fires. *Weatherwise* 15:149–52.

Fujita, T. 1967. Mesoscale aspects of orographic influences on flow and precipitation patterns. Pp. 131–46 in *Proc. Symp. on mountain meteorology*, ed. E. R. Reiter and J. L. Rasmussen. Atmosph. Sci. Pap. 122. Fort Collins, Colo.: Dept. Atmos. Sci., Colorado State Univ. *p.98*

Furrer, G., and Fitze, P. 1970. Treatise on the permafrost problem in the Alps. *Vierteljahrsschrift der naturforschenden Gesellschaft in Zurich* 115(3):353–68. (Trans. D. A. Sinclair, Nat. Res. Council Canada, Tech. Trans. 1657, 1973.)

Gade, D. W. 1969. Vanishing crops of traditional agriculture: The case of Tarwi (*Lupinus mutabilis*) in the Andes. *Proc. Assoc. Amer. Geog.* 1:47–51.

————. 1970. Coping with cosmic terror: The earthquake cult in Cuzco, Peru. *Amer. Benedictine Rev.* 21(2):218–23.

————. 1975. *Plants, man and the land in the Vilcanota Valley of Peru*. The Hague: Junk. 240 pp.

————. 1978. Windbreaks in the lower Rhône Valley. *Geog. Rev.* 68(2):127–44.

Gale, J. 1972. Elevation and transpiration: Some theoretical considerations with special reference to Mediterranean-type climate. *J. Appl. Ecol.* 9:691–702.

Gallimore, R. G., Jr., and Lettau, H. H. 1970. Topographic influence on tornado tracks and frequencies in Wisconsin and Arkansas. *Wisconsin Acad. Sci. Arts and Letters* 58:101–27.

Gambo, K. 1956. The topographical effect upon the jet stream in the westerlies. *Meteor. Soc. Japan J.* (Ser. 2) 34(1):24–28.

Gardner, J. 1967. Notes on avalanches, icefalls, and rockfalls in the Lake Louise District, July and August 1966. *Can. Alpine J.* 50:90–95.

———. 1969. Snow patches: Their influence on mountain wall temperatures and the geomorphic implications. *Geog. Ann.* 51A:114–20.

———. 1970a. Rockfall: A geomorphic process in high mountain terrain. *Albertan Geog.* 6:15–21.

———. 1970b. A note on the supply of material to debris slopes. *Can. Geog.* 14:369–72.

———. 1970c. Observations of surficial talus movement. *Zeits. für Geomorph.* 13:317–23.

———. 1971. Morphology and sediment characteristics of mountain debris slopes in Lake Louise District (Canadian Rockies). *Zeits. für Geomorph.* 15:390–403.

———. 1973. The nature of talus shift on alpine talus slopes: An example from the Canadian Rocky Mountains. Pp. 95–105 in *Research in polar and alpine geomorphology*, ed. B. D. Fahey and R. D. Thompson. 3rd Guelph Symp. on Geomorph. 206 pp.

Gardner, N. C., and Judson, A. 1970. *Artillery control of avalanches along mountain highways*. U.S. Dept. Agri. For. Serv. Res. Pap. RM-61. Fort Collins, Colo. 26 pp.

Garner, H. F. 1959. Stratigraphic-sedimentary significance of contemporary climate and relief in four regions of the Andes mountains. *Geol. Soc. Amer. Bull.* 70:1327–68.

———. 1965. Base-level control of erosional surfaces. *Arkansas Acad. Sci. Proc.* 19:98–104.

———. 1974. *The origin of landscapes*. New York: Oxford Univ. Press. 734 pp.

Garnett, A. 1935. Insolation, topography and settlement in the Alps. *Geog. Rev.* 25:601–17.

———. 1937. Insolation and relief, their bearing on the human geography of alpine regions. *Proc. Inst. British Geog.* 5, 910:6–159.

Garnier, B. J., and Ohmura, A. 1968. A method of calculating the direct shortwave radiation income of slopes. *J. Appl. Meteor.* 7:796–800.

———. 1970. The evaluation of surface variations in solar radiation income. *Solar Energy* 13:21–34.

Gates, D. M., and Janke, R. 1966. The energy environment of the alpine tundra. *Oecol. Planta.* 1:39–62.

Geiger, R. 1965. *The climate near the ground*. Cambridge, Mass.: Harvard Univ. Press. 611 pp.

———. 1969. Topoclimates. Pp. 105–38 in *World survey of climatology*, Vol. 2, ed. H. E. Landsberg. Amsterdam: Elsevier. 266 pp.

Geikie, A. 1912. *Love of nature among the Romans*. London: J. Murray, ed. 394 pp.

Geist, V. 1971. *Mountain sheep: A study in behavior and evolution*. Chicago: Univ. of Chicago Press. 383 pp.

Gersmehl, P. 1971. Factors involved in the persistence of southern Appalachian treeless balds. *Proc. Assoc. Amer. Geog.* 3:56–61.

———. 1973. Pseudo-timberline: The southern Appalachian grassy balds (summary). *Arctic and Alpine Res.* 5(3):(Pt. 2) A137–38.

Gilbert, G. K. 1904. Systematic asymmetry of crest lines in the High Sierra of California. *J. Geol.* 12:579–88.

Gill, P. W., Smith, J. H., and Ziurys, E. J. 1954. *Fundamentals of internal combustion engines*. Annapolis, Md.: U.S. Naval Institute.

Gillison, A. N. 1969. Plant succession in an irregularly fired grassland area, Doma Peaks region, Papua. *J. Ecol.* 57:415–28.

———. 1970. Structure and floristics of a montane grassland-forest transition, Doma Peaks Region, Papua. *Blumea* 18:71–86.

Glass, M., and Carlson, T. N. 1963. The growth characteristics of small cumulus clouds. *J. Atmosph. Sci.* 20:397–406.

Glenn, C. L. 1961. The chinook. *Weatherwise* 14:175–82.

Glennie, E. A. 1941. Supposed cannibalism among spiders in high altitudes. *J. Bombay Nat. Hist. Soc.* 42(3):667.

Godley, A. D. 1925. Mountains and the public. *Alpine J.* 37:107–17.

Goldberg, S. R. 1974. Reproduction in mountain and lowland populations of the lizard *Sceloporus occidentalis*. *Copeia* 1:176–82.

Goldstein, M. C. 1976. Fraternal polyandry and fertility in a high Himalayan valley in northern Nepal. *Human Ecol.* 4(3):223–33.

Goldthwait, R. P. 1969. Patterned soils and permafrost on the Presidential Range (abs.).

P. 150 in *Resumés des communications*. Paris: 8th INQUA Cong.

———. 1970. Mountain glaciers of the Presidential Range in New Hampshire. *Arctic and Alpine Res.* 2(2):85–102.

Gómez-Ibáñez, D. A. 1975. *The western Pyrenees*. Oxford: Clarendon Press. 162 pp.

———. 1977. Energy, economics and the decline of transhumance. *Geog. Rev.* 67(3):284–98.

Good, R. 1953. *The geography of the flowering plants*. 2nd ed. London: Longmans, Green. 452 pp.

Goodell, B. C. 1966. *Snowpack management for optimum water benefits*. ASCE Water Resource Eng. Conf. Pap. 379. Denver, Colo., May 1966. 14 pp.

Gorbunov, A. P. 1978. Permafrost investigations in high-mountain regions. *Arctic and Alpine Res.* 10(2):283–94.

Gradwell, M. W. 1954. Soil frost studies at a high-country station. Vol. I. *New Zealand Jour. Sci. Tech.* (Sec. B) 36:240–57.

Graf, W. L. 1976. Cirques as glacier locations. *Arctic and Alpine Res.* 8(1):79–90.

Grahn, D., and Kratchman, J. 1963. Variation in neonatal death rate and birth weight in the United States and possible relations to environmental radiation, geology, and altitude. *Amer. J. Hum. Genet.* 15:329–52.

Grant, L. D., and Kahan, A. M. 1974. Weather modification for augmenting orographic precipitation. Pp. 282–317 in *Weather and climate modification*, ed. W. N. Hess. New York: John Wiley and Sons. 842 pp.

Grant, M. C. 1980. Acid precipitation in the western United States. *Science* 207(4427): 176–77.

Grant, M. C., and Mitton, J. B. 1977. Genetic differentiation among growth forms of Engelmann spruce and subalpine fir at treeline. *Arctic and Alpine Res.* 9(3):259–63.

Grard, R., and Mathevet, P. 1972. *Extension des précipitations "De Lombarde" sur les Alpes françaises*. Vol. II. Geilo, Norway: Proc. Int. Symp. World Meteor. Organ. 587 pp.

Grauer, C. T. 1962. High altitude pole line. *Elec. Light and Power* 40(5):34–36.

Gray, J. T. 1972. Debris accretion on talus slopes in the central Yukon Territory. Pp. 75–84 in *Mountain geomorphology*, ed. O. Slaymaker and H. J. McPherson. Vancouver, B.C.: Tantalus Research. 274 pp.

———. 1973. Geomorphic effects of avalanches and rock-falls on steep mountain slopes in the central Yukon Territory. Pp. 107–17 in *Research in polar geomorphology*, ed. B. D. Fahey and R. D. Thompson. 3rd Guelph Symp. Geomorph. Guelph, Ontario. 206 pp.

Green, C. V. 1936. Observations on the New York weasel, with remarks on its winter dichromatism. *J. Mammal.* 17:247–49.

Greller, A. M., Goldstein, M., and Marcus, L. 1974. Snowmobile impact on three alpine plant communities. *Envir. Consv.* 1(2):1–110.

Gribble, F. 1899. *The early mountaineers*. London: Unwin, T. Fisher. 338 pp.

Griggs, D. T. 1936. The factor of fatigue in rock exfoliation. *J. Geol.* 44:781–96.

Griggs, R. F. 1934. The problem of arctic vegetation. *J. Wash. Acad. Sci.* 24(4):153–75.

———. 1938. Timberlines in the northern Rocky Mountains. *Ecol.* 19:548–64.

Grinnell, G. B. 1922. The medicine wheel. *Amer. Anthrop.* 24:299–310.

Grinnell, J. 1923. The burrowing rodents of California as agents in soil formation. *J. Mammal.* 4(3):137–49.

Grove, J. M. 1972. The incidence of landslides, avalanches, and floods in western Norway during the Little Ice Age. *Arctic and Alpine Res.* 4(2):131–39.

Grover, R. F. 1974. Man living at high altitudes. Pp. 817–30 in *Arctic and alpine environments*, ed. J. D. Ives and R. G. Barry. London: Methuen. 999 pp.

Grover, R. F., Reeves, J. T., Grover, E. G., and Leathers, J. E. 1967. Muscular exercise in young men native to 3100 m altitude. *J. Appl. Physiol.* 22:555–64.

Grubb, P. J. 1971. Interpretation of the Massenerhebung effect on tropical mountains. *Nature* 229:44–45.

———. 1974. Factors controlling the distribution of forest types on tropical mountains: New facts and a new perspective. Pp. 1–25 in *Altitudinal zonation in Malesia*, ed. R. Flenley, Jr. Univ. Hull Dept. Geog. Misc. Ser. 16. Hull, Eng.: Univ. Hull. 109 pp.

———. 1977. Control of forest growth and distribution on wet tropical mountains. *Ann. Rev. Ecol. and Systematics* 8:83–107.

Grubb, P. J., and Tanner, E. V., Jr. 1976. The montane forests and soils of Jamaica:

A reassessment. *J. Arnold Arbor.* 57:313–68.

Grunow, J. 1955. Der Niederschlag im Bergwald. *Forstwiss Centrabl.* 74:21–36.

———. 1960. The productiveness of fog precipitation in relation to the cloud droplet spectrum. Pp. 110–17 in *Physics of precipitation*, ed. H. Weickmann. Geophysical Monogr. 5. Washington, D.C.: Amer. Geophys. Union. 435 pp.

Gutenberg, B., Buwalda, J. P., and Sharp, R. P. 1956. Seismic explorations on the floor of Yosemite Valley. *Geol. Soc. Amer. Bull.* 67: 1051–78.

Gutman, G. J., and Schwerdtfeger, W. 1965. The role of latent and sensible heat for the development of a high pressure system over the subtropical Andes in the summer. *Meteor. Rund.* 18:69–75.

Haantjens, H. A. 1970. Soils of the Goroka-Mount Hagen area. Pp. 80–103 in *Lands of the Goroka-Mount Hagen area, Papua, New Guinea*. Land Res. Ser. 27. Melbourne, Australia: Commonwealth Sci. and Indus. Res. Organ. 159 pp.

Haantjens, H. A., and Rutherford, G. K. 1965. Soil zonality and parent rock in a very wet tropical mountain region. Pp. 493–500 in *Proc. 8th Int. Congr. Soil Sci.*, Vol. 5. Bucharest, Romania.

Haas, J. D. 1976. Prenatal and infant growth and development. Pp. 161–79 in *Man in the Andes: A multidisciplinary study of high-altitude Quechua*, ed. P. T. Baker and M. A. Little. Stroudsburg, Pa.: Dowden, Hutchinson and Ross. 482 pp.

Habeck, J. R. 1972a. *Fire ecology investigations in Selway-Bitterroot Wilderness.* U.S. For. Serv. Publ. R1-72-001. Missoula, Mont.: Univ. of Montana. 119 pp.

———. 1972b. Glacier's Logan Pass: A case of mismanagement. *Nat. Parks and Consv. Mag.* 46(5):10–14.

Hack, J. T. 1960. Origin of talus and scree in northern Virginia (abs.). *Geol. Soc. Amer. Bull.* 71:1877–78.

Hack, J. T., and Goodlett, J. C. 1960. *Geomorphology and forest ecology of a mountain region in the central Appalachians.* U.S. Geol. Surv. Prof. Pap. 347. 66 pp.

Hackman, W. 1964. On reduction and loss of wings in Diptera. *Not. Ent. Helsinki* 46:73–93.

Hafeli, H. 1968–69. The alpine salamander. Pp. 166–74 in *The mountain world*, ed. M. Barnes. Swiss Found. for Alpine Res. London: George Allen and Unwin. 188 pp.

Hahn, D. G., and Manabe, S. 1975. The role of mountains in the South Asian monsoon circulation. *J. Atmosph. Sci.* 32(8):1515–41.

Hales, W. B. 1933. Canyon winds of the Wasatch Mountains. *Bull. Amer. Meteor. Soc.* 14:194–96.

Hall, F. G. 1937. Adaptations of mammals to high altitudes. *J. Mammal.* 18:468–72.

Hall, F. G., Dill, D. B., and Guzman-Barron, E. S. 1936. Comparative physiology in high altitudes. *J. Cell. Comp. Physiol.* 8:301–13.

Hallam, A. 1975. Alfred Wegener and the hypothesis of continental drift. *Sci. Amer.* 232(2): 88–97.

Hamann, R. R. 1943. The remarkable temperature fluctuations in the Black Hills region. *Mon. Wea. Rev.* 71(1):29–32.

Hammel, H. T. 1956. Infrared emissivities of some arctic fauna. *J. Mammal.* 37(3):375–81.

Hammond, A. L. 1975. Minerals and plate tectonics: A conceptual revolution. *Science* 189 (4205):779–81.

Hammond, E. H. 1964. Analysis of properties in landform geography: An application to broad-scale landform mapping. *Annals Assoc. Amer. Geog.* 54(1):11–19.

Hampel, R., Figala and Praxl. 1960. Forest practices in control of avalanches, floods and soil erosion in the Alps. Pp. 1625–29 in *Proc. Fifth Forestry Cong.*, Vol. 3. Seattle: Univ. Washington.

Hanawalt, R. B., and Whittaker, R. H. 1976. Altitudinally coordinated patterns of soil and vegetation in the San Jacinto Mountains, California. *Soil Sci.* 121(2):114–24.

———. 1977. Altitudinal patterns of Na, K, Ca, and Mg in soils and plants in the San Jacinto Mountains, California. *Soil Sci.* 123(1):25–36.

Hann, J. 1866. Zur Frage über den Ursprung des föhn. *Z. Ost. Ges. Meteor.* 1:257–63.

———. 1903. *Handbook of climatology.* Part 1. Trans. R. De C. Ward. London: Macmillan. 437 pp.

Hanna, J. M. 1974. Coca leaf use in southern Peru: Some biological aspects. *Amer. Anthrop.* 76:281–96.

———. 1976. Drug use. Pp. 363–78 in *Man in the Andes: A multidisciplinary study of high-altitude*

Quechua, ed. P. T. Baker and M. A. Little. Stroudsburg, Pa.: Dowden, Hutchinson and Ross. 482 pp.

Hansen, W. R., and Eckel, E. B. 1966. *The Alaskan earthquake, March 27, 1964: Field investigations and reconstruction effort.* U.S. Geol. Surv. Prof. Pap. 541. 37 pp.

Hardin, G. 1969. The economics of wilderness. *Nat. Hist.* 78(6):20–27.

Hardon, H. J. 1936. Podzol-profiles in the tropics. *Natuurweten-Schappelijk Tijdschrift voor Neder-landsch Indie* 96:25–41.

Hardy, J. T., and Curl, H., Jr. 1972. The candy-colored, snow-flaked alpine biome. *Nat. Hist.* 81:74–78.

Hargens, A. R. 1972. Freezing resistance in polar fishes. *Science* 176(4031):184–86.

Harr, R., Harper, W. C., Krygier T., and Hsieh, F. S. 1975. Changes in snow hydrographs after road building and clear-cutting in the Oregon Coast Range. *Water Resources Res.* 11(3):436–44.

Harris, S. A. 1971. Podzol development on volcanic ash deposits in the Talamanca Range, Costa Rica. Pp. 191–209 in *Paleopedology: Origin, nature and dating of paleosols*, ed. D. H. Yaalon. Jerusalem: Int. Soc. Soil Sci. and Israel Univ. Press. 350 pp.

Harrison, G. A., Kuchenmann, C. F., Moore, M. A. S., Bouce, A. J., Baju, T., Mourant, A. E., Godber, M. J., Glasgow, B. G., Lopec, A. C., Tills, D., and Clegg, E. J. 1969. The effects of altitudinal variation in Ethiopian populations. *Phil. Trans. Roy. Soc. London* (Ser. B) 256(805):147–82.

Harrison, H. T., and Beckwith, W. B. 1951. Studies on the distribution and forecasting of hail in western United States. *Bull. Amer. Meteor. Soc.* 32(4):119–31.

Harrison, J. V., and Falcon, N. L. 1937. The Said-marreh landslip, southern Iran. *Geog. J.* 89:42–47.

―――. 1938. An ancient landslip at Saidmarreh in southwestern Iran. *J. Geol.* 46:296–309.

Harrold, T. W., Bussell, R., and Grinsted, W. A. 1972. The Dee Weather Radar Project. Vol. II, pp. 47–61 in *Distribution of precipitation in mountainous areas.* Geilo, Norway: Proc. Int. Symp. World Meteor. Organ. 587 pp.

Hart, J. S. 1956. Seasonal changes in insulation of the fur. *Can. J. Zool.* 34:53–57.

Harwood, M., and Treshow, M. 1975. Impact of ozone on the growth and reproduction of understory plants in the aspen zone of western U.S.A. *Envir. Consv.* 2(1):17–23.

Hastenrath, S. 1967. Rainfall distribution and regime in Central America. *Archiv. Meteor. Geophys. Biokl.* 15:202–41.

―――. 1968. Certain aspects of the three dimensional distribution of climate and vegetation belts in the mountains of Central America and southern Mexico. Pp. 122–30 in *Geoecology of the mountainous regions of the tropical Americas*, ed. C. Troll. Proc. UNESCO Mexico Symp. Aug. 1966. Bonn: Ferd. Dümmlers Verlag. 223 pp.

―――. 1973. Observations on the periglacial morphology of Mts. Kenya and Kilimanjaro, East Africa. Pp. 161–79 in *Quaternary geomorphology*, ed. J. Hovermann and K. Kaiser. *Zeits. für Geomorph.* Suppl. 16. Berlin. 203 pp.

―――. 1977. Observations on soil phenomena in the Peruvian Andes. *Zeits. für Geomorph.* 21(3):357–62.

Havlik, D. 1969. Nachweis und Begründung der hochreichenden Niederschlagszunahme in den Westalpen. *Freiburger Geographische* 7.

Hayano, D. M. 1973. Individual correlates of coffee adoption in the New Guinea highlands. *Human Org.* 32(3):305–13.

Hayes, G. L. 1941. *Influence of altitude and aspect on daily variations in factors of forest-fire danger.* Circular 591. Washington, D.C.: U.S. Dept. Agri. 38 pp.

Headley, J. T. 1855. *The sacred mountains.* New York: C. Scribner. 175 pp.

Hedberg, O. 1951. Vegetation belts of the East African mountains. *Svensk. Bot. Tidskr.* 45:140–202.

―――. 1961. The phytogeographical position of the afroalpine flora. *Rec. Adv. Botany* 1:914–19.

―――. 1964. Features of afroalpine plant ecology. *Acta Phytogeographica Suecica* 49:1–144.

―――. 1965. Afroalpine flora elements. *Webbia* 19:519–29.

―――. 1969. Evolution and speciation in a tropical high mountain flora. *Biol. J. Linnean Soc.* 1(1):135–48.

―――. 1971. Evolution of the afroalpine flora. Pp. 16–23 in *Adoptive aspects of insular evolution*, ed. W. L. Stern. Pullman, Wash.: Washington State Univ. Press. 85 pp.

―――. 1972. On the delimitation and subdivision of the high mountain region of Eurasian high mountains. Pp. 107–9 in *Geoecology of the high mountain regions of Eurasia,* ed. C. Troll. Wiesbaden: Franz Steiner. 300 pp.

————. 1975. Studies of adaptation and speciation in the afro-alpine flora of Ethiopia. *Boissiera* 24:71–74.

Heede, B. H. 1975. Mountain watersheds and dynamic equilibrium. Pp. 407–20 in *Watershed management symposium; ASCE Irrigation and Drainage Div.* Logan, Utah, Aug. 11–13, 1975.

Heer, D. M. 1967. Fertility differences in Andean countries: A reply to W. H. James. *Pop. Stud.* 21:71–73.

Heine, E. M. 1937. Observations on the pollination of New Zealand flowering plants. *Royal Soc. New Zealand, Trans.* 67:133–48.

Heinrich, B. 1974. Thermoregulation in endothermic insects. *Science* 185(4153):747–56.

Heinrich, B., and Raven, P. H. 1972. Energetics and pollination ecology. *Science* 176(4035): 597–602.

Heinselman, M. L. 1970. Preserving nature in forested wilderness areas and National Parks. *Nat. Parks and Consv. Mag.* 44(276):8–14.

Heirtzler, J. R. 1968. Sea floor spreading. *Sci. Amer.* 219(6):60–70.

Heizer, R. F. 1966. Ancient heavy transport, methods and achievements. *Science* 153(3738): 821–30.

Hellriegel, K. O. 1967. Health problems at altitude. Paper presented at the WHO/PAHO/ IBP Meeting of Investigators on Population Biology of Altitude, 13–17 Nov. Washington, D.C.

Hembree, C. H., and Rainwater, F. H. 1961. *Chemical degradation on opposite flanks of the Wind River Range, Wyoming.* U.S. Geol. Surv. Water Supply Pap. 1534 E. 9 pp. p.174

Hendee, J. C. 1974. A scientist's views on some current wilderness management issues. *Western Wildlands* (Spring):27–32. p.439

Hendee, J. C., and Lucas, R. C. 1973. Mandatory wilderness permits: A necessary management tool. *J. Forestry* 71(4):206–9. p.440

Hendee, J. C., and Stankey, G. H. 1973. Biocentricity in wilderness management. *BioScience* 23(9):535–38.

Hendee, J. C., Stanley, G. H., and Lucas, R. C. 1978. *Wilderness management.* U.S. Dept. Agri. For. Serv. Misc. Pub. 1365. Washington, D.C. 381 pp. p.439

Henrie, R. L., and Ridd, M. K. 1977. Environmental hazards and development on the Wasatch Front. Pp. 35–49 in *Perceptions of Utah: A field guide,* ed. D. C. Greer. Prepared for 1977 Nat. Meetings Assoc. Amer. Geog., Salt Lake City, Utah. Ogden, Utah: Weber State College. 115 pp. p.387

Henry, A. J. 1919. Increase of precipitation with altitude. *Mon. Wea. Rev.* 47:33–41.

Henshaw, R. E., Underwood, L. S., and Casey, T. M. 1972. Peripheral thermoregulation: Foot temperature in two arctic canines. *Science* 175(4025):988–90.

Henz, J. F. 1972. An operational technique of forecasting thunderstorms along the lee slopes of a mountain range. *J. Appl. Meteor.* 11(8): 1284–92.

Herbert, D., and Bardossi, F. 1968. *Kilauea: A case history of a volcano.* New York: Harper and Row. 191 pp.

Herrmann, R. 1970. Vertically differentiated water balance in tropical high mountains— with special reference to the Sierra Nevada de Santa Marta, Colombia. Pp. 262–73 in *Symposium on world water balance.* Int. Ass. Sci. Hydrol. Pub. 93. Vol. 2. Brussels: UNESCO.

Hess, S. L., and Wagner, H. 1948. Atmospheric waves in the northwestern United States. *J. Meteor.* 5(1):1–19.

Hesse, R., Allee, W. C., and Schmidt, K. P. 1951. *Ecological animal geography.* New York: John Wiley and Sons. 715 pp.

Hewitt, K. 1968. The freeze-thaw environment of the Karakoram Himalaya. *Can. Geog.* 12:85–98. p.186

————. 1972. The mountain environment and geomorphic processes. Pp. 17–36 in *Mountain geomorphology,* ed. O. Slaymaker and H. J. McPherson. Vancouver, B.C.: Tantalus Research. 274 pp. p.172, 212, 221, 230, 423

————. 1976. Earthquake hazards in the mountains. *Nat. Hist.* 85(5):31–37.

Hewlett, J. F., and Helvey, J. D. 1970. Effects of forest clear-felling on the storm hydrograph. *Water Resources Res.* 6(3):768–82.

Hickman, J. C. 1974. Pollination by ants: A low-energy system. *Science* 148(4143):1290–92. p.297

Highman, B., and Altland, P. D. 1964. Immunity and resistance to pathogenic bacteria at high altitude. Pp. 177–80 in *The physiological effects of high altitude,* ed. W. H. Weihe. New York: Macmillan. 351 pp.

Higuchi, K., and Fujii, Y. 1971. Permafrost at the

summit of Mount Fuji, Japan. *Nature* 230 (5295):521.

Hill, L. E. 1924. *Sunshine and the open air: Their influence on health, with special reference to alpine climate.* London: E. Arnold. 132 pp.

Hill, M. R. 1965. Earth hazards—an editorial. *Mineral Info. Serv. Calif. Div. Mines and Geol.* 18(4):57–59.

Hindman, E. E. 1973. Air currents in a mountain valley deduced from the break-up of a stratus deck. *Mon. Wea. Rev.* 101(3):195–200.

Hingston, R. W. G. 1925. Animal life at high altitudes. *Geog. J.* 65(3):185–98.

Hirao, Y., and Patterson, C. C. 1974. Lead aerosol pollution in the high Sierra overrides natural mechanisms which exclude lead from a food chain. *Science* 184:989–92.

Hobbs, P. V., and Radke, L. F. 1973. Redistribution of snowfall across a mountain range by artificial seeding: A case study. *Science* 181 (4104):1043–45.

Hock, R. J. 1964a. Animals in high altitudes: Reptiles and amphibians. Pp. 841–42 in *Handbook of physiology.* Sec. 4: *Adaptation to the environment,* ed. D. B. Dill, E. F. Adolph, and C. G. Wilber. Washington, D.C.: Amer. Physiol. Soc. 1056 pp.

———. 1964b. Terrestrial animals in cold: Reptiles. Pp. 357–60 in *Handbook of physiology.* Sec. 4: *Adaptation to the environment,* ed. D. B. Dill, E. F. Adolph, and C. G. Wilber. Washington, D.C.: Amer. Physiol. Soc. 1056 pp.

———. 1964c. Physiological responses of deer mice to various native altitudes. Pp. 59–72 in *The physiological effects of high altitude,* ed. W. H. Weihe. New York: Macmillan. 351 pp.

———. 1965. An analysis of Gloger's Rule. *Hvalradet Skrifter* (Oslo) 48:214–26.

———. 1970. The physiology of high altitude. *Sci. Amer.* 222(2):53–62.

Hocking, B. 1968. Insect-flower associations in the high arctic with special reference to nectar. *Oikos* 19:359–88.

Hodge, W. H. 1949. Tuber foods of the old Incas. *Nat. Hist.* 58(10):464–70.

Hoff, C. C. 1957. A comparison of soil, climate, and biota of conifer and aspen communities in the central Rocky Mountains. *Amer. Midl. Nat.* 58:115–40.

Hoff, C. J., and Abelson, A. E. 1976. Fertility. Pp. 128–46 in *Man in the Andes: A multidisciplinary study of high-altitude Quechua,* ed. P. T. Baker

and M. A. Little. Stroudsburg, Pa.: Dowden, Hutchinson and Ross. 482 pp.

Hoffmann, R. S. 1974. Terrestrial vertebrates. Pp. 475–568 in *Arctic and alpine environments,* ed. J. D. Ives and R. G. Barry. London: Methuen. 999 pp.

Hoffmann, R. S., and Taber, R. D. 1967. Origin and history of Holarctic tundra ecosystems, with special references to their vertebrate faunas. Pp. 143–70 in *Arctic and alpine environments,* ed. W. H. Osburn and H. E. Wright, Jr. Bloomington, Ind.: Indiana Univ. Press. 308 pp.

Hogan, A. W. 1972. Snowmelt delay by oversnow travel. *Water Resources Res.* 8:174–75.

Hoham, R. W. 1975. Optimum temperatures and temperature ranges for growth of snow algae. *Arctic and Alpine Res.* 7(1):13–24.

Hoinkes, H. C. 1964. Glacial meteorology. *Res. Geophys.* 2:391–424.

———. 1968. Glacial variation and weather. *J. Glaciol.* 7(49):3–19.

Hoinkes, H. C., and Rudolph, R. 1962. Mass balance studies on the Hintereisferner, Otztal Alps, 1952–1961. *J. Glaciol.* 4:266–80.

Holdich, T. H. 1901. *The Indian borderland.* London: Methuen. 402 pp.

Holdridge, L. R. 1957. *Life zone ecology.* San Jose, Costa Rica: Tropical Science Center. 206 pp.

Höllermann, P. 1973. Some reflections on the nature of high mountains, with special reference to the western United States. *Arctic and Alpine Res.* 5(3):(Pt. 2)A149–60.

Holmes, A. 1931. Radioactivity and earth movements. *Geol. Soc. Glasgow Trans.* 18:559–606.

———. 1965. *Principles of physical geology.* 2nd ed. New York: Ronald Press. 1288 pp.

Holmes, R. T. 1966. Molt cycle of the Redbacked sandpiper (*Calidris alpina*) in western North America. *Auk* 83:517–33.

Holtmeier, F. K. 1972. The influence of animal and man on the alpine timberline. Pp. 93–97 in *Geoecology of the high mountain regions of Eurasia,* ed. C. Troll. Wiesbaden: Franz Steiner. 299 pp.

———. 1973. Geoecological aspects of timberlines in northern and central Europe. *Arctic and Alpine Res.* 5(3):(Pt. 2)45–54.

Hope, G. S. 1976. The vegetational history of Mt. Wilhelm, Papua, New Guinea. *J. Ecol.* 64(2): 627–64.

Hope, J. 1968. The king besieged. *Nat. Hist.* 77(9):52–57.

Horton, R. E. 1934. Water-losses in high latitudes and at high elevations. *Trans. Amer. Geophys. Union* (Pt. II):351–79.

Horvath, S. M. 1972. Physiology of work at altitude. Pp. 183–90 in *Physiological adaptations, desert and mountain*, ed. M. K. Yousef, S. M. Horvath, and R. W. Bullard. New York: Academic Press. 258 pp.

Hough, A. F. 1945. Frost pockets and other microclimates in forests of the northern Allegheny plateau. *Ecol.* 26:235–50.

— House, J. W. 1959. The Franco-Italian boundary in the Alps Maritimes. *Trans. and Pap. Inst. British Geog.* 26:107–31. ρ·376

Houston, C. S. 1964. Effects of high altitude (oxygen lack). Pp. 469–93 in *Medical climatology*, ed. S. Licht. Baltimore: Waverly Press. 753 pp. ρ·314

———. 1972. High-altitude pulmonary and cerebral edema. *Amer. Alpine J.* 18(1):83–92.

Houston, D. 1971. Ecosystems of national parks. *Science* 172:648–51.

Hovind, E. L. 1965. Precipitation distribution around a windy mountain peak. *J. Geophys. Res.* 70:3271–78.

Howard, A. D. 1967. Drainage analysis in geologic interpretation: A summation. *Amer. Assoc. Petrol. Geol. Bull.* 51:2246–59.

Howard, G. E. 1949. Alpine uplift. *Alpine J.* 57 (278):1–9.

Howard, R. A. 1971. The "alpine" plants of the Antilles. Pp. 24–28 in *Adoptive aspects of insular evolution*, ed. W. L. Stern. Pullman, Wash.: Washington State Univ. Press. 85 pp.

Howe, E. 1909. *Landslides in the San Juan Mountains, Colorado: Including a consideration of their causes and their classification*. U.S. Geol. Surv. Prof. Pap. 67. 58 pp.

Howe, J. 1971. Temperature readings in test bore holes. *Mt. Washington Observatory News Bull.* 12(2):37–40. ρ·181

Howell, W. E. 1953. Some measurements of ablation, melting, and solar absorption on a glacier in Peru. *Trans. Amer. Geophys. Union* 34(6): 883–88.

Hsu, K. J. 1975. Catastrophic debris streams (Sturzstroms) generated by rockfalls. *Geol. Soc. Amer. Bull.* 86:129–40.

Hudson, G. V. 1905. Notes on insect swarms on mountain tops in New Zealand. *Royal Soc. New Zealand, Trans.* 38:334–36.

Hunt, C. B. 1958. *How to collect mountains*. San Francisco: W. H. Freeman. 38 pp.

Hurd, W. E. 1929. Northers of the Gulf of Tehuantepec. *Mon. Wea. Rev.* 57:192–94.

Hurley, P. 1968. The confirmation of continental drift. *Sci. Amer.* 218(4):52–64.

Hurtado, A. 1955. Pathological aspects of life at high altitudes. *Military Med.* 117:272–84.

———. 1960. Some clinical aspects of life at high altitudes. *Ann. Int. Med.* 53:247–58.

———. 1964. Animals in high altitudes: Resident man. Pp. 843–60 in *Handbook of physiology*. Sec. 4: *Adaptation to the environment*, ed. D. B. Dill, E. F. Adolph, and C. G. Wilber. Washington, D.C.: Amer. Physiol. Soc. 1056 pp.

Husted, W. M. 1965. Early occupation of the Colorado Front Range. *Amer. Antiquity* 30(4): 494–98.

———. 1974. Prehistoric occupation in the Rocky Mountains. Pp. 857–72 in *Arctic and alpine environments*, ed. J. D. Ives and R. G. Barry. London: Methuen. 999 pp.

Huxley, T. 1978. Tourism—Uses and abuses of mountain resources. Pp. 199–208 in *The use of high mountains of the world*. Wellington, N.Z.: Dept. Lands and Survey Head Office, Private Bag (in assoc. with Tussock Grasslands and Mountain Lands Inst., P.O. Box 56, Lincoln College, Canterbury, N.Z., for Int. Union Cons. Nature). 223 pp. ρ·430

Hyde, W. W. 1915–16. The ancient appreciation of mountain scenery. *Classical J.* 11:70–84.

———. 1917. The development of the appreciation of mountain scenery in modern times. *Geog. Rev.* 3:107–18.

Imeson, A. C. 1976. Some effects of burrowing animals on slope processes in Luxembourg Ardennes. *Geog. Ann.* 58A(1–2):115–25.

Imhof, E. 1900. Die Waldgrenze in der Schweiz. *Beiträge zur Geophysic* 4:241–330.

Ingles, L. G. 1952. The ecology of the mountain Pocket gopher, *Thomomys monticola. Ecol.* 33(1): 87–95.

Irving, L. 1960. Human adaptation to cold. *Nature* 185:572–74.

———. 1964. Terrestrial animals in cold: Birds and mammals. Pp. 361–78 in *Handbook of physiology*. Sec. 4: *Adaptation to the environment*, ed. D. B. Dill, E. F. Adolph, and C. G. Wilber. Washington, D.C.: Amer. Physiol. Soc. 1056 pp.

————. 1966. Adaptations to cold. *Sci. Amer.* 214:94–101.

————. 1972. *Arctic life of birds and mammals.* New York: Springer-Verlag. 192 pp.

Irving, L., and Krog, J. 1955. Temperature of skin in the Arctic as a regulator of heat. *J. Appl. Physiol.* 7:355–64.

Irving, L., Krog, H., and Monson, M. 1955. Insulation and metabolism of some Alaskan animals in winter and summer. *J. Physiol. Zool.* 28:173–85.

Isacks, B., Oliver, J., and Sykes, L. R. 1968. Seismology and the new global tectonics. *J. Geophys. Res.* 73(18):5855–99.

I.U.C.N. 1978. *The use of high mountains of the world.* Wellington, N.Z.: Dept. Lands and Survey, Head Office, Private Bag (in assoc. with Tussock Grasslands and Mountain Lands Inst., P.O. Box 56, Lincoln College, Canterbury, N.Z., for Int. Union Cons. Nature), 223 pp.

Ives, J. D. 1958. Mountain top detritus and the extent of the last glaciation in northeastern Labrador-Ungava. *Can. Geog.* 12:25–31.

————. 1966. Blockfields, associated weathering forms on mountain tops and the Nunatak hypothesis. *Geog. Ann.* 48A:220–23.

————. 1973. Permafrost and its relationship to other environmental parameters in a midlatitude, high-altitude setting, Front Range, Colorado Rocky Mountains. Pp. 121–25 in *North Amer. Contr. Perm. Second Int. Conf.* Washington, D.C.: Nat. Acad. Sci.

————. 1974a. Permafrost. Pp. 159–94 in *Arctic and alpine environments,* ed. J. D. Ives and R. G. Barry. London: Methuen. 999 pp.

————. 1974b. Biological refugia and the Nunatak hypothesis. Pp. 605–36 in *Arctic and alpine environments,* ed. J. D. Ives and R. G. Barry. London: Methuen. 999 pp.

————. 1974c. The UNESCO Man and the Biosphere Programme and INSTAAR. *Arctic and Alpine Res.* 6(3):241–44.

————. 1974d. The UNESCO Man and the Biosphere Programme (MAB) Project 6: Regional Meeting, La Paz, June 9 to 16, 1974. *Arctic and Alpine Res.* 6(4):419–20.

————. 1974e. The impact of motor vehicles. Pp. 907–10 in *Arctic and alpine environments,* ed.

J. D. Ives and R. G. Barry. London: Methuen. 999 pp.

————. 1975. The development of mountain environments, Munich International Workshop. *Arctic and Alpine Res.* 7(1):101–2.

————. 1979. Applied high altitude geoecology: Can the scientist assist in the preservation of the mountains? Pp. 9–45 in *High altitude geoecology,* ed. P. J. Webber. Amer. Assoc. Adv. Sci. Selected Symp. 12. Boulder, Colo.: Westview Press. 188 pp.

Ives, J. D., and Barry, R. G., eds. 1974. *Arctic and alpine environments.* London: Methuen. 999 pp.

Ives, J. D., and Bovis, M. J. 1978. Natural hazards maps for land-use planning, San Juan Mountains, Colorado, U.S.A. *Arctic and Alpine Res.* 10(2):185–212.

Ives, J. D., Mears, A. R., Carrara, P. E., and Bovis, M. J. 1976. Natural hazards in mountain Colorado. *Annals Assoc. Amer. Geog.* 66(1):129–44.

Ives, R. L. 1941. Vegetative indicators of solifluction. *J. Geom.* 4:128–32.

————. 1950. Frequency and physical effects of chinook winds in the Colorado high plains region. *Annals Assoc. Amer. Geog.* 40:293–327.

Jackson, E. P. 1930. Mountains and the aborigines of the Champlain lowland. *Appalachia* 24(70):121–36.

Jacobs, A. H. 1965. African pastoralists: Some general remarks. *Anthrop. Quart.* 38:144–54.

Jahn, A. 1967. Some features of mass movement on Spitsbergen slopes. *Geog. Ann.* 49A:213–25.

James, P. E. 1959. *A geography of man.* 2nd ed. Boston: Ginn and Co. 656 pp.

James, W. H. 1966. The effect of high altitude on fertility in Andean countries. *Pop. Stud.* 20:97–101.

Janetschek, H. 1956. Das problem de inneralpinen Eiszeitsüberdauerung durch Tiere: Ein Beitrag zur Geschichte der nival Fauna. *Osterr. Zool. Inst.* 6(3/5):421–596.

Janzen, D. H. 1967. Why mountain passes are higher in the tropics. *Amer. Nat.* 101(919):233–49.

————. 1973. Rate of regeneration after a tropical high elevation fire. *Biotropica* 5(2):117–22.

Jaworowski, Z., Bilkiewicz, J., Dobosz, E., and Wodkiewicz, L. 1975. Stable and radioactive pollutants in a Scandinavian glacier. *Envir. Pollut.* 9(4):305–16.

Jenny, H. 1930. Hochgebirgsboden. Pp. 96–118 in *Handbuch de Bodenlehre,* Vol. 3, ed. E. Blanck. Berlin.

———. 1941. *Factors of soil formation.* New York: McGraw-Hill. 281 pp.

———. 1946. Arrangement of soil series and types according to functions of soil forming factors. *Soil Sci.* 61:375–91.

———. 1948. Great soil groups in the equatorial regions of Colombia, South America. *Soil Sci.* 66:5–28.

———. 1958. Role of the plant factor in the pedogenic functions. *Ecol.* 39:5–16.

Jerstad, L. 1969. *Mani-Rimdu: A Sherpa dance drama.* Seattle: Univ. Wash. Press. 192 pp.

Johnson, D. D., and Cline, A. J. 1965. Colorado mountain soils. *Adv. Agronomy* 17:233–81.

Johnson, D. R. 1976. Mountain caribou: Threats to survival in the Kootenay Pass region, British Columbia. *Northwest Sci.* 50(2):97–101.

Johnson, D. R., and Maxwell, M. H. 1966. Energy dynamics of Colorado pikas. *Ecol.* 47:1059–61.

Johnson, D. W., Cole, D. W., Gessel, S. P., Singer, M. J., and Minden, R. V. 1977. Carbonic acid leaching in a tropical temperate, subalpine and northern forest soil. *Arctic and Alpine Res.* 9(4): 329–43.

Johnson, J. P. 1973. Some problems in the study of rock glaciers. Pp. 84–94 in *Research in polar and alpine geomorphology,* ed. B. D. Fahey and R. D. Thompson. 3rd Guelph Symp. on Geomorphology. Guelph, Ontario.

Johnson, N. K. 1975. Controls of number of bird species on montane islands in the Great Basin. *Evolution* 29:545–67.

Johnson, P. C., and Denton, R. E. 1975. *Outbreaks of the western spruce budworm in the American northern Rocky Mountain area from 1922 through 1971.* U.S. Dept. Agri. For. Serv. Gen. Tech. Rep. INT-20. Ogden, Utah. 144 pp.

Johnson, R. E. 1968. Temperature regulation in the white-tailed ptarmigan, *Lagopus leucurus. Comp. Biochem. Physiol.* 24:1003–14.

Johnson, W. D. 1931. *Stream sculpture on the At-lantic slope.* New York: Columbia Univ. Press. 142 pp.

Johnson, W. M. 1965. *Rotation, rest-rotation, and season-long grazing on a mountain range in Wyo-ming.* U.S. For. Serv. Res. Pap. RM-14. Fort Collins, Colo. 16 pp.

Johnston, R. S., Brown, R. W., and Cravens, J. 1975. Acid mine rehabilitation problems at high elevations. Pp. 66–79 in *Proc. Amer. Soc. Civ. Eng. Watershed Management Symp.,* Logan, Utah. New York.

Jonca, E. 1972. Winter denudation of molehills in mountainous areas. *Acta Theriologica* 17(31): 407–12.

Judson, A. 1965. *The weather and climate of a high mountain pass in the Colorado Rockies.* U.S. For. Serv. Res. Paper RM-16. Fort Collins, Colo. 28 pp.

Julian, R. W., Yevjevich, V., and Morel-Seytoux, H. J. 1967. *Prediction of water yield in high moun-tain watersheds based on physiography.* Hydrol. Pap. 22. Fort Collins, Colo.: Colorado State Univ. 20 pp.

Juvik, J. O., and Perreira, D. J. 1974. Fog inter-ception on Mauna Loa, Hawaii. *Proc. Assoc. Amer. Geog.* 6:22–25.

Juvik, J. O., and Ekern, P. C. 1978. *A climatology of mountain fog on Mauna Loa, Hawaii Island.* Water Resources Center Tech. Rep. 118. Manoa, Hawaii: Univ. Hawaii. 63 pp.

Kaith, D. C. 1960. Forest practices in control of avalanches, floods, and soil erosion in the Himalayan Front. Pp. 1640–43 in *Proc. Fifth World Forestry Cong.,* Vol. 3. Seattle: Univ. Washington. 1341–2066 pp.

Kalabukov, N. J. 1937. Some physiological ad-aptations of the mountain and plain forms of the Wood mouse (*Apodemus sylvaticus*) and of other species of mouse-like rodents. *J. Animal Ecol.* 6:254–74.

Karan, P. P. 1960a. *Nepal: A cultural and physical geography.* Lexington, Ky.: Univ. of Kentucky Press. 101 pp.

———. 1960b. The India-China boundary dis-pute. *J. Geog.* 59:16–21.

———. 1963. *The Himalayan kingdoms: Bhutan, Sikkim and Nepal.* Princeton, N.J.: Van Nos-trand. 144 pp.

———. 1967. *Bhutan: A physical and cultural geog-raphy.* Lexington, Ky.: Univ. of Kentucky Press. 103 pp.

———. 1973. The changing geography of Tibet. *Asian Profile* 1(1):39–48.

———. 1976. *The changing face of Tibet: The impact of Chinese Communist ideology on the landscape.* Lexington, Ky.: Univ. of Kentucky Press. 114 pp.

Karan, P. P., and Mather, C. 1976. Art and geography: Patterns in the Himalaya. *Annals Assoc. Amer. Geog.* 66(4):487–515.

Karlstrom, E. L. 1962. *The toad genus* Bufo *in the Sierra Nevada of California.* Univ. Calif. Publ. Zool. 62. Berkeley, Ca. 104 pp.

Karrasch, H. 1972. The planetary and hypsometric variation of valley asymmetry. Pp. 31–33 in *International geography 1972,* Vol. 1, ed. W. P. Adams and F. M. Helleiner. 22nd Int. Geog. Cong. Toronto: Univ. of Toronto Press. 694 pp.

———. 1973. Microclimatic studies in the Alps. *Arctic and Alpine Res.* 5(3):(Pt. 2)55–64.

Kasahara, A. 1967. The influence of orography on the global circulation patterns of the atmosphere. Pp. 193–221 in *Proc. symp. mountain meteor.,* Atmos. Sci. Paper 122. Fort Collins, Colo.: Dept. of Atmos. Sci., Colorado State Univ.

Kaushic, S. D. 1959. Human settlement and occupational economy in Garhual-Bhot Himalayas. *J. Asiatic Soc.* 1(1):23–34.

Keeler, C. M. 1969. Snow accumulation on Mount Logan, Yukon Territory, Canada. *Water Resources Res.* 5:719–23.

Keenlyside, F. H. 1957. The influence of mountains upon the development of human intelligence. *Alpine J.* 62(295):192–94.

Kehrlein, O., Serr, S., Tarble, R. D., and Wilson, W. T. 1953. High Sierra snow ablation observations. Pp. 47–50 in *Proc. Amer. Met. Soc.* Fort Collins, Colo.: Western Snow Conf.

Kelsall, J. P., and Telfer, E. S. 1971. Studies of the physical adaptations of big game for snow. Pp. 134–46 in *Proc. snow and ice in relation to wildlife and recreation symp.* Ames, Iowa: Iowa State Univ. 280 pp.

Kendeigh, S. C. 1932. A study of Merriam's temperature laws. *Wilson Bull.* 44(3):129–43.

———. 1954. History and evaluation of various concepts of plant and animal communities in North America. *Ecol.* 35:152–71.

———. 1961. *Animal ecology.* Englewood Cliffs, N.J.: Prentice-Hall. 468 pp.

———. 1969. Tolerance of cold and Bergmann's Rule. *Auk* 86:13–25.

Kendrew, W. G. 1961. *The climates of the continents.* 5th ed. Oxford: Clarendon. 608 pp.

Kennedy, B. A. 1976. Valley-side slopes and climate. Pp. 171–202 in *Geomorphology and climate,* ed. E. Derbyshire. London: John Wiley and Sons. 512 pp.

Kennedy, B. A., and Melton, M. A. 1972. Valley asymmetry and slope forms of a permafrost area in the Northwest Territories, Canada. Pp. 107–21 in *Polar geomorphology,* ed. R. J. Price and D. E. Sugden. Spec. Pub. 4. London: Inst. Brit. Geog. 215 pp.

Kent, P. E. 1966. The transport mechanism in catastrophic rock falls. *J. Geol.* 74:79–83.

Kesseli, J. E. 1941. Rock streams in the Sierra Nevada, California. *Geog. Rev.* 31:203–27.

Khurshid Alam, F. C. 1972. Distribution of precipitation in mountainous areas of west Pakistan. Vol. II, pp. 290–306 in *Distribution of precipitation in mountainous areas.* Geilo, Norway: World Meteor. Organ. 587 pp.

Kikkawa, J., and Williams, W. T. 1971. Altitudinal distribution of land birds in New Guinea. *Search* 2:64–69.

Kilgore, B. M., and Briggs, G. S. 1972. Restoring fire to high elevation forests in California. *J. Forestry* 70(5):266–71.

King, L. C. 1967. *The morphology of the earth.* Edinburgh: Oliver and Boyd. 726 pp.

———. 1976. Planation remnants upon high lands. *Zeits. für Geomorph.* 20(2):133–48.

King, R. H., and Brewster, G. R. 1976. Characteristics and genesis of some subalpine podzols (spodosols), Banff National Park, Alberta. *Arctic and Alpine Res.* 8(1):91–104.

Kirby, M. J., and Statham, I. 1975. Surface stone movement and scree formation. *J. Geol.* 83(3):349–62.

Klein, W. H. 1974. From Zermatt to Utah: Autofree environment in ski resort areas. *Amer. Forests* 80(7):14–18.

Klikoff, L. G. 1965. Microenvironmental influence on vegetational pattern near timberline in the central Sierra Nevada. *Ecol. Monogr.* 35(2):187–211.

Klock, G. 1973. *Mission Ridge: A case history of soil disturbance and revegetation of a winter sports area development.* U.S. Dept. Agri. For. Serv. Res. Note PNW-199. Portland, Or. 10 pp.

Köhler, H. 1937. Rauhreifstudien. *Bull. Geol. Inst. Uppsala* 26:279–308.

Kollias, J., Buskird, E. R., Akers, R. F., Prokop, E. K., Baker, P. T., and Picon-Reategui, E. 1968. Work capacity of long time residents and newcomers to altitude. *J. Appl. Physiol.* 24:792–99.

Komarkova, V. 1974. Plant ecology of mylonitic soils in the alpine belt of the Tatra Mountains

(Carpathians). *Arctic and Alpine Res.* 6(2):205–16.

Krader, L. 1955. Ecology of Central Asian pastoralism. *Southwestern J. Anthrop.* 11(4):301–26.

———. 1959. The ecology of nomadic pastoralism. *Int. Soc. Sci. J.* 11:499–510.

Kruckeberg, A. R. 1954. The ecology of serpentine soils. III: Plant species in relation to serpentine soils. *Ecol.* 35:267–74.

———. 1969. Plant life on serpentinite and other ferromagnesian rocks in northwestern North America. *Syesis* 2:15–114.

Krüger, H., and Arias-Stella, J. 1970. The placenta and the newborn infant at high altitude. *Amer. J. Obstet. Gynec.* 106:486–551.

Kubiena, W. L. 1953. *The soils of Europe.* London: Thomas Murphy. 317 pp.

———. 1970. *Micromorphological features of soil geography.* New Brunswick, N.J.: Rutgers Univ. Press. 254 pp.

Kulas, M. W. 1950. Food preparation at high altitudes. *J. Amer. Diet. Assoc.* 26:510–13.

LaChapelle, E. 1966. The control of snow avalanches. *Sci. Amer.* 214:92–101.

———. 1968. Snow avalanches. Pp. 1020–25 in *The encyclopedia of geomorphology,* ed. R. W. Fairbridge. New York: Reinhold. 1295 pp.

———. 1969. *Field guide to snow crystals.* Seattle: Univ. of Washington Press. 101 pp.

LaChapelle, E., Johnson, J. B., Langdon, J. A., Morig, C. R., Sackett, E. M., and Taylor, P. L. 1976. *Alternate methods of avalanche control.* Res. Prog. Rep. 19.2. Olympia, Wash.: Wash. State Highway Dept. 95 pp.

LaChapelle, E., Bell, D. B., Johnson, J. B., Lindsey, R. W., Sackett, E. M., and Taylor, P. L. 1978. *Alternate methods of avalanche control, final report, phase IV.* Res. Prog. Rep. 19.3. Olympia, Wash.: Wash. State Highway Dept. 54 pp.

Lachman, R., and Bonk, W. 1960. Behavior and beliefs during the recent volcanic eruption at Kapoho, Hawaii. *Science* 13(3407):1095–96.

Lack, D. 1948. The significance of clutch size. III: Some interspecific comparisons. *Ibis* 90:25–45.

———. 1954. *The natural regulation of animal numbers.* Oxford: Oxford Univ. Press. 343 pp.

Lackey, E. E. 1949. Mountain passes in the Colorado Rockies. *Econ. Geog.* 25:211–15.

Lahiri, S., Milledge, A. S., Challopadhyay, H. T.,

Bhattacharyya, A. K., and Sinha, A. K. 1967. Respiration and heart rate of Sherpa highlanders during exercise. *J. Appl. Physiol.* 23:545–54.

LaMarche, V. C., Jr. 1967. Spheroidal weathering of thermally metamorphosed limestone and dolomite, White Mountains, California. Pp. C32–37 in *U.S. Geol. Surv. Prof. Pap.* 575-C.

LaMarche, V. C., Jr., and Mooney, H. A. 1972. Recent climatic change and development of the Bristlecone pine (*P. longaeva Bailey*) krummholz zone, Mt. Washington, Nevada. *Arctic and Alpine Res.* 4(1):61–72.

Lamb, H. H. 1965. The early medieval warm epoch and its sequel. *Paleogeog., Paleoclimatol., Paleoecol.* 1:13–37.

Landsberg, H. 1962. *Physical climatology.* 2nd ed. DuBois, Penn.: Gray Printing. 439 pp.

Lange, I. M., and Avent, J. C. 1973. Ground based thermal infrared surveys as an aid in predicting volcanic eruptions in the Cascade Range. *Science* 182(4109):279–81.

Langtvet, O. 1974. The farm-seter system in Ausdal, Norway: An analysis of change. *Norsk. Geografisk Tidsskrift* 28:167–80.

Lauer, W. 1973. The altitudinal belts of the vegetation in the central Mexican highlands and their climatic condition. *Arctic and Alpine Res.* 5(3):(Pt. 2)A99–114.

Lawrence, D. B. 1938. Trees on the march. *Mazama* 20(12):49–54.

———. 1939. Some features of the vegetation of the Columbia River Gorge with special reference to asymmetry in forest trees. *Ecol. Monogr.* 9:217–57.

Lawrence, D. B., and Lawrence, E. G. 1958. Bridge of the Gods legend: Its origin, history, and dating. *Mazama* 40:33–41.

Laycock, W. A., and Richardson, B. Z. 1975. Long-term effects of Pocket gopher control on vegetation and soils of a subalpine grassland. *J. Range Management* 28(6):458–62.

Leaf, A. 1973. Every day is a gift when you are over 100. *Nat. Geog. Mag.* 143(1):93–119.

Leaf, C. F. 1966. *Sediment yields from high mountain watersheds, Central Colorado.* U.S. Dept. Agri. For. Serv. Res. Pap. RM-23. Fort Collins, Colo. 15 pp.

———. 1974. More water from mountain watersheds. *Colo. Rancher Farmer* 28(7):11–12.

———. 1975. *Watershed management in the Rocky*

Mountain subalpine zone: The status of our knowledge. U.S. Dept. Agri. For. Serv. Res. Pap. RM-137. Ft. Collins, Colo. 31 pp.

Le Drew, E. F. 1975. The energy balance of a mid-latitude alpine site during the growing season, 1973. *Arctic and Alpine Res.* 7(4):301–14.

Lee, C. H. 1911. Precipitation and altitude in the Sierra. *Mon. Wea. Rev.* 39:1092–99.

Lee, R. 1972. An optographic technique for evaluating the exposure of precipitation gauge sites in mountainous areas. Vol. II, pp. 62–72 in *Distribution of precipitation in mountainous areas*. Geilo, Norway: Proc. Int. Symp. World Meteor. Organ. 587 pp.

Lefevre, R. 1972. Aspect de la pluriométrie dans la region du Mont Cameroun. Vol. II, pp. 373–82 in *Distribution of precipitation in mountainous areas*. Geilo, Norway: Proc. Int. Symp. World Meteor. Organ. 587 pp.

Leopold, A. S., Cain, S. A., Cottam, C. H., Gabrielson, I. N., and Kimball, T. L. 1963. Wildlife management in the National Parks. *Amer. Forests* 69(4):32–35, 61–63.

Leopold, L. B., and Miller, J. P. 1956. *Ephemeral streams—hydraulic factors and their relation to the drainage net*. U.S. Geol. Surv. Prof. Pap. 282-A. 32 pp.

Leopold, L. B., Wolman, M. G., and Miller, J. P. 1964. *Fluvial processes in geomorphology*. San Francisco: W. H. Freeman. 522 pp.

Lester, P. F., and Fingerhut, W. A. 1974. Lower turbulent zones associated with mountain lee waves. *J. Appl. Meteor.* 13(1):54–61.

Lettau, H. H. 1967. Small to large-scale features of boundary layer structure over mountain slopes. Pp. 1–74 in *Proc. symp. mountain meteor.*, ed. E. R. Reiter and J. L. Rasmussen. Atmosph. Sci. Paper 122. Fort Collins, Colo.: Dept. of Atmosph. Sci., Colorado State Univ.

Levi, W. 1959. Bhutan and Sikkim: Two buffer states. *The World Today* 15(12):492–500.

Lewis, N. N. 1953. Lebanon—The mountains and its terraces. *Geog. Rev.* 43(1):1–14.

Lewis, W. V. 1939. Snow-patch erosion in Iceland. *Geog. J.* 94:153–61.

Lichtenberger, E. 1975. *The eastern Alps*. London: Oxford University Press. 48 pp.

Lichty, J. A., Ting, R. Y., Burns, P. D., and Dyar, E. 1957. Studies of babies born at high altitude. *Amer. Med. Assoc. J. Dis. Child* 93:666–67.

Likens, G. E., and Bormann, F. H. 1974. Acid rain:

A serious regional environmental problem. *Science* 184:1176–79.

Lilly, D. K. 1971. Observation of mountain induced turbulence. *J. Geophys. Res.* 76(27): 6585–88.

Linares, O. F., Sheets, P. D., and Rosenthal, E. J. 1975. Prehistoric agriculture in tropical highlands. *Science* 187(4172):137–45.

Lipman, P. W., Prostka, H. J., and Christiansen, R. L. 1971. Evolving subduction zones in the western United States, as interpreted from igneous rocks. *Science* 174(4011):821–25.

List, R. J. 1958. *Smithsonian meteorological tables*. Pub. 4014. Washington, D.C.: Smithsonian Institution. 527 pp.

Little, M. A. 1970. Effects of alcohol and coca on foot temperature responses of highland Peruvians during a localized cold exposure. *Amer. J. Phys. Anthrop.* 32:233–42.

Little, M. A., and Baker, P. T. 1976. Environmental adaptations and perspectives. Pp. 405–28 in *Man in the Andes: A multidisciplinary study of high-altitude Quechua*, ed. P. T. Baker and M. A. Little. Stroudsburg, Pa.: Dowden, Hutchinson and Ross. 482 pp.

Livingston, D. A. 1963. *Chemical composition of rivers and lakes*. U.S. Geol. Surv. Prof. Pap. 440G. 64 pp.

Lliboutry, L. 1953. Internal moraines and rock glaciers. *J. Glaciol.* 2:296.

————. 1977. Glaciological problems set by the control of dangerous lakes in Cordillera Blanca, Peru. II: Movement of a covered glacier embedded within a rock glacier. *J. Glaciol.* 18(79):255–73.

Lliboutry, L., Morales Arnao, B., Pautre, A., and Schneider, B. 1977. Glaciological problems set by the control of dangerous lakes in Cordillera Blanca, Peru. I: Historical failures of morainic dams, their causes and prevention. *J. Glaciol.* 18(79):239–54.

Lobeck, A. K. 1939. *Geomorphology*. New York: McGraw-Hill. 731 pp.

Lockhart, J. A., and Franzgrote, U. B. 1961. The effects of ultraviolet radiation on plants. Pp. 532–54 in *Encyclopedia of plant physiology*, ed. W. Ruhland. Berlin: Springer-Verlag.

Lomnitz, C. 1970. Casualties and behavior of population during earthquakes. *Bull. Seismol. Soc. Amer.* 60:1309–13.

Longacre, L. L., and Blaney, H. F. 1962. Evaporation at high elevations in California. *J. Irrig. Drainage Div.* (Proc. Amer. Soc. Civil Engr.) 3172:33–54.

Longley, R. W. 1966. The frequency of chinooks in Alberta. *Albertan Geog.* 3:20–22.

———. 1967. The frequency of winter chinooks in Alberta. *Atmos.* 5(4):4–16.

Lopez, M. E., and Howell, W. E. 1967. Katabatic winds in the equatorial Andes. *J. Atmosph. Sci.* 24:29–35.

Lord, R. D., Jr. 1960. Litter size and latitude in North American mammals. *Amer. Midl. Nat.* 64(2):488–99.

Lorenz, K. 1975a. High altitude food preparation and processing. *CRC Critical Reviews in Food Technology* (April):403–41.

———. 1975b. High altitude cooking, baking: Some tips for the housewife. Pp. 281–88 in *That we may eat.* Washington, D.C.: U.S. Dept. Agri. 362 pp.

Lorenz, K., Bowman, F., and Maga, J. 1971. High altitude baking. *Bakers' Digest* 45(2):39–41, 44–45, 73.

Loucks, O. L. 1970. Evaluation of diversity, efficiency, and community stability. *Amer. Zool.* 10:17–25.

Love, D. 1970. Subarctic and subalpine: Where and what? *Arctic and Alpine Res.* 2:63–73. *C·258*

Lucas, R. C. 1973. Wilderness: A management framework. *J. Soil and Water Conserv.* 28(4): 150–54. *C·434*

Luckman, B. H. 1971. The role of snow avalanches in the evolution of alpine talus slopes. Pp. 93–110 in *Inst. British Geog. Spec. Pub. 3.* London.

———. 1972. Some observations on the erosion of talus slopes by snow avalanches in Surprise Valley, Jasper National Park, Alberta. Pp. 85–92 in *Mountain geomorphology,* ed. H. O. Slaymaker and H. J. McPherson. Vancouver, B.C.: Tantalus Research. 274 pp.

———. 1976. Rockfalls and rockfall inventory data: Some observations from Surprise Valley, Jasper National Park, Canada. *Earth Surface Processes* 1(3):287–98.

———. 1978. Geomorphic work of snow avalanches in the Canadian Rocky Mountains. *Arctic and Alpine Res.* 10(2):261–76.

Ludlam, F. H., and Scorer, R. S. 1953. Convection in the atmosphere. *Quart. J. Royal Meteor. Soc.* 79:317–41.

Luft, U. C. 1972. Principles of adaptations to altitude. Pp. 143–56 in *Physiological adaptations, desert and mountain,* ed. M. K. Yousef, S. M. Horvath, and R. W. Bullard. New York: Academic Press. 258 pp.

Lull, H. W., and Ellison, L. 1950. Precipitation in relation to altitude in central Utah. *Ecol.* 31: 479–84.

Lunn, A. H. M. 1912. An artist of mountains— C. J. Holmes. Pp. 3–34 in *Oxford mountaineering essays,* ed. A. H. M. Lunn. London: Edward Arnold.

———. 1939. Alpine mysticism and cold philosophy. *Alpine J.* 51(259):284–92.

———. 1950. Alpine puritanism. *Alpine J.* 57(280): 341–51.

Lynch, D. L. 1974. *An ecosystem guide for mountain land planning, Level I.* Fort Collins, Colo.: Colorado State For. Serv., Colorado State Univ. 94 pp.

Lynott, Robert E. 1966. Weather and climate of the Columbia Gorge. *Northwest Sci.* 40:129–32.

MacArthur, R. H. 1972. *Geographical ecology.* New York: Harper and Row. 269 pp.

McClain, E. P. 1952. Synoptic investigation of a typical chinook situation in Montana. *Bull. Amer. Meteor. Soc.* 33:87–94.

———. 1958. *Some effects of the western cordillera of North America on cyclonic activity in the United States and southern Canada.* Tech. Rep. 12. Tallahassee, Fla.: Dept. Meteorology, Florida State Univ.

McClung, J. 1969. *Effects of high altitude on human birth.* Cambridge, Mass.: Harvard Univ. Press. 150 pp.

McConnell, R. G., and Brock, R. W. 1904. *Report on the great landslide at Frank, Alberta.* Canada Dept. Interior Ann. Rep. 1902–1903, Pt. 8. 17 pp.

McCraw, J. D. 1962. Sequences in the mountain soil pattern of central and western Otago. *New Zealand Soc. Soil Sci. Proc.* 5:1–3.

MacCready, P. B. 1955. High and low elevations as thermal source regions. *Weather* 10:35–40.

McDonald, A. H. 1956. Hannibal's passage to the Alps. *Alpine J.* 61(292):93–101.

Macdonald, G. A. 1972. *Volcanoes.* Englewood Cliffs, N.J.: Prentice-Hall. 510 pp. *C·381*

McFarland, R. A. 1972. Psychophysiological implications of life at altitude and including the role of oxygen in the process of aging. Pp. 157–82 in *Physiological adaptations, desert and mountain*, ed. M. K. Yousef, S. M. Horvath, and R. W. Bullard. New York: Academic Press. 258 pp.

McKain, W. C. 1967. Are they really that old? *Gerontol.* 7(1):70–72, 80.

McKay, G. A., and Thompson, H. A. 1972. Mapping of snowfall and snowcover in North America. Vol. I, pp. 598–607 in *The role of snow and ice in hydrology*. Proc. Banff Symp., Sept. 1972. Paris: UNESCO.

Mackay, J. R., and Mathews, W. H. 1974. Needle ice striped ground. *Arctic and Alpine Res.* 6(1): 79–84.

Maclean, S. F., Jr., and Pitelka, F. A. 1971. Seasonal patterns of abundance of tundra arthropods near Barrow. *Arctic* 24:19–40.

McNab, B. K. 1971. On the ecological significance of Bergmann's Rule. *Ecol.* 52:845–54.

MacNeish, R. S. 1971. Early man in the Andes. *Sci. Amer.* 224(4):36–55.

McPherson, H. J. 1971a. Dissolved, suspended and bedload movement patterns in Two O'Clock Creek, Rocky Mountains, Canada, summer 1969. *J. Hydrol.* 12:221–33.

———. 1971b. Downstream changes in sediment character in a high energy mountain stream channel. *Arctic and Alpine Res.* 3:65–79.

McPherson, H. J., and Hirst, F. 1972. Sediment changes on two alluvial fans in the Canadian Rocky Mountains. Pp. 161–76 in *Mountain geomorphology*, ed. H. O. Slaymaker and H. J. McPherson. Vancouver, B.C.: Tantalus Research. 274 pp.

McVean, D. N. 1968. A year of weather records at 3,480 m on Mt. Wilhelm, New Guinea. *Weather* 23:377–81.

———. 1974. Mountain climates of the Southwest Pacific. Pp. 47–58 in *Altitudinal zonation in Malesia*, ed. R. Flenley, Jr. Misc. Ser. 16. Univ. Hull Dept. Geog. Hull, Eng.: Univ. Hull. 109 pp.

Macior, L. W. 1970. The pollination ecology of *Pedicularis* in Colorado. *Amer. J. Bot.* 57:216–78.

Maga, J., and Lorenz, K. 1972. Effect of altitude on taste thresholds. *Percept. Motor Skills* 34:667–70.

Major, J., and Bamberg, S. A. 1967. Comparison of some North American and Eurasian alpine ecosystems. Pp. 89–118 in *Arctic and alpine environments*, ed. W. H. Osburn and H. E. Wright, Jr. Bloomington, Ind.: Indiana Univ. Press. 308 pp.

Man and Biosphere. 1973a. *Impact of human activities on mountain ecosystems*. Man and Biosphere Report 8, Programme on Man and the Biosphere (MAB). Expert Panel on Project 6, Salzburg, 29 Jan.–4 Feb. 1973. Final Report, May 1973. Paris: UNESCO. 69 pp.

———. 1973b. *Conservation of natural areas and of the genetic material they contain*. Man and Biosphere Report 12, Programme on Man and the Biosphere (MAB). Expert Panel on Project 8, Morges, 25–27 Sept. 1973. Final Report, 27 Dec. 1973. Paris: UNESCO. 64 pp.

———. 1974a. *Impact of human activities on mountain and tundra ecosystems*. Man and Biosphere Report 14, Programme on Man and the Biosphere (MAB). Working Group on Project 6, Lillehammer, 20–23 Nov. 1973. Final Report, March 1974. Paris: UNESCO. 132 pp.

———. 1974b. *Criteria and guidelines for the choice and establishment of biosphere reserves*. Man and Biosphere Report 22, Programme on Man and the Biosphere (MAB). Task Force, Paris, 20–24 May, 1974. Final Report, 30 July 1974. Paris: UNESCO. 61 pp.

———. 1975. *Impact of human activities on mountain and tundra ecosystems*, ed. J. D. Ives and Ann Stites, Man and Biosphere Final Report, Programme on Man and the Biosphere (MAB). Project 6, Proc. Boulder, Colo., Workshop, July 1974. Boulder, Colo.: INSTAAR Spec. Pub. 122 pp.

Mani, M. S. 1962. *Introduction to high altitude entomology*. London: Methuen. 302 pp.

———. 1968. *Ecology and biogeography of high altitude insects*. The Hague: Junk. 527 pp.

Manning, H., ed. 1967. *Mountaineering: The freedom of the hills*. Seattle, Wash.: The Mountaineers. 485 pp.

Manville, R. H. 1959. The Columbian ground squirrel in northwestern Montana. *J. Mammal.* 40:26–45.

Marchand, D. E. 1970. Soil contamination in the White Mountains, eastern California. *Geol. Soc. Amer. Bull.* 81(8):2497–505.

———. 1971. Rates and modes of denudation, White Mountain, eastern California. *Amer. J. Sci.* 270:109–35.

————. 1974. Chemical weathering, soil development, and geochemical fractionation in a part of the White Mountains, Mono and Inyo counties, California. Pp. 379–424 in *U.S. Geol. Surv. Prof. Pap.* 352-J.

Marchand, W. 1917. Notes on the habits of snowfly (Chiona). *Psyche* 24:142–53.

Marcus, M. G. 1969. Summer temperature relationships along a transect in the St. Elias Mountains. Vol. 1, pp. 23–32 in *Icefield Ranges Res. Proj. sci. results*, ed. V. C. Bushnell and R. H. Ragle. Amer. Geog. Soc. and Arctic Inst. of N.A. Washington, D.C. 234 pp.

————. 1974a. Investigations in alpine climatology: The St. Elias Mountains, 1963–1971. Vol. 4, pp. 13–26 in *Icefield Ranges Res. Proj. sci. results*, ed. V. C. Bushnell and M. G. Marcus. Amer. Geog. Soc. and Arctic Inst. of N.A. Washington, D.C. 385 pp.

————. 1974b. A note on snow accumulation and climatic trends in the Icefield Ranges, 1969–1970. Vol. 4, pp. 219–24 in *Icefield Ranges Res. Proj. sci. results*, ed. V. C. Bushnell and M. G. Marcus. Amer. Geog. Soc. and Arctic Inst. of N.A. Washington, D.C. 385 pp.

Marcus, M. G., and Ragle, R. H. 1970. Snow accumulation in the Icefield Ranges, St. Elias Mountains, Yukon. *Arctic and Alpine Res.* 2(4):277–92.

Marcus, M. G., and Brazel, A. 1974. Solar radiation measurements at 5365 meters, Mt. Logan, Yukon. Vol. 4, pp. 117–210 in *Icefield Ranges Res. Proj. sci. results*, ed. V. C. Bushnell and M. G. Marcus. Amer. Geog. Soc. and Arctic Inst. of N.A. Washington, D.C. 385 pp.

Mark, A. F., and Bliss, L. C. 1970. The high-alpine vegetation of central Otago, New Zealand. *New Zealand J. Bot.* 8(4):381–451.

Marr, J. W. 1961. *Ecosystems of the east slope of the Front Range in Colorado.* Univ. Colorado Stud. Ser. Biol. 8. Boulder, Colo. 134 pp.

————. 1964. Utilization of the Front Range tundra, Colorado. Pp. 109–18 in *Grazing in terrestrial and marine environments*, ed. D. J. Crisp. Oxford: Blackwells Scientific Publications.

————. 1967. *Data on mountain environments.* I: *Front Range, Colorado, sixteen sites, 1952–1953.* Univ. Colorado Stud. Ser. Biol. 27. Boulder, Colo. 110 pp.

Marr, J. W., Johnson, W., Osburn, W. S., and Knorr, O. A. 1968b. *Data on mountain environments.* II: *Front Range, Colorado, four climax re-gions, 1953–1958.* Univ. Colorado Stud. Ser. Biol. 28. Boulder, Colo. 170 pp.

Marr, J. W., Clark, J. M., Osburn, W. S., and Paddock, M. W. 1968a. *Data on mountain environments.* III: *Front Range, Colorado, four climax regions, 1959–1964.* Univ. Colorado Stud. Ser. Biol. 29. Boulder, Colo. 181 pp.

Marsell, R. E. 1972. Cloudburst and snowmelt floods. Pp. N1–18 in *Environmental geology of the Wasatch Front.* Salt Lake City, Utah: Utah Geol. Assoc.

Marsh, J. S. 1969. Maintaining wilderness experience in Canada's National Parks. Pp. 313–23 in *Vegetation, soils, and wildlife*, ed. J. G. Nelson and M. J. Chambers. Toronto: Methuen. 372 pp.

Marticorena, E., Ruiz, L., Severino, J., Galvez, J., and Penaloza, D. 1969. Systemic blood pressure in white men born at sea level: Changes after long residence at high altitudes. *Amer. J. Cardiol.* 23:364–68.

Martin, W. P., and Fletcher, J. E. 1943. Vertical zonation of great soil groups on Mt. Graham, Arizona, as correlated with climate, vegetation, and profile characteristics. Pp. 89–153 in Univ. Arizona Agr. Exp. Sta. Tech. Bull. 99. Tucson.

Martinelli, M., Jr. 1960. Moisture exchange between the atmosphere and alpine snow surfaces under summer conditions. *J. Meteor.* 17:227–31.

————. 1967. Possibilities of snowpack management in alpine areas. Pp. 225–31 in *Int. symp. on forest hydrology*, ed. W. E. Sopper and H. W. Lull. Oxford: Pergamon. 818 pp.

————. 1972. *Simulated sonic boom as an avalanche trigger.* U.S. Dept. Agri. Serv. Res. Note RM-224. Fort Collins, Colo. 7 pp.

————. 1974. *Snow avalanche sites.* U.S. Dept. Agri. For. Serv. Agr. Info. Bull. 360. Washington, D.C. 27 pp.

————. 1975. *Water-yield improvement from alpine areas: The status of our knowledge.* Dept. Agri. For. Serv. Res. Pap. RM-138. Fort Collins, Colo. 16 pp.

————. 1976. Meteorology and ski area development and operation. Pp. 142–46 in *Proc. Fourth Nat. Conf. Fire and Forest Meteorology*, St. Louis, Mo. U.S. Dept. Agri. For. Serv. Gen. Tech. Rep. RM-32. Fort Collins, Colo. 239 pp.

Martof, B. S., and Humphries, R. L. 1959. Geographic variation in the wood frog, *Rana sylvatica. Amer. Midl. Nat.* 6:350–89.

Mason, A. C., and Foster, H. L. 1953. Diversion of lava flows at O Shima, Japan. *Amer. J. Sci.* 251:249–58.

Math, F. A. 1934. Battle of the chinook at Havre, Montana. *Mon. Wea. Rev.* 62(2):54–57.

Mathews, W. H. 1955. Permafrost and its occurrence in the southern coast mountains of British Columbia. *Can. Alpine J.* 28:94–98.

Matley, I. M. 1968. Transhumance in Bosnia and Herzegovina. *Geog. Rev.* 58(2):231–61.

Matthes, F. E. 1934. Ablation of snow-fields at high altitudes by radiant solar heat. *Trans. Amer. Geophys. Union* (Pt. II):380–85. *p.89*

———. 1937. Exfoliation of massive granite in the Sierra Nevada of California. *Geol. Soc. Amer. Proc. 1936*, pp. 342–43.

———. 1938. Avalanche sculpture in the Sierra Nevada of California. Pp. 631–37 in Int. Union Geod. and Geophys., Int. Assoc. Sci. Hydrology *Bull.* 23. Beltsville, Md.

Mayer-Oakes, W. J. 1963. Early man in the Andes. *Sci. Amer.* 208(5):117–28.

Mayr, E. 1956. Geographical character gradients and climatic adaptation. *Evolution* 10:105–8.

Mayr, E., and Diamond, J. M. 1976. Birds on islands in the sky: Origin of the montane avifauna of Northern Melanesia. *Proc. Natl. Acad. Sci.* (U.S.A.) 73(5): 1765–69.

Mazess, R. B. 1965. Neonatal mortality and altitude in Peru. *Amer. J. Phys. Anthrop.* 23:209–14.

———. 1968. The oxygen cost of breathing in man: Effects of altitude, training, and race. *Amer. J. Phys. Anthrop.* 29:365–75.

Meade, R. H. 1969. Errors in using modern stream-load data to estimate natural rates of denudation. *Geol. Soc. Amer. Bull.* 80:1265–74.

Medvedev, Z. A. 1974. Caucasus and Altai longevity: A biological or social problem. *Gerontol.* 14:381–87.

Megahan, W. F. 1972. Sedimentation in relation to logging activities in the mountains of central Idaho. Pp. 74–82 in *Present and prospective technology for predicting sediment yields and sources.* Proc. Sediment-Yield Workshop, U.S. Dept. Agri. Sediment Lab. U.S. Agri. Res. Serv. Rep. ARS-S-40. Oxford, Miss. 285 pp.

Megahan, W. F., and Kidd, W. J. 1972. Effects of logging and logging roads on erosion and sediment deposition from steep terrain. *J. Forestry* 70:136–41.

Meier, M. F. 1962. Proposed definitions for glacier mass budget terms. *J. Glaciol.* 4:252–65. *p.136*

———. 1965. Glaciers and climate. Pp. 795–805 in *The quaternary of the United States*, ed. H. E. Wright and D. G. Frey. Princeton, N.J.: *p.137* Princeton Univ. Press. 922 pp.

———. 1969. Seminar on the causes and mechanics of glacier surges, St. Hilaire, Canada, September 10–11, 1968: A summary. *Can. J. Earth Sci.* 6(4):987–89. *p.137*

Meinertzhagen, R. 1928. Some biological problems connected with the Himalaya. *Ibis* (Ser. 12) 4:480–533.

Melton, M. A. 1960. Intravalley variations in slope angles related to microclimate and erosional environment. *Geol. Soc. Amer. Bull.* 71:133–44.

Merriam, A. C. 1890. Telegraphing among the ancients. *Pap. Amer. Arch. Inst.* III:1–32.

Merriam, C. H. 1890. *Results of a biological survey of the San Francisco mountain region and desert of the Little Colorado.* North American Fauna No. 3, U.S. Dept. Agri. Washington, D.C.: U.S. Govt. Printing Off. 136 pp.

———. 1894. The geographic distribution of animals and plants in North America. Pp. 203–14 in *U.S. Dept. Agri. Yearbook.* Washington, D.C.: U.S. Govt. Printing Off.

———. 1898. Life zones and crop zones of the United States. Pp. 9–79 in *U.S. Dept. Agri. Biol. Surv. Bull. No. 10.* Washington, D.C.: U.S. Govt. Printing Off.

Mesinger, J. 1973. The living cultural landscape in National Parks. Pp. 49–53 in *Alpine landscape preservation in Slovenia.* Syracuse Univ. Envir. Policy Rep. Syracuse, N.Y. 53 pp.

Messerli, B. 1973. Problems of vertical and horizontal arrangement in the high mountains of the extreme arid zone (Central Sahara). *Arctic and Alpine Res.* 5(3):(Pt. 2)A139–48. *p.269*

Messerli, B., Messerli, P., Pfister, C., and Zumbuhl, H. J. 1978. Fluctuations of climate and glaciers in the Bernese Oberland, Switzerland, and their geoecological significance, 1600 to 1975. *Arctic and Alpine Res.* 10(2):247–60. *p.137*

Meyerhoff, H. A., and Olmsted, E. W. 1934. Wind gaps and water gaps in Pennsylvania. *Amer. J. Sci.* (Ser. 5) 27:410–16.

Mielke, P. W., Jr., Grant, L. O., and Chappell, C. F. 1970. Elevation and spatial variation in effects from wintertime orographic cloud seeding. *J. Appl. Meteor.* 9:476–88. *p.99*

Mikesell, M. W. 1969. The deforestation of Mount Lebanon. *Geog. Rev.* 59(1):1–28.

Miles, S. R., and Singleton, P. C. 1975. Vegetative history of Cinnabar Park in Medicine Bow National Forest, Wyoming. *Soil Sci. Soc. Amer. Proc.* 39:1204–8.

Miller, A. H. 1961. Molt cycles in equatorial Andean sparrows. *Condor* 63:143–61.

Miller, D. H. 1955. *Snow cover and climate in the Sierra Nevada, California.* Univ. of Calif. Publ. in Geog. II. Berkeley, Ca. 218 pp.

———. 1959. Transmission of insolation through pine forest canopy, as it affects the melting of snow. *Mitteilungen der Schweizerischen Anstalt für das forstliche Versuchswesen* 35(1):57–79.

———. 1965. The heat and water budget of the earth's surface. Vol. II, pp. 176–302, in *Advances in geophysics*, ed. H. E. Landsberg and J. Van Mieghem. New York: Academic Press. 349 pp.

———. 1977. *Water at the surface of the earth.* New York: Academic Press. 557 pp.

Miller, J. P. 1958. *High mountain streams: Effect of geology on channel characteristics and bed material.* Socorro, N.M.: New Mexico State Bur. Mines and Mineral Resources Mem. 4. 53 pp.

———. 1961. *Solutes in small streams draining single rock types, Sangre de Cristo Range, New Mexico.* U.S. Geol. Surv. Water Supply Pap. 1535-F. 23 pp.

Miller, P. C. 1970. Age distributions of spruce and fir in beetle-killed forests on the White River Plateau, Colorado. *Amer. Midl. Nat.* 83:206–12.

Miller, R. P., Parmeter, J. R., Jr., Taylor, O. C., and Cardiff, E. A. 1963. Ozone injury to foliage of *Pinus ponderosa. Phytopathology* 53:1072–76.

Milne, L. J., and Milne, M. 1962. *The mountains.* New York: Life Nature Library, Time-Life. 192 pp.

Minger, T. 1975. The Vail story. Pp. 31–36 in *Man, leisure and wildlands: A complex interaction.* Proc. 1st Eisenhower Consortium Res. Symp., Vail, Colo. 286 pp.

Mishkin, B. 1940. Cosmological ideas among the Indians of the southern Andes. *J. Amer. Folklore* 53:225–41.

Mitchell, A. H., and Reading, H. G. 1971. Evolution of island arcs. *J. Geol.* 79:253–84.

Mitchell, W. P. 1976. Irrigation and community in the central Peruvian highlands. *Amer. Anthrop.* 78:25–44.

Mohr, E. C. J. 1945. The relationship between soil and population density in the Netherlands Indies. Pp. 254–62 in *Science and scientists in the Netherlands Indies*, ed. P. Honig and F. Ver-

doorn. New York: Board for the Netherlands Indies, Surinam and Curacao. 491 pp.

Molloy, B. P. J. 1964. Soil genesis and plant succession in the subalpine and alpine zones of Torlesse Range, Canterbury, New Zealand. Part 2: Introduction and description. *New Zealand J. Bot.* 1:137–48.

Molloy, B. P. J., Burrows, C. J., Cox, J. E., Johnston, J. A., and Wardle, P. 1963. Distribution of subfossil forest remains, eastern South Island, New Zealand. *New Zealand J. Bot.* 1:68–77.

Monge, C. M. 1948. *Acclimatization in the Andes.* Baltimore: Johns Hopkins Press. 130 pp.

Monge, C. M., and Monge, C. C. 1966. *High-altitude diseases, mechanism and management.* Springfield, Ill.: Charles C. Thomas. 97 pp.

Montieth, J. L. 1965. Evaporation and environment. *Symp. Soc. Exp. Biol.* 19:205–34.

Mooney, H. A., and Billings, W. D. 1961. Comparative physiological ecology of arctic and alpine populations of *Oxyria digyna. Ecol. Monogr.* 31:1–29.

Moorbath, S. 1977. The oldest rocks and the growth of continents. *Sci. Amer.* 236(3):92–105.

Moores, E. M., and Vine, F. J. 1971. The Troodoes Massif, Cyprus, and other ophiolites as oceanic crust: Evaluation and implications. *Phil. Trans. Roy. Soc. London* (Ser. A.) 268:443–66.

Moreau, R. E. 1951. The migration system in perspective. Pp. 245–48 in *Proc. 10th Int. Ornith. Cong.* (1950).

———. 1966. *The bird faunas of Africa.* New York: Academic Press. 424 pp.

Morgan, W. J. 1972. Deep mantle convection plumes and plate margins. *Amer. Assoc. Petrol. Geol. Bull.* 56:203–13.

Morris, E. A. 1976. The Colorado Mountains: An aboriginal refuge during periods of climatic fluctuation. P. 154 in Amer. Quat. Assoc. *Abstract* of 4th biennial meeting. Tempe, Ariz.: Ariz. State Univ. 170 pp.

Morrison, P. R. 1964. Wild animals at high altitudes. Pp. 49–55 in *The biology of survival*, ed. O. G. Edholm. London: Zool. Soc. London Symp. 13.

———. 1966. Insulative flexibility in the guanaco. *J. Mammal.* 47:18–23.

Morrison, P. R., and Elsner, R. 1962. Influence of altitude on breathing rates in some Peruvian rodents. *J. Appl. Physiol.* 17:467–70.

Morrison, P. R., Kerst, K., and Rosenmann, M. 1963a. Hematocrit and hemoglobin levels in some Chilean rodents from high and low altitude. *Inter. J. Biometeor.* 7:44–50.

Morrison, P. R., Kerst, K., Reynafarje, C., and Ramos, J. 1963b. Hematocrit and hemoglobin levels in some Peruvian rodents from high and low altitude. *Inter. J. Biometeor.* 7:51–58.

Morrow, P. A., and LaMarche, V. C., Jr. 1978. Tree ring evidence for chronic insect suppression of productivity in subalpine eucalyptus. *Science* 201(4362):1244–46.

Morton, N. E., Yasuda, N., Miki, C., and Yee, S. 1968. Population structure of the ABO blood groups in Switzerland. *Amer. J. Hum. Genet.* 20:420–29. p367

Moyer, D. B. 1976. Acclimatization and high altitude medical problems in Antarctica. *U.S. Navy Med.* 67(11):19–21. p353

Müller, H. 1969. North America. Pp. 147–229 in *Pre-Colombian American religions,* ed. W. Krickenberg, H. Trimborn, W. Müller, and O. Zerries. Trans. S. Davis. New York: Holt, Rinehart and Winston. 365 pp.

Muller, S. W. 1947. *Permafrost or permanently frozen ground and related engineering problems.* Ann Arbor, Mich.: Edwards Bros. 231 pp.

Mullikin, M. A., and Hotchkis, A. M. 1973. *The nine sacred mountains of China.* Hong Kong: Vetch and Lee. 156 pp.

Mumm, A. L. 1921. A history of the Alpine Club. *Alpine J.* 34(223):1–18.

Murphy, T. D., and Schamach, S. 1966. Mountain versus sea level rainfall measurements during storms at Juneau, Alaska. *J. Hydrol.* 4(1):12–20. p103

Murra, J. 1965. Herds and herders in the Inca state. Pp. 185–216 in *Man, culture, and animals: The role of animals in human ecological adjustments,* ed. A. Leeds and A. Vayda. Amer. Assoc. Adv. Sci. Pub. 78. Washington, D.C. 304 pp.

Murray, G. 1912. *Greek and English tragedy: A contrast.* Pp. 7–24 in *English literature and the classics.* Oxford: Oxford Univ. Press.

Myers, A. M. 1962. Airflow on the windward side of a large ridge. *J. Geophys. Res.* 67:4267–91.

Myers, C. W. 1969. The ecological geography of cloud forest in Panama. *Amer. Museum Novitates* 2396:1–52. p258

Myers, J. S. 1976. Erosion surfaces and ignimbrite eruption, measures of Andean uplift in northern Peru. *J. Geol.* 11(1):29–44.

Nagel, J. F. 1956. Fog precipitation on Table Mountain. *Quart. J. Royal Meteor. Soc.* 82:452–60. p99

Nanson, G. C. 1974. Bedload and suspended-load transport in a small, steep, mountain stream. *Amer. J. Sci.* 274(5):471–86. p215

Nash, R. 1973. *Wilderness and the American mind.* Rev. ed. New Haven, Conn.: Yale Univ. Press. 300 pp.

Nebesky-Wojkowitz. 1956. *Where the gods are mountains.* London: Weidenfeld and Nicolson. 256 pp.

Netting, R. 1972. Of men and meadows: Strategies of alpine land use. *Anthrop. Quart.* 45(3): 132–44.

———. 1976. What alpine peasants have in common: Observations on communal tenure in a Swiss village. *Human Ecol.* 4(2):135–46.

Newcomb, R. M. 1972. Has the past a future in Denmark? The preservation of landscape history within the Nature Parks. *Geoforum* 3:61–67.

Newman, M. T. 1956. Adaptation of man to cold climates. *Evolution* 10:101–5.

———. 1958. Man and the heights: A study of response to environmental extremes. *Nat. Hist.* 67:9–19.

Nicholls, J. M. 1973. *The airflow over mountains: Research 1958–1972.* World Meteor. Org. Tech. Note 127, WMO 355. Geneva, Switzerland. 73 pp.

Nicolson, M. H. 1959. *Mountain gloom and mountain glory.* New York: W. W. Norton. 403 pp.

Nienaber, J. 1972. The Supreme Court and Mickey Mouse. *Amer. Forests* 78(7):28–43. p435

Nilsson, M. P. 1972. *Mycenaean origins of Greek mythology.* Berkeley: Univ. of Calif. Press. 258 pp.

Nimlos, T. J., and McConnell, R. C. 1962. The morphology of alpine soils in Montana. *Northwest Sci.* 36:99–112.

North Carolina Dept. Admin. 1974. *A quest for mountain resources management policies.* Raleigh, N.C.: (North Carolina Dept. Admin., Office State Planning. 83 pp.

Noyce, W. 1950. *Scholar mountaineers, pioneers of Parnassus.* London: Dennis Dobson. 164 pp.

Oakeshott, G. B. 1976. *Volcanoes and earthquakes, geologic violence.* New York: McGraw-Hill. 143 pp.

Oberlander, T. 1965. *The Zagros streams: A new interpretation of transverse drainage in an orogenic zone.* Syracuse Geographical Series 1. Syracuse, New York: Syracuse Univ. Press. 168 pp.

Ogden, H. V. S. 1945. Thomas Burnet's *Telluris theoria sacra* and mountain scenery. *English Lit. Hist.* 14:139–50.

Ohi, J. M. 1975. Colorado's winter resource management plan: The state's responsibility for comprehensive planning. Pp. 127–33 in *Man, leisure, and wildlands: A complex interaction.* 1st Eisenhower Consortium Res. Symp., Vail, Colo. 286 pp. *p. 435*

Olgeirson, E. 1974. Parallel conditions and trends in vegetation and soil on a bald near tree line, Boreas Pass, Colorado. *Arctic and Alpine Res.* 6(2):185–204.

Ollier, C. D. 1969a. *Volcanoes.* Cambridge, Mass.: M.I.T. Press. 177 pp.

———. 1969b. *Weathering.* Edinburgh: Oliver and Boyd. 304 pp.

———. 1976. Catenas in different climates. Pp. 137–70 in *Geomorphology and climate,* ed. E. Derbyshire. London: John Wiley and Sons. 512 pp. *p. 259*

Oosting, H. J. 1956. *The study of plant communities.* San Francisco: W. H. Freeman. 440 pp.

Orowan, E. 1969. The origin of the oceanic ridges. *Sci. Amer.* 221(5):102–19.

Orr, H. K. 1975. *Watershed management in the Black Hills: The status of our knowledge.* Dept. Agri. For. Serv. Res. Pap. RM–141. Fort Collins, Colo. 12 pp.

Orville, H. D. 1965. A photogrammetric study of the initiation of cumulus clouds over mountainous terrain. *J. Atmosph. Sci.* 22(6):700–709.

Osburn, W. S. 1963. The dynamics of fallout distribution in a Colorado alpine snow accumulation ecosystem. Pp. 51–71 in *Radioecology,* ed. V. Schultz and A. W. Klement. New York: Reinhold. 746 pp.

———. 1967. Ecological concentration of nuclear fallout in a Colorado mountain watershed. Pp. 675–709 in *Radioecological concentration processes,* ed. B. Aberg and F. P. Hungate. Proc. Int. Symp., Stockholm, April 1966. London: Pergamon. 1040 pp.

———. 1974. Radioecology. Pp. 875–903 in *Arctic and alpine environments,* ed. J. D. Ives and R. G. Barry. London: Methuen. 999 pp.

Östrem, G. 1964. Ice-cored moraines in Scandinavia. *Geog. Ann.* 64A:228–337.

———. 1971. Rock glaciers and ice-cored moraines, a reply to D. Barsch. *Geog. Ann.* 53A(3–4): 207–13.

———. 1973. The transient snowline and glacier mass balance in southern British Columbia and Alberta, Canada. *Geog. Ann.* 55A(2):93–106.

———. 1974. Present alpine ice cover. Pp. 225–52 in *Arctic and alpine environments,* ed. J. D. Ives and R. G. Barry. London: Methuen. 999 pp.

Outcalt, S. I. 1971. An algorithm for needle ice growth. *Water Resources Res.* 7:394–400.

Ovington, J. D. 1978. The rational use of high mountain resources in timber harvesting and other consumptive uses of natural plant products. Pp. 184–90 in *The use of high mountains of the world.* Wellington, N.Z.: Dept. Lands and Survey Head Office, Private Bag (in assoc. with Tussock Grasslands and Mountain Lands Inst., P.O. Box 56, Lincoln College, Canterbury, N.Z., for Int. Union Cons. Nature). 223 pp. *p. 429*

Pagliuca, S. 1937. Icing measurement on Mount Washington. *J. Aeronautical Serv.* 4:399–402.

Palmieri, R. P. 1976. Domestication and exploitation of livestock in the Nepal Himalaya and Tibet: An ecological, functional, and culture historical study of yak and yak hybrids in society, economy and culture. Unpub. Ph.D. dissertation, Dept. of Geog., Univ. of Calif., Davis. 304 pp. *p. 403*

Pant, S. D. 1935. *The social economy of the Himalayans.* London: G. Allen and Unwin. 264 pp.

Papp, R. P. 1978. A nival aeolian ecosystem in California. *Arctic and Alpine Res.* 10:117–31. *p. 291*

Parizek, E. J., and Woodruff, J. F. 1957. Mass wasting and the deformation of trees. *Amer. J. Sci.* 255:63–70. *p. 191*

Park, O. 1949. Application of the converse Bergmann Principle to the carabid beetle, *Dicaelus purpuratus. Physiol. Zool.* 22:359–72.

Parsons, R. B. 1978. Soil-geomorphology relations in mountains of Oregon. *Geoderma* 21: 25–39.

Paterson, W. S. B. 1969. *The physics of glaciers.* London: Pergamon. 250 pp. *p. 137*

Patric, J. H., and Reinhart, K. G. 1971. Hydrologic effects of deforesting two mountainsheds in

West Virginia. *Water Resources Res.* 7(5):1182–88.

Pattie, D. L. 1967. Observations on an alpine population of Yellow-bellied marmots (*Marmota flaviventris*). *Northwest Sci.* 41:96–102.

Pattie, D. L., and Verbeek, N. A. M. 1966. Alpine birds of the Beartooth Mountains. *Condor* 67:167–76.

———. 1967. Alpine mammals of the Beartooth Mountains. *Northwest Sci.* 41:110–17.

Pawson, I. G. 1972. Growth and development in a Himalayan population. *Amer. J. Phys. Anthrop.* 37:447–48.

Pears, N. V. 1968. The natural altitudinal limit of forest in the Scottish Grampians. *Oikos* 19:71–80.

Pearsall, W. H. 1960. *Mountains and moorlands.* London: Collins. 312 pp.

Pearson, O. P. 1948. Life history of mountain viscachas in Peru. *J. Mammal.* 29:345–74.

———. 1951. Mammals of the highlands of southern Peru. *Harvard Univ. Museum Comp. Zool. Bull.* 106:117–74.

———. 1954. Habits of the lizard *Liolaemus multiformis multiformis* at high altitudes in southern Peru. *Copeia* 2:111–16.

Pearson, O. P., and Bradford, D. F. 1976. Thermoregulation of lizards and toads at high altitudes in Peru. *Copeia* 1:155–69.

Pearson, O. P., and Ralph, C. P. 1978. *The diversity and abundance of vertebrates along an altitudinal gradient in Peru.* Memorias del Museo de historia natural "Javier Prado" 18. Lima, Peru. 97 pp.

Peattie, R. 1929. Andorra: A study in mountain geography. *Geog. Rev.* 19:218–33.

———. 1931. Height limits of mountain economies. *Geog. Rev.* 21:415–28.

———. 1936. *Mountain geography.* Cambridge, Mass.: Harvard Univ. Press. 239 pp.

Peck, E. L. 1972. Relation of orographic winter precipitation patterns to meteorological parameters. Vol. II, pp. 234–42 in *Distribution of precipitation in mountainous areas.* Geilo, Norway: Proc. Int. Symp. World Meteor. Organ. 587 pp.

———. 1972b. Discussion of problems in measuring precipitation in mountainous areas. Vol. I, pp. 5–16 in *Distribution of precipitation in mountainous areas.* Geilo, Norway: Proc. Int. Symp. World Meteor. Organ. 228 pp.

Peck, E. L., and Brown, M. J. 1962. An approach to the development of isohyetal maps for mountainous areas. *J. Geophys. Res.* 67(2):681–94.

Peck, E. L., and Pfankuch, D. J. 1963. Evaporation rates in mountainous terrain. Pp. 267–78 in *Int. Assoc. Sci. Hydrol. Pub. 62.* Beltsville, Md.

Peltier, L. 1950. The geographic cycle in periglacial regions as it is related to climatic geomorphology. *Annals Assoc. Amer. Geog.* 40:214–36.

Penaloza, D., Sime, F., Banchero, N., Gamboa, R., Cruz, J., and Martiocorena, E. 1963. Pulmonary hypertension in healthy man born and living at high altitudes. *Amer. J. Cardiol.* 11:150.

Penck, A. 1919. Die Gipfelflur der Alpen. *Sitzungsber. preuss. Akad.* 17:256–68.

Perla, R. 1978. Artificial release of avalanches in North America. *Arctic and Alpine Res.* 10(2):235–40.

Perla, R., and Martinelli, M. 1976. *Avalanche handbook.* U.S. Dept. Agri. Handbook 489. Washington, D.C. 238 pp.

Perov, V. F. 1969. Block fields in the Khibiny Mtns. *Biuletyn Peryglacjalny* 19:381–89.

Perry, T. S. 1879. Mountains in literature. *Atl. Monthly* 44:302–11.

Perry, W. J. 1916. The geographical distribution of terraced cultivation and irrigation. *Mem. and Proc. Manchester Literary Phil. Soc.* 60(6):1–25.

Pewe, T. L. 1970. Altiplanation terraces of early Quaternary age near Fairbanks, Alaska. *Acta Geog. Lodz.* 24:357–63.

Phillips, E. L. 1972. The climate of Washington. Pp. 935–60 in *Climates of the states. 2: Western states.* Port Washington, N.Y.: Water Information Center Inc. 481–975 pp.

Phipps, R. L. 1974. The soil-creep-curved tree fallacy. *J. Res. U.S. Geol. Surv.* 2(3):371–78.

Pierce, W. G. 1957. Heart Mountain and South Fork detachment thrusts of Wyoming. *Amer. Petrol. Geol. Bull.* 41:591–626.

———. 1961. Permafrost and thaw depressions in a peat deposit in the Beartooth Mountains, northwestern Wyoming. Pp. 154–56 in *U.S. Geol. Surv. Prof. Pap. 424-B.*

Pinczes, Z. 1974. The cryoplanation steps in the Tokai Mountains. *Studia Geomorphologica Carpatho-Balcania* 8:27–46.

Plafker, G. 1965. Tectonic deformation associated with the 1964 Alaska earthquake. *Science* 148(3678):1675–87.

Platt, C. M. 1966. Some observations on the climate of Lewis Glacier, Mount Kenya, during the rainy season. *J. Glaciol.* 6(44):267–87.

Platts, W. S. 1970. The effects of logging and road construction on the aquatic habitat of the South Fork Salmon River, Idaho. Pp. 182–85 in *Proc. 50th ann. conf. Western Assoc. State Game and Fish Comm.* Sacramento, Calif.

Plesnik, P. 1973. La limite supérieure de la forêt dans les hautes Tatras. *Arctic and Alpine Res.* 5(3):(Pt. 2)A37–44.

———. 1978. Man's influence on the timberline in the West Carpathian Mountains, Czechoslovakia. *Arctic and Alpine Res.* 10(2):491–504.

Pollock, R. 1970. What colors the mountain snow? *Sierra Club Bull.* 55:18–20.

Polunin, N. 1960. *Introduction to plant geography.* New York: McGraw-Hill. 640 pp.

Porter, S. C. 1975a. Glaciation limit in New Zealand's Southern Alps. *Arctic and Alpine Res.* 7(1):33–38.

———. 1975b. Weathering rinds as a relative-age criterion: Application to subdivision of glacial deposits in the Cascade Range. *Geol.* 3(3):101–4.

———. 1977. Present and past glaciation threshold in the Cascade Range, Washington, U.S.A.: Topographic and climatic controls, and paleoclimatic implications. *J. Glaciol.* 18(78): 101–15.

Posamentier, H. W. 1977. A new climatic model for glacier behavior of the Austrian Alps. *J. Glaciol.* 18(78):57–65.

Potter, N., Jr. 1969. Tree-ring dating of snow avalanche tracks and geomorphic activity of avalanches, northern Absaroka Mountains, Wyoming. Pp. 141–65 in *U.S. contributions to Quaternary research,* ed. S. A. Schumm and W. C. Bradley. Geol. Soc. Amer. Spec. Pap. 123.

———. 1972. Ice-cored rock glacier, Galena Creek, northern Absaroka Mountains, Wyoming. *Geol. Soc. Amer. Bull.* 83:3025–57.

Potter, N., Jr., and Moss, J. H. 1968. Origin of the Blue Rocks block field and adjacent deposits, Berks County, Pennsylvania. *Geol. Soc. Amer. Bull.* 79:255–62.

Potts, A. S. 1970. Frost action in rocks: Some experimental data. *Inst. British Geog. Trans.* 49:109–24.

Powell, J. W. 1876. *Report on the geology of the eastern portion of the Uinta Mountains.* U.S. Geol. and Geog. Survey Terr. 218 pp.

Preston, D. A. 1969. The revolutionary landscape of highland Bolivia. *Geog. J.* 135(1):1–16.

Price, L. W. 1969. The collapse of solifluction lobes as a factor in vegetating blockfields. *Arctic* 22(4):395–402.

———. 1970. Up-heaved blocks: A curious feature of instability in the tundra. *Proc. Assoc. Amer. Geog.* 2:106–10.

———. 1971a. *Biogeography field guide to Cascade Mountains, transect along U.S. Highway 26 in Oregon.* Occ. Pap. in Geog. Pub. 1. Portland, Or.: Portland State Univ. 35 pp.

———. 1971b. Vegetation, microtopography, and depth of active layer on different exposures in subarctic alpine tundra. *Ecol.* 52(4): 638–47.

———. 1971c. Geomorphic effect of the arctic ground squirrel in an alpine environment. *Geog. Ann.* 53A(2):100–106.

———. 1972. *The periglacial environment, permafrost and man.* Assoc. Amer. Geog. Resource Pap. 14. Washington, D.C. 88 pp.

———. 1973. Rates of mass wasting in the Ruby Range, Yukon Territory. Pp. 235–45 in *North American contr. permafrost, second int. conf.* Washington, D.C.: Nat. Acad. Sci. 783 pp.

———. 1978. Mountains of the Pacific Northwest: A study in contrast. *Arctic and Alpine Res.* 10(2): 465–78.

Price, R., and Evans, R. B. 1937. Climate of the west front of the Wasatch Plateau in central Utah. *Mon. Wea. Rev.* 65:291–301.

Price, R. J. 1973. *Glacial and fluvialglacial landforms.* Edinburgh: Oliver and Boyd. 242 pp.

Price Zimmerman, T. C. 1976. The AAC and American mountaineering. *Amer. Alpine News* 138(3):9–14.

Prohaska, F. 1970. Distinctive bioclimatic parameters of the subtropical-tropical Andes. *Inter. J. Biometeor.* 14(1):1–12.

Pruitt, W. O., Jr. 1960. Animals in the snow. *Sci. Amer.* 203(1):61–68.

———. 1970. Some ecological aspects of snow. Pp. 83–99 in *Ecology of the subarctic regions.* Proc. Helsinki Symp. Paris: UNESCO. 364 pp.

Pugh, L. G. C. E. 1963. Tolerance to extreme cold at altitude in a Nepalese pilgrim. *J. Appl. Physiol.* 18:1234–38.

———. 1964. Muscular exercise at great altitudes. Pp. 209–10 in *The physiological effects of high altitude,* ed. W. H. Weihe. New York: Macmillan. 351 pp.

Putnam, W. C. 1971. *Geology.* 2nd ed., rev. Ann B. Bussett. New York: Oxford Univ. Press. 586 pp.

Quaritch-Wales, H. G. 1953. *The mountain of God.* London: B. Quaritch. 174 pp.

Rall, C. 1965. Soil fungi from the alpine zone of the Medicine Bow Mountains, Wyoming. *Mycologia* 57:872–81.

Rao, K. S., Wyngaard, J. C., and Cote, O. R. 1975. Local advection of momentum, heat, and moisture in microclimatology. *Bound. Layer Meteor.* 7:331–48.

Rapp, A. 1960. Recent development of mountain slopes in Karkevagge and surroundings, northern Scandinavia. *Geog. Ann.* 42(2–3): 65–201.

———. 1974. Slope erosion due to extreme rainfall, with examples from tropical and arctic mountains. Pp. 118–36 in *Geomorphologische Prozesse und Prozesskombinationen unter verschiedenen Klimabedingungen,* ed. H. Poser. Gottingen: Abhand. der Akademie der Wissenschaften.

Rapp, A., Berry, L., and Temple, P., eds. 1972. Studies of soil erosion and sedimentation in Tanzania. *Geog. Ann.* 54(3–4):105–379.

Rapp, A., and Strömquist, L. 1976. Slope erosion due to extreme rainfall in the Scandinavian Mountains. *Geog. Ann.* 58A(3):193–200.

Raven, P. H. 1973. Evolution of subalpine and alpine plant groups in New Zealand. *New Zealand J. Bot.* 11:177–200.

Rees, R. 1975a. The taste for mountain scenery. *History Today* 25(5):305–12.

———. 1975b. The scenery cult: Changing landscape tastes over three centuries. *Landscape* 19(3):39–47.

Reger, R. D., and Pewe, T. L. 1976. Cryoplanation terraces: Indicators of a permafrost environment. *Quat. Res.* 6(1):99–110.

Reider, R. G. 1975. Morphology and genesis of soils on the Prairie Divide Deposit (Pre-Wisconsin), Front Range, Colorado. *Arctic and Alpine Res.* 7(4):353–72.

Reider, R. G., and Uhl, P. J. 1977. Soil differences within spruce-fir forested and century-old burned areas of Libby Flats, Medicine Bow

Range, Wyoming. *Arctic and Alpine Res.* 9(4): 383–92.

Reinelt, E. R. 1968. The effect of topography on the precipitation regime of Waterton Lakes National Park. *Albertan Geog.* 4:19–30.

Reiners, W. H., Marks, R. H., and Vitousek, P. M. 1975. Heavy metals in subalpine and alpine soils of New Hampshire. *Oikos* 26:264–75.

Reiter, E. R. 1963. *Jet-stream meteorology.* Chicago: Univ. of Chicago Press. 515 pp.

Reiter, E. R., Beran, D. W., Mahlman, J. D., and Wooldridge, G. 1965. *Effect of large mountain ranges on atmospheric flow patterns as seen from Tiros satellites.* Atmos. Sci. Tech. Pap. 69. Fort Collins, Colo.: Colorado State Univ. 111 pp.

Reiter, E. R., and Foltz, H. P. 1967. The prediction of clear air turbulence over mountainous terrain. *J. Appl. Meteor.* 6(3):549–56.

Rensch, B. 1959. *Evolution above the species level.* London: Methuen. 419 pp.

Retzer, J. L. 1954. Glacial advances and soil development, Grand Mesa, Colorado. *Amer. J. Sci.* 252:26–37.

———. 1965. Alpine soils of the Rocky Mountains. *J. Soil Sci.* 7:22–32.

———. 1962. *Soil Survey, Fraser Alpine Area, Colorado.* U.S. Dept. Agri. Ser. 1956, no. 20. Washington, D.C. 47 pp.

———. 1965. Present soil-forming factors and processes in arctic and alpine regions. *Soil Sci.* 99(1):38–44.

———. 1974. Alpine soils. Pp. 771–804 in *Arctic and alpine environments,* ed. J. D. Ives and R. G. Barry. London: Methuen. 999 pp.

Reynolds, R. C. 1971. Clay mineral formation in an alpine environment. *Clays and Clay Minerals* 19:361–74.

Reynolds, R. C., and Johnson, N. M. 1972. Chemical weathering in the temperate glacial environment of the northern Cascade Mountains. *Geochim. et Cosmochim. Acta* 36:537–54.

Ricciuti, E. R. 1976. Mountains besieged. *Int. Wildlife* 6(6):24–34.

Richards, P. W. 1966. *The tropical rain forest: An ecological study.* Cambridge: Cambridge Univ. Press. 450 pp.

Richmond, G. M. 1962. *Quaternary stratigraphy of the La Sal Mountains, Utah.* U.S. Geol. Surv. Prof. Pap. 324. 135 pp.

Riehl, H. 1974. On the climatology and mechanism of Colorado chinook winds. *Bonner Met. Abh.* 17:493–504.

Roberts, D. 1968. Occurrences of weathering pits from Sørøy, northern Norway. *Geog. Ann.* 50(1):60–63.

Rochow, T. F. 1969. Growth, caloric content, and sugars in *Caltha leptosepala* in relation to alpine snow melt. *Bull. Torrey Bot. Club* 96:689–98.

Rodda, J. C. 1971. *The precipitation measurement paradox—the instrument accuracy problem.* Rep. 16. Geneva, Switzerland: WMO/IHD World Meteor. Organ.

Roderick, J., and Roderick, D. 1973. Africa's puzzle animal. *Pacific Discovery* 26(4):26–28.

Romashkevich, A. I. 1964. Micromorphological indications of the processes associated with the formation of the krasnozems (red earths) and the red-coloured crust of weathering in the Transcaucasus. Pp. 261–68 in *Soil micromorphology,* ed. A. Jongerius. Amsterdam: Elsevier. 540 pp.

Rona, P. A. 1973. Plate tectonics and mineral resources. *Sci. Amer.* 231 (July):86–95.

Rooney, J. F. 1969. The economic and social implications of snow and ice. Pp. 389–401 in *Water, earth, and man,* ed. R. J. Chorley. London: Methuen. 206 pp.

Rosenfeld, C. L., and Schlicker, H. G. 1976. The significance of increased fumarolic activity at Mount Baker, Washington. *Ore Bin* 38(2):23–35. (Pub. by Oregon Dept. Geol. Min. Ind., Portland.)

Roundy, R. W. 1976. Altitudinal mobility and disease hazards for Ethiopian populations. *Econ. Geog.* 52:103–15.

Roy, S. B., and Singh, I. 1969. Acute mountain sickness in Himalayan terrain: Clinical and physiologic studies. Pp. 32–41 in *Biomedicine of high terrestrial elevations,* ed. A. H. Hegnauer. Natick, Mass.: U.S. Army Res. Inst. Envir. Med. 323 pp.

Rubey, W. W. 1951. Geologic history of sea water—an attempt to state the problem. *Geol. Soc. Amer. Bull.* 62:1111–47.

Rudberg, S. 1968. Wind erosion—preparation of maps showing the direction of eroding winds. *Biuletyn Peryglacjalny* 17:181–94.

Rumney, G. R. 1968. *Climatology and the world's climates.* New York: Macmillan. 656 pp.

Rusinow, D. I. 1969. *Italy's Austrian heritage, 1919–1946.* London: Oxford Univ. Press. 423 pp.

Ruskin, J. 1856. *Modern painters.* Vol. 3, part 4. Chicago: Belford Clarke. 431 pp.

Russell, R. J. 1933. Alpine landforms of western United States. *Geol. Soc. Amer. Bull.* 44:927–50.

Rutherford, G. K. 1964. The tropical alpine soils of Mt. Giluwe, Australian New Guinea. *Can. Geog.* 8:27–33.

Ruxton, B. P., and McDougall, I. 1967. Denudation rates in northeast Papua from potassium-argon dating of lavas. *Amer. J. Sci.* 265: 545–61.

Saint Girons, H., and Duguy, R. 1970. Le cycle sexuel de *Lacerta muralis* L. en plaine et en montagne. *Bull. Mus. Nat. d'Hist. Natur.* 42: 609–25.

Sakai, A. 1970. Mechanism of desiccation damage of conifers wintering in soil-frozen areas. *Ecol.* 51:657–64.

Salisbury, F. B., and Spomer, G. G. 1964. Leaf temperatures of alpine plants in the field. *Planta.* 60:497–505.

Salmon, J. T. 1975. The influence of man on the biota. Chapter 17 in *Biogeography and ecology in New Zealand,* ed. G. Kuschel. The Hague: Junk. 689 pp.

Salt, G. 1954. A contribution to the ecology of Upper Kilimanjaro. *J. Ecol.* 42:375–423.

Salt, R. W. 1956. Influence of moisture content and temperature on cold hardiness of hibernating insects. *Can. J. Zool.* 34:283–94.

———. 1961. Principles of insect cold-hardiness. *Ann. Rev. Entomol.* 6:55–74.

———. 1969. The survival of insects at low temperatures. Pp. 331–50 in *Dormancy and survival, 23rd symp. soc. exper. biol.* London: Cambridge Univ. Press. 599 pp.

Samson, C. A. 1965. A comparison of mountain slope and radiosonde observations. *Mon. Wea. Rev.* 93:327–30.

Sarker, R. P. 1966. A dynamic model of orographic rainfall. *Mon. Wea. Rev.* 94(9):555–72.

———. 1967. Some modifications in a dynamical model of orographic rainfall. *Mon. Wea. Rev.* 95:673–84.

Sauer, C. 1936. American agricultural origins: A consideration of nature and culture. Pp. 279–97 in *Essays in anthropology,* ed. A. L. Kroeber. Berkeley, Ca.: Univ. of Calif. Press.

Sawkins, F. J. 1972. Sulfide ore deposits in relation to plate tectonics. *J. Geol.* 80:377–97.

Sawyer, J. S. 1956. The physical and dynamical problems of orographic rain. *Weather* 11(12): 375–81.

Sayward, P. 1934. High points of the forty-eight states. *Appalachia* 20(78):206–15.

Scaëtta, H. 1935. Les avalanches d'air dans les Alps et dans les hautes montagnes de l'Afrique centrale. *Ciel et Terre* 51:79–80.

Schaerer, P. A. 1972. Terrain and vegetation of snow avalanche sites of Rogers Pass, British Columbia. Pp. 215–22 in *Mountain geomorphology*, ed. O. Slaymaker and H. J. McPherson. Vancouver, B.C.: Tantalus Research. 274 pp.

Schell, I. I. 1934. Differences between temperatures, humidities, and winds on the White Mountains and in the free air. *Trans. Amer. Geophys. Union* (Pt. I):118–24.

———. 1935. Free air temperatures from observations on mountain peaks with application to Mt. Washington. *Trans. Amer. Geophys. Union* (Part I):126–41.

———. 1936. On the vertical distribution of wind velocity over mountain summits. *Bull. Amer. Meteor. Soc.* 17:295–300.

Schlesinger, W. H., Reiners, W. A., and Knopman, D. S. 1974. Heavy metal concentrations and deposition in bulk precipitation in montane ecosystems of New Hampshire, U.S.A. *Envir. Pollut.* 6:39–47.

Schmid, E. 1972. A mousterian silex mine and dwelling-place in the Swiss Jura. Pp. 129–32 in *The origin of homo sapiens*, ed. F. Bordes. Paris: UNESCO. 321 pp.

Schmid, J. M., and Frye, R. H. 1977. *Spruce beetle in the Rockies*. U.S. Dept. Agri. For. Serv. Gen. Tech. Rep. RM-49. Fort Collins, Colo: Rocky Mt. Forest and Range Experiment Station. 38 pp.

Schmid, W. D. 1971. Modification of the subnivean microclimate by snowmobiles. Pp. 251–57 in *Proc. snow and ice symp.* Ames, Iowa: Iowa State Univ. 250 pp.

Schmidt, K. P. 1938. A geographic variation gradient in frogs. *Zool. Ser. Field Mus. Nat. Hist.* 20:377–82.

Schmidt, W. 1934. Observations on local climatology in Austrian mountains. *Quart. J. Royal Meteor. Soc.* 60:345–51.

Schmoller, R. 1971. Nocturnal arthropods in the alpine tundra of Colorado. *Arctic and Alpine Res.* 3(4):345–52.

Scholander, P. F. 1955. Evolution of climatic adaptation in homeotherms. *Evolution* 9(1): 15–26.

———. 1957. The wonderful net. *Sci. Amer.* 196:97–107.

Scholander, P. F., Hock, R., Walters, V., and Irving, L. 1950a. Adaptation to cold in arctic and tropical mammals and birds in relation to body temperature, insulation, and basal metabolic rate. *Biol. Bull.* 99:259–71.

Scholander, P. F., Hock, R., Walters, V., Johnson, F., and Irving, L. 1950b. Heat regulation in some arctic and tropical mammals and birds. *Biol. Bull.* 99:237–58.

Scholander, P. F., Walters, V., Hock, R., and Irving, L. 1950c. Body insulation of some arctic and tropical mammals and birds. *Biol. Bull.* 99:225–36.

Schramm, J. R. 1958. The mechanism of frost heaving of tree seedlings. *Proc. Amer. Phil. Soc.* 102(4):333–50.

Schumm, S. A. 1956. The movement of rocks by wind. *J. Sed. Pet.* 26:284–86.

———. 1963. The disparity between present rates of denudation and orogeny. Pp. 1–13 in *U.S. Geol. Surv. Prof. Pap. 454H*.

Schweinfurth, U. 1972. The eastern marches of high Asia and the river gorge country. Pp. 276–87 in *Geoecology of the high mountain regions of Eurasia*, ed. C. Troll. Wiesbaden: Franz Steiner. 300 pp.

Scorer, R. S. 1952. Soaring in Spain. *Weather* 7:373–76.

———. 1955. The growth of cumulus over mountains. *Archiv. Meteor. Geophys. Biokl.* (Ser. A) 8:25–34.

———. 1961. Lee waves in the atmosphere. *Sci. Amer.* 204:124–34.

———. 1967. Causes and consequences of standing waves. Pp. 75–101 in *Proc. symp. mountain meteor.*, ed. E. R. Reiter and J. L. Rassmussen. Atmosph. Sci. Pap. 122. Fort Collins, Colo.: Dept. of Atmosph. Sci., Colorado State Univ. 221 pp.

Scorer, R. S., and Klieforth, H. 1959. Theory of mountain waves of large amplitude. *Quart. J. Royal Meteor. Soc.* 85(364):131–43.

Scott, D., and Billings, W. D. 1964. Effects of environmental factors on standing crop and productivity of an alpine tundra. *Ecol. Monogr.* 34:243–70.

Scott, J. D. 1962. What do snow worms eat? *Summit* (Big Bear City, Calif.) 8:8–9.

Scott, W. H. 1958. A preliminary report on upland rice in northern Luzon. *Southwestern J. Anthrop.* 14:87–105.

Scotter, G. W. 1975. Permafrost profiles in the continental divide region of Alberta and British Columbia. *Arctic and Alpine Res.* 7(1):93–96.

Seidensticker, J. C., Hornock, M. G., Wiles, W. V., and Messick, J. P. 1973. *Mountain lion social organization in the Idaho Primitive Area.* Wildlife Monogr. 35. 60 pp.

Seligman, G. 1936. *Snow structure and ski fields; with an appendix on alpine weather by C. K. M. Douglas.* London: Macmillan. 555 pp.

Semple, E. C. 1897. The influence of the Appalachian barrier upon colonial history. *J. of School Geog.* 1:33–41.

———. 1911. *Influences of geographic environment.* New York: Henry Holt. 683 pp.

———. 1915. The barrier boundary of the Mediterranean Basin and its northern breaches as factors in history. *Annals Assoc. Amer. Geog.* 5:27–59.

Sevruk, B. 1972. Precipitation measurements by means of storage gauges with stereo and horizontal orifices in Baye de Montreaux watershed. Vol. II, pp. 86–102 in *Distribution of precipitation in mountainous areas.* Geilo, Norway: Proc. Int. Symp. World Meteor. Organ. 587 pp.

Sharp, R. P. 1942. Mudflow levees. *J. Geom.* 5:222–27.

———. 1949. Pleistocene ventifacts east of the Big Horn Mountains, Wyoming. *J. Geol.* 57:175–95.

———. 1960. *Glaciers.* Eugene, Or.: Univ. of Oregon Press. 78 pp.

Sharpe, C. F. S. 1938. *Landslides and related phenomena.* New York: Columbia Univ. Press. 137 pp.

Shaw, C. H. 1909. Causes of timber line on mountains: The role of snow. *Plant World* 12:169–81.

Shaw, R. B. 1872. Religious cairns of the Himalayan region. *British Assoc. Advancement Sci. Rep.* 42:194–97.

Shields, E. T. 1913. Omei San: The sacred mountain of West China. *Royal Asiatic Soc., North China Branch, J.* 44:100–109.

Shields, O. 1967. Hilltopping. *J. Res. Lepidoptera* 6:71–178.

Shreve, F. 1915. *The vegetation of a desert mountain range as conditioned by climatic factors.* Pub. 217. Washington, D.C.: Carnegie Inst. 112 pp.

Shreve, R. L. 1966. Sherman landslide, Alaska. *Science* 154:1639–43.

———. 1968. Leakage and fluidization in air-layer lubricated avalanches. *Geol. Soc. Amer. Bull.* 79:653–58.

Shryock, J. 1931. *The temples of Anking and their cults.* Paris: Librairie Orientaliste P. Guethner. 206 pp.

Shulls, W. A. 1976. Microbial population of the Colorado alpine tundra. *Arctic and Alpine Res.* 8(4):387–91.

Siiger, H. 1952. A cult for the god of Mount Kanchenjunga among the Lepcha of northern Sikkim. Vol. 2, pp. 185–89, in *Congress. Int. Des. Sci. Anthro. et Ethnol.* Vienna, 1–9 Sept., Actes Dv. IV.

Sillitoe, R. H. 1972. A plate tectonics model for the origin of porphyry copper deposits. *Econ. Geol.* 67:184–97.

Simoons, F. J. 1960. *Northwest Ethiopia, peoples and economy.* Madison, Wis.: Univ. Wisconsin Press. 250 pp.

Simpson, B. B. 1974. Glacial migrations of plants: Island biogeographical evidence. *Science* 185:698–700.

———. 1975. Pleistocene changes in the flora of the high tropical Andes. *Paleobiology* 1(3):273–94.

Singer, M. and Ugolini, F. C. 1974. Genetic history of two well-drained subalpine soils formed on complex parent materials. *Can. J. Soil Sci.* 54:475–89.

Singh, I., Khanna, P. K., Srivastava, M. C., Lal, M., Roy, S. B., and Subramanyan, C. S. V. 1969. Acute mountain sickness. *New Eng. J. Med.* 280:175–84.

Slaymaker, H. O. 1972. Sediment yield and sediment control in the Canadian cordillera. Pp. 235–45 in *Mountain geomorphology,* ed. O. Slaymaker and H. J. McPherson. Vancouver, B.C.: Tantalus Research. 274 pp.

———. 1974. Alpine hydrology. Pp. 133–58 in *Arctic and alpine environments,* ed. J. D. Ives and R. G. Barry. London: Methuen. 999 pp.

Slaymaker, H. O., and McPherson, H. J. 1977. An overview of geomorphic processes in the Canadian cordilerra. *Zeits. für Geomorph.* 21(2):169–86.

Sleeper, R. A., Spencer, A. A., and Steinhoff, H. W. 1976. Effects of varying snowpack on small mammals. Pp. 437–85 in *Ecological impacts of snowpack augmentation in the San Juan Mountains, Colorado*, ed. H. W. Steinhoff and J. D. Ives. Colo. State Univ., prepared for U.S. Bur. of Reclamation. Springfield, Va.: Nat. Tech. Info. Serv. PB255 012. 489 pp.

Sleumer, H. 1965. The role of *Ericaceae* in the tropical montane and subalpine forest of Malaysia. Pp. 179–84 in *Symposium on ecological research in humid tropics vegetation*. Paris: UNESCO.

Smith, A. T. 1974. The distribution and dispersal of pikas: Consequences of insular population structure. *Ecol.* 55(5):1112–19.

———. 1978. Comparative demography of pikas (*Ochotona*): Effect of spatial and temporal age-specific mortality. *Ecol.* 59(1):133–39.

Smith, A. V. 1958. The resistance of animals to cooling and freezing. *Biol. Rev.* 33:197–253.

Smith, A. W. 1975. Mineral King. *Nat. Parks and Consv. Mag.* 49(6):2.

Smith, D. R. 1969. *Vegetation, soils, and their interrelationships at timberline in the Medicine Bow Mountains, Wyoming*. Sci. Monogr. 17. Laramie, Wyo.: Agri. Exp. Sta., Univ. Wyoming. 13 pp.

Smith, H. T. U. 1953. The Hickory Run boulder field, Carbon County, Pennsylvania. *Amer. J. Sci.* 251:625–42.

———. 1973. Photogeologic study of periglacial talus glaciers in northwestern Canada. *Geog. Ann.* 55A(2):69–84.

Smith, J. M. B. 1975. Mountain grasslands of New Guinea. *J. Biogeog.* 2(1):27–44.

———. 1977a. Vegetation and microclimate of east- and west-facing slopes in the grasslands of Mt. Wilhelm, Papua, New Guinea. *J. Ecol.* 65:39–53.

———. 1977b. An ecological comparison of two tropical high mountains. *J. Trop. Geog.* 44: 71–80.

Smith, M. E. 1966. Mountain mosquitos of the Gothic, Colorado, area. *Amer. Midl. Nat.* 76: 125–50.

Smith, R. B. 1976. The generation of lee waves by the Blue Ridge. *J. Atmosph. Sci.* 33(3):507–19.

Sneddon, J. I., Lavkulich, L. M., and Farstad, L. 1972. The morphology and genesis of some alpine soils in British Columbia, Canada. I: Morphology, classification, and genesis. II:

Physical, chemical, and mineralogical determinations and genesis. *Soil Sci. Soc. Amer. Proc.* 36:100–110.

Soil Survey Staff. 1960. *Soil classification, a comprehensive system (7th approximation)*. Washington, D.C.: U.S. Dept. Agri. Soil Cons. Serv. 265 pp.

———. 1974. *Soil taxonomy, a basic system of soil classification for making and interpreting soil surveys*. Handbook 436. Washington, D.C.: U.S. Dept. Agri. 754 pp.

Solon, L. R., Lowder, W. M., Shambon, A., and Blatz, H. 1960. Investigations of natural environmental radiation. *Science* 131(3404):903–6.

Sömme, A. 1949. Recent trends in transhumance in Norway. *Comptes Rendus du Congr. Int. de Geog., Lisbonne* 3:83–93.

Sommerfeld, R., and LaChapelle, E. 1970. The classification of snow metamorphism. *J. Glaciol.* 9(55).3–17.

Soons, J. M. 1968. Erosion by needle ice in the southern Alps, New Zealand. Pp. 217–28 in *Arctic and alpine environments*, ed. W. H. Osburn and H. E. Wright, Jr. Bloomington, Ind.: Indiana Univ. Press. 308 pp.

Soons, J. M., and Rayner, J. N. 1968. Micro-climate and erosion processes in the Southern Alps, New Zealand. *Geog. Ann.* 50A:1–15.

Sowerby, A. 1940. *Nature in Chinese Art*. New York: John Day. 203 pp.

Spalding, J. B. 1979. The aeolian ecology of White Mountain Peak, California: Windblown insect fauna. *Arctic and Alpine Res.* 11(1):83–94.

Spencer, A. W., and Steinhoff, H. W. 1968. An explanation of geographic variation in litter size. *J. Mammal.* 49:281–86.

Spencer, J. E., and Hale, G. A. 1961. The origin, nature and distribution of agricultural terracing. *Pacific Viewpoint* 2(1):1–4.

Spurr, J. E. 1923. *The ore magmas*. New York: McGraw-Hill. 915 pp.

Standley, S. 1975. The Aspen story. Pp. 17–19 in *Man, leisure, and wildlands: A complex interaction*. Proc. 1st Eisenhower Consortium Res. Symp., Vail, Colo. 286 pp.

Stankey, G. H. 1971. Wilderness carrying capacity and quality. *Naturalist* 22(3):7–13.

———. 1973. *Visitor perception of wilderness recreation carrying capacity*. U.S. Dept. Agri. For. Serv. Res. Pap. INT-142. Ogden, Utah. 61 pp.

Stankey, G. H., Lucas, R. C., and Lime, D. W.

1976. Crowding in parks and wilderness. *Design and Environment* 7:1–3.

Stankey, G. H., and Baden, J. 1977. *Rationing wilderness use: Methods, problems, and guidelines.* U.S. Dept. Agri. For. Serv. Res. Pap. INT-192. Ogden, Utah. 20 pp.

Starkel, L. 1976. The role of extreme (catastrophic) meteorological events in contemporary evolution of slopes. Pp. 203–46 in *Geomorphology and climate,* ed. E. Derbyshire. London: John Wiley and Sons. 512 pp.

Stauffer, T. R. 1965. The economics of nomadism in Iran. *Middle East J.* 19:284–302.

Steinhoff, H. W., and Ives, J. D., eds. 1976. *Ecological impacts of snowpack augmentation in the San Juan Mountains, Colorado.* Colo. State Univ., prepared for the U.S. Bur. Reclamation. Springfield, Va.: Nat. Tech. Info. Serv. PB-255 012. 489 pp.

Steward, J. H. 1955. Introduction: The irrigation civilizations. Pp. 1–6 in *Irrigation civilizations: A comparative study,* ed. J. H. Steward et al. Soc. Sci. Monogr. 1. Washington, D.C.: Pan Amer. Union. 78 pp.

Stewart, G. R. 1960. *Ordeal by hunger: The story of the Donner Party.* Boston: Houghton Mifflin. 394 pp.

Stewart, J. H., and LaMarche, V. C., Jr. 1967. *Erosion and deposition produced by the flood of December 1964 on Coffee Creek, Trinity County, California.* U.S. Geol. Surv. Prof. Pap. 422-K. 22 pp.

Stewart, N. R., Belote, J., and Belote, L. 1976. Transhumance in the Central Andes. *Annals Assoc. Amer. Geog.* 66(3):377–97.

Stoecker, R. E. 1976. Pocket gopher distribution in relation to snow in the alpine tundra. Pp. 281–88 in *Ecological impacts of snowpack augmentation in the San Juan Mountains, Colorado,* ed. H. W. Steinhoff and J. D. Ives. Colo. State Univ., prepared for U.S. Bur. of Reclamation. Springfield, Va.: Nat. Tech. Info. Serv. PB-255 012. 489 pp.

St.-Onge, D. A. 1969. *Nivation landforms.* Geol. Surv. Can. Pap. 69-30. 12 pp.

Storey, H. C., and Wilm, H. G. 1944. A comparison of vertical and tilted rain gauges in estimated precipitation on mountain watersheds. *Trans. Amer. Geophys. Union* 3:518–23.

Strahler, A. N. 1965. *Introduction to physical geography.* New York: John Wiley and Sons. 455 pp.

Street, J. M. 1969. An evaluation of the concept of carrying capacity. *Prof. Geog.* 21:104–7.

Strickland, M. D., and Diem, K. 1975. The impact of snow on mule deer. Pp. 135–74 in *The Medicine Bow ecology project.* Prepared for Off. U.S. Atmosph. Water Resources. Laramie, Wyo.: Univ. of Wyoming, in cooperation with Rocky Mtn. Forest and Range Experiment Station. 397 pp.

Strickler, G. S. 1961. *Vegetation and soil condition changes on a subalpine grassland in eastern Oregon.* U.S. Dept. Agri. For. Serv. Pac. N.W. Range Expt. Sta. Res. Pap. 40. Portland, Or. 46 pp.

Strong, D. F., ed. 1976. *Metallogeny and plate tectonics.* Geol. Assoc. Can. Spec. Pap. 14. 660 pp.

Strong, J. 1894. *The exhaustive concordance of the Bible.* New York: Abingdon-Cokesbury Press. 1545 pp.

Strutfield, H. E. M. 1918. Mountaineering as a religion. *Alpine J.* 32:241–47.

Stuart, D. G. 1975. Community and regional implications of large scale resort developments: Big Sky of Montana. Pp. 121–26 in *Man, leisure, and wildlands: A complex interaction.* Proc. 1st Eisenhower Consortium Res. Symp., Vail, Colo. 286 pp.

Sullivan, M. 1962. *The birth of landscape painting in China.* Berkeley, Ca.: Univ. of Calif. Press. 213 pp.

Sushkin, P. 1925. Outlines of the history of the Recent fauna of Palearctic Asia. *Proc. Natl. Acad. Sci.* 11:299–302.

Sutton, C. W. 1933. Andean mud slide destroys lives and property. *Eng. News-Record* 110:562–63.

Suzuki, S. 1965. On the mechanism of a miniature frost shelter. *Meteor. Runds.* 17:171–73.

Svihla, A. 1956. The relation of coloration in mammals to low temperature. *J. Mammal.* 37:378–81.

Swan, L. W. 1952. Some environmental conditions influencing life at high altitudes. *Ecol.* 33:109–11.

_____. 1961. The ecology of the high Himalayas. *Sci. Amer.* 205:68–78.

_____. 1963a. Aeolian zone. *Science* 140:77–78.

_____. 1963b. Ecology of the heights. *Nat. Hist.* 72:22–29.

_____. 1967. Alpine and aeolian regions of the world. Pp. 29–54 in *Arctic and alpine environments,* ed. H. E. Wright and W. H. Osburn,

Jr. Bloomington, Ind.: Indiana Univ. Press. 308 pp.

_____. 1970. Goose of the Himalayas. *Nat. Hist.* 79(10):68–75.

Swan, L. W., and Leviton, A. E. 1962. The herpetology of Nepal: A history, checklist, and zoogeographical analysis of the herpetofauna. *Calif. Acad. Sci. Proc.* 32:103–47.

Swanson, E. 1955. Terrace agriculture in the Central Andes. *Davidson J. Anthrop.* 1(2):123–32.

Swanson, F. T., and Dyrness, C. T. 1975. Impact of clear-cutting and road construction on soil erosion by landslides in the western Cascade Range, Oregon. *Geol.* 3(7):393–96.

Swanston, D. N. 1974. *Slope stability problems associated with timber harvesting in mountainous regions of the western United States.* U.S. Dept. Agri. For. Serv. Gen. Tech. Rep. PNW-21. Portland, Or. 14 pp.

Sweeney, J. M., and Steinhoff, H. W. 1976. Elk movements and calving as related to snow cover. Pp. 415–36 in *Ecological impacts of snowpack augmentation in the San Juan Mountains, Colorado*, ed. H. W. Steinhoff and J. D. Ives. Colo. State Univ., prepared for U.S. Bur. of Reclamation. Springfield, Va.: Nat. Tech. Info. Serv. PB-255 012. 489 pp.

Swift, L. W., Jr. 1976. Algorithm for solar radiation on mountain slopes. *Water Resources Res.* 12(1):108–12.

Taber, S. 1929. Frost heaving. *J. Geol.* 37:428–61.

_____. 1930. The mechanics of frost heaving. *J. Geol.* 38:303–17.

Tanner, C. B., and Fuchs, M. 1968. Evaporation from unsaturated surfaces: A general combination method. *J. Geophys. Res.* 73:1299–1304.

Tanner, J. T. 1963. Mountain temperatures in the southeastern and southwestern U.S. during late spring and early summer. *J. Appl. Meteor.* 2:473–83.

Taylor-Barge, B. 1969. *The summer climate of the St. Elias mountain region.* Arctic Inst. N.A. Res. Pap. 53. 265 pp.

Tazieff, H. 1970. The Afar triangle. *Sci. Amer.* 222(2):32–40.

Tedrow, J. C. F., and Brown, J. 1962. Soils of the northern Brooks Range, Alaska: Weakening of the soil forming potential at high arctic altitudes. *Soil Sci.* 93:254–61.

Teichert, C. 1939. Corrasion by wind-blown snow in polar regions. *Amer. J. Sci.* 237:146–48.

Terborgh, J. 1971. Distribution on environmental gradients: Theory and a preliminary interpretation of distributional patterns in the avifauna of the Cordillera Vilcabamba, Peru. *Ecol.* 52: 23–40.

Terjung, W. H., Kickert, R. N., Potter, G. L., and Swarts, S. W. 1969a. Energy and moisture balances of an alpine tundra in mid-July. *Arctic and Alpine Res.* 1:247–66.

_____. 1969b. Terrestrial, atmospheric, and solar radiation fluxes on a high desert mountain in mid-July: White Mtn. Peak, California. *Solar Energy* 12:363–75.

Terzaghi, K. 1950. Mechanism of landslides. Pp. 83–123 in *Geol. Soc. Amer., Berkley Volume.* New York.

Thams, J. C. 1961. The influence of the Alps in the radiation climate. Pp. 76–91 in *Progress in photobiology*, ed. B. Christensen and B. Buchmann. Proc. 3rd Int. Congr. Photobiol. Amsterdam: Elsevier. 628 pp.

Thomas, R. B. 1976. Energy flow at high altitude. Pp. 379–404 in *Man in the Andes: A multidisciplinary study of high-altitude Quechua*, ed. P. T. Baker and M. A. Little. Stroudsburg, Pa.: Dowden, Hutchinson and Ross. 482 pp.

Thomas, W. H. 1972. Observations on snow algae in California. *J. Phycol.* 8:1–9.

Thompson, A. H. 1967. Surface temperature inversions in a canyon. *J. Appl. Meteor.* 6(2): 287–96.

Thompson, B. W. 1966. The mean annual rainfall of Mount Kenya. *Weather* 21:48–49.

Thompson, W. F. 1960–61. The shape of New England mountains. *Appalachia* 33:145–59, 316–35, 458–78.

_____. 1962a. Preliminary notes on the nature and distribution of rock glaciers relative to true glaciers and other effects of the climate on the ground in N.A. Pp. 212–19 in *Int. Assoc. Sci. Hydrol. Symp. of Obergurgl Pub.* 58. Paris.

_____. 1962b. Cascade alp slopes and gipfelfluren as climageomorphic phenomena. *Erdkunde* 16:81–93.

_____. 1964. How and why to distinguish between mountains and hills. *Prof. Geog.* 16(6): 6–8.

_____. 1967. Military significance of mountain environmental studies. *Army Res. and Develop. News Mag.* (May issue):1–2.

————. 1968. New observations on alpine accordances in the western United States. *Annals Assoc. Amer. Geog.* 58(4):650–69.

————. 1970. Airmobile warfare in the mountains. *Military Rev.* 50(7):57–62.

Thorington, J. M. 1957. As it was in the beginning. *Alpine J.* 62(295):4–15.

Thorn, C. E. 1975. Influence of late-lying snow on rock-weathering rinds. *Arctic and Alpine Res.* 7(4):373–78.

————. 1976. Quantitative evaluation of nivation in the Colorado Front Range. *Geol. Soc. Amer. Bull.* 87(8):1169–78.

————. 1978a. The geomorphic role of snow. *Annals Assoc. Amer. Geog.* 68(3):414–25.

————. 1978b. A preliminary assessment of the geomorphic role of Pocket gophers in the alpine zone of the Colorado Front Range. *Geog. Ann.* 60A(3–4):181–87.

————. 1979a. Bedrock freeze-thaw weathering regime in an alpine environment, Colorado Front Range. *Earth Surface Processes* 4:211–28.

————. 1979b. Ground temperatures and surficial transport in colluvium during snowpatch meltout, Colorado Front Range. *Arctic and Alpine Res.* 11(1):41–52.

Thornbury, W. D. 1965. *Regional geomorphology of the United States.* New York: John Wiley and Sons. 609 pp.

————. 1969. *Principles of geomorphology.* New York: John Wiley and Sons. 594 pp.

Thornthwaite, C. W. 1961. *The measurement of climatic fluxes.* Tech. Rep. 1. Centerton, N.J.: Lab. Climatol. 19 pp.

Thornthwaite, C. W., and Mather, J. R. 1951. The role of evapotranspiration in climate. *Archiv. Meteor. Geophys. Biokl.* (Ser. B) 3:16–39.

Thorp, J. 1931. The effects of vegetation and climate upon soil profiles in northern and northwestern Wyoming. *Soil Sci.* 32:283–301.

Thorp, J., and Bellis, E. 1960. Soils of the Kenya highlands in relation to landforms. Vol. 4, pp. 329–34, in *Trans. 7th Int. Cong. Soil Sci.* Madison, Wis.

Timiras, P. S. 1964. Comparison of growth and development of the rat at high altitude and at sea level. Pp. 21–32 in *The Physiological effects of high altitude,* ed. W. H. Weihe. New York: Macmillan. 351 pp.

Toksoz, M. N. 1975. The subduction of the lithosphere. *Sci. Amer.* 233(5):88–101.

Tolbert, W. W., Tolbert, V. R., and Ambrose, R. E. 1977. Distribution, abundance, and biomass of Colorado alpine tundra arthropods. *Arctic and Alpine Res.* 9(3):221–34.

Townsend, C. H. T. 1926. Vertical life zones of Northern Peru with crop correlations. *Ecol.* 7:440–44.

Tozer, H. F. 1935. *A history of ancient geography.* Cambridge: Cambridge Univ. Press. 370 pp.

Tranquillini, W. 1964. The physiology of plants at high altitudes. *Ann. Rev. Plant Physiol.* 15:345–62.

————. 1979. *Physiological ecology of the Alpine timberline.* New York: Springer-Verlag. 137 pp.

Tricart, J. 1969. *Geomorphology of cold environments.* Trans. E. Watson. London: Macmillan. 320 pp.

————. 1974. *Structural geomorphology.* New York: Longman. 305 pp.

Tricart, J., et collaborateurs. 1961. Mécanismes normaux et phénomènes catastrophiques dans l'évolution des versants du bassin du Guil (Hautes-Alpes, France). *Zeits. für Geomorph.* 5:276–301.

Trimble, S. W. 1977. The fallacy of stream equilibrium in contemporary denudation studies. *Amer. J. Sci.* 277:876–87.

Trimborn, H. 1969. South Central America and the Andean civilizations. Pp. 83–146 in *Pre-Colombian American religions,* ed. W. Krickeberg, H. Trimborn, W. Müller, and O. Zerries. New York: Holt, Rinehart and Winston. 365 pp.

Troll, C. 1948. Der asymmetrische Aufbau der Vegetationszonen und Vegetationsstufen auf der Nord- und Sudhalbkugel. *Ber. Geobot. Forsch. Inst. Rubel.* 1947:46–83.

————. 1952. Die Lokalwinde der Tropengebirge und ihr Einfluss auf Niederschlag und Vegetation. *Bonner Geog. Abh.* (Köln) 9:124–82.

————. 1958a. *Structure soils, solifluction, and frost climates of the earth.* Trans. H. E. Wright and associates. U.S. Army Snow, Ice and Permafrost Res. Est. Trans. 43. Wilmette, Ill.: Corps of Engineers. 121 pp.

————. 1958b. Tropical mountain vegetation. *Proc. 9th Pac. Sci. Cong.* 20:37–45.

————. 1959. Die tropischen Gebirge. Ihre dreidimensionale Klimatische und pflanzengeographischen Zonierung. *Bonner Geog. Abh.* 25:1–93.

————. 1960. The relationship between climates and plant geography of the southern cold temperate zone and of the tropical high mountains. *Proc. Roy. Soc. Medicine, London* B-152: 529–32.

———. 1968. The cordilleras of the tropical Americas: Aspects of climatic, phytogeographical and agrarian ecology. Pp. 15–56 in *Geoecology of the mountainous regions of the tropical Americas,* ed. C. Troll. Proc. UNESCO Mexico Symp. Aug. 1966. Bonn: Ferd. Dümmers Verlag. 223 pp.

———. 1972a. Geoecology and the world-wide differentiation of high mountain ecosystems. Pp. 1–16 in *Geoecology of the high mountain regions of Eurasia,* ed. C. Troll. Wiesbaden: Franz Steiner. 300 pp.

———. 1972b. The three-dimensional zonation of the Himalayan system. Pp. 264–75 in *Geoecology of the high mountain regions of Eurasia,* ed. C. Troll. Wiesbaden: Franz Steiner, 300 pp

———. 1972c. The upper limit of aridity and the arid core of high Asia. Pp. 237–43 in *Geoecology of the high mountain regions of Eurasia,* ed. C. Troll. Wiesbaden: Franz Steiner. 300 pp.

———. 1973a. The upper timberlines in different climatic zones. *Arctic and Alpine Res.* 5(3): (Pt. 2)3–18.

———. 1973b. High mountain belts between the polar caps and the equator: Their definition and lower limit. *Arctic and Alpine Res.* 5(3): (Pt. 2)19–28.

Tuan, Y. 1964. Mountains, ruins, and the sentiment of melancholy. *Landscape* 14(1):27–30.

———. 1974. *Topophilia: A study of environmental perception, attitudes, and values.* Englewood Cliffs, N.J.: Prentice-Hall. 260 pp.

Tuck, R. 1935. Asymmetrical topography in high altitudes resulting from glacial erosion. *J. Geol.* 43:530–38.

Turner, G. T., Hansen, R. M., Reid, V. H., Tietjen, H. P., and Ward, A. L. 1973. *Pocket gophers and Colorado mountain rangeland.* Colo. State Univ. Exp. Sta. Bull. 5545. Fort Collins, Colo. 90 pp.

Turner, H. 1958a. Uber das Licht und Strahlungsklima einer Hanglage der Otztaler Alpen bei Obergurgl und seine Auswirkung auf das Mikroklima und auf die Vegetation. *Archiv. Meteor. Geophys. Biokl.* (Ser. B.) 8:273–325.

———. 1958b. Maximaltemperaturen oberflachennaher Bodenschichten am der alpinen Waldgrenze. *Wetter und Leben* 10:1–12.

Turner, P. R. 1977. Intensive agriculture among the highland Tzeltals. *Ethnol.* 16(2):167–74.

Twidale, C. R. 1971. *Structural landforms.* Cambridge, Mass.: M.I.T. Press. 247 pp.

———. 1976. *Analysis of landforms.* New York: John Wiley. 572 pp.

Tyler, J. E. 1930. *The Alpine passes, the Middle Ages (962–1250).* Oxford, England: Basil Blackwell. 188 pp.

Udvardy, M. D. F. 1969. *Dynamic zoogeography.* New York: Van Nostrand Reinhold. 445 pp.

Ugolini, F. C., and Tedrow, J. C. F. 1963. Soils of the Brooks Range, Alaska. 3: Rendzina of the Arctic. *Soil Sci.* 96:121–27.

Uhlig, H. 1969. Hill tribes and rice farmers in the Himalayas and southeast Asia. *Inst. British Geog. Trans.* 47:1–23.

———. 1978. Geoecological controls on high-altitude rice cultivation in the Himalayas and mountain regions of southeast Asia. *Arctic and Alpine Res.* 10(2):519–29.

U.S. Dept. Agriculture. 1968. *Snow avalanches.* U.S. Dept. Agri. Handbook 194. Revised. Washington, D.C. 84 pp.

———. 1972. *Snow survey and water supply forecasting.* U.S. Dept. Agri. Soil Cons. Ser., Nat. Engr. Handbook Sec. 22. Washington, D.C.

———. *Avalanche protection in Switzerland.* U.S. Dept. Agri. For. Serv. Gen. Tech. Pap. RM-9. Fort Collins, Colo. 168 pp.

U.S. Dept. Army. 1972. *Medical problems of man at high terrestrial elevations.* U.S. Dept. Army Tech. Bull. TB MED 288. 21 pp.

U.S. Dept. Interior. 1904–1970. *Public use of the National Parks: A statistical report.* U.S. Dept. Interior, Nat. Park Serv. Washington, D.C. 1904–1940, 12 pp.; 1941–1953, 7 pp.; 1960–1970, 11 pp.

U.S. Dept. Transportation. 1977. *F.A.A. seeks advice on ozone irritation.* Washington, D.C.: U.S. Dept. Trans., Off. Pub. Affairs, 18 Oct. 1977. 2 pp.

Utah Geol. Assoc. 1972. *Environmental geology of the Wasatch Front,* Pub. 1. Salt Lake City, Utah: Utah Geol. Assoc.

Valcarcel, L. E. 1946. Indian markets and fairs in Peru. Pp. 477–82 in *Handbook of South American Indians,* ed. J. Steward. Washington, D.C.: Smithsonian Institution.

Van Buren, E. D. 1943. Mountain-gods. *Orientalia* 12:76–84.

Vance, J. E. 1961. The Oregon Trail and the Union Pacific Railroad—a contrast in purpose. *Annals Assoc. Amer. Geog.* 51(4):357–79.

Vandeleur, C. R. P. 1952. The love of mountains. *Alpine J.* 58(284):505–10. *p. 72*

Van der Hammen, T. 1968. Climatic and vegetational succession in the equatorial Andes of Colombia. Pp. 187–94 in *Geoecology of the mountainous regions of the tropical Americas*, ed. C. Troll. Proc. UNESCO Mexico Symp., Aug. 1966. Bonn: Ferd. Dümmers Verlag. 223 pp.

Vander Wall, S. B., and Balda, R. P. 1977. Co-adaptations of the Clark's nutcracker and the Pinon pine for efficient seed harvest and dispersal. *Ecol. Monogr.* 47:89–111.

Van Dyke, E. C. 1919. A few observations on the tendency of insects to collect on ridges and mountain snow fields. *Ent. News* 30(9):241.

Van Ryswyk, A. L., and Okazaki, R. 1979. Genesis and classification of modal subalpine and alpine soil pedons of south-central British Columbia, Canada. *Arctic and Alpine Res.* 11(1): 53–67. *p. 238*

Van Steenis, C. G. G. J. 1934. On the origin of the Malaysian mountain flora. Part 1: Facts and statements of the problem. *Bull. Jardin Botan. Buitenzorg.* 13(2):135–262.

———. 1935. On the origin of the Malaysian mountain flora. Part 2: Altitudinal zones, general considerations and renewed statement of the problem. *Bull. Jardin Botan. Buitenzorg.* 13(3):289–417.

———. 1961. An attempt towards an explanation of the effect of mountain mass elevation. *Proc. Koninklijke Nederlandse Akademie van Wetenschappen* (Ser. C) 64:435–42.

———. 1962. The mountain flora of the Malaysian tropics. *Endeavor* 21:183–93.

———. 1964. Plant geography of the mountain flora of Mt. Kinabalu. *Proc. Roy. Soc. London* (Ser. B) 161:7–38.

———. 1972. *The mountain flora of Java.* Amsterdam: Brill. 90 pp.

Vaughan, T. A. 1969. Reproduction and population densities in a montane small mammal fauna. Pp. 51–74 in Univ. of Kansas Misc. Pub. 51. Lawrence, Kansas.

Vaurie, C. 1972. *Tibet and its birds.* London: H. F. Witherby. 407 pp.

Veblen, T. T. 1975. Alien weeds in the tropical highlands of western Guatemala. *J. Biogeog.* 2(1):19–26. *p. 431*

Verbeek, N. A. M. 1970. Breeding ecology of the water pipit. *Auk* 87:425–51.

VerSteeg, K. 1930. Wind gaps and water gaps of the northern Appalachians. *Ann. N.Y. Acad. Sci.* 32:87–220.

Vitaliano, D. B. 1973. *Legends of the earth: Their geologic origins.* Bloomington, Ind.: Indiana Univ. Press. 320 pp.

Vitousek, P. M. 1977. The regulation of element concentration in mountain streams in the northeastern United States. *Ecol. Monogr.* 47(1):65–87.

Vogelmann, H. W. 1973. Fog precipitation in the cloud forests of eastern Mexico. *BioScience* 23:96–100.

Vogelmann, H. W., Siccama, T., Leedy, D., and Ovitt, D. C. 1968. Precipitation from fog moisture in the Green Mountains of Vermont. *Ecol.* 49:1205–7.

Von Muralt, A. 1964. Introduction: Where are we? A short review of high altitude physiology. Pp. xvii–xxiii in *The physiological effects of high altitude*, ed. W. H. Weihe. New York: Macmillan. 351 pp.

Vuilleumier, B. S. 1971. Pleistocene changes in the fauna and flora of South America. *Science* 173:771–80.

Vuilleumier, F. 1969. Pleistocene speciation in birds living in the high Andes. *Nature* 223: 1179–80.

———. 1970. Insular biogeography in continental regions. I: The northern Andes of South America. *Amer. Nat.* 104:373–88.

Waddell, E. 1975. How the Enga cope with frost: Response to climatic perturbations in the central highlands. *Human Ecol.* 3(4):249–73.

Wade, L. K., and McVean, D. N. 1969. *Mt. Wilhelm Studies. I: The alpine and subalpine vegetation.* Research School of Pacific Studies Pub. BG/1. Canberra: Australian Natl. Univ. 225 pp.

Wagar, J. A. 1964. *The carrying capacity of wild lands for recreation.* Forest Sci. Monogr. 7. Washington, D.C. 24 pp.

Wahl, E. W. 1966. *Windspeed on mountains.* Final Report AF 19(628)–3873. Madison: Univ. of Wisconsin. 57 pp.

Wahrhaftig, C. 1965. Stepped topography of the southern Sierra Nevada, California. *Geol. Soc. Amer. Bull.* 76:1165–90.

Wahrhaftig, C., and Cox, A. 1959. Rock glaciers in the Alaska Range. *Geol. Soc. Amer. Bull.* 70: 383–436.

Waibel, K. 1955. Die meteorologischen Bedingungen fur Nebelfrostablagerungen an Hochspannungsleitungen im Gebirge. *Archiv. Meteor. Geophys. Biokl.* (Ser. B) 7:74–83.

Walshingham, L. 1885. On some probable causes of a tendency to melanic variation in Lepidoptera of high altitudes. *Entomologist* 18:81–87.

Walter, H. 1971. *Ecology of tropical and subtropical vegetation.* Trans. D. Mueller-Dombois. New York: Van Nostrand Reinhold. 539 pp.

Ward, A. L., Diem, K., and Weeks, R. 1975. The impact of snow on elk. Pp. 105–33 in *The Medicine Bow ecology project.* Prepared for Off. U.S. Atmosph. Water Resources. Laramie, Wyo.: Univ. of Wyoming in cooperation with Rocky Forest and Range Experiment Station. 397 pp.

Ward, R. T., and Dimitri, M. J. 1966. Alpine tundra on Mt. Cathedral in the southern Andes. *New Zealand J. Bot.* 4:42–56.

Wardle, P. 1963. Growth habits of New Zealand subalpine shrubs and trees. *New Zealand J. Bot.* 1:18–47.

———. 1965. A comparison of alpine timber lines in New Zealand and North America. *New Zealand J. Bot.* 3:113–35.

———. 1968. Engelmann spruce (*Picea engelmannii engel.*) at its upper limits on the Front Range, Colorado. *Ecol.* 49:483–95.

———. 1971. An explanation for alpine timberline. *New Zealand J. Bot.* 9:371–402.

———. 1973a. New Guinea: Our tropical counterpart. *Tuatara* 20(3):113–24.

———. 1973b. New Zealand timberlines. *Arctic and Alpine Res.* 5(3):(Pt. 2)A127–36.

———. 1974. Alpine timberlines. Pp. 371–402 in *Arctic and alpine environments*, ed. J. D. Ives and R. G. Barry. London: Methuen. 999 pp.

Warren-Wilson, J. 1952. Vegetation patterns associated with soil movement on Jan Mayen Island. *J. Ecol.* 40:249–64.

———. 1958. Dirt on snow patches. *J. Ecol.* 46: 191–98.

———. 1959. Notes on wind and its effects in arctic alpine vegetation. *J. Ecol.* 47:415–27.

Washburn, A. L. 1956. Classification of patterned ground and review of suggested origins. *Geol. Soc. Amer. Bull.* 67:823–66.

———. 1967. Instrumental observations of mass wasting in the Mesters Vig district, northeast Greenland. *Meddelelser om Grønland* 166(4). 296 pp.

———. 1969. Weathering, frost action, and patterned ground in the Mesters Vig district, northeast Greenland. *Meddelelser om Grønland* 176(4). 301 pp.

———. 1970. An approach to a genetic classification of patterned ground. *Acta Geog. Lodz.* 24:437–46.

———. 1973. *Periglacial processes and environments.* London: Edward Arnold. 320 pp.

Waters, A. C. 1973. The Columbia River Gorge: Basalt stratigraphy, ancient lava dams, and landslide dams. Pp. 133–62 in *Geologic field trips in northern Oregon and southern Washington.* Oregon State Dept. Geol. Min. Ind. Bull. 77. Portland. 206 pp.

Watson, J. B. 1965. From hunting to horticulture in the New Guinea highlands. *Ethnol.* 4:295–309.

Watson, R. A., and Wright, H. E., Jr. 1969. The Saidmarreh landslide, Iran. Pp. 115–40 in *United States contributions to Quaternary research,* ed. S. A. Schumm and W. C. Bradley. Geol. Soc. Amer. Spec. Pap. 123. New York. 305 pp.

Way, A. B. 1976. Morbidity and postneonatal mortality. Pp. 147–60 in *Man in the Andes: A multidisciplinary study of high-altitude Quechua,* ed. P. T. Baker and M. A. Little. Stroudsburg, Pa.: Dowden, Hutchinson and Ross. 482 pp.

Weatherwise. 1961. Waiting for the chinook. *Weatherwise* 14(5):174.

Webber, P. J. 1974. Tundra primary productivity. Pp. 445–73 in *Arctic and alpine environments*, ed. J. D. Ives and R. G. Barry. London: Methuen. 999 pp.

Webber, P. J., Emerick, J. C., May, D. C., and Komarkova, V. 1976. The impact of increased snowfall on alpine vegetation. Pp. 201–64 in *Ecological impacts of snowpack augmentation in the San Juan Mountains, Colorado,* ed. H. W.Steinhoff and J. D. Ives. Colorado State Univ., prepared for U.S. Bur. of Reclamation. Springfield, Va.: Nat. Tech. Info. Serv. PB-255 012. 489 pp.

Webber, P. J., and May, E. E. 1977. The distribution and magnitude of belowground plant structures in the alpine tundra of Niwot Ridge, Colorado. *Arctic and Alpine Res.* 9(2):157–74.

Weber, W. A. 1965. Plant geography in the southern Rocky Mountains. Pp. 453–68 in *The Quaternary of the United States,* ed. H. E. Wright and D. G. Frey. Princeton, N.J.: Princeton Univ. Press. 922 pp.

Webster, G. L. 1961. The altitudinal limits of vascular plants. *Ecol.* 42:587–90.

Webster, S. 1973. Native pastoralism in the south Andes. *Ethnol.* 12:115–33.

Wedel, W. R., Husted, W. M., and Moss, J. H. 1968. Mummy Cave: Prehistoric record from Rocky Mountains of Wyoming. *Science* 160:184–86.

Weertman, J. 1957. On the sliding of glaciers. *J. Glaciol.* 3:33–38.

———. 1964. The theory of glacial sliding. *J. Glaciol.* 5:287–303.

Wegener, A. 1924. *The origin of continents and oceans.* London: Methuen. 212 pp.

Weinberg, D. 1972. Cutting the pie in the Swiss Alps. *Anthrop. Quart.* 45(3):125–31.

———. 1975. *Peasant wisdom: Cultural adaptations in a Swiss village.* Berkeley, Ca.: Univ. Calif. Press. 214 pp.

Weisbecker, L. W. 1974. *The impacts of snow enhancement: Technology assessment of winter orographic snow augmentation in the upper Colorado River basin.* Norman, Okla: Univ. Oklahoma Press. 624 pp.

Weischet, W. 1969. Klimatologische Regeln zur Vertikalverteilung der Niederschläge in Tropengebirgen. *Die Erde* 100:287–306.

Weisskopf, V. F. 1975. Of atoms, mountains, and stars: A study in qualitative physics. *Science* 187(4177):605–12.

Welin, C. 1974. Cultural problems and approaches in a ski area. Pp. 64–70 in *Proc. workshop on revegetation of high-altitude disturbed lands,* ed. W. A. Berg, J. A. Brown, and R. L. Cuany. Info. Ser. 10, Envir. Resources Center. Fort Collins, Colo.: Colorado State Univ. 88 pp.

Went, F. W. 1948. Some parallels between desert and alpine flora in California. *Madrono* 9:241–49.

Wertz, J. B. 1966. The flood cycle of ephemeral mountain streams in the southwestern United States. *Annals Assoc. Amer. Geog.* 56(4):598–633.

Westervelt, W. D. 1963. *Hawaiian legends of volcanoes.* Rutland, Vt.: Charles F. Tuttle. 205 pp.

White, C. L., and Renner, G. T. 1936. *Geography: An introduction to human ecology.* New York: Appleton-Century. 790 pp.

White, R. M. 1949. The role of mountains in the angular momentum balance of the atmosphere. *J. Meteor.* 6(5):353–55.

White, S. E. 1971a. Rock glacier studies in the Colorado Front Range, 1961 to 1968. *Arctic and Alpine Res.* 3(1):43–64.

———. 1971b. Debris falls at the front of Arapaho rock glacier, Colorado Front Range, U.S.A. *Geog. Ann.* 53A(2):86–91.

———. 1976a. Is frost action really only hydration shattering? A review. *Arctic and Alpine Res.* 8(1):1–6.

———. 1976b. Rock glaciers and block fields, review and new data. *Quat. Res.* 6(1):77–98.

Whitehead, L. 1968. Altitude, fertility, and mortality in Andean countries. *Pop. Stud.* 22:335–46.

Whitney, M. I., and Dietrich, R. V. 1973. Ventifact sculpture by windblown dust. *Geol. Soc. Amer. Bull.* 84:2561–82.

Whittaker, R. H. 1954. The ecology of serpentine soils. IV: The vegetational response to serpentine soils. *Ecol.* 35:275–88.

Whittaker, R. H., Buol, S. W., Niering, W. A., and Havens, Y. H. 1968. A soil and vegetation pattern in the Santa Catalina Mountains, Arizona. *Soil Sci.* 105:440–51.

Wilbanks, T. J., Mioric, P., and Gerson, J. 1973. Economic development and scenic landscape preservation: The case of Bovec. Pp. 16–35 in *Alpine landscape preservation in Slovenia.* Syracuse, N.Y.: Syracuse Univ. Envir. Policy Proj. 53 pp.

Wilcox, R. E. 1959. Some effects of recent ash falls, with especial reference to Alaska. Pp. 409–76 in *U.S. Geol. Surv. Bull. 1028-N.*

Willard, B. E., and Marr, J. W. 1970. Effects of human activities on alpine tundra ecosystems in Rocky Mountain National Park, Colorado. *Biol. Conserv.* 2(4):257–65.

———. 1971. Recovery of alpine tundra under protection after damage by human activities in the Rocky Mountains, Colorado. *Biol. Conserv.* 3(3):181–90.

Williams, H. 1942. *The geology of Crater Lake National Park, Oregon.* Publ. 540. Washington, D.C.: Carnegie Inst. 162 pp.

———. 1951. Volcanoes. *Sci. Amer.* 185(5):45–53.

Williams, H., and Goles, G. 1968. Volume of the Mazama ash-fall and the origin of the Crater Lake, Oregon. Pp. 37–41 in *Andesite Conf. Guidebook,* Or. Dept. Geol. Min. Ind. Bull. 62. Portland, Or.

Williams, J. E. 1949. Chemical weathering at low temperatures. *Geog. Rev.* 39:129–35.

Williams, J. H. 1911. *The mountain that was God.*

New York: G. P. Putnam's Sons. 142 pp.

Williams, K. 1975a. *The snowy torrents: Avalanche accidents in the United States 1967–71.* U.S. Dept. Agri. For. Serv. Gen. Tech. Rep. RM-8. Fort Collins, Colo. 190 pp.

————. 1975b. *Avalanche fatalities in the United States, 1950–1975.* U.S. Dept. Agri. For. Serv. Res. Note RM-300. Fort Collins, Colo. 4 pp.

Williams, P., Jr., and Peck, E. L. 1962. Terrain influences on precipitation in the intermountain West as related to synoptic situation. *J. Appl. Meteor.* 1:343–47.

Williams, P. J. 1957. Some investigations into solifluction features in Norway. *Geog. J.* 72: 42–58.

Wilson, J. T. 1966. Did the Atlantic close and then reopen? *Nature* 211(5050):676–81.

————, ed. 1976. *Continents adrift and continents aground: Readings from Scientific American.* San Francisco: W. H. Freeman. 230 pp.

Windom, H. L. 1969. Atmospheric dust records in permanent snowfields: Implications to marine sediments. *Geol. Soc. Amer. Bull.* 80:761–82.

Winterhalder, B., Larsen, R., and Thomas, R. B. 1974. Dung as an essential resource in a highland Peruvian community. *Human Ecol.* 2(2):

Wittfogel, K. A. 1955. Developmental aspects of hydraulic societies. Pp. 43–52 in *Irrigation civilizations: A comparative study*, ed. J. H. Steward et al. Soc. Sci. Monogr. 1. Washington, D.C.: Pan Amer. Union. 78 pp.

Woillard, G. M. 1978. Grande Pile peat bog: A continuous pollen record for the last 140,000 years. *Qual. Res.* 9(1):1–2.

Wolf, E. R. 1970. The inheritance of land among Bavarian and Tyrolese peasants. *Anthropologica* N.S. 12(1):99–114.

Wolman, M. G., and Miller, J. P. 1960. Magnitude and frequency of forces in geomorphic processes. *J. Geol.* 68:54–74.

Wood, T. G. 1970. Decomposition of plant litter in montane and alpine soils on Mt. Kosciusko, Australia. *Nature* 226:541–62.

————. 1974. The distribution of earthworms in relation to soils, vegetation and altitude on the slopes of Mt. Kosciusko, Australia. *J. Animal Ecol.* 43(1):87–106.

Woodcock, A. H. 1974. Permafrost and climatology of a Hawaii crater. *Arctic and Alpine Res.* 6:49–62.

Woodcock, A. H., Furumoto, A. S., and Woollard, G. P. 1970. Fossil ice in Hawaii. *Nature* 226:873.

Woodman, D. 1969. *Himalayan frontiers.* New York: Frederick A. Praeger. 423 pp.

Wooldridge, G. L., and Ellis, R. I. 1975. Stationarity of mesoscale airflow in mountainous terrain. *J. Appl. Meteor.* 14(1):124–218.

Worsley, P., and Harris, C. 1974. Evidence for neoglacial solifluction at Okstindan, north Norway. *Arctic* 27(2):128–44.

Wright, H. E., Jr. 1974. Landscape development, forest fires, and wilderness management. *Science* 186:487–95.

Wright, H. E., Jr., and Osburn, W. H. 1968. *Arctic and alpine environments.* Bloomington, Ind.: Indiana Univ. Press. 308 pp.

Wright, H. E., Jr., and Heinselman, M. L., eds. 1973. The ecological role of fire in natural conifer forests of western and northern America. *Quat. Res.* 3(3):317–513.

Wright, J. B., ed. 1977. *Mineral deposits, continental drift, and plate tectonics.* New York: Dowden, Hutchinson and Ross. 416 pp.

Wright, K. R., and Fricke, O. W. 1966. Waterfreezing problems in mountain communities. Pp. 447–49 in *Permafrost international conference, Lafayette, Ind., 1963.* Proc. Natl. Acad. Sci. Natl. Res. Coun. Pub. 1287. Washington, D.C. 563 pp.

Wulff, H. E. 1968. The qanats of Iran. *Sci. Amer.* 218:94–105.

Wyllie, P. J. 1975. The earth's mantle. *Sci. Amer.* 232(3):50–63.

Yeend, W. E. 1972. Winter protalus mounds: Brooks Range, Alaska. *Arctic and Alpine Res.* 4(1):85–88.

Yen, D. E. 1974. *The sweet potato and Oceania.* Bernice P. Bishop Museum Bull. 236. Honolulu, Hawaii: Bishop Museum Press. 389 pp.

Yoshino, M. M. 1964a. Some aspects of air temperature climate of the high mountains of Japan. Pp. 147–53 in *Sonderdruck aus Carinthia II*, 24. Sonderheft, Bericht Über die VIII. International Tagung für Alpine Meteorologie, Villach, 9–12 Sept. 1964.

————. 1964b. Some local characteristics of the winds as revealed by wind-shaped trees in the Rhône Valley in Switzerland. *Erdkunde* 18: 28–39.

————. 1975. *Climate in a small area.* Tokyo: Univ. of Tokyo Press. 549 pp.

Young, G. W. 1943. Mountain prophets. *Alpine J.* 54(267):97–116.

———. 1957. *The influence of mountains upon the development of human intelligence.* Glasgow University Publ., W. P. Ker Memorial Lecture 17. Glasgow: Jackson, Son and Co. 30 pp.

Young, N. E. 1912. The mountains in Greek poetry. Pp. 59–89 in *Oxford mountaineering essays*, ed. A. H. M. Lunn. London: E. Arnold.

Young, T. C., and Smith, P. E. L. 1966. Research in the prehistory of central western Iran. *Science* 153(3734):386–91.

Zeman, L. J., and Slaymaker, H. O. 1975. Hydrochemical analysis to discriminate variable runoff source areas in an alpine basin. *Arctic and Alpine Res.* 7(4):341–52.

Zeuner, F. E. 1949. Frost soils on Mt. Kenya and the relation of frost soils to aeolion deposits. *J. Soil Sci.* 1:20–32.

Zimina, R. P. 1967. Main features of the fauna and ecology of the alpine vertebrates of the U.S.S.R. Pp. 137–42 in *Arctic and alpine environments*, ed. W. H. Osburn and H. E. Wright, Jr. Bloomington, Ind.: Indiana Univ. Press. 308 pp.

———. 1973. Upper forest boundary and the subalpine belt in the mountains of the southern U.S.S.R. and adjacent countries (summary). *Arctic and Alpine Res.* 5(3):(Pt. 2)A29–32.

———. 1978. The main features of the Caucasian natural landscapes and their conservation, U.S.S.R. *Arctic and Alpine Res.* 10(2):479–88.

Zimina, R. P., and Panfilov, D. V. 1978. Geographical characteristics of the high-mountain biota within nontropical Eurasia. *Arctic and Alpine Res.* 10(2):435–39.

Zimmermann, A. 1953. The highest plants in the world. Pp. 130–36 in *The mountain world*. New York: Harper. Swiss Foundation for Alpine Research.

Index

Designer: Al Burkhardt
Compositor: Dharma Press
Printer: Halliday Lithograph
Binder: Halliday Lithograph
Text: Fototronic Elegante
Display: Typositor Neil Bold
Cloth: Joanna Arrestox A 41000
Paper: 70 lb. Glatco Smooth